THE OXFORD HANDBOOK OF

SKEPTICISM

THE OXFORD HANDBOOK OF

SKEPTICISM

Edited by

JOHN GRECO

OXFORD

UNIVERSITY PRESS

2008

OXFORD
UNIVERSITY PRESS

Oxford University Press, Inc., publishes works that further
Oxford University's objective of excellence
in research, scholarship, and education.

Oxford   New York
Auckland   Cape Town   Dar es Salaam   Hong Kong   Karachi
Kuala Lumpur   Madrid   Melbourne   Mexico City   Nairobi
New Delhi   Shanghai   Taipei   Toronto

With offices in
Argentina   Austria   Brazil   Chile   Czech Republic   France   Greece
Guatemala   Hungary   Italy   Japan   Poland   Portugal   Singapore
South Korea   Switzerland   Thailand   Turkey   Ukraine   Vietnam

Copyright © 2008 by Oxford University Press, Inc.

Published by Oxford University Press, Inc.
198 Madison Avenue, New York, New York 10016

www.oup.com

Oxford is a registered trademark of Oxford University Press

Library of Congress Cataloging-in-Publication Data

The Oxford handbook of skepticism / edited by John Greco.
p. cm.
Includes bibliographical references.
ISBN 978-0-19-518321-4
1. Skepticism.   I. Greco, John.
B837.O94 2008
149'.73—dc22
2007043349

1 3 5 7 9 8 6 4 2
Printed in the United States of America
on acid-free paper

For my father, a good sort of skeptic.

Thanks to Ben Hart for his help with
the manuscript and the index.

Contents

Contributors

ROBERT AUDI is professor of philosophy and David E. Gallo Professor of Business Ethics at the University of Notre Dame.

GUY AXTELL is lecturer in philosophy at the University of Nevada, Reno.

MICHAEL BERGMANN is professor of philosophy at Purdue University.

JOSÉ LUIS BERMÚDEZ is professor of philosophy with a joint appointment as director of the Philosophy-Neuroscience-Psychology program and director of the Center for Programs in Arts and Sciences at Washington University of St. Louis.

STEWART COHEN is professor of philosophy at Arizona State University.

TERENCE CUNEO is assistant professor of philosophy at Calvin College.

BRYAN FRANCES is associate professor of philosophy at Fordham University.

RICHARD FUMERTON is F. Wendell Miller Professor of Philosophy at the University of Iowa.

PETER J. GRAHAM is associate professor of philosophy at the University of California, Riverside.

JOHN GRECO is Leonard and Elizabeth Eslick Professor of Philosophy, Saint Louis University.

CHRISTOPHER HOOKWAY is professor of philosophy at the University of Sheffield.

MARK KAPLAN is professor of philosophy at Indiana University, Bloomington.

PETER KLEIN is professor of philosophy at Rutgers University.

JONATHAN KVANVIG is Distinguished Professor of Philosophy at Baylor University.

MARKUS LAMMENRANTA is professor of philosophy at the University of Helsinki.

NOAH LEMOS is Leslie and Naomi Legum Professor of Philosophy at the College of William and Mary.

MARIE MCGINN is professor of philosophy and Chairman of the Philosophy Research Committee at the University of York.

ALAN MILLAR is professor of philosophy at the University of Stirling.

PAUL K. MOSER is professor of philosophy and chairperson of the Department of Philosophy at Loyola University of Chicago.

GEORGE PAPPAS is professor of philosophy at Ohio State University.

DUNCAN PRITCHARD is chair in Epistemology at the University of Edinburgh.

ROBERT STERN is department head and professor of philosophy at the University of Sheffield.

JAMES VAN CLEVE is professor of philosophy at the University of Southern California.

JONATHAN VOGEL is professor of philosophy at the University of California, Davis.

RUTH WEINTRAUB is professor of philosophy at Tel-Aviv University.

MICHAEL WILLIAMS is a Krieger-Eisenhower Professor of Philosophy and Chair of the Department of Philosophy at Johns Hopkins University.

THE OXFORD HANDBOOK OF

SKEPTICISM

INTRODUCTION

JOHN GRECO

PHILOSOPHERS have long been concerned with various kinds of skepticism. They have explored reasons for and against various skeptical positions, and they have argued about the consequences of adopting various skeptical stances. Today's philosophers are no exception. In fact, in recent years there has been renewed interest in skepticism and skeptical arguments. New work has been done on the nature and structure of various skeptical arguments and on historically important responses to skepticism. Contemporary epistemologists have also crafted new strategies for responding to skepticism, often drawing on recent developments in other fields, such as metaphysics, the philosophy of mind, and the philosophy of language.

This volume explores the results of this new work. Part I of the volume looks at several varieties of skepticism, including some important varieties of skeptical argument. Part II examines some historically important responses to skepticism, such as Berkeley's idealism, Reid's "commonsense" view, and Peirce's pragmatism. Part III reviews several contemporary issues, including some new strategies for responding to skepticism of various sorts. Each chapter is self-contained and offers a detailed but accessible treatment of its topic. The volume as a whole will serve as a fairly comprehensive introduction to skeptical thought and thought about skepticism.

The remainder of this introduction is structured as follows. Section 1 briefly discusses some varieties of skepticism. Section 2 offers some remarks about how skepticism has been approached in different philosophical periods. Section 3 frames skepticism as a theoretical problem, as is the usual approach today.

1. VARIETIES OF SKEPTICISM

Skepticism involves doubt, or at least a reluctance to commit. If I am skeptical about what my government is telling me about the war, then I have my doubts that the government's claims are true. If you are skeptical that the Red Sox will win the pennant, then you have your doubts that they will. Or perhaps you are a rabid Red Sox fan and psychologically incapable of entertaining doubts about your team's chances. Nevertheless, you might be reluctant to commit, for example with a bet.

These kinds of skepticism are limited in scope and, as such, are commonplace. Skepticism is of philosophical interest when it becomes more general. For example, some people are moral skeptics, claiming that no one can know what is right or wrong. Other people are religious skeptics, claiming that no one can know what God is like, what God wills, or whether God exists at all. Here we have more general claims, about the possibility of a general kind of knowledge: "There is no moral knowledge," or "There is no knowledge of God." Skepticism can be more general still. Some skeptics claim that there is no knowledge beyond how things appear, or of the world "outside our minds." Even more generally, some skeptics claim that there is no knowledge at all.

The different kinds of skepticism just mentioned differ in their scope. Skeptical positions can also differ in their degree. For example, some skeptics claim that there is no knowledge of some general kind. Others claim, less strongly, that there is no certainty. Others claim, more strongly, that there is no reasonable or rationally preferable belief. Varieties of skepticism can also differ in their "level." Thus some skeptics claim that no one knows, whereas others claim that no one knows that one knows. All these varieties will be discussed in the chapters that follow.

2. SKEPTICISM THROUGH THE AGES

In the ancient world, skepticism was recommended as a way of life. The general claim was that living with an attitude of skeptical doubt is superior to living with an attitude of dogmatic certainty. This recommendation might be framed in practical terms: a life lived in skeptical doubt is happier than a life lived in dogmatic certitude, perhaps because skepticism involves a more peaceful or tranquil state of mind. Alternatively, the recommendation might be framed as moral: a skeptical life is morally superior to a dogmatic one, perhaps because the former is more open-minded and tolerant. Ironically, skepticism in the modern world (i.e., the 1600s through the 1800s) was more often treated as a practical problem. Skeptical doubt was considered a state of mind to be avoided or overcome, and considerable philosophical energy was put into strategies for doing so.

Whatever the merits of the ancient and modern approaches, nowadays skepticism is more often framed as a theoretical problem than as a practical or moral one. For contemporary philosophers, skepticism is of interest insofar as there are good arguments or reasons for thinking that skepticism might be true. Contemporary philosophers tend to focus on the merits of those arguments rather than on the practical or moral value of a skeptical way of life. The chapters in this volume reflect this contemporary point of view. That is, their emphasis is on the merits of skeptical arguments or skeptical reasoning. Their concern is to closely consider the best arguments for skepticism and to explore how best to respond to them.

How should we understand this shift toward the theoretical and away from the practical and moral? First, it should be noted that this is a shift in emphasis. Certainly, ancient and modern writers were concerned with the merits of skeptical arguments and with the truth or falsity of skeptical conclusions. And certainly, contemporary writers, including ones in this volume, are concerned with the moral and practical consequences of various forms of skepticism. Second, the shift to a theoretical focus can be partly understood as professional: contemporary philosophers, especially in English-speaking traditions, take arguments to be the proper focus of philosophical inquiry in general. Qua philosophers, they consider themselves better qualified to examine and evaluate arguments than to offer psychological advice or recommendations for living.

However, there is perhaps a more important explanation for the shift to a theoretical focus. Namely, contemporary philosophers tend to be unimpressed with both the ancient recommendations and the modern worries. Put differently, contemporary philosophers tend to be unimpressed with the efficacy of skeptical arguments either to engender doubt or to inspire behavior. This attitude can be traced back to Hume, who noted that his skeptical doubts held sway only in the study. The activities of ordinary life are sufficient to dispel skeptical doubt. In a famous passage, Hume writes:

> The *intense* view of these manifold contradictions and imperfections in human reason has so wrought upon me, and heated my brain, that I am ready to reject all belief and reasoning, and can look upon no opinion even as more probable or likely than another.... Most fortunately it happens, that since reason is incapable of dispelling these clouds, nature herself suffices for that purpose, and cures me of this philosophical melancholy and delirium.... I dine, I play a game of backgammon, I converse, and am merry with my friends; and when after three or four hour's amusement, I wou'd return to these speculations, they appear so cold, and strain'd, and ridiculous, that I cannot find in my heart to enter into them any farther.
>
> (*A Treatise of Human Nature*, bk.1, pt.4, sec.7)

More generally, and again following Hume, contemporary philosophers hold "reason" in less regard than did many of their ancient or modern counterparts. Perhaps most important, the power of reason to control thought and action is seen as far more restricted. From this general point of view, the impotence of skeptical reasoning is merely a special case.

3. SKEPTICISM AS A THEORETICAL PROBLEM

Suppose, then, that skepticism is more properly of theoretical interest than of moral or practical interest. Or less strongly, suppose that skepticism is primarily of theoretical interest. What does it mean to say that skepticism is theoretically interesting? One thing that it means has already been suggested: skepticism is theoretically interesting (or philosophically interesting) insofar as there are good arguments that skepticism might be true. Suppose that someone were to claim that no one knows anything. Or somewhat less radically, that you do not know that you have two hands, or that there is a table in front of you. Such claims by themselves would not be interesting. But suppose that there were good reasons for thinking that no one knows anything, or that you do not know that you have two hands. That is, suppose that there were reasons that looked good, and that it was not obvious where or why they were wrong. Now that would be interesting even if we were not inclined to take the skeptical claims seriously. It would be interesting to examine the skeptical reasons more closely and to see if we could find a mistake in them. Of course, there is a flip side to this: having seen the skeptical arguments in question, some people (including some in this volume) will want to take some skeptical claims very seriously, and will want to defend the arguments in their favor.

There is another sense in which skepticism is theoretically interesting. As things turn out, responding to skeptical arguments often requires substantive theoretical commitments. Suppose that we are faced with a skeptical argument that concludes that no one knows anything. Somewhat less radically, suppose that we are faced with an argument that no one knows right from wrong, or that other persons exist, or that any scientific claim is true. Presumably something is wrong with any such skeptical argument. But what is wrong? Where exactly is the mistake? In many cases, that turns out to be very hard to say. And in trying to say, philosophers end up making surprising and controversial philosophical claims—they make claims about the nature of reality, the nature of mind, the nature of morality, and much more. To a surprising extent, the history of philosophy is the history of philosophical theory in response to skeptical arguments. Put differently, thinking about skepticism inspires philosophical theory. As we will see in the chapters to come, it can inspire epistemology, ontology, philosophy of mind, philosophy of language, moral philosophy, and philosophy of religion. That being the case, skepticism is interesting indeed.

PART I

VARIETIES OF SKEPTICISM AND SKEPTICAL ARGUMENTS

CHAPTER 1

THE PYRRHONIAN PROBLEMATIC

MARKUS LAMMENRANTA

CURRENT discussion about skepticism focuses on Cartesian skepticism. There is an older and perhaps more fundamental skeptical problematic documented in the works of Sextus Empiricus. It is at least arguable that this is the problematic to which Descartes himself and other early modern philosophers responded. However, it is not at all clear what this problematic—the Pyrrhonian problematic—really is. I will give a rational reconstruction of it, considering three possible interpretations of the problematic, and argue that only the last one provides a serious skeptical challenge and explains the huge influence that the problematic had on early modern philosophy.[1]

In contemporary analytical epistemology, skeptical problems are taken to be theoretical in nature. They are composed of skeptical arguments for the impossibility of knowledge or justified belief. Rather than making us accept the conclusion, these arguments are thought to teach us something about knowledge or justified belief. They offer test cases for our theories of knowledge and justification. Because the conclusion is intuitively implausible, our theories must explain what goes wrong in the premises. Typically, the fault is seen to be in the epistemic premises. So our theory must explain why these are false, and thus how knowledge or justified belief is, after all, possible.[2] In this tradition, the Pyrrhonian problem is identified with a skeptical argument purporting to show that it is impossible for finite beings like us to have any justified beliefs. Various theories of justification then try to explain what is wrong with this argument, and how finite beings can have justified beliefs.

There is another common way of understanding the Pyrrhonian problematic. As scholars of Hellenistic philosophy emphasize, ancient skeptics used to argue both for and against a proposition. Because the arguments are of equal force, we are unable to decide whether the proposition is true or false. Here the problem is seen to be practical or psychological rather than theoretical. We are unable to decide between the alternatives because they are equally plausible. It is the skeptics' ability to find such equipollent oppositions that leads them to suspend all belief.

There is a third interpretation not as fully defended in the literature as the other two. According to it, the problem is dialectical rather than theoretical or psychological: we seem to be unable to resolve disagreements about the nature of reality without begging the question at issue. This problem does not presuppose any theoretical assumptions about knowledge or justification, but neither does it concern a purely psychological inability to decide between conflicting propositions. It just assumes that in order to rationally resolve a disagreement, we should not beg the question.

When Sextus wrote his texts, ancient skepticism already had a long history with a variety of different positions. That is why it may be hard to find a coherent description of a single skeptical problem there. Perhaps there are several such problems, so it may not be difficult to find some textual evidence for each of these interpretations. However, rather than Sextus's own stance, I am interested in the skeptical problems that an educated reader may find in his work and in evaluating their epistemological significance. This may help us understand modern epistemology, which, ever since Descartes, has tried to respond to the problems found there. But even more important, it may help us see a serious skeptical problem for which we may still lack a satisfactory solution.

I will start by considering the first two interpretations and argue that neither of them provides a serious skeptical challenge to our beliefs: neither has a tendency to induce suspension of belief, which the arguments of the ancient skeptics were supposed to do. Then I will try to explicate the dialectical problem, which will prove to be much harder. Only this fully explains the skeptical crisis created by the rediscovery of Sextus's books during the Renaissance and the responses of early modern philosophers to it. I will try to show that not even contemporary analytical epistemologists have sufficient resources for resolving it.

1. THE REGRESS PROBLEM

The core of the Pyrrhonian problematic is often taken to be an argument for the impossibility of justified beliefs. This argument is found in the five modes of Agrippa and is called the regress argument. It is an argument for a very strong form of global skepticism that denies the possibility of any justified beliefs. Suspension of belief would then seem to be the appropriate attitude to every proposition: if we are not justified in believing anything, we should not believe anything.

It was once common to interpret the Pyrrhonian skeptic as advocating this argument and basing her suspension of belief on its negative epistemic conclusion. This raised the accusation of self-refutation. If the conclusion of the argument is true, no one can be justified in believing anything, not even the premises of the argument itself, and thus they cannot be used to justify the conclusion. No one can thus effectively argue for the conclusion that there cannot be justified beliefs. So why should anybody take the argument seriously?

Many recent scholars of Hellenistic philosophy take this to be a misinterpretation of the dialectical strategy of ancient skeptics.[3] The arguments of ancient skeptics are ad hominem arguments. They are directed at us, the dogmatists, and use only premises that we accept. The regress argument poses a problem for us because we are inclined to accept the premises and take the argument to be valid, though we are not willing to accept the conclusion. As many contemporary epistemologists see it, a genuine skeptical problem is a kind of paradox: we are inclined to accept the premises and the denial of the conclusion, though they form an inconsistent set of propositions.[4]

On the other hand, Sextus says that the skeptics welcome the self-refuting nature of their arguments. Their arguments are like a ladder that we throw away once we have climbed up it, or like fire that after consuming the fuel also destroys itself.[5] However, as Hume noticed, our beliefs tend to come back when we lose our reasons for giving them up. But then, the skeptic may point out, we also return to the arguments that make us reject the beliefs once again. So the skeptical arguments at least create instability in our beliefs. This may be enough to make them a serious skeptical challenge to our beliefs.[6]

In order to pose a genuine paradox, the regress argument must have plausible premises. As Michael Williams points out, they should not be based on theoretical ideas that we are not bound to accept. They should be based on our ordinary intuitions about justification and knowledge.[7] Does the regress argument have such intuitively plausible premises? This is the standard formulation of the argument:

1. In order to be justified in believing something, one must believe it on the basis of good reasons.
2. Good reasons must themselves be justified beliefs.
3. Therefore, in order to be justified in believing something, one must believe it on the basis of an infinite number of good reasons.
4. No human being can have an infinite number of good reasons.
5. Therefore, it is humanly impossible to have justified beliefs.

Most epistemologists have not found all the premises plausible. There are several ways of criticizing the argument. Indeed, epistemologists use the argument typically just to classify the possible theories of justification. These are distinguished by virtue of which premise or step in the argument they deny: Circular (linear) coherentists deny the step from premises 1 and 2 to 3 because they think that a circular chain of reasons can justify a belief. Wittgensteinian contextualists think that the chain of good reasons can terminate in beliefs that are not themselves justified, and thus they deny premise 2. Foundationalists think that the chain terminates in basic beliefs that are justified but do not derive all their justification from their inferential relations to other justified beliefs.[8] They deny premise 1.

The skeptical conclusion is essentially based on the infinitist lemma (3) that only an infinite chain of reasons can justify a belief. All other theories except dogmatic infinitism deny this. Though Peter Klein, who has recently defended the position, argues that infinitism need not lead to skepticism, the skeptic has a strong position if infinitism is true. Indeed, Klein acknowledges that skepticism is a serious possibility for the infinitist.[9]

The regress argument thus provides a real paradox and a skeptical challenge only if infinitism is an intuitively plausible account of justification. Initially, it does not seem to be plausible. Why should we possess a concept of justification that is not applicable to any finite being? So the skeptic must do something to convince us of the truth of infinitism.

In his reconstruction of skeptical reasoning, Michael Williams appeals to our practice of giving and asking for reasons: Suppose I claim to know something. You can ask me how I know it. As a reply, I give my reasons for believing what I claim to know. But then you can ask how I know my reasons, and so on. Williams's skeptic admits that in real life this process of justification has an end. It ends when my interlocutor is satisfied with my reasons. In spite of this, Williams's skeptic insists that the regress goes on. Whether or not anybody really challenges my reasons, they can reasonably be challenged, and so I must go on giving reasons. The skeptic concludes that I do not know what I originally claimed unless I have first completed an infinite number of prior justifications, which is, of course, impossible.[10] But is this really the intuitive conclusion to draw from our practice of justifying knowledge claims?

Klein imagines a similar dialogue between Fred, the foundationalist, and Sally, the skeptic. Sally asks Fred his reasons for believing that p. Fred gives as his reason his belief that q. Then Sally asks his reasons for q, and the regress continues until Fred gives a reason that he takes to be a basic belief, which, according to foundationalism, is justified independently of reasons. Now Sally asks why Fred thinks that the basic belief is true. In order to avoid arbitrariness, Fred says that his basic belief has property P, and that all beliefs having P are likely to be true. But then Sally insists that the regress does not stop, and asks Fred for his reasons for the meta beliefs that his belief has P and that beliefs having P are probably true. Klein concludes that nobody is completely justified in believing anything because this would require going through an infinite number of reasons, but that people can still be provisionally justified in believing things because such infinite chains are in a relevant sense available to them.[11]

Neither infinitist conclusion from our ordinary practices is intuitive. We see this more clearly if we think about the point of our practice of giving and asking for reasons. The point seems to be to evaluate each other as potential informants. When you claim to know something, I ask your reasons because I want to decide whether I can trust you and learn from you. In this sort of case, I already have many beliefs about the world and your situation. I use these beliefs in evaluating your trustworthiness, and I do not expect you to justify them. So the regress may very well terminate in basic beliefs because these are the kind of beliefs I take to be probably true in your circumstances. You need not justify them to me. This also explains why we sometimes attribute knowledge to small children and nonhuman animals though they cannot justify their beliefs at all.

If we imagine that the practice of giving and asking for reasons is conducted between the skeptic and us, the situation is different. The skeptic does not accept any beliefs as being justified or true. There is no way to convince her because she does not accept any reasons that we could give, so there is no way out of the regress. But why should this show that it is impossible for us to have justified beliefs and knowledge? Our justificational practice does not aim at convincing the skeptic. It aims at convincing someone who already has many beliefs and is able to use these beliefs for evaluating the given reasons. The fact that we cannot justify our beliefs to the skeptic is of no epistemological importance.

So the skeptical strategy of arguing ad hominem from the infinite regress of reasons has no chance of succeeding. Our ordinary epistemic concepts and practices cannot be used to support it. It is thus hard to see how it could have created the skeptical crisis in early modern philosophy and played such an important role in shaping modern epistemology. Neither does it explain how the Pyrrhonian skeptics themselves became skeptics. Sextus does have a story about this, and this story seems to give us an independent skeptical problem.

2. THE PRACTICAL PROBLEM

Sextus starts his *Outlines of Scepticism* by distinguishing three kinds of outcomes that any inquiry may have: (1) it may result in discovery, (2) it may result in the denial of discovery and the confession that the truth cannot be discovered, (3) or it may just continue. According to Sextus, there are three kinds of philosophers corresponding to these outcomes: (1) the dogmatists think that they have discovered the truth, (2) the Academics think that the truth cannot be discovered, and (3) the skeptics continue inquiry.[12] If discovering the truth amounts to knowing the truth, we can say that the dogmatists think that they know the truth, the Academics deny the possibility of knowledge, and the skeptics suspend judgment both about their actually knowing anything and about the possibility of knowledge.

Here Sextus wants to distinguish real skepticism—Pyrrhonism—from Academic skepticism. The latter is itself one sort of dogmatism—negative dogmatism—because it defends the dogma that nothing can be known. Presumably, this negative thesis is based on a positive epistemology: nothing can be known because the conditions of knowledge put forth by this epistemology cannot be satisfied. So both dogmatists and Academics need an epistemology: the former need it for defending their knowledge claims, and the latter for defending their claim about the impossibility of knowledge.

Sextus ignores here the fact that the skeptics in Plato's Academy typically argue ad hominem: they use their opponents', the Stoics', epistemology to argue against it. Yet the message is clear. The Pyrrhonist neither needs nor possesses any epistemology. She suspends judgment about both the nature and the possibility of knowledge. So her suspension of judgment is not based on any theory or epistemological thesis, such as infinitism. It is based rather on her inability to resolve disagreements among different dogmatists—including the disagreement about the possibility of knowledge.

This is how Sextus describes the way one becomes a skeptic:

> Sceptics began to do philosophy in order to decide among appearances and to apprehend which are true and which false, so as to become tranquil; but they came upon equipollent dispute, and being unable to decide this they suspended judgement. And when they suspended judgement, tranquillity in matters of opinion followed fortuitously.[13]

According to Sextus, the skeptics were originally inquirers who were seeking truth, but who realized that there were disagreements about truth that they could not resolve. They were therefore forced to suspend judgment. To their surprise, they achieved in this way the tranquility to which they originally aspired by trying to find the truth.

Sextus also describes skepticism as an ability:

> an ability to set out oppositions among things which appear and are thought of in any way at all, an ability by which, because of the equipollence in the opposed objects and accounts, we come first to suspension of judgement and afterwards to tranquillity.[14]

So skepticism, as Sextus understands it, is not a thesis about the impossibility of knowledge or justified belief. It is an ability to find equipollent oppositions and the practice of using this ability to induce suspension of belief.

It is common to understand this account of skepticism in purely psychological terms. Thus from Julia Annas and Jonathan Barnes's translation we get the following explanation of the relevant terms:

> By equipollence we mean equality with regard to being convincing or unconvincing. Suspension of judgement is a standstill of the intellect, owing to which we neither reject nor posit anything. Tranquillity is freedom from disturbance or calmness of soul.[15]

This psychological interpretation is also defended in Michael Williams's article "Skepticism without Theory." He objects to the view that Pyrrhonian skepticism is based on any epistemological thesis. Pyrrhonian skepticism arises from practice. It depends on acquiring an ability, not on proving or even assenting to a thesis. Skepticism is an ability to oppose any thesis or argument with a countervailing thesis or argument of equal force. Williams emphasizes that no epistemological commitments are buried in this notion of equal force, which is to be understood as equal convincingness or plausibility. There is no implication of equal evidential force.[16]

In spite of some textual support, this psychological interpretation makes the Pyrrhonian problem completely trivial. Of course, if there is a question with conflicting answers that are equally convincing, we suspend judgment about which answer is correct. For example, there seems to be no convincing reason to believe that there is an even number of stars rather than an odd number of stars. What else could we do but suspend belief about the matter? But in many cases, we do not find the answers equally convincing. We are inclined to find one of the answers more plausible than the others.

If the skeptic really finds such equally convincing oppositions everywhere, this requires that she attend only to arguments that are equally strong on both sides of the issue, and manage to forget arguments that do not balance in this way. But why should anybody try to do this? If we aim at truth, we should rather take all arguments on both sides of the issue into account, and these arguments typically do not balance. The only answer seems to be that the skeptic is convinced that she can attain tranquility only by suspending belief, and that suspension of belief requires her to do so. But such a skeptic hardly poses any problems for those who do not believe that this is the way to attain tranquility, and who are still interested in truth.

3. The Ten Modes

In order to induce global suspension of judgment, the Pyrrhonists have general modes—strategies or arguments—that can be used in any topic. However, these modes do not save the psychological interpretation. A closer look at these modes, especially the ten modes of Aenesidemus and the five modes of Agrippa, shows that they do not work if "equipollent dispute" is understood psychologically. I will argue that they finally reveal a genuine and serious skeptical problematic that cannot be as easily wiped out as the versions considered so far.

The ten modes of Aenesidemus share the following common structure:

1. x appears F relative to a.
2. x appears F^* relative to b.
3. x cannot be both F and F^* (F and F^* being incompatible properties).
4. We cannot decide whether x really is F or x really is F^*.
5. We must suspend judgment about the real nature of x.

Sextus spends most of the time giving examples of 1 and 2, thus establishing that things appear differently to different animals, to different people, in different sense organs, in different perceptual circumstances, and so on. Then, in very much the same way, he proceeds to show that we cannot decide between the conflicting appearances and concludes that we must suspend judgment.[17]

I have intentionally formulated the "conclusion" in an ambiguous way. Are we to understand the word "must" in a psychological and causal way, or are we to understand it as a normative "must" or "should"? Sextus's text seems to be ambiguous on this point.

The psychological interpretation favors the former reading. It assumes that my considering the conflicting appearances and being unable to favor one over the others causes me to suspend judgment about the nature of reality. So the ten modes are not exactly arguments. Rather, they are general strategies that are supposed to help find conflicting appearances or equipollent disputes and to induce suspension of judgment causally.

If we look at the details, however, we see that the modes cannot work in this way. What is supposed to cause suspension of judgment, according to this view, is the fact that I find the alternatives that x is F and that x is F^* equally convincing. The problem is that the conflicting appearances that Sextus considers are not equally convincing in this way. The first mode appeals to the fact that things appear differently to animals of different species. Of course, I am not aware of how things appear to cows or dogs, for example, so I cannot compare my appearances with their appearances and find both equally convincing. Surely I find my own appearances more convincing than those I am not even aware of. After all, it is only those appearances that I am aware of that causally affect my beliefs.

Sextus is also quite aware that the dogmatists do not find the appearances of other animals and human beings as convincing as their own. He does not deny this psychological fact. His point is rather that when they prefer their own appearances to those of other animals and human beings, they make a mistake. There is something wrong with doing so:

> For we shall not be able ourselves to decide between our own appearances and those of other animals, being ourselves a part of the dispute and for that reason more in need of someone to decide than ourselves able to judge.[18]

> When the self-satisfied Dogmatists say that they themselves should be preferred to other humans in judging things, we know that their claim is absurd. For they are themselves a part of the dispute, and if it is by preferring themselves that they judge what is apparent, then by entrusting the judging to themselves they are taking for granted the matter being investigated before beginning the judging.[19]

Here Sextus clearly thinks that the mistake of the dogmatists is a dialectical one. When dogmatists judge that their own appearances are true while those of other animals and other people are false, they simply assume what they are supposed to prove. They beg the question against their opponents' conflicting judgments. So our inability to decide between conflicting appearances is not a psychological matter but an inability to do so without violating the rules of dialectic. It is an inability to resolve disagreements without begging the question at issue.

This shows that the conclusions in the ten modes are, after all, normative. We should suspend judgment because we cannot decide between conflicting appearances without begging the question. The equipollence of oppositions is thus not a matter of equal convincingness. It is a matter of neither participant in the dispute having dialectically effective reasons for her own position. Neither can defend herself against the other without begging the question. Sextus suggests that we should suspend judgment in this sort of situation.

4. THE MODES OF AGRIPPA

The considerations that Sextus relies on in supporting (4) are systematized in the five modes of Agrippa. We can see that the dialectical interpretation also fits very well with how they work. According to Sextus, every object of investigation can be brought under the following five modes:

> According to the mode deriving from dispute, we find that undecidable dissension about the matter proposed has come about both in ordinary life and among philosophers. Because of this we are not able either to choose or to rule out anything, and we end up with suspension of judgement. In the mode deriving from infinite regress, we say that what is brought forward as a source of conviction for the matter proposed itself needs another such source, which itself needs another, and so on *ad infinitum*, so that we have no point from which to begin to establish anything, and suspension of judgement follows. In the mode deriving from relativity, as we said above, the existing object appears to be such-and-such relative to the subject judging and to the things observed together with it, but we suspend judgement on what it is like in its nature. We have the mode from hypothesis when the Dogmatists, being thrown back *ad infinitum*, begin from something which they do not establish but claim to assume simply and without proof in virtue of a concession. The reciprocal mode occurs when what ought to be confirmatory of the object under investigation needs to be made convincing by the object under investigation; then being unable to take either in order to establish the other, we suspend judgement about both.[20]

Sextus describes here five modes that are supposed to induce suspension of judgment about any object of inquiry. We may call them the modes of (1) disagreement, (2) infinite regress, (3) relativity, (4) hypothesis, and (5) circularity. It is not clear how they are to be understood. Usually they are thought to work together: the modes of disagreement and relativity challenge us to justify our beliefs by revealing that there are competing claims about the matter, and then the rest of the modes show that the process of justification cannot be completed in a satisfactory way. All attempts to justify a belief lead either to an infinite regress, an arbitrary assumption, or circularity. Often the challenging modes are seen to be unnecessary because the skeptic is thought to assume implicitly that our concept of justification requires noncircular and nonarbitrary reasons. So the three modes of infinite regress, hypothesis, and circularity—the so-called Agrippa's trilemma—alone form the problem that can be identified with the regress argument against the possibility of justified beliefs.[21]

I have argued that this interpretation of Agrippa's problem does not make it a serious skeptical challenge to our beliefs. It also misses the dialectical nature of the problem. According to the dialectical interpretation, it is the mode of disagreement that is the central one, and the others are subordinate to it. Its structure is very much the same as in the ten modes, and we may regard it as a generalization of them. Suppose we have a question to which there are just two possible answers, p and $\sim p$. Then the mode of disagreement works as follows:

1. S_1 believes that p.
2. S_2 believes that $\sim p$.
3. At most one of them is right.
4. The disagreement between S_1 and S_2 is irresolvable.
5. We should suspend judgment about p.

So the mode of disagreement alone is supposed to induce suspension of judgment. The other modes are used if the dogmatist wants to deny 4, that the disagreement is irresolvable. He is then asked how the disagreement is to be resolved. If he gives a reason r for his belief that p, it is pointed out that there is also an irresolvable disagreement about r. If he admits this, he also admits the irresolvability of the original disagreement. If he denies it, he is asked how the disagreement about r is resolved, and so on. By repeating the mode of disagreement, the dogmatist is led into Agrippa's trilemma. Modes 2, 4, and 5 cannot resolve the disagreement: modes 4 and 5 are clearly question begging, and nobody can complete an infinite chain of reason required by mode 2.[22]

The dogmatist may also try to appeal to a criterion of truth, but he is told that there is an irresolvable disagreement about it. If he tries to resolve this disagreement by appealing to a new criterion of truth, he is led into a regress. If he appeals to the same criterion again, he is in a circle. And if he just assumes a criterion, the mode of hypothesis applies to him.[23]

Sextus clearly assumes that in order to avoid skepticism, the dogmatist must be able to resolve all disagreements there are or could be about the object of inquiry and the reasons he appeals to. This requirement may seem too strong. We will see, however, that it arises from presuppositions that are quite plausible.

5. THE DIALECTICAL PROBLEM

The Pyrrhonian problematic is, after all, composed of an argument. We saw that suspension of judgment cannot be based on equal convincingness of contradictory propositions. So it must be based on an argument for the normative conclusion that we should suspend judgment. Notice that this conclusion is not based on epistemic premises and the lemma that justified belief is impossible. It is based on our inability to resolve disagreements without begging the question and the normative principle that we should suspend judgment in such conditions. So the argument does not presuppose any epistemology, and therefore it cannot be opposed by rejecting that epistemology.

How plausible is the normative principle? In order to answer this question, we must keep in mind that the argument is meant to be an ad hominem argument, the targets of which are inquirers seeking truth. As Sextus tells us, the skeptics were originally talented people who were seeking truth and were puzzled about the disagreements they found. Disagreement would hardly be a problem unless we were interested in truth. So we can assume that the target audience of the argument is truth-seekers. And it includes the skeptics themselves—at least before they became skeptics.

So how plausible is the requirement that inquirers should avoid begging the question under inquiry? It is very plausible indeed. We can see this by considering two sorts of cases in which disagreements arise. The principle says essentially that inquirers should treat them similarly, and this accords very well with our intuitions about the cases:

1. The inquirer is an impartial observer who is attending to a dispute between two persons. The dispute ends in a tie. Neither can convince the other because their arguments beg the question. The inquirer does not have her own opinion about the matter under dispute and does not have independent grounds regarding either side. So she has no choice but to suspend judgment about the matter.

2. The situation is similar, except now the inquirer is herself one participant in the dispute. Being a participant, she naturally has her own beliefs about the matter. Otherwise, there would be no dispute. Once again, she realizes that the dispute ends in a tie. Neither position can be defended without begging the question. What should she do in this situation? It seems that she should give up her beliefs about the matter under dispute.

It is clear that the inquirer should suspend judgment in the first case: she has no ground for choosing one rather than the other of the opposed views. But why should the outcome be different in the second case? The only relevant difference is that the inquirer is in this case a participant in the dispute. If she were to prefer her own view in this case, she would seem to choose it simply because it is her own. But how could she then hope to find the truth? It is quite accidental which party in the dispute she happens to be.[24]

The two cases are thus in all normatively relevant respects similar. It does not make a normative difference that the inquirer is herself a participant in the dispute. If she should suspend judgment in one case, she should do the same in the other. The implicit normative assumption is that it is wrong to beg the question, so one should not prefer one's own position simply on the ground that it is one's own.

One should look for impartial grounds for one's beliefs. This, at least, is what the skeptic's dialectical norm suggests, and it does have considerable intuitive force.

In brief, the problem is that there are equally good arguments for both sides of the dispute. They may not be equally good from the perspectives of the participants, who both take the argument of the other party to be unsound. But they are equally good from the point of view of the impartial observer, who sees how both arguments beg the question against each other. For her, the choice between the two sides would be completely arbitrary. The intuition is that the sincere truth-seeker should view the dispute from this impartial point of view and suspend judgment.

6. Appearance and Reality

The dialectical argument also relies on a general distinction between appearance and reality. In early modern philosophy, the distinction is typically made ontologically, between mental objects—ideas or sense data—and physical objects in the external world. But this is not the distinction that is present in the ancient skeptical problematic. The ancient distinction does not concern just sensory appearances and external objects. It is a topic-neutral distinction that applies to any object of inquiry. About any topic we can ask what appears to be the case and what is in fact the case. For example, an argument may appear valid but not in fact be valid.[25]

I suggest that the distinction is to be understood as a distinction between how things are represented and how they are in themselves. In this way, we get the general distinction that covers both sensory experiences and beliefs. Both represent the world, and the world may differ from the way it is represented. What makes the modes of Aenesidemus and Agrippa such a serious problem is that they apply to both our sensory and our doxastic appearances. We cannot decide which of our appearances are true by appealing to other appearances—be they sensory or doxastic—because the same problem of variability of appearances concerns these appearances.

Though the received view among analytical epistemologists is that skeptical problems depend on dubious epistemological presuppositions, it is also common to think that skepticism presupposes realism. This seems to be true of the Pyrrhonian problem as it is understood here. The distinction between appearance and reality is realistic. It presupposes two moderate forms of realism. As William Alston points out, we must distinguish between alethic realism and metaphysical realism. Alethic realism is a thesis about truth. It says that a belief or a perceptual content is true if and only if the world is the way it is represented by it. Metaphysical realism is the thesis that the world is mind independent, that is, independent of the way it is represented.[26]

In short, alethic realism says that appearances represent reality, and metaphysical realism says that reality is independent of its appearances. Both theses are mere platitudes and were taken to be such during the greater part of the history of Western philosophy. But once we accept both theses, we have a problem: if our only access to reality is through its appearances, and these vary in the way suggested, how can we ever decide which of the appearances are true and which are false?

Of course, if we were allowed to beg the question in favor of some of them, the matter would be easy. But then anybody could defend the truth of any appearance in the same way. The task is to distinguish true appearances from false ones without begging the question, and this seems to be impossible.

If the dialectical interpretation is correct, we have three main options to avoid the skeptical conclusion. (1) We may try to produce non-question-begging reasons for our beliefs and show how disagreements could thus be resolved. (2) We may reject the dialectical principle. (3) Or we may reject either of the realistic theses. Cartesian foundationalism seems to be motivated by the first option. Contemporary internalist and externalist epistemologists typically choose the second one. They take epistemology to be independent of dialectical issues. Relativists take dialectic more seriously. They think that we can avoid skepticism only by rejecting realism. We will see that none of these options should satisfy us. This makes the dialectical problem a more difficult and serious skeptical problem than those given by the other interpretations.

7. CARTESIAN FOUNDATIONALISM

I have formulated the Pyrrhonian problematic without presupposing any epistemological theories—or at least any theories of knowledge or justified belief. This is not to say that such theories could not be offered as a response to the problematic. On the contrary, traditional theories of knowledge and justification seem to be motivated by the attempt to respond to it.

This is how the problematic is connected to knowledge and justification. We just take knowledge to be the state that truth-seeking inquirers want to attain. This is a natural and traditional use of the term. We want to discover the truth, that is, to know the truth. When we now face the Pyrrhonian problematic, the natural intuition is that we cannot know until we can give non-question-begging justification for the truth of our belief. This seems to motivate, for example, Descartes, who writes in his *Rules for the Direction of the Mind*:

> Whenever two persons make opposite judgments about the same thing, it is certain that at least one of them is mistaken, and neither, it seems, has knowledge. For if the reasoning of one of them were certain and evident, he would be able to lay it before the other in such a way as eventually to convince his intellect as well.[27]

So we want to have knowledge, and we believe that we cannot have it if we do not have non-question-begging reasons for the truth of our beliefs. What kind of reasons are these? In the same work, Descartes says that intuition and deduction are the only sources of knowledge. In his later works, he speaks about clear and distinct perception.

What Descartes and other Cartesian foundationalists have in mind is some sort of direct intuitive awareness of certain facts or truths. It seems that without a faculty like this, we cannot have the required reasons. We cannot resolve disagreements by appealing to further beliefs that are themselves under dispute. We must get outside our beliefs directly to the facts that make them true. We can thus ensure the truth of some of our beliefs by direct awareness of their truth-makers. Other beliefs are then inferred from this foundation by deduction or, as empiricists allow, by deduction or induction. Also, the conclusions of these inferential steps must be ensured to be true or highly probable by our intuitive grasp of the inferential relations.

It may seem that this sort of Cartesian foundationalism would be the only fully satisfactory response to the problematic. The required direct awareness of certain facts or truth-makers of our beliefs and necessary inferential relations between beliefs would provide an impartial standpoint from which to judge which beliefs are true without just begging the question. Furthermore, it was supposed that this direct awareness removes all doubt about the existence of those facts and guarantees the truth or probable truth of the beliefs based on it. So anybody who is aware of the relevant facts would have to follow the reasoning and become convinced of the conclusion. Disagreements could therefore be resolved by a careful use of our faculty of intuitive reason.

What directly accessible truths are there? In order to answer this question, Descartes uses the method of doubt. If we could find some completely indubitable propositions, these would be the ones that we can just see to be true. Others, like Berkeley and Russell, use also Sextus's strategy in the ten modes. Their conclusion from the variability of sensory appearances is not that we should suspend judgment. They conclude that in perception we are not aware of physical object at all but only of our own ideas or sense data.[28]

The upshot of both strategies is that there are at most two subjects that we can be directly aware of: the present contents of our own mind and obvious necessary truths, including truths about necessary inferential relations between propositions. This creates the notorious problem of our knowledge about the external world. The relation of our mind to the external world seems to be contingent rather than necessary. So there is no intuitively accessible inferential relation from the mind to the external world. Cartesian foundationalism leads to Cartesian skepticism.

There is a more fundamental worry, and Wilfrid Sellars presents it as a dilemma: either the kind of direct awareness in question is propositional in content, in which case it itself needs justification, or it is nonpropositional, in which case it is unable to provide justification. In neither case can it be used to stop the regress of reasons in a non-question-begging way.[29] There are other worries, but together these two problems form a strong case against Cartesian foundationalism.[30]

I have presented Cartesian foundationalism as a possible response to the Pyrrhonian problematic. Post-Cartesian epistemological theories can be seen as reactions to the failure of the Cartesian program rather than as attempts to resolve the original Pyrrhonian problematic. Theories in the analytical tradition appeal to our ordinary epistemic concepts and practices and argue that Cartesian epistemology has got them wrong. They suggest standards of knowledge and justification that are less stringent and psychologically more realistic but at the same time not strong enough to settle our disputes. This reaction may help us avoid Cartesian skepticism, but, I will argue, it does not give a satisfactory response to the original Pyrrhonian problematic.

8. INTERNALISM

There are two ways of weakening the Cartesian requirements. The first of these keeps the requirements that the reasons or the factors that make our beliefs justified are something we can be directly aware of by introspection or reflection. They are factors that we must be able to appeal to in justifying our beliefs. What this suggestion rejects is the requirement that justification be truth conducive. After all, this is not something we can be directly aware of. There is also an intuition that supports this weakening:

> Imagine that you are deceived by a Cartesian demon that arranges things so that all your experiences, beliefs and other mental states are the same as they are now but the external world is completely different from what you believe. When you now form a perceptual belief based on sense experience and you have no reason to doubt the belief, the intuition is that your belief is justified. The facts that your belief is false and that your experience is not a reliable indication of truth do not affect your being justified in your belief. So external factors, such as truth and reliability, do not affect your being justified in your beliefs.[31]

Let us grant that there is such an internal sense of justification. Justification is a function of factors that are internal to the believing subject. External factors, like truth and reliability, do not affect justification. We may assume simply that these internally accessible factors are the subject's nonfactive mental states.[32] Internalism then makes justification the function of the subject's beliefs and experiences. Externalism takes justification to depend also on factors external to the mind.

What does internalism say about irresolvable disagreements? If we assume that both participants are reflective and careful in attending to their own internal evidence, it seems that they can both be justified in their beliefs, though at most one of them is right. For example, a theist may very well be internally justified in believing that God exists, while an atheist may be equally internally justified in believing that God does not exist. Though neither of them can rationally convince the other, both can still be justified in their beliefs. So contemporary internalism, unlike Cartesian foundationalism, does not require non-question-begging reasons for justified belief. We can justifiably persist in our beliefs irrespective of irresolvable disagreements with others.

Internalism does allow that the evidence that both the theist and the atheist have about their opponent's beliefs and reasons may undermine or defeat their own justification, in which case they are not justified in their beliefs. If this were the case, they should both give up their beliefs, and the skeptic would win.[33] However, assuming that both are sophisticated enough, they may also have as part of their evidence a theory that explains why the other party is wrong and why its evidence is misleading. In this case, they both can sustain their justification for their beliefs. But would not the skeptic win in this case too? If the conflicting beliefs of the theist and the atheist really are equally justified, it is arbitrary to favor one over the other. They should rather both give up their beliefs.

An internalist may point out that this is not the way things appear from the participant's subjective point of view, and it is this that determines internal justification. It may be that from each participant's point of view, the other participant is not justified in his or her belief. They may both be justified in believing that the other party has made a mistake, has a blind spot, or has in some other way evaluated the evidence incorrectly.[34] So both participants in a dispute not only may have justified beliefs but also may be justified in believing that the other participant's belief is not justified. In this case, neither of them has any reason for suspending belief.

Though the participants in a dispute could not recognize the equal justification of their conflicting beliefs, an impartial observer who is aware of the relevant internal facts could surely do that. From her point of view, their beliefs are epistemically on a par, and it would be impossible for her to say who is right and who is wrong. So at least she would have to suspend judgment, having no independent reasons for either side. The skeptic's point is that it is this impartial point of view that a sincere inquirer or truth-seeker should take.

An internalist may insist that we should stick to our own subjective point of view and decide what to believe from that.[35] But can I really stick to my subjective point of view once I have realized that from the objective and impartial point of view, my opponent and I are equally justified in our beliefs? I have realized that things appear differently from different points of view, and that there is no impartial way of choosing between them. Can I now go back to my own subjective point of view and be happy with how things appear from that point of view? Surely, I cannot if I am seriously interested in truth. As a truth-seeker, I should rather conclude that internal justification is not what I want.

9. EXTERNALISM

The second way of weakening the Cartesian program retains the truth-conducivity of justification but rejects the awareness requirement. It is enough for justification that the sources of belief are reliable. The subject need not know or be aware of what those sources are and whether they are reliable. According to a typical form of externalism, reliabilism, justification is a function of the reliable causal origin of belief. So justification and knowledge do not require non-question-begging reasons. Indeed, they do not require reasons at all. They require that the belief be caused in a reliable way.

Reliabilism would be an easy answer to the first version of the Pyrrhonian problematic. The regress of reasons terminates in beliefs that have some other reliable source than reasoning. Of course, it is possible for finite beings to have such beliefs. So reliabilism easily explains how it is possible for us to have justified beliefs. But what is in question in the dialectical version is not merely the possibility of justified belief and knowledge. The problem is to decide who in fact knows or is justified in his or her beliefs. So even if we were to grant that reliabilism is the right answer to the possibility question, we do not yet have an answer to the actuality question.

Let us assume that we want to have knowledge, and that we understand knowledge as a true belief that has a reliable source. According to Sextus, our situation is similar to that of the people in the following simile:

> Let us imagine that some people are looking for gold in a dark room full of treasures. It will happen that each will grasp one of the things lying in the room and think that he has got hold of the gold. But none of them will be persuaded that he has hit upon the gold even if he *has* in fact hit upon it. In the same way, the crowd of philosophers has come into the world, as in a vast house, in search of truth. But it is reasonable that the man who grasps the truth should doubt whether he has been successful.[36]

Let us assume that those people in the dark room who have hit upon the gold have not done so accidentally. They happen to have some reliable way of detecting pieces of gold. They thus resemble inquirers or truth-seekers who have arrived at a true belief in a reliable way. So, according to Sextus, even people who have in fact hit upon the gold or come to know the truth—in the reliabilist sense—should doubt whether they have done so.

Why should inquirers doubt their knowledge? They should do so because none of them has any non-question-begging way of deciding which of them really know and which of them do not. None of them is able to produce a non-question-begging argument for the truth of his or her own beliefs or the reliability of his or her own sources of belief. Because there are disagreements both about the truth of beliefs and the reliability of the sources of belief, they cannot argue from the truth of some particular beliefs to the reliability of their sources or the other way around without begging the question. There is no impartial way of saying who is right and who is wrong. So everybody is left in the dark about his or her really knowing anything.

Reliabilists typically point out that there is nothing in reliabilism that prevents one from attaining knowledge about reliability and thus knowing that one knows. If our sources of belief really are reliable, we can use these sources to attain knowledge about their own reliability. Though this is surely possible if reliabilism is true, it does not help with the present problem, which concerns the actuality of knowledge rather than its possibility. Arguing for the reliability of a source from premises based on the very same source begs the question at issue: because the premises are based on the source in question, we cannot be justified in accepting them unless the source really is reliable. When we thus use the argument to justify the conclusion, we assume implicitly that the conclusion is true. This begs the question concerning the reliability of the source.[37]

A reliabilist might think that some questions simply need to be begged, and that the reliability of one's sources of belief is such a question. But if it were permissible to beg this question, then it would be very easy to defend almost any source of belief. Religious people could defend the reliability of religious experience by arguing from premises based on religious experience. Crystal-ball gazers could defend the reliability of the crystal ball by arguing from premises based on the crystal ball. Any intelligent madman could offer his favorite source and defend its reliability in the same way. Indeed, people would not even need to do this. They could simply assert without argument that the source in question is reliable.

If he is really aiming at truth, the reliabilist should not be willing to beg the question concerning reliability. He should suspend judgment about the scope of his knowledge and the reliability of his sources of belief. He, like anybody else, is in the dark and has no impartial grounds for preferring some particular set of sources to others.

10.   RELATIVISM AND ANTIREALISM

It seems that there is no satisfactory epistemological resolution of the Pyrrhonian problematic. Perhaps we should rather focus on its realistic presuppositions. A radical Protagorean relativist avoids the problem by denying that there are genuine disagreements about reality. If I believe that p and you believe that $\sim p$, we are both right because p is true for me and $\sim p$ is true for you. There is no disagreement between us. Indeed, there can be no disagreements because every belief or appearance is true. If truth is relative in this way, everybody can retain his or her beliefs without begging the question against others.

The traditional objection is that relativism is self-referentially incoherent: when the relativist says that relativism is true, she may mean that relativism is absolutely true or that relativism is relatively true. In the former case, she contradicts her own view that truth is relative. In the latter case, she acknowledges that relativism is true only for the relativist. It is not true for the absolutist. This is dialectically inefficient. She cannot argue the absolutist out of his position.

If we take relativism to be a response to the Pyrrhonian problem, the objection is misdirected. The problem is composed of an ad hominem argument against the absolutist. Because the absolutist accepts the premises of this argument, he cannot avoid the conclusion that he should suspend belief. If, in spite of this, he continues to hold to his beliefs, it is his position that is incoherent. The relativist avoids the skeptical conclusion and the possible incoherence that it produces by denying the premise that there are genuine disagreements. There is no reason for her to suspend belief.[38]

However, because it denies the possibility of error and disagreement, Protagorean relativism is extremely implausible. A more plausible form of alethic relativism—relativism about truth—relativizes truth to something other than singular persons, such as social groups or cultures. If truth is relative to something that can be shared by different persons, error and disagreement are possible for them. This shared background also provides the neutral basis for resolving their disagreements. When the background is not shared, there can be no genuine disagreements. So alethic relativism gives some hope for resolving the Pyrrhonian problematic.

Alethic relativism denies alethic realism that many philosophers take to be a mere truism. According to alethic realism, it is an obvious necessary truth that a proposition that p is true if and only if p. It follows from this that one and the same proposition cannot be true for some people and false for others. So the truth-value of a proposition cannot vary in the way that alethic relativism suggests. For these philosophers, this is a sufficient reason for rejecting alethic relativism.[39]

Another form of relativism denies metaphysical realism rather than alethic realism. Instead of truth, it relativizes facts or reality. According to metaphysical relativism, there are no facts simpliciter or absolute facts. There are facts only relative to conceptual scheme, culture, or some other parameter. So beliefs that appear to ascribe incompatible properties to the same object may all be made true by different relative facts. Metaphysical relativism explains how people who appear to disagree about the same absolute fact can all be right by interpreting their beliefs as being about different relative facts.

Though alethic relativism and metaphysical relativism promise to resolve the Pyrrhonian problematic, both are problematic if they are taken to be global in scope. The problem of global relativism is not self-referential incoherence or dialectical indefensibility but vicious regress. In the case of metaphysical relativism, we get the regress as follows. Assuming that a is an object, F is a property and $P_1, \ldots, P_\infty$ is a sequence of parameters, metaphysical relativism says that there are no facts of the form:

1. a is F.

There are only facts of the form:

2. *a* is *F* relative to P_1.

We can now ask whether this relational fact is itself an absolute fact or a relative fact. If it is an absolute fact, global metaphysical relativism is false. But if it is a relative fact, we get a more complex relational fact:

3. The fact that *a* is *F* relative to P_1 is relative to P_2.

If this is also a relative fact, there must be a more complex relational fact, and so on ad infinitum. Thus global metaphysical relativism entails the absurd view that all facts are infinitely long.[40] Clearly, global alethic relativism entails a similar regress.[41]

We can avoid the problem by restricting the scope of relativism to some particular subject matter, such as aesthetic, moral, or epistemic truths or facts. For example, epistemic relativism says that there are no absolute epistemic facts. There are no epistemic facts of the form: *S* is justified in believing that *p*. There are only facts of the form: *S* is justified in believing that *p* relative to the system of epistemic rules that ascriber *A* accepts. This relational fact is not really an epistemic fact. It is a mental fact about *S*'s and *A*'s beliefs. And because this is an absolute fact, there is no regress. So epistemic relativism avoids the regress by allowing absolute nonepistemic facts to make epistemic judgments true.

There is a current debate about the coherence of even this sort of local relativism. Paul Boghossian argues that it cannot be coherently formulated, but there are others who disagree.[42] We need not resolve this disagreement here. It is enough to note that these forms of local relativism can, at most, resolve disagreements about those subject matters that they are restricted to. As we have seen, the Pyrrhonian problem is general: it concerns any object of inquiry. So the local forms of relativism cannot resolve it.

It may be objected that there is a sense in which epistemic relativism is quite general: about any disagreement, we can ask what the participants are justified in believing. Epistemic relativism allows that each participant can be justified in his or her belief even if he or she cannot rationally convince the other participants. Each can be justified relative to different epistemic rules. So epistemic relativism explains how people can justifiably or rationally disagree and persist in their beliefs even though they cannot rationally resolve their disagreements. Does this resolve the Pyrrhonian problematic?

We saw earlier that the Pyrrhonian problematic presupposes that we take an impartial point of view toward our disagreements. The problem is that, from this point of view, we cannot rationally decide who is right and who is wrong and we are forced to suspend belief. The relativist comes to our rescue by pointing out that the disputing parties can all be right relative to different parameters. So the problem of deciding between them disappears. However, the epistemic relativist cannot say this. She can say at most that when the participants take themselves to be justified in their beliefs, they are right relative to their respective epistemic rules.

This does not help us, the impartial observers, to say who is right in the original disagreement about the absolute facts.

Relativism is thus unable to resolve the Pyrrhonian problematic. Global relativism has absurd consequences, and local forms of relativism—assuming that they can be coherently formulated—can at most handle some disagreements. Disagreements about most matters we care about are left unresolved.

11. The Skeptical Moral

I have discussed three interpretations of the ancient Pyrrhonian problematic and have argued that only the last one, the dialectical interpretation, provides a serious skeptical challenge to our beliefs. There seems to be no satisfactory nonskeptical response to it. Should we thus accept the skeptical conclusion and stop believing anything? This is what the Pyrrhonists are traditionally thought to suggest. The traditional objection, made by Hume, is that it is impossible to live without beliefs. On the one hand, action requires beliefs: without beliefs, we would be like vegetables that need someone else to take care of their needs. On the other hand, we cannot just give up our beliefs. This is psychologically impossible. Belief is simply not under our voluntary control.[43]

Hume seems to be right. We cannot live without beliefs. But this does not get us off the hook. Remember that the skeptic gives us an ad hominem argument. It is we who are committed to the conclusion, and it is our problem if we cannot follow its recommendation. Nevertheless, Sextus thinks that it is possible to be a skeptic. The skeptic lives by appearances, he says. So we still need to consider whether there could be a plausible skeptical resolution of the problematic.

The received view is that the Pyrrhonian skeptic really intends to live without beliefs by relying on appearances understood in some nondoxastic way. Whether there is such a sense of "appearance" and whether it helps us respond to Hume's challenge is controversial.[44] We need not, however, go into this debate because the dialectical interpretation of the problematic does not support this view of skepticism. It is rather the epistemological and psychological interpretations that do so, but these do not make it a serious challenge to our beliefs.

The moral of the first, theoretical, interpretation is clear. If there can be no justified beliefs, the suspension of belief should be global. But this demand only concerns the infinitist. If we are not infinitists, there is no moral for us. We can keep all our beliefs. The same is true of the skeptics who do not accept the infinitist dogma.

Also, the psychological interpretation suggests that the skeptic lives without beliefs. If the reasons for and against a proposition are equally strong psychologically, then we are forced to suspend belief in it. The objection was that it is extremely difficult to maintain such a balance in most cases. Furthermore, the attempt to do so seems to be unmotivated. In any case, the scope of skepticism would in fact be very restricted under this interpretation. Surely, at least our commonsense beliefs are safe from doubt in this psychological sense.

According to the dialectical interpretation, the proper scope of Pyrrhonian skepticism is things we have disagreements about. Since we do not disagree about appearances, they fall outside this scope. So the skeptic may very well retain her beliefs about the world insofar as she does not take those beliefs to be true. This is something that is disputed, not the fact that she has beliefs or that things appear to her in some way.

So one possible skeptical moral deriving from the dialectical interpretation is that we should suspend judgment about the truth of our beliefs. The scope of suspension of judgment is restricted to the higher level propositions about the truth of lower level propositions. When the skeptic thus asserts something, she just expresses the proposition that she believes something. She does not suggest that the belief is true or that she knows anything. Because she does not want to beg any questions, her utterances can be understood as including an implicit indexical element, "It appears to me that," and expressing her current belief about the matter. In this way, she avoids contradicting others who may have conflicting beliefs about the same matter.

There is tension or instability in this sort of skepticism. Because of the obvious necessary truth "it is true that p if and only if p," it may be hard to believe that p without also believing that it is true that p, provided that it is even logically possible. Some commentators suggest that instead of restricting the scope of doubt, the skeptic distinguishes between two kinds of assent or propositional attitudes.[45] Let us call them belief and acceptance. Belief is a passive state produced in us by various causal processes and is not under our direct voluntary control. Acceptance is a voluntary act of judging something to be true, and it needs to be based on reasons. When the skeptic thus suspends judgment, she refrains from accepting anything as true. At the same time, she goes on forming beliefs involuntarily. Yet this may not avoid all instability: The skeptic believes involuntarily that p and that it is true that p, but she also believes involuntarily that there are others who disagree with her and that she has no impartial reasons for accepting her own belief that p to be true. Why should these latter beliefs have no causal effect on the former beliefs?

So there seems to be no satisfactory response to the dialectical version of the Pyrrhonian problematic. Perhaps this is just an initial appearance, and we can work out such a response. It is more probable, however, that philosophers will continue debating the matter without reaching a consensus.[46]

NOTES

1. See Richard Popkin, *The History of Scepticism from Erasmus to Spinoza* (Berkeley: University of California Press, 1979); Charles Schmitt, "The Rediscovery of Ancient

Skepticism in Modern Times," in *The Skeptical Tradition*, ed. M. F. Burnyeat (Berkeley: University of California Press, 1983).

2. See, for example, John Greco, *Putting Skeptics in Their Place* (Cambridge: Cambridge University Press, 2000).

3. See, for example, Michael Frede, "The Sceptic's Two Kinds of Assent and the Question of the Possibility of Knowledge," in *The Original Sceptics: A Controversy*, ed. M. Burnyeat and M. Frede (Indianapolis: Hackett, 1997), 127–131; Julia Annas and Jonathan Barnes, *The Modes of Scepticism* (Cambridge: Cambridge University Press, 1985), 45.

4. See, for example, Stewart Cohen, "How to Be a Fallibilist," *Philosophical Perspectives* 2 (1988): 93–94.

5. Sextus Empiricus, *Against the Logicians*, trans. R. G. Bury (Cambridge, Mass.: Harvard University Press, 1935), 487–489 (M VIII, 480–481).

6. Michael Williams, *Problems of Knowledge* (Oxford: Oxford University Press, 2001), 66.

7. Michael Williams, "Skepticism," in *The Blackwell Guide to Epistemology*, ed. J. Greco and E. Sosa (Oxford: Blackwell, 1999), 35–36.

8. Because holistic coherentism rejects the idea that justification depends on a linear chain of reasons, we may classify it as a special case of foundationalism that takes all justified beliefs to be basic beliefs.

9. Peter Klein, "Human Knowledge and the Infinite Regress of Reasons," *Philosophical Perspectives* 13 (1999): 297–325.

10. Williams, "Skepticism," 39.

11. Peter Klein, "The Failures of Dogmatism and a New Pyrrhonism," *Acta Analytica* 15 (2000): 14–17; Klein, "Human Knowledge and the Infinite Regress of Reasons," 312–316.

12. Sextus Empiricus, *Outlines of Scepticism*, ed. J. Annas and J. Barnes (Cambridge: Cambridge University Press, 2000), 3 (PH I, 1–4).

13. Ibid., 10 (I, 26).

14. Ibid., 4 (I, 8).

15. Ibid., 5 (I, 10).

16. Michael Williams, "Skepticism without Theory," *Review of Metaphysics* 41 (1988): 554–555.

17. Sextus Empiricus, *Outlines of Scepticism*, 11–40 (PH I, 35–163). For commentary, see Annas and Barnes, *Modes of Scepticism*; R. J. Hankinson, *The Sceptics* (London: Routledge, 1995), chap. 9.

18. Sextus Empiricus, *Outlines of Scepticism*, 17 (I, 59).

19. Ibid., 25 (I, 90).

20. Ibid., 40–41 (I, 165–169).

21. This is the standard way of understanding the modes of Agrippa among analytical epistemologists. See, for example, Robert Fogelin, *Pyrrhonian Reflections on Knowledge and Justification* (Oxford: Oxford University Press, 1994), pt. 2; Greco, *Putting Skeptics in Their Place*, chap. 5; Ernest Sosa, "How to Resolve the Pyrrhonian Problematic: A Lesson from Descartes," *Philosophical Studies* 85 (1997): 229–249; Williams, "Skepticism"; Williams, *Problems of Knowledge*, chap. 5.

22. One mystery of Agrippa's problem is the mode of relativity. It also appears as one of the ten modes, and Sextus says that it is the most general of them. One possibility is that it just spells out the conclusion of the mode of disagreement: We can say how things appear to the participants in the dispute, but we cannot say how they are in themselves. The object of dispute is not how things appear. It is how they are in their real nature. The other interpretation is that Sextus confuses skepticism and relativism. Richard Bett argues that Aenesidemus was really a relativist. If Sextus took Aenesidemus to be a skeptic, the

relativistic phrases may have been left in the text by mistake. See Bett, "What Does Pyrrhonism Have to Do with Pyrrho?" in *Ancient Scepticism and the Sceptical Tradition*, ed. J. Sihvola (Helsinki: Acta Philosophica Fennica, 2000).In any case, relativism is a possible response to Agrippa's problem. It denies 3. See section 10.

23. Sextus Empiricus, *Outlines of Scepticism*, 72 (II, 20).

24. Gary Gutting argues in a similar way in his *Religious Belief and Religious Skepticism* (Notre Dame, Ind.: University of Notre Dame Press, 1982), 83–87. However, he thinks that we get the skeptical conclusion only if the disputing parties are epistemic peers—that is, equals in intelligence, perspicacity, honesty, thoroughness, and other relevant epistemic virtues. Thomas Kelly argues that we should further restrict the set of peers: only people sharing the same evidence count. See his "Epistemic Significance of Disagreement," *Oxford Studies in Epistemology* 1 (2005): 173–175. The skeptic seems to be more liberal. She counts even animals of nonhuman species as our peers. Though animals cannot defend themselves by arguments, we understand that the truth of their appearances can be defended as effectively as our own human appearances. So what is crucial is not equal epistemic virtue or evidence but the fact that both sides can be equally well defended—that they are dialectically on a par.

25. Myles Burnyeat, "Can the Sceptic Live His Skepticism?" in Burnyeat and Frede, *The Original Sceptics*, 37–41; Benson Mates, *The Skeptic Way: Sextus Empiricus's Outlines of Pyrrhonism* (Oxford: Oxford University Press, 1996), 6.

26. William Alston, *A Realistic Conception of Truth* (Ithaca, N.Y.: Cornell University Press, 1996).

27. *The Philosophical Writings of Descartes*, vol. 1, ed. J. Cottingham, R. Stoothoff, and D. Murdoch (Cambridge: Cambridge University Press, 1985), 11.

28. Kenneth Winkler, "Berkeley, Pyrrhonism, and the *Theaetetus*," in *Pyrrhonian Skepticism*, ed. W. Sinnott-Armstrong (Oxford: Oxford University Press, 2004), 48–54; Bertrand Russell, *The Problems of Philosophy* (Oxford: Oxford University Press, 1967), chap. 1.

29. Wilfrid Sellars, "Empiricism and the Philosophy of Mind," in *Science, Perception and Reality* (London: Routledge, 1963), 128–129. For a more accessible formulation, see Laurence BonJour, *The Structure of Empirical Knowledge* (Cambridge, Mass.: Harvard University Press, 1985), 69.

30. There have been attempts to rehabilitate Cartesian foundationalism, especially by Laurence BonJour and Richard Fumerton. See M. DePaul, ed., *Resurrecting Old-Fashioned Foundationalism* (Lanham, Md.: Rowman & Littlefield, 2001).

31. See Keith Lehrer and Stewart Cohen, "Justification, Truth, and Coherence," *Synthese* 55 (1983): 191–192; Richard Foley, "What's Wrong with Reliabilism?" *Monist* 68 (1985): 192–193.

32. "Perceiving that" is a factive propositional attitude because perceiving that *p* entails that *p*. Nonfactive mental states do not entail the truth of their content and thus anything about the external world.

33. Richard Feldman draws this conclusion from disagreements between epistemic peers who have shared their evidence. See his "Epistemological Puzzles about Disagreement," in *Epistemology Futures*, ed. S. Hetherington (Oxford: Oxford University Press, 2006), 216–236.

34. See Alvin Plantinga, "Pluralism: A Defense of Religious Exclusivism," in *The Philosophical Challenge of Religious Exclusivism*, ed. P. L. Quinn and K. Meeker (Oxford: Oxford University Press, 2000), 184.

35. See Kelly, "Epistemic Significance of Disagreement," 179, and Richard Foley, *Intellectual Trust in Oneself and Others* (Cambridge: Cambridge University Press, 2001), 79.

36. Sextus Empiricus: *Against the Logicians*, 27 (M VII, 52). The translation is from Jonathan Barnes, *Toils of Scepticism* (Cambridge: Cambridge University Press, 1990), 138–139.

37. William Alston calls arguments of this sort epistemically circular in *The Reliability of Sense Perception* (Ithaca, N.Y.: Cornell University Press, 1993), 15–17. For a more detailed discussion of the reliabilist responses, see Markus Lammenranta, "Reliabilism, Circularity, and the Pyrrhonian Problematic," *Journal of Philosophical Research* 28 (2003): 315–332.

38. Because the relativist therefore has no need to defend relativism for the absolutist, she may very well concede that relativism is only relatively true.

39. Alston, *Realistic Conception of Truth*, 180.

40. See Paul Boghossian, *Fear of Knowledge: Against Relativism and Constructivism* (Oxford: Clarendon Press, 2006), 54–57.

41. See Frederick F. Schmitt, *Truth: A Primer* (Boulder, CO: Westview Press, 1995), 68–71.

42. Boghossian, *Fear of Knowledge*, chap. 6. The coherence of epistemic relativism is defended by Ram Neta in "In Defense of Epistemic Relativism," *Episteme* 4 (2007): 30–48; and by Gideon Rosen in "The Case against Epistemic Relativism: Reflections on Chapter 6 of *Fear of Knowledge*," *Episteme* 4 (2007): 10–29. See also Boghossian's response in "The Case against Epistemic Relativism: Replies to Rosen and Neta," *Episteme* 4 (2007): 49–65.

43. David Hume, *Inquiries Concerning Human Understanding and Concerning the Principles of Morals*, ed. L. A. Selby-Bigge, rev. P. H. Nidditch (Oxford: Oxford University Press, 1975), 160.

44. See Burnyeat, "Can the Sceptic Live His Scepticism?" and Bredo Johnsen, "On the Coherence of Pyrrhonian Skepticism," *Philosophical Review* 110 (2001): 521–561.

45. Frede, "Sceptic's Two Kinds of Assent"; Gisela Striker, "Historical Reflections on Classical Pyrrhonism and Neo-Pyrrhonism," in Sinnott-Armstrong, *Pyrrhonian Skepticism*, 17.

46. I wish to thank Robert Audi, Mario De Caro, John Greco, Raul Hakli, Timo Kajamies, Marja-Liisa Kakkuri-Knuuttila, Kirk Ludwig, Marie McGinn, Alan Millar, Sami Pihlström, Duncan Pritchard, Walter Sinnott-Armstrong, Ernest Sosa, Emidio Spinelli, Leopold Stubenberg, and Timothy Williamson for helpful comments or discussion, as well as audiences at the University of Helsinki, the University of Rome "La Sapienza," the University of Notre Dame, the University of Tartu, and the University of Stirling.

CHAPTER 2

THE PROBLEM OF
THE CRITERION

RICHARD FUMERTON

THE problem of the criterion in epistemology raises certain fundamental questions concerning the methods a philosopher ought to use in arriving at both analyses of epistemic concepts and conclusions concerning legitimate principles of reasoning and justification. The answers one gives to these questions are thought to bear directly on the challenge of skepticism. The outcome of battles is often determined by the ground occupied by opposing forces. Interest in the problem of the criterion is often a function of the desire to occupy favorable ground in the battle with the skeptic.

Despite the title of this chapter, there are, I believe, at least two different problems one might associate with "the criterion." One is perhaps best known through the work of Roderick Chisholm, whose various editions of *Theory of Knowledge* all devote a chapter to it. As Chisholm develops the problem, it concerns methodological questions concerning how to identify *sources* of knowledge or justified belief. But there is a closely related question concerning how to identify necessary and sufficient conditions for the application of epistemic *concepts* like knowledge and justified belief. In the following discussion, I shall distinguish these two methodological issues. I begin by looking at the question of how one should go about discovering the correct analysis of epistemic concepts.

1. METAEPISTEMOLOGY AND THE PROBLEM OF THE CRITERION

Metaepistemological questions seek to uncover through philosophical analysis the nature of fundamental epistemic concepts or properties. In metaepistemology, we are interested in getting an account of what knowledge, evidence, and justified belief are. To be sure, philosophers do not agree with each other about exactly what is involved in coming up with a correct philosophical analysis. Many analytic philosophers in the first part of the twentieth century thought that their task was to discover *analytically* necessary and sufficient conditions for the application of concepts. So if we were concerned with analyzing knowledge, our task was to discover some set of conditions, each of which is analytically necessary for knowledge and all of which together are analytically sufficient for knowledge. The classic test for whether a condition for knowledge, say, the truth of what is believed, is analytically necessary is whether it is absolutely *inconceivable* that someone has knowledge while failing to satisfy the condition. The test for whether a conjunction of conditions X is jointly sufficient for knowledge is whether we can conceive of X obtaining without knowledge.[1]

Even philosophers who are more or less committed to the central role of thought experiments in testing proposed analyses disagree with each other profoundly over exactly what the *object* of an analysis is. Some think that they are analyzing the meanings of words or sentences, some think that they are analyzing concepts or thoughts into their "parts," and still others think that they are analyzing properties, states of affairs, or facts into their constituents.

These days, matters are even more complicated because of currently fashionable externalist theories of reference and meaning. At least some externalists toy with the idea of modeling philosophical analysis on scientific "analysis."[2] The scientist investigates the world in an attempt to discover the fundamental nature of various "natural" phenomena—water, heat, or lightning, for example. Water turns out to be H_2O, heat turns out to be molecular motion, and lightning turns out to be an electrical discharge. No one thinks that it was possible to discover these familiar facts about the natural world through thought experiments. Would that science were that easy. Still, many direct-reference theorists will argue, the truths just described are in some important sense necessary. The molecular structure of water, for example, is not just a contingent feature of water. It is an essential feature of the stuff we call water that it has that molecular structure. Stuff that looks, tastes, and smells like water would not be water, the argument goes, unless it had the right molecular structure. If we can discover the essential nature of so-called natural kinds like water through empirical investigation, then perhaps we can discover the essential nature of knowledge, or justified belief, through empirical investigation.

2. METHODOLOGICAL INTERNALISM AND ANALYSIS

Given the radical differences between these conceptions of philosophical analysis, we must be careful in characterizing the problem of the criterion as it relates to the way in which one tests proposed analyses. Let us begin, however, by presupposing the more traditional conception of analysis as conceptual analysis—the sort of task a philosopher could complete from the armchair, employing the method of thought experiment. Presupposing this framework, we are trying to discover necessary and sufficient conditions for the application of epistemic concepts. Let us use the concept of knowledge as our example. Put starkly, the problem of the criterion is this: Does one first decide what one knows and then try to learn from paradigmatic examples of knowledge the necessary and sufficient conditions for knowledge? Or does one discover first the necessary and sufficient conditions for knowledge and apply what one learns to discover what one knows? Or should one perhaps conclude that it is a mistake to suppose that either sort of discovery takes priority over the other? Following Chisholm's terminology, we can describe those who give priority to particular knowledge claims as particularists. Those who insist that we be guided by antecedent conclusions about the correct analysis of knowledge we can call generalists or methodists. The compromise position is most naturally associated with the method of reflective equilibrium made most famous by Rawls, but I shall reserve discussion of this view until my concluding remarks.[3]

The questions just posed are difficult to answer. Each approach may seem prima facie plausible. On the one hand, if we look at how philosophers actually do test proposed analyses of knowledge (or other epistemic concepts), they do seem to rely critically on the method of counterexample and "intuitions" about particular cases. There is no argument form used more frequently by philosophers than modus tollens, and the kind of modus tollens most favored by philosophers is the reductio ad absurdum. Reductio ad absurdum is just modus tollens with appropriate histrionics employed in the denial of the consequent—if P, then Q, but (for God's sake, anyone in his right mind knows that) not-Q, so not-P. And nowhere is reductio ad absurdum employed more often than in the attempt to argue against proposed philosophical analyses. In Plato's *Republic* (331c), after Socrates takes Cephalus to be suggesting that right conduct is just telling the truth and returning what you owe to others, Socrates immediately rejects the view by pointing out that you obviously should not return weapons you have borrowed from a man who has gone mad. All kinds of twentieth-century epistemologists thought that we have knowledge whenever and only when we have justified true belief. Gettier (1963) described a couple of cases in which people have justified true beliefs but do not have knowledge, and almost everyone abandoned the view.[4] So it certainly looks as if our search for correct analyses of epistemic concepts is guided by particular judgments we make about what does and does not satisfy the concepts in question.

Still, one must wonder how philosophers who lack the correct analysis of knowledge are in a position to decide what people do or do not know. Furthermore, on the traditional view, one is supposed to be able to know a priori the necessary and sufficient conditions for knowledge. That we know this or that proposition is always a contingent matter. But a priori knowledge is usually thought to be more secure than knowledge of contingent truths. So why would the traditional analytic philosopher let a priori knowledge of analytic truths be held hostage to contingent truths about knowledge of particular cases?

Again, one might suppose that the position one takes on this issue has significant implications for the way in which one approaches the challenge of skepticism. If we emulate Moore and assume at the outset that we know all sorts of particular truths about the past, the physical world, and the future, using that assumption to guide our analysis of knowledge, the skeptic obviously cannot win. We *start* with the rejection of skepticism, and we defend that starting point by arguing that philosophical methodology requires it. Philosophy cannot proceed without a healthy sense of what is absurd, and radical skepticism, the argument goes, is clearly absurd.

The details of our defense of the particularist starting point will be shaped by our particular metaphilosophical view of analysis. For example, if we think that analysis is a matter of discovering the meanings of words, we might defend the particularist's starting point by arguing for the slogan that meaning is use and by pointing out that we do in fact use the term "know" frequently and unapologetically to describe our relation to all sorts of truths. To offer an account of knowledge that makes all or most paradigmatic knowledge claims false is to exhibit a failure to understand what it is for an expression to have meaning. Paradigmatic uses of an expression *determine* its meaning.

However attractive the particularist's approach to traditional philosophical analysis might initially seem, at least one version of the view does not stand up to close examination. It is, in fact, a bit misleading to suggest that on the traditional view, one evaluates one's proposed analyses of epistemic concepts by testing them against "intuitions" about which particular propositions we know or are justified in believing. We have already had occasion to note that conceptual analysis is guided by *thought* experiments. Gettier did not wander around looking for someone who believed falsely that Jones owned a Ford while randomly forming a belief in a disjunctive proposition involving Brown and Barcelona. He asked us to *imagine* a situation and filled in the details of that imaginary situation as he pleased. The nice thing about thought experiments is that one gets to assign the properties of the imagined situation as one pleases. Now to be sure, we do seem to discover *something* in thinking about the hypothetical situation. We discover, I would suggest, something about how we use the term "know"—we discover something about our linguistic dispositions. Specifically, we discover that we would not describe the particular situations Gettier describes as cases of knowledge.

I have argued elsewhere (Fumerton 1983) that it is a mistake to suppose that one can divorce philosophical analysis from language. The idea that when one is engaged in philosophical analysis, one begins by getting before one's mind a nonlinguistic concept, property, state of affairs, or fact and then performs a philosophical dissection of it is phenomenologically wildly implausible. If that is how philosophical analysis were to proceed, it would be utterly mysterious how philosophers come to such radically different positions concerning the analysis of such issues as knowledge, causation, justified belief, and moral obligation. Rather, in trying to discover what knowledge, say, is, I think that the philosopher is trying to discover facts about which possible situations would be correctly described using the term "know." More precisely still, I think that each philosopher is trying in the first instance to discover facts about his or her own linguistic dispositions—conclusions that we typically presume will inform others about *their* linguistic dispositions.

I cannot convince you here of my own view of philosophical analysis. The first point I want to stress, though, is that however one thinks of *traditional* philosophical analysis, one does not, and should not, test analyses against particular *empirical* claims about what is known or not known. To convince yourself of this, suppose that you are actually in a Gettier situation. You are looking at a broken clock that reads 3:00 P.M. just as it happens to be 3:00 P.M.[5] Because you do not know that the clock is broken, you naturally enough form the true belief that it is 3:00. Now also since you do not know that you are in a Gettier situation, I suppose that if you were inclined to make Moore-style pronouncements, you might insist that this is a clear example of knowledge, and that it better turn out that any plausible analysis of knowledge implies that you know this proposition. Clearly, though, were you to discover relevant contingent features of your actual situation, you would recant your insistence that this turns out to be a case of knowledge. The moral to draw is that you never really were relying critically on *this* being a case of knowledge. The most you were doing in using this example was to conjure up a *kind* of hypothetical situation of which you took this particular example to be an instance. But it did not matter whether it was or was not an instance of the kind. It was the hypothetical situation—the situation *thought of* in a certain way—against which you were testing your intuitions. And the *conditional* statement "if a belief were to satisfy the description in question, it would be knowledge," if true, is every bit as analytic as the general statement "S knows that P iff X."

Indeed, once it becomes apparent that it is *subjunctives* the truth-value of which is guiding our proposed analysis, it is not at all clear that we can still so easily draw the distinction between the generalist who insists on the priority of knowledge of philosophical analyses and the particularist who insists on the priority of knowledge of particular truths about what we know. Even if subjunctive conditionals contain expressions that appear to pick out particular objects, it is often the case that their truth conditions are just as general as the truth conditions of general propositions. Suppose, for example, that I tell you that if this (pointing to my pencil) were metal, then it would expand when heated. In one sense, it looks as if the claim is one about a particular object—the pencil. But further reflection surely suggests that it is more plausibly construed as a claim about lawful or causal connection between *properties*. After all, the fact that I picked out the pencil in making the claim is utterly irrelevant to the truth of the subjunctive. I could have pointed to my phone, my arm, the water in my glass, or anything else, for that matter, and it would not have affected in the slightest the truth of my statement. What makes it true that if the pencil (my phone, my arm, the water in my class) were metal, it would expand when heated is the general truth that metal expands when heated. I am suggesting that the truths involving hypothetical situations that guide our claims about how to analyze knowledge are like the "particular" subjunctive truth about the pencil. If it is true that a particular belief would count as knowledge if and only if it possesses characteristics X, what makes it true will be the fact that we can analyze knowledge as beliefs with characteristics X.

Still, this account seems to leave mysterious the force that counterexamples have for philosophers. It certainly seems that we often do find a given analysis of some concept plausible, only to be convinced by consideration of some *more* detailed hypothetical situation that our initial view was mistaken. Remember the Gettier counterexamples. So what is going on? The best way to answer the question, it seems to me, is to think carefully about what happens when you do get convinced by a counterexample. You start out, let us say, thinking that you would be prepared to describe as knowledge all and only strongly justified true beliefs. You then think of a possible situation in which it is pretty obvious that a strongly justified true belief is present, even though you would not describe it as a case of knowledge. What you discover, it seems to me, is that you do not have the disposition that you thought you had. That discovery, of course, does not tell you what features of the situation entertained are prompting your refusal to characterize the belief in question as knowledge. There are all sorts of properties posited in the description of the situation. You might have withheld the judgment that the belief is knowledge because the situation entertained was one in which you reasoned through a falsehood. Or you might have been influenced by the fact that the imaginary situation involved defeaters. Or perhaps the situation might have reminded you forcefully that your justification did not satisfy appropriately strong Cartesian requirements for knowledge. And you need not be *consciously* aware of any of these features of the posited situation in order for them to play a causal role in your withholding an ascription of knowledge. That you had only implicitly filled out the imaginary situation with certain properties present seems to leave unaffected the capacity of their presence to affect your judgment. Just as we can feel uneasy about some action we are thinking about undertaking without understanding what makes us uneasy, so also, it seems that we can realize that we are uneasy about calling a given belief knowledge even if we are not sure what is making us uneasy. Again, when consideration of some hypothetical situation affects us in this way, we come to realize that we do not follow the semantic rule we thought we followed governing knowledge.[6]

So on the traditional conception of analysis, it seems that we can discover facts about our dispositions that are relevant to the truth of our proposed analyses by careful consideration of thought experiments. We can, if we like, call this a version of particularism. It is important to stress again, however, that it is a *thought* experiment that plays the evidential role in testing the analysis. It is *not* empirical conclusions concerning our actual knowledge or justified belief about some particular proposition that guides our analyses.

3. Methodological Externalism and Analysis

One might suppose that the above arguments will leave untouched the new "particularists" who are determined to model philosophical analysis on scientific discovery. But considerations raised earlier tell against this conception of analysis as well. To pursue the scientific model, one surely must begin with "samples" of the epistemic kind we are going to empirically investigate. One cannot perform an empirical assay of a kind without having samples of the kind to assay. So just as on one caricature of the view we run across some relatively clear, odorless, liquid in bodies we call rivers and lakes, presume that it is all of the same kind, and proceed to investigate empirically the kind, so also, I suppose, the idea is that we run across some true beliefs that we take to be of the same fundamental kind and begin to empirically investigate the nature of that kind.

To state the view clearly is to see the obvious difficulties it encounters. Precisely how are we to pick out the samples? The literature suggests at least three possibilities: (1) Our reference to knowledge, justified belief, evidence, and the like might piggyback on the successful reference of others to such "stuff"—perhaps the experts in the field; (2) we might "fix the reference" of expressions such as "knowledge" and "justified belief" with definite descriptions, where the samples to be investigated are those things denoted by the definite descriptions; (3) we might demonstratively refer to the samples we are interested in investigating as we run across them. Consider each in turn.

We surely cannot rely on experts to pick out the samples of epistemic properties the nature of which we want to empirically investigate. Who are the experts to whom we would defer when it comes to the referents of such terms as "knowledge" and "justified belief?" Would they include Descartes? Or perhaps Hume? Or maybe Goldman? The problem, of course, is that these philosophers do not agree with each other on what should be included in the class of knowledge and justified belief. And no self-respecting epistemologist is going to defer to another philosopher when it comes to presuppositions about what counts as a paradigmatic instance of knowledge or justified belief.

I have argued elsewhere (Fumerton 1989) that the very idea of reference fixing is an illusion. We can assign a name (for a particular or a kind) the meaning of a definite description, but we cannot wave a definite description magically over a symbol and create thereby a "pure" referring expression. But suppose (contrary to fact) that we can use a definite description to mystically breathe referential life into an expression like "knowledge" or "justified belief," and that we can do this without assigning the terms the meaning of the definite description. Precisely what definite description should we use to fix the reference of "knowledge," say? Is knowledge the intentional state that is of fundamental interest to epistemologists? Hardly. There are lots of intentional states that are of fundamental interest to epistemologists. Is knowledge the belief state that precludes the possibility of error? Maybe. Is knowledge the true belief that results from a properly functioning belief-producing process that is operating in precisely the environment for which it was designed? Perhaps. Is knowledge the intentional state directed at truth and supported by evidence that contains no essential falsehoods? Could be. But these suggestions are precisely the controversial suggestions that we need to evaluate in our search for a plausible account of knowledge. They are not uncontroversial *preliminary* moves that enable us to begin an empirical investigation into the nature of knowledge.

The same problem affects an attempt to secure our samples through demonstrative reference. You might pick out as one of the samples of knowledge to investigate your belief that you will be alive tomorrow. Another philosopher might well claim that such a belief is hardly an instance of knowledge. We beg all sorts of interesting questions at the outset by our selection of the samples to be investigated. But it is not just the controversial character of knowledge claims that creates problems for our search for the right samples. Whatever we choose as our paradigm of knowledge might not be knowledge *even by our own lights*. Suppose, once again, that you were unlucky enough to choose your samples of "knowledge" while trapped in a Gettier situation. You make such declarations as that if anything is a case of knowledge, *this* is. We start investigating the situation and discover that we relied on inferences from justifiably believed falsehoods in reaching our "paradigm" of knowledge. Letting the chips fall where they may, should we then conclude as a result of our empirical investigation that knowledge apparently involves inference from justifiably believed falsehoods? Of course not. Our empirical discovery will lead us to abandon our original declaration. The reason is again simple. We never were willing to let an empirical investigation decide what would or would not count as a case of knowledge—at least not an empirical investigation of the sort envisioned by the philosopher modeling an analysis of knowledge on the scientific "analysis" of water or lightning. When we try to understand our concept of knowledge, we think of all sorts of hypothetical situations and try to figure out the common denominators to all the belief states that we would call knowledge in an effort to learn something about our epistemic concepts.

4. Sources of Knowledge and the Problem of the Criterion

As I indicated in my introductory comments, the more familiar problem of the criterion, the problem most often associated with the work of Chisholm, concerns not the analysis of epistemic *concepts*, but the search for "sources" of knowledge and justified belief. So, as Chisholm describes the opposing views, the particularist, relying on so-called common sense, decides that we know and are justified in believing all sorts of commonplace propositions and uses this as a datum to argue for the necessity of recognizing either certain sorts of justification as noninferential or for recognizing the legitimacy of various sorts of inference. The "generalist" or the "methodist," by contrast, decides what kinds of beliefs are noninferentially justified and what kinds of inferences are legitimate and is willing to let the chips fall where they may when it comes to implications concerning what we do and do not know or are justified in believing. Once again, the methodology favored by the particularist seems simply to rule out the possibility that skepticism might be true. The particularist decides at the very outset that the correct epistemology will ensure that we know and are justified in believing most of what we think we know and are justified in believing. We shall "give ourselves" whatever principles of justification we need in order to arrive at the antiskeptical destination we are determined to reach. Most of the classical skeptics, by contrast, were methodists. Hume, for example, advanced a view about how one can legitimately move from premises to conclusions and argued from that view for skepticism.[7]

Following Chisholm, let us illustrate the particularist's strategy for dealing with skepticism by looking at a couple of skeptical arguments. Consider skepticism with respect to the external world. Hume famously argued that the only way to justifiably believe that there are objective, enduring physical objects is to *infer* their existence from what we know directly about the character of fleeting subjective appearance. He further argued that the only way to get legitimately from knowledge of appearance[8] to knowledge of objective reality is to inductively establish the occurrence of the former as evidence for the existence of the latter. But, Hume argued, we cannot correlate appearance with something other than appearance— we have no direct access to anything but appearances. We have, therefore, no justification for believing that physical objects exist.

Or consider the problem of memory. I seem to remember having had a headache earlier today and reach the conclusion that I did have the headache. No one my age needs to be convinced that seeming to remember doing *X* does not entail having done *X*. But once again, the prospect of inductively establishing memory as a reliable indicator of the past seems hopeless. Any inductive argument would rely on *past* correlations of memory "experiences" with the events we took them to be signs of, and without relying on the legitimacy of the very memory under skeptical attack, we would have no access to such past correlations. The radical empiricist seeking to identify foundational justification with internally accessible infallible justification and committed to the view that the only sort of nondeductive inference that is legitimate is inductive inference will inevitably be led to a radical skepticism about the past.

The particularist with whom Chisholm sympathizes responds that if Hume is right and we cannot use either deduction or enumerative induction to legitimately infer the existence of physical objects or to reach conclusions about the past, then there must be some other source of justified belief. It is simply absurd, the particularist argues, to deny that we have the knowledge or justified belief under skeptical attack. If we are not going to use modus tollens *here* to reject a philosophical position, we shall never use it. Chisholm, for example, agrees with Hume that we are not getting where we want to go by relying exclusively on deduction and induction from infallibly believed foundations, and he is willing to infer from this that we had better recognize additional epistemic principles that will sanction the beliefs under skeptical attack. So in the third edition of *Theory of Knowledge*, for example, Chisholm advances the following principles, tailor-made to counter the skeptic:

> For any subject S, if S believes, without grounds for doubt, that he is perceiving something to be F, then it is beyond reasonable doubt for S that he perceives something to be F.
>
> (p. 76)

> For any subject S, if S believes, without grounds for doubt, that he remembers perceiving something to be F (where F is a sensible characteristic) then it is beyond reasonable doubt for S that he does remember perceiving something to be F.
>
> (p. 81)

5. Particularism, Methodism, or Reflective Equilibrium

5.1. Epistemological Internalism and the Problem of the Criterion

So who has the correct approach to the philosophical investigation of sources of knowledge and justification? Is it the particularist or the methodist? Or should we reject both as extreme positions and sign on to the method of reflective equilibrium, an approach that recommends that we try to maximize coherence between our "intuitions" about the legitimacy of methods and our "intuitions" about particular cases of knowledge and justified belief?

It is important, I think, that however one answers these questions, one does so in a principled way that is consistent with one's other epistemological views.

Chisholm, for example, seems to me to be in a precarious position. According to Chisholm, coherence among one's beliefs can increase the level of epistemic justification those beliefs enjoy. But he is, in the final analysis, a confirmed foundationalist. There are beliefs that enjoy foundational justification, and all other beliefs owe their justification in part to these foundationally justified beliefs. Furthermore, like most classical foundationalists, Chisholm includes among the candidates for foundational justification necessary truths knowable a priori. That brings us back to epistemic principles. For Chisholm, epistemic principles describe conditions under which a belief enjoys a certain positive epistemic status (the terms of epistemic appraisal are all defined in terms of the primitive "being more reasonable to believe than"). So what is the modal status of an epistemic principle, and what is the nature of our justification for believing an epistemic principle?

It is clear from the corpus of Chisholm's work that he does not take an epistemic principle to describe *contingent* circumstances under which beliefs enjoy an epistemic status. He takes epistemic principles to state necessary truths and presumably allows that one can know such truths a priori. If there is any doubt about this, one need only reflect on Chisholm's commitment to access internalism. Chisholm holds that one always has the ability to directly access the epistemic status of one's beliefs (1977, p. 116).[9] That is because he thinks that the epistemic status of beliefs depends on subjective states that are self-presenting and on the truth of epistemic principles that one can know a priori.

So what business does Chisholm have embracing the particularist's position? He should be the paradigm of a philosopher who endorses the claim that one can acquire unproblematic knowledge of epistemic principles and employ such knowledge in reaching conclusions about what we know and are justified in believing. He really should let the chips fall where they may. Of course, you might suppose that the question whether Chisholm can consistently endorse particularism is at best a matter of historical interest. But my observations about what Chisholm is committed to extend to any philosopher who embraces a similar sort of access internalism. I have argued elsewhere (Fumerton 1996, 2004) that one cannot consistently embrace plausible internalist access requirements unless one takes the principles that sanction inference to be synthetic necessary truths knowable a priori.[10] If one accepts, for example, the view that I call *inferential internalism* and argues that to justifiably infer P from E, one needs justification for believing that E makes probable P, the only way to avoid a vicious regress is to acknowledge that there are some propositions of the form E makes probable P that are knowable a priori. I do not see how one can take that position without rejecting the view that one should hold one's conclusions about epistemic principles hostage to conclusions about particular claims to knowledge and justified belief, at least when those particular claims involve inferential knowledge or justification. After all, according to the inferential internalist, inferential justification/knowledge is parasitic upon prior justification for accepting epistemic principles concerning evidential connections.

In arguing for this position, I want to emphasize again a point made earlier in connection with the particularist/generalist controversy over the nature of our access to the truth of philosophical analyses. It is doubtless true that in trying to discover plausible epistemic principles, one might well consider particular *inferences* (in contrast to particular claims about what we know or are justified in believing). Think about how you try to teach undergraduates the rules of deductive inference. To be sure, one could just trot out general principles like modus ponens and modus tollens and tell the students to think carefully about the principles until they start seeming pretty obvious. This might work. But it often helps to ask students to think about particular applications of modus ponens and modus tollens as a heuristic device. The fallacy of affirming the consequent might not seem like a fallacy until one thinks about inferring that Chisholm was a dolphin from the fact that if he were a dolphin, he would have lungs, and he does have lungs. Put another way, it might be easier to "see" probabilistic connections in the context of contemplating particular pairs of propositions. But this is not an argument for Chisholmian particularism. We are not trying to reach conclusions about principles of reasoning from particular claims about what we know or are justified in believing. We are trying to get the students to discover a priori the legitimacy of a particular inference in an effort to get them to see a priori the more general principle of reasoning instantiated in this particular inference. Our discovery of the general principle is arrived at through consideration of the particular inference only in the sense in which our original "seeing" that two plus two equals four was aided by our kindergarten teacher's illustrating that a priori truth with the truth about the four apples arranged on the desk.

5.2. Epistemological Externalism and the Problem of the Criterion

I have argued that most classical internalists, ironically the very kind of internalists of whom Chisholm was a paradigm, should place themselves firmly in the generalist's camp. But what of the increasingly popular externalisms embraced by many contemporary epistemologists? The vast majority of externalists reject the claim that all epistemic principles are necessary truths.[11] The reliabilist, for example, is clearly committed to the view that once we leave deduction, the legitimacy of an inference is a matter of contingent fact. Should such a philosopher embrace particularism or methodism?

For me, the question is difficult to answer because I have never been sure how externalists decide which beliefs are or are not justified, or why they place such confidence in their "intuitions" about which particular beliefs are justified. Again, let us take as our paradigmatic externalist the reliabilist. We certainly shall not get very far by trying to discover where reliabilists' sympathies lie by looking at their practice. As far as I can tell, most reliabilists seem to take for granted that most of what they take to be justified beliefs are in fact justified, and they sometimes seem to be guided by these "intuitions" when it comes to addressing problems raised both for their analysis of justification and for their views about what should count as a reliable belief-producing process. In this respect, they look a bit like the particularist Chisholm describes. On the other hand, reliabilists seem to me to have equally confident, unswerving faith in the reliability of such commonly used process types like perception, memory, and induction. Again, it is just not clear to me what they think their epistemic license is to place such faith in the reliability of the various belief-producing mechanisms they employ.

Rather than look to the externalist's practice for insight, let us instead try to figure out how a consistent externalist, a reliabilist, for example, should go about reaching conclusions about the epistemic status of particular beliefs and the legitimacy of various sources of justification.[12] Consider memory. As I said earlier, most reliabilists I have read are quite certain that most of what they seem to remember happened, that most of their beliefs based on an apparent memory are justified, and that memory is a more or less reliable source of information about the past. To be sure, any careful discussion of the issues would require the reliablist to address head-on now-familiar problems facing their account of justification. In particular, before one assesses either the justificatory status of a memory-produced belief or the general reliability of memory, it would be critical to address the well-known generality problem. Empirical research indicates that there are radically different kinds of memory, and one sort may be much more reliable than another. Furthermore, common sense itself suggests that we may want to treat as a different kind of process memory-induced belief in old people and memory-induced beliefs in younger people. For all I know, the reliabilist will end up with memory after an all-night bender being a different belief-producing process from memory after taking a course on how to improve one's memory. Thankfully, I am not a reliabilist, so I do not have to worry about how to divvy up possible belief-producing processes about the past. There is the further complication that verbs like "remember" probably are usually used to report factive states.[13] If my belief that I put the keys on the table results from remembering that I did in this factive sense, then, trivially, the belief-producing process is 100 percent reliable. For any interesting epistemological discussion of memory, we will need to identify memory-induced beliefs as those whose input is something more like seeming to remember, where seeming to remember is perfectly compatible with the apparent memory being nonveridical.

With all that as preliminary, let us suppose that we have identified a belief-producing process that takes as its input something like seeming to remember having done X and has its output the belief that X occurred. We ask the reliabilist to justify both his belief that the belief that X occurred is justified and his belief that the input/output mechanism that results in that belief is reliable—it is a legitimate source of justification. How should the reliabilist proceed? Well, I suppose that he might try an inductive argument. He might claim to remember seeming to remember a great many things where most of the time the apparent memory turned out to be accurate. I seemed to remember seeming to remember having put the keys on the table, and the keys were there. I seemed to remember having had cornflakes for breakfast, and I did. Get enough of these correlations, and we are in business generalizing to the reliability of apparent memories.

One does not have to be in the clutches of skepticism to wonder whether this argument is not suspect. To inductively infer that the belief-producing process in question is reliable, we need justified beliefs in the premises of our argument. According to reliabilism, we may be justified in believing that the keys were on the table, and we may be justified in believing that we seemed to remember having put the keys on the table, but only if the relevant sort of memory upon which we rely is reliable. But that is precisely what we are trying to establish. Our belief in the conclusion of our argument based on our acceptance of the premises is only as justified as our belief in the premises, and that justification presupposes that the conclusion is true. I have argued elsewhere (Fumerton 1996) that none of this should bother the consistent reliabilist. The facts about inputs and reliabilities that determine the epistemic status of our beliefs, according to the reliabilist, are in-dependent of our access to those facts. Given this view, the justification of first-level beliefs does not require any beliefs about the reliability of methods by which the beliefs were acquired. It is enough that the world cooperate so as to supply the relevant correlations. And, of course, if the metaepistemological view is correct, the matter should be no different when it comes to the epistemic status of second-level beliefs about the epistemic status of first-level beliefs. It is simply not necessary that we have any sort of epistemic access to the legitimacy of whatever methods we employ in reaching our conclusions about the epistemic status of first-level beliefs.

Again, I have argued in a number of places that the sort of epistemic justifi-cation in which philosophers are interested is tied to getting *assurance* of truth, and I do not see how satisfying the reliabilist's conditions for epistemic justification gets anyone assurance of anything. If I start worrying that my memory is getting very bad, I do not think that I can assure myself that it is really not so bad by apparently remembering all sorts of recent successful employment of memory (though I can, perhaps, confirm my fears by seeming to remember all sorts of unsuccessful reliance on memory). But here I am interested primarily in the issue of where the externalist, in this case represented by the reliabilist, should stand on the particularist/generalist controversy concerning the problem of the criterion.

The upshot of this discussion suggests initially that the reliabilist is *some* sort of generalist/methodist. Again, given the reliabilist's understanding of epistemic justification, one must discover something about the source of a belief to reach a conclusion about its epistemic status. To be sure, the track-record argument dis-cussed earlier employs premises that describe particular instances of memory and particular conclusions about the past, but it does *not* involve particular claims about the epistemic status of our beliefs in these propositions. To be sure, without justification for believing the premises of the argument, we have no justification for believing the conclusion of the argument, but that does not alter the fact that the premises make no claim about the epistemic status of particular beliefs. Chisholm's particularist employs premises describing the epistemic status of various beliefs in order to reach conclusions about the legitimacy of epistemic principles.

But if the reliabilist is a kind of generalist, it is important to recognize the difference between this sort of generalist and the sort that Chisholm had in mind.

Given reliabilism, it is *trivially* true that every conclusion about the epistemic status of a belief involves a conclusion about the "legitimacy" of its source, but only because a conclusion about the epistemic status of a belief just *is* a conclusion about its having the right kind of source.[14] That position does not imply that one reaches conclusions about the epistemic status of beliefs through prior or independent knowledge of the legitimacy of epistemic principles. The consistent reliabilist will insist that one need not know much of anything about the *specific* nature of the particular belief-producing mechanism that leads to a belief in order to reach a justified conclusion about that belief's epistemic status. As I have pointed out many times, the reliabilist places no a priori restrictions on what beliefs can be justified, even justified noninferentially. I might be so constituted that when I entertain the proposition that a belief is justified, I instinctively respond with either an endorsement or a rejection of its having positive epistemic status, and I might be almost always right. I might be the epistemic counterpart of the infamous "chicken sexer" much discussed in the literature.[15] If I am, and if the reliabilist is correct, then I can come to know that various beliefs are justified, and I can do so without even understanding *how* I am reaching these conclusions. If the reliabilist is right, a conclusion about the epistemic status of a belief *is equivalent in meaning* to a conclusion about the belief's having the right sort of cause, but reaching the conclusion does not involve an examination or investigation of that cause. If the *robust* generalist/methodist thinks that one can only reach legitimate conclusions about the epistemic status of beliefs by *first* finding out which specific epistemic principles are legitimate, then the reliabilist (and, more generally, the externalist) is neither a robust generalist nor a particularist. As far as I can see, on this controversy, the externalist does not have a dog in the hunt.

5.3. Reflective Equilibrium and the Problem of the Criterion

In the preceding discussion, the method of reflective equilibrium has been conspicuous by its absence. Given the widespread use of that method, this might seem a bit odd. In the final analysis, however, it seems to me that one can deal with the method of reflective equilibrium in short order. Whether one is searching for a correct analysis or trying to discover the sources of knowledge and justified belief, one can legitimately employ the method of reflective equilibrium only if the coherence theory of justification is true. And it is not. Let me explain.

According to proponents of bringing beliefs into reflective equilibrium, one takes beliefs one has about particular beliefs being justified, one takes one's beliefs about various epistemic principles being justified or unjustified, and one makes whatever adjustments will allow one to maximize retention of beliefs. When the smoke clears and the dust settles, however, what could possibly justify this approach to arriving at the truth of the matter but the idea that justification is a function of coherence? The beliefs that survive the winnowing process presumably are justified in virtue of occupying a place in a system of beliefs that coheres. We do not have the space here to engage in a full-scale evaluation of the coherence theory of justification. I have argued elsewhere (Fumerton, 1994), however, that a coherence theory comes in either an externalist or an internalist version. On the externalist version of the view, my beliefs are justified provided that they do in fact cohere (in whatever sense of coherence the coherence theorist develops), and I do not need any access to the fact that the beliefs do cohere. This version of the coherence theory is vulnerable to devastating counterexamples. One need only imagine a person who whimsically chooses to believe a great many propositions based on bizarre hunches and who by sheer happenstance ends up believing propositions that mutually support each other in ways that only a master logician could discover. Such a person has coherent beliefs but also has wildly irrational beliefs.

If in the face of this objection one turns to an internalist coherence theory and allows that one must have access to coherence among one's beliefs in order for those beliefs to be justified, one faces the regress argument that BonJour (1985) made famous. One's access to coherence will involve access to one's belief states, an access that is either foundational (and thus inconsistent with the coherentist's position) or dependent on relations of coherence to which one needs access—the beginning of the regress.

In short, I am not interested in whether someone rests comfortably with a belief system in reflective equilibrium, regardless of the subject matter of those beliefs. I have known many a philosopher, and the odd paranoid schizophrenic, with wonderfully coherent belief systems where I am quite convinced that the beliefs are mostly false and mostly irrational.

6. CONCLUSION

I have been primarily interested in exploring connections between metaepistemological views and the approach one would most naturally take to the problem of the criterion. The implication of the positions one takes on skepticism is a complicated issue. With respect to the metaepistemological problem of the criterion, there is a version of particularism that would seem to require at least the presupposition that skepticism is false. But as we also saw, that version of particularism is exceedingly implausible. When we turned our attention to the problem of the criterion as it relates to the question of how, if at all, we can discover epistemic principles (principles concerning sources of knowledge and justified belief), I argued that the inferential internalist is committed to the view that if we have any inferential knowledge or justification, it had better be possible to justify belief in propositions describing evidential connections without having to rely on knowledge of the epistemic status of beliefs reached through inference. Because I think that inferential internalism is true (for at least the most philosophically interesting senses of justification), and because I think that getting the relevant knowledge of epistemic principles is, at best, problematic, the spectre of skepticism looms large. Epistemic externalists, by contrast, face no insuperable skeptical difficulties posed by the problem of the criterion. Most externalists place no a priori restrictions on what can be known or how it can be known. As far as I can see, the externalist should allow that one can get knowledge of epistemic principles that does not rely on knowledge of which particular beliefs are justified, and one can get knowledge of which beliefs are justified that does not rely on justified beliefs about the legitimacy of any particular rules of inference. Externalism is, in general, a great comfort to those fighting classical arguments for skepticism. Unfortunately, I do not think that it is true.

NOTES

I would like to thank the faculty (particularly Laurence BonJour and Ann Baker) and the graduate students at the University of Washington for their valuable criticisms and comments on an earlier draft of this chapter. Michael Bergmann's and John Greco's comments were also most helpful. Although I am not sure that he will remember it, I would also like to thank Richard Feldman for an interesting conversation we once had on some of the issues discussed here.

1. I carefully talk of conceivability as a *test*. The modal operator implicitly contained in talk of what is conceiv*able* precludes, I believe, an analysis of any sort of possibility in terms of conceivability.

2. See Kornblith (2002).

3. There is a fourth possible view. One might hold that the problem is insuperable, and for that reason we must be skeptics about whether we have knowledge or justified belief. This position is rarely held, and I shall not be discussing it in this chapter, either here or in the section focusing on methods.

4. Though not, of course, the spirit of the view. There continues the (seemingly never-ending) search for a Gettier-proofing condition to add to the traditional analysis of knowledge.

5. Russell's (1948, p. 154) example, given long before Gettier.

6. Compare the thought experiments a linguist employs in testing hypotheses about the syntactic rules we follow in speaking a language. There is a marked similarity between these thought experiments and the thought experiments that test hypotheses about semantic rule following. Just as consideration of a given sentence can reveal that we do not follow a generalized syntactic rule, so also consideration of a given hypothetical situation can reveal that we do not follow a generalized semantic rule.

7. As I noted earlier, it is also possible to argue for a kind of skepticism from the premise that the problem of the criterion is insoluble. The idea would be that there simply is no way of reaching conclusions about particular cases of what we know without

knowledge of methods, and there is no way of arriving at knowledge of methods without the guidance provided by particular claims about what we know. So we can never be in a position to know what we know (even if we have first-level knowledge). Again, I shall not be discussing this view in this chapter. Note that the philosopher arguing for skepticism this way would presumably need to know, or at least justifiably believe, that the problem is insoluble, and this would contradict the skeptical conclusion of the argument. It may not be correct to dismiss arguments that are epistemically self-refuting in this way, but that is a long story.

8. Chisholm (1977) would prefer "self-presenting states."

9. The principle here is advanced concerning knowledge, but it is clear that Chisholm would apply it to all other epistemic properties of one's beliefs.

10. I think that this is one of the main thrusts of BonJour's (1998) defense of the a priori.

11. Even externalists will allow that some belief-producing processes are necessarily truth conducive—processes that realize the rules of deductive inference, for example. To be sure, most externalists will distinguish analytic truths about the necessary and sufficient conditions for a belief to be justified from the kind of *normative* epistemic principles I am characterizing as contingent truths. According to most reliabilists, for example, it is a necessary truth that a belief is justified only if it is reliably produced. But the claim that memory, induction, perception, and other commonsense "sources" of knowledge are reliable sources of information is contingent.

12. It what follows, I am going to use the reliabilist as the paradigm of an externalist in epistemology. I believe that all of what I say will apply, mutatis mutandis, to other versions of externalism.

13. A psychological state directed at an object is factive if the truth of the statement describing the state entails that the object exists. My seeing a table is factive in that my doing so (arguably) requires the existence of the table. My fearing ghosts is not, because the fear can exist without the ghosts.

14. In this sense, the classic internalist might also be trivially committed to a form of generalism when it comes to reaching conclusions about inferential justification. The classic recursive analysis of justification might define inferential justification in terms of legitimate inference from noninferentially justified belief.

15. The chicken sexer is supposed to have the uncanny ability to look at a chick and predict its sex even though (according to the story) he cannot tell how he arrives at his conclusion.

REFERENCES

BonJour, Laurence. 1985. *The Structure of Empirical Knowledge.* Cambridge, MA: Harvard University Press.

———. 1998. *In Defense of Pure Reason.* London: Cambridge University Press.

Chisholm, R. M. 1977. *Theory of Knowledge.*2nd ed. Englewood Cliffs, NJ: Prentice-Hall.

Fumerton, Richard. 1983. "The Paradox of Analysis." *Philosophy and Phenomenological Research* 43: 477–97.

———. 1989. "Russelling Causal Theories of Reference." In *Rereading Russell,* ed. Wade Savage and Anthony Anderson. Minneapolis: University of Minnesota Press, 108–18.

————. 1994. "The Incoherence of Coherence Theories." *Journal of Philosophical Research* 19: 89–102.

————. 1996. *Metaepistemology and Skepticism*. Boston: Rowman and Littlefield.

————. 2004. "Epistemic Probability." *Philosophical Issues* 14: 149–64.

Gettier, Edmund. 1963. "Is Justified True Belief Knowledge?" *Analysis* 23: 121–23.

Kornblith, Hilary. 2002. *Knowledge and Its Place in Nature*. Oxford: Oxford University Press.

Russell, Bertrand. 1948. *Human Knowledge: Its Scope and Limits*. New York: Simon and Schuster.

CHAPTER 3

CARTESIAN SKEPTICISM: ARGUMENTS AND ANTECEDENTS

JOSÉ LUIS BERMÚDEZ

THE most frequently discussed skeptical arguments in the history of philosophy are to be found in the tightly argued twelve paragraphs of Descartes' Meditation 1. There is considerable controversy about how to interpret the skeptical arguments that Descartes offers; the extent to which those arguments rest upon implicit epistemological and/or metaphysical presuppositions; their originality within the history of skepticism; and the role they play within Cartesian philosophy and natural science. This chapter begins by tracing the complex argumentation of Meditation 1. The second section explores the differences between Cartesian skeptical arguments and the skeptical arguments discussed in the ancient world, while the third section considers whether there might be medieval antecedents for the radical doubts that end Meditation 1. The final section suggests that the radical nature of the doubts raised in Meditation 1 has its sources in two fundamental characteristics of Cartesian science: the radical error that Cartesian science posits in our everyday experience of the world and the hypothetical and (only) morally certain nature of the scientific edifice that is proposed to replace the commonsense view of the world enshrined in Aristotelian science.

1. MEDITATION 1: ARGUMENTS AND PRESUPPOSITIONS

1.1. Foundationalism in Meditation 1?

In the first paragraph of Meditation 1, Descartes announces his intention to "demolish" all his beliefs and "start again from the foundations."[1] To do this, he continues in the next paragraph, there is no need to consider them individually: "Once the foundations of a building are undermined, anything built on them collapses of its own accord; so I will go straight for the basic principles on which all my former beliefs rested."[2]

According to Michael Williams, this innocent-sounding suggestion is deeply theory-laden:

> The epistemological systematicity implied by the metaphor of "foundations" allows beliefs to be undermined in a "topic-neutral" way; that is, independently of their particular content, the current state of collateral knowledge, and all concrete problem-situations and contexts of inquiry in which they might be examined. But the possibility of this kind of doubt is a requirement, not a discovery. There is no argument anywhere in Descartes' *Meditations* to show that common sense recognises the conception of justification, embodied in the metaphor of foundations, on which Descartes' definitive doubt depends.
>
> (Williams, 1986, 124–125)

Williams stresses how Descartes' procedure differs from that of classical skepticism, which he describes as essentially open ended, considering and posing counterarguments to particular knowledge-claims rather than considering general epistemological principles. His charge is that Descartes is tacitly rejecting the modesty of ancient skepticism in favor of an illegitimate foundationalism that underwrites the possibility of just the sort of global skepticism that he wants to introduce.

It is not clear, however, that Williams is right to claim that Descartes' rejection of the piecemeal approach of the ancients is, as he puts it, a requirement rather than a discovery. The whole of Meditation 1 is a complicated set of moves designed to introduce reasons for doubt that are increasingly broad and eventually culminate in the global doubt associated with the malicious-demon hypothesis. It is not the case that these moves are only possible once the piecemeal approach is rejected. Rather, they add up to a long argument against the piecemeal approach. Admittedly, Descartes does express himself as if he knows in advance that it is possible and useful to attack basic principles rather than individual beliefs, but this is not part of the argument. The real argumentative work is done by the arguments that *show* that basic principles can be attacked, and because of this, Meditation 1 would be completely unaffected if the passages to which Williams takes exception were cut.

Nonetheless, Descartes does appear to be making the ostensibly foundationalist claim that everything he has accepted as most true has been acquired either from the senses or through the senses.[3] How innocuous is this? The first point to make is that it cannot be his considered opinion. Such a quasi-empiricist epistemology is clearly incompatible with his belief in innate ideas and, on some interpretations, with his conviction that only the intellect can be a source of clear and distinct ideas. Obviously, then, he cannot be smuggling it into the *Meditations*. Second, Descartes is not saying that he knows that he has a class of perceptual beliefs that are, in some foundationalist sense, the basis for all his other beliefs. He is making no stronger claim than that the senses are, in some very loose sense, involved in the genesis of all his beliefs, which is obviously very different from the foundationalist empiricist claim that all beliefs are either perceptual beliefs or inferred from them. The involvement of the senses in every belief does not mean that every belief involves some sort of corresponding perceptual belief, but just that without sensory experience, such a belief could never have arisen. All this rules out is, first, the idea that certain beliefs can be acquired through some sort of intellectual intuition that operates in complete independence of the senses, and, second, beliefs that are innate. Both of these are more epistemologically controversial than the idea that all beliefs ultimately involve the senses, and Descartes would be begging the question far more if he assumed that beliefs could be acquired in either of these two ways than he does by assuming the converse.

Harry Frankfurt (and many others) have plausibly argued that the epistemological position under investigation in Meditation 1 is that of common sense, and that the basic principles of sensory evidence Descartes subjects to skeptical doubt are those typically appealed to by an "ordinary man" (Frankfurt, 1970). Certainly, this would explain why Descartes should have adopted such a quasi empiricism, given that he did not actually hold it himself, and it adds to the "naturalness" of Meditation 1 if one sees it as a critique of commonsense epistemology on its own terms. But it is also helpful to bear in mind the connection between an Aristotelian sense-based epistemology and a commonsense reliance on the testimony of the senses (Clarke, 1992; Garber, 1986, 1992; Hatfield, 1986; Rozemond, 1996). It is not just common sense that comes up with the various criteria of sensory evidence canvassed in Meditation 1 (the idea, for example, that the senses are reliable when operating in favorable conditions). These are also the criteria that an Aristotelian scientist would come up with. One reason for stressing this aspect of Meditation 1 is that it helps explain the obvious conflict between the quasi-empiricist principle that all the meditator's beliefs are derived either from or through the senses and his recognition that those beliefs include mathematical beliefs. On the Scholastic/Aristotelian philosophy of mathematics, beliefs about mathematics are indeed derived through the senses by a process of abstraction from experience of material objects.[4] It would be stretching plausibility, however, to ascribe to common sense any comparable theory about the apprehension of mathematical truths.

We shall return to the complex relations between Aristotelian science, Cartesian science, and the skepticism of Meditation 1 in section 4. The remainder of this section retraces the skeptical dialectic of Meditation 1.

1.2. The First Level of Doubt

Descartes begins the skeptical movement of Meditation 1 with the comment that "from time to time I have found that the senses deceive, and it is prudent never to trust completely those who have deceived us even once."[5] This is all he says in Meditation 1, but in Meditation 6 he fleshes things out a little more:

> Sometimes towers which looked round from a distance appeared square from close up; and enormous statues standing on their pediments did not seem large when observed from the ground. In these and countless other such cases, I found that the judgements of the external senses were mistaken.[6]

These examples of perceptual error are the familiar ones, canvassed by classical skeptics as often as modern ones. But he immediately goes on to cite examples of introspective error, which appear far less frequently in the skeptical literature. The passage in Meditation 6 continues:

> And this applied not just to the external senses, but to the internal senses as well. For what can be more internal than pain? And yet I had heard that those who had had an arm or a leg amputated sometimes still seemed to feel pain intermittently in the missing part of the body. So even in my own case it was apparently not quite certain that a particular limb was hurting even if I felt pain in it.[7]

Descartes is not suggesting that we can be mistaken about whether or not we are in pain. What he is questioning is the inference from "I feel pain" to "my leg is hurting" as a parallel to the inference from "the tower looks round" to "the tower is round."

What might seem perplexing, however, is the conclusion he draws from this. If when Descartes maintains that "it is prudent never to trust completely those who have deceived us even once," he means that we should completely withdraw our assent from anything that we appear to learn through the senses, then his position is clearly fallacious. But of course Descartes is not making this rather elementary error. He does not suggest that we should never in any circumstances trust those who have once deceived us. What he says is that we should never trust *completely* those who have once deceived us, and he immediately goes on to specify when it does seem that we can trust the senses:

> Yet although the senses occasionally deceive us with respect to objects which are very small or in the distance, there are many other beliefs about which doubt is quite impossible, even though they are derived from the senses—for example, that I am here, sitting by the fire, wearing a winter dressing-gown, holding this piece of paper in my hands, and so on. Again, how could it be denied that these hands or this whole body is mine?[8]

In the case of perceptual experience, what Descartes offers is a precursor of the familiar "preferential-conditions" response to the argument from illusion.[9] Although perceptual error does occur, he is saying, this does not mean that it always can occur. There are situations in which the conditions of perceptual experience are so optimal that it does not make sense to suppose that perceptual error can exist. Perceptual error only takes place, he suggests, when perceptual conditions are unfavorable, as when the objects of perception are far away or very small.

Interestingly, Descartes does not offer a parallel argument in the case of erroneous inferences from bodily experience, where there seems room for a version of the preferential-conditions response. He could, for example, suggest that mistakes like those made by people suffering from phantom limb occur only in unusual circumstances, such as the aftermath of amputations. In normal circumstances, when we are healthy and our bodies are functioning normally, bodily experience is a reliable guide to what is going on in our bodies. But this is not what he actually does. Instead of isolating conditions under which error does not occur, he points to judgments based on bodily experience that he thinks cannot be mistaken—"Again, how could it be denied that these hands or this whole body are mine?"

Be that as it may, however, these two lines of response close the first level of doubt in Meditation 1. Descartes has grounds for thinking that not all his perceptual beliefs are immune to error, whether they are beliefs about his body or about non-bodily objects. Nonetheless, he has what seems to be a perfectly sensible damage-limitation strategy. Although not all perceptual beliefs are immune to error, perceptual beliefs acquired in suitably favorable conditions are immune. So too are certain classes of general belief about the body derived from bodily experience.

1.3. The Second Level of Doubt

Descartes quickly realizes that this damage-limitation strategy is seriously flawed. He offers two reasons for thinking so, one for each set of stable beliefs left in play after the first level of doubt. He starts with the general beliefs about the body derived from bodily experience:

> Again, how could it be denied that these hands or this whole body are mine? Unless perhaps I were to liken myself to madmen, whose brains are so damaged by the persistent vapours of melancholia that they firmly maintain they are kings, when they are paupers, or say they are dressed in purple when they are naked, or that their heads are made of earthenware, or that they are pumpkins, or made of glass.[10]

For perceptual beliefs, Descartes considers not the possibility that he might be insane but the possibility that he might be dreaming:

> How often, asleep at night, am I convinced of just such familiar events—that I am here in my dressing-gown, sitting by the fire—when in fact I am lying undressed in bed![11]

Dreaming is problematic because it introduces the possibility of error even when perceptual conditions seem to be optimal. Descartes brings this out very clearly. He initially tries to respond to the dreaming possibility by putting forward the damage-limitation strategy that worked in the first level of doubt:

> Yet at the moment my eyes are certainly wide awake when I look at this piece
> of paper; I shake my head and it is not asleep; as I stretch out and feel my hand I do
> so deliberately, and I know what I am doing. All this would not happen with
> such distinctness to someone asleep.[12]

As he instantly realizes, however, no appeal to optimal conditions can work in this
case:

> Indeed! As if I did not remember other occasions when I have been tricked by
> exactly similar thoughts while asleep! As I think about this more carefully, I see
> plainly that there are never any sure signs by means of which being awake can
> be distinguished from being asleep.[13]

The dream argument is, I take it, directed at the possibility that any given experience that I take to be a waking experience could be a dreaming experience. It is not
directed at the possibility that I might be dreaming all the time.[14] Nor is it based on
the implausible premise that waking experience and dreaming experience are
qualitatively identical. Descartes is simply pointing out that he has often been taken
in by dreams, in the sense that he has believed himself to be awake when he was not
and had to correct himself retrospectively. The reason he has been taken in by
dreams in this way is that, as he puts it, there are no distinguishing marks that will
infallibly identify any given experience as either a waking experience or a dreaming
experience.

As in the first level of doubt, Descartes goes on to consider possible damage-
limitation strategies. His first move is to draw a comparison between a dreamer's
imagination and a painter's imagination, suggesting that both produce visions that
must in some sense be based on things that are real and have been experienced.
Both dreamers and painters have to work with preexisting materials. Descartes
gives the following list of what those "simpler and more universal things" might be:

> This class appears to include corporeal nature in general, and its extension; the
> shape of extended things; the quantity, or size and number of these things; the
> place in which they may exist, the time through which they may endure, and
> so on.[15]

The context makes clear Descartes' belief that these "simpler and more universal
things" can account for putative dream visions about both the external world and
one's own body. But, of course, his point is not just one about the workings of the
imagination. He continues:

> So a reasonable conclusion from this might be that physics, astronomy, medicine,
> and all other disciplines which depend on the study of composite things, are
> doubtful; while arithmetic, geometry and other subjects of this kind, which deal
> only with the simplest and most general things, regardless of whether they actually
> exist in nature or not, contain something certain and indubitable.[16]

So, Descartes seems to be saying, even the dream argument cannot cast doubt upon
the truths of mathematics.

Two things are immediately striking here. First, Descartes started out with the thought that we could only be dreaming now if we had some basic materials from which to construct our dreams. But how could the truths of mathematics be the basic materials that the dreaming imagination works from? Second and relatedly, the list of "simpler and more universal things" that Descartes gives comprises more or less the objects of Cartesian physics. It is a very natural assumption that the basic materials from which the dreaming imagination could, if necessary, construct a dream of the external world will be the basic materials of a veridical physics. The view that Descartes' damage-limitation response to the dreaming argument implicitly relies upon Cartesian physics has been most prominently adopted by Martial Guéroult.[17] According to Guéroult, the "simpler and more universal things" mentioned in Meditation 1 are the simple natures that Descartes thinks are ontologically basic. This allows the dream argument to be seen as a way of supporting what would now be described as a scientific realist view of the world, on which commonsense perception is systematically mistaken but can be corrected by physics. On this sort of view, the dream argument has an important heuristic function, focusing attention on precisely the features of physical objects that are essential on Descartes' scientific assumptions. But however plausible this reading might be, it seems to be ruled out when Descartes confines certainty to mathematics and explicitly says that physics is uncertain.

The key to understanding what is going on here, however, is to note that Descartes also says something else about physics that is rather peculiar. He classifies it together with astronomy and medicine as a discipline that deals with composite things rather than simples. As a description of Cartesian physics, this is patently false. Cartesian physics is corpuscular. It tries to show how the behavior of composite physical objects can be predicted and explained in terms of the behavior of their parts, which are themselves understood in terms of simples. On the other hand, however, this does seem to be a fair description of Aristotelian/Scholastic physics, where explanation proceeds in terms of the potentialities and formal principles pertaining to composite physical objects. If we take it that Descartes is claiming that Aristotelian/Scholastic physics is rendered unstable by the dream argument, then we can retain the thought that the dream argument leaves some elements of Cartesian science unscathed without doing violence to the text.

1.4. The Third Level of Doubt

Descartes begins by introducing a new type of doubt, starting from his belief that there is an omnipotent God and then posing the question "How do I know that he has not brought it about that there is no earth, no sky, no extended thing, no shape, no size, no place, while at the same time ensuring that all these things appear to me to exist just as they do now?"[18] The first scenario that he envisages is one in which God has arranged matters so that he is completely deceived about everything, including what he had earlier described as the transparent truths of mathematics:

> What is more, since I sometimes believe that others go astray in cases where they think they have the most perfect knowledge, may I not similarly go wrong every time I add two and three or count the sides of a triangle, or in some other even simpler matter, if that is imaginable?[19]

This is not, however, Descartes' considered formulation of the skeptical problem. The fact that he has placed the responsibility for possible deception on God immediately suggests to him two damage-limitation strategies. The first foreshadows what will eventually become his antiskeptical line of argument in the main part of the *Meditations*, namely, that complete deception seems to be incompatible with the divine goodness. At this stage in the argument, however, Descartes immediately realizes that this strategy is not available because occasional deception seems just as incompatible with the divine goodness as complete deception, and yet it obviously occurs. It is not until he develops his theory of judgment and error in Meditation 4 that he finds an answer to this problem.

The second damage-limitation strategy is initially more promising. It too exploits the role that God plays in generating Descartes' first attempt at global skepticism. "Perhaps there are some," he wonders, "who would prefer to deny the existence of so powerful a God rather than believe that everything else is uncertain."[20] What is interesting, and not often noticed by commentators on Meditation 1, is that Descartes does actually accept this strategy. For the sake of argument, he accepts that there is no God. But his conclusion from this is that it makes skeptical worries more rather than less threatening:

> Let us not argue with them, but grant them that everything said about God is a fiction. According to their supposition, then, I have arrived at my present state by fate or chance or a continuous chain of events, or by some other means; yet since deception and error seem to be imperfections, the less powerful they make my original cause, the more likely it is that I am so imperfect as to be deceived all the time.[21]

What is particularly interesting is that Descartes clearly thinks that these apparently rather tenuous thoughts suffice to render all his beliefs unstable. He continues:

> I have no answer to these arguments, but am finally compelled to admit that there is not one of my former beliefs about which a doubt may not properly be raised; and this is not a flippant or ill-considered conclusion, but is based on powerful and well thought-out reasons. So in future I must withhold my assent from these former beliefs just as carefully as I would from obvious falsehoods, if I want to discover any certainty.[22]

Descartes has now reached the ultimate degree of skepticism. Strikingly, however, he reaches this conclusion two paragraphs before there is any mention of the malicious-demon hypothesis, which is usually taken to provide Descartes' considered reason for withdrawing assent from all his previous beliefs. Just before introducing the malicious-demon hypothesis, Descartes emphasizes that the skeptical conclusion has already been established to his satisfaction. He refers to "the fact that they [all his opinions] are in a sense doubtful, as has just been shown," and goes on to say, "But it is not enough merely to have noticed this; I must make an effort to remember it."[23] The malicious-demon hypothesis is part of the "effort to remember." It is a device he introduces to stop himself wavering rather than an argument in support of the conclusion that all his beliefs are unstable.

2. Cartesian Skepticism and Classical Skepticism

2.1. The Basic Differences

It is widely accepted that there are fundamental differences between the skepticism with which Descartes engages in Meditation 1 and the various forms of skepticism at play in the ancient world.[24] Hellenistic skepticism was, for at least some of its defenders, an ethically driven doctrine. For Pyrrhonists, the suspension of belief (*epoche*) inspired by skeptical argumentation is the only way of attaining the state of tranquility and freedom from disquiet (*ataraxia*) in which true happiness consists.[25] In the debates between the Stoics and the followers of the Academy, the crucial premise on which all parties agreed was that the man of true wisdom would never have false beliefs.[26] The Stoics believed that it was (in principle, although not in practice) possible for the wise man to avoid assenting to falsehoods. Academics such as Arcesilaus and Carneades thought that a man who assented to some propositions would not be able to avoid assenting to falsehoods and hence concluded that the wise man would not assent to anything. Some scholars accordingly have held that the characteristic feature of ancient skepticism is that skeptical concerns and arguments are not in any way *insulated* from everyday judgments and knowledge-claims, whereas modern skepticism is concerned with doubts that are "purely philosophical."[27]

There are certainly significant continuities between the skeptical *devices* employed by ancient skeptics and the devices that Descartes brings into play in Meditation 1. It was a common strategy, then as now, to make a distinction between optimal and suboptimal perceptual conditions in response to arguments from the possibility of perceptual error, just as Descartes does when he offers his perceptual belief that he is sitting beside the fire as immune from perceptual error.[28] It was equally common to draw attention to the possibility of thinking that one is awake when one is in fact dreaming. Socrates raises the problem in the *Theaetetus* (particularly at 158b–c), noting that it applies equally to illness and to madness, while a well-known and dismissive passage in Aristotle's *Metaphysics* lumps it together with arguments from perceptual error in a way that shows clearly how commonly discussed at the time these problems were.[29]

Nonetheless, pointing out that there are parallels in the *skeptical devices* used by Descartes and the ancient skeptics is not at all to say that there are parallels in the *skeptical arguments* in which those devices are put to work. There are many different ways of employing worries about perceptual error and dreams, and the arguments employed by Descartes and the ancient skeptics are very different in structure and intent.

2.2. Cartesian Skepticism and the Modes of Skepticism

Pyrrhonian skeptical arguments tend to take a standard form. They point out two different ways in which things can appear, either to different people or to the same person at different times, observe that there is no way of deciding between them, and hence conclude that the appropriate response is to suspend judgment. For Descartes, in contrast, the general pattern of skeptical argumentation is to offer a specimen belief or set of beliefs together with a possible source of doubt and then to take the possibility of doubt as sufficient reason to reject the belief or beliefs. Pyrrhonian-style arguments depend upon the two alternatives offered being equally credible, whereas this clearly does not hold for much of Meditation 1. It is, after all, part of the definition of hyperbolic doubt that it involves doubting *propositions that are for all practical purposes indubitable.* Pyrrho of Elis and Aenesidemus think that no sane and rational person would have grounds for thinking one appearance to be true rather than the other. Descartes, however, thinks that no sane and rational person could have any reason for actually believing the skeptical possibilities that he entertains.

2.3. Cartesian Arguments and Classical Arguments: Globalizing versus Nonglobalizing Skeptical Arguments

In developing the second level of Cartesian skepticism, Descartes proposes (and appears to endorse) the principle that any given perceptual experience might be false on the grounds that (as he puts it) "there are never any sure signs by means of which being awake can be distinguished from being asleep" (AT VII 19, CSM II 13). The epistemological principle driving this argument is that if, for any perceptual experience, it is possible that there could be a nonveridical but phenomenally indistinguishable experience, then the first perceptual experience cannot be trusted to be veridical. The skeptical arguments of the Academy feature a very similar organizing principle. Here, for example, is how Cicero describes the debate between the Stoic Zeno and the Academic skeptic Arcesilaus. According to Zeno, the wise man would always have knowledge rather than opinions, provided that he confined his assent to a certain class of presentations:

So what kind of presentation? Zeno defined it as a presentation which came from an existing thing and which was formed, shaped and moulded exactly as that thing was. Next question: could a true presentation be of the same quality as a false one? Here Zeno was quite sharp and saw that no presentation could be perceived if, though it came from something which exists, it could be of the same quality as that which came from something which does not exist. Arcesilaus agreed that the addition to the definition was correct, since what is false cannot be perceived and neither can what is true if it is just like what is false. The burden of his argument in those debates was to show that there in fact existed no presentation coming from something true which was not such that one of the same quality could have come from something false.[30]

Let me term the principle making it inadmissible to endorse a perceptual experience for which there might exist a phenomenally indistinguishable but non-veridical counterpart Zeno's principle in honor of its most famous exponent. Zeno's principle makes considerable sense in Descartes' framework and in the context of the debate between Stoics and Academics. Descartes was committed to rejecting any belief for which there is a possibility of error, and both the Stoics and Academics accepted the general principle that the wise man would never assent to a falsehood.

The difference between the doubts of the dreaming argument and the doubts associated with what is usually but misleadingly called the malicious-demon argument is quite straightforward. It is the transition from

(A) It is possible that any of my perceptual beliefs might be mistaken

to

(B) It is possible that all my perceptual beliefs might be mistaken.

In Descartes' hands, Zeno's principle is extended from individual perceptual beliefs to the set of all perceptual beliefs and indeed to almost all beliefs about the external world. Whereas in the dreaming argument and in the debates between Academics and Stoics what is at issue is the possibility of a single perception having a phenomenally indistinguishable but nonveridical counterpart, third-level skepticism trades on the possibility of a completely nonveridical set of perceptual beliefs serving as a phenomenally indistinguishable counterpart to all our current perceptual beliefs. This, in Descartes' eyes, gives us reason to doubt or withhold assent from all our beliefs about the world, whether perceptual or not.

This globalization of the indistinguishability argument is the distinctive feature of Cartesian skepticism. It is a simple matter of fact that no such globalization took place in the ancient world.[31] The interesting philosophical question, however, is why this should be. Is it simply a contingent fact about the ancient skeptics that they failed to draw the most powerful conclusions from the skeptical arguments and skeptical devices available to them? Or is there something inherent to the philosophical context within which Descartes was operating that made available to him types of skeptical argument unavailable to ancient skeptics?

2.4. Williams on Skepticism and the Cartesian Conception of the Mental

We have already observed that an important feature of the local indistinguishability arguments that feature prominently in Academic skepticism is that the possibility of there being two (or more) indistinguishable perceptions is motivated in causal terms. We can have indistinguishable perceptions because we can have perceptions that are caused by indistinguishable objects. According to Williams, this reflects a deep fact about Academic skepticism, rooted in how the Academics think about sensations:

> The Academic skeptics think of sensation in partly causal-physical terms, as an affection of the living organism. Accordingly, they think of similar perceptions as perceptions of (caused by) similar objects. This precludes uniting their arguments so as to raise the question of whether there is any external world at all.
>
> (Williams, 1986, 134–35)

For the Academic skeptics, sensations are thought of primarily as products of the senses, and the senses are thought of as means by which we become aware of the world around us. Descartes, in contrast, assimilates sensations to thoughts and allows them to become detached from their causes, thereby opening up the possibility of a gap between the content of a perceptual experience and the causes of that perceptual experience. Descartes' skeptical arguments work by exploiting this gap, which is itself an artifact of what is often called, according to Williams, the "Cartesian conception of the mental."

It is true that the globalization of the indistinguishability argument involves severing the link between the content of perception and the causal origins of perception, since it depends upon the possibility that the entirety of our perceptual experience might have a radically deviant causal origin. But it seems arbitrary to claim that the link must be severed before the globalization of the indistinguishability argument can be undertaken. Perhaps, on the contrary, the globalization of the indistinguishability argument is what severs the link. After all, what better grounds might there be for thinking that content and causal origins can come apart than the conceivability of a radical skeptical scenario in which they do come apart? But then the argumentative weight is borne by the conceivability of the skeptical scenario, and the question remains: Why was the radical skeptical scenario conceivable to Descartes in a way that it was not to the Academic skeptics?

2.5. Burnyeat's Reading of Ancient Skepticism

Myles Burnyeat (1982) is firmly of the view that the Pyrrhonist and Academic skeptics were just not bold enough. They had everything that they needed to make the move from (A) to (B), but just did not push hard enough:

> It is possible, contrary to Stoic theory, that even the most luminously clear and distinct perceptions are in fact false. But there the argument stops. The general-

isation which for us lies so readily to hand is not made. At no point is it suggested, as Descartes does suggest, that the malignant demon might have made every perception false (the whole totality), and every deliverance of our reasoning faculties false as well, so that we are deceived in everything. This is the "hyperbolical" doubt which alone poses in an absolutely general way the problem of the existence of the external world. . . . If this is the result of Descartes's rehash of ancient scepticism, the implied claim is that the traditional material supports a doubt more radical than the traditional sceptic had dared suppose. *So far as I can see, that claim is correct.*

(Burnyeat, 1982, 37, emphasis mine)

Since the type of skeptical worry envisaged in (A) does not entail the skeptical worry envisaged in (B), things cannot be quite as straightforward as Burnyeat suggests by talking about the "generalisation which for us lies so readily to hand." Any such generalization would have to be argued for.

Prima facie, the two *major* types of skeptical argument current in antiquity (the nodes [*tropoi*] of skepticism central to Pyrrhonism and the arguments from Zeno's principle deployed by the Academics to attack the Stoics) support (A)-type worries but not (B)-type worries. The aim of the modes of skepticism is to illustrate an undecidable opposition among appearances (*ta phainomena*—which may or may not be perceptual) that will precipitate the suspension of judgment. Here is a schematic presentation of a typical Pyrrhonian argument:[32]

1. *x* appears *F* in situation *S*.
2. *x* appears *F** in situation *S**.
3. There is no epistemic reason to trust *S* over *S**, or vice versa.
4. We can neither affirm nor deny that *x* is really *F* or really *F**.

This form of skeptical argument is clearly committed to the existence of the *x* that is being discussed. The issue is whether that *x* really has a given property or not.[33]

Academic arguments drawing upon Zeno's principle seem a more promising source, and it is these that Burnyeat himself discusses. These arguments are not quite as standardized as the modes of skepticism, but the following is a fairly common argument form (and is described as such in Cicero's *Academica* II 40):

1. Some cognitive impressions are true and others false.
2. No false cognitive impressions can be perceived.
3. Every true cognitive impression is such that there can be a qualitatively identical false cognitive impression.
4. With cognitive impressions such that there is no difference between them, it cannot be that some are perceived and others not [an application of Zeno's principle].
5. Therefore, no cognitive impressions are perceived.

This clearly supports (A)-type skeptical worries. But does it support (B)-type skeptical worries? In defending (3), the Academic philosophers made much of the possibility of a cognitive impression being caused by one member of an indistinguishable pair. Stock examples of such indistinguishable pairs include eggs, twin brothers, and the like. There are no qualitative ways of telling whether one is perceiving an egg from this hen or that hen—or which of the famous identical Servilius twins is in front of one.

The crucial issue is how far one is prepared to take the notion of an indistinguishable pair. (B)-type skeptical worries arise if and only if the possibility is entertained that, to put it in the relevant terms, the total set of all my current cognitive impressions might be caused in one of two different ways—a standard way, whereby they would be veridical, or a nonstandard way, whereby they would be false. If the notion of an indistinguishable pair is given this sort of global reading, then (B)-type skeptical worries can indeed emerge from a suitably reconstructed version of (3). It will be useful to have a name for this. Let me distinguish the *local indistinguishability argument* from the *global indistinguishability argument* and term the move from one to the other the *globalization of the indistinguishability argument*.

If the indistinguishability argument is to be globalized, some sort of coherent story has to be told about how and why the total set of my current cognitive impressions might be being caused in a nonstandard way. Did the ancients have anything comparable to Descartes' *malin génie* at their disposal? Burnyeat appeals to the second book of Cicero's *Academica*, where Lucullus, in the course of an attack on Academic skepticism, attributes to his opponents what might well seem to be a prototype of the *malin génie* argument:

> They [the Academics] first attempt to show the possibility that many things may appear to exist that are absolutely non-existent, since the mind is deceptively affected by non-existent objects in the same manner as it is by real ones. For, they say, when your school asserts that some presentations are sent by the deity—dreams, for example, and the revelations furnished by oracles, auspices and sacrifices (for they assert that the Stoics against whom they are arguing accept these manifestations)—how possibly, they ask, can the deity have the power to render false presentations probable and not have the power to render probable those which approximate absolutely most closely to the truth? or else, if he is able to render these also probable, why cannot he also render probable those which are distinguishable, although only with extreme difficulty, from false presentations? and if these why not those which do not differ from them at all?[34]

However, as Lucullus himself goes on to point out, the argument is really a type of sorites argument. It attempts to move in a series of uncontroversial steps, each of which seems unexceptional on its own terms, from a starting point that would be happily accepted by those to whom it is directed. Starting with the premise that the deity can bring it about that we are convinced of false cognitive impressions (the equivalent of the premise that a man with no hair is bald), the argument moves to the conclusion that the deity can bring it about that we are convinced of cognitive impressions that not only are false but that we are in principle unable to identify as false (which, at least to the Stoics, would be the equivalent of the conclusion that a man with a full head of hair is bald). Each step in the argument effectively takes the form of asking why the difference between *this* class of cognitive impressions and *that* class of cognitive impressions should be relevant to the power of the deity (just as one might ask why the addition of a single hair should make a man who is bald not bald).

The conclusion of the sorites argument is that all cognitive impressions are individually subject to arguments from Zeno's principle, which is a form of an (A)-type skeptical worry. It does not bring us to the possibility that the totality of cognitive impressions might be subject to arguments from Zeno's principle. Nor, pace Burnyeat, does the generalization lie easily to hand. There is no easy sorites-like step that leads from the possibility of any of my cognitive impressions being false to the possibility of all my cognitive impressions being false. What I think misleads Burnyeat here is the thought that a powerful deity who sometimes deceives is all that is required to motivate (B)-type skeptical worries. But that seems quite wrong. (B)-type skeptical worries will not emerge until we also have, first, reasons to think that the deity is sufficiently powerful to bring about the reality of global error and, second, reasons to take seriously the possibility that the deity might be responsible for such global error. Lucullus himself points out that an opponent of the Academic arguments from the deity would attack under both heads. "For who will have granted you, he asks, either that the deity is omnipotent, or that even if he can do as described he will...?"[35]

Merely believing in a deity who occasionally deceives is not sufficient to motivate (B)-type skepticism. Something more is required. The next two sections consider different possibilities. Section 3 considers the possibility of motivating (B)-type skepticism through the idea of an omnipotent creator, while section 4 suggests that a more profitable place to look for the motivation for (B)-type skepticism is in the distinctive nature and status of Cartesian science.

3 · CARTESIAN SKEPTICISM AND MEDIEVAL ANTECEDENTS

3.1. Skeptical Arguments in the Medieval Period

Scholars have been giving increasing attention to the much-neglected history of skepticism and skeptical arguments in the medieval period. Although Burnyeat's influential collection *The Skeptical Tradition* (1983) moves straight from Augustine at the end of the fourth century and beginning of the fifth century A.D. to the Renaissance rediscovery of the Hellenistic skeptical texts a thousand years later, and Popkin's even more influential history of skepticism (2003) begins only with Savonarola in the fifteenth century, scholars are becoming increasingly aware that skeptical arguments and positions were hotly debated during the medieval period

(Gregory 1974; Lagerlund 2007; Perler, forthcoming). It has even been suggested that when Descartes famously introduces his final level of doubt in Meditation 1 by referring to "the long-standing opinion [*vetus opinio*] that there is an omnipotent God who made me the kind of creature that I am" (AT VII 21, CSM II 14), he is deliberately harking back to these debates.[36]

In works of a number of philosophers, skeptical arguments played what might be termed a dialectical role. A good example is the Franciscan Peter John Olivi (Pasnau, 1997), who made use of skeptical arguments to attack the Aristotelian doctrine of intelligible species. Olivi's objection to intelligible species is, in essence, that the intelligible species stands as a barrier between mind and object. It is part of the Aristotelian doctrine of intelligible species that what is represented in the mind is exactly the same universal form that is instantiated in the cognized object. However, Olivi argues, the Aristotelian doctrine rests upon a substantive ontological assumption, namely, that whenever we cognize an intelligible species, there is a corresponding object instantiating the same form. This ontological assumption is open to skeptical challenge:

> Let us suppose that God presents such a species to our [intellectual] gaze without there existing a thing or without there being a thing actually present. In that case something would appear as well as in the case in which a thing exists or is actually present. In fact, no more or less would something appear in that case.[37]

In the terminology introduced previously, Olivi is employing a local form of the indistinguishability argument. Skepticism, and epistemology more generally, is not his primary interest, however. Olivi's main concern is with motivating a form of direct realism that dispenses with intelligible species and other representational intermediaries.

We find another version of the local indistinguishability argument discussed by John Duns Scotus in book 1, distinction 3, question 4 of the *Ordinatio* when he considers "whether any certain and unadulterated truth can be known naturally by the intellect of a person in this life without the special illumination of the Uncreated Light."[38] Scotus's general topic is the scope of unaided human knowledge as opposed to the knowledge that might come from divine illumination, but nonetheless his discussion of the illuminationist views of Henry of Ghent shows a clear sensitivity to the type of local indistinguishability arguments canvassed by the Academic skeptics (with whom he, like Henry of Ghent, was familiar through Augustine). In fact, in the first article of the question he argues that the very arguments that Henry uses to defend the need for divine illumination lead to Academic skepticism, which he then sets out to refute in article 2.[39]

There is an even more explicitly epistemological engagement with skeptical arguments in the debate between Bernard of Arezzo and Nicholas of Autrecourt (de Rijk, 1994). Bernard of Arezzo's writings have not come down to us, but Nicholas characterizes them as highly skeptical:

> And thus, when we review and sum up your position, it appears that you have to admit that you are not certain of those things which are outside of you. And so you

do not know if you are in the sky or on earth, in fire or in water.... Similarly you do not know what things exist in your immediate surroundings, as to whether you have a head, a beard, hair, and the like.... Furthermore, your position seems to lead to the destruction of civic and political life, because if witnesses testify to what they have seen, it does not follow "We have seen it therefore it has happened". Likewise, if we reason along these lines, I ask you how the Apostles were sure that Christ suffered on the cross, that He has risen from the dead, and so on.[40]

In opposition to Bernard, Nicholas maintains a form of what is often termed "mitigated skepticism." He defends the reliability of sense perception but withholds certainty from judgments that go beyond the evidence of the senses, particularly judgments that make claims about causal relations between objects. In defending this mitigated skepticism, Nicholas discusses various forms of the argument from illusion and a version of the dreaming argument.

It does not seem, however, that anything along the lines of the (B)-type skeptical argument envisaged by Descartes was entertained during the medieval period. Even the extreme skepticism attributed by Nicholas to Bernard of Arezzo seems to be an (A)-type skepticism. This poses a puzzle, since there is a clear sense in which at least some of the machinery that Descartes employed to motivate (B)-type skeptical worries was very much in the air toward the end of the medieval period, particularly in the debates about the possible epistemological ramifications of divine omnipotence that occurred in the schools of London and Paris during the late thirteenth and early fourteenth centuries. These debates are well known to historians of medieval thought,[41] but rather less so to Descartes scholars and hardly at all to philosophers of skepticism.

3.2. Debates about Divine Omnipotence

The defining feature of late medieval philosophy (chronologically, the thirteenth and fourteenth centuries) was the incorporation of the main texts of the Aristotelian corpus into the curricula of the newly formed universities.[42] By the middle of the thirteenth century, Aristotle's works were widely known and taught. However, several of Aristotle's doctrines could not be reconciled with orthodox interpretations of Christian theology. Particularly problematic were Aristotle's belief in the eternity of the world, his necessitarianism, and his doctrine of the active intellect, which seemed to be incompatible with the doctrine of the creation and the doctrine of the immortality of the soul. These tensions gave rise to a range of controversies in the 1250s and 1260s covering not just the truth or otherwise of Aristotle's claims but also the more general question of how to demarcate the boundaries between philosophy and theology. These eventually gave rise to two important condemnations in 1270 and more significantly in 1277.[43]

A significant number of the propositions condemned in 1277 placed limits on divine omnipotence. Particularly influential in subsequent debates on divine omnipotence were propositionss 67 and 69:

That the first principle cannot produce generable things immediately because they are new effects and a new effect requires an immediate cause that is capable of being otherwise.

That God cannot produce the effect of a secondary cause without the secondary cause itself.[44]

Etienne Gilson has argued that the conception of divine omnipotence in play after 1277 not only provided the resources for (B)-type skeptical worries but actually precipitated them.[45] The key notion here is the principle associated with the condemned proposition 69, namely, that whatever God can bring about through secondary causes he can bring about directly, since our experience of the world, both sensory and intellectual, is a clear example of something that God brings about through the operation of a secondary cause. The possibility that divine omnipotence might operate in this sphere was famously noted by William of Ockham when he argued that God could bring about intuitive knowledge of a nonexistent object. It is apropos of this claim of Ockham's that Gilson writes:

> If God can conserve in us the intuition of something that is not actually existing, how shall we ever be sure that what we are perceiving as real is an actually thinking thing? In other words, if it is possible for God to make us perceive as real an object that does not really exist, have we any proof that this world of ours is not a vast phantasmagoria behind which there is no reality to be found?
>
> (Gilson, 1937, 80–81)

It is generally held that this interpretation of Ockham is based on a misreading.[46] Ockham's conception of intuitive apprehension requires it to give rise to evident judgments, which cannot be false. If, therefore, God were to create in us an intuitive cognition of a nonexistent object, we would (according to Ockham) come to the true judgment that the nonexistent object in question does *not* exist.[47] Nonetheless, one might be forgiven for thinking that Ockham's position is wildly implausible, and that the natural position would be that in such a situation we would have the false judgment that the nonexistent object *does* exist. This indeed was the view taken by several of the so-called Ockhamists, such as Robert Holcot.[48] Moreover, Ockham himself is clearly of the view that God could cause in us a so-called creditive act of a nonexistent object that, although not an intuitive cognition, would be indistinguishable from one and would lead us to judge that the nonexistent object exists.[49]

It might seem very easy to put this conception of divine omnipotence to work to globalize the indistinguishability argument, since an omnipotent God is limited only by the principle of contradiction, and there is nothing contradictory about the suggestion that God might bring about a state of affairs in which all my perceptual beliefs are false. Certainly, the use of an omnipotent God to motivate (B)-type skeptical arguments rests upon the possibility that God might be a radical deceiver, and many theologians and philosophers of the time were inclined to think that this is theologically impossible in virtue of being directly in conflict with the divine goodness. But there was nothing like a consensus in the thirteenth and fourteenth centuries that God's power is limited by his nature in the way that Descartes was later to suggest. Ockham has a characteristically subtle account of how, in at least one sense, God could be a deceiver, based on the distinction between absolute and connotative terms. He accepts that God cannot be a deceiver, but he understands this as a limitation not on God's power, but on descriptions of God's actions. God cannot sin, for example, because (on Ockham's view) to sin is to act against one's obligations, and God has no obligations toward his creatures. However, this does not mean that there is some action that God cannot perform, merely that there is some description that cannot be applied to God's actions.

One possible explanation for the absence of globalizing versions of the indistinguishability argument, even in the light of this radical notion of divine omnipotence, is the distinction frequently drawn in this period between God's absolute power (*potentia absoluta*) and his ordained power (*potentia ordinata*).[50] The distinction had its origin in debates about divine freedom—debates taking the form of asking whether God can do more than he wills to do.[51] Should we hold, with Anselm, that divine freedom does not require divine choice but merely the absence of compulsion?[52] Or should we follow Peter Damian in maintaining that the divine freedom is a freedom of choice and hence dependent upon God's being able to do things other than those that he willed?[53] In its classic form, the distinction between *potentia absoluta* and *potentia ordinata* reconciled these two different notions of divine freedom. We can think of God's power without thinking about how he has created the world and the laws he has laid down. Thus, considered with respect to his *potentia absoluta*, God has the power to do anything that is not contradictory. Alternatively, we can think about God's power in terms of what in fact God has chosen to do. This gives us the divine *potentia ordinata*, which considers divine freedom as constrained by the world he has created and the laws he has ordained (including the miracles that he has ordained).

This distinction gives us two different notions of possibility. There is nothing self-contradictory about the suggestion that it is possible for God to bring about a state of affairs in which all my beliefs about the physical world are mistaken. But it would be very reasonable for a late medieval philosopher to take the view that a state of affairs that is possible *de potentia absoluta* is not *really* possible in any sense that should cause us grave epistemic concern. Suppose that we ask, then, whether my being in a state of global error is possible *de potentia ordinata*. If we put any faith at all in divine revelation, then the possibility of God bringing about global error seems slim indeed. If we adopt Aquinas's reading of *potentia ordinata* as whatever God has ordained to come to pass,[54] there is no indication in the Bible that it is part of God's ordained plan that everything that I believe and that I believe myself to have been told about the physical world should be mistaken—and indeed there is every indication that God's ordained plan contains nothing of the sort. On Scotus's reading of *potentia ordinata* in terms of compatibility with the laws that God has ordained, the prospects for skepticism are little better. What we know of the general laws that God has ordained seems clearly incompatible with God's bringing things about in a way that would make me globally deceived about the nature of the physical world.

How can we be confident about our knowledge of God's ordained plan? The theologians who took divine omnipotence most seriously were also those least convinced of the powers of human reason to establish truths about the nature and existence of God. The conception of divine omnipotence that played so central a role in late medieval philosophy was derived quite straightforwardly from faith and revelation. This comes across very clearly in Ockham's famous discussion of the possibility of intuitive knowledge of nonexistent objects in Quodlibet 6, question 6. He states that there are two conclusions that he seeks to establish:

> The first is that there can be by the power of God intuitive knowledge concerning a non-existent object; this I prove first by an article of faith; I believe in God, father almighty; which I understand thus, that everything which does not involve a manifest contradiction is to be attributed to the divine power.
>
> (McKeon, 1931, 373)

The appeal to faith is explicit and is echoed by others of the so-called doctors of the absolute.[55] The dependence of our conceptions of God and his omnipotence upon faith and revelation place severe limitations on the extent to which we can *coherently* and *consistently* doubt what God has revealed about how he has created the world and his plans for it. What the doctors of the absolute thought they knew about divine omnipotence was too inextricably linked with what they thought they knew about God's ordained plan for the world for it to be possible for them to disregard revelation as comprehensively as it would need to be disregarded to take seriously the possibility that (B)-type global error might fall within the scope of the divine *potentia ordinata*.[56]

4. CARTESIAN SKEPTICISM
AND CARTESIAN SCIENCE

Sections 2 and 3 have brought out how the distinctive and original feature of the skeptical arguments in Meditation 1 is the possibility that Descartes envisages of globalizing the indistinguishability arguments. The real innovation that appears with Descartes is the (B)-type skeptical possibility that our experience could be just the way it is even if it were no guide whatsoever to the real nature of the external world—and even if there were no external worlds. As we saw in discussing ancient skepticism, (B)-type skeptical worries cannot be derived from local versions of the indistinguishability argument. Nor is it enough to motivate those worries, the medieval period seems to show, that one accept the existence of an omnipotent creator unconstrained by anything except the principle of contradiction. So, it is natural to ask, why should the (B)-type skeptical scenario have been a "live" possibility for Descartes (albeit in a hyperbolic sense) in a way that it was not for his ancient and medieval predecessors?

No doubt there is a range of contributing factors. I end this survey, however, with some remarks on the connection between the (B)-type skeptical hypothesis and Descartes' extraordinarily innovative and influential natural philosophy. Historians of early modern philosophy are increasingly emphasizing the importance of Descartes' scientific work for understanding his philosophical views and arguments.[57] By and large, however, this historiographical trend has led to a downplaying of the importance for Descartes of "traditional" philosophical problems, such as skepticism about the external world. In a number of respects, the pendulum seems to me to have swung too far. Epistemological skepticism is a prime example.[58] There is a way of seeing Descartes' preoccupation with (B)-type skeptical worries as a very natural concomitant of two central features of his scientific work (features that have come very much to the fore in recent Descartes scholarship).

First, unlike Scholastic natural philosophy, which is underpinned by a faith in the senses, Cartesian science reveals our commonsense perceptions of the world to be mistaken. It shows that there is systematic and pervasive error in our experience, most obviously by making what is effectively a distinction between primary and secondary qualities and maintaining that the latter are ultimately reducible to the differential motion of "packets" of a continuous extended substance.[59] Descartes discusses how uncritical reliance on the senses is a prime cause of scientific error in the "Replies to the Sixth Objections," giving the example of gravity. The sense-based temptation is to treat gravity as a "real quality" inhering in bodies that somehow "knows" where the center of the earth is and impels bodies toward it.[60] Similarly, the testimony of the senses seems to compel belief in the existence of the vacuum because air looks empty, in conflict with the principle that space is identical to body.

Nonetheless, the existence of systematic error in everyday experience is not itself a *compelling* reason for embracing the possibility of global error. If our science is good enough, then we can account for systematic error within science.[61] This brings us to the second feature of Cartesian science. As many historians of philosophy have noted, Cartesian science is ineliminably hypothetical.[62] It offers explanations that can ultimately be warranted only by their predictive success and explanatory power because "the supreme craftsman of the real world could have produced all that we see in several different ways."[63] Such *morally certain* explanations cannot offer the sort of correction of systematic perceptual error that is required by Cartesian science's repudiation of our "manifest image" of the world. We can only respond to skeptical worries from within science if we have confidence in the scientific solutions that we are providing. It is no use claiming that our commonsense view of the world is completely mistaken and then offering a hypothetical physics and metaphysics that will explain how that comprehensive error fits into a complete account of the world. As soon as a world of orbiting planets and moving particles is put forward as a hypothesis to explain the familiar world of everyday experience, one possible and perhaps inevitable consequence is the skeptical suggestion that perhaps another, even more counterintuitive, hypothesis will explain the phenomena just as well. And that just is the (B)-type skeptical scenario that marked Descartes' original contribution to the history of skepticism.

Cartesian science generates skepticism precisely because it is predicated on the existence of radical error in the commonsense view of the world and yet cannot provide anything more than a hypothetical replacement for the commonsense view of the world. It is here that we must locate the sources of the originality of Cartesian skepticism. Descartes' own scientific work opened up for him the possibility of (B)-type skeptical worries that had not been available to his medieval and ancient predecessors. There is much truth in the traditional view that Descartes' discussion of epistemological skepticism was the defining and originating moment in modern philosophy, but we need to appreciate his epistemological innovation against the background of his own scientific work and, more generally, in the context of the radical divergence between appearance and reality opened up by the New Science. Only then will we appreciate the gulf that separates Cartesian skepticism from the far more circumscribed skepticism of the ancient and medieval periods.

NOTES

1. AT VII 17, CSM II 12. References to Descartes' writings in the text are given in the standard manner to the Adam and Tannery edition of the *Oeuvres de Descartes*, 12 vols. (Paris: Cerf, 1897–1913), cited as AT, and to the translation by John Cottingham, Robert Stoothof, Dugald Murdoch, and Anthony Kenny of the *Philosophical Writings of Descartes*, 3 vols. (Cambridge: Cambridge University Press, 1985–1991). Volumes I and II are cited as CSM I and II, and Volume III as CSMK. This paper draws in part on Bermúdez 1997 and 2000.

2. AT VII 18, CSM II 12.

3. The distinction between beliefs acquired from the senses and beliefs acquired through the senses is the distinction between beliefs derived from personal experience and beliefs derived from testimony; cf. *Conversation with Burman*, AT V 146, CSMK 332.

4. For Aristotle, see, for example, Lear, 1988.

5. AT VII 18, CSM II 12.

6. AT VII 76, CSM II 53.

7. AT VII 77, CSM II 53.

8. AT VII 18, CSM II 13.

9. As employed, for example, in Ayer, 1940, chap. 5.

10. AT VII 18–19, CSM II 13.

11. AT VII 19, CSM II 13.

12. Ibid.

13. Ibid.

14. This is the interpretation most famously canvassed and attacked in Walsh, 1963. It is criticized comprehensively in Curley, 1988, and Frankfurt, 1970.

15. AT VII 20, CSM II 14.

16. Ibid.

17. Guéroult, 1968, vol. 1, pp. 34–35.

18. AT VII 21, CSM II 14.

19. Ibid.

20. Ibid.

21. Ibid.

22. AT VII 21–22, CSM II 14–15.

23. AT VII 22, CSM II 15.

24. See, for example, Burnyeat, 1982; Williams, 1986; Everson, 1991; and Broughton, 2002. For an opposed view, see Fine, 2003.

25. See, for example, Sextus Empiricus, *Outlines of Pyrrhonism* 1.12. The idea that the distinctive motivation of Greek skepticism was the perceived ethical advantages of suspension of assent is persuasively presented in Sedley, 1983.

26. Cicero, *Academica* 2.67; Sextus Empiricus, *Adversus Mathematicos* 7.156–158.

27. E.g., Annas and Barnes, 1985, chap. 1. Burnyeat, 1984, accepts the first part of the claim but not the second. He sees the provisional morality that Descartes offers in part 3 of the *Discourse* as a sign that he was deeply concerned with the possible effects of skeptical argument on ground-level judgments and beliefs (Burnyeat, 1984, 247–248).

28. See Cicero, *Academica* 2.19, for example.

29. Aristotle, *Metaphysics* 1010b2–12.

30. Cicero, *Academica* 2.77 (translated in In wood, 1983, 163).

31. Even Fine (2003), who argues that Pyrrho espoused a form of external-world skepticism, is clear that he does not deploy anything like the indistinguishability argument.

32. See Annas and Barnes, 1985, for general discussion of the form of the modes of skepticism.

33. Fine, 2003, rejects the standard *de re* reading of statements about appearances.

34. Cicero, *Academica* II 47–48 (trans. H. Rackham in the Loeb Classical Library).

35. Cicero, *Academica* II 50.

36. See Gregory, 1974. The crux of the matter seems to be how we read the Latin word *vetus*. Does he mean long-standing in him or long-standing in the intellectual atmosphere? The second reading might well indicate a tacit reference to long-standing debates on divine omnipotence. The Latin is ambiguous, but the French text (personally checked and approved by Descartes) reads "il y a longtemps que j'ai eu dans mon esprit une certaine opinion." This is clearly autobiographical.

37. Translated by Perler from Olivi's *Quaestiones in secundum librum Sententiarum*. See Perler, forthcoming, n. 23.

38. Latin text with a parallel translation in Duns Scotus and Wolter, 1987. Also translated in McKeon, 1931, 313–350.

39. Henry of Ghent had also engaged directly with Academic arguments at the very beginning of his *Summae quaestionum ordinariarum*. See Adams, 1987, 552–571, for a clear exposition of Henry's views, and see Pasnau, 1995, for Henry's illuminationism.

40. Translated in de Rijk, 1994, 55, #14.

41. Rudavsky, 1985, is an extremely useful collection of articles on the evolution of thought about divine omnipotence in the Middle Ages. Classic discussions of the epistemological ramifications of the debates in Oxford and Paris in the fourteenth century will be found in the essays by the Polish historian Konstanty Michalski collected in Michalski, 1969.

42. For details on the medieval appropriation of Aristotle, see Dod, 1982. See also the chapters by Jacquart and Maccagnolo in section 4 of Dronke, 1988.

43. See Wippel, 1977, 1995, as well as Hissette, 1977. A selection of the 219 propositions condemned in 1277 is translated in Hyman and Walsh, 1983.

44. Translated in Hyman and Walsh, 1983, 587.

45. Gilson, 1937. See also Michalski's "Le Criticisme et le Scepticisme dans la Philosophie du XIVème Siècle," in Michalski, 1969.

46. This was emphatically argued in Boehner, 1945, reprinted (minus the appended edited texts) in Boehner, 1958. See also Adams, 1970, and Adams, 1987, where she modifies her earlier view to make Ockham even less skeptical.

47. This is clearly stated in the prologue to *Ordinatio* Q. 1, where Ockham writes: "If the divine power were to conserve a perfect intuitive cognition of a thing no longer existent, in virtue of this non-complex knowledge the intellect would know evidently that this thing does not exist" (translated in Boehner, 1958, 23).

48. See Kennedy, 1983, 1993.

49. William of Ockham, *Quodlibetal Questions* Q. 6 question 6.

50. See Courtenay, 1985, for a historical survey and Oberman, 1963, for an application of the distinction to debates over the scope of skepticism in the fourteenth century.

51. See Normore, 1982, and Boh, 1985.

52. Anselm, *De concordia praescientiae et praedestinatione et gratiae dei cum libero arbitrio*, edited and translated in Anselm, Hopkins, and Richardson, 1974.

53. Cantin, 1972.

54. Thomas Aquinas, *Summa Theologica* I, 25, 5.

55. The phrase is William Courtenay's.

56. This, of course, does leave (A)-type error as a genuine possibility *de potentia ordinata*.

57. The importance of the scientific background for a proper understanding of Descartes' philosophical work has been stressed by a number of influential recent commentaries. See, for example, Clarke, 1982; Garber, 1978; Gaukroger, 1995; and the essays collected in Gaukroger, 1980.

58. See Bermúdez, 1997, where the central themes of this concluding section are discussed in more detail.

59. For a fascinating account of Descartes' mathematical physics, see Garber, 1992.

60. AT VII 442, CSM II 298.

61. This is the strategy adopted in our own day by Quine and somewhat earlier by Locke. For a discussion of the background to Locke's imperviousness to skeptical worries, see Bermúdez, 1992.

62. See Clarke, 1982, for a detailed discussion of Descartes' philosophy of science.

63. AT VIIIA 327, CSM I 289.

REFERENCES

Adams, M. M. (1970). "Intuitive Cognition, Certainty, and Skepticism in William Ockham." *Traditio* 26: 389–398.

———. (1987). *William Ockham*. Notre Dame, Ind.: University of Notre Dame Press.

Annas, J., and Barnes, J. (Eds.). (1985). *The Modes of Skepticism: Ancient Texts and Modern Interpretations*. Cambridge: Cambridge University Press.

Ayer, A. J. (1940). *The Foundations of Empirical Knowledge*. London: Macmillan.

Bermúdez, J. L. (1992). "The Adequacy of Simple Ideas in Locke." *Locke Newsletter* 23: 25–58.

———. (1997). "Skepticism and Science in Descartes." *Philosophy and Phenomenological Research* 58: 743–772.

———. (2000). "The Originality of Cartesian Skepticism." *History of Philosophy Quarterly* 17, 333–360.

Boehner, P. (1945). "The Notitia Intuitiva of Non-existents According to William of Ockham." *Traditio* 1: 223–275.

———. (1958). *Collected Articles on Ockham.* St. Bonaventure, N.Y: Franciscan Institute (St. Bonaventure University).

Boh, I. (1985). "Divine Omnipotence in the Early Sentences." In T. Rudavsky (Ed.), *Divine Omniscience and Divine Omnipotence in Medieval Philosophy.* Dordrecht: D. Reidel.

Broughton, J. (2002). *Descartes's Method of Doubt.* Princeton, N.J.: Princeton University Press.

Burnyeat, M. (1982). "Greek Philosophy and Idealism: What Descartes Saw and Berkeley Missed." *Philosophical Review* 90: 3–40.

———. (Ed.). (1983). *The Skeptical Tradition.* Berkeley: University of California Press.

———. (1984). "The Skeptic in His Place and Time." In R. Rorty, J. B. Schneewind, and Q. Skinner (Eds.), *Philosophy in History.* Cambridge: Cambridge University Press.

Cantin, A. (Ed.). (1972). *Pierre Damien: Lettre sur la toute-puissance divine. Introduction, texte, critique, traduction, et notes.* Paris: Les Editions du Cerf.

Clarke, D. M. (1982). *Descartes' Philosophy of Science.* Manchester: Manchester University Press.

———. (1992). "Descartes' Philosophy of Science and the Scientific Revolution." In J. Cottingham (Ed.), *The Cambridge Companion to Descartes.* Cambridge: Cambridge University Press.

Courtenay, W. J. (1985). "The Dialectic of Omnipotence in the High and Late Middle Ages." In T. Rudavsky (Ed.), *Divine Omniscience and Divine Omnipotence in Medieval Philosophy.* Dordrecht: D. Reidel.

Curley, E. (1988). *Descartes against the Skeptics.* Cambridge, Mass.: Harvard University Press.

de Rijk, L. M. (Ed.). (1994). *Nicholas of Autrecourt: His Correspondence with Master Giles and Berhard of Arezzo; A Critical Edition and English Translation.* Leiden: Brill.

Dod, B. (1982). "Aristoteles Latinus." In N. Kretzmann (Ed.), *Cambridge History of Late Medieval Philosophy.* Cambridge: Cambridge University Press.

Dronke, P. (1988). *A History of Twelfth-Century Western Philosophy.* Cambridge: Cambridge University Press.

Duns Scotus, J. (1987). *Philosophical Writings: A Selection,* A. B. Wolter (Ed.). Indianapolis: Hackett.

Everson, S. (1991). "The Objective Appearance of Pyrrhonism." In S. Everson (Ed.), *Companion to Ancient Thought: Psychology.* Cambridge: Cambridge University Press.

Fine, G. (2003). "Sextus and External World Skepticism." *Studies in Ancient Philosophy* 24: 341–385.

Frankfurt, H. (1970). *Demons, Dreamers, Madmen: The Defense of Reason in Descartes's Meditations.* Indianapolis: Bobbs-Merrill.

Garber, D. (1978). "Science and Certainty in Descartes." In M. Hooker (Ed.), *Descartes: Critical and Interpretive Essays.* Baltimore: John Hopkins University Press.

———. (1986). "Semel in Vita: The Scientific Background to Descartes' *Meditations.* In A. O. Rorty (Ed.), *Essays on Descartes'* Meditations. Berkeley: University of California Press.

———.(1992). *Descartes' Metaphysical Physics*. Chicago: University of Chicago Press.

Gaukroger, S. (1980). *Descartes: Philosophy, Mathematics and Physics*. Brighton, Sussex: Harvester Press

———. (1995). *Descartes : An Intellectual Biography*. Oxford: Clarendon Press

Gilson, E. (1937). "The Road to Skepticism." In *The Unity of Philosophical Experience*. New York: Charles Scribner.

Gregory, T. (1974). "Dio ingannatore e genio maligno: Nota in margine alle *Meditatione* de Descartes." *Giornale critico della filosofia italiana*, 477–516.

Guéroult, M. (1968). *Descartes selon l'ordre des raisons*. Paris: Aubier.

Hatfield, G. (1986). "The Senses and the Fleshless Eye: The *Meditations* as Cognitive Exercises." In A. O. Rorty (Ed.), *Essays on Descartes'* Meditations. Berkeley: University of California Press.

Hissette, R. (1977). *Enquête sur les 219 articles condamnés à Paris le 7 mars 1277*. Louvain: Publications universitaires.

Hopkins, J., and Richardson, H. W. (Trans.) (1974). *Anselm of Canterbury*. 2nd American ed. Toronto: Edwin Mellen Press.

Hyman, A., & Walsh, J. J. (1983). *Philosophy in the Middle Ages: The Christian, Islamic, and Jewish Traditions*. 2nd ed. Indianapolis: Hackett.

Inwood, B., and Gerson, L. P. (Ed.). (1983). *Hellenistic Philosophy: Introductory Readings*. Indianapolis: Hackett.

Kennedy, L. A. (1983). "Philosophical Skepticism in England in the Mid-Fourteenth Century." *Vivarium* 21: 35–57.

———. (1993). *The Philosophy of Robert Holcot, Fourteenth-Century Skeptic*. Lewiston, N.Y: Edwin Mellen Press.

Lagerlund. H. (2007). *Representation and Objects of Thought in Medieval Philosophy*. Aldershot: Ashgate.

Lear, J. (1988). *Aristotle: The Desire to Understand*. Cambridge: Cambridge University Press.

McKeon, R. (1931). *Selections from Medieval Philosophers*.Vol. 2, *Roger Bacon to William of Ockham*. London: C. Scribner's.

Michalski, K. (1969). *La Philosophie au XIVe siècle*. Frankfurt: Minerva.

Normore, C. (1982). "Future Contingents." In N. Kretzmann, A. Kenny, J. Pinborg, and E. Stump (Eds.), *Cambridge History of Later Medieval Philosophy*. Cambridge: Cambridge University Press.

Oberman, H. A. (1963). *The Harvest of Medieval Theology: Gabriel Biel and Late Medieval Nominalism*. Cambridge, Mass.: Harvard University Press.

Pasnau, R. (1995). "Henry of Ghent and the Twilight of Divine Illumination." *Review of Metaphysics* 49, no. 1: 49–75.

———. (1997). *Theories of Cognition in the Later Middle Ages*. Cambridge: Cambridge University Press.

Perler, D. (Forthcoming). "Skepticism." In *Cambridge History of Medieval Philosophy*. Cambridge: Cambridge University Press.

Popkin, R. (2003). *The History of Skepticism from Savonarola to Bayle*. Oxford: Oxford University Press.

Rozemond, M. (1996). "The First Meditation and the Senses." *British Journal for the History of Philosophy*, 1996, no. 4: 21–52.

Rudavsky, T. (Ed.). (1985). *Divine Omniscience and Divine Omnipotence in Medieval Philosophy*. Dordrecht: D. Reidel.

Sedley, D. (1983). "The Motivation of Greek Skepticism." In M. Burnyeat (Ed.), *The Skeptical Tradition*. Berkeley: University of California Press.

Walsh, W. H. (1963). *Metaphysics*. London: Hutchison.

Williams, M. (1986). "Descartes and the Metaphysics of Doubt." In A. O. Rorty (Ed.), *Essays on Descartes's* Meditations. Berkeley: University of California Press.

Wippel, J. F. (1977). "The Condemnations of 1270 and 1277 at Paris." *Journal of Medieval and Renaissance Studies* 7, no. 2: 169–201.

————. (1995). *Medieval Reactions to the Encounter between Faith and Reason*. Milwaukee: Marquette University Press.

CHAPTER 4

HUME'S SKEPTICISM

MICHAEL WILLIAMS

By all that has been said the reader will easily perceive, that the
philosophy contained in this book is very sceptical.

(Hume)[1]

1. INTRODUCTION

By Hume's own account, the philosophy contained in *A Treatise of Human Nature*
is "very sceptical." His later book *An Enquiry Concerning Human Understanding* is
in some ways even more openly skeptical than its predecessor.[2] At the same time, it
is clear that Hume sees himself as in some respects a critic of skepticism and, indeed,
as a constructive philosopher. So the questions arise, how skeptical is Hume's
philosophy, and in what ways? In pursuing these questions, with respect to which
there is little agreement among Hume's commentators, I shall be mainly concerned
with the *Treatise*. However, I shall have something to say about the *Enquiry* where
the later work points to significant developments in Hume's thought.

Three preliminary points concerning the goal, task, and apparent outcome of
Hume's investigations will enable us to formulate some more definite questions
concerning Hume's skepticism.

The goal of the *Treatise*, announced in the introduction, is a reform of the
Republic of Letters, which Hume sees as driven by interminable disputes. "There is
nothing which is not the subject of debate, and in which men of learning are not of
contrary opinions." If a temporary victory is won, "'tis not reason, which carries

the prize, but eloquence" (T 3). A reformist goal animates the *Enquiry* too, though in the later book Hume suggests that not *all* subjects are matters of interminable dispute, problematic claims being found principally in "a considerable part of metaphysics" and in "popular superstitions" (E 91). This more focused complaint reflects Hume's increasingly overt religious skepticism.

To improve the state of learning, we must become "thoroughly acquainted with the extent and force of human understanding" (T 4). We will then be able to determine what we can profitably investigate (our understanding's *extent*) and the degree of certainty we can reasonably expect to achieve in our several inquiries (its *force*). Equipped with this epistemological self-understanding, we will acknowledge that our minds are not fitted to inquire into certain "remote and abstruse subjects" (E 92). Hume's project thus implies a measure of *critical* or *selective* skepticism.[3] It also has *normative implications*, offering prescriptions for good epistemic conduct.

We see from this that although Hume's *goal* is a general reform of the sciences, his *task* is the development of a particular science: the science of man. The aim of this science, with respect to the understanding, is to "explain the nature of the ideas we employ, and the operations we employ in our reasonings." This is "the sole end of logic" (T 4). But "as the science of man is the only solid foundation for the other sciences, so the only solid foundation we can give this science itself must be laid on experience and observation" (T 4). Logic thus becomes a division of empirical psychology. This *naturalistic* aspect of Hume's philosophical outlook also appears to reflect definite skeptical commitments. Hume is often taken to argue that since our fundamental beliefs and inferential tendencies have no basis in "Reason," they are best explained in terms of the workings of the "imagination." His thought is supposed to be that since these beliefs and tendencies cannot be *justified*, they can only be *explained* in causal-psychological terms. In this way, skepticism clears the way for naturalism.[4]

Already we encounter problems. In contrast to the selective skepticism integral to Hume's critical project, the skepticism (allegedly) deployed to support the naturalization of epistemology ("logic") seems to be *general*. But if *no one's* beliefs are justified, why are not "bad reasoners," as Hume calls them, just psychologically *different* rather than epistemologically *deficient*? How can a general skeptic offer epistemic advice? It is as if Hume wants to say that while all beliefs are groundless, some are more groundless than others.

The question of Hume's relation to deep and general forms of skepticism gains force as his investigation proceeds. In the case of the *Treatise*, it can seem that Hume started to write one book and finished by writing another. Although the introduction to the *Treatise* announces a bold critical-explanatory project, the conclusion to book 1 offers a dramatic narrative of a complete skeptical collapse. In the *Enquiry*, Hume is more ironic than despairing. He notes the "whimsical condition of mankind, who must act and reason and believe; though they are not able, by the most diligent enquiry, to satisfy themselves concerning the foundation of these operations, or to remove the objections, which may be raised against them" (E 207). But although the tone is different, the doctrine may not be. Early and late, there is at least a suspicion that the *outcome* of Hume's epistemological reflections investigations is *ultimately wholly skeptical.*[5]

These remarks suggest three questions that an account of Hume's skepticism should address.

1. What is the connection between skeptical argumentation and Hume's naturalistic science of man? (Answered in section 5.)
2. How does Hume's naturalism subserve his critical project? In particular, insofar as naturalism is associated with general skepticism, can Hume be both a general and a selective skeptic? (Answered in section 6, with further relevant discussion in section 7.)
3. Do Hume's skeptical tendencies get out of hand? (Answered in section 7.)

However, putting ourselves in a position to answer these questions requires some preliminary work. We need to understand the various ways in which forms of skepticism can differ (section 2) and then, building on this understanding, to characterize the general tendencies of Hume's skeptical thinking (sections 3–4). But once our questions are answered, we will have a clearer sense of the distinctiveness and complexity of the role played by skepticism in Hume's philosophical project.[6]

2. VARIETIES OF SKEPTICISM

In the *Treatise*, Hume offers no systematic account of what he understands by "scepticism." This is one of the principal points of difference from the *Enquiry*. There Hume offers two distinctions for classifying forms of skepticism: "antecedent" versus "consequent" and extreme versus moderate. But while this is a step forward, Hume still exploits more distinctions than he explicitly makes. So rather than simply following Hume's classificatory scheme, I shall offer a more fine-grained account of the ways in which skeptical outlooks can differ.

One important distinction is between two genres of skepticism: *epistemological* and *conceptual*. Epistemological skepticism is concerned principally with knowledge, justification, and belief. By contrast, conceptual skepticism, although it has implications for belief, revolves around issues of meaning. So where an epistemological skeptic may argue that certain beliefs are unjustified, so perhaps we should give them up, a conceptual skeptic will deny that certain words are so much as meaningful, so they cannot be used to express any genuine beliefs at all.[7]

The significance of epistemological skepticism can be *methodological* or *plain*. A methodological skeptic uses skeptical problems as tools for investigation. Descartes is the paradigm: he marshals skeptical considerations in order to discover truths that resist skeptical undermining, which truths can serve as foundations for scientific knowledge. Treated this way, skepticism is taken up only to be overcome and is thus *provisional* rather than *final*. In a way, then, a methodological skeptic is not a skeptic at all. By contrast, a plain skeptic incorporates skepticism into his own philosophical outlook.

Hume's science of man investigates the force and extent of human understanding. This distinction can usefully be applied to forms of skepticism.

The force of skepticism can be either *theoretical* or *practical*. A theoretical skeptic accepts (or at least does not deny) some skeptical *thesis*: for example, that inductive inference has no rational basis, or that we have no knowledge of external objects. I say "or at least does not deny" because a plain skeptic's attitude to his skepticism can be either *dogmatic* (when skepticism is unqualifiedly endorsed) or *skeptical* (when it is neither endorsed nor repudiated). A practical skeptic does more than assent to a philosophical thesis: he takes on distinctive attitudes or practices. He may cultivate doubt or uncertainty. Typically, he renounces something, eschewing claims to knowledge or, at the extreme, suspending judgment altogether.[8] Obviously, this is a distinction, not a dichotomy. A philosopher may be both a theoretical and a practical skeptic. Indeed, it is natural to suppose that philosophers become practical skeptics in virtue of endorsing theoretical skepticism.

Both theoretical and practical forms of skepticism can vary in their extent. There are three ways in which forms of skepticism can be more or less extensive: *depth*, *range*, and *context*.

The depth of a philosopher's skepticism depends on his epistemic targets. Skepticism that impugns knowledge, leaving open the possibility of justification, is relatively shallow. How shallow depends on the conception of knowledge in play: the higher the standards for knowledge, the shallower the skepticism.[9] A deeper form of skepticism more deeply questions the possibility of *justification*, though justification skepticism too can be more or less deep, depending on how demanding a conception of epistemic justification the skeptic has in mind. In Hume's case, there is a conception of epistemic justification especially worth noting, which we can call "rational-foundational" ("rf"). This conception is *evidentialist* and *internalist*: a belief is rf justified only if it is either noninferentially justified (evident in itself, intrinsically credible) or evidently supported by other justified beliefs. I shall call the form of skepticism that denies that our beliefs are justified according to this demanding conception *antirationalism*. Since the sort of justification it excludes is stringent, antirationalism is a *moderate* form of justification skepticism and contrasts with *radical* justification skepticism, which denies that our beliefs are epistemically justified *in any sense at all*.

So far, I have discussed depth in connection with theoretical skepticism. With regard to practical skepticism, a practical knowledge skeptic will give up claiming to *know* anything. A practical justification skeptic will desist from representing his beliefs as justified. A practical belief skeptic will try to have no beliefs. In connection with Hume, this is a form of skepticism that we must bear very much in mind. In principle, a theoretical skeptic, too, can have reservations about belief, justified or not. However, since Hume has no such worries, we can ignore this possibility.

The range of a given form of skepticism concerns what commitments the skeptic has in his sights. At the limit, skepticism is *universal*: nothing we believe (or suppose ourselves to know) is exempt. Other forms of skepticism are *restricted*: skepticism with respect to inductively based beliefs or beliefs about the external world. But even restricted forms of skepticism are hypergeneral in that, within the broad domains to which they apply, they are emphatically *nonselective*. No inductive conclusions yield knowledge (or justified belief). The most elementary claims about the world are as badly off as the most arcane. Prima facie, then, both universal and restricted forms of skepticism preclude such narrow forms of skepticism as skepticism about miracle reports or about claims concerning the existence and nature of God, as inferred from the order and harmony of the universe, insofar as these turn on (allegedly) *bad* inductive reasoning.

Finally, skepticism can be subject to *contextual* limitations. For example, Descartes ties his methodological skepticism to a highly unusual form of inquiry devoted to uncovering fundamental principles. Outside this special investigative context, in which all practical considerations have been set aside, extreme skeptical doubts would be inappropriate, even mad. So skepticism is *contextually constrained* if it is essentially connected with certain special circumstances.

Let us examine Hume's skepticism in the light of these distinctions.

3. EPISTEMOLOGICAL AND CONCEPTUAL SKEPTICISM

In both the *Treatise* and the *Enquiry*, Hume's first order of business is to argue that all simple "ideas" are derived from simple "impressions"—experiences of red or of the taste of a pineapple—that they copy or "represent." Hume is not yet dealing with judgments but with components of judgments: something like concepts. Hume's "copy principle" is thus not a theory of knowledge or belief but of *conception.* But since, in Hume's view, words are meaningful insofar as they are proxies for ideas, this theory of conception has the potential to function as a criterion of significance. It is therefore tempting to suppose that conceptual skepticism is the key to Hume's critical project. On this reading, Hume intends to trace the lack of progress in certain subjects, such as abstruse metaphysics, to an uncritical use of technical terms that lack clear meaning. Thus, as he writes in the *Abstract*,

> Our author thinks, that "no discovery cou'd have been made more happily for deciding all controversies concerning ideas, than this, that impressions always take the precedency of them, and that every idea, with which the imagination is furnished, first makes its appearance in the correspondent impression. . . . " And

when he suspects that any philosophical term has no idea annexed to it (as is too common) he always asks, *From what impression that pretended idea is derived?* And if no impression can be produced, he concludes that the term is altogether insignificant. 'Tis after this manner he examines our idea of *substance* and *essence.*

(T 409)

Apparently, Hume's critical skepticism draws the line between good and bad philosophy (or science) on conceptual rather than epistemological grounds.

It would be absurd to claim that there is no element of conceptual skepticism in Hume's outlook. But it is not absurd to insist that epistemological skepticism is far more important, and that Hume's conceptual skepticism is both more re-stricted and more nuanced than the passage just quoted might suggest. For al-though Hume does go in for conceptual skepticism—the cases of substance and essence are paradigms—skepticism of this kind is something of a threat to his main goals. There is a tendency for conceptual skepticism to get out of hand, a tendency rooted in the inadequacy of Hume's version of the theory of ideas. Hume has great difficulty distinguishing between concepts and judgments; indeed, he is inclined to pour scorn on the distinction (see T 67, n. 20). But this gives some of his skeptical arguments a dangerous duality: failures to find an "impression" for an "idea" can be read as raising a problem either about the sensory basis of a concept or about the observational evidence for a belief. The duality is dangerous because although Hume is eager to question the epistemological credentials of commonsense beliefs, he has no interest in impugning their contentfulness. On the contrary, Hume wants to explain the psychological bases of our everyday beliefs; and since he takes beliefs to be "lively" ideas, commonsense beliefs demand ideas to be enlivened. Thus if conceptual skepticism ever threatens to spill over into common sense, he must find some way of containing it. This is why, surprising as it may sound, Hume devotes considerable energy to *warding off* conceptual skepticism, even at the cost of departing from the strict conceptual empiricism he seems to espouse.

The clearest example of Hume's problem is found in his discussion of the notion of "body" (external objects). The senses, he argues,

are incapable of giving rise to the notion of the continu'd existence of their objects, after they no longer appear to the senses. For that is a contradiction in terms, and supposes that the senses continue to operate, even after they have ceased all manner of operation.

(T 126)

But "continued" existence is an essential component in the concept of "body." So what is Hume's point: that we have no observational grounds for *believing* that bodies exist, or that the very *concept* of body is problematic? The answer is "both." However, since the belief in body is a natural belief and so in a sense not to be questioned, Hume must resist Berkeley's conclusion that so far as objects go, there is no distinction between *esse* and *percipi*. Accordingly, we find Hume going to great lengths to explain how certain features of our impressions lead the imagi-nation to draw this distinction, thereby creating the "fiction" of external things.

Whatever its merits, this explanation does not begin to fit the simple theory of conception enshrined in the "copy principle," but it does allow him to detach the threat of conceptual skepticism from the epistemological arguments he endorses.

This raises an obvious question: how can Hume abandon the copy principle and still go in for conceptual skepticism? The answer is that the basis of Hume's conceptual skepticism is what he calls "one of the greatest and most valuable discoveries that has been made of late in the Republic of Letters": Berkeley's discovery that there are no abstract ideas (T 17). However, a serious defense of this claim would take me too far afield.[10] I want instead to turn to epistemological skepticism, which is where Hume's interest mostly lies.

4. METHODOLOGICAL AND PLAIN SKEPTICISM

It is clear that Hume is some kind of plain skeptic: his skepticism is not *merely* methodological. But does Hume dabble in methodological skepticism at all? Can he? It is tempting to claim that he cannot. If skeptical arguments are to underwrite naturalism, their conclusions must be allowed to stand. So we might argue that Hume must eschew methodological skepticism *because* he is a plain skeptic.

This account of Hume's intentions seems to be confirmed by the *Enquiry*, where Hume distinguishes two "species" of skepticism. The first is "*antecedent* to all study and philosophy" and is

> much inculcated by DES CARTES and others, as a sovereign preservative against error and precipitate judgment. It recommends an universal doubt, not only of all our opinions and principles, but also of our very faculties; of whose veracity, say they, we must assure ourselves by a chain of reasoning, deduced from some original principle, which cannot possibly be fallacious or deceitful.
>
> (E 199)

The second species is "*consequent* to science and enquiry" and arises

> when men are supposed to have discovered, either the absolute fallaciousness of their mental faculties, or their unfitness to reach any fixed determination in all those curious subjects of speculation, about which they are commonly employed. Even our very senses are brought into dispute, by a certain species of philosophers; and the maxims of common life are subjected to the same doubt as the most profound principles or conclusions of metaphysics and theology.
>
> (E 200)

Hume's distinction corresponds roughly to our distinction between *methodological* and *plain* skepticism.[11]

Cartesian skepticism is *extreme* methodological skepticism in that it sets the bar for accepting a proposition very high: a proposition is to be accepted only if it is certified by an infallible principle. But the idea that we could use skepticism to identify such a principle is a nonstarter, since

> neither is there any such original principle, which has a prerogative above others, that are self-evident and convincing. Or if there were, could we advance a step beyond it, but by the use of those very faculties of which we are supposed to be already diffident. The CARTESIAN doubt, therefore, were it ever possible to be attained by any human creature (as it plainly is not) would be entirely incurable; and no reasoning could ever bring us to a state of assurance and conviction upon any subject.

> (E 199)

This argument—that attempts to validate basic epistemological principles are apt to prove circular—is a classic Pyrrhonian trope: the *dialellos* or "wheel." This argument is central to the ancient problem of the criterion, and Hume suggests that it has no theoretical solution. If this is right, plain skepticism makes methodological skepticism useless. But on closer examination, Hume's relation to Cartesian methodological skepticism is more complex than it first seems and may be more problematic than Hume himself realized.

To be sure, Hume rejects the Cartesian idea of rationally reconstructing human knowledge on secure foundations and hands over the question of the "extent and force" of human understanding to his naturalistic science of man. But his conception of the science of man retains Cartesian undertones. More or less without argument, Hume identifies the naturalistic successor to Cartesian epistemology with individual psychology. And although he makes a passing allusion to "my Lord Bacon" (T 5), he has none of Bacon's interest in either experimental procedures or the social and institutional aspects of scientific research. Thus although Hume is not wholly oblivious to the social dimension of knowledge, he remains very much a methodological individualist, indeed, a Cartesian subjectivist. However, Cartesian subjectivism has its roots in Cartesian methodological skepticism: in particular, in skepticism concerning knowledge of the external world.

Hume's discussion of external-world skepticism highlights his essentially "Cartesian" understanding of his otherwise naturalized epistemology. Contemporary naturalists have no hesitation in using our knowledge of the world to explain how such knowledge is acquired. We might think that Hume got there first. Introducing the topic of "scepticism with regard to the senses," he advises us:

> We may well ask, *What causes induce us to believe in the existence of body?* But t'is vain to ask, *Whether there be body or not?* That is a point, which we must take for granted in all our reasonings.

> (T 125)

But Hume does not "take for granted" the existence of body, if taking the existence of body for granted means feeling free to invoke it for explanatory purposes. All he means by claiming that we must take the existence of body for granted is that we are going to believe in an external world, come what may. The most that philosophy can do is explain why.

What Hume does take for granted is a fundamental tenet of the theory of ideas: that the "immediate" objects of consciousness are *perceptions* (impressions and ideas). He welcomes this tenet because it allows him to argue that we have no immediate perceptual knowledge of external reality:

> That our senses offer not their impressions as the images of something . . . external, is evident; because they convey to us nothing but a single perception, and never give us the least intimation of any thing beyond.
>
> (T 126)

This means that an argument for the existence of body would have to involve an inference from what we do know, that we have impressions of various kinds; and according to Hume, no such inference is available. This skeptical lemma points us toward an investigation of the causes of our belief in external bodies, which Hume locates in certain temporal patterns displayed by impressions, their "constancy and coherence." Hume's causal explanation starts from the same subjective basis as his argument that our belief in body cannot be justified.

Why are impressions thus privileged if the Cartesian project has been abandoned? The answer is that Hume takes it to be obvious that our immediate awareness of our own thoughts and sensations is incorrigible:

> For since all actions and sensations of the mind are known to us by consciousness, they must necessarily appear what they are, and be what they appear. Every thing that enters the mind, being in *reality* a perception, 'tis impossible anything shou'd to *feeling* appear different. This were to suppose, that even where we are most intimately conscious, we might be mistaken.
>
> (T 127; italics in the original)

Since impressions are the source of all ideas, causal explanations must start from them: impressions are thus both genetically primitive and epistemically privileged. So although Hume often questions things that we are psychologically incapable of doubting, in the case of our immediate awareness of our impressions or sensations he does not allow even the possibility of error. This is a Cartesian argument in all but name. But since Hume does not acknowledge this use of methodological skepticism, its implications are not carefully thought through.[12]

5. FORCE: SKEPTICISM AND NATURALISM

Hume sees a close connection between skepticism and naturalism. There is a straightforward way of explaining the connection. Skeptical arguments show that inductive expectations, or beliefs implying the existence of an external world, cannot be justified. It follows that they can only be explained causally, in terms of psychological mechanisms.[13] Since these mechanisms operate for the most part automatically, wide-ranging practical skepticism is psychologically impossible. Far from encouraging us to be practical skeptics, theoretical skepticism shows why practical skepticism is a nonstarter, and a naturalistic theory of belief provides the crucial link. In the words of Robert Fogelin, while Hume "accepts a theoretical scepticism that is wholly unmitigated," he "further holds that only on his theory of belief can we explain (though not justify) the occurrence of any belief whatsoever."[14] But although this account of Hume's move from skepticism to naturalism might seem to fit the *Enquiry*, as a way of characterizing Hume's argument in the *Treatise*, it is quite wrong. It does not fit at all well with one of the *Treatise*'s central themes: the basis of inductive inference.

Hume is famous for discovering (or inventing) the problem of induction. But Hume's understanding of the problem differs from modern understandings in several ways. I mention two. First, Hume's main interest is in projective inference (why do we believe that the sun will rise tomorrow?) rather than generalizing inference (why do we believe the sun always rises?). Second, Hume does not speak of induction but of reasoning concerning causes and effects. His treatment of (what we call) inductive inference is thus closely interwoven with his discussion of the idea of necessary connection, which he takes to be part of our ordinary concept of causality. Examining individual cases of cause-effect relations, Hume finds no impression of necessary connection. With a little imagination, we can detach any cause from its customary effect, which we could not do if cause and effect were perceptibly bound together. Looking beyond individual cases, Hume finds only constant *conjunction*, effects consistently following causes, but still without any discernible necessity. Where, then, does the idea of necessary connection come from?

This interest in the idea of necessary connection suggests that Hume's problem is conceptual. As usual, however, Hume's interests are primarily epistemological. Hume is strongly inclined to restrict "knowledge" to truths that are intuitively or demonstratively certain and hence necessary. "Knowledge," he tells us, is "the assurance arising from the comparison of ideas" (T 86). Given this conception of knowledge, the fact that there is no perceptible necessary connection between cause and effect entails that we have no (intuitive or demonstrative) knowledge of causal relations.[15] This result sets the stage for the "sceptical" argument of *Treatise* 1.3.6, "Of the Inference from the Impression to the Idea." Since there is no demonstrative knowledge of causal relations, "the transition from an impression present to the memory or senses to the idea of an object, which we call cause or effect, is founded on past *experience*, and on our remembrance of their constant conjunction" (T 62; italics in the original). The question is therefore "whether experience produces the idea by means of the understanding or imagination; whether we are determin'd by reason to make the transition, or by a certain association and relation of perceptions?" Call this "Hume's dilemma."

Having set up his dilemma, Hume argues by elimination. If the inference depended on reason, "it wou'd proceed upon that principle, *that instances, of which we have had no experience, must resemble those of which we have had experience, and that the course of nature continues always uniformly the same*" (T 62; italics in the original). The question is now whether there is a good argument for the principle. Hume thinks that there could not be. Since the principle could be false, it cannot be "derived from knowledge," that is, demonstrated. It must therefore be supported by an argument from "probability." To be convincing, this argument must proceed from empirical evidence, "the impressions of our senses and memory" (T 63). This means that it must be based on *past* experience. But since the argument's conclusion extends to future cases, and since the fact that experience has been a certain way so far does not entail that it must continue to be that way in the future, the argument must presuppose the very principle in question. Hume sums up:

> Probability is founded on the presumption of a resemblance betwixt those objects, of which we have had experience, and those, of which we have had none; and therefore 'tis impossible this presumption can arise from probability. The same proposition cannot be both the cause and effect of another.
>
> (T 63)

In a nutshell, we can neither *demonstrate* the inductive principle nor argue for it inductively, which would be circular. (This is another example of Hume's fondness for the Pyrrhonian wheel.) Anyway, having argued that inductive inference is not guided by "reason," Hume embraces his dilemma's second horn. Experience of the constant conjunction of two "objects" leads to their ideas becoming associated in the "imagination." When the idea of one occurs to us, the idea of the other is apt to come along automatically; and when we get an *impression* of one, we get a *lively* idea of the other, that is, a belief. Inductive inference does not presuppose belief in the uniformity principle.

According to my taxonomy, Hume's thesis that inductive inference is not guided by reason is a skeptical claim, though one of as-yet-undetermined depth. However, Hume does not describe the claim as "sceptical" at all. The only mention of skepticism in the whole of book 1, part 3, is a passing reference to "sceptics" in 1.3.13, which we shall discuss later. Skepticism does not come to the fore until *Treatise* 1.4.1, "Of Scepticism with Regard to Reason," where the topic is demonstrative reasoning. In the demonstrative sciences, Hume tells us, though "the rules are certain and infallible . . . , when we apply them, our fallible and uncertain faculties are very apt to depart from them and fall into error" (T 121). For this reason, even demonstrative reasoning is subject to skeptical doubts in that our confidence in a supposedly demonstrated conclusion should be no greater than our (inductively based) confidence in our reliability as demonstrative reasoners (T 121f). Indeed, even this judgment is hostage to a further judgment concerning our reliability in estimating our own reliability, and so on ad infinitum. Hume thinks that reflecting on this regress of probability estimates threatens to reduce our initial confidence to zero. Ignoring the details of this argument, which appears to be fallacious, we must ask whether Hume endorses this explicitly skeptical result (his first). Harking back to his problem about inductive inference, Hume insists that he is *not* rehearsing the argument in order to establish a skeptical conclusion:

> Shou'd it here be asked me, whether I sincerely assent to this argument, which I seem to take such pains to inculcate, and whether I be really one of those sceptics, who hold that all is uncertain, and that our judgment is not in *any* thing possest of *any* measures of truth and falsehood; I shou'd reply, that this question is entirely superfluous, and that neither I, nor any other person was ever sincerely and constantly of that opinion. Nature, by an absolute and uncontroulable necessity has determin'd us to judge as well as to breathe and feel; nor can we any more forbear viewing certain objects in a stronger and fuller light, upon account of their customary connexion with a present impression, than we can hinder ourselves from thinking as long as we are awake, or seeing the surrounding bodies, when we turn our eyes towards them in broad sunshine. Whoever has taken the pains to refute the cavils of this *total* scepticism, has really disputed without an antagonist, and endeavour'd by arguments to establish a faculty, which nature has antecedently implanted in the mind, and render'd unavoidable.
>
> (T 123; italics in the original)

"Total" skepticism is *practical, radical, wide-ranging belief skepticism.* No matter what the subject matter is, the total skeptic sees no beliefs as better than others and thus avoids judgment altogether. This is the form of skepticism that Hume takes most seriously and that he emphatically rejects. But there are several points to make about this important passage.

One point to notice is that Hume avoids talk of "sceptical arguments," preferring "the arguments of that fantastic sect." This distancing device indicates that he does not endorse radical, wide-ranging skepticism *even as a purely theoretical conclusion.* The reason is that for Hume, notions like "evidence" and "certainty" are not just terms of epistemic evaluation but *always* have a psychological dimension. To Hume's way of thinking, if something strikes us as evident, we must be strongly inclined to believe it. Let us not forget that Hume takes beliefs to be "lively" ideas: ideas infused with a greater "force and vivacity." This greater livelinesss, which Hume connects with "evidence," is not just a phenomenal glow: it gives our ideas "more force and influence; makes them appear of greater importance, infixes them in the mind; and renders them the governing principles of all our actions" (T 68). Beliefs are thus ideas that we rely on: we make inferences from them; crucially, they guide our actions. It follows that if anyone sincerely assented to the radically skeptical conclusion that everything is uncertain, he would be plagued with real doubts. Not knowing what to think, he would be incapable of action. In other words, sincere assent to a radically skeptical conclusion would be expressed in the practical belief skepticism that Hume regards as a psychological impossibility.

The upshot of Hume's discussion is that skeptical arguments, while not (so far as we can tell) unsound, are unpersuasive. We cannot assent to a radically skeptical conclusion. It follows that Hume cannot argue from radical theoretical skepticism to his naturalistic theory of belief. Pace Fogelin, Hume has a quite different way of connecting skepticism with naturalism. Hume continues:

> My intention . . . in displaying so carefully the arguments of that fantastic sect, is only to make the reader sensible of the truth of my hypothesis, that all our reasonings concerning causes and effects are deriv'd from nothing but custom; and that belief is more properly an act of the sensitive, than of the cogitative part of our natures. . . . If belief . . . were a simple act of thought . . . , it must infallibly destroy itself, and in every case terminate in a total suspence of judgment. But as experience will convince any one, who thinks it worth while to try, that tho' he can find no error in [the skeptics'] arguments, yet he still continues to believe, and think, and reason as usual, he may safely conclude, that his reasoning and belief is some sensation or peculiar manner of conception, which 'tis impossible for mere ideas and reflection to destroy.
>
> (T 123)

If belief were "a simple act of thought," it would be wholly under our control. In that case, we could give or withhold assent depending on a claim's epistemic credentials. This means that if we could find no error in the skeptic's argument, we would assent to his conclusion, inducing a near-universal suspension of judgment. Since such an annihilation of belief is impossible, it follows that belief is not in general a "simple act of thought." Hume's argument for naturalism is not based on the truth of the skeptic's conclusions but on the unpersuasiveness of his arguments. However, I must stress the limited character of this claim. The fact that Hume's argument for naturalism is not based on an endorsement of radical skepticism does not settle the question whether ultimately Hume is some kind of radical skeptic.

Whether or not Hume is ultimately a *radical* skeptic, it is hard to resist the feeling that even by this stage of his argument he is a theoretical skeptic of some kind. Even if his claim that "belief is more properly an act of the sensitive, than of the cogitative part of our natures" is not deduced from a skeptical lemma, it seems skeptical in itself. Hume came to agree. Thus section 4 of the *Enquiry*, in which he introduces the problem of induction, bears the heading "Sceptical Doubts Concerning the Operations of the Understanding" (E 108); and the ensuing section, in which he argues that a propensity to form inductive expectations is a fundamental feature of human psychology, is headed "Sceptical Solution of These Doubts." Here Hume exploits the theoretical/practical distinction. The doubts are "sceptical" in that they express a form of theoretical justification skepticism. The solution is "sceptical" in that it finds no flaw in the skeptical argument. The solution is a solution only in that it denies the skeptic any move from theoretical to practical skepticism.

In the *Enquiry*, then, Hume bases his naturalism on an explicit theoretical skepticism. The earlier strategy of arguing for naturalism from the unpersuasiveness of skeptical arguments still finds an echo in Hume's summary of his skeptical conclusion, which is that the mental operations underlying inferences from experience are "a species of natural instincts, which no reasoning or process of the thought and understanding is able, either to produce or to prevent" (E 123–24). The reasoning Hume has in mind is skeptical argumentation, which, though theoretically impeccable, cannot suppress basic cognitive propensities. The idea recurs in section 12, "Of the Academic or Sceptical Philosophy," where Berkeley's arguments are characterized as "merely sceptical" on the grounds that they "admit of no answer and produce no conviction" (E 203, n. 32). But the argument from unpersuasiveness now shares the stage with an argument that goes through an avowedly skeptical lemma.

The change in Hume's presentation reflects a sharpened sense of how skepticism can vary in range and depth. In the *Treatise*, skepticism is always total. By contrast, in the *Enquiry*, total skepticism, now called "Pyrrhonism," is just one kind of skepticism. More precisely, it is the extreme form of "scepticism consequent to enquiry," as Cartesian skepticism is the extreme form of antecedent or methodological skepticism. Both antecedent and consequent skepticism are impossible when taken to extremes. Equally, however, both are salutary in a moderate form. This raises a question: how would a moderate theoretical skepticism find practical expression? This brings us to the critical dimension of Hume's skeptical naturalism.

6. Depth and Range: Critical Skepticism and the Goal of Inquiry

I have argued that between the *Treatise* and the *Enquiry*, Hume developed a more nuanced understanding of skepticism, which in turn allowed him to modify his account of the connection between skepticism and naturalism. However, the modification is not without its problems. In the *Enquiry*, Hume retains his views about belief unmodified. Is he not therefore still committed to the unpersuasiveness of skeptical conclusions? And if so, how can he endorse theoretical skepticism? The answer is that he can endorse such skepticism *provided that it is not radical.*

Again pace Fogelin, there is a case to be made that Hume's skepticism is far from "unmitigated." Radical, general skepticism not only would preclude selective skepticism, short-circuiting Hume's critical project, but also would undermine the science of man itself. Hume seems to have decided that the *Treatise* gave a misleading impression of the depth of his skepticism. Thus at the very beginning of the *Enquiry*, section 1, he is at pains to distance himself from any form of skepticism that would compromise his philosophical ambitions. He insists that we can have no doubts about the feasibility of an investigation of our powers and faculties "unless we should entertain such a scepticism as is entirely subversive of all speculation, and even action" (E 93). This theme is picked up in section 12 (E 199–200), where, exploiting his new scheme for classifying forms of skepticism, he identifies himself with skepticism of a moderate or "mitigated" variety. But even at the time of the *Treatise*, if Hume had acknowledged his antirationalist account of inductive inference as in some way skeptical, there is ample evidence that he would not have seen it as radically so. A radical skeptic does not make invidious epistemological distinctions. But at 1.3.15, Hume offers "Rules by Which to Judge of Causes and Effects," a brief summation of his inductive methodology. Subsequently, when Hume argues that belief in "body" is not the product of "reason," he takes "reason" to include inductive inference, suitably methodized. This more liberal use of "reason" makes sense only on the assumption that Hume takes himself to have vindicated inductive inference: not, of course, absolutely, by Cartesian standards of certainty, but relative to other ways of acquiring beliefs.

Of course, this only pushes the problem one stage back. Perhaps Hume *wants* to make invidious epistemological distinctions, but how *can* he? His rejection of total skepticism does not answer this question. The claim that nature has determined us to judge, as well as to breathe and feel, entails only that we will inevitably have many beliefs. It does not explain why some beliefs or some methods of acquisition are better than others.[16]

At this point, we must be clear just how moderate a form of theoretical skepticism Hume's antirationalist conception of inductive inference commits him to. To have a basis in "reason," inductive inference would have to depend on intuitively evident relations of necessitation or perhaps probabilification. As we have seen, Hume thinks that he can show that there are no such relations and that, in consequence, inductive inference turns on an empirical presupposition—the uniformity of nature—that cannot be justified in a noncircular way. However, all this shows is that inductively based conclusions are not rf justified. It does not imply that they are not justified *in any way at all*. Hume's moderate theoretical skepticism leaves him plenty of room for maneuver.

To see how Hume's antirationalist naturalism acquires a critical edge, we need to recall his ultimate goal of reforming the Republic of Letters. The need for reform arises from persistent, irresolvable controversy: there is nothing about which "men of learning are not of contrary opinions" (T 3). Good methods of inquiry would lead to disputes being settled. One way to settle disputes would be to use methods that prove that our beliefs are certainly true. Hume's anti-Cartesian temperament leads him to recoil from this suggestion. But there is no need to be so ambitious. It will be sufficient for Hume's purpose if he can find methods that produce agreement. For Hume, the goal of inquiry is stable consensus.[17] He is not scrupulous about distinguishing truth from certainty (demonstrated truth). Hume's proposal is that long-term consensus replace truth as the goal of inquiry.

That this is Hume's strategy is evident from his discussion of inductive inference. Hume recognizes three "natural" relations, that is, relations capable of inducing associations between ideas: resemblance, contiguity and cause, and cause and effect. Of these, the last—the foundation of inductive reasoning—has a special connection with what Hume calls "the system of the judgment." As we have seen, judgment depends on the impressions of the senses and memory. Of these, "we form a kind of system," every member of which "we are pleas'd to call a reality." However,

> the mind stops not here. For finding, that with this system of perceptions, there is another connected by custom, or . . . the relation of cause and effect . . . it forms them into a new system, which it likewise dignifies with the title of *realities*.

> (T 75)

Hume does not claim that our beliefs are true. Instead, he finesses the issue of truth, remarking that we may "draw inferences from the coherence of our perceptions, whether they be true or false; whether they represent nature justly, or be mere illusions of the senses" (T 59). What we can be confident of is that, by producing a coherent belief-system, causal inference "peoples the world, and brings us acquainted with such existences, as by their removal in time and place, lie beyond the reach of the sense and memory" (T75). Causal inference produces a system of beliefs, coherent and thus stable. By contrast, in the absence of constant conjunction, the influence of resemblance or contiguity is "very feeble and uncertain" (T 76). Since resemblances are everywhere, we can associate anything with anything: our conclusions are a matter of "caprice," easily destabilized.

There are two objections to this account of Hume's strategy that need to be considered. First, it may seem that Hume is only aiming at stable belief on the part of each individual, and thus not at stable consensus.[18] Second, it may seem that Hume is speaking only descriptively and not normatively.

On the first point, it is true that Hume sees the way to consensus as going through the cultivation, on the part of individuals, of suitable habits of reasoning. But this is not to say that he values individual doxastic stability *as such*, no matter what its source or no matter whose beliefs are in question. Lacking an inquiring temperament, "country gentlemen" have stable beliefs; but Hume does not pretend "to make philosophers of them." As indicated in the introduction to the *Treatise*, Hume aims to foster agreement within the community of inquirers.

As for the second objection, Hume is sensitive to the charge that his antirationalist stance compromises his ability to make normative distinctions. Having criticized the "antient philosophers" for their talk of substance and essence, Hume anticipates the objection

> that the imagination, according to my own confession, being the ultimate judge of all systems of philosophy, I am unjust in blaming the antient philosophers for makeing use of that faculty, and allowing themselves to be entirely guided by it in their reasonings.

However, the principles of the imagination are not all of a piece. We must distinguish between

the principles which are permanent, irresistable and universal; such as the customary transition from causes to effects, and effects to causes: And the principles,
which are changeable, weak and irregular. . . . The former are the foundation of all
our thoughts and actions, so that upon their removal human nature must immediately perish and go to ruin. The latter are neither unavoidable to mankind,
nor necessary, or so much as useful in the conduct of life; . . . and being opposite to
the other principles of custom and reasoning, may easily be subverted by a due
contrast and opposition.

(T 148)

This passage connects the indulgence of capricious associations with instability and
hence with the disputatiousness of much philosophy. The principles of the
imagination that foster doxastic stability *even in the curious* also foster long-term
consensus. Since such consensus is the goal of inquiry, the distinction between the
two kinds of principles acquires the requisite normative edge.

From the standpoint of combining naturalism with selective skepticism, this is
perhaps Hume's most prized result. In his final summing up at the very end of
book 1 of the *Treatise*, Hume connects the different sorts of principles with two
tendencies: the speculative, which runs wild, and the commonsensical, which
cleaves to experience. Hume does not want to *eliminate* our tendency to indulge
speculative inclinations, turning us into country gentlemen. Instead, he hopes to
temper the fieriness of the speculative temperament with the earthiness of common sense. This way,

we might hope to establish a system or set of opinions, which if not true (for that,
perhaps, is too much to be hop'd for) might at least be satisfactory to the human
kind, and might stand the test of the most critical examination.

(T 177)

Hume sees his inductive methodology as embodying the wished-for synthesis. But
again, this proposal for methodological reform does not embody a consensus
theory of truth: interpersonally stable belief is an alternative to truth.

Hume's position in the *Enquiry* is harder to discern. Not only is explicit
interest in doxastic stability far less evident, but also Hume introduces an argument
not to be found in the *Treatise*: a protoreliabilist vindication of causal reasoning.
Since causal reasoning is grounded in experience of observed regularities, he
claims, it reflects

a kind of pre-established harmony between the course of nature and the succession of our ideas. . . . Custom is the principle by which this correspondence has
been effected; so necessary to the subsistence of our species, and the regulation
of our conduct.

(E 129)

This strategy has obvious advantages over the consensus-oriented approach of the
Treatise. It is easy to see how a tendency to form true beliefs can aid survival, which
could not be said of a tendency toward either mere doxastic stability or mere

agreement. However, whether Hume was conscious of making a serious break with his position in the *Treatise* is unclear. In any case, as we shall see, there are reasons why Hume cannot exploit a reliabilist strategy in a fully general way.

A further change in the *Enquiry* is that the distinction between speculative and commonsensical temperaments gives way to one between *dogmatic* and *skeptical* tendencies. This new spin is another reflection of Hume's more developed understanding of the varieties of skepticism. Having introduced the antecedent/consequent and extreme/moderate distinctions, he is able to represent his methodological stance as itself a kind of moderate skepticism. Although the extreme methodological skepticism of Descartes is pointless, Cartesian skepticism can be understood in "a very reasonable sense":

> To begin with clear and self-evident principles, to advance by timorous and sure steps, to review frequently our conclusions, and examine accurately all their consequences; though by these means we shall make both a slow and a short progress in our systems; are the only means, by which we can ever hope to reach truth, and attain a proper stability and certainty in our opinions.
>
> (E 200)

In other words, the key to reforming the Republic of Letters is *moderate methodological skepticism.*[19]

With regard to "consequent" skepticism, the "chief and most confounding objection to excessive scepticism" is that

> no durable good can ever result from it; while it remains in its full force and vigour. We need only ask such a sceptic, *What his meaning is? And what he proposes by all these curious researches?* He is immediately at a loss, and knows not what to answer. . . . [A] PYRRHONIAN cannot expect, that his philosophy will have any constant influence on the mind: Or if it had, that its influence would be beneficial to society. On the contrary, he must acknowledge, if he will acknowledge anything, that all human life must perish, were his principles universally and steadily to prevail. All discourse, all action would immediately cease; and men remain in a total lethargy, till the necessities of nature, unsatisfied, put an end to their miserable existence.
>
> (E 206–7)

Again, however, there is a moderate or "mitigated" skepticism that results when the "undistinguished doubts" of the Pyrrhonist are "in some measure corrected by common sense and reflection." This mitigated skepticism is invaluable because "the greater part of mankind are naturally apt to be affirmative and dogmatical in their opinions; . . . they see objects only on one side, and have no idea of any counterpoising arguments" (E 207). This claim about our predilection for dogmatism echoes Hume's grounds for commending moderate antecedent skepticism. Such skepticism is "a necessary preparative to the study of philosophy" in virtue of "preserving a proper impartiality in our judgments" (E 200). The slow progress made by the moderate antecedent skeptic contrasts sharply with the rush to judgment characteristic of the general run of men. But no one escapes altogether from such general human tendencies. So how do we achieve impartiality, given a natural tendency to dogmatism and precipitate judgment? The answer is that

> could such dogmatical reasoners become sensible of the strange infirmities of human understanding, even in its most perfect state, and when most accurate and cautious in its determinations; such a reflection would naturally inspire them with more modesty and reserve. . . . In general, there is a degree of doubt, and caution, and modesty, which, in all kinds of scrutiny and decision, ought ever to accompany a just reasoner.
>
> (E 208)

That is, the epistemic scrupulousness of the moderate *antecedent* skeptic—his willingness to consider alternate opinions and to follow where the argument leads—is the natural result of a serious thinking through the paradoxes of *consequent* skepticism.

The antecedent skeptic's progress is "slow" *and* "short." In addition to avoiding precipitate judgment, he limits the scope of his inquiries to the sorts of questions that we can reasonably hope to settle. In practice, adopting this moderate skeptical outlook entails avoiding most abstruse metaphysics. But this outlook cannot be acquired at the drop of a hat. Again, achieving it involves exploiting an encounter with excessive skepticism to overcome a natural tendency. Our imagination, Hume tells us, is "naturally sublime, delighted with whatever is remote and extraordinary." By contrast,

> A correct *Judgment* observes a contrary method, and avoiding all distant and high enquiries, confines itself to common life, and to such subjects as fall under daily practice and experience; leaving the more sublime topics to the embellishment of poets and orators, or to the arts of priests and politicians. To bring us to so salutary a determination, nothing can be more serviceable, than to be once thoroughly convinced of the force of the PYRRHONIAN doubt.
>
> (E 208)

The proper attitude with which to approach philosophy—an attitude in that sense "antecedent to philosophy"—is moderate methodological skepticism. But as I have stressed, this is not an attitude that we can just *take up* but rather one that we *induce* by exposing ourselves to the force of arguments for consequent skepticism in its excessive form. Appreciating the limits to epistemological self-understanding reinforces the moderate theoretical skepticism (antirationalism) exploited in Hume's consideration of the basis of causal reasoning, a form of skepticism that then finds practical expression in a modestly skeptical methodological stance. In contrast to the *Treatise*, however, the *Enquiry* offers no detailed inductive methodology.

7 · ULTIMATE SKEPTICISM (OF A KIND)

We have found three elements in Hume's philosophical outlook: moderate theoretical skepticism, moderate practical skepticism, and naturalism. Though not without its difficulties, this combination of ideas is not evidently incoherent either. But we have yet to deal with our final question: is Hume ultimately some kind of radical skeptic after all? Or, as I phrased the question at the outset, do his skeptical tendencies get out of hand?

Repudiating total skepticism, Hume says that no one was ever "sincerely and constantly of that opinion" (T 123). A philosopher can be a sincere radical skeptic, but only intermittently. The conclusion to the *Treatise* narrates just such a temporary skeptical breakdown:

> The intense view of these manifold contradictions and imperfections in human reason has so wrought upon me, and heated my brain, that I am ready to reject all belief and reasoning, and can look upon no opinion even as more probable or likely than another.
>
> (T 175)

How do such episodes come about, and what is their significance?

We have seen that Hume does not argue for naturalism by endorsing radical skepticism, even as a purely theoretical position. Whatever their differences, the *Treatise* and the *Enquiry* are at one in this respect. If Hume is driven in the end to radical skepticism, it must be because radically skeptical tendencies emerge within Hume's naturalistic theory of reasoning and belief.

We noted in passing that in the *Treatise*, book 1, part 3, the first reference to "sceptics" occurs in section 13, "Of Unphilosophical Probability." The context is a discussion of "general rules." Hume thinks that if we once become convinced of a general rule, we are apt to ignore or discount apparent counterevidence. On the one hand, this tendency is the source of prejudice. We can be so sure that "an Irishman cannot have wit or a Frenchman solidity" that neither the most agreeable Irishman nor the most judicious Frenchman will shake our opinion: "they most be dunces or fops in spite of sense or reason" (T 100). On the other hand, since appearances can be misleading, it can be a good idea to resist an otherwise natural causal inference when it conflicts with well-established principles. This is particularly so when we recognize the case as one resembling situations in which we have previously gone wrong. We can even form methodological principles to guide us in making such judgments. (Hume's "Rules by Which to Judge of Causes and Effects" are largely concerned with this.) Hume concludes that one and the same tendency—to override experience in the interest of preserving a well-entrenched generalization—is both the source of unreasonable prejudice and an indispensable restraint on overhasty causal inference.[20] The upshot is that "our general rules are in a manner set in opposition to another." The vulgar tend to generalize from superficial resemblances, making hasty inferences and showing a liability to prejudice. This is the first influence of general rules. Wise men reject such inferences as contrary to "the more general and authentic operations of the understanding." Meanwhile,

> the sceptics may here have the pleasure of observing a new and signal contradiction in our reasoning, and of seeing all philosophy ready to be subverted by a principle of human nature, and again sav'd by a new direction of the very same principle. The following of general rules is a very unphilosophical species of probability; and yet 'tis only by following them that we can correct this, and all other unphilosophical probabilities.
>
> (T 102)

Hume does not elaborate on why the skeptics should be so pleased. The method may be surprising; but if philosophy is saved in the end, where is the skepticism? The answer, I think, is that Hume does not want to elevate even the principles of his own inductive methodology to the status of inviolable rules. Of two kinds of influence exerted by general rules—going with obvious resemblances while ignoring potentially important differences versus resisting such inferences under the influence of metainductive principles or deeply entrenched commitments— "sometimes the one, sometimes the other prevails, according to the disposition and character of the person" (T 102). There is no rule to tell us when to follow a rule. But if we let experience be our guide, then, bearing in mind that inquiry will involve persons of various characters, we can entertain modest hopes of converging on consensual views.

In its first appearance, the idea of conflict within the fundamental principles of reasoning and belief shows itself in a benign guise, introducing an element of modesty into Hume's critical skepticism. However, the idea reveals its seriously skeptical potential once Hume turns to skepticism with regard to the senses. We have seen that Hume does not really take the existence of body for granted. What he means by saying that we must take it for granted is that belief in the existence of body is a bedrock principle of human nature, a belief that no skeptical reasoning can permanently undermine. However, in Hume's eyes, there is a vital difference between causal reasoning and belief in external bodies. The former is (in a sense) ultimately unjustifiable: rf unjustifiable. But the latter is *false*.

Hume holds that in its most basic or "vulgar" form, belief in "body" takes the form of what we would call "direct realism." In the opinion of the vulgar—"all of us, at one time or another" (T 136)—perception acquaints us directly with bodies. Bodies enjoy "continued and distinct" existence: unlike, say, pains, bodies are supposed to exist whether or not anyone is aware of them. But as we noted in our initial discussion of methodological skepticism, Hume never questions the Cartesian doctrine that the objects of immediate awareness are our own "perceptions." Combining this philosophical doctrine with vulgar direct realism, Hume concludes that the vulgar belief in body involves attributing mind-independent existence to (what are in fact) perceptions:

> Almost all mankind, and even the philosophers themselves for the greatest part of their lives, take their perceptions to be their only objects, and suppose, that the very being, which is intimately present to the mind, is the real body or material existence.

(T 137)

Anticipating his theory that a mind is nothing but a bundle of perceptions, Hume argues that "there is no absurdity in separating any particular perception" from "that connected mass of perceptions, which constitute a thinking being" (T 138). But although the vulgar belief is not *necessarily* false, simple experiments refute it. For example:

> When we press one eye with a finger, we immediately perceive all the objects to become double. But as we do not attribute a continu'd existence to both these perceptions, and as they are both of the same nature, we clearly perceive, that all our perceptions are dependent on our organs, and the disposition of our nerves and animal spirits.

(T 140)

From cases like this, we conclude that "our sensible perceptions are not possest of any distinct or independent existence" (T 140).

This lemma should lead us to conclude that "objects" do not enjoy continued existence either. However, our commitment to the existence of material bodies is so deeply rooted that it blocks this inference. *Something* must be capable of continued and independent existence; and if the immediate objects of awareness do not measure up, something else must do so. Under the influence of this thought, we draw for the first time a fully general distinction between perceptions and objects (as opposed to the distinction that we draw within the phenomenal world between things like pains and things like stones). Direct realism gives way to representative realism.

Lacking all basis in reason, this "philosophical" system does not constitute an epistemological advance:

> As no beings are ever present to the mind but perceptions; it follows that we may observe a conjunction or a relation of cause and effect betwixt different perceptions, but can never observe it betwixt perceptions and objects.

(T 141)

Worse, it proves no more stable than the vulgar view it supplants. In its initial version, representative realism postulates objects exactly resembling the perceptions they give rise to. But considerations similar to those that led to the demise of direct realism readily undermine this idea, spawning further philosophical theories. Ancient philosophy explains how a succession of shifting appearances can represent properties united in an unchanging object by postulating "something unknown and invisible." This postulation of an "unintelligible something" called "a substance" is a mere verbal subterfuge (T 146). "The modern philosophy," which is supposed to rest on far more solid ground, takes a different tack. It distinguishes between secondary qualities such as color, which are avowedly dependent on the state of the perceiver, and primary qualities such as extension and solidity, which are the mind-independent properties of physical existences. But according to Hume, there are no grounds for this distinction. As perceived, the primary qualities are as observer dependent as the secondary qualities and indeed are inseparable from them: for example, we cannot conceive a shape without some kind of color boundary marking it out. But "an extension, that is neither tangible nor visible, cannot possibly be conceived" (E 203). Yet take away all "intelligible qualities" from matter, secondary and primary, and "you in a manner annihilate it, and leave only a certain unknown, inexplicable something, as the cause of perceptions; a notion so imperfect, that no sceptic will think it worth while to contend against it" (E 203). Like the ancient philosophy, the modern suffers conceptual collapse. It just takes a bit longer.

To an extent, Hume welcomes this account of the collapse of philosophical theories of matter. The account fits well with Hume's critical skepticism, which encourages an instrumentalist view of scientific theories. Thus, "As long as we confine our speculations to the appearances of objects to our senses, without entering into disquisitions concerning their real nature and operations, we are safe from all difficulties" (T 46, n. 12). More problematic is the fact that the collapse begins with the instability of the *vulgar* belief in external objects. This is the source of our natural tendency to *radical* skepticism. The crucial point is that the vulgar belief in body is destabilized by *simple causal reasoning*, which implies that the two great principles of natural belief—causal reasoning and the principle underlying our belief in external reality—are in fundamental and irresolvable tension. Hume does not hesitate to draw this conclusion:

> This sceptical doubt, both with respect to reason and the senses, is a malady which can never be radically cur'd, but must return upon us every moment, however we may chace it away, and sometimes may seem entirely free from it.' Tis impossible upon any system to defend either our understanding or senses; and we but expose them farther when we endeavour to justify them in that manner. As the sceptical doubt arises naturally from a profound and intense reflection on those subjects, it always encreases, the farther we carry our reflections whether in opposition or conformity to it. Carelessness and inattention alone can afford us any remedy.
>
> (T 144)

Hume returns to this theme in the conclusion to the *Treatise*: it is impossible "to reason justly and regularly from causes and effects, and at the same time believe the continu'd existence of matter" (T 173). It is vital to be clear that the skepticism here described is not merely theoretical. Rooted in the conflict between fundamental *natural* propensities, it is the source of recurrent and severe "Pyrrhonian" episodes, at least for anyone with a philosophical turn of mind. Hume thus appears to settle for what I have called "biperspectivism." In our philosophical moods, if we think rigorously, we are driven to radical skepticism, not as a *mere* theoretical conclusion but as a total, if temporary, breakdown of belief:

> The intense view of these manifold contradictions and imperfections in human reason has so wrought upon me, and heated my brain, that I am ready to reject all belief and reasoning, and can look upon no opinion even as more probable than another.

(T 175)

Notice, too, that an appeal to general rules of reasoning is no help here. As Hume has argued, one factor that normally saves us from skepticism is the difficulty we find in "entering into remote views," that is, of sustaining the intense reflection from which skepticism derives. But we cannot make it a principle that "no refin'd or elaborate reasoning" is ever to be entertained: to do so would be to "cut off entirely all science and philosophy." This means that we have "no choice left but betwixt a false reason and none at all" (T 174). We have to do our best, but without ultimate guarantees.

Here Hume deftly picks up his point about general rules. Reason alone being no help,

> Most fortunately it happens, that . . . nature herself . . . cures me of this philosophical melancholy and delirium, either by relaxing this bent of mind, or by some avocation, and lively impression of my senses, which obliterate all theses chimeras. I dine, I play a game of backgammon, I converse.

(T 175)

As I once put it, "Scepticism has the air of a deep yet curiously evanescent insight," deep because it is wholly at variance with everyday convictions, but evanescent because it is incapable of surviving detachment from the peculiar context of intense philosophical reflection.[21] So although radical skepticism is not refutable, it is severely contextually constrained.

When one encounters the passages just cited, it is easy to sympathize with readers who think that, ultimately, Hume is *just* a skeptic. Hume represents the philosophically minded as fated to oscillate between phases of untroubled commonsense believing and skeptical despair. But we may well suspect that Hume's treatment of the two perspectives—common sense and skepticism—is not even-handed. After all, "Reason" is on the side of skepticism, not common sense. One can escape skepticism's destructive insights only through "carelessness and inattention," that is, by averting one's gaze from what would otherwise be a compelling train of thought. A return to common sense involves an "indolent belief in general maxims of the world" (T 175), which is as good as to say a considerable degree of thoughtlessness. It is hard to escape the suspicion that the skeptical perspective is rationally privileged, albeit psychologically unsustainable. Even though we cannot "sincerely and constantly" assent to skeptical conclusions, the skeptics are *right*.

I would not say that this view is wholly wrong. But we need to be careful here. Although Hume often sounds as though he is giving the last word to the skeptics, he also reminds us that such endorsements of skepticism are no more than "the sentiments of my spleen and indolence" (T 175). In giving voice to such sentiments, Hume is illustrating the descent into skepticism that he finds to be inherent in the quest for philosophical understanding. But precisely because of this, whenever his thoughts take a radically skeptical turn, he is only speaking for the mood of the moment. Seeing the impossibility of defending any view of the external world, he announces, "I feel myself *at present* . . . more inclined to repose no faith at all in my senses" (T 144; italics in the original). And although refined speculations ought generally to have little influence on us, "This opinion I can scarce forbear retracting and condemning from my present feeling and experience" (T 175). But one's mood is always the mood of the moment. In consequence, there is no overarching perspective from which we could accord the final honors either to skepticism or to common sense. Hume records his sentiments at various stages of his argument and leaves it at that, though with this qualification: commonsense beliefs reflect our dominant tendencies.

There is, then, a kind of ultimate skepticism in Hume. However, it is not *philosophical skepticism*, the straightforward view that none of our beliefs are justified. Rather, Hume's ultimate skepticism is *skepticism about the philosophical enterprise itself*. Interestingly, this ultimate skepticism is more shown than stated. Hume's skepticism about philosophy is revealed by his phenomenological account of his alternation between stretches of commonsense believing and radically skeptical breakdowns of belief.

That said, the contours of Hume's skepticism about philosophy are clear enough. Philosophy, as Hume understands it, seeks to uncover ultimate principles, whether of knowledge, man, or nature. The lesson of skepticism is that no such understanding is to be had. With respect to human knowledge, we are on the way to a skeptical conclusion as soon as we start to ask philosophical questions. This does not mean that we can say that skepticism is unqualifiedly true. The point is simply that skepticism is the destiny of attempts to philosophize about human knowledge. But this does not mean that philosophy can simply be avoided either. Hume seems to think that the urge to keep asking for reasons is embedded in human understanding itself.

Why is the quest for philosophical understanding fated to fail? There seem to be several reasons. Most fundamentally, perhaps, our desire for philosophical understanding could be sated only by principles that are self-evidently necessarily true, but Hume thinks that there are no such principles, and that those who claim to have discovered them are suffering from a lack of imagination. Worse still, the search for such principles has the effect of weakening the only factors that effectively stabilize beliefs: the particulars of experience and memory, and the habits they sustain. The very enterprise of philosophical reflection cuts us off from ordinary interests and social support: "I feel all my opinions loosen and fall of themselves, when unsupported by the approbation of others" (T 172).

There is much more that could be said about all this. In my view, the Achilles' heel of Humean biperspectivalism is Hume's conception of philosophy. Hume thinks that skepticism awaits the philosopher because he is driven to ask questions that push him beyond the constraints of everyday belief formation: "the understanding, when it acts alone, and according to its most general principles, entirely subverts itself." Crucial to this conception of philosophy is the idea that philosophical questioning has no presuppositions of its own and so is "unnatural" only in being unconstrained. However, as we saw in discussing Hume's unacknowledged debt to Cartesian methodological skepticism, Hume's attempt at understanding human understanding is shot through with Cartesian presuppositions about the mind. Following through on this thought would allow us to see that the Humean condition is not the human condition.[22] But this is a long story. Hume's view is not, as many readers have supposed, driven by irreconcilable tensions. On the contrary, Hume offers one of the most complex and intriguing articulations of a skeptical outlook to be found in skepticism's long history, a challenging vision that continues to haunt us today.[23]

NOTES

1. David Hume, "An Abstract of a Book Lately Published Entitled *A Treatise of Human Nature*," reprinted in David Hume, *A Treatise of Human Nature*, edited by David Fate Norton and Mary J. Norton (Oxford: Oxford University Press, 2000), p. 413. Subsequent references to this edition of the *Treatise* are given in the text by "T" and page number.

2. David Hume, *An Enquiry Concerning Human Understanding*, edited by Tom L. Beauchamp (Oxford: Oxford University Press, 1999). References are given in the text by "E" and page number.

3. The critical, antimetaphysical, and antireligious aspects of Hume's philosophy are emphasized by philosophers who see themselves as belonging to a broadly empiricist tradition and who are therefore admirers of Hume, for example, Anthony Flew, *Hume's Philosophy of Belief* (London: Routledge, 1961); Jonathan Bennett, *Locke, Berkeley, Hume* (Oxford: Oxford University Press, 1971); and A.J. Ayer, *Hume* (New York: Hill and Wang, 1980).

4. Hume's naturalism is stressed by Norman Kemp Smith, *The Philosophy of David Hume* (London: Macmillan, 1941); John Passmore, *Hume's Intentions* (London: Duckworth, 1952); and Barry Stroud, *Hume* (London: Routledge, 1977).

5. Kemp Smith called the radically skeptical reading of Hume the "Beattie-Reid-Green" interpretation after three of Hume's most trenchant critics. See James Beattie, *An Inquiry into the Nature and Immutability of Truth*, 4th ed. (London: Edward and Charles Dilly, 1773); Thomas Reid, *Essays on the Intellectual Powers of Man*(University Park: Pennsylvania State University Press, 2002), essay 2, chap. 14; and T.H. Green in the introduction to his edition of Hume's works, reprinted as *Thomas Hill Green's Hume and Locke*, edited by Ramon M. Lemos (New York: Thomas Crowell, 1968). More recent versions of this reading have been given by Richard Popkin and Robert Fogelin. See Popkin, "Hume's Pyrrhonism and His Critique of Pyrrhonism," in *Hume*, edited by V.C. Chappell (Garden City, NY: Doubleday, 1966); and Fogelin, *Skepticism in Hume's Treatise of Human Nature* (London: Routledge, 1985).

6. For more detailed discussion of how to reconcile the critical, naturalistic, and skeptical aspects of Hume's philosophy, see Michael Williams, "The Unity of Hume's Philosophical Project," *Hume Studies*30, no. 2 (November, 2004). The essay is an extended critical response to Louis Loeb, *Stability and Justification in Hume's "Treatise"*(Oxford: Oxford University Press, 2002).

7. Whether a philosopher connects epistemological with conceptual skepticism will depend on his other views. For example, if he is tempted by a verificationist conception of meaning, epistemological skepticism will readily induce conceptual concerns.

8. To head off a possible misunderstanding, I emphasize that the theoretical/practical distinction, as I intend it, has nothing to do with what the skeptic is skeptical about, such as theoretical as opposed to practical (e.g., moral) matters. Rather, the distinction is concerned exclusively with skepticism's force, distinguishing skepticism as an epistemic doctrine from skepticism as an attitude, stance, or practice.

9. In the *Treatise*, Hume defines knowledge as "the assurance arising from the comparison of ideas" (T 86), thus revealing a lingering attachment to the idea, typical of early modern philosophy, that "knowledge" is restricted to truths that are intuitively or demonstratively certain. This conception of knowledge leads to the shallowest form of knowledge skepticism.

10. For more details, see Michael Williams, "Hume's Criterion of Significance," *Canadian Journal of Philosophy* 15, no. 2 (June 1986): 273–304.

11. But only roughly. Hume's account of Cartesian skepticism is a travesty. Descartes does not arbitrarily take up a policy of doubting anything and everything; rather, he represents his general doubt as buttressed by "well-considered reasons." Indeed, although Descartes does employ skeptical considerations in his quest for certainty, the skepticism of Meditation 1, particularly as it concerns our knowledge of the external world, grows out of the kind of reflection on our epistemic situation that belongs to skepticism consequent to inquiry. Descartes' skepticism thus seems to straddle Hume's distinction. The trouble is that in contrasting antecedent skepticism with consequent skepticism, Hume has a second distinction in play, having to do with how skepticism arises. Is skepticism a stance to be adopted voluntarily and without argument? Or does skepticism reflect a surprising discovery, one that arises out of an *investigation* of our epistemic situation? And while this distinction can be made to line up with that between methodological and plain skepticism, it does not have to be treated this way. There is no reason why skeptical paradoxes—the skeptic's apparent discoveries—cannot themselves be used as tools of investigation. This is just how Descartes uses them.

12. Hume's commitment to the transparency of the mind gets him into difficulties, since he also likes to argue that we are liable to natural confusions. For example, in accounting for our belief in the necessary connection between cause and effect, he postulates two confusions. (1) we mistake the involuntariness of habit-based inferences for the rational compulsion involved in demonstrative reasoning; and (2) because of the "mind's great propensity to spread itself on external objects" (T 112), we mistake this internal impression of compulsion for a link between outer objects. So impressions can appear to feeling to be other than what they are in reality. It can take effort to see them for what they are: in fact, the kind of effort involved in a skeptical examination of our ideas and beliefs.

13. Thus Stroud, *Hume*, sees Hume's discussion of induction, belief in the external world, and personal identity as analyzable into a "negative phase," in which the pretensions of Reason are undermined, and a "positive phase," in which a naturalistic explanation is given in lieu of an epistemological vindication.

14. Fogelin, *Skepticism*, p. 22.

15. The true origin of the idea of necessary connection or power, it turns out, is internal:

> Tho' the several resembling instances, which give rise to the idea of power . . . can never produce any new quality *in the object*, which can be the model of that idea, yet the observation of this resemblance produces a new impression *in the mind*, which is its real model. For after we have observed the resemblance in a sufficient number of instances, we immediately feel a determination of the mind to pass from one object to its usual attendant. . . . Necessity . . . is nothing but an internal impression of the mind, or a determination to carry our thoughts from one object to another.
>
> (T 111; italics in the original)

However, because of the mind's "propensity to spread itself on external objects" (T 112), we tend to read our own inferential compulsions into the world, thereby being led to think of "power" as something in the object.

On this account, our thought is (naturally) prone to some measure of confusion: a skeptical point. Nevertheless, Hume has at least the germ of an eminently defensible account of modally inflected causal talk: that in speaking of "power" or "necessity," we give voice to our commitment to the goodness of a material inference (from the perceived cause to its expected effect). Or to make the point in Hume's more psychological idiom, we see things as connected to the extent that we are already inclined to take perceiving the one as grounds for expecting the other. Either way, we do not make the inference because of an antecedent perception of the necessary connection between a cause and its customary effect. Rather, "the necessary connexion depends on the inference, instead of the inference's depending on the necessary connexion" (T 62). Since talk of necessity reflects commitment to the goodness of an inference, it cannot explain or justify that commitment.

16. By far the most thorough and penetrating recent attempt to show the critical and epistemological import of Hume's science of the understanding is Loeb, *Stability and Justification in Hume's "Treatise."*

17. Contrast Loeb's emphasis on stability, ibid.

18. This is Louis Loeb's view. See his "Reply to Williams," *Hume Studies* (2006).

19. Notice that in these passages, Hume advances his critical project independently of any form of conceptual skepticism.

20. Hume connects this with the contrast between steady and capricious principles: "The general rule is attributed to our judgment; as being more extensive and constant. The exception to the imagination; as being more capricious and uncertain" (T 101).

21. Michael Williams, *Unnatural Doubts* (Princeton, NJ: Princeton University Press, 1996), p. 8.

22. This is the burden of Williams, *Unnatural Doubts*.

23. For discussion of contemporary neo-Humean conceptions of skepticism, see ibid.

CHAPTER 5

SKEPTICISM ABOUT THE EXTERNAL WORLD

JOHN GRECO

A skeptic about the external world thinks that knowledge of the external world is impossible. But what is meant by "the external world"? One way to understand this is to consider a familiar skeptical argument. Let us grant, says the skeptic, that you can know how things appear to you. For example, you can know that things appear visually as if you are sitting at a desk, as if there is an open book before you, and so on. But how do you know that the way things appear is the way things are? After all, things could appear to you visually in just the same way if you were dreaming, and if you were actually lying in bed with no book at all. Or worse, suppose that your entire life is a dream. Suppose, for example, that you are a disembodied spirit, deceived by a powerful demon into thinking that you are embodied and living in a material world. Or suppose that you are a mere brain floating in a vat of chemical nutrients, your severed nerve endings hooked up to a supercomputer and stimulated so as to have just the sensory experiences that you are having now. Since you cannot rule these possibilities out, argues the skeptic, you cannot know that you are sitting at a desk and reading a book. In fact, you cannot know anything about the external world because the same considerations undermine any such knowledge whatsoever.

I am not interested at this point in evaluating the skeptic's reasoning—we will look more closely at that issue later. Here I am interested in understanding the skeptic's conclusion. More specifically, I am interested in understanding what the skeptic means by "the external world" when he denies that knowledge of the external would is possible. One natural reading of "the external world" is "the world of things outside my body," or "the world of things spatially external to me." But this geographical reading is not quite right. After all, the skeptic means to deny that you can have knowledge even of your own body or your own spatial location.

A better way to understand "the external world" is in relation to how things appear. Specifically, the external world is *the world as it really is, independently of appearances*. Again, the skeptic about the external world grants that you can know how things appear to you. What he denies is that you can know how things are in fact.

An example will help clarify further. Suppose that you and a friend are looking at a tower from different distances. From your perspective, the tower appears to be cylindrical. From your friend's perspective, the tower appears to be rectangular. The skeptic about the external world grants that each of you can know how the tower appears to you individually. That is, each of you can know the character of your own visual experience. What he denies is that either of you can know what the shape of the tower really is—that is, what its shape actually is, appearances aside.

Why should someone be interested in skepticism about the external world? After all, is it not just crazy to think that no one knows anything about how the world really is? For example, is it not crazy to think that I cannot know that there is a tower and that it has a certain shape, even after I get a close look? And do you not know right now that you are seated at a desk and reading a book (assuming that you are)? In my opinion, skepticism about the external world does indeed present an interesting problem, although it is important to get clear what sort of problem it is. Certainly there is no practical problem regarding skepticism about the external world. For example, no one is paralyzed from action by reading about skeptical considerations or evaluating skeptical arguments. Even if one cannot figure out where a particular skeptical argument goes wrong, life goes on just the same. Similarly, there is no "existential" problem here. Reading skeptical arguments does not throw one into a state of existential dread. One is not typically disturbed or disconcerted for any length of time. One does not feel any less at home in the world, or go about worrying that one's life might be no more than a dream. As skeptics themselves have often admitted, skeptical doubts have no staying power, and so do not pose a practical or existential threat.

Rather, skepticism about the external world constitutes an interesting *theoretical* problem. More exactly, skeptical *arguments* constitute interesting theoretical problems. This is because, when skeptical arguments are constructed in their most plausible form, it is not at all obvious where they go wrong. Even if we assume that skeptical arguments do go wrong somewhere—even if we assume that knowledge of the external world is indeed possible—it is not at all obvious which premise of an argument is false or what step in the reasoning is invalid. In fact, the best skeptical arguments have the following interesting structure: they begin with premises that seem pretheoretically plausible, even obvious, and proceed by valid reasoning to a conclusion that is outrageous—for example, that I cannot know that I am seated at a desk or reading a book. The conclusion *must* be false, one wants to say. The trick is to find out which of the seemingly obvious premises is mistaken. It is in that sense that arguments for skepticism about the external world constitute interesting theoretical problems.

If this is the nature of a skeptical problem, then there are various kinds of solutions. A minimal sort of solution would be to identify a premise in the skeptical argument that we need not accept. If the argument really does depend on this premise, and if accepting the premise forces us to an outrageous conclusion, then we should take the lesson that an initially plausible assumption was in fact misguided. That minimal sort of solution teaches something, but it is not very satisfying in and of itself. Rather, we want good reasons for rejecting the skeptical premise other than that it leads to an unwanted conclusion. A second sort of solution provides such reasons, by giving us an independent argument for rejecting the premise in question. But even this sort of solution is not the best we could have, for we also want an explanation why the skeptic's premise is false. That is, we want a theory that gives us some insight into what knowledge is and what having knowledge requires, and that *explains* why a premise that looked pretheoretically plausible is in fact mistaken. This is another sense in which skeptical problems are theoretically interesting: the analysis of skeptical arguments drives epistemological theory. Skeptical arguments force us to reconsider pretheoretically plausible but mistaken assumptions about the nature of knowledge, and to replace them with something better.[1]

The discussion that follows will proceed in that spirit. Section 1 of this chapter reconstructs several lines of skeptical argument, puts them in their most powerful form, and considers some relations among them. Section 2 considers several popular but misguided replies to skepticism about the external world. These replies are misguided in that they fail to appreciate the force of the most powerful skeptical arguments and therefore misdiagnose the nature of the skeptical problem at hand. For example, it is common to think that skepticism about the external world depends on a mistaken ontology, but I will show that the best skeptical arguments require no contentious ontological commitments. Section 3 considers a more promising approach to external-world skepticism: semantic contextualism. Here I argue that, even if contextualism is correct about the semantics of "knows" and related language, it fails to give us the sort of explanation we want in a satisfying response to skepticism. In particular, contextualism fails to give us a theory of knowledge. and therefore fails to explain where and why skeptical arguments are mistaken. In section 4, I defend an approach to external-world skepticism that does provide the sort of explanation we are looking for. If we think of knowledge as deriving from intellectual powers or abilities, we can locate the places where various skeptical arguments go wrong, and we can explain how knowledge of the external world is indeed possible.

1. SOME ARGUMENTS FOR SKEPTICISM ABOUT THE EXTERNAL WORLD

I have said that skeptical arguments are theoretically interesting because they have the following structure: they begin with premises that seem initially plausible or even obvious, and they proceed by valid reasoning to conclusions that seem

outrageous. In this light, consider a skeptical argument that has received a lot of attention in the recent literature:
(S)

1. I know that I have a hand only if I can know that I am not a brain in a vat.
2. I cannot know that I am not a brain in a vat.

Therefore,

3. I cannot know that I have a hand. (1, 2)

Premise 1 of the argument is plausible enough in its own right and is supported by plausible "closure principles," for example, that knowledge is closed under known entailments. In general, it would seem, if I know that p is the case and I know that p entails q, then I can know that q is the case. Premise 1 is simply an instance of some such general principle.

But what about premise 2? Is that premise initially (or pretheoretically) plausible? It seems to me that it is not. In fact, it seems to me that it is initially obvious that I *do* know that I am not a brain in a vat. That is not to deny that there might be good reasons in favor of premise 2. That is, the skeptic might very well have good arguments that would make (2) plausible. For example, perhaps I cannot know that I am not a brain in a vat because my sensory experience cannot rule out the possibility that I am. The present point is only that (2) is not plausible in the absence of some such argument. Pretheoretically, that is, before such arguments are brought to bear, premise 2 is not plausible at all.

If this is right, then argument S is parasitic on other skeptical arguments. That is, premise 2 of (S) is plausible only insofar as other skeptical arguments are plausible. Accordingly, we should focus our attention on those other arguments.

1.1. Hume's Argument

The first such argument I want to consider is inspired by David Hume. The argument begins with the assumption that our beliefs about the external world are at least partly based on how things appear. For example, I believe that I am presently seated at my desk at least partly because that is the way things visually appear to me. But that cannot be the whole story, the argument continues. I must also be assuming, at least implicitly, that the way things appear is a good indication of the way things really are. If I were not relying on that assumption, Hume argues, then the fact that things appear to me a certain way would not be a reason for thinking that they are that way. But now how am I to justify this assumption about the reliability of appearances? How can I know that the way things appear is a good indication of the way things really are? According to Hume, there is no way to justify that assumption. For example, suppose I were to rely on appearances, reasoning that as far as I can tell, the way things appear to me appears to be a reliable indication of the way things really are. This, of course, would be to argue in a circle, taking for granted the very thing at issue. Here is Hume's argument put more formally:

(H)

1. All my beliefs about the external world depend for their evidence on both (a) the way things appear to me, and (b) an assumption that the way things appear to me is a reliable indication of the way things really are.
2. But the assumption in question cannot be justified.

Therefore,

3. All my beliefs about the external world depend for their evidence on an unjustifiable assumption. (1, 2)
4. Beliefs that depend for their evidence on an unjustifiable assumption do not count as knowledge.

Therefore,

5. None of my beliefs about the external world count as knowledge. I do not know anything about the external world.(3, 4)

Clearly, an important point in this argument is premise 2: that an assumption regarding the reliability of appearances cannot be justified. In support of premise 2, Hume considers various possibilities for justifying the assumption in question. One consideration that Hume emphasizes is that the assumption is itself a contingent claim about the external world. That is, the assumption claims that sensory appearances are, as a matter of contingent fact, related to the way things are in a particular way. This suggests that the assumption can be justified, if at all, only in the way that contingent claims about the external world are justified in general— that is, by relying on the way things appear. But this, of course, would be to argue in a circle, taking for granted the very thing at issue. Here again is the reasoning in support of (2):

(H2)

1. All my beliefs about the external world depend for their evidence on both (a) the way things appear to me, and (b) an assumption that the way things appear to me is a reliable indication of the way things really are.
2. The assumption in question is itself a belief about the external world.

Therefore,

3. The assumption depends on itself for its evidence. (1, 2)
4. Beliefs that depend on themselves for their evidence cannot be justified.

Therefore,

5. The assumption in question cannot be justified.(3, 4)

A natural thought is that the assumption that appearances are a reliable guide to reality can be justified in some other way, perhaps by some sort of a priori reflection that proceeds independently of appearances. But Hume thinks that this line of reasoning is a dead end. This is because the assumption in question makes a contingent claim about the way things are—it is a matter of contingent fact, and not a matter of necessity, that appearances do or do not reflect the way things really are. But that sort of fact cannot be known through a priori reflection. In short, a priori reflection gives us knowledge of necessary truths rather than contingent truths.

Finally, let us return to premise 2 of argument S. Does Hume's argument provide independent support for that premise? Clearly, it does. Insofar as my belief that I am not a brain in a vat involves a claim about the external world, Hume's argument applies. In sum, I cannot know that I am not a brain in a vat because my evidence for that belief essentially involves an assumption that appearances to this effect are a reliable indication of reality. But there is no way to justify that assumption without going in a circle, and so my belief that I am not a brain in a vat depends on inadequate evidence.[2]

1.2. Descartes' Argument

The next skeptical argument I want to consider is inspired by Descartes' Meditation 1, and in particular by Barry Stroud's reading of that meditation.[3] To understand the argument, consider the claim that one sees a goldfinch in the garden, based on one's observation that the bird is of a particular size and color and with a tail of a particular shape. Suppose now that a friend challenges one's claim to know, pointing out that woodpeckers also are of that size and color and also have tails with that shape. As Stroud points out, this seems to be a legitimate challenge to one's claim to know that the bird is a goldfinch. More generally, if one's evidence for one's belief that the bird is a goldfinch is consistent with the possibility that it is in fact a woodpecker, then one does not know on the basis of that evidence that it is a goldfinch. On the basis of this sort of reasoning, the skeptic proposes the following plausible principle:

1. A person knows that p on the basis of evidence E only if E rules out alternative possibilities to p.

Further support for this sort of principle comes from reflection on scientific inquiry. Suppose that there are several competing hypotheses for explaining some phenomenon, and suppose that these various hypotheses are "live" in the sense that current evidence does not rule them out as possibilities. It would seem that one cannot know that one of the hypotheses is true until further evidence rules out the remaining ones. Again, principle 1 looks plausible.

The second step in the skeptical argument is to point out that there are various possibilities that are inconsistent with what we claim to know about the external world. For example, it is possible that things appear to me visually just as they do now, but that I am actually lying in my bed asleep rather than sitting at my desk awake. It is possible that things appear to Descartes just as they do, but that he is actually the victim of an evil demon, a disembodied spirit who only dreams that he inhabits a material world and is presently seated by the fire. To be clear, it is no part of the skeptical argument that such alternative possibilities are true, or even that they are somewhat likely. The point is only that they are possibilities, and so undermine our knowledge if our evidence does not rule them out.

The third step in the skeptical argument is to claim that our evidence does not in fact rule these possibilities out. The gist of the present claim is something like this: these possibilities are consistent with all the evidence that we have or could have at our disposal. Even if, practically speaking, we do not usually give such possibilities a thought, upon reflection, we have no evidence available to us that counts against them and in favor of our preferred beliefs.

If we put these three claims together, we have the materials for a powerful skeptical argument. Here is the argument stated more formally:
(D)

1. A person knows that p on the basis of evidence E only if E rules out alternative possibilities to p. (Principle 1 stated earlier)
2. It is a possibility that I am not sitting at my desk awake but am merely dreaming that I am.

Therefore,

3. I know that I am sitting at my desk only if my evidence rules out the possibility that I am merely dreaming. (1, 2)
4. But my evidence does not rule out this possibility.

Therefore,

5. I do not know that I am sitting at my desk. (3, 4)

Of course, the skeptical argument is supposed to generalize. That is, it is supposed to apply to beliefs about the external world in general. We therefore have the following:

6. The same line of reasoning can be brought to bear against any belief about the external world.

Therefore,

7. No one knows anything about the external world.(5, 6)

I have said that this is a powerful argument. The argument is not powerful in the sense that it is convincing—we should not start to worry that we really do not know anything about the external world. Rather, the argument is powerful in the sense that it is not easy to see where it goes wrong.

One place to look for a weakness in the argument is premise 4. What does it mean, exactly, to say that my evidence does not rule out the possibility that I am dreaming? The most common way that philosophers interpret the premise is epistemically, so that it says, in effect, that I cannot *know* that I am not dreaming. But this way of understanding premise 4, I have suggested, robs the skeptical argument of its force. This is because it is pretheoretically implausible that one cannot know that one is not dreaming. Insofar as this is the case, the argument is not theoretically interesting in the sense outlined previously. There are at least two other ways to interpret premise 4 that do make the argument interesting, however. I turn to those now.

One way to understand the notion of "ruling out" a possibility is as follows: a body of evidence E rules out a possibility q if and only if E supports not -q in a noncircular way. Here "support" cannot be understood epistemically if we are to avoid the problem just raised. Rather, we can understand support as a semantic notion: Evidence E supports proposition p, in the relevant sense, just in case E entails p or E makes p probable. Putting these ideas together, we get the following interpretation of premise 4 of argument D:

> 4a. My evidence for my belief that I am sitting at my desk neither entails nor makes probable (in a noncircular way) the proposition that I am not dreaming.

Why might one accept premise 4a? One reason for accepting (4a) is the considerations put forward by Hume's argument, discussed earlier. That is, one might think that my evidence for believing that I am sitting at my desk is the way things appear to me, together with my assumption that the way things appear to me is a reliable indication of the way things are. But as Hume's reasoning shows, there is no noncircular way to justify the assumption in question, and therefore there is no good evidence for either that assumption or further beliefs that are based on it. In particular, my evidence cannot entail or even make probable (in a noncircular way) the proposition that I am not dreaming. Insofar as this is the reasoning behind (4a), argument D is parasitic on argument H.

There is, however, another way to understand the notion of evidence ruling out alternative possibilities. On this understanding, a body of evidence E rules out alternative possibilities to p just in case E discriminates the state of affairs represented by p from alternative states of affairs. For example, hearing my wife coming in the door from work, my auditory experience rules out the possibility that it is my children coming home from school or a burglar coming in through a window. I have the capacity to "tell the difference," so to speak, and this is what allows me to know that it is my wife who has just come in the house. On this understanding of "ruling out," it does seem plausible that my evidence must rule out alternative possibilities in order to ground knowledge. For example, how can I know that my wife has just come home, on the basis of hearing her come through the door, if I cannot discriminate that state of affairs from my daughter's coming through the door? Moreover, premise 4 of argument D becomes plausible on this understanding of "ruling out." We now have the following:

> 4b. My evidence does not discriminate my sitting at my desk from my merely dreaming that I am sitting at my desk.

One might think that this claim is obviously right.

Finally, we may note that either reading of "ruling out" yields an argument that lends support for premise 2 of argument S. That premise claims that I cannot know that I am not a brain in a vat. One might think that this is so because my evidence does not support the negation of alternative hypotheses. In particular, it does not support the negation of the hypothesis that I *am* a brain in a vat. Alternatively, one might think that (2) is true because my evidence does not discriminate the case where I am not a brain in a vat from the case where I am.

2. SOME MISGUIDED RESPONSES TO EXTERNAL-WORLD SKEPTICISM

Having reconstructed several arguments for skepticism about the external world, we are now in a position to see that several popular responses to this kind of skepticism are misguided. Some of these responses are "dismissive," in that they reject the conclusions of skeptical arguments without seriously considering the reasoning that leads up to them. Another kind of response is not dismissive in this sense. Nevertheless, I will argue, it misdiagnoses the mistake that skeptical arguments make.

2.1. Dismissive Responses

It is often alleged that the skeptic's standards for knowledge are too high. The skeptic is demanding absolute certainty, or infallibility, or some such thing, and so we can reject skeptical arguments simply by rejecting these implausible standards. A cursory look at the skeptical arguments in section 1 shows that this sort of response is mistaken, however. In short, none of the premises in those arguments can be read as requiring absolute certainty, or infallibility, or some other high-powered epistemic status. For example, argument H requires that knowledge be grounded on assumptions that are "justified," and insists that circular reasoning does not yield justification. Argument D requires that evidence "rule out" alternative possibilities, where this notion is understood either in terms of discrimination or in terms of deductive or inductive support. I assume that (H) and (D) go wrong somewhere—that is a working assumption of our methodology. But the arguments do not seem to trade on standards for knowledge that are "too high."

Another kind of dismissive response to external-world skepticism is "pragmatic." Pragmatic responses allege that skepticism about the world entails some practical difficulty, and that this effectively refutes the position. This sort of skepticism "cannot be lived," it is said, as the skeptic himself must reveal when he avoids an oncoming bus. A closely related kind of response is "rhetorical." These responses imply that skepticism can be refuted by making some rhetorical point about the skeptic's position in a debate. Thus Locke famously wrote, "If all be a dream, then he doth but dream, that he makes the question; and so it is not much matter, that a waking man should answer him."[4]

On the present understanding of the skeptical problem, however, these kinds of response miss the mark. As we noted earlier, skepticism presents a theoretical problem rather than a practical or existential problem. It is a problem because some skeptical arguments begin with premises that seem plausible and proceed by valid reasoning to a conclusion that is implausible. The way to solve this sort of problem is to find the mistake in the argument; that is, to find which of the initially plausible premises must in fact be rejected. Claims about how the skeptic must act or what the skeptic must say are irrelevant.

Pragmatic and rhetorical responses to skepticism are therefore misguided. Another way to see this point is to consider the following: skeptical arguments would lose none of their force if we could find no one willing to defend them. That is, skeptical arguments are philosophically interesting because their premises look good to *us*. If they contain some sort of mistake, it is a mistake that we are making in *our* pretheoretical intuitions about the nature of justified belief and knowledge. It is in this sense that skeptical arguments require a theoretical solution: they require a theoretical stance that explains why some of our pretheoretical assumptions are mistaken, and that replaces those assumptions with something better. Put another way, it is skeptical *arguments* that are interesting—not skeptical persons.[5]

2.2. Ontological Responses

Ontological responses to external-world skepticism allege that skeptical arguments assume a mistaken ontology. For example, it is often claimed that skeptical arguments assume a dualism between mental knower and material object of knowledge. Thus Heidegger writes, "Only then can the problem arise of how this knowing subject comes out of its inner 'sphere' into one which is 'other and external' . . . of how one must think of the object itself so that eventually the subject knows it without needing to venture a leap into another sphere."[6] Once this sort of ontological gulf between subject and object is in place, Heidegger thinks, it is impossible to bridge. On the other hand, if we reject this sort of dualism between knower and object of knowledge, skeptical arguments no longer get off the ground.

Another kind of ontological response blames realism rather than dualism for skepticism about the external world. So long as material objects are deemed to be mind independent, this response goes, it will seem impossible for the mind to know them. Perhaps the most explicit advocate of this diagnosis is Bishop Berkeley. He writes:

> So long as men thought that real things subsisted without the mind, and that their knowledge was only so far forth *real* as it was conformable to *real things*, it follows,

they could not be certain that they had any real knowledge at all. . . . All this scepticism follows, from our supposing a difference between *things* and *ideas*, and that the former have a subsistence without the mind, or unperceived.[7]

A closer look at skeptical arguments makes these diagnoses implausible, however. In short, the skeptical arguments reconstructed in section 1 can be run without assuming either dualism or realism. In fact, the arguments can be run on any number of ontologies and therefore do not depend on one ontology or another. One way to show this is to note that both arguments H and D can be run even on Berkeley's radical idealism.

According to Berkeley's idealism, all that exist are minds and ideas. Leaving aside the niceties, objects such as tigers and trees are essentially well-ordered bundles of ideas. But even here we have a distinction between "real" objects and mere appearances. For example, Berkeley's ontology makes a distinction between actual tigers and hallucinations of tigers. The latter are not well ordered—they lack the coherence and stability that bundles of ideas constituting "real" tigers possess. But then what is our evidence, on Berkeley's view, that there is a real tiger before us? In cases of perception, it has to be the sensory appearances that we have *at the moment*. But of course, momentary appearances, even if they are over several moments, can be deceiving. What appears to be a real tiger need not be, since initial stability and coherence might later give way to the incoherence of an illusion. In short, even Berkeley's radical idealism maintains a distinction between appearance and reality, as any ontology must in order to be even minimally plausible. But with that distinction in place, the skeptical arguments have the resources they need to get up and running. According to argument H, there is no good inference from present appearances to extended stability and coherence. According to argument D, present appearances do not rule out the possibility of pending instability and incoherence. For example, present appearances do not discriminate between those that will lead to the stability and coherence of "real" objects and those that will give way to the instability and incoherence of illusion.

The lesson to be learned here is this: the skeptical arguments run on a minimal distinction between appearance and reality rather than on any particular way of cashing out that distinction. But this sort of minimal distinction is innocent— it is a platitude that things are not always as they appear, that appearance and reality can come apart. This cannot be the mistake that skeptical arguments make.[8]

3. SEMANTIC CONTEXTUALISM

Another approach to skepticism, one that has garnered a lot of attention in recent years, is not dismissive of the skeptic's arguments. In fact, contextualists pride themselves on taking the skeptic's arguments seriously, and on explaining why such arguments have the force that they do. To properly understand the contextualist approach, it is first necessary to distinguish between contextualism as a semantic thesis and contextualism as a response to skepticism.

3.1. The Semantic Thesis

Contextualism is first and foremost a thesis about the semantics of "knows" and related language. Specifically, it is the thesis that the semantic value of " knows" and related language is variable across attributor contexts. In the paradigmatic case, the sentence "S knows that p" can be true in one context and false in another, for the very same S and p and at the very same time.

An example will illustrate. Suppose that it is very important that a particular train stops in Kingston. Suppose that our lives depend on it. In this context, we overhear a passerby say, "I know that the next train stops in Kingston," basing his claim on the fact that he has just read the schedule posted on the station wall. In the present "high-stakes" context, we might very well deny that the passerby's claim to know is true. Given that train schedules change, and given that our lives depend on his being right, we might very well think that better evidence is required. However, suppose that the passerby is himself in a "low-stakes" situation. Suppose that for him and his conversation partner, nothing very important depends on whether the train stops in Kingston—nothing more than the usual inconvenience in missing one's stop. In this context, the passerby's partner might very well think that the claim to know is true.

The contextualist thesis is that all of us can be right. In other words, it is possible that relative to our high-stakes context, the passerby's claim that he "knows" is false, while at the same time, relative to the passerby's low-stakes context, the claim that he "knows" is true. In this respect, contextualists claim, the verb "knows" acts like an indexical. For example, the claim "Joe is here" can be true relative to one context of utterance and false relative to another. Even better, "knows" acts in a similar way to gradable adjectives, such as "tall" and "flat." For example, relative to normal contexts, the claim "Joe is tall" is true, since Joe's height is 6 feet, and that counts as tall in normal contexts. However, in the context of a National Basketball Association game, the standards for what counts as "tall" go up, and so the claim "Joe is tall" is false relative to that context.

3.2. Contextualism as a Response to Skepticism

Suppose that the contextualist semantic thesis is right. How is this relevant to the problem of skepticism? Contextualists typically focus on skeptical argument S:

1. I know that I have a hand only if I can know that I am not a brain in a vat.
2. I cannot know that I am not a brain in a vat.

Therefore,

> 3. I cannot know that I have a hand.

Contextualists agree that both (1) and (2) are highly plausible pretheoretically. On the other hand, (3) is highly implausible pretheoretically, although (3) can become plausible once we are in the grips of a skeptical argument. Contextualism promises to explain all this by invoking the semantics of "knows" described previously. Specifically, in normal contexts, the standards for "knows" are relatively low, and therefore knowledge claims about the external world, such as "I know I have a hand," typically meet those standards. In contexts where we are considering skeptical arguments, however, the standards for "knows" get driven higher, and so in those contexts, knowledge claims about the external world are typically false. According to this diagnosis, argument S is actually sound relative to the skeptic's high standards for what counts as "knowledge." This result does not have unwanted skeptical consequences, however, since the skeptical argument is *not* sound relative to normal standards. In particular, premise 2 of (S) is false, since relative to normal standards I do know that I am not a brain in a vat. Put another way, most of our knowledge claims are true relative to the contexts in which we make them.[9]

One objection that has been raised against the contextualist response to skepticism is that it concedes too much. In particular, it seems to many people that the skeptic is wrong when he claims that we cannot "know" things about the external world; that is, wrong even relative to contexts in which the skeptic (or someone on the skeptic's behalf) is speaking. Put another way, it seems to many people that, even in contexts where we are considering a skeptical argument, our claims that we "know" things about the external world are true, and the skeptic's claims that we "do not know" are false. The contextualist response to skepticism does not give us that result, and it is in that sense, some have argued, that it concedes too much.

A second objection to the contextualist response comes from the other direction, however. Namely, contextualism does not explain why skeptical arguments are *not* sound relative to low-stakes contexts. For example, the contextualist claims that premise 2 of argument S is false relative to normal, low-stakes contexts. But contextualism as such does not explain why that should be the case. In other words, contextualism does not explain how I know that I am not a brain in a vat, even relative to the standards that are relevant to my normal low-stakes context. The problem becomes more apparent when we consider skeptical arguments H and D. Which premises of those arguments does contextualism allow us to deny? In other words, which premises of those arguments are supposed to be false relative to normal, low-stakes contexts? Suppose that the contextualist means to deny premise 2 of argument H: that our assumption that appearances are reliable cannot be justified. In that case, what is wrong with argument H2, which the skeptic gives in support of that premise? Contextualism as such does not say.

What about argument D? Presumably, contextualists will deny premise 2, claiming that in low-stakes contexts my evidence does rule out the possibility that I am merely dreaming. But how so? Does my evidence entail or make probable that I am not dreaming? Does it discriminate my dreaming from my sitting at a desk? It is not clear that either is the case, and contextualism as such does not make it clear.

More generally, contextualism as such does not explain why skeptical arguments are unsound relative to normal low-stakes contexts. Even if contextualism is right about the semantics of "knows," it does not give us a theory of knowledge, and therefore does not explain how we know things when we do. In short, contextualism leaves more work to do.[10]

4. Where Skeptical Arguments Go Wrong

We are looking for a particular sort of response to skepticism about the external world: one that identifies which premise of a skeptical argument makes a mistake, and that explains why it is a mistake. That is, a satisfying response to skepticism ought to say something about what knowledge is, explaining why skeptical assumptions about what knowledge requires are wrong, and replacing those assumptions with something better. With this goal in mind, let us take a closer look at the skeptical arguments set out earlier.

4.1. Where Humean Skepticism Goes Wrong

Let us begin with argument H. Premise 1 of that argument is as follows:

1. All my beliefs about the external world depend for their evidence on both (a) the way things appear to me, and (b) an assumption that the way things appear to me is a reliable indication of the way things really are.

In effect, (1) says that the assumption mentioned in clause b must be part of my evidence for my beliefs about the external world. If it were not, Hume argues, then the fact that things appear to me a certain way would not be a reason to think that they are that way. Premise 1 looks innocent enough; pretheoretically, it might even seem obvious. I will argue that premise 1 is mistaken, however. In particular, the assumption mentioned in clause b—that appearances are a reliable indication of reality—does not function as a part of our evidence for beliefs about the external world. And because it does not, that assumption need not be justified for beliefs about the world to be justified. The skeptical reasoning in argument H is therefore unsound. To make this case, however, we must first look at the skeptic's reasoning more closely.

Why does Hume think that the assumption in clause b must be part of our evidence for beliefs about the world? He says that if it were not, then the fact that things appear a particular way would not count as a reason for believing that they are that way. For example, if I were not assuming that appearances are a reliable guide to reality, then the fact that the tower visually appears to be rectangular would not be (for me) a reason for thinking that it really is rectangular. A natural thought here is that one's evidence has the structure of an argument, with appearances serving as premises and beliefs about the world serving as conclusions. Hume's thought, then, is that the premises have to support the conclusion, and that they do not unless they include some further premise to the effect that appearances are a reliable guide to reality—that the way things appear is a good indication of the way things are. For example, my evidence for my belief about the tower would look like this:

(R)

a. It appears to me visually as if the tower is rectangular.
b. The way things appear to me is a reliable indication of the way things really are.

Therefore,

c. (At least probably) the tower is rectangular.

But if we are thinking of my evidence this way, then it is a further natural thought that each of the premises must be justified for the evidence to be any good. Of course, both these natural thoughts are supposed to be quite general. In general, our beliefs about the external world depend on some such assumption for their evidence, and therefore we must be justified in believing some such assumption if we are to have knowledge of the external world.

Again, this way of thinking about knowledge is natural enough, and might even seem obvious. It is entirely mistaken, however, or so I want to argue. Here is a different way of thinking that is incompatible with it: In the typical case, I know that the tower is rectangular because I can see that it is, and seeing that the tower is rectangular is nothing like having an argument that it is. Put another way, perceptual evidence does not have the structure of an argument for a conclusion. Put yet another way, perceptual evidence is not inferential. In particular, perception does not involve an inference from premises about appearances to a conclusion about reality.

Suppose we think about knowledge as deriving from reliable powers or abilities. Thus we have abilities to remember things about the past, within certain ranges, and to reason about the future, again within ranges. We also have powers of perception—we come to know things about the world by seeing, hearing, tasting, and so on. One way to think about our cognitive powers is to use an information-processing model: we have powers of information uptake (perception), information retrieval (memory), and information processing (reasoning). Another way to think about our cognitive powers, not incompatible with the first, is as involving agency. On this model, perceiving, remembering, and reasoning are things that we do—they are various forms of activity, involving various sorts of intention and control. Now the relevant thought is this: not all these powers, not all these activities, involve arguments or inferences. Reasoning from prior beliefs to further conclusions is only one kind of intellectual activity, involving one kind of intellectual power. Reasoning *does* involve inferring conclusions from prior premises, as in an argument. But perception is a different sort of power, involving a different sort of activity.

To be sure, perception does involve a sort of information processing. It takes sensory appearances as inputs and operates on them so as to produce beliefs about the world as outputs. But it is a mistake to think of this sort of processing as an inference from premises to a conclusion. For one thing, inferences operate on propositions. When one reasons from premises to a conclusion, one does so on the basis of inference rules that are sensitive to propositional contents and structures. That is why Hume thought that an assumption about the reliability of appearances was required in the reasoning set out in (R): it is just the sort of thing that is needed to make the content of (a) relevant to the content of (c). But perception does not operate on propositional contents and structures. On the contrary, perception takes properties of appearances, such as intensities and contrasts, and operates on them so as to produce object-level representations. The outputs of perception are therefore propositional—perceptual representations have the sort of content and structure that are appropriate to propositions. But the inputs of perception are not propositional, and therefore perceptual processing is not inferential processing.

A second reason for denying that perceptual processing involves inference is that inference seems to be an "executive" function, whereas perceptual processing is not. When a cognitive agent infers a conclusion from premises, she herself is sensitive to the content and structure of the premises in question. Even if she lacks the ability to articulate those meanings and structures clearly, she is in some way sensitive to them. For example, people can usually reconstruct their reasoning, at least to some degree, even when the reasoning was originally unconscious or otherwise unarticulated. Likewise, people have some ability to judge instances of reasoning valid or invalid, even if they cannot explicitly articulate the correct rule or the fallacy involved. By contrast, perceptual processing is largely subpersonal. Perceptual representations are built up from information that is, for the most part, not available at all to the perceiver. Put another way, much of the information serving as the inputs for perceptual processing is not represented at the level of belief. So, for example, people do not typically have beliefs about the qualities of light on the retina, or even about the qualities of their visual experience. Rather, they have beliefs about desks, books, and towers, without considering appearances at all.

This is not to say that prior beliefs play no part at all in perception. But the part they play is not that of premises in an inference to a conclusion. It is perfectly correct, for example, to say that prior beliefs "shape" or otherwise influence perception. Thus the way we see the world partly depends on what we already believe about it. But that is a far cry from saying that perception involves inference, or even that perception has the structure of an inference.

Here is an example of how belief might influence perception, but in a way that is entirely different from acting as a premise, or as any sort of evidence for the perceptual belief that results. Suppose that S believes that there are snakes in the building, and suppose that this belief is entirely irrational. Let us say that S has no good reason at all to believe that there are snakes there and every reason to believe that there are not. Nevertheless, S holds to his belief irrationally. Now suppose that because this background belief is in place, S is sensitive to perceptual cues that allow him to see clearly that there is a snake in the corner of the room. We can suppose that had S lacked his belief about there being snakes in the building, along with its attendant expectations, he would never have picked up on these perceptual cues and would never have seen the snake. Nevertheless, now that S does see clearly that there is a snake in the room, S knows that there is a snake in the building.

Clearly, S's prior belief that there were snakes in the building influenced his perception of the snake. The way I told the story, his belief was essential in enabling the perception. Nevertheless, it is clear that S did not infer his perceptual belief that there is a snake in the room from his prior belief that there are snakes in the building.

One might object as follows: S's prior belief is acting as evidence for his perceptual belief, and so his evidence has the *structure* of an inference, even if there is no actual inference involved in the production of S's perceptual belief. But not even that is true. Consider that S *knows* that there is a snake in the room—he sees it clearly. But he could not know it if that belief were evidentially based on his prior belief that there are snakes in the building, for *that* belief is entirely irrational, and knowledge cannot be based on evidence that is held irrationally.

It is better to give up the idea that perception has an inferential structure, and that the evidence of perception is to be understood on an inferential model. But once we give up that idea, argument H loses its force. In particular, we have no reason to accept premise 1 of H, and we have good reason to reject it.

4.2. Where Cartesian Skepticism Goes Wrong

Let us turn now to argument D, and in particular to that version of the argument that interprets "ruling out" alternative possibilities in terms of discrimination.[11] Taking a lesson from the previous section, we will no longer talk in terms of S's *evidence* discriminating among alternative possibilities. Rather, it is more natural to say that S *herself* discriminates among alternative possibilities, on the basis of her power of perception. (Putting things this way begs no question against evidentialists about perception, since they can say that S discriminates by means of her evidence discriminating. The present formulation allows alternatives to evidentialism, however.)

The argument now goes as follows:
(D2)

1. S can know that *p* on the basis of perception only if S can discriminate the state of affairs that *p* from alternative possibilities.
2. It is a possibility that I am not sitting at my desk awake, but merely dreaming that I am.

Therefore,

3. I can know that I am sitting at my desk (on the basis of perception) only if can perceptually discriminate that state of affairs from the possibility that I am merely dreaming. (1, 2)
4. I cannot perceptually discriminate my sitting at my desk from my merely dreaming that I am sitting at my desk

Therefore,

5. I cannot know (on the basis of perception) that I am sitting at my desk. (3, 4)

We may now slightly revise premise 6 to draw the more general skeptical conclusion:

6. If I cannot know by perception that I am sitting at my desk, then I cannot know anything about the external world.

Therefore,

7. I cannot know anything about the external world.(5, 6)

The mistake in argument D2, I want to argue, is again in premise 1. To motivate this diagnosis, consider that (1) is supposed to be read with a universal quantifier: the idea is that perceptual knowledge requires that the perceiver can discriminate the state of affairs that *p* from *all* alternative possibilities whatsoever. But the considerations that we saw in favor of (1) do not license this strong claim. Those considerations involved some observations about our ordinary practices of making and accepting knowledge claims, and about the scientific practice of evaluating alternative hypotheses. But those practices do not license the claim that knowledge requires an ability to discriminate from all alternative possibilities whatsoever. Consistent with those practices is a weaker claim: that knowledge that *p* requires the ability to discriminate the state of affairs that *p* from some restricted class of possibilities. In keeping with one common approach to skepticism about the external world, we might say that perceptual knowledge that *p* requires the ability to perceptually discriminate the state of affairs that *p* from "relevant" alternative possibilities.

This seems like a good thought, but can we invoke a plausible theory of knowledge to back it up? For that, let us return to the idea that knowledge derives from reliable abilities or powers. In the case of perceptual knowledge, knowledge derives from reliable perceptual abilities or powers. But what is required for a perceptual ability or power to be reliable? Presumably, it requires the ability to discriminate perceptual truths from relevant alternatives. Thus I can hear (or see) that my wife has just come home only if I can perceptually discriminate that state of affairs from my daughter's coming home and from my neighbor's coming over to borrow a cup of sugar. But need I be able to discriminate my wife's coming home from any alternative possibility whatsoever, including possibilities involving deceiving demons and brains in vats? That would be a stretch. Presumably, I have reliable perception just in case my perceptual abilities do the usual sort of job in the usual sorts of circumstances.

The present point about perceptual abilities is confirmed by considerations about abilities in general. To attribute an ability to someone is to say that he or she has reliable success (of the relevant sort) in circumstances that are appropriate for excercising the sort of ability in question. For example, to say that Derek Jeter has the ability to hit baseballs is to say that Jeter hits baseballs with reliable success in circumstances that are appropriate for playing baseball. It is not required, for example, that he can hit baseballs into the next city, or that he can literally rip the cover off the ball. Neither is it required that he can hit baseballs in the dark, or when he is drunk, or while someone is shooting at him.

Accordingly, we have a principled reason for denying premise 1 of (D2). Namely, knowledge in general is grounded in reliable intellectual abilities or powers. Perceptual knowledge in particular is grounded in reliable perceptual powers. But our perceptual powers are reliable, in the relevant sense, insofar as they reliably discriminate perceptual truths from the usual alternatives in the usual circumstances. The stronger requirement laid down in premise 1 is too strong.

One issue remains, however. A skeptic might agree with these points about our perceptual abilities and about what perceptual knowledge requires but insist that dreaming is a relevant possibility that occurs in normal circumstances. That is, the skeptic might insist that people dream things about the external world all the time, and that we lack an ability to perceptually discriminate between this sort of dreaming and states of affairs in the external world. In effect, the skeptic would be arguing as follows:

(D3)

1. S can know that p on the basis of perception only if S can discriminate (here and now) the state of affairs that p from an appropriately restricted set of alternative possibilities.
2. The possibility that I am not sitting at my desk awake but am merely dreaming that I am is a member of the appropriately restricted set.

Therefore,

3. I can know that I am sitting at my desk only if I can perceptually discriminate (here and now) the state of affairs that I am sitting at my desk from the possibility that I am merely dreaming. (1, 2)

4. I cannot here and now perceptually discriminate my sitting at my desk from my merely dreaming that I am sitting at my desk

Therefore,

5. I cannot know that I am sitting at my desk. (3, 4)

But here I think that the skeptic is on shaky grounds. For if "this sort of dreaming" means actual dreaming while asleep in one's bed, then it is true that this sort of dreaming happens all the time, but false that we lack an ability to perceptually discriminate waking life from mere dreaming. Our ability in this regard is not perfect—it is not infallible. But certainly it is highly reliable. Premise 4 of argument D3 is false. On the other hand, suppose that "this sort of dreaming" is meant to include dreams involving deceiving demons and brains in vats. In that case, it is not true that the possibility that I am merely dreaming is a member of an appropriately restricted set. On this reading of (D3), premise 2 is false.

In sum, we may grant the skeptic that we lack an ability to perceptually discriminate waking life from dreaming, at least in circumstances where we *are* dreaming in these special ways. But that does not count against our ability to reliably perceive things about the external world here and now. That is, it does not count against our ability to perceive the usual sorts of things in the usual sorts of circumstances.

NOTES

1. For more on the nature of skeptical problems, see John Greco, *Putting Skeptics in Their Place: The Nature of Skeptical Arguments and Their Role in Philosophical Inquiry* (New York: Cambridge University Press, 2000), especially chap. 1. See also Michael Williams, *Unnatural Doubts* (Princeton: Princeton University Press, 1996).

2. For more on Hume's skepticism, see the chapters by Ruth Weintraub and Michael Williams in this volume.

3. See Barry Stroud, *The Significance of Philosophical Scepticism* (Oxford: Clarendon Press, 1984). See also the chapter by José Luis Bermúdez in this volume.

4. John Locke, *An Essay Concerning Human Understanding*, ed. Peter Nidditch (Oxford: Oxford University Press, 1975), p. 634.

5. For more on dismissive responses to skepticism, see Greco, *Putting Skeptics in Their Place*, chap. 3.

6. Martin Heidegger, *Being and Time* (New York: Harper and Row, 1962), p. 87.

7. George Berkeley, *A Treatise Concerning the Principles of Human Knowledge* (Oxford: Oxford University Press, 1998), p. 134 (emphases in original).

8. For more on ontological responses to skepticism, see Greco, *Putting Skeptics in Their Place*, chap. 4. See also the chapters by George Pappas and Robert Stern in this volume.

9. Variations on this theme are possible. For example, contextualists can disagree about what it takes for the skeptic to drive standards higher and about whether skeptics are typically successful in doing so.

10. Typically, contextualists do go on to explain how a person knows relative to normal contexts. But at that point they are moving beyond semantic contextualism and offering a substantive theory of knowledge. For more on contextualist responses to skepticism, see Stewart Cohen, "How to Be a Fallibilist," *Philosophical Perspectives* 2 (1988): 91–123.; Keith DeRose, "Solving the Skeptical Problem," *Philosophical Review* 104 (1995): 1–52; and Cohen's chapter in this volume.

11. If we interpret "ruling out" in terms of deductive or inductive support, then argument D is akin to argument H, incorporating the idea that perceptual evidence must have an inferential structure. In that case, we can respond to the argument along the lines of the previous section.

CHAPTER 6

SKEPTICISM ABOUT INDUCTION

RUTH WEINTRAUB

THE term "induction" is sometimes (Swinburne, 1974, p. 1; Lipton, 1991; Howson, 2000) applied to all nondeductive (ampliative) inferences. I shall use it more narrowly to denote only inferences from a sample to the whole population or to the next case. On my (more customary) usage, we reason inductively when we infer that the sun will rise tomorrow on the basis of daily sunrises in the past. The belief in Newton's second law of motion ($F = Ma$), by way of contrast, is not inductively based. We do not have the requisite evidence from which to generalize because neither the force acting on a body nor its mass is observable. Our belief is warranted (if at all) by the fact that it best explains such phenomena as planetary motion, the tides, falling bodies, and motion on inclined planes.

Inductive skepticism is the claim that no inductive argument is reasonable. Like any skepticism worth its salt, it has to be based on an argument rather than merely issue a challenge. Instead of *asking*, "How is it possible that there should be knowledge of general propositions in cases where we have not examined all the instances"? (Russell, 1912, p. 81), or *challenging* us to justify a prior probability distribution (Howson, 2000), the skeptic should undertake *to show* that there cannot be such knowledge; that the inference from numerous sunrises to the sun's rising tomorrow, or to its always rising, does not yield knowledge and, indeed, is not even warranted.

True, Hume *wonders* whether the "effects and influences" of bodies might not "change, without any change in their sensible qualities." "What logic," he asks, "secures you against this supposition?" (1777, p. 38). But the question is just a rhetorical flourish. He has just presented *an argument* to show that the only reply is "No logic"; that induction is irrational.

1. THE FIRST ARGUMENT

Sextus Empiricus, the ancient Greek skeptic, adduces an argument in the form of a dilemma to "set aside the method of induction":

> [W]hen they propose to establish the universal from the particulars by means of induction, they will effect this by a review either of all or of some of the particular instances. But if they review some, the induction will be insecure, since some of the particulars omitted in the induction may contravene the universal; while if they are to review all, they will be toiling at the impossible, since the particulars are infinite and indefinite.
>
> (*OP*, p. 283)

If Sextus is right, our expectation that the sun will rise tomorrow is *completely unfounded*. His conclusion, that induction is unjustified, seems even more outrageous because it pertains even to what seems the paradigm of rationality, science, putting it on a par with astrology and soothsaying. No wonder Broad (1952, p. 143) labels induction "the glory of science and the scandal of philosophy" and inductive skepticism "a skeleton in the cupboard of Inductive Logic."

How should we respond to the skeptical argument? If we are to reject its conclusion in a principled way, the argument must be rebutted, and this is easily done. We can concede that the conclusion of an inductive argument may be false even if its premises are true, and that in this, induction differs from, indeed, falls short of, deduction. But that does not mean, as the skeptic is (implicitly) assuming, that inductive grounds do not provide good reasons. The term 'reason', we will point out (Edwards, 1949), does not mean "logically conclusive," and inductive grounds, despite being logically inconclusive, may well provide perfectly good reasons, thereby rendering their conclusions *rational* ("secure"). Taking a risk, we will remind the skeptic, may be eminently reasonable. It is rational, for instance, to take a medicine one thinks is very likely, although uncertain, to cure one of a horrible disease even if it sometimes has pretty unpleasant side effects.

Note that since our aim is to rebut the skeptical argument, we are not required to *show* that induction is like the medicine; that it yields overall more truths than falsehoods. The skeptic has claimed that induction is irrational because it involves the risk of inferring a false conclusion from true premises. In response, we may simply point out that *this* is not a good reason for eschewing it; that it is sometimes quite reasonable—as is attested by familiar situations—to take risks.

This does not complete our response to the skeptical argument. We also want to disprove the argument's conclusion, that is, show that the inductive inference *is* justified. Although we have rebutted the argument, its conclusion may nonetheless be true. Whether or not this task can be accomplished remains to be seen. We must first respond to a second skeptical argument.

2. A Better Skeptical Argument

Hume's argument against induction is more sophisticated and persuasive. It is presented in the course of his (complex) discussion of causality in the *Treatise* (1739, I.3.vi), and more succinctly and perspicuously in the *Enquiries* (1777, pp. 35–36):

1. The conclusion of an inductive argument is not logically entailed by its premises. "Concerning matter [*sic*] of fact and existence," Hume claims (1777, p. 35), "there are no demonstrative arguments . . . since it implies no contradiction that the course of nature may change. . .and the trees will flourish in December. . . . If we be, therefore, engaged by arguments to put trust in past experience . . . these arguments must be probable only."
2. Every inductive argument assumes that nature is *uniform*; "that the future will be conformable to the past."
3. The principle of uniformity, which must be warranted if induction is to be justified, cannot be justified a priori.
4. The principle of uniformity cannot be justified a posteriori, since such a justification would be circular. It would itself be inductive, inferring nature's uniformity *tout court* from its uniformity in the past, thus presupposing—like *any* inductive argument—that nature is uniform.

3. Hume's First Premise

Is Hume right when he says that "it implies no contradiction that . . . the trees will flourish in December"? It might be objected that anything that flourished in December would not be a tree. But this ploy is both implausible and ineffectual (von Wright, 1957, pp. 48–50). It is implausible since trees simply are not defined as not flourishing in December. That they do not is an *empirical* claim about them.

The definitional gambit *is* plausible in some cases. It might be claimed, for instance, that water is defined as H_2O. This means that the generalization "Water is H_2O" is a *conceptual* truth and, does not, therefore, satisfy the skeptical premise. But even if plausible in this case, this response will not silence the inductive skeptic. There *are* empirical generalizations pertaining to water: that it freezes at $0°$ C, for instance. And of these the skeptical premise *is* true.

Similarly, suppose that we grant the definition of the term 'tree' as applying only to things that do not flourish in December. Then what we would (now) describe as a tree flourishing in December will have to be described—in the face of this maneuver—as something that *looked* like a tree and flourished in December. But as in the case of water, the skeptic will cite *other* empirical generalizations about trees to which the first premise in his argument applies. For instance, he can formulate his premise in terms of what things *look like*. There are no demonstrative arguments from past appearances to future ones: even if things have never looked as if trees flourished in December, it is logically possible that they suddenly should.

4. HUME'S SECOND PREMISE

Does every inductive argument assume that "the future will be conformable to the past" (Hume, 1777, p. 35)? Should inductive arguments be construed as enthymematic, with the principle of uniformity as a suppressed premise? To answer this question, the principle of uniformity must be properly formulated.

First, it must not be construed as essentially pertaining to the future. Although it is often assumed that induction involves an inference "from the past to the future," some inductive arguments extrapolate to past or present (unobserved) cases. So the requisite principle is that unobserved cases, whether future or not, resemble observed ones. Indeed, this is one of Hume's formulations in the *Treatise* (1739, p. 89): "that instances, of which we have had no experience, must resemble those, of which we have had experience."

Second, Hume seems to think that the principle of uniformity, when conjoined with a statement of some observed regularity, logically entails predictions about unobserved cases, so that its addition to an inductive argument renders it deductively valid. It "implies no contradiction," he says (1777, p. 35), "that the course of nature may change, and that an object, seemingly like those which we have experienced, may be attended with different or contrary effects. May I not clearly and distinctly conceive that a body, falling from the clouds, and which, in all other respects, resembles snow, has yet the taste of salt or feeling of fire?" Hume is illustrating the principle by giving an example of its violation, from which we can see that he thinks that if nature were assumed to be uniform, it would *follow* that all snowflakes would resemble observed ones (in all relevant respects). If we add the principle of uniformity to a statement of our (restricted) experience of snow like flakes, Hume thinks, we would get a logically valid argument, whose conclusion is that the next snow like flake will be cold, tasteless, and so on.[1]

Hume's construal of the principle of uniformity renders it far too powerful. As Ayer (1972, pp. 20–21) points out, we do not take a counterexample to an inductive prediction to refute the principle of uniformity: we continue to extrapolate from observed cases to unobserved ones even after encountering a white raven. Ayer concludes from this that there is no principle of uniformity to be invoked, but this is surely precipitate. We should instead substitute a weakened but still substantive (albeit vague) principle according to which unobserved cases are *sufficiently often* reliable guides to unobserved ones. From this principle no *particular* inductive prediction follows, but it nonetheless fulfills an important function: justifying the inference from an observed regularity to an unobserved case. Even if the inference is not deductively valid, it is reasonable, since sufficiently many like it have true conclusions. Unlike deduction, induction sometimes leads us astray. But—thanks to the (weakened) uniformity principle—this is atypical.

Third, Hume seems to think that we project every observed regularity onto unobserved cases: "We remember to have had frequent instances of the existence of one species of objects; and also remember, that the individuals of another species of objects have always attended them. . . . Without any farther ceremony, we . . . infer the existence of the one from that of the other" (1739, p. 87). But here, too, he ascribes an inflated content to the principle of uniformity. We have learned from Goodman (1955) that we do not always project regularities onto unobserved cases. We predict that the next emerald will be green if those that we have observed have been green, but we do not predict that the next emerald will be grue, although those that we have observed have been grue. (An emerald is grue if it is green and the time is no later than 2010, or it is blue and the time is after 2010.) Similarly, we do not predict that all emeralds are observed even if all observed emeralds have been observed. The principle of uniformity should therefore be construed to take account of our "discriminatory" extrapolative practice: *some* observed regularities are reliable guides to unobserved cases.

Here is the last clarificatory point, which I will present by considering Howson's defense of Hume's premise. Without "a patent of trustworthiness—a soundness argument—for a putative rule," Howson (2000, pp. 28–29) argues, "you have no reason for confidence in any reasoning which employs it." Howson's claim can be made quite plausible by considering the following analogy. My taking some unpleasant medicine is irrational unless I *believe* that it is efficacious, sufficiently efficacious, that is, to offset the unpleasant side effects. Similarly, someone who reasons inductively while thinking that induction is not reliable or being agnostic about its reliability does not seem (intuitively) justified (reasonable) in his inductively based beliefs, and this is so even if induction is reliable (BonJour, 1985, 3.3).

But a qualification is needed to meet a natural objection. Someone who reasons inductively while thinking that induction is not reliable is intuitively unjustified in his inductively based beliefs because plausibly, one should not believe something to which one has, *to one's knowledge*, no reliable means of epistemic access. But an (unsophisticated) agent who does not have the concept of reliability (uniformity) may be justified in reasoning inductively although he does not believe that induction is reliable. So the skeptic will have to restrict his premise to sophisticated agents. But this is not a devastating concession.

With these clarificatory points in mind, we can now consider the cogency of Hume's second premise. Perhaps Hume's reason for thinking that induction requires a principle of uniformity is not convincing. According to van Cleve (1984) and Mackie (1979), Hume thinks that the principle of uniformity is crucial because it is supposed to render "probable reasoning" deductively valid. This suggestion, we have just seen, is misguided: we do *not* expect an inductive argument to entail its conclusion. But this, of course, does not show that Hume's second premise is wrong: we do not disprove a claim by rebutting an argument for it. And even if (plausibly) inductive arguments involve a sui generis (nondeductive) inference rule, they might, in addition, presuppose nature's uniformity. Indeed, the supposition, properly construed, is eminently plausible. Without a justified belief in nature's uniformity, an observed regularity will not even give *inductive* support to a prediction.

All of the following accounts of induction deny Hume's intuitively compelling second premise, and this must count against them. First, externalists about justification think that a belief (inference rule) may be justified in virtue of facts that need not be known (or even believed) by the agent to obtain. In particular, the inductive principle is justified because, given true premises, it yields true conclusions sufficiently often (Braithwaite, 1953; van Cleve, 1984)[2] or is grounded in virtuous (reliable) cognitive dispositions (Greco, 2000), and the agent does not—contrary to Hume's second premise—need to believe this so as to be justified in reasoning inductively.

Second, Goodman (1955, p. 64) thinks that the rules of inference we employ and particular inferences we make, whether deductive or inductive, are adequately justified by "being brought into agreement with each other," the "agreement achieved . . . [being] the only justification needed for either,"

Third, according to the so-called analytic defense of induction (Edwards, 1949; Strawson, 1952, chap. 9; Barker, 1974; Kyburg 1974), induction is constitutive of rationality. "It is an analytic proposition . . . that . . . other things being equal, the evidence for a generalization is strong in proportion as the number of favorable instances . . . is great . . . plac[ing] reliance on inductive procedures . . . is what 'being reasonable' *means*" (Strawson, 1952, pp. 256–257; emphasis in the original).

Finally, Carnap (1950, p. 30), Sen (1980, chap. 5) and Stove (1986) think that it is a logical truth that the sun rising tomorrow is rationally believed on the basis of previous sunrises.[3] Call this the "logical" defense of induction. Its claim is weaker than that of the "analytic" defense since not all logical truths are analytic (true in virtue of their meaning).

Further objections can be cited against the latter three proposals; that is, Goodman's, the "analytic," and the "logical" defenses of induction. If the analyticity claim were correct, Blackburn (1973, pp. 20–21) argues, the question "What reason do we have for believing according to inductive grounds?" would not arise: to have inductive grounds just *means* to have a good reason. But the question does arise, so the analyticity claim must be false. Fumerton (1995, p. 194) argues in a similar vein. If the statement "Induction is rational" were analytic, the skeptic would be contradicting himself. Since his claim *is* intelligible (even if implausible), the analytic defense, Fumerton concludes, fails.

In response, it may be claimed that not all analytic statements are trivial, and mistakes about them can be made (Weintraub, 2004). There may be unknown conceptual truths, since we are not omniscient about meaning. Witness disagreements about the meaningfulness of the positivists' metaphysical bogeys such as Bradley's "The absolute enters into, but is itself incapable of, evolution and progress." Remember, too, the disputes about the correctness of philosophical analyses of some terms. It is not just that we cannot come up with an analysis: *that* is not surprising. We find it difficult to determine whether a *given* analysis is correct. Does 'knowledge' mean "true justified belief"? Does the meaning of the terms 'cause' and 'effect' preclude an effect from preceding its cause? Do ethical propositions report the objective obtaining of ethical facts, or does the statement "Murder is wrong" mean "I disapprove of murder"? Some of these questions seem irresolvable; none are trivial.

Here is an objection to both the "analytic" and "logical" defenses of induction. As I will show, it can easily be modified to apply to Goodman's proposal as well. If induction's rationality is a logical truth (and, in particular, if it is analytic), it would be justified no matter what the circumstances are. But, as Strawson admits (1952, p. 261), the reliability of induction is contingent. So we can envisage circumstances in which it is less reliable than some rival. And, the objection continues, in such circumstances it would be irrational to infer inductively. This, the objection concludes, shows that the rationality of induction is not logically guaranteed.

But, the proponents of the "analytic" and "logical" defenses of induction may reply, such circumstances *cannot* be envisaged. We can, to be sure, imagine that induction has *hitherto* been less reliable than a rival, but that does not mean that we will judge it to be unreliable *simpliciter*. This judgment requires a nondeductive inference induction: we invoke induction's (bad) track record and infer (inductively) that it is an unreliable method. But then, the reply continues, the conclusion is unstable: it undermines the inference rule that engenders it.

This does not rebut the objection to the "analytic" and "logical" defenses. We do not actually need to imagine ourselves judging induction to be unreliable. The very fact that it is not *self-certifying* (in the envisaged circumstances) means that its use is not (then) rational (Lewis, 1971).

Goodman thinks that induction is rational only if it "agrees" (coheres) with our particular inferences. So how can his proposal be vulnerable to a difficulty that is engendered by the claim that induction is *necessarily* rational? Well, in fact, the objection only invokes the possibility of circumstances in which induction is not self-certifying, yet is classified by a proposal as rational. The possibility suffices of a world in which our inductions are more often than not refuted by our experience, yet the inductive rule of inference and particular inductive inferences we make are in reflective equilibrium.

I think that the proponents of all three defenses of induction can meet this objection by slightly retreating. Even if induction is not necessarily rational, it may be claimed, it is prima facie rational. If there is no reason for suspecting that induction is not reliable, its invocation is reasonable; there is no need to invoke a uniformity principle. And this is enough to rebut Hume's premise.

Here is another, more powerful objection to the latter three attempts to rebut Hume's second premise, Goodman's, the "analytic," and the "logical" defenses of induction. These proposals all deny that there is a conceptual link between justification and reliability. Without such a link, it might be claimed, the value of "justification" ("rationality") is called into question. "The distinguishing characteristic of epistemic justification is . . . its *essential* or internal relation to the cognitive goal of truth" (BonJour, 1985, p. 8; my italics).

The point can be reinforced by considering the analogy Strawson draws between induction and the law. It "makes no sense," he claims, "to inquire in general whether . . . the legal system as a whole, is or is not legal. For to what legal standards are we appealing?" (1952, p. 257). Analogously, he argues, the only standard by which induction can be assessed is the one set by induction itself and relative to which it is trivially justified.

Strawson's analogy misfires. True, there are no standards by which to judge the law *illegal*. But the law, being a *motivated* practice (designed to achieve justice, public order, and so on), must be believed to be *efficacious*, well suited to its aims, rather than merely *legal* if we are to be justified in adhering to it. For instance, a system incorporating a law disenfranchising women is legal but unfair. Now substitute "induction" for "the law" and "truth" for "justice" and see how Strawson's defense of induction collapses. Induction is a goal-oriented practice, and we want to know whether it is *sufficiently often truth-preserving*. Conforming to one inductive practice in preference to another will certainly make a difference, possibly a considerable one, in the verisimilitude of the beliefs we form. This is why the problem of induction is a pressing one. And a "justification" that has no implications about its reliability does not provide us with a reason for using it.

5. HUME'S THIRD PREMISE

Here is Hume's argument in support of the claim that the principle of uniformity cannot be justified a priori. "We can at least conceive a change in the course of nature; which sufficiently proves, that such a change is not absolutely impossible" (1739, p. 89).

Whatever we can conceive, Hume argues, is logically possible. But how are we to construe the conceivability that is supposed to be a criterion of logical possibility? If conceiving is "entertaining in one's mind," then the criterion looks too liberal. It seems that we can entertain both Goldbach's conjecture and its negation, yet, since the propositions are mathematical, one of them (we know not which) is impossible (Kneale, 1949, pp. 79–80). So even if Hume can conceive of nature changing its course, he will not have shown that it is logically possible for it to do so. Perhaps, alternatively, we are mistaken in thinking that we can entertain both

Goldbach's conjecture and its negation. But then "'conceivable' is taken to mean 'non-contradictory', [and]...no non-circular test for contradictoriness...or possibility has been given" (Stroud, 1977, p. 50). The conceivability criterion turns out to be either inadequate or vacuous and cannot be invoked to uphold Hume's claim that nature may (logically) be nonuniform.

In light of Hume's failure to provide an argument against the possibility of grounding nature's uniformity a priori, we should consider whether any of the several attempts thus to ground nature's uniformity succeeds.

5.1. Williams

The term 'reliable', which is used in Hume's third premise, is vague. This means that attempts to ground induction's reliability may be more or less ambitious, depending on how they construe it. Williams's attempt (1947) is very ambitious, aiming as it does to show that inductive conclusions (based on sufficiently large samples) are *typically true*.

At least one inductive principle, Williams claims, can be (deductively) derived from evident a priori principles. The principle, call it I, is the following:
(I)

m/n of a large sample of A's are B.

About m/n of the population of A's are B.

The two (a priori) principles from which I is supposed to follow are the law of large numbers and the "statistical syllogism." According to (a very rough formulation of) the law of large numbers, most samples are typical: for any property A, the proportion of A's in most (sufficiently large) samples is very close to their proportion in the entire population.

The statistical syllogism, SS, is the following inference rule:
(SS)

Most P's are Q's
a is P

(Probably) a is Q

How is I derived? Consider a sample of A's, S, m/n of which are B, and invoke the statistical syllogism, substituting for P and Q, respectively, "is a sample" and "is typical with respect to B":
(SS₁)

Most samples are typical with respect to B.
S is a sample.

(Probably) S is typical with respect to B.

But (since in S the proportion of B's is m/n) this means that the proportion of B's in the population is (probably) close to m/n. And we have managed to derive this from the law of large numbers in conjunction with the statistical syllogism. It seems that we have an a priori justification of the inductive inference rule I.

Here is Ayer's (1972, pp. 41–42) objection to the invocation of the law of large numbers in defense of induction. The law may be invoked, Ayer claims, if we assume that our sample is randomly selected—as likely to be drawn as any other. This assumption, he thinks, is clearly warranted if we suppose "that the distribution of properties in the spatiotemporal region which is accessible to us reflects their distribution in the continuum as a whole." But this (uniformity) assumption, Ayer claims, is unjustified: "We should not be very surprised to learn that many matters were very differently ordered in other parts of the universe."

Even if Ayer's criticism is cogent, it is partial: it is only relevant when we are trying to extrapolate to those far reaches of the universe. But even thus restricted, the criticism is not cogent. Although randomness justifies the assumption that our sample is typical, it is not necessary. Indeed, it is seldom satisfied when we project from a sample. Our samples, even those on which scientific research is based, are seldom random: members of the population do *not* have an equal chance of being selected. Some ravens, for instance, are dead; others are not yet living. And we do not refrain from generalizing about ravens on the basis of those we have encountered.

Random sampling is not intrinsically desirable. It is a means of increasing the likelihood that the sample is *representative* of the entire population (Fisher, 1935, chap. 8). If we think that our (nonrandomly chosen) sample of ravens is varied geographically, we can (cautiously) assume that it is representative of the entire population and conclude that all ravens—including future ones, which *cannot* be examined—are black. We allow ourselves to omit future ravens from our sample because we think that ravens are not likely to change their color. Similarly, we do not bother to include in our sample ravens hatched on both odd and even days of the week because we think that this factor is not correlated with color. So long as the sample is thought to be representative, for which randomness is merely evidence, the projection is legitimate.

Here is the real difficulty with William's attempt to derive the inductive principle. Consider a sample of black ravens. Since it is probably typical, we may infer that (probably) all ravens are black. But the reasoning can be applied to the predicate "shmblack," which is satisfied by an object iff it has been observed to be black or has not been observed and is white. By the statistical syllogism, our sample is (probably) typical with respect to *this* property. This means that (probably) in the entire population all ravens are shmblack, that is, that all unobserved ravens are white. Our seemingly impeccable inference principle yields incompatible predictions.

Stove (1986, p. 77), who defends Williams's proposal, is aware of the difficulty. Inductive validity, he claims in response, is not formal, and only some instances of I are warranted. Of course, he is right, and we already know this. Now the law of large numbers is beyond reproach, so how has Williams managed to derive the sweeping (and contradictory) principle I? The trouble must lie with the statistical syllogism. Some of its instances are legitimate, and others are not. The following two instances cannot both be valid.

(SS$_2$)

> Most samples are typical with respect to blackness.
> S is a sample of ravens.
> _____
>
> S is typical with respect to blackness.

(SS$_3$)

> Most samples are typical with respect to shmblackness.
> S is a sample of ravens.
> _____
>
> S is typical with respect to shmblackness.

We think that only the first is warranted, and, of course, a complete account of induction, which we do not as yet have, will elucidate (and hopefully justify) our (selective) practice, our preference for "black" over "shmblack." But pending such an account, we simply cannot assume that we can identify the legitimate instances of SS (and I) a priori. So we have not been given an a priori justification for I.

5.2. BonJour

BonJour's argument is also an ambitious attempt to prove induction reliable because it purports to show that inductive conclusions are typically true (if the premises are). This is so, BonJour (1998, 7.7) claims, because it is the best explanation of the regularities we observe. For instance, that all ravens are black best explains why the ravens we have observed have been black. The explanatorily inferior alternatives are that our observations are the result of mere coincidence and "non-standard inductive explanations," such as "Some ravens are blue, but they sleep during the day, and are, therefore, never observed." The probable existence of a "normal inductive explanation" for the regularity we observe, furthermore, is guaranteed a priori.

Of the two difficulties I will cite, the first is more of a challenge. BonJour persuasively argues for the existence of a priori knowledge, but the a priori knowledge of the principle he invokes, a special instance of inference to the best explanation, seems more problematic than that of logical truths, for instance. The probability claim that is supposed to be a priori is construed frequentistically: in most worlds there exists an explanation for the observed regularities. For instance, in most worlds in which only black ravens have been observed, *all* the ravens are black. Thus construed, the claim is very substantive, and, pace BonJour (1998, p. 208), far from "evident." So pending some further argument, we have a promissory note, not an actual defense of induction.

The second objection is one that BonJour anticipates (1998, p. 214) but does not, I think, manage to rebut. The suspicion he attempts to quell is that the "standard inductive evidence," the regularities we have observed, only warrants the claim that induction has been reliable *hitherto*. His response is that a "Humean constant conjunction ['All ravens living hitherto are black,' e.g.] amounts to just a restatement and generalization"of the standard inductive evidence ['All ravens observed hitherto have been black'], but has no real capacity to explain the occurrence of that evidence" (1998, p. 214), whereas the more "robust," law like regularity, which "involve[s] by its very nature a substantial propensity to persist into the future" (1998, p. 214), does explain the occurrence. And in virtue of being the *best* explanation, the nomological regularity is made probable, establishing induction's reliability in the future.

To see the inadequacy of this response, we should understand what it is that induction's reliability is supposed to explain. It is not that the objects picked out by the description "ravens observed by me" are black. *This* fact is not explained by the generalization "All ravens are black"—whether nomological or accidental. A proper explanation will cite genetic makeup, evolutionary adaptation, etc.

The fact that induction's reliability *can* explain pertains to our *observations*: that all the events picked out by the description "observation of a raven" have been observations of a black raven. *This* fact is explained equally well by the (temporally restricted) constant conjunction and the "robust" law like statement. To see this, consider a similar case, in which an explanation is sought for the fact that the coin I drew at random out of my pocket was a penny. Here it is perfectly adequate to cite the fact that all the coins in my pocket *when the coin was drawn* were pennies. The regularity, note, is accidental and has no implications regarding the future.

Returning now to induction, we do not improve the explanation of our observations by supposing that the regularities (in nature) are nomological. The explanation that appeals to accidental regularities *obtaining hitherto* is equally good. And if the temporally restricted regularity explains equally well, explanatory considerations will only warrant a *restricted* conclusion, that induction has *hitherto been reliable*. But the conclusion we are seeking to establish to justify our reliance on induction *in the future* is that induction is reliable *tout court*.

5.3. The Pragmatic Justification of Induction

Reichenbach's (1949, sec. 87) justification of induction invokes the claim—supposedly an a priori truth—that induction will succeed if any method will. So we see that it is less ambitious than those we have considered: unlike them, it does not purport to show that induction is reliable *tout court*.

To assess its cogency, two questions must be answered. Does the claim provide an adequate justification of induction? Is the claim true? I will consider them in turn.

The skeptic might object that the claim is hypothetical and therefore insufficient to justify induction (BonJour, 1998, p. 195). But this objection is misguided. We do not need, when justifying an action under uncertainty, to show that its consequences are good. It is enough that the action is the best available option. And if Reichenbach is correct, he will have shown that induction is the best prediction policy, our best hope for finding the truth, and, therefore, rational. But is he correct?

When we reason inductively, Reichenbach assumes, we infer that the limit of the relative frequency of an attribute in an infinite sequence approximates within a small interval the relative frequency of that attribute in the observed section of the sequence. If nature is uniform, Reichenbach argues, induction will enable us to make veridical predictions on the basis of our observations. Uniformity means that there is a limit, that is, that there exists some number such that the observed relative frequency in any sufficiently long initial section of the sequence matches that number as closely as we like. So a persistent use of the rule applied to larger and larger initial sections of the sequence will establish the limit within any desired interval of accuracy.

If, on the other hand, nature is not uniform, there is no limit to be discovered, and, of course, no method will succeed. Induction, Reichenbach concludes, is demonstrably the best method, although it may be quite poor (if nature is inauspicious).

This argument fails because there are infinitely many other rules that will "ultimately" reveal the limit if it exists: if I_n is the value posited by the inductive rule after n observations, then for any sequence $\{y_n\}$ that converges to 0, $I_n + y_n$ will also converge to the limit. This only shows that induction is not unique in discovering the limit. Unfortunately, the possibility that its short-term deliverances are much worse than those of some rivals and indeed are very poor cannot be ruled out a priori. Even if the sequence $\{I_n\}$ converges to a limit, the initial segment (the observed relative frequencies) may take a very long time to approach it. When this happens, induction will be a very poor method in the short term—the only term that interests us. And other methods will be much better.

5.4. Savage

Savage's justification of induction is probabilistic, so a short explanation of probabilistic, "Bayesian" justification is in order. Bayesians think that belief comes in (real-numbered) degrees that satisfy the probability calculus and change by conditionalizing. When new evidence E is acquired, the new probability of each proposition T changes to its old probability conditional on E, $P(T/E)$. Within the Bayesian framework, the problem of induction takes the form of justifying the assignment of prior probabilities. To take a proposition about an unobserved case, E_2, as confirmed by an observed one, E_1, is to assign a higher (subjective) probability to E_2 conditional on E_1 than to E_2 *simpliciter*.

The Bayesian assumptions are unrealistic. True, belief comes in degrees, and our inductions may increase our confidence while still leaving us in (some) doubt about the truth of our predictions. But our degrees of belief are seldom precise enough to be assigned real numbers and often violate the probability calculus, which would have us, for instance, assigning probability 1 to all logical truths. Nonetheless, this idealization is useful. It provides us with a mathematically tractable characterization of inductive inferences for agents whose beliefs are often partial. And if the problem of induction can be solved for Bayesian agents, the solution might work, mutatis mutandis, for humans too.

In his Bayesian response to the "problem of induction," Savage (1954, p. 49) attempts to show that induction is (sufficiently) reliable. In fact, *any* assignment of prior probabilities is justified, he argues, since they all converge, in the long run, on the truth. Invoking a (stable-estimation) theorem of the probability calculus, Savage argues that accumulating evidence *swamps* prior probabilities. In the long run, as the agent conditionalizes on more and more evidence propositions, his probabilities will tend to be concentrated on true propositions.

We seem to have a deductive demonstration of the reliability of our inductive practice and, indeed, of any other. But do we? Unfortunately, the answer is no. To begin with, the theorem does nothing to vindicate our confidence about our *current* predictions: *different* inductive practices may greatly diverge in the short run. And in Keynes's words, we are all dead in the long run. Worse, the theorem does not even provide a long-run deductive vindication of induction. If we observe *all* the instances of a generalization, we will establish its truth. But this will be deduction: in induction the conclusion goes beyond the premises. And so long as our evidence is incomplete, the result established with the aid of the theorem is probabilistic rather than categorical. "The theorem does not tell us that in the limit any rational Bayesian will assign probability 1 to the true hypothesis and probability 0 to the rest; it only tells us that rational Bayesians are certain that he will" (Glymour, 1980, p. 73). This is because we cannot deductively infer the truth of a proposition from its having probability 1.[4] Savage's Bayesian attempt to justify induction a priori, I conclude, fails.

6. HUME'S FOURTH PREMISE

Hume's fourth premise needs to be fleshed out. It rules out an empirical justification of induction because of its circularity. But Hume is (implicitly) assuming that an empirical justification must be inductive. To justify this assumption, the possibility must be ruled out that nature's uniformity is—although empirical— *basic, noninferentially justified*. But this can easily be done (Fumerton, 1995; van

Cleve, 2003). The claim that nature is uniform is very sweeping. Of course, very general claims ("Triangles have three sides," for instance) may be basic. But the justification of general *empirical* claims must be inferential. And Hume's fourth premise is concerned with the possibility that the principle of uniformity is contingent.

Hume peremptorily dismisses the possibility of justifying induction inductively. This is eminently plausible. He has endorsed (in the second premise) the supposition that induction's reliability is a *presupposition* of any inductive argument, so he thinks that an inductive justification of induction's reliability will have its conclusion as a premise. And this circularity is vicious because it renders justification nondiscriminating: *any* proposition can be "justified" if it is allowed as a premise in a justificatory argument.

Things are very different, though, if Hume's second premise is rejected. The reliabilist endorsement of an inductive justification of induction's reliability deserves serious consideration. For the justification of an inductive inference, it is enough that induction is (sufficiently) reliable. So induction's reliability is not a premise in justified inductive arguments. In particular, it is not a premise in an inductive argument for induction's reliability based on its track record.

This is not merely a *formal* point. It is important to note that—unlike the circular justification of *propositions*—the reliabilist circular justification of the reliability of inference rules is *discriminating*. Even if we are allowed to invoke an inference rule in its own justification, success is not guaranteed. The horoscope *may* predict the unreliability of its predictions and the superiority of an alternative method of prediction (Lewis, 1971). The same is true of the circular justification of induction. Consider the inductive rule I_1:

(I_1)

> Most observed A's have been B's.
> _____
> (Probably): the next A will be B.

The rule I_1 can be defended by invoking the following inductive argument, using I_1 itself:

> Most applications of I_1 have been successful.
> _____
> (Probably) the next use of I_1 will be successful.

Note that the premise is contingent, and the self-supporting defense could (logically) fail. Indeed, it does fail in the case of the following inductive rule, I_2:

(I_2)

> All observed A's have been B's.
> _____
> (Probably) the next A will be B.

The (circular) justification fails, since the requisite premise is false:

All applications of I_2 have been successful.

(Probably) the next use of I_2 will be successful.

It might be objected that the nontriviality of the circular justification of inference rules does not suffice to vindicate it. Crazy rules can be invoked in their own defense (Salmon, 1957, p. 46). Consider the anti-inductive rule AI, which allows us to infer from "All observed A's have been B's" that the next A will *not* be a B.[5] We can construct an argument using AI to show that AI will be successful:

Most applications of AI have not been successful.

(Probably) the next use of AI will be successful.

The objection fails. Reliabilists do not claim that (nontrivial) self-support is sufficient for justification. The inductive justification of induction is epistemically efficacious, they will remind us, because induction is *reliable*. The self-supporting argument in defense of AI, by way of contrast, is bogus (even if its proponents are taken in by it): AI simply is not reliable.

My conclusion is that there is nothing wrong with the reliabilist's circular justification of induction. The trouble is with reliabilism itself. I have already criticized reliabilism for violating the intuitively plausible internalist requirement (section 5). There are, in addition, several very telling counterexamples to it. My favorite is Vogel's (2000, pp. 313–314) Roxanne. Her car has a reliable gas gauge, and she forms beliefs about how much gas there is in the tank. She also forms beliefs about the gauge's readings by looking at it. Both beliefs are reliably acquired: the gauge and perception are (sufficiently) reliable. By conjoining these two types of belief, Roxanne forms several beliefs of the form "The gauge reads 'F' ('E') and F (E)." Now Roxanne reasons inductively from these conjunctions and concludes that the gauge is reliable. Since induction is reliable, her belief is justified by reliabilist lights, but it is intuitively (resoundingly) unjustified.[6]

7. Accepting the Skeptical Conclusion with Equanimity: Popper

Even if the skeptical conclusion is correct, it does not follow that we are irrational. For *that*, it must also be assumed that we rely on induction. And this (seemingly truistic) assumption may be denied.

Popper (1972) claims that induction is dispensable. Science progresses by formulating bold hypotheses and subjecting them to rigorous tests, and the only mode of reasoning it requires is deduction. Predictions ("observation statements") are deductively derived from hypotheses, and when they are observationally refuted, the theory is *deductively* falsified: if $T \vdash E$, then $\sim E \vdash \sim T$. If this is so, we may cheerfully concede the skeptical conclusion that induction is irrational. Since science does not invoke induction, its rational credentials are not thereby impugned.

This attempt to take the sting out of Hume's argument is unsuccessful because even on Popper's account, induction is indispensable to the scientific method (Newton-Smith, 1981, chap. 3). First, inductive considerations must be invoked in locating a theory's Achilles' heel to determine whether a test is really severe. A theory's prediction is more vulnerable the *less likely* it is. But judgments about likelihood are based on inductive reasoning. Suppose I predict that the sun will rise from now on only on Tuesdays. Watching for the sun on Wednesday morning (but not on Tuesday morning) is a severe test because my prediction about that day contravenes our supposition that the sun rises daily. And this supposition is *inductively* based—inferred from past sunrises.

Second, as Popper himself concedes, we are fallible and can never know with certainty the truth of any factual assertion, even an "observation statement." This means that we must invoke inductive considerations in deciding what our observations are, so as to see which theories they falsify.

Induction also comes in at a later stage in the scientific inquiry. We do not rest content with having "on our books" a theory that has withstood rigorous attempts at refutation. If we rely on theories in action, we must at least believe (if only tentatively) their empirical consequences to be (very probably) true. Unlike the inference from the existence of a falsifying instance to the falsity of the theory, the inference from a theory's having withstood rigorous tests to it continuing to do so is not deductively valid. And it is the latter that is required to ground our reliance on the theory. Similarly, we can only partake of our theories' nonpractical virtues (verisimilitude, explanatory strength) if we take them to be (probably) true. This belief, too, is not logically entailed by their surviving stringent tests.

We must conclude that Popper's attempt to show that science does not essentially depend on induction fails. Skeptical arguments against induction cannot be shrugged aside.

8. DIAGNOSIS

Hume's skeptical argument against induction seems cogent, but its conclusion is implausible. Must we accept it nonetheless? The (dialectical) situation is familiar. Like Zeno, our (reasoning) skeptic presents us with a *paradox*, "an apparently unacceptable conclusion derived by apparently acceptable reasoning from apparently acceptable premises" (Sainsbury, 1988, p. 1). To solve the (skeptical) paradox, we must either reject (at least one of) the premises or accept the conclusion. But both alternatives flout strong intuitions. So how are we to avoid a stalemate?

The symmetry is specious, Greco (2000) suggests. The skeptical conclusion, he thinks, is so incredible that no skeptical argument can establish it. The conjunction of the premises, on the other hand, is not incontrovertible. So a solution to the paradox must reject at least one of them.

I am inclined to disagree. Greco likens the skeptical argument to Zeno's "proof" that motion is impossible. Zeno's conclusion is so preposterous that it can only force us to find the fallacy in the reasoning. And perhaps initially, the mathematical theory that avoided the conclusion (the infinitesimal calculus) seemed very unintuitive. (To some, it still does.) But its acceptance was nonetheless warranted because it was the least implausible way of denying Zeno's conclusion.

The analogy is not apt. We *see* motion all the time. But attributions of justification (knowledge) are theoretical, and the claim that they are never (or seldom) true is not preposterous. The skeptic may well have exposed our error in making them, and we cannot simply assume that the (intuitive) premises that engender the skeptical conclusion are jointly false.

My (tentative) conclusion is that we have reached an impasse. Perhaps we do not have a veritable "skeleton in the cupboard of Inductive Logic": the skeptical conclusion has not been established. But we do have an unsolved paradox.

NOTES

I am very grateful to John Greco for his painstaking and helpful comments.

1. I side here with Mackie (1980, p. 15) and van Cleve (1984) against Howson (2000, p. 13) and Greco (2000, pp. 145–159), who think that Hume recognizes nondeductive forms of justification. Hume's "probabilistic reasoning" is deductive. It differs from "demonstrative reasoning," which involves the comparison of ideas, only with respect to its *premises*, at least some of which are contingent and (sometimes) uncertain.

2. The formulation is intentionally vague. Does "sufficiently often" mean "more often than not," "most of the time," or "more than any other method"? The choice does not matter, because we are concerned with the viability of the *very idea* that the reliability of induction could constitute justification.

3. Carnap seems to lose the courage of his convictions and invokes various other considerations by way of justifying the probability distribution (confirmation function) he favors. He narrows the field down to two functions that "are most simple and suggest themselves as the most natural ones" (1950, p. 565).

4. The inference is not a theorem of the probability calculus because in any nondenumerable probability space there will be nonempty events assigned probability 0.

5. Van Cleve (1984, n. 16) and Plantinga (1993, p. 127, n. 8) suggest that anti-induction is inconsistent. For instance, if all observed ravens have been black, then, since they have

been observed to be not red and not green, anti-induction will predict that the next raven will be both red and green. But without restricting the predicates we project, induction, too, will be inconsistent. This is the lesson we have learned from Goodman. So, similarly, "anti-induction" is not a formal rule, sanctifying the reversal of *every* observed regularity. Of course, I do not have a proposal as to how anti-induction is to be restricted so as to be rendered consistent, but we may assume that it can be done. At least, the problem is no more difficult than that of characterizing induction in light of Goodman's new riddle.

6. Conjunctions of reliabilistically acquired beliefs are not as reliable as the conjuncts. Two methods may count as reliable by reference to some threshold, yet the reliability rate of the combined method might fall below it. But we may suppose that *overall*, conjunction is (sufficiently) reliable.

REFERENCES

Ayer, A.J. 1972. *Probability and Evidence*. London: Macmillan.

Barker, S.F. 1974. "Is There a Problem of Induction?" In R. Swinburne (ed.), *The Justification of Induction*. Oxford University Press.

Blackburn, S. 1973. *Reason and Prediction*. Cambridge: Cambridge University Press.

BonJour, L. 1985. *The Structure of Empirical Knowledge*. Cambridge, Mass.: Harvard University Press.

———. 1998. *In Defense of Pure Reason*. Cambridge University Press.

Braithwaite, R.B. 1953. *Scientific Explanation*. Cambridge University Press.

Broad, C.D. 1952. "The Philosophy of Francis Bacon." In C.D. Broad, *Ethics and the History of Philosophy*. London: Routledge and Kegan Paul, pp. 117–143.

Carnap, R. 1950. *Logical Foundations of Probability*. London: Routledge and Kegan Paul.

Edwards, P. 1949. "Russell's Doubts about Induction." *Mind* 68: 141–163.

Fisher, R.A. 1935. *The Design of Experiments*. 8th ed.

Fumerton, R. 1995. *Metaepistemology and Skepticism*. Lanham, Md.: Rowman and Littlefield.

Glymour, C. 1980. *Theory and Evidence*. Cambridge University Press.

Goodman, N. 1955. *Fact, Fiction and Forecast*. Indianapolis, IN: Bobbs-Merrill.

Greco. J. 2000. *Putting Skeptics in their Place*. Cambridge University Press.

Howson, C. 2000. *Hume's Problem*. Oxford: Clarendon Press.

Hume, D. 1739. *A Treatise of Human Nature*. Edited by L.A. Selby-Bigge. 2nd ed. Oxford: Clarendon Press, 1975.

———. 1777. *Enquiries Concerning Human Understanding*. Edited by L.A. Selby-Bigge. 3rd ed. Oxford: Clarendon Press, 1978.

Kneale, W. 1949. *Probability and Induction*. Oxford: Clarendon Press.

Kyburg, H. 1974. "Comments on Salmon's 'Inductive Evidence.'" In R. Swinburne (ed.), *The Justification of Induction*. Oxford University Press.

Lewis, D. 1971. "Immodest Inductive Methods." *Philosophy of Science* 38: 54–63.

Lipton, P. 1991. *Inference to the Best Explanation*. 2nd ed. London: Routledge.

Mackie, J.L. 1979. "A Defence of Induction." In G.F. Macdonald (ed.), *Perception and Identity*. London: Macmillan.

———. 1980. *The Cement of the Universe*. Oxford: Clarendon Press.

Newton-Smith, W. 1981. *The Rationality of Science*. London: Routledge and Kegan Paul.

Plantinga, A. 1993. *Warrant and Proper Function*. Oxford University Press.

Popper, K.R. 1972. *The Logic of Scientific Discovery*. 4th ed. London: Hutchinson.

Reichenbach, H. 1949. *The Theory of Probability*. Berkeley: University of California Press.

Russell, B. 1912. *The Problems of Philosophy*. Oxford University Press.

Sainsbury, M. 1988. *Paradoxes*. Cambridge University Press.

Salmon, W.C. 1957. "Should We Attempt to Justify Induction?" *Philosophical Studies* 8: 33–48.

Savage, L.J. 1954. *The Foundations of Statistics*. London: Chapman and Hall.

Sen, P.K. 1980. *Logic, Induction and Ontology*. Delhi: Macmillan.

Sextus Empiricus. 1933. *Outlines of Pyrrhonism*. Trans. R.G. Bury. Loeb Classical Library. London: W. Heinemann. Cited as *OP*.

Stove, D.C. 1986. *The Rationality of Induction*. Oxford: Clarendon Press.

Strawson, P.F. 1952. *Introduction to Logical Theory*. London: Methuen.

Stroud, B. 1977. *Hume*. London: Routledge and Kegan Paul.

Swinburne, R. 1974. *The Justification of Induction*. Oxford University Press.

van Cleve, J. 1984. "Reliability, Justification and Induction." *Midwest Studies in Philosophy* 9: 555–567.

———. 2003. "Is Knowledge Easy—or Impossible? Externalism as the Only Alternative to Skepticism." In S. Luper (ed.), *The Sceptics*. Ashgate.

Vogel, J. 2000. "Reliabilism Leveled." *Journal of Philosophy* 97: 602–623.

Von Wright, G.H. 1957. *The Logical Problem of Induction* 2nd ed. Oxford: Blackwell.

Weintraub, R. 2004. "On Sharp Boundaries for Vague Predicates." *Synthese* 138: 233–245.

Williams, D.C. 1947. *The Ground of Induction*. Cambridge, Mass.: Harvard University Press.

CHAPTER 7

SKEPTICISM ABOUT A PRIORI JUSTIFICATION: SELF-EVIDENCE, DEFEASIBILITY, AND *COGITO* PROPOSITIONS

ROBERT AUDI

A priori justification is commonly taken to be a kind based on reason rather than on experience. Our justification for believing elementary logical truths, such as the principle of noncontradiction, is often considered a priori. But there are propositions whose classification as a priori is disputed, and there are many interpretations of "based on experience" and "based on reason." This chapter will clarify the ideas these phrases point to. It will also assess the skeptical view that no genuinely substantive proposition is a priori, and that, accordingly, reason has far less power to reveal truth than has been supposed by a great many philosophers.

Skepticism may extend even to truths of logic. For one thing, these have been regarded as only empirical rather than a priori, and justification for believing them has been argued to be defeasible.[1] These claims pave the way for countenancing unjustified and even false beliefs of propositions in the categories in question. One could, to be sure, hold that there *is* knowledge of some a priori truths, but that they are simply not known to be a priori in the strong traditional sense that has been thought to imply necessary truth and a ground for epistemic certainty. With regard to candidates for the nonformal a priori—roughly, for propositions whose negation does not entail (by principles of formal logic) a contradiction—there is widespread skepticism about their a priori status, even if not about their truth. It is common for empiricists from Hume onward to deny the apriority of such propositions.

Substantive a priori propositions are now widely taken to include mathematical propositions, as well as at least three other kinds: propositions expressing relations between universals, say, that everything green is colored or that nothing round is square; simple philosophical propositions, for instance, that beliefs are not processes; and moral principles of a kind that may be considered in a sense basic, say, that it is prima facie wrong to kill people.[2] My focus will be the question whether we can be justified in believing substantive propositions of these sorts. I call them *substantive* because I assume that they are not formal truths and that they have content important for their subject matters, such as mathematics, philosophy, or ethics. Many points made here will apply to knowledge, as well as to justification, but I will concentrate on justification. This is both to confine the inquiry to a single chapter and because, if the kind of case that emerges for the possibility of substantive priori justification (i.e., justification for believing substantive a priori propositions) is sound, much of what needs to be said in defense of the possibility of a priori knowledge will be clear.

1. THE DOMAIN OF THE A PRIORI

Skepticism comes in many forms and cuts across the distinction between the a priori and the empirical. It may, for instance, concern knowledge or justification; and it may be unrestricted as to subject matter or confined to a particular topic, such as morality. In one way, my concern is with a specific kind of skepticism—skepticism about the possibility of substantive a priori justification—but in another way, it is quite general, since I do not restrict consideration to either mathematics or philosophy or ethics or any particular subject matter. For ease of reference, we might speak of *justification skepticism* where the focus is justification and of *knowledge skepticism* (or epistemic skepticism) where the focus is knowledge. We might also speak of *general skepticism,* which applies to any kind of proposition whatever, and *domain-specific skepticism* where there is a particular subject matter or specific kind of proposition in question. Many other useful distinctions can be made among kinds of skepticism (and are made in this volume), but these will suffice here.[3]

1.1. The Self-Evident and the A Priori

The notion of the self-evident can be treated as basic in the concept of the a priori. Self-evidence has been widely misunderstood, and in part for that reason, its potentially central role in explicating the a priori has not been generally appreciated. What follows is the core of an account of the self-evident that will be useful in understanding skepticism about the substantive a priori.[4]

Consider first the idea that a self-evident proposition is one whose truth is in some way evident "in itself." This idea is plausible, given what one would expect from the meanings of the parts of the compound, *self-evidence,* and it accords with standard uses of the term. Now if a proposition, *p,* is evident in itself, one would think that there is a way of "looking at it" that reveals positive status—at least truth. I take it that looking at it in a way appropriate to seeing its truth (or to appreciating its being evident) requires at least understanding it.

If the self-evident is evidently true, one might think that what must be revealed by proper consideration of such a proposition is that it *is* evidently true.[5] *Being evident,* however, is an epistemic notion, often taken to be equivalent to being manifestly true; and one could have a proper cognitive response to a self-evident proposition, *p,* say that nothing round is square, without conceptualizing the proposition as *evident*—and probably without even having the concept of the evident. A young child learning elementary logic grasps, through understanding the proposition, that if Ellie is taller than Yu-chi, then he is shorter than she. What, then, is revealed by the kind of comprehending consideration of a self-evident proposition that concerns us?

Consider what is meant when it is said to be "evident to everyone" that, say, the car is emitting dark smoke. What is standardly meant is that to everyone (suitably positioned) this seems *true,* not that this seems evident. In this case, however, it is manifestly true not in itself but on the basis of the ease with which it is believed to be true true (as opposed, e.g., to being believed to be true on the basis of inferring it). Even if, by reflection, we may also discern the proposition's higher order property of being evident, its being evident is not what is revealed when we simply come to know the proposition. I take *self*-evidence to be a special kind of manifest truth of a proposition in itself, not the higher order property of being manifestly evident in itself. Given its self-evidence, one can come to know *it*—here, that *p*—by appropriately considering it. If one could also come to know its status by such consideration—say, to know that *p is evident*—this is a different matter.

1.2. The Basic Kind of Self-Evidence

Given these and other points about the notion of the self-evident, I construe the basic kind of self-evident proposition as (roughly) a truth such that any adequate understanding of it meets two conditions: (a) in virtue of having that understanding, one is justified in believing the proposition (i.e., has justification for believing it, whether one in fact believes it or not); and (b) if one believes the proposition on the *basis* of that understanding of it, then one knows it.[6] More briefly (even if not exactly equivalently), *p* is self-evident provided an adequate understanding of it grounds (1) being justified in believing it and (2) knowing it if one believes it on the basis of that understanding. Here the grounding role of understanding the proposition—whereby no other ground is needed to be justified in believing it—clarifies the idea of a self-evident proposition's being manifestly true "in itself." Understanding a proposition need not connect it with something else needed as evidence or as independent justification. Three elements need clarification here: the relation between the understanding in question and believing *p*; the notion of the adequacy of that understanding; and the need for the second, knowledge condition in the account.

First, as (a) indicates, it does not follow from the self-evidence of a proposition that it is psychologically *compelling*: that if one understands (and considers) it, then one believes it.[7] Granted, insofar as we are rational, if we comprehendingly consider a self-evident proposition that we adequately understand, we *tend* to believe it, more or less upon so considering it. This tendency indeed seems partly constitutive of what it is to *be* a rational person. But a tendency is not an entailment. Skepticism, caution, and slow uptake can explain delay in, and resistance to, belief formation. None of these entails lesser rationality. Quite apart from how much of a deficiency in rationality may be indicated by certain persistent failures to form beliefs in such cases, there are (as we shall see) instances in which one can see *what* a self-evident proposition says—and thus understand it—before seeing *that*, or how, it is true. Moreover, skepticism, at least, is a basis on which some people might withhold or even disbelieve a self-evident proposition.

Another way to see the plausibility of a non-belief-entailing conception of self-evidence is to note that we can fail initially to "see" a self-evident truth, so that the proposition does not seem clearly true at all, yet later grasp it in just the way we grasp the truth of a paradigmatically self-evident proposition: one that is obvious in itself the moment we comprehendingly consider it. Take, for instance, a self-evident proposition that, to many people, is not immediately obvious: first cousins share a pair of grandparents. Or consider a proposition that is not at all obvious, that initially seems false to most people who consider it, and that is hard for many to see to be true without help from someone else: a man may be both grandfather and father of the same person. Perhaps one reason this is especially likely to seem false is that on the basis of ordinary cases, we tend to think of the relation *parent of* as intransitive, so that if *x* is a parent of *y*, and *y* is a parent of *z*, then *x* is not a parent of *z*.[8]

Second, the notion of adequate understanding needs elucidation. I offer no full analysis, but it may suffice to draw some contrasts, provide some suggestive examples, and distinguish some different types of understanding. I should add that we might also speak of *full* understanding to avoid the suggestion that adequacy implies sufficiency for some specific purpose. Neither term is ideal, but "full" may suggest maximality, which is also inappropriate.

Adequate understanding contrasts with (doubtless among other things) mistaken, insufficient, distorted, clouded, and equivocal understanding. One would *misunderstand* the proposition about grandchildren if one took a generation of people to require a span of at least thirty years. The original proposition does not even entail that there are three such "generations." The other four inadequacies are better illustrated by a more complex example, say the proposition that knowledge entails true belief. Call this *k*. One would *insufficiently understand k* if one conceived of it as equivalent to the nonmodal proposition that if someone knows something, it is true (where this is also an indicative, nonmaterial conditional). One would see the implication of truth but would miss the modal point that this *must* hold. This understanding would thus be not merely insufficient but also *partial* (since it embodies part of the conceptual content of *k*).

Partial understanding also contrasts with complete understanding, and such comprehensional completeness (whatever that is) is not a requirement for adequate understanding.[9] One would have a *distorted understanding* of *k* if one took *k* to entail that there is a precise minimal level of confidence appropriate to knowledge and that the entailed belief must be accompanied by the subject's attributing a corresponding numerical probability to the proposition known. This complex idea is compatible with *k* but not entailed by it, and it indicates mistaking *k* for a different proposition, one that is at best an interpretation of *k* that does not account for the full range of ascriptions of knowledge. Suppose, however, that one took knowledge to be a pattern in the brain and true belief to be an instance of the pattern that enables one to see some aspect of reality. Here one's understanding of *k* would be *clouded* (as well as, perhaps, distorted); one would see it through conceptually extraneous, though not necessarily inapplicable, concepts. For that reason, one would not grasp *k* clearly, even in the inadequate way the person who merely ascribes distorting properties to knowledge and belief may.

Equivocation may also vitiate adequate understanding. Consider a woman worried about whether a friend knows that the friend's husband is having an affair. If, solely on the ground that the woman truly believes this, one would say that she knows it, one might be conceiving knowledge as simply true belief. One could employ this conception—call it a *verisimilitude* conception—however, and yet, when the question whether one's daughter has cancer comes up, shift ground and say that owing to insufficient evidence of it, no one knows that she does. This would indicate a conception of knowledge—an *evidential* conception— on which adequate evidence is required for knowledge. A person who employs both conceptions in question could have an equivocal understanding of knowledge, one liable to cause shifts from the verisimilitude conception to the evidential one or viceversa. As it happens, either conception would make it possible to take "knowing entails believing" to express a truth; but on one interpretation, the truth would be the trivial proposition that true belief entails belief, and on the other, it would be substantive, say, that a presumption that p based on adequate evidence entails believing p. In some contexts, moreover, a truth about knowledge would not be seen by someone with an equivocal understanding of the concept of knowledge, or would be seen on the wrong basis, because the person shifts from one conception of it to the other.

There are, then, limits to how deficient an understanding of a proposition, p, can be if the subject, S, is to be able to believe it at all. Any of the four deficiencies in understanding just described can push its inadequacy so low that S cannot believe p at all, as opposed, say, to believing some proposition S confuses with it. In that case, since knowledge requires belief S cannot know that p on the basis of understanding it. But understanding is not an all-or-nothing affair. For at least most kinds of propositions, belief is possible with a level of adequacy of understanding that is insufficient to provide a basis for justification or knowledge of the kinds in question. This point applies especially to certain kinds of deep or complex a priori propositions.

Adequate understanding of a proposition, then, is more than simply getting the general sense of a sentence expressing it, as where one can parse the sentence grammatically, indicate, through examples, something of what it means, and perhaps correctly translate it into another language one knows well. This last point is of special importance. It shows that—as our kinship examples indicate—even a good understanding from a *linguistic* point of view does not entail an adequate understanding from a *conceptual* point of view. The latter is the point of view central for explicating the a priori. Adequate conceptual understanding of a proposition implies not only (1) seeing what the proposition says but also (2) being able to apply it (illustratively) to, and withhold its application from, an appropriately wide range of cases and (3) being able to (a) see some of its logical implications, (b) distinguish it from a certain range of close relatives, and (c) comprehend its elements and some of their relations.

Having an adequate understanding of a self-evident proposition does not, of course, require being able to see *all* its logical implications. Some are distant, or difficult to discern, in ways that can make them incomprehensible to a person with a minimally adequate understanding. Others are trivial, such as the entailment, by the proposition that nothing is round and square, of the proposition that either that is true or I am not reading. An inadequate understanding of a proposition might suffice for seeing this kind of entailment. A greater inadequacy in understanding would be a failure to see, upon considering the propositions that this page is rectangular and that it has a shape, that the former is (in fact) true. Missing this even more evident connection would betray an inadequate understanding of that proposition so severe that the understanding, even given an adequate understanding of "being round," would probably not ground justification for believing that nothing is round and rectangular. An inadequate understanding of a self-evident proposition is not sufficient to justify believing it, nor can beliefs of the proposition based (wholly) on such an understanding constitute knowledge.[10]

Something should also be said about the need for the second, knowledge condition in the proposed account of self-evidence. It is not obvious that this second condition is not entailed by the first, in which case it is in some logical sense redundant. For reasons given in detail elsewhere (Audi, 1999), I am inclined to doubt that this entailment holds. One could also take the knowledge condition to entail the justification condition.[11] Let us consider these matters in turn.

Suppose that the knowledge condition can be shown to be logically redundant (a possibility I do not claim can be decisively ruled out). It does not follow that, philosophically, we are better off deleting it. Logical redundancy does not entail either semantic or conceptual redundancy. Moreover, the condition captures something apparently essential to the common notion of the self-evident: that it is knowable "in itself." The condition may also be needed to do justice to the notion of a proposition's being *evident* in itself.

A case can also be made that the knowledge condition, even if no more important than the justification condition, entails it, which would make the latter logically redundant. This entailment claim is not self-evident but is plausible. If a self-evident proposition is understood as one knowable if it is believed on the basis of an adequate understanding, our account still makes essential use of the notion of adequate understanding. If, in addition, knowability implies the possibility of knowledge, then self-evident propositions can (possibly) be adequately understood.[12] If adequate understanding of them entails being justified in believing them, then the knowability condition, in turn, entails the justification condition. Let us suppose this. Still, even if one of the conditions is logically redundant, the account can be both correct and conceptually more illuminating than it would be with only one of them.

1.3. Self-Evidence, Apriority, and Necessity

It should be clear that if (adequate) understanding of a self-evident proposition constitutes justification for believing it, then self-evident propositions are justifiable a priori: if all one needs to acquire justification for believing p is understanding of it—which is a matter of the use, or at least the capacity, of reason to comprehend it as an object of thought—surely p is justifiable a priori in the sense (roughly) that reason alone, as directed toward p, is sufficient to justify believing it, at least if reason is used extensively enough and with adequate care. We may also say that the proposition itself is a priori, meaning simply that it admits of a priori justification in the minimal sense that acquiring an adequate understanding of it provides one with a justification for believing it.

It is important to see that the minimal case of a priori justifiability as sketched here contrasts with the perhaps more common case of justifiability in which it implies the possibility of a justificatory argument *from premises*.[13] The availability of such an argument is not an appropriate constraint for self-evident propositions: it is at best difficult to see why they should be seen as *self*-evident if this constraint held, and self-evident propositions are regarded by those who countenance them as precisely the kind capable of serving as justifiedly held premises that can provide support for other propositions without themselves needing support (or even potential support) from prior premises.[14]

What still needs attention is the relation of the self-evident (and the a priori as based on it) to the necessary, since it has often been held that ("by definition") both self-evident and a priori propositions are such that understanding them entails grasping, or suffices to enable one to grasp, their necessity.[15] As I have characterized the self-evident, the notion is *nonmodal*, at least in this sense. It is not analyzed explicitly in terms of a modal notion, and (the point relevant here) its application to a proposition does not immediately entail that the proposition is a necessary truth. Neither the point that (adequate) understanding is a ground for justification nor even the point that belief on the basis of such understanding constitutes knowledge immediately entails that the self-evidence of a proposition requires its necessity. In denying an immediate entailment here, I mean roughly that the claim that self-evident propositions are necessary is neither self-evident (in any preanalytic, intuitive sense) nor self-evidently entailed (in any such sense) by any philosophically uncontroversial account of self-evidence. Self-evidence, as I conceive it, is a matter of *how* a truth can be seen, not a matter of seeing what *kind* of truth it is.

This absence of an immediate entailment from the self-evident to the necessary is a desirable result of my characterization. Not only is there dispute about whether every a priori proposition is necessary,[16] it also seems possible to see the truth of a self-evident proposition without either seeing that it is necessary or even having the concept of necessity.[17] These are among the reasons why it is desirable for an account of the self-evident to leave room for a theoretically interesting account of why the self-evident is necessary—and for debate about whether it is.

I cannot develop such an account now, but a promising beginning is made by reflection on how, for a contingent proposition, there could be the requisite kind of a priori justification. Suppose that p is only a contingent truth and hence is false in some possible worlds. It is at least not clear (for reasons that will emerge in section 4) how an adequate understanding of the *content* of p, as opposed to, for instance, a grasp of facts about what is required to have the thought that p, might suffice to justify believing it. But suppose that this does suffice. It would still be at best mysterious how such understanding would suffice for knowing that p. How, for instance, would the relevant understanding rule out one's being in a world where p is false? By contrast, if at least part of what is understood when a self-evident truth is adequately understood is relations between concepts, and if concepts are abstract entities existing in all possible worlds, then (on certain additional assumptions, above all, that the relevant relations of abstract entities are unchanging across worlds)[18] two important points follow: that the truth in question holds (and may in some cases be seen to hold) in all possible worlds, and that understanding the relevant conceptual relations can ground knowledge of it. The concept of categorial exclusion, for instance, is (intrinsically and self-evidently) symmetrical. Hence (adequately) understanding it to obtain between the concept of a dog and that of a cat is sufficient to ground knowing that it is necessary that no dogs are cats, and conversely.

As this suggests, my conception of the a priori is compatible with the existence of a *de re* (hence objectual and nonpropositional) grasp of at least some kinds of necessity, for instance of the necessary connection between being square and being rectangular or of the entailment relation between the premises and the conclusion of a valid syllogism. Children can presumably grasp these relations even before conceptualizing them in the way required for believing, *de dicto, that* they hold, say, that a syllogism is valid. It is also compatible with some such grasp being a necessary noninferential basis of a priori justification, rather as seeing *the rectangularity* of something may be an essential basis of one's justification for believing the proposition *that it is rectangular.*[19] But if a priori propositions are by their very nature necessary, their being so does not depend on the possibility of a *de re* grasp of necessity. (The possible case of a priori knowledge of contingent propositions in Cartesian *cogito* cases will be considered later.)

1.4. Three Cases of the A Priori

I have so far indicated the plausibility of taking self-evident propositions to be a priori. Some are indeed paradigms of the a priori: clear instances of what we think of as (a priori) axioms or at least axiomatic truths.[20] I now want to go further.

I suggest that the self-evident may be plausibly viewed as the base and hence the fundamental case of the a priori. The idea is this: a priori propositions are those that are either (a) self-evident in the sense specified earlier (we may call these *directly self-evident* or *a priori in the narrow sense*); (b) though not self-evident in the narrow sense, self-evidently entailed by at least one proposition that is (we may call these *indirectly self-evident*, since there is a self-evident path to them from something self-evident in the narrow sense); or (c) neither directly nor indirectly self-evident but *provable* by self-evident steps, possibly a great many, from a proposition that is self-evident (we may call these *ultimately a priori*). We might call cases of (b) or (c) *a priori in the broad sense.*

A common general notion of an a priori proposition, clearly applicable to the first two cases, is roughly the notion of a truth that either is a self-evident proposition or is self-evidently entailed by one.[21] (A related notion, to be described shortly, applies to the third kind.) Knowledge of propositions that are a priori in the broad sense, however, unlike knowledge of those that are a priori in the narrow sense, depends on knowledge of some self-evident proposition as a ground. But neither kind of knowledge depends in this inferential way on knowledge of any empirical proposition, and in that sense both kinds meet the common conception of the a priori as "independent of experience."

2. EMPIRICIST SKEPTICISM ABOUT THE A PRIORI

It is widely known that Hume took reason to concern two kinds of proposition: propositions regarding matters of fact and those regarding "relations of ideas."[22] There is dispute about the extent of his skepticism about the possibility of knowledge or justification regarding the former; but in some places he apparently took it that we can have both knowledge and justification concerning the latter. He did not, however, countenance knowledge or (though this is perhaps not explicit in his writings) justification of substantive a priori propositions. This might be because he held what we might call a *syntactic theory of thought*: "All this creative power of the mind amounts to no more than the faculty of compounding, transposing, augmenting, or diminishing the materials afforded us by the senses and experience" (1777/1977, p. 11). It is precisely because causal connections cannot be understood in terms of any such syntactic operations that Hume took any knowledge we may have of them to be based on experience. His argument seems to be that since (1) all reasonings concerning matter of fact (inductive reasonings) are founded on the relation of cause and effect (1777/1977, p. 16), and (2) knowledge of this relation is never a priori but arises from experience of "constant conjunction" (p. 17), (3) if inductive reasoning yields any knowledge, it is from experience of constant conjunction.

Another source of skepticism concerning substantive a priori justification (and one consistent with Hume's theory of thought) is the epistemological naturalism proposed by W. V. Quine in "Epistemology Naturalized" (1969) and foreshadowed in his "Two Dogmas of Empiricism" (1951), a view on which all knowledge is based on experience, and any claim to knowledge must face "the tribunal of experience" in a way that gives sense perception, as distinct from understanding of propositions and concepts, a central grounding role. This view may be considered a version of empiricism and remains widely held.[23]

A different source of skepticism about substantive a priori propositions is a view about the connection between meaning and a priori truth. Insofar as one thinks of a priori truths as propositions (or other truth-valued entities) true by virtue of meaning, and insofar as one's paradigms of such truths are those that are commonly said to hold "by definition," such as the truth that all bachelors are unmarried, one might think that the only a priori propositions are the analytic ones. These are commonly conceived as reducible through the use of definitions to instances of formal truths. Our example, for instance, becomes the following: all unmarried adult human males are unmarried, which is an instance of the formal truth that whatever is *F* and *G* is *F*.

This view—which we might call *definitionalism about the a priori*— does not adequately represent the a priori[24] What gives the view plausibility is the quite different view that there are some truths one can *come* to know (or at least clearly see to be true) by reflection on the meanings of sentences expressing those truths or of individual terms in those sentences, such as "bachelor." This view indicates a route to knowing these truths; it is not an account of what kind of truth they are or of their grounds. The route may, for instance, begin on a semantic path and take one to a conceptual path.

There is another reason for skepticism about the substantive a priori, and indeed about any a priori justification. If a priori propositions are conceived as, in the basic cases, self-evident, then an adequate understanding of their content is sufficient for justification for believing them. Suppose we add the assumption that the concepts that must be understood in such cases are abstract and that their relations ground the truth of the propositions in question. Empiricists will want to know how the facts in question can causally ground the supposed knowledge. So will anyone who takes knowledge that *p* to depend on some reliable connection between, on the one hand, the fact that *p* and, on the other hand, any individual belief that *p* constituting knowledge that *p*. The fact must, as it were, underlie the corresponding belief if that belief is to constitute knowledge. Given the conception of the a priori I have sketched, what can be said in reply to this?

In addition to leaving open—at the outset, at least—the possibility of a contingent self-evident truth, my account is moderate in not requiring any special faculty for knowing the self-evident. Proponents of an external causal condition on all knowledge might deny this.[25] Suppose, for instance, that to know a proposition, one must be causally affected by some object(s) it is about. Then it might be argued that knowledge can be grounded in understanding a proposition only if some abstract entity, such as a constituent in that proposition, causally affects the mind, which—if possible at all—entails our having a special faculty to respond to the distinctive inputs.

I cannot see either that such a causal condition is needed for a priori knowledge or that if some kind of causal condition is needed, a special faculty is required to meet it (unless such a faculty simply is the capacity in question, in which case it may be considered at least no more difficult to understand than ordinary perception). To understand abstract entities *is* in part to be in some kind of contact with them; this is presumably a basic capacity of the mind, whether the capacity is in some sense causal or not.[26] This point does not imply, however, that a belief can constitute a priori knowledge without meeting *any* causal condition. Let me explain.

What makes the causal condition on knowledge plausible may be more than its apparent application to all empirical knowledge. Perhaps the requirement is best conceived as a special case of the wider requirement that knowledge must be grounded in something appropriately connected with that in virtue of which a belief constituting knowledge is true. We might call this the *external requirement on knowledge* provided we note that *self*-knowledge (which includes knowledge of one's mental states) need not be grounded in something external to the *mind* but only external to the belief in question.[27] If the properties and relations of abstract entities are external to the mind, knowledge of self-evident propositions meets the external requirement.[28] On the other hand, because those properties and relations are *accessible* to the mind, justification, conceived on epistemologically internalist lines, is also possible for self-evident propositions. The proposed characterization of self-evidence thus connects it with both internal and external epistemological requirements; and in the light of the previous sketch of understanding as a ground of justification and knowledge, it should be clear how, for self-evident propositions, both are possible on the basis of internally accessible grounds.

A further point can be made here. Suppose that understanding of abstract entities and their relations—say, of circles and spaces and of the inclusion relation between them—entails a kind of direct contact with them, indeed, a kind such that these entities form an essential part of the very content of that understanding. Then they play an indispensable, if indirect, role in sustaining beliefs that are justified a priori or constitute a priori knowledge. These beliefs, then, have understanding as a causal sustaining ground; the relevant understanding in a sense contains the abstract facts that ground the truths known; and through this apprehensional causal grounding of the beliefs, they are *reliably* based on the facts they represent.

The relevant kind of understanding is in some sense conceptual and is not reducible to understanding terms in any particular language. The conceptual knowledge in question may be reached *through* such linguistic understanding and perhaps even through a certain kind of mental imaging; but it is not constituted by understanding any particular language (and arguably not essentially linguistic at all) or by mental imaging. Moreover, the knowledge it grounds is not groundable in a definition of any linguistic expressions and need not be groundable through the kind of analysis of concepts that (let us assume for the sake of argument) enables us to reduce the proposition that all bachelors are unmarried to the formal truth that all unmarried males are unmarried. No parallel analysis is available for the concepts central for substantive a priori truths, such as the concepts of a circle, of redness, and, arguably, of moral obligation.

This view does not entail that abstract entities have causal power. They do not play a direct causal role in grounding (roughly, producing or sustaining) justified a priori beliefs (beliefs grounded in adequate understanding of the a priori propositions that are their objects). But abstract entities do play an essential role in what does causally ground such beliefs: they are essential elements in the kind of understanding that plays a direct grounding role in which it does the ordinary causal work of producing or sustaining belief. The indirect–or perhaps we should say *adjunctive*–causal role of abstract entities can preserve truth as well as any ordinary causal role; and it is the need for preservation of truth that chiefly motivates the causal requirement in the first place.

3. MODERATE RATIONALISM, SKEPTICISM, AND INTELLECTUAL HUMILITY

In setting out a conception of the a priori, I have noted that certain philosophical burdens need not be borne by a rationalist view—understood in the minimal sense of a view that affirms the existence of substantive a priori propositions and the possibility of our justification for believing them. One burden is requiring a grasp of necessity as a condition for such justification. Another is implying a special faculty for cognizing the truths in question. Still another is positing knowledge or justification that cannot be based, in a way that essentially involves causation, on a ground of the truths in question. Removing these burdens helps in meeting skepticism about a priori justification, but it does not go the entire distance. Indeed, some of the points needed to make the proposed conception of the a priori plausible may also open the way to the very skepticism I seek to rebut.[29]

One point here is that even justification for believing a self-evident proposition is defeasible. Defeasibility, as here understood in reference to justification, is liability to the relevant justification's being overridden, say, by plausible argumentation against the justified belief in question or undermined, for instance, by the discovery that the grounds underlying the belief are inadequate. Defeasibility will not be well understood if it is taken to be equivalent to a notion that is found in Quine's work and still frequently appears: that of "revisability."[30] It is certainly true that experiences may lead us to revise our view, and that if our justification for believing even an a priori truth is undermined, we may cease to affirm it and, using a revised formulation, affirm something else. Such cases are common in both mathematics and philosophy. But what is revised is not a *proposition* (or belief, conceived as individuated by propositional content); it is something, such as a sentence or a pattern of assertive utterances, that expresses propositions. This point needs explanation.

What might it *be* to revise a proposition? Take the proposition that Juan married Maria. If one wanted to emphasize Maria's part in the marriage, one might revise a *report* of it so that the report expresses the proposition that Maria married Juan. Has one revised the original proposition or simply stated it differently? And suppose, in response to the kinds of evidence that defeat justification, we revise what we hold, we would surely then hold a *different* proposition (hence a different belief), or the problem would not be met. We might pacify an objector by offering an equivalent point in a new formulation; but we cannot in general meet a substantive objection to a proposition by a revision that results in stating an equivalent: what falsifies or disconfirms p will falsify or disconfirm any equivalent of p. The notions of revision and revisability properly apply to what can change significantly and retain its identity.[31]

Talk of revising propositions, then, or the corresponding beliefs (or statements) that have them as contents, is misleading. It is not clear what may be properly called revising a proposition, as opposed to formulating a different one. Revising a formulation, on the other hand, may or may not yield an expression of the same proposition; and if, as where it succeeds in meeting apparent counterevidence, it does not yield the same proposition, then far from having the same proposition revised, as we can have the same theory revised or an insurance claim for damages revised, we have expressed a different proposition. It is not revisability but the quite different notion of *defeasibility* that is needed to dissipate the objections of those who have taken the existence of substantive (or other) a priori truths to imply indefeasible justification and thereby to violate the "revisability" requirement.[32]

Reflection on the defeasibility of substantive a priori justification leads to another possible source of skepticism about it. I call this the *dissensus problem* (Audi, 2004). It is the problem of maintaining justification for believing a substantive a priori proposition, given the realization or justified belief that others who are rational and consider the proposition reject it. This problem is common not only in ethical matters but also in philosophy. Recall the philosophical proposition that belief is not a process. Suppose that someone denied this. Our first thought might be that the person has misunderstood. A nonnative speaker of English, for instance, might perhaps reason as follows: since believing is thinking and thinking is a process, believing is, too. Pointing out that to believe does not entail thinking in this occurrent process sense might solve the problem. But there are other routes to such an error, such as confusing the concept of believing with that of coming to believe or with the concept of neural phenomena that may be taken to underlie belief.

Moreover, the strategy just illustrated—eliminating dissensus by dispelling confusion—is at least not readily applicable to many other cases. Take the principle that killing persons is prima facie wrong. What is to be said to someone who claims that when one is being gratuitously and lethally attacked, killing in self-defense is not morally negative *at all*? We now have a substantive disagreement. We can point out that the prima facie qualification does not entail that there can be no justification for killing, but only that there is some reason to avoid it such that if, for instance, one can as effectively protect oneself by using mace, this is normally preferable to killing. This will not convince every disputant—especially if skeptical—to accept the principle. If both parties give plausible arguments, can *both* be justified in their incompatible conclusions, or is neither justified?

A skeptic is likely to say that *neither* is justified; a nonskeptic is likely to say that, at least where each has a rational account of how the other may be plausible yet mistaken, *both* may be justified to some significant degree. I find the former reaction understandable but favor the latter.[33] Neither reaction, however, requires concluding that there is no truth of the matter or that if there is, truth is either empirical or, on the other hand, a priori but reducible to a formal truth. These are, however, each views for which some plausible argument may be given. I cannot assess these views here. My conclusion at this point is simply that certain kinds of defeasibility and certain cases of dissensus should induce intellectual humility but do not warrant skepticism about a priori justification. Skepticism is a serious challenge to the view that we have substantive a priori justification. It should not be lightly dismissed.

4. THE COGITO AND THE CASE FOR A PRIORI EXISTENTIAL KNOWLEDGE

One great hope for refuting a completely general skepticism and, at the same time, establishing the power of reason is Descartes' *cogito* argument. This is popularly identified with arguments having the form "I think, therefore I am," but those forms apparently do not represent Descartes' most mature formulation of his *cogito* argument.[34] That formulation comes in his *Meditations* and has as its crucial line "[W]e must come to the definite conclusion that this proposition: I am, I exist, is necessarily true each time that I pronounce it, or that I mentally conceive it" (Meditation 2). Unlike the popular argument, this statement does not even categorically assert the proposition that I (Descartes) exist. In my view, it is best not taken to be a proof of his existence in any straightforward sense.[35]

The *cogito* argument in the *Meditations* (which Descartes presents elliptically, to be sure) might be better understood as a proof of the indubitability of his existence. It might be rendered roughly as follows: (a) it is necessary that if I pronounce or mentally conceive the proposition that I exist, then I do exist (so this is "necessarily true every time that I pronounce it"); (b) I cannot doubt that I exist without pronouncing or mentally conceiving the proposition that I exist; (c) any proposition (such as that I exist) the very doubting of which self-evidently entails its truth cannot be rationally doubted. Hence (d) *that I exist* is indubitable for me, that is, cannot be rationally doubted by me. All the premises may appear self-evident; but "I" occurs referentially in (b), which is thus contingent and therefore cannot be considered a priori *if* only necessary propositions are a priori. All the premises, however, may be plausibly considered noninferentially justified for the person reasoning from them to (d), even if they are not self-evident (as some might claim they are).

Might we construct an a priori argument here (which I here take to be a valid one having only a priori premises)? Consider the parallel argument:

1. It is necessary that if a person pronounces or mentally conceives the proposition that that very person exists, then the person does exist.
2. A person cannot doubt that that very person exists without pronouncing or mentally conceiving this proposition.
3. Any proposition the very doubting of which self-evidently entails its truth cannot be *rationally* doubted by any person doubting it.
4. That I myself exist is such a proposition.

Hence,

5. That I myself exist is indubitable for me, that is, cannot be rationally doubted by me.

This argument also does not prove the existence of the reasoner; that a proposition is indubitable (for me or anyone else) does not entail its truth. But—on the assumptions that (1) all its premises are either self-evident (in the narrow sense) or (more plausibly) at least justifiably believable without prior premises and (2) its conclusion follows from them—the argument does something perhaps equally important from the point of view of skepticism.[36] It establishes a very high epistemic status for the proposition that Descartes (or any person arguing in exactly the same way) exists; it shows that he (or that other person) cannot rationally doubt his own existence. If, for each of us, the proposition that we ourselves exist cannot be rationally doubted by us, we may justifiedly use that proposition as a premise in further arguments. This permits our justifiably relying on the proposition, and it does so very much as our proving it would.

This reading of Descartes enables us to see the *cogito* argument as cogent but does not require taking any a priori proposition to entail the existence of any concrete entity. Granted, the (contingent) proposition that I myself exist is special in a way that makes it seem a good candidate for a proposition that is a priori in the basic way self-evident propositions are. For unlike my understanding of contingent truths in general, my understanding of this one rules out my being in a world in which the proposition understood is false. But why is this? It is not because of my understanding of this proposition in particular—at least not if it is the one expressed by "Robert Audi exists," since others can understand that without thereby being justified in believing it.

The kind of understanding of "I myself exist" that makes it seem a priori is, moreover, apparently not the kind that grounds a priori justification for believing a self-evident proposition. Nor is my justification for believing that I exist clearly an appropriate kind of exercise of reason; it is not a justification grounded in my understanding of the proposition (as an object of thought that in principle two or more persons can entertain), as opposed to my acquaintance with myself as its subject. Thus, no one else's understanding of it entails being justified in believing it (or its truth), whereas anyone who adequately understands a self-evident proposition thereby has justification for believing it.[37]

The same points apply generally to what might be called "*cogito* propositions," such as the propositions that I am thinking and that I am considering whether I exist. Compare "Something exists," which is also *truth-sufficient*: it is not a *cogito* proposition (since it is not first-personal) but also cannot be thought by someone without thereby expressing a truth.[38] If I have this thought and am, as would be normal, aware that there is something being thought or someone thinking it, then I am correct. I am even justified in believing this and can know that something exists. But the understanding of the content alone does not justify my believing the proposition; unlike understanding the proposition that I exist, understanding the proposition that something exists does not entail acquaintance with any referent *that one is asserting to exist*. In both cases, however, there is nothing about the concepts figuring in the proposition that grounds their truth, as is plain for the clear cases of the a priori. What justifies my believing the proposition is my acquaintance with an element in my experience, such as my thinking something. Indeed, as in the *cogito* argument as interpreted earlier, I am even relying on a premise justified by that experiential acquaintance, say, that there is a thought that something exists.

The view that the self-evident apparently does not extend to contingent truths (a view I do not claim to have shown here) should not be taken to require undervaluing *cogito* examples. There is an important property possessed by the proposition that I exist that should not be assimilated to self-evidence but has great epistemological importance. For each of us, the first-person *expression* of the proposition that we exist, whether silent or spoken, is *epistemically self-sufficient*: it is such that reflection on the proposition conceived as expressed by us, together with adequate understanding of it as thus expressed, *entails* justification for believing it. It implies this because one cannot in this case help becoming self-aware or even seeing in an experiential way that one exists. But the ground of the justification is not understanding of abstract content alone; it is the self-awareness acquired in arriving at that understanding. To be sure, if the content is taken to *include* the person, as on some views of singular propositions expressed by sentences containing proper names, then we do indeed have a special category of contingent self-evident propositions. I prefer not to take this line, but my account could be qualified to accommodate it as a special case. One might then say, of *cogito* propositions, that they represent the *first-personal a priori* and may be contingent, whereas impersonal a priori propositions—the kind found in logic and pure mathematics—do not entail the existence of any contingent being and may be plausibly argued to be necessary.[39]

5. The Regressiveness of Skepticism

In crediting Descartes with a powerful antiskeptical argument—indeed, one with some substantive a priori premises—I do not mean to imply that simply by reflecting on it we can refute either skepticism about a priori justification or even unrestricted skepticism. But there is something important to be learned from it. Imagine a cautious skeptical challenge that runs as follows: "I do not claim to know or have any justification for taking you to lack knowledge, but *show* me that you know anything at all." Is there any criterion of showing that makes good sense here and is not satisfied by replying with a self-evident proposition or one self-evidently entailed by some self-evident proposition? I do not see that there is one. But suppose Descartes, in response, *presents* the *cogito* argument I just formulated on his behalf. The skeptic may still intelligibly rejoin with "Show me that your premises *are* indeed self-evident or otherwise justifiable." After all, even if they are, it need not be self-evident *that* they are.

At this point, we may have no self-evident premises for our premises. We might ask the skeptic to go through the argument in the first person; but this will at best convince skeptics that *they* each know or justifiably believe something. This might quell some of their skeptical worries; but if they are skeptical about other minds, they may still doubt that they have heard any more than a parroting of the *cogito* argument and demand self-evident premises for the proposition their apparently animate interlocutor purportedly showed by the argument. Suppose one did find self-evident premises. The same challenge could still be issued regarding those.

What we are seeing here is the possibility of a dialectical regress. If skeptics can intelligibly challenge us to show the truth of propositions that are self-evident, there is likely to be no way to stop this regress to their satisfaction. Both justification skepticism and knowledge skepticism appear to be unscathed. We cannot even justifiably reply that the skeptic's demand is unintelligible, since there *cannot* be a premise for something self-evident. This sweeping impossibility claim does not follow from the notion of the self-evident and seems mistaken.[40] However, there is also good reason to think that a proposition's being self-evident does not entail that there *are* self-evident premises for it that can ground knowledge of or justification for it. Why should a reasonable person feel rational pressure to go on with the dialectic, given a proposition such that adequate understanding of it yields justification for believing it?

One answer is that even if understanding does yield adequate justification for belief, it does not automatically yield knowledge that one has this justification. And when challenged to show that *p*, one wants to believe that one knows it, and perhaps even that one has shown it. Showing that *p*, however, does not entail knowing that one has shown it, any more than knowing that *p* entails knowing that one knows it. If, moreover, one gives in to the temptation to claim credit for one's achievement and says that one has shown that *p*, one takes responsibility for a higher-level proposition than the one originally challenged. Another regress looms, this time one of demonstration. Can anything be said to provide a rationale for stopping?

It is surely of some help to distinguish between showing *that* we know something and *exhibiting* our knowledge *of* it. If, in a certain sound way— paradigmatically illustrated by the Cartesian *cogito* argument—we do show that *p* (and believe it on the basis of the premises of our argument), we exhibit our knowledge of it. The same holds for our justification for believing *p*. This two-fold achievement—showing that *p* and exhibiting our knowledge of it and our justification for believing it—does not, however, entail showing the higher-order propositions that we know it or that we are justified in believing it. But particularly where a proposition is justifiable by an a priori argument, I see no need to show this (apart from intellectual courtesy to doubters and aside from special reasons for doubt, which do not follow from general skeptical considerations). The skeptic asks for our credentials, and we show them. We may know that we will next be asked to authenticate them; but their authenticity does not depend on our ability to show it, and indeed the authenticating authority can be challenged as well. If we claim no more cognitive authority than our credentials warrant, why should we have to authenticate them too?

It may also be of some help to say that an intelligible challenge presupposes certain standards for meeting it. We may ask the skeptic what these are. We may then challenge them. If the standards are so strict that they rule out showing even what self-evidently follows from self-evident premises (and hence is a priori), we can push the skeptic down the same regressive pathways. We can ask to be shown that the standards are, by the criteria those standards set, sound; we can then ask the same of the premises for conclusion that they are sound; and so forth.

What emerges here is that there is a logic of dialogue itself, and that it seems to require as a presupposition of intelligibility that for showing a proposition p, no higher standard than provision of something self-evident should be demanded, at least no higher than providing a self-evident proposition that self-evidently entails the proposition in question.[41] To be sure, a weaker standard, such as constructing a good inductive argument, is often adequate for showing a proposition. Moreover, explaining the self-evidence of p itself may be an element in the process of "providing" a self-evident premise for a disputed claim or in showing, in one important sense, that a proposition is self-evident. One might argue that this is not showing p but only demonstrating, in a way, that it does not stand in need of being shown. Suppose that this is so. It does not imply—and I would emphatically deny—that the self-evident should never be defended. But a defense of a proposition need not be shoring it up from below, with premises prior to it in the epistemic order; a defense may be shedding light on a proposition, displaying its fruits, removing obstacles to accepting it, and casting off burdens that those embracing it need not carry.

The a priori may be conceived as grounded in the self-evident, with the basic case being self-evident propositions themselves. This will hold even if some a priori propositions are taken to be contingent, since the good candidates for this status may be argued, with no less plausibility, to be self-evident. Knowledge of the self-evident, in turn, may be conceived as grounded in a kind of understanding. This kind of understanding both causally grounds beliefs constituting knowledge of the self-evident and characteristically puts us in direct contact with elements that form a sufficient basis of the truth of the a priori propositions it justifies us in believing and enables us to know. These elements are most plausibly conceived as abstract, but the account of the a priori I have presented does not require that conception. That there are a priori propositions self-evident in the sense clarified here is intuitively plausible; that we can have justified beliefs even of many substantive ones is also plausible. In arguing for these points, I have been defending a region of common sense. But my defense has been, in a way, negative: I have sought to show that there is no compelling reason to deny the existence of substantive a priori justification. I have not claimed to provide a positive defense, one that shows that there is such justification. I may, however, have succeeded in exhibiting such justification. Perhaps this chapter contains, or points the way to, raw materials sufficient for a cogent positive defense. But skepticism is a powerful, if limited, position. Keeping it at bay may be sufficient to liberate the philosophical conscience and license the affirmation of a priori justification in many substantive matters.[42]

NOTES

1. In Quine's famous "Two Dogmas of Empiricism" (Quine, 1951) he says, "Any statement may be held true come what may, if we make drastic enough adjustments elsewhere in the system.... Conversely, by the same token, no statement is immune to revision. Revision even of the logical law of the excluded middle has been proposed as a means of simplifying quantum mechanics; and what difference of principle is there between such a shift and the shift whereby Kepler superseded Ptolemy or Einstein Newton or Darwin Aristotle?" (sec. 6).

2. I have explicated such prima facie principles and defended their apriority in *The Good in the Right* (Audi, 2004), esp. chap. 2.

3. Many kinds of skepticism and many bibliographical references are contained in this volume. My own account of its status is given in Audi (2003, chap. 10);for detailed appraisals contrasting both with mine and with each other, see Greco (2000) and Sinnott-Armstrong (2006).

4. Much of the material in this section is based on or closely follows my account of self-evidence in Audi (1999).

5. Propositions may even be said to present themselves *as self-evident* in specifying criteria for accepting propositions "as self-evident," Sidgwick maintains that "a collision [between two formulae supposed to be genuine intuitions] is absolute proof that at least one of the formulae needs qualification" and suggests a doubt whether the correctly qualified proposition will present itself with the same self-evidence as the simpler but inadequate one" (1907, p. 341). Here and elsewhere Sidgwick suggests that self-evident propositions present themselves as such (though even false propositions may also do so), and in places he appears to think that such a presentation is at least a major element in an intuitive grasp of them.Cf. BonJour: "Do direct challenges to serious *a priori* claims even in fact occur? Is a claim that seems rationally self-evident ever flatly and unambiguously contradicted by experience?" (1997, p. 122). It appears that he regards at least the very clear cases of a priori propositions as seeming ("rationally") self-evident, whether or not he takes their so seeming to be crucial for a priori justification regarding them, as the kindred notion of grasp of necessity has been taken to be.

6. Four clarifications will help. First, if the belief is based on anything *other* than understanding the proposition, that understanding must still be a *sufficient* basis (in a sense I cannot explicate now). Second, the relevant-basis relation precludes a wayward causal

chain: the understanding must not produce the belief in certain abnormal ways. (I assume that the belief in question *constitutes* knowledge, but there is no need to build this assumption into the account.) Third, although the formulation allows that two people have different understandings of *p*, if both are adequate, they will in a certain way overlap. Fourth, the conditionals implicit in the account are neither material nor strict implications, and they imply subjunctives.

7. This characterization contrasts with a common one in which a self-evident proposition is one "self-evidently true, in the sense in which 'rock-bottom' basic axioms of mathematics and logic may well be. . . propositions which are necessarily such that if they are understood or grasped, they are known to be true" (Anderson, 1993, p. 10).

8. Consider Jocasta in Sophocles' *Oedipus Rex*. By virtue of her incestuous marriage to her (biological) son, she is both grandmother and mother of their children. The case I presented is exactly parallel. There, as elsewhere, gender makes no difference.

9. I leave open the possibility that understanding of a self-evident proposition could be insufficient for adequacy on a ground other than being partial, but this is the main case.

10. It should be added that quite apart from differences in how good an understanding is, understanding may be either occurrent or dispositional. The former case is illustrated by comprehending a proposition one is entertaining, the latter by such comprehension as is retained in memory, say, after our attention turns elsewhere. A distinct, weaker dispositional case is illustrated by "She understands such ideas," uttered when one has in mind something like this: she may or may not have ever entertained them but would (occurrently) understand them upon considering them. I leave further subtleties aside; the crucial point is that in my characterization of self-evidence, understanding in clause (a) may be of any of the three kinds indicated so long as justification is understood accordingly. If S occurrently understands a self-evident proposition *p*, S has occurrent justification for it, roughly, justification grounded at least largely in elements in S's consciousness, such as awareness of a relation between concepts. If S has strong dispositional understanding of *p*, S has dispositional justification, roughly in the sense that S can bring justifying elements into consciousness in an appropriate way by suitable reflection (but does not at the time have them in consciousness). If S has weak dispositional understanding of *p*, S has *structural justification* for it: roughly, S does not have occurrent or strong dispositional justification for it, but there is an appropriate path leading from justificatory materials accessible to S to an occurrent justification for *p*. I assume that when knowledge of a self-evident proposition is based on understanding it, the understanding must be occurrent or strongly dispositional, but there may be, and one could certainly devise, a conception of knowledge more loosely connected with understanding. In chapter 8 of Audi (2003), the notion of virtual knowledge is described in a way that lends itself to playing this role.

11. Jackson (2000) characterizes "an a priori (true) sentence" as "one such that understanding it is sufficient for being able to see that it is true" (p. 324). He apparently takes seeing that *p* to entail knowing that *p* or something close to knowing it (this is in any case required for the plausibility of the account); and he apparently takes seeing that *p* to entail justification for believing it. His account differs from mine in giving justification no explicit role in the account, in applying justification to sentences rather than to propositions, and in leaving implicit the role of knowledge in it. Cf. David Chalmers's view that a thought can be "justified a priori" "when there is a possible reasoning process that conclusively justifies the thought with justification independent of experience" (2002, p. 609). This view is compatible with mine so long as, in the basic cases of the a priori

(which are instances of self-evidence), the justification need not be *inferential* (as one might assume from the reference to reasoning); inferences of certain kinds are admissible here, as noted in Audi (1999).

12. My account does not entail that self-evident propositions can be understood by just *any* rational person; it is required only that understanding of them is possible for some (actual or possible) "mind." We can, however, use the account to define "self-evident *for S*"; this will accommodate the point that some self-evident propositions are beyond the understanding of some people. Once one sees why the self-evident need not be obvious, one should find that point obvious.

13. This is worded so as to leave open the possibility that there might be strongly axiomatic self-evident propositions, an Aristotelian kind such that there is nothing prior to them in the order of justification by appeal to which they could be justified. They would of course be justifiably *inferable* from premises, but not all inference is justificatory (e.g., the inference of *q* from *p* and *q*). I also leave open the possibility that, assuming that the content of a justificatory understanding of *p* is that in virtue of which it justifies believing *p*, it may in some cases be impossible (at least for everyone who has such an understanding) to frame premises adequate for a justificatory argument for *p*.

14. Epistemological coherentists may, partly for this reason, deny that there are self-evident propositions. I am here supposing that there are, but I have argued at length against such a strong version of coherentism in chapter 4 of Audi (1993). It is worth adding that self-evidence does not imply (as some coherentists, as well as other philosophers, may have thought) self-justification—a notion that is at best unclear. Cf. Burge's remark, in explicating Frege, that Frege took primitive truths to be "self-evident or self-justifying" (2000, p. 17).

15. See, e.g., BonJour (1997), esp. chap. 4. Cf. Butchvarov's view that what is crucial for justification for propositions of the kind we are considering is the unthinkability of mistake (see esp. 1970, pp. 76–88). Brooke goes so far as to hold that "for him [Kant], necessity is the prior notion, and he uses it to construct a criterion, in fact the only criterion he offers in the Introduction, of apriority—'If we have a proposition which in being thought is thought as *necessary*, it is an *a priori* judgment . . .' (B 3)" (1992, p. 220). Kantian passages like this may have been highly influential in later characterizations of the a priori and the self-evident, perhaps including Butchvarov's and BonJour's. See esp. Kant (1781–87/1963), e.g., pp. 48–51.

16. See, e.g., Saul Kripke's discussion of the standard meter bar (1972, p. 275). BonJour (1997, pp. 12–13) provides a valuable short discussion of the case. Boghossian and Peacocke mention other examples (from Kripke and David Kaplan) that they take to show the possibility of apriority without necessity (2000, p. 3). An instructive discussion of the issue from the point of view of modal logic is provided by Anderson (1993).

17. I leave open the possibility of a preconceptual, *de re* kind of grasp of necessity. Perhaps a child could see the necessity of the proposition that if *x* is taller than *y*, then *y* is shorter than *x*, but (lacking the relevant concepts) not have a belief that this is necessary. That necessity is grasped might be evidenced by how the child treats denials of the proposition, say with "I don't understand," by contrast with how the child treats certain denials of contingent propositions.

18. It is not easy to specify the relevant relations between abstract entities, but we must rule out such relations as *being instantiated by three things*; this is the kind of relation that, e.g., the property of weighing exactly a trillion tons would have to the (say) three

items with this weight, and it can vary within a world over time or across worlds. If, as is natural, we explain why the relevant relations are unchanging because abstract entities themselves are, then we must distinguish *concepts* as abstract and *conceptions,* which, as psychological, can change.

19. Cf. BonJour's view that "such an apparent rational insight [the kind that 'seems to provide an entirely adequate epistemic justification for believing or accepting the proposition in question'] purports to be nothing less than a direct insight into the necessary character of reality.... What, after all, could be a better reason for thinking that a particular proposition is true than that one sees... that it reflects a necessary feature that reality could not fail to possess?" (1997, p. 107). The view is apparently that a *de re* grasp of a necessary feature is prior to seeing that a proposition is a priori, and that seeing this may be cited as a reason for believing the proposition. Elsewhere BonJour speaks as if to believe an a priori proposition *is* to believe that it cannot fail to be true: "consider the proposition that there are no round squares, *that is,* that no surface or demarcated part of a surface that is round can also be square" (p. 103; emphasis added). The shift from "are" to "can be" leads one to wonder whether the a priori proposition in question is modal. Despite other passages that raise a similar doubt, I take the considered view to be that a grasp of necessity is a nonpropositional *ground* of a priori justification but does not imply modal content in all a priori propositions (or perhaps even in the basic cases—a further matter that BonJour's discussion also leaves unsettled).

20. Not in Roderick Chisholm's sense of 'axiom', in which "h is an axiom = Df h is necessarily such that (1) it is true and (2) for every S, if S accepts h, then h is certain for S." That is a technical sense yielding a strong notion with limited uses outside his epistemology. See Chisholm (1989, p. 28). An indication of some different ways in which axioms may be conceived is provided in Audi (1999).

21. Two points of clarification may help here. (1) In a broader usage, a falsehood can be called an a priori proposition provided it is an a priori *truth* that it is false. This less common usage raises no special problems but presents a terminological complication I ignore in the text. (2) As argued in Audi (1999), provability *by self-evident steps* from a self-evident proposition does not entail *self-evident entailment* by it (think, e.g., of how many steps there might be and how difficult they might be to discover).

22. See Hume (1777/1977), p. 15.

23. For Michael Devitt (2005), "It is overwhelmingly plausible that *some* knowledge is empirical, justified by experience. The attractive thesis of naturalism is that *all* knowledge is" (p. 105). Louise Antony argues, regarding this second claim, that it "conflates naturalism with *empiricism*" (2004, p.1). I myself have argued that naturalism is not committed to empiricism (Audi, 2000), but the view that all knowledge is empirical is widely held and ably defended. See, e.g., Kitcher (2000), who supports what he calls "factualism in epistemology" (p. 87), and, for a short version of her defense of naturalism in the same Quinean tradition, Maddy (2000).

24. A similar view was expressed by Ayer (1936, p. 85): "Our knowledge that no observation can even confute '$7 + 5 = 12$' depends simply on the fact that the symbolic expression '$7 + 5$' is synonymous with '12', just as our knowledge that every oculist is an eye-doctor depends on the fact that 'oculist' is 'synonymous' with eye-doctor'." I have criticized this kind of *linguisticism,* as we might call it, and definitionalism about the a priori in general, in Audi (2003). For different but compatible objections, see Horwich (2000).

25. Paul Benacerraf's "Mathematical Truth" (1973) comes to mind here as a leading statement of the causal requirement. Cf. James Robert Brown's ascription to "contemporary empiricism" of the view that *"knowledge of X is based on sensory experience for which there is an underlying physical causal connection between the knower and X; there are no other sources of knowledge"* (1992, p. 253).

26. Plantinga suggests that if indeed there are no causal relations of the relevant kind, still, any plausible causal requirement on knowledge does not rule out a priori knowledge (1993, pp, 113–17).

27. This may need qualification for certain cases of self-reference, e.g., knowing that all of one's knowledge is partly constituted by psychological properties, but that would not affect my main point, which concerns knowledge of the other kinds (virtually all of it).

28. These entities are presumably not even mind dependent unless, as some philosophers hold, they depend on the mind of God, in which case they could be as external as any other object of human knowledge.

29. I am taking *rebutting* a skeptical thesis to imply only showing the case for it to be unsound, which does not require showing that there *is* the kind of justification or knowledge it challenges us to show is genuine. The latter would count as *refuting* the relevant skeptical thesis (or challenge). In Audi (2003, chap. 10), I describe rebuttal and refutation in some detail and associate the former with a negative defense of common sense and the latter with a positive defense of it.

30. I have already cited Quine (1951) as speaking of revision of a statement. Employments of some notion of revisability are found in many later discussions of the a priori. See, e.g., Hanson and Hunter (1992, p. 36); Friedman (2000, p. 383); Peacocke (2004, p. 30); and Field (2005, pp. 71–72).The central thrust of Peacocke's discussion of revisability, however (pp. 31–33), is couched (quite properly, for some of the reasons I have given) in terms of defeasiblity.

31. Even talk of revising a sentence can be misleading. If I revise the third sentence on a given page, do I have the same sentence? I have revised my essay in that place; but if there is an important question whether a given sentence appears twice (say, because of a plagiarism charge), a "revised sentence" would not count as the same (identical) one. Sentences are not the only kind of thing for which there are individuation problems; but with them there need not be the kind of pitfall opened up by the idea that a proposition (or statement conceived as similarly truth-valued) can be revised.

32. Cf. Quine's remark that "truth in general depends on both language and extralinguistic fact. The statement 'Brutus killed Caesar' would be false if the world had been different in certain ways, but it would also be false if the word 'killed' happened rather to have had the sense of 'begat'" (1951, sec. 4). Compare saying that the *sentence* "Brutus killed Caesar" would have expressed a different, and false, proposition. Has Quine provided any reason to think that the *statement* in question—understood as the historical truth we express using the sentence—would have been false if the English word "killed" had meant "begat"? I see none. For an instructive discussion of the importance of distinguishing among sentences, statements, and propositions, see Cartwright (1962).

33. This is not to imply that *one* person can be justified in believing that *p* and also that not-*p*. For detailed discussion of the status of rational disagreement, see Audi (forthcoming).

34. In Descartes' *Replies to Objections* (Second Replies), he responds to Mersenne as follows:

When someone says, "I am thinking, therefore I am, or exist", he does not deduce existence from thought by a syllogism, but, recognizes it as something self-evident by a simple intuition of the mind. This is clear from the fact that if he were deducing it from a syllogism, he would have to have had previous knowledge of the major premise . . . yet in fact he learns it from experiencing in his own case that it is impossible that he should think without existing.

(Cottingham, Stoothoff, Murdock, and Kenny 1984–91, VII 140, II 100)

35. My suggestion is not uncontroversial. Yablo (2000), e.g., goes so far as to say that "the only easy existence proof we know of in philosophy is Descartes' *cogito ergo sum*" (p. 197). A detailed account of the *cogito* argument seen in historical perspective is provided by Markie (1992).

36. Whether this argument is a priori depends on how (4) is to be interpreted. Does "I" occur referentially in "That I myself exist"? This is presumably not a specification of a proposition referring to me under a definite description that might be satisfied by someone in another possible world. Statement 4 is still epistemically self-sufficient in the sense characterized later in the text, and I indicate later that it might be considered a priori in a "first-personal" sense.

37. I bypass the issue of whether the sense in which I believe that I exist can be the same as that in which someone else believes that I exist; and I grant that there is a *relativized* and perhaps loose sense of "self-evident" in which it can be self-evident *to* one that one exists. Nothing major turns on these matters here. A major issue that remains is how to deal with sentences containing other indexicals or proper names, such as "Hesperus is Phosphorous." I believe that the proposed conception of self-evidence can accommodate the relevant data in such cases, but doing so requires considerable analysis and cannot be undertaken here.

38. This example (among others I cannot address here) was suggested to me by Walter Sinnott-Armstrong.

39. An important question here is whether (using my own case as representative) believing myself to exist is *believing a proposition* at all, as opposed to something that might be called *ascribing existence* to myself. If apriority (and self-evidence) are properties of propositions, the latter interpretation would explain why understanding of a proposition is not the basis of justification for believing myself to exist. For discussion of the indicated difference between objectual (*de re*) and propositional (*de dicto*) beliefs, see Audi (2007, pp. 231–38).

40. In chapter 2 of Audi (2004), I argue against this unprovability claim, but I also make sense of it for a special kind of self-evident proposition, which I call "strongly axiomatic." This is apparently the kind Aristotle had in mind in *Posterior Analytics* 72b, under the heading of the "indemonstrable," and Frege had in mind for basic a priori truths. As Burge (2000) puts it, "Frege writes that the axioms 'neither need nor admit of proof' " (p. 16).

41. A stricter rule is defensible: one might say that intelligible discourse should be relativized to a given level of conceptual sophistication and then require that the appropriate demand is for one or more premises self-evident *at that level* (i.e., to persons at that level) whose self-evident entailment of *p* is also at that level.

42. Earlier versions of this chapter have benefited from discussions at Colgate University, Dalhousie University, Mankato State University, Ohio State University, the University of Helsinki, University of Siena, and Washington University. I would particularly like to thank Paul Audi, Michele Cargol, Peter J. Graham, John Greco, John Heil, Markus

Lammenranta, Keith McPartland, Sandro Nannini, Walter Sinnott-Armstrong, Raimo Tuomela, Giuseppe Varnier, and Thomas Vinci for helpful comments on earlier versions.

REFERENCES

Anderson, C. Anthony (1993). "Toward a Logic of A Priori Knowledge." *Philosophical Topics* 21, no. 2: 1–20.

Antony, Louise (2004). "A Naturalized Approach to the *A Priori*." In *Epistemology. Philosophical Issues* 14 (a supplement to *Nous*): 1–17.

Audi, Robert (1993). *The Structure of Justification* (Cambridge: Cambridge University Press).

———— (1999). "Self-Evidence." *Philosophical Perspectives* 13: 204–28.

———— (2000). "Philosophical Naturalism at the Turn of the Century." *Journal of Philosophical Research* 25: 27–45.

———— (2003). *Epistemology* (London: Routledge).

———— (2004). *The Good in the Right: A Theory of Intuition and Intrinsic Value* (Princeton: Princeton University Press).

————. (2007). "Justifying Grounds, Justified Beliefs, and Rational Acceptance." In Mark Timmons, John Greco, and Alfred R. Mele, eds., *Rationality and the Good: Critical Esssays on the Ethics and Epistemology of Robert Audi* (Oxford: Oxford University Press).

———— (forthcoming). "Rational Disagreement as a Challenge to Ethical Theory and Moral Objectivity." In Quentin Smith, ed., *Epistemology: New Essays* (Oxford. Oxford University Press).

Ayer, A. J. (1936). *Language, Truth and Logic* (London: Gollancz).

Benacerraf, Paul (1973). "Mathematical Truth." *Journal of Philosophy* 70: 661–79.

Boghossian, Paul, and Christopher Peacocke, eds. (2000). *New Essays on the A Priori* (Oxford: Oxford University Press).

BonJour, Laurence (1997). *In Defense of Pure Reason* (Cambridge: Cambridge University Press).

Brooke, J. A. (1992). "Kant's A Priori Methods for Recognizing A Priori Truths." In Hanson and Hunter, 1992, 215–52.

Brown, James Robert (1992). "EPR as A Priori Science." In Hanson and Hunter, 1992, 253–72.

Burge, Tyler (2000). "Frege on Apriority." In Boghossian and Peacocke, 2000, 11–42.

Butchvarov, Panayot (1970). *The Concept of Knowledge* (Evanston: Northwestern University Press).

Cartwright, Richard (1962). "Propositions." In R. J. Butler, ed. *Analytical Philosophy* (Oxford: Blackwell), 81–103.

Chalmers, David J. (2002). "The Components of Content." In his *Philosophy of Mind* (Oxford: Oxford University Press), 608–33.

Chisholm, Roderick M. (1989). *Theory of Knowledge*. 3rd ed. (Englewood Cliffs, N.J.: Prentice-Hall).

Cottingham, John, ed. (1992). *The Cambridge Companion to Descartes* (Cambridge: Cambridge University Press).

Cottingham, John, Robert Stoothoff, Dugald Murdock, and Anthony Kenny, eds. 1984/91. *The Philosophical Writings of Descartes*, 3 vols. (Cambridge: Cambridge University Press).

Davidson, Donald, and Gilbert Harman, eds., (1972). *Semantics of Natural Language* (Dordrecht: D. Reidel).

Descartes, René. 1641/1993. *Meditations on First Philosophy*. Donald A. Cress, trans. (Indianapolis: Hackett).

Devitt, Michael (2005). "There Is No *a Priori*." In Steup and Sosa, 2005, 105–115.

Field, Hartry (2005). "Recent Debates about the A Priori." *Oxford Studies in Epistemology* 1: 69–88.

Friedman, Michael (2000). "A Neo-Kantian Perspective." In Boghossian and Peacocke, 2000, 367–83.

Greco, John (2000). *Putting Skeptics in Their Place* (Cambridge: Cambridge University Press).

Hanson, Philip, and Bruce Hunter, eds. (1992). *Return of the a Priori. Canadian Journal of Philosophy*, supplementary volume 22.

Horwich, Paul (2000). "Stipulation, Meaning, and Apriority." In Boghossian and Peacocke, 2000, 150-169.

Hume, David (1777/1977). *An Enquiry Concerning Human Understanding* (Indianapolis: Hackett).

Jackson, Frank (2000). "Representation, Scepticism, and the A Priori." In Boghossian and Peacocke, 2000, 320–32.

Kant, Immanuel (1781–87/1963). *Critique of Pure Reason*. Norman Kemp Smith, trans. (London: Macmillan, 1963).

Kitcher, Philip (1983). *Mathematical Knowledge* (Oxford: Oxford University Press).

——— (2000). "A Priori Knowledge Revisited." In Boghossian and Peacocke, 2000, 65–91.

Kripke, Saul (1972)."Naming and Necessity." In Davidson and Harman, 1972,

Maddy, Penelope (2000). "Naturalism and the A Priori." In Boghossian and Peacocke, 2000, 92–116.

Markie, Peter (1992). "The *Cogito* and Its Importance." In Cottingham, 1992, 140–73.

Peacocke, Christopher (2004). *The Realm of Reason* (Oxford: Oxford University Press).

Plantinga, Alvin (1993). *Warrant and Proper Function* (Oxford: Oxford University Press).

Quine, W. V. (1951). "Two Dogmas of Empiricism." *Philosophical Review* 60: 20–43.

——— (1969). "Epistemology Naturalized." In his *Ontological Relativity and Other Essays* (New York: Columbia University Press), 69–90.

Sidgwick, Henry (1962). *The Methods of Ethics*. 7th ed. (Chicago: University of Chicago Press).(Originally published 1907.)

Sinnott-Armstrong, Walter (2006). *Moral Skepticisms* (Oxford: Oxford University Press).

Smith, Quentin (forthcoming). *Epistemology: New Essays*. Oxford: Oxford University Press.

Steup, Matthias, and Ernest Sosa, eds. (2005). *Contemporary Debates in Epistemology* (Oxford: Blackwell).

Yablo, Stephen (2000). "Apriority and Existence." In Boghossian and Peacocke, 2000, 197–228.

CHAPTER 8

MORAL REALISM, QUASI REALISM, AND SKEPTICISM

TERENCE CUNEO

A recognizable pattern marks the debates between realists and antirealists. Consider, in this regard, the debate between realists and antirealists regarding the external world. Realists about the external world claim that things such as mountains and fish exist in a robustly objective sense, according to which they do not owe their existence or nature to human cognitive activity. Antirealists about these things often respond by pointing out that if entities such as mountains and fish were to exist in this sense, then, for one or another reason, it would be impossible to gain epistemic access to them. According to the antirealists, realism engenders skepticism about the external world. Since skepticism of this sort is highly undesirable, antirealists counsel us to surrender realism in favor of an antirealist position regarding the external world, according to which it is possible to gain knowledge of such things as mountains and fish (or dissolves altogether the need to have knowledge of them).

This pattern of debate replicates itself in the moral domain. On the one hand, there are moral realists, who believe that moral facts exist in a full-blooded, objective sense.[1] Particularly, "robust" moral realists, who are my concern in this chapter, maintain not only that moral facts objectively exist, but also that they are not part of the natural world. As such, according to robust realists, moral facts fail to play any sort of causal explanatory roles. On the other hand, there are moral antirealists, who find robust moral realism fantastic, a relic of outmoded Platonist views in ethics. The antirealists present an epistemic challenge to robust realism which runs something like this:

Robust moral realists hold that there are moral facts and that these facts play no sort of causal explanatory role. But if this were true, it is difficult to see how we could secure "mental reference" to such facts—get them well enough in mind to form true thoughts about them. For what else other than causal relations of various kinds could explain our being able to gain epistemic access to these facts? Robust realists offer us no answer to this question—no story that explains how facts about what ought to be the case impinge upon our cognitive faculties so as to produce the corresponding states of knowledge. And it is difficult to imagine what type of story could be told. In light of this failure, it is best to conclude that there is no explanation available. On the further assumption that if we had epistemic access to moral facts, some explanation of this would be available, it follows that we have good reason to believe that we do not have access to moral facts. Arguably, however, moral beliefs display epistemic merits such as *being justified, being reliably formed*, and *being a case of knowledge* only if we can secure mental reference to moral facts. It follows that we have strong reason to believe that, were robust moral realism true, our moral beliefs would fail to display epistemic merits. Moral knowledge, were robust realism true, would be impossible.[2]

This argument, in my judgment, deserves a mixed verdict. On the one hand, the argument is not a decisive reason to reject robust realism. For suppose the worst case scenario were true of robust realism: realists of this sort have no informative account of how we gain epistemic access to moral facts. Even if this were true, the epistemic challenge depends on a controversial application of the inference schema "no relation we know of accounts for our being able to secure mental reference to moral facts" to "probably, there is no relation that accounts for our being able to secure mental reference to moral facts." The present application of this inference schema is controversial because it is not apparent that we should expect to know of any relation that accounts for our being able to gain epistemic access to moral facts. For all we reasonably believe, it may be that even if there were noncausal relations that allow us to gain epistemic access to moral facts, we would be unable to say much that would be illuminating about them—the problem being that, given the inherent limitations of our epistemic faculties, these relations are "cognitively closed" to us. Unlike some philosophers, I am not inclined to dismiss this response to the epistemic challenge as "mystery mongering." It may be that far less than we have supposed is amenable to genuine philosophical explanation.[3]

On the other hand, I think that the foregoing response to the epistemic challenge is one that should be accepted only as a last resort. After all, realists would like to say *something* illuminating about how we gain epistemic access to moral facts; complete silence on this issue is something that realists should like to avoid if they could. And, presumably, it would be desirable if we could model ethical knowledge on other fairly well-understood approaches, such as reliabilism. Yet the foregoing response appears to rule this out. Because of this, robust realism appears to be at a decided disadvantage in relation to its rivals. For if a rival view were to specify how we gain epistemic access to moral facts (or dissolve the need for an explanation altogether), that view would be, in this respect, considerably preferable to realism.

Suppose, then, that we accept the mixed verdict: the epistemic challenge, while not decisive, counts against robust moral realism. How heavily it counts against robust realism, however, is a function of (among other things) how well other views account for moral knowledge. After all, if other rival views do no better on this score, then robust realists face no special problem regarding moral knowledge. So let us raise the question: when we compare robust realism with rival views, does it offer us a less satisfactory account of the character of moral knowledge than these other views?

In my estimation, an especially intriguing rival to robust realism is the broadly expressivist position that Simon Blackburn calls "moral quasi-realism."[4] The reason this position seems intriguing to me is not simply that it shares extensive commitments with robust realism, such as the suspicion that ordinary moral thought cannot be understood as many moral naturalists believe. It is also because quasi realism promises to reap the benefits of moral realism at a fraction of the theoretical cost, for central to quasi realism is the claim that we can explain the realist-seeming appearances of ordinary moral thought and discourse, including attributions of moral knowledge, from an antirealist expressivist basis.[5] The question I wish to put to quasi realism in this chapter is whether it offers us a more satisfactory account of moral knowledge than moral realism. Quasi realism's advocates, such as Simon Blackburn, claim that it does.[6] I am going to argue, by contrast, that it does not.

As it turns out, however, arguing for this claim is fairly complicated, for quasi realism is not a unified position but admits of multiple variations. So, in what follows, I am going to set for myself three tasks. First, I am going to lay out a central reason why quasi realists believe that they can explain and justify the realist-seeming appearances of ordinary moral thought and discourse. Second, having done this, I will distinguish three different varieties of quasi realism, noting that they are not simply minor variants of one another. Third, I will argue that none of these positions does a more satisfactory job of explaining the acquisition of moral knowledge than does robust realism. To anticipate, my claim is that some varieties of quasi realism fail to comport with platitudes central to our ordinary understanding of knowledge, while others do so comport but fail to explain the acquisition of moral knowledge in a way that is more illuminating than robust realism.

If my overall assessment is correct, moral realists should take heart. For, presumably, if any type of moral realism were to have trouble accounting for moral knowledge, it would be robust moral realism. But if even robust moral realism does at least as well as one of its most important rivals in accounting for the acquisition of moral knowledge, this is good news for moral realists of all varieties.

1. Moral Quasi Realism

In his official description of the view, Blackburn writes that quasi realism is

> the enterprise of explaining why our discourse has the shape it does, in particular by way of treating evaluative predicates like others. . . . It thus seeks to explain, and justify, the realistic-seeming nature of our talk of evaluations. . . . Technically, in the philosophy of language, it tries mainly to justify what I call the "propositional surface" of ethics, or the fact that we voice our reactions in very much the way in which we describe facts.[7]

Quasi realism, then, is an explanatory project. When applied to the moral domain, it instructs us to begin our theorizing by assuming the truth of expressivist antirealism, according to which moral thought and discourse function not to represent moral facts but to express attitudes, sentiments, degrees of confidence, action plans, or the like toward nonmoral reality. From this starting point, we "earn the right" to speak as realists and allow ourselves to talk of moral propositions, moral truth, and moral facts.[8] But how, according to quasi realists, do we earn the right to speak this way?

In large measure, we do so by "going deflationary." That is, quasi realists maintain that they, as antirealists, can also claim that moral judgments express moral propositions, that some such propositions are true, and that there are moral facts—so long as we understand these notions in a sufficiently deflationary sense. What deflationary sense is this? Elsewhere, I have suggested that the best way to find out is by taking a closer look at what I call the quasi realist's "deflationary package," which is a set of claims about moral propositional content, truth, and facthood that explicates these notions in a deflationary way.[9] On this occasion, however, a brief description of the deflationary package will have to do. According to this brief description, the best way to understand the deflationary package is by reflecting for a moment on the concept of representation.

Suppose we assume that representation is a genuine, robust "aboutness" relation that holds between mental states (or their content) and objects. It is natural to ask: what is the link between propositional content, truth, and facts, on the one hand, and representation, on the other? Many philosophers believe that the connection is intimate. The propositional content of beliefs, these philosophers claim, is such that it purports to represent the world. Truth consists in a belief (or its content) accurately representing the world. And facts are what are represented by the content of true beliefs (or are identical therewith). Advocates of the deflationary package claim that these philosophers are mistaken. The concepts of propositional content, truth, and facthood, say deflationists, are much less substantive than many have supposed; none of them is conceptually tied to the notion of representation in the ways just noted.

More specifically, advocates of the deflationary package accept one of two deflationary positions. Some philosophers accept what I will call "radical" deflationism about a given domain. According to these philosophers, sentences in that domain express "nondescriptive" propositional contents. These contents, it is said, do not purport to represent the world but rather play grammatical or logical roles very similar to those played by ordinary "descriptive" propositions, such as embedding in propositional attitude ascriptions (e.g., "I believe that p"). Accordingly, radical deflationists claim that, strictly speaking, nondescriptive propositional contents neither are true nor correspond to correlative facts in that domain. Nonetheless, radical deflationists maintain that we can *say* that these contents are true or correspond to the facts. But talk of this type is to be understood in a very minimalist fashion. For example, according to this view, to say "It is true that killing is wrong" is simply to repeat or endorse the (nondescriptive) proposition *that killing is wrong.*

Other philosophers, however, endorse what I will call "sober" deflationism about a given domain. Advocates of this view also hold that the sentences in that domain express nondescriptive contents, but unlike their radical cousins, they maintain that these contents can be true. Granted, sober deflationists maintain that there is little to say about the truth property: it neither plays any robust explanatory roles nor consists in a proposition's corresponding to a fact (or consists in any other "substantive" relation, for that matter). But still, according to sober deflationists, there is such a property—properties, according to this view, coming for free with the existence of well-behaved predicates. Since, however, there is a truth property, sober deflationists maintain that there are truths. And since there are truths, there are facts. To this it should be added that these facts are taken to be simply the "semantic shadows" of the true sentences of a given domain. They are not in any interesting sense truth-makers or what is represented by propositions.

The differences between the radical and sober deflationary packages are important. They imply that were quasi realists to accept the sober deflationary package, they would be committed to the existence of moral truths and facts, albeit of a nonsubstantive sort. By contrast, were quasi realists to accept the radical deflationary package, they would be committed to no such thing. So long as we accept some fairly widely held, broadly Quinean claims about quantification and existence, the fact that sober deflationary views quantify over moral facts (or properties) implies that sober and radical deflationary positions are not mere notional variants of one another—at least no more so than realists and nominalists about properties are stylistic variants of one another.[10] So which version of the deflationary package do moral quasi realists accept? Are they better understood to be radical or sober deflationists with respect to the moral domain?

2. THE MANY FACES OF QUASI REALISM

Let me approach this question by assembling a series of passages in which quasi realists address how they understand the character of moral truth and facthood. I divide these passages (most of which are from Blackburn) into three groups.

Group 1:

To think that a moral proposition is true is to concur in an attitude to its subject. To say that a moral judgement is true is to repeat that judgement.

If I assert "That pleasure is worth having is a fact," that is no more than a fancy way of saying that pleasure is worth having.... The same goes for truth: "that peas are yucky is the truth" just means that peas are yucky.

Moral realism is the view that the truth of moral utterances is to consist in their correspondence with some fact or state of affairs.... Certainly there is a sense in which the quasi-realist is opposed to giving an ontological status to moral...facts.

[Quasirealism] is visibly anti-realist, for the explanations make no irreducible or essential appeal to the existence of moral "properties" or "facts"; they demand no "ontology" of morals.[11]

Group 2:

The propositional surface of the discourse means that we have moral predicates, and where we have predicates, we ascend to properties.

Even if we sorted truth into TRUTH and truth...and decided that there was no moral TRUTH, this would only mean that you don't walk into rights and duties, or that they can't be cubic or solid or seen under a microscope.

Obviously there will be some differences between "ethical facts" and the others. The fact that there is a cannonball on the cushion explains why it is sagging in the middle. The fact that kindness is good explains no such thing.

Yes, I am an anti-realist; no, this does not mean that there are no facts of an ethical or normative kind....

Quasi-realism...refuses to give ethical facts a typical explanatory role. This is already heralded when we turn our backs on ethical representation. A representation of something as F is typically explained by the fact that it is F. A representation *answers to* what is represented. I hold that ethical facts do not play this explanatory role.[12]

Group 3:

It seems that the quasi-realist inhabits a familiar but highly suspect philosophical world: one where we know what we mean by descriptive versus non-descriptive theories, by objectivity, or by realism versus anti-realism. Not only would many philosophers deny that we can make good sense of these oppositions, but quasi-realism itself can offer them support. For if, from the non-descriptive starting point, it is successful in capturing some propositional feature of our discourse, then that feature can no longer be used as a litmus test such that if we allow it we are realists and if we do not then we are expressivists. If it can do this for all proposed features, then there is no point at which our *use* of ethical language supports realism rather than expressivism (or vice versa); if that is so, it is tempting to conclude that the debate is unreal, since there is no methodology for conducting it.[13]

These passages strongly suggest that quasi realism comes in at least three different varieties. The first group of quotations indicates that quasi realists sometimes accept what I have called the "radical" deflationary package, according to which the truth term does not function as a genuine predicate and there are, strictly speaking, no moral facts. Because views of this sort embrace the radical deflationary package, I will call them "radical" versions of quasi realism. The second group of passages suggests, however, that in other cases quasi realists adopt what I have called the "sober" deflationary package, according to which there is a truth property and there are moral facts, albeit the nature of these entities is "nonsubstantial." (Note, for example, that the first quotation from this group articulates the same line of thought embraced by proponents of the sober deflationary view of truth: properties come for free with well-behaved predicates.) I will call positions of this kind "sober" versions of quasi realism. Finally, the quotation that makes up the third group suggests that quasi realists sometimes embrace a very radical, "quietest" position, according to which moral "realism" and "antirealism" are empty tags because there is no distinction to draw between these positions. If quietism is true, the mimicry in which quasi realists engage is so complete that there is no point at which we can say that realists are committed to a given set of claims while antirealists are not; the alleged distinctions simply dissolve. Views of this variety I will call versions of "quietest" quasi realism.

Robust moral realism, I acknowledged earlier, faces some difficult questions about how we could acquire moral knowledge. In the next three sections, I want to raise the question whether any of the quasi-realist positions I have identified do better. However, let me say at the outset that I am not going to give equal attention to each of these views. Most of my attention will be focused on radical quasi-realism, since the main issues that I wish to consider emerge when we explore this view.[14]

3. RADICAL QUASI REALISM

The project in which I am engaged is to determine whether quasi realism offers us a more adequate account of moral knowledge than robust moral realism. The first version of quasi realism I wish to consider—what I have called "radical quasi realism"—attempts to formulate a more satisfactory account of moral knowledge by defending a recognizably antirealist position in ethics. According to radical quasi realists, moral judgments do not purport to represent moral reality, as they express nondescriptive moral propositional content.[15] Moreover, although we may say such things as "It is true that murder is wrong," no such judgment involves the predication of a truth property, as the content of moral judgments does not admit of such a property. Finally, while we may make apparent reference to moral facts, all such apparent reference is merely apparent, for there are, strictly speaking, no moral facts. (As quasi realists sometimes put the point, from the engaged, "internal" perspective, we speak of moral truths and facts. But from the disengaged, "external" perspective, there are no such truths or facts.)[16] None of this, radical quasi realists maintain, should lead us to believe that ordinary moral thought and discourse are mistaken. As Blackburn emphasizes, there could be a mistake only if there were some type of mismatch between the content of ordinary moral judgments and moral reality. A mismatch of this sort, however, is precisely what quasi realism is designed to avoid, since, according to quasi realists, moral judgments are not even in the business of purporting to represent moral reality.[17]

Suppose, for the sake of argument, that we agree that radical quasi realism is positioned to capture many of the realist-seeming features of ordinary moral thought. Can radical quasi realism also capture the idea that we know moral truths?

There are passages indicating that quasi realists believe as much. Consider the following passage from Blackburn:

> So the question for the expressivist is whether sometimes our situation in making evaluations is one in which we are reliably situated, and in which there is no chance that an improvement in our position would undermine the evaluation. And the answer to this question is that surely we sometimes are in such a position. Consider firstly a middle-size, clear-cut judgment: regardless of danger, at some cost, but successfully, alone among the spectators, Alaric jumped in to save the drowning Bertha; and I commend his action, judging that he behaved well.... Am I reliable? If Alaric had not behaved well I should not be going around thinking that he did. The close possible worlds in which he did not behave well are ones, presumably, in which Bertha was not in the water, or in which she was but he averted his eyes or slunk away, and if these things had happened I would not be thinking that he behaved well. Furthermore, there may be no chance that further acquaintance with the situation reverses my verdict: there are not hidden wrinkles waiting to turn up, proving that the whole thing was a publicity stunt or whatever. So I know that Alaric behaved well.[18]

Allan Gibbard, although more guarded about whether quasi realism can vindicate the claim that there is normative knowledge, develops an account similar to Blackburn's:

> In effect, then, Hera's plans include judgments of what it takes to be a reliable judge of what to live for. Being reliable is a matter of being someone to rely on, and so thinking someone reliable amounts to planning to rely on which people.... Can we, then, sometimes know what to do? When we do, is this real knowledge; is it knowledge in the same sense as with natural features of our surroundings? Knowledge or quasi-knowledge—which it is I won't try saying. In crucial respects, though, plan-laden judgments can at least parallel the clearest and most literal cases of knowledge. Plan-laden judgments may be true, in a minimal sense, and they can be formed in a way to rely on.... If planning judgments to trust are still not fully cases of knowing, they share many features with full knowing. The parallels extend far.[19]

The strategy in both cases is as follows. Assume that moral judgments express nondescriptive moral propositional content.[20] Assume, furthermore, that there is a sense in which we can say that such content is true. Assume, finally, that the acceptance of such content can be reliably formed. In Blackburn's case, that means appealing to the idea that in a sufficiently wide range of close possible worlds, this content is true and one would also accept it (and, indeed, no further information would change this latter fact). In Gibbard's case, we appeal to the claim that decisions to act in a certain way—what he calls "plan-laden" judgments—can be reliable (or the people who make them can be reliable) in the sense that we can rely on them. The suggestion is that if we grant these assumptions, quasi realists can maintain that we have moral knowledge, as the latter is simply true, reliably formed moral belief (plus, perhaps, some condition to address Gettier-style considerations).

The passages I have just presented contain interesting proposals. But it seems to me that neither proposal is satisfactory; each omits something that is central to our ordinary (and philosophical) understanding of knowledge. For fundamental to our ordinary understanding of knowledge is what I will call the knowledge platitude:

> The knowledge platitude: The concept "being a case of knowledge that p" properly applies to some mental state only if and because it (or its content) purports to represent that p.[21]

This platitude is arguably just one example of a large network of platitudes, each of which expresses the idea that epistemic concepts, including justification, warrant, reliability, and so forth, are intimately tied to the notion of representation. Put somewhat roughly, these platitudes tell us that we can properly apply epistemic merit concepts such as these to mental states only if the latter (or their contents) purport to represent or represent reality. The difficulty with both Blackburn's and Gibbard's proposals—at least if we read them as attempts to defend a radical quasi-realist position—is that they fall afoul of the knowledge platitude. Both, admittedly, offer an account of what it is for a normative judgment to be reliably formed. But neither offers an account of what it is for a normative judgment to be reliably formed in the *epistemic* sense, according to which reliability is intimately linked with accurate representation. It is this sense of reliability, however, that is at issue when we say that an agent's belief is reliably formed or is a case of knowledge.

Earlier I suggested that a helpful way to understand the deflationary project is to see it as one that endeavors to divorce concepts such as propositional content and truth from that of representation. But if the objection I am now pressing is on target, this divorce has undesirable consequences when we try to understand moral knowledge in a quasi-realist fashion. For suppose we assume that we have moral knowledge. And suppose we concede that robust realism has no explanatorily informative account about how we acquire such knowledge, since it offers no account of how we gain epistemic access to moral reality. Suppose, furthermore, we admit that this is a demerit of the view. Even if we concede all this, radical quasi realism does not look any better than robust realism. If radical quasi realism were true, it would also imply that we have no explanatorily informative account of how we acquire moral knowledge since, if we take the knowledge platitude seriously, it implies that we could not acquire such knowledge at all.

This is a result with which quasi realists would not be happy. As I emphasized earlier, quasi realism is an attempt not to revise but to *vindicate* our ordinary views about morality, and ordinary morality chafes at the idea that moral knowledge is impossible. That said, I believe that there are several responses to the foregoing objection that lie close at hand. According to one response, the present objection to quasi realism works only if we take representation to be a robust "aboutness" relation between mind (or its content) and world. But, it might be said, we need not assume this. After all, there is nothing that prohibits quasi realists from adding another component to the deflationary package by deflating representation itself. For example, Blackburn writes that quasi realists can be deflationists about representation too, so long as they appropriate what he calls "Ramsey's ladder":

> Because of the minimalism [i.e., deflationism] we can have for free what looks like a ladder of philosophical ascent: "*p*", "it is true that *p*," "it is really and truly a fact that *p*." . . . None of these terms . . . marks an addition to the original judgment. . . . *p* is true means that *p*. . . . "represents the facts" means no more than: "is true."[22]

Call the thesis that expressions such as "*p*," "it is true that *p*," "it is a fact that *p*," and "'*p*' represents the facts" are identical in meaning the "equivalence thesis." Blackburn's contention is that since the equivalence thesis is true, quasi realists should have no difficulty being deflationists about representation. If this is right, however, radical quasi realists no less than realists can honor the knowledge platitude. They too can say that moral belief purports to represent the facts.

I have two concerns about this response. On the one hand, I believe that the equivalence thesis is false. On the other hand, it seems to me that even if it were true, radical quasi realism would not offer us an account of moral knowledge that is more satisfactory than robust realism.

Let us begin with the first concern. The equivalence thesis is an ambitious claim about meaning equivalences. It also seems to me suspect in several ways. In the first place, it appears as if the sentences that it says are identical in meaning are not. After all, on the face of it, to say that something is a fact and to say that it represents the facts is to say two very different things. Moreover, as stated, the equivalence thesis proves difficult to evaluate. According to the thesis, the sentences "It is true that murder is wrong" and "'Murder is wrong' is true" are supposed to mean the same thing. Arguably, however, the second sentence commits us to the claim that sentences are truth evaluable, while the first does not. (The first sentence, for example, is compatible with a view according to which "true" functions as an adverb that modifies only beliefs.) Given that the equivalence thesis fails to tell us how to interpret sentences such as these, how are we to determine whether they mean the same thing?

Those who are skeptical of the equivalence thesis, such as I, would like to have a method for testing whether the thesis is true. Although I doubt that there is such a test, there is, I believe, a test by which we can determine whether claims about truth, facthood, and representation are *not* identical in meaning. The test is this: formulate schemata with regard to truth, facthood, and representation of the same logical form. Then see whether their substitution instances are at least logically equivalent.[23] If their substitution instances are not logically equivalent, then we have excellent reason to believe that the equivalence thesis should be rejected. Let us refer to this strategy as "the schema test."

The best way to apply the schema test, in my judgment, is to start with three basic truth schemata to which philosophers appeal when elucidating the notion of truth. We then model schemata for facthood and representation on these three schematatypes. I claim that when we do this, we find that their substitution instances are not logically equivalent and, hence, not identical in meaning. Admittedly, this approach has the demerit of not being exhaustive in character; there are truth schemata other than the ones I consider. Still, I think that our survey offers strong reasons for rejecting the equivalence thesis.

Consider, first, schema (Tp), which is a schema for propositional truth. Were we to formulate schemata concerning facthood and representation modeled on (Tp), we would have the following trio of statement schemata:

(Tp) The proposition that p is true iff p.

(Fp) The proposition that p is a fact iff p.

(Rp) The proposition that p represents the fact that p iff p.

Taken at face value, these schemata are not acceptable to radical quasi realists. The basic problem is that if radical deflationism were true, then we should be able to delete "is true" without loss of meaning from any substitution instance of (Tp). But a sentence such as

The proposition that murder is wrong iff murder is wrong

does not make any sense. Schema (Tp) has the wrong sort of logical form for the purposes of radical deflationism.

Consider, then, the second type of truth schema to which discussions of truth often appeal, which is the so-called disquotational truth schema. Were we to formulate a trio of schemata regarding truth, facthood, and representation along disquotational lines, we would have the following:

(Td) "p" is true iff p.

(Fd) "p" is a fact iff p.

(Rd) "p" represents the fact that p iff p.

The primary difference between schemata (Td) and (Tp) is that the former takes not propositions but sentence tokens to be truth-bearers.[24] This maneuver has advantages for radical quasi realists. For one thing, it looks as if we can eliminate "is true" from substitution instances of (Td) without loss of meaning.[25] Moreover, it is plausible to hold that substitution instances of (Td) and (Rd) are logically equivalent. But if appealing to sentences rather than propositions has theoretical advantages, it also has serious disadvantages. Consider a substitution instance of (Fd) such as the following:

"Murder is wrong" is a fact iff murder is wrong.

This claim does not have much to recommend it. There is no use of the term "fact" of which I am aware according to which linguistic items such as sentence tokens are identical with facts. They are simply not of the right ontological category. (We would find it very odd, I think, if someone were to maintain that the wrongness of murder resides, say, in a concatenation of chalkmarks.) Something similar is not true of sentences, however. According to many analyses, they are (or at least many of them are) plausibly viewed as being identical with truths. If so, we have good reason to believe that substitution instances of (Td) and (Fd) are not logically equivalent.

Let us turn now to the third type of schema invoked in discussions of truth, which is the so-called bearerless truth schema. Were we to formulate schemata regarding truth, facthood, and representation that employ the bearerless approach, we would have the following three statement schemata:

(T) It is true that p iff p.

(F) It is a fact that p iff p.

(R) It represents the fact that p iff p.

As it turns out, there are two different ways to interpret these schemata. According to the first approach, the phrases "it is true that" and "it is a fact that" function as sentential operators. This approach will also be attractive to radical quasi realists, as these sentential operators can be eliminated from any sentence in which they embed without loss of meaning. Still, according to this reading, it is not very plausible to hold that substitution instances of (R) are logically equivalent to substitution instances of (T) and (F). After all, a substitution instance of (R) such as

It represents the fact that murder is wrong iff murder is wrong

makes no more sense than

The proposition that murder is wrong iff murder is wrong.

Both sentences are grammatically malformed. The problem with the first sentence is that unlike the phrase "it is true that," the expression "it represents the fact that" is not a sentential operator of any sort. Nor, as far as I can see, does any modification of this phrase function as a sentential operator. That is why we cannot simply preface a noun phrase such as "that murder is wrong" with it and thereby construct a well-formed sentence.

The second way to read the trio of schemata just formulated is to hold that the phrase "it is true that" functions not as a sentential operator but as a "prosentence." According to advocates of this approach, a prosentence is very much like a pronoun inasmuch as its function is to make anaphoric reference to a noun phrase in a sentence in which it embeds (or some other sentence). If this view is correct, instances of these schemata should be read as follows:

> (T*) *P*. That is true iff *p*.
>
> (F*)*P*. That is a fact iff *p*.
>
> (R*)*P*. That represents the fact that *p* iff *p*.

Like the bearerless approach to truth, there is reason for radical quasi realists to find the prosentential view attractive. Substitution instances of (T*) and (R*) appear, after all, to be logically equivalent. However, the problem with the prosentential approach, at least in the present context, is that substitution instances of (F*) and (R*) such as

> Murder is wrong. That is a fact iff murder is wrong

and

> Murder is wrong. That represents the fact that murder is wrong iff murder is wrong

are not logically equivalent. The first claim appears to be about facts, while the second is not about facts themselves but about what represents them—facts not being the sort of thing that purport to represent themselves.

To sum up, radical quasi realists embrace the equivalence thesis since doing so appears to allow them to honor the knowledge platitude. I have suggested that the way to evaluate this thesis is by applying what I have called the "schema test." If what I have claimed is correct, when we apply this test, we find that sentences that quasi realists claim are identical in meaning are not even logically equivalent, let alone identical in meaning. And this, I have argued, gives us strong reason to believe that the equivalence thesis is false.

Suppose for the sake of argument, however, that further investigation were to reveal that the equivalence thesis can be defended satisfactorily. The second concern I want to raise is that even if this were true, radical quasi realism does not furnish a satisfactory account of why certain beliefs satisfy the knowledge platitude.

The knowledge platitude says that we can properly apply the concept "being a case of knowledge that *p*" to a mental state only if its content purports to represent the fact that *p*. According to a natural reading of this platitude, the concept "being a case of knowledge" properly applies to a mental state only if its content has the property *being such as to purport to represent the fact that* p. This reading, however, is not one that radical quasi realists can accept since, according to their view, moral propositional content is nondescriptive. Yet the knowledge platitude is supposed to be a platitude. So, one suspects that there has to be a reading of the platitude that is acceptable to radical quasi realists. What would it be?

Allan Gibbard has stressed recently that much of what philosophers want to say by making apparent reference to properties can be said equally well by making reference to concepts.[26] If so, realists and quasi realists can agree on the following:

> The concept "being a case of knowledge that *p*" properly applies to some mental state *M* only if and because the concept "being such as to purport to represent *p*" properly applies to its content.

Once we state the platitude in this fashion, however, we can distinguish two ways of reading it.

According to what I will call the "restrictive" reading of the knowledge platitude, concepts are paired with correlative properties: the concept "*F*-ness" properly applies to a thing only if it is the type of entity that can display the correlative property *being* F. If this view is right, it is appropriate to think of the content of a mental state as being representative only if that content is the sort of thing that can display the correlative property *being such as to purport to represent the facts*. According to what I will term the "expansive" reading, however, concepts need not be paired with correlative properties, since some concepts are nondescriptive. If this view is true, a nondescriptive concept "*F*-ness" can properly "pertain" to a thing even when that thing is not the sort of entity that can display the correlative property *being* F. According to this position, it is appropriate to think of the content of a mental state as representative even if that content is not the sort of thing that can display the correlative property *being such as to purport to represent the facts*.

Moral realists accept the restrictive reading of the knowledge platitude. Radical quasi realists do not, opting instead for the expansive reading. Their reasons for doing so are clear: if the expansive reading can be maintained, then they too can claim that moral knowledge satisfies the knowledge platitude. Are quasi realists right about this?

Yes, but not for the right reasons. Consider the fact that we hold that there is a difference between knowledge and mere belief. Some beliefs, we assume, are such that it is appropriate to think of them as being cases of knowledge, while others are not. We assume this, presumably, because we think that some beliefs enjoy features that qualify them as being cases of knowledge that other beliefs fail to enjoy. We appear, then, to assume that something like the following principle is true:

> For any propositional content *p* of some mental state *M*, there must be some feature (or set of features) of *p* that renders it appropriate to apply the concept "being a case of knowledge that *p*" to *M* rather than the concept "being a case of mere belief."

Advocates of what I have called the "restrictive" reading of the knowledge platitude hold that they can identify the relevant features. Central among those features that render it appropriate to think of a belief as a case of knowledge is this: that its content accurately represents reality (or that we have strong grounds for believing that it does). There does seem to be something right about this response. Any attempt to identify what distinguishes knowledge from mere belief must appeal to the claim that, necessarily, beliefs that are cases of knowledge accurately represent reality, while mere beliefs do not, of necessity, accurately represent reality. If we follow the trajectory of our discussion thus far, radical quasi realists will also offer an answer along these lines but will translate apparent reference to properties into reference to concepts. If pressed on the issue of why it is appropriate to think of a mental state as a case not of mere belief but of knowledge, the quasi-realist answer should be: because it is proper to apply the concept "being such as to accurately represent reality" to that mental state but not others.

The problem with this reply, in my judgment, is this: we want an explanation of why it is appropriate to apply the concept "being a case of knowledge" to some moral beliefs but not others. Radical quasi realists offer an explanation, but of the wrong sort. Recall what it is, according to the radical deflationary view, to say that some nondescriptive content represents the facts: it is merely to endorse or repeat that content. Surely, however, the fact that it is appropriate to endorse or repeat a particular propositional content is not what *explains* why it is appropriate to think of it as a case of knowledge rather than mere belief. Even if it were true that all and only those propositional contents that it is proper to endorse or repeat are such that they are properly thought of as being cases of knowledge—and I see no reason to believe this—this would shed no light on why it would be appropriate to think of them as being cases of knowledge. And although I suppose that there might be some further property (or set of properties) that explains why all and only those propositional contents that it is proper to endorse or repeat are such that they are properly thought of as being cases of knowledge, I do not know what this property could be. (At least, I do not know what it could be unless it were a property such as *being correct* or *accurately representing reality*, which are properties that nondescriptive contents do not display.) If this is true, it may be that radical quasi realism offers an account of knowledge that satisfies the knowledge platitude. But to the question "Why is it appropriate to think of a given nondescriptive content as a case not of mere belief but of knowledge?" it fails to offer a satisfactory reply.

Let me summarize what I have argued in this section. Any adequate account of moral knowledge, I have claimed, must satisfy the knowledge platitude. At first glance, radical quasi realism does not offer an account of moral knowledge that satisfies this platitude, since it denies that moral beliefs purport to represent moral reality. There seems, however, to be no reason that radical quasi realists could not defend a deflationary account of representation itself—one according to which expressions such as "'p' represents the facts" are identical in meaning with expressions such as "it is true that p." I raised two objections to this response. First,

I claimed that the purported meaning equivalences fail to hold. And, second, I argued that even if they do hold, radical quasi realism does not offer an adequate account of why some beliefs satisfy the knowledge platitude while others do not.

To this, let me add a final comment. Earlier I said that there are several radical quasi-realist responses to the charge that their view fails to satisfy the knowledge platitude. I spent most of this section exploring a response that appeals to a radical deflationary account of representation. In closing, let me note that there is another response, according to which radical quasi realists can simply agree that their view fails to satisfy the knowledge platitude but deny that this is as problematic as I have claimed. The reason there is no problem, it might be maintained, is that radical quasi realism is an effort to account not for moral knowledge but for what is going on when we *think* that something is a case of moral knowledge or *ascribe* such knowledge to someone—an account, it should be added, that does not commit ordinary moral agents to moral beliefs that are systematically mistaken. According to this understanding of radical quasi realism, it is neither here nor there whether their view fails to satisfy the knowledge platitude.

I myself doubt that this response evades the objection I have pressed. But even if it does, let me make the following point. We have seen that the knowledge platitude can be stated in such a way that it merely offers conditions for the proper application of epistemic concepts. If what I have argued is correct, in the event that radical quasi realists maintain that moral thought does not purport to represent moral reality, it falls afoul of the knowledge platitude thus understood. It would be a conceptual mistake to apply an epistemic concept such as "being a case of knowledge" to a moral judgment if the content of that judgment does not even purport to represent moral reality.[27]

4. Sober Quasi Realism

An explanatory strategy binds together the various versions of quasi realism. This strategy, recall, is one in which we begin our theorizing about the moral domain by assuming that moral judgments do not endeavor to describe or represent moral reality. From this starting point, we explain how it is that nondescriptive attitudes could nonetheless mimic descriptive ones to such an extent that it is appropriate to say of them that they express moral propositions, that they are true, that they represent moral reality, and so on. Radical quasi realists, we have seen, pursue this explanatory project only to a certain point. While radical quasi realists maintain that it is appropriate to say such things, they maintain that saying these things does not commit us either to the existence of moral facts or to beliefs whose content purports to represent them. Sober quasi realists, by contrast, are willing to take the explanatory project a step further. According to their view, quasi realists should maintain not only that we can say that there are moral truths and facts, but also, strictly and literally speaking, that there *are* such facts and truths—this latter claim being simply an implication of the claim that entities such as moral properties "come for free" with well-behaved moral predicates.

Sober quasi realists, then, hold that there are moral facts. In this sense, their view is a close cousin to realism. Nonetheless, sober quasi realists think of these facts rather differently than realists do. As realists think of them, moral facts play at least one of the following explanatory roles: they are what make the content of our beliefs true or what are represented by this content. (Granted, if one is a correspondence theorist about truth, these two roles coincide.) Sober deflationists, by contrast, deny that moral facts play these roles. To return to a passage from Blackburn I quoted earlier: "Quasi-realism . . . refuses to give ethical facts a typical explanatory role. This is already heralded when we turn our backs on ethical representation. A representation of something as F is typically explained by the fact that it is F. A representation *answers to* what is represented. I hold that ethical facts do not play this explanatory role" (Blackburn, 1999, 216). To which we might add that if sober deflationism is true, not only do moral facts not play this role, they fail to play *any* sort of robust explanatory role.

I think that we should acknowledge that sober quasi realism is more plausible than its radical counterpart, if only because it is not committed to the equivalence thesis. But does it offer us a more satisfactory account of the character of moral knowledge than realism? I hold that it does not. My reason for holding this is that sober quasi realism is subject to the following dilemma.

Suppose that sober quasi realists were to accept the sober deflationary package with its relatively robust account of propositional content, truth, and facthood. Suppose, furthermore, we were to interpret the passage just quoted from Blackburn in such a way that it says that there is no sense in which the content of moral judgments purports to represent moral reality—this denial being what distinguishes quasi-realist from realist positions. If we assume these things, then sober quasi realism's account of moral knowledge falls afoul of the knowledge platitude. That is, if sober quasi realism were true, it would imply that moral knowledge is impossible because there would be no sense in which the content of moral belief purports to represent (let alone succeeds in representing) a correlative state of affairs. However, if knowledge of this sort is impossible, then sober quasi realism does not offer us a more attractive account of moral knowledge than robust realism. In fact, the sober quasi realist's view looks considerably less attractive than the position defended by robust realists. Robust realists may be saddled with philosophical mysteries, such as how we gain epistemic access to moral facts. But their view (at least if what I said earlier about the limitations of the epistemic challenge is true) does not yield a version of skepticism according to which moral knowledge is unattainable.

There is, however, an alternative to this first option available to sober quasi realists, which is to read the passage from Blackburn in such a way that it implies not that moral facts cannot be represented, but only that they cannot be represented in any substantive sense of "represent." Suppose, then, we were to read the passage quoted from Blackburn in this way. Suppose, furthermore, that sober quasi realists were to expand their version of the deflationary package so that it includes a deflationary account of representation. If our understanding of sober quasi realism has been on the mark, its understanding of representation mirrors its understanding of truth: to the question "Is there a representation relation such that moral beliefs can be among its relata?" sober quasi realists would answer yes. There is, strictly and literally speaking, such a relation. To the further question "Does this relation have a nature that can be unpacked by philosophical or scientific analysis?" sober quasi realists would answer no. If sober quasi realists are correct, the representation relation is not a causal relation, a teleofunctional relation, a sui generis "aboutness" relation, or anything of that sort. To use Paul Horwich's words, representation is a "relation [that] has no underlying nature."[28] That there is a representation relation is merely a consequence of a view according to which properties and relations come for free with well-behaved predicates such as "represents" and "refers." But, according to deflationists, there is nothing to say about these properties and relations beyond the fact that they are the semantic values of predicates that play certain grammatical or logical roles.

According to what I have called the "epistemic challenge," robust realism is problematic because it has nothing illuminating to say about how moral beliefs could represent moral facts. Since moral facts are not causally efficacious, the worry is, we are in the dark about how we could gain epistemic access to them. I have conceded that this is a legitimate concern to raise about robust realism. But if it is a legitimate concern to raise about robust realism, it is also a legitimate concern to raise about sober quasi realism. Sober quasi realists, after all, do not deny that moral knowledge consists in a moral belief's representing moral reality—so long as we understand the representation relation in a deflationary manner. But they do deny that moral facts are causally efficacious. And they do deny that there is anything illuminating to say about how we represent moral reality. In their view, there is nothing illuminating to say about the representation relation. In these respects, sober quasi realism is very similar to robust realism, with this exception: it is in principle possible that robust realists could say more that is genuinely informative about the representation relation operative in moral thought than they often do. For example, it is in principle possible for robust realists to make the case that the (robust) representation relation operative in moral thought is no different from other fairly well-understood (robust) representation relations operative in other nonmoral domains. In this respect, robust realism differs from sober quasi realism. For if what I have claimed is true, sober quasi realists accept an explanatory embargo on notions such as representation, which stipulates that there is nothing informative to say about that in virtue of which moral claims represent reality. Robust realists, if I am right, do not face an embargo of this kind, and that, arguably, is to their advantage.

That is one concern. Here is another. In the previous section, I said that it is a truism that if some beliefs are cases of knowledge, then they enjoy features that qualify them as such—features that other beliefs fail to enjoy. Among these features, I further claimed, is that beliefs that count as cases of knowledge necessarily represent reality, while mere beliefs do not. Radical quasi realism, I argued earlier, has a difficult time explaining why it makes sense to apply the concept "being a case of knowledge" to some moral beliefs but not to others. Recall that the argument went as follows: one feature that qualifies a belief as a case of knowledge is that it is proper to apply the concept "being such as to accurately represent the facts" to it. But, according to radical deflationists, to apply this concept to a moral belief is simply to endorse or repeat the content of that belief. And it is difficult to see why a belief's being such that it is appropriate to endorse or repeat its content should explain why it is appropriate to think of it as being a case of knowledge rather than mere belief.

I suggest that we can raise a similar concern about sober quasi realism. Let us agree that for sober quasi realists it is appropriate to apply the concept "being a case of knowledge" to some moral beliefs. Let us further agree that it is appropriate to apply this concept only when and because it is appropriate to apply the concept "being such as to represent accurately the relevant moral facts" to those same beliefs. However, if sober deflationary views are true, it is appropriate to apply this latter concept not because the contents of moral beliefs bear any sort of "aboutness" relation to moral facts but rather for the same reason we apply the concept "being true" to some beliefs: to thereby make linguistic maneuvers of certain kinds, such as generalizations. For example, suppose I wished to attest to Smith's reliability about some subject matter X. I might reel off a long list of claims that Smith makes about X, such as "Smith said p and p," "Smith said q and q," and so on. Or, to make things easy, I might simply say, "Everything that Smith says about X represents the facts." According to sober deflationists, the phrase "represents the facts" allows us to make this generalizing maneuver in a very economical way.

Call a concept that plays a generalizing function of this variety a "generalizing concept." Now, in certain cases when we use representation concepts, such as when we say that a singular proposition represents the facts, these concepts do not play a generalizing function. Whatever else its merits, then, sober quasi realism does not offer a *general* account of how representation concepts work.[29] But suppose that in ordinary moral discourse, representation concepts function as generalizing concepts much of the time. Then we are left with the following puzzle: it is appropriate to apply the concept "being a case of knowledge" (and not simply "being a case of mere belief") to some moral judgment only if and because it is appropriate to apply the concept "being such as to represent the relevant moral facts" to its content. But, according to sober deflationism, to apply the concept "being such as to represent the relevant moral facts" is simply to apply a generalizing concept of a certain kind. But why should the fact that it is appropriate to apply a generalizing concept of this kind to the propositional content of a mental state explain why it is appropriate to think of that mental state as a case of knowledge rather than a mere belief? As best I can tell, this is a question that does not have a satisfactory answer. The fact that representation concepts play a generalizing role seems to have nothing to do with why it is appropriate to think that a mental state to whose content we apply such a concept counts as a case of knowledge rather than mere belief. If this is right, our conclusion regarding sober quasi realism mirrors our conclusion regarding radical quasi realism: the sober quasi-realist account of moral knowledge may satisfy the knowledge platitude, but the reasons that are offered for believing this are of the wrong sort.

My aim in this section has been to see whether sober quasi realism offers us an account of moral knowledge that is more satisfactory than radical quasi realism. I have claimed that it does not. To recapitulate, I have claimed, first, that sober quasi realists offer an account of how we represent moral reality that is no more informative than that of robust realists. This, I have said, is an implication of "going deflationary" about representation. Second, I have argued that sober quasi realists do not offer a satisfactory explanation of why it is appropriate to apply epistemic concepts of certain kinds, such as "being a case of knowledge," to mental states if they are representational in a merely deflationary sense.[30]

5. QUIETEST QUASI REALISM

Robust moral realists, I have conceded, may have to swallow philosophical mysteries, such as how we gain epistemic access to moral reality. Quasi realism, I have suggested, is alluring because it promises to do better than this. If quasi realists are right, we can dispel the mystery surrounding moral knowledge. My argument in the last two sections has been that the quasi-realist promise remains unfulfilled. Provided we accept certain platitudes about knowledge and representation, quasi realism does not offer us a more adequate account of moral knowledge than robust realism. And this, I suggested, is good news for moral realists of all sorts.

Quietist quasi realism—the third and final version of quasi realism I wish to consider—does not claim that it can better account for certain puzzling phenomena in the moral domain. Rather, it claims something much more radical: that the quasi realist's ability to mimic various realist-sounding claims simply dissolves any distinctions we might have thought to exist between realism and quasi realism in the first place. The success of the quasi-realist project, according to quietest quasi realists, is not the vindication of expressivist antirealism but the destruction of the moral realist/antirealist debate. The apparent debate, to return to a passage from Blackburn quoted earlier, "is unreal, since there is no methodology for conducting it" (Blackburn, 1993a, 4).

In his recent book *Truth: A Guide*, Blackburn gives a fuller indication of why he thinks that quasi realism threatens to deconstruct the debate between moral realists and antirealists. For any area of discourse, says Blackburn, realists have a story to tell about what it is to be a realist with respect to that area of discourse. The story goes like this:

> (Story) The commitments in question are capable of strict and literal truth; they describe the world; they answer to or represent (independent) facts of a particular kind; there is a way in which the world is that makes them true or false. These facts are discovered, not created, and they have their own "ontological" and "metaphysical" natures, about which reflection can inform us.

Blackburn maintains that realists must add a further clause to this story. In particular, realists must stipulate that:

> (Meta Story) The terms of Story themselves mark out *the* substantive philosophical position, or theory about the area; they are the terms in which to define the best view of it. There are bad people out there who oppose Story, but they are wrong.[31]

It is crucial, according to Blackburn, to add this further comment on the original Story because "the words of Story might come very cheaply—so cheaply that anybody who voices commitments in the area can say them. They might represent no second-order theoretical stance, but simply be available as a high-flown way of expressing ordinary commitment within the area."[32] In other words, the words of Story can be given a quasi-realist construal. According to the quasi-realist construal of Story, what appear to be second-order theoretical claims about some area of discourse are really expressions of first-order attitudes *within* that area of discourse that carry no commitment to realism. That quasi-realist construals of this kind are available should, Blackburn reminds us, be obvious. We need only remember the lesson taught us by Ramsey's ladder, which is that "*p*" and "it is true that *p*... mean ... the same thing."[33] So, although realists may believe that they are articulating a discernible position when they say "according to our view, *p* really represents the facts," they are not. "Ramsey's ladder," as Blackburn puts it, "raises you nowhere."[34] If this is right, quietest quasi realists believe, we have powerful reason to maintain that moral realists do not mark out a distinctive theory about the moral domain. Since nothing that realists say carves out a discernible position, we simply have no grip on what it is that is supposed to distinguish realist views from their rivals.

There is a great deal to say about quietest quasi realism. For present purposes, I will restrict myself to the following observation: if Blackburn is correct, quietest quasi realism is tempting because expressions such as "*p*," "it is true that *p*," "it is a fact that *p*," and " '*p*' represents the facts" are identical in meaning. I labeled this claim about meaning equivalence "the equivalence thesis." Quietest quasi realists maintain that the equivalence thesis is true. But if our earlier discussion is on the mark, we have excellent reason to believe that this thesis is not true. In fact, it looks pretty clearly false. However, if it is false, then it is not a reason for accepting quietest quasi realism. Admittedly, this is to cast doubt on only one reason to accept quietest quasi realism. But, to my knowledge, it is the only reason that quasi realists offer for accepting quietism. If so, it seems that there is little reason to believe that the debate between moral realists and their rivals will disappear.[35]

NOTES

1. For an account of what the objectivity in question amounts to, see Cuneo (2007), chap. 1, and Enoch (2007). I borrow the term "robust realism" from Enoch. Enoch (forthcoming), Shafer-Landau (2003), and Parfit (forthcoming) offer defenses of robust moral realism.

2. See Oddie (2005), 26, for a statement of a similar argument. Oddie, let me add, is a moral realist.

3. McGinn (1993) defends an approach of this variety.

4. Blackburn (1984, chaps. 5 and 6; 1993a, 1998), Gibbard (2003), Horgan and Timmons (2000), and Timmons (1999) all develop variants of quasi realism.

5. See Gibbard (2003), 20 and 191.

6. See Blackburn (1993a), 7 and chap. 2, (1993b), and (1996).

7. Blackburn (1984), 180, and (1996), 83–84. See also Blackburn (1993a), 4.

8. The phrase is Blackburn's. See Blackburn (1993a), 186, and Wright (1992), 149.

9. See Cuneo (2007), chap. 6.

10. Despite what some quasi realists and commentators seem to claim. See Dreier (2004), 26, and Blackburn (1998), 75.

11. The passages are from Blackburn (1993a), 129; (2002), 128; Gibbard (2003), 18; and Blackburn (1993a), 111 and 175, respectively.

12. The passages are from Blackburn (1996), 92; (1998), 319; (1998), 80; and (1999), 216, respectively.

13. The passage is from Blackburn (1993a), 4.

14. In Cuneo (2007. chap. 6), I consider what I here call "sober" quasi realism in more detail.

15. See Blackburn (1996), 83, for example.

16. See, for example, Blackburn (1993a), chap. 9, and Timmons (1999), chap. 4.

17. Blackburn (1993a), 56.

18. Blackburn (1996), 88.

19. Gibbard (2003), 233, 235.

20. Gibbard's view is presented as an account not of the content of moral judgments but of the content of normative judgments about what, on the whole, one ought to do. Still, Gibbard indicates that he takes his basic approach to transfer to the moral arena. See Gibbard (2003), 8.

21. Three points: First, I assume that the contents of the mental states in question are predicative in character (i.e., of the form there is some x that is F). Second, I shall use expressions of the form "being F" to stand for concepts. By using this convention, I do not mean to suggest that concepts are linguistic entities. Third, unless the context indicates otherwise, when I use the term "represents," I mean "accurately represents."

22. Blackburn (1998), 78, 79, and (1999), 214.

23. I assume that the same noun phrase will be substituted for the schematic letter "p" in each schema.

24. For the argument that according to the disquotational view, it is not sentence types but tokens that are truth bearers, see David (1994), chap. 2, as well as Alston (1996), chap. 1, and Soames (1997).

25. Although I believe that here appearances deceive. See David (1994), chap. 2.

26. See Gibbard (2003), chap. 2.

27. See Cuneo (2007), chap. 5. Some philosophers, such as Chrisman (forthcoming), suggest that there is a sharp difference between theoretical knowledge, which is representational, on the one hand, and practical knowledge, which is not, on the other. Moral knowledge, it is suggested, is not theoretical in character but practical in nature; it is knowledge of how to act. If this view of moral knowledge were correct, one might believe that the knowledge platitude does not govern our understanding of moral knowledge because moral knowledge is not descriptive. I do not have the space to consider this view here. But it seems to me that reflection on the character of games such as baseball reveals the distinction to be overly sharp. Knowledge of how to play baseball is both theoretical and practical; it is knowledge of the relevant norms or rules that govern participation in the game.

28. Horwich (1998a), 123.

29. How, then, do representation concepts work, according to sober quasi realists, when they are applied to singular propositions? Presumably, they work the same way that radical quasi realists believe they work all the time. If this is right, sober quasi realism is subject to the second concern I raised about radical quasi realism.

30. Here is an objection that might be raised: "Your objection supposes that deflationists are in the business of offering explanations of how we acquire moral knowledge. But this is illegitimate. Deflationary views are not in the explanation-giving business. They are designed to vindicate the possibility of moral knowledge without having to explain how moral beliefs represent moral reality." My short reply is this: First, the second objection I raised concerns only why it is appropriate to apply epistemic *concepts* of certain kinds. This, however, is not something that deflationists say resists explanation. Second, the objection I have raised supposes not that deflationary views must explain how we acquire knowledge, but only that their views about knowledge acquisition are assessable from an explanatory point of view. That is, it assumes only that it is legitimate to ask whether deflationism honors well-entrenched assumptions about knowledge, whether it coheres well with the answers we give to "In virtue of what do we know *p*?" questions in other domains, and so forth.

31. Blackburn (2005), 117 and 118.

32. Ibid., 120.

33. Ibid., 121, 70.

34. Ibid., 121.

35. Megan Berglund, Marian David, Rebecca Konyndyk DeYoung, David Enoch, Bill FitzPatrick, John Greco, Brad Majors, Christian Miller, Russ Shafer-Landau, and audiences at the University of British Columbia and the University of Vermont offered helpful comments on an earlier draft of this chapter. I express to them my thanks.

REFERENCES

Alston, William. 1996. *A Realist Conception of Truth.* Ithaca, NY: Cornell University Press.
Blackburn, Simon. 1984. *Spreading the Word.* Oxford: Oxford University Press.
———. 1993a. *Essays in Quasi-Realism.* Oxford: Oxford University Press.
———. 1993b. "Realism: Quasi or Queasy?" In Crispin Wright and John Haldane, eds.,- *Reality, Representation, and Projection.* Oxford: Oxford University Press.

———. 1996. "Securing the Nots." In Walter Sinnott-Armstrong and Mark Timmons, eds., *Moral Knowledge?* Oxford: Oxford University Press.

———. 1998. *Ruling Passions.* Oxford: Oxford University Press.

———. 1999. "Is Objective Moral Justification Possible on a Quasi-realist Foundation?" *Inquiry* 42: 213–28.

———. 2002. "Précis of Ruling Passions." *Philosophy and Phenomenological Research* 65: 124-35.

———. 2005. *Truth: A Guide.* Oxford: Oxford University Press.

Chrisman, Matthew. Forthcoming. "Expressivism, Inferentialism, and Saving the Debate." *Philosophy and Phenomenological Research.*

Cuneo, Terence. 2007. *The Normative Web: An Argument for Moral Realism.* Oxford: Oxford University Press.

David, Marian. 1994. *Correspondence and Disquotation.* Oxford: Oxford University Press.

Dreier, James. 2004. "Meta-ethics and the Problem of Creeping Minimalism." In John Hawthorne, ed., *Philosophical Perspectives, 18, Ethics.* Oxford: Blackwell, 23–44.

Enoch, David. 2007."An Outline of an Argument for Robust Metanormative Realism." In Russ Shafer-Landau, ed., *Oxford Studies in Metaethics*, vol. 2. Oxford: Oxford University Press.

Gibbard, Allan. 2003. *Thinking How to Live.* Cambridge, MA: Harvard University Press.

Horgan, Terence, and Mark Timmons. 2000. "Nondescriptivist Cognitivism: Framework for a New Metaethic." *Philosophical Papers* 99: 121–53.

Horwich, Paul. 1998a. *Meaning.* Oxford: Clarendon Press.

McGinn, Colin. 1993. *Problems in Philosophy.* Oxford: Blackwell.

———. 1996. *Ethics, Evil, and Fiction.* Oxford: Oxford University Press.

Oddie, Graham. 2005. *Value, Reality, and Desire.* Oxford: Oxford University Press.

Parfit, Derek. Forthcoming. *Climbing the Mountain.*

Shafer-Landau, Russ. 2003. *Moral Realism: A Defence.* Oxford: Oxford University Press.

Soames, Scott. 1997. "The Truth about Deflationism." In Ernest Sosa and Enrique Villanueva, eds. *Philosophical Issues, 8, Truth.* Boston: Blackwell.

Timmons, Mark. 1999. *Morality without Foundations.* Oxford: Oxford University Press.

Wright, Crispin. 1992. *Truth and Objectivity.* Cambridge, MA: Harvard University Press.

CHAPTER 9

RELIGIOUS SKEPTICISM

PAUL K. MOSER

SKEPTICISM comes in many different shapes and sizes. Skeptics have doubted the reality of the external world, (other) minds, God, abstract objects, history, the future, causation, and so on. In addition, skeptics have disavowed various cognitively important states: certainty, knowledge, justified belief, and reliable belief, among others. Skepticism can also come in different strengths. *Modal* skeptics disavow that a cognitive state, such as knowledge, is even possible, and *actuality* skeptics disavow that a cognitive state, such as knowledge, is actual. This is just the beginning of distinctions about skepticism, but we will not delay with more taxonomy. Instead, we will turn directly to religious skepticism and its prospects.

We will see that religious skepticism is not as easy and comfortable as many philosophers have supposed. In particular, we will see that we have no easily generalizable support for religious skepticism about the reality of God. Even if a person were to lack adequate evidence for God's reality, this person would have no ready way to generalize to the truth of religious skepticism for people in general.

1. SKEPTICISM AND RELIGION

A version of skepticism is unclear to the extent that its object (namely, what the skepticism is *about*) is unclear. *Religious* skepticism is skepticism about religion. What, however, is religion? The term "religion" is as unclear as any in the English language. When is something a religion, and when is it not? English language users sometimes call even a sport or a hobby a religion: "Baseball is his religion," or

"Knitting is her religion." How, then, could all of the following qualify as religion: Judaism, Christianity, Islam, Buddhism, Hinduism, Confucianism, Taoism, baseball, knitting? They clearly lack a common goal or object. Perhaps, however, they sometimes share an underlying attitude. That is, a distinctive kind of *commitment* may be common to these diverse phenomena, namely, a *religious* commitment.

We now shift the question. When is a *commitment* religious, and when is it not? Whatever the answer, this shift redirects skepticism to concern a particular kind of commitment. In doing so, the shift makes skepticism question something about a psychological attitude. Let us suppose, if only for the sake of discussion, that a commitment is religious for a person if and only if the commitment is intrinsic (that is, not merely instrumental toward something else) and intended to be life defining (that is, intended to be essential to living) for that person. We can imagine a person for whom baseball or knitting is, however strangely, an object of religious commitment in this sense. (In reality, there are T-shirts in Chicago and elsewhere that proclaim, "Baseball is Life"; see also Evans and Herzog 2002.) Religious skeptics, in this case, would express doubt about a religious commitment. The doubt could concern the commitment in question in this way, for instance: is the commitment ill advised rather than well advised? This is a question about value, in effect: is the religious commitment in question *bad* rather than *good*?

Goodness and badness, like many normative realities, come in different species. We can distinguish *moral* goodness, *cognitive* goodness, *prudential* goodness, *aesthetic* goodness, and so on. (For details, see Moser 1989, chap. 5; 1993, chap. 4.) Religious skeptics can disavow various species of value with respect to religious commitment. A religious commitment could be *factually* bad with regard to capturing reality. We may say that it lacks "factual" goodness in that case. A religious commitment could also be *cognitively* bad in virtue of lacking the status of knowledge or of justified belief (perhaps owing to inadequate evidential support, even if it turns out to be factual, i.e., true). In addition, a religious commitment could be *morally* bad in virtue of bringing about moral harm, such as social injustice or individual selfishness. Religious skepticism regarding factual goodness and cognitive goodness has dominated philosophical discussion. It will occupy our attention here.

We will set aside *semantic* religious skepticism, the position that dismisses religious claims on the ground that they are semantically meaningless. Nothing whatever speaks in favor of such semantic skepticism regarding prominent religious claims. One could, with as much plausibility, reject religious skepticism on the ground that it is itself semantically defective, that is, meaningless. A certain lack of imagination underlies semantic religious skepticism regarding prominent religious claims. The skeptic who reports that he cannot imagine, for instance, that the God of traditional monotheism exists needs remedial attention in the area of imagining circumstances. The deficiency here lies with the skeptic, not with the semantic status of monotheism. Sometimes this deficiency is accompanied by a dubious approach to semantic meaning, such as Humean empiricism or positivist verificationism about meaning. We are, in any case, well advised to move on.

The factuality of the object of a religious commitment serves as a common target for religious skeptics. In the case of baseball or knitting, skeptical doubt would be strange indeed. People involved in modern society do not usually doubt the reality of baseball or knitting. When they do, we are inclined to question their sanity or at least their sense of humor. A skeptic might introduce global doubt that bears on baseball or knitting, but that would be a dramatic move well beyond religious skepticism. (It would definitely upset baseball and knitting fans too, given the price of admission these days.) We will not wander into that far-flung region where anything whatever seems to go (see Moser 2000, 2004b). Our topic is much closer to home, where our decisions make a very important difference.

For current purposes, a certain irrelevance characterizes skepticism about religious commitments that have no peculiar object. Consider, for instance, a morality-focused nontheistic religious commitment held by some contemporary proponents of Confucianism. Their religious commitment focuses on moral virtues and has no role for a personal god or any other supernatural object. (This was evidently not the attitude of Confucius himself, for what it is worth.) Suppose that a skeptic questioned the factuality of the object of these Confucianists' religious commitment. This would amount to *moral* skepticism. Our topic, however, is *religious* skepticism that does not reduce to moral skepticism. The most common target of such skepticism is *theistic* religious commitment. As a result, we will focus on skepticism about theistic religious commitment, in particular, skepticism about its object: God. This focus includes doubt about the reality of God and doubt about the cognitive value of endorsements of God's reality.

2. GOD AND EVIDENCE

The term "God" is as unclear as the term "religion." At times, it seems that each person has his or her own distinctive understanding of the term. Actually, however, the situation is not quite so fractured. Many people use the term "God" as a *title* that signifies an authoritatively and morally perfect creator who is worthy of worship, including full adoration, love, and trust. If the term "God" is a title rather than a name, it can be fully intelligible even if there is no titleholder, that is, even if God does not exist. This use of the term thus allows for the intelligibility of familiar skeptical questions about the existence of God. It also fits with some prominent understandings of the monotheism of Judaism and Christianity. Let us, then, use the term in that manner, as a preeminent title that may or may not be satisfied by an actual titleholder. To avoid even the appearance of begging the main question against skeptics, I will typically talk of what God "would" do or be like, where this is short for "would if God actually exists."

Religious skeptics about God usually raise doubt that there is a titleholder for the term "God." This is, indeed, central to their calling as religious skeptics. Their familiar allegation is that people lack *adequate evidence* (for cognitively reasonable belief) that God exists. This charge is particularly cognitively bold if it concerns *all* people. The allegation is cognitive in that it concerns evidence, and the alleged lack of adequate evidence underlies doubt regarding *the reality* of God, that is, doubt that God exists. These religious skeptics assume that if we lack adequate evidence of the reality of God, then, from a cognitive viewpoint, we should doubt (i.e., suspend judgment) that God exists. If we define "adequate evidence" suitably broadly, this assumption is true and even cognitively compelling. We will not quarrel with skeptics on this front.

Belief that God exists would be evidentially arbitrary and thus cognitively irrational in the absence of adequate supporting evidence, even if it is true that God exists. Mere factuality does not yield *cognitive* merit for a person's belief; many claims are true but still without cognitive merit. So, the requirement of adequate evidence is cognitively impeccable, at least if its notion of adequate evidence is suitably broad and free of unduly narrow empiricist and rationalist strictures. Since a concern about adequate evidence defines mainline religious skepticism, this chapter will be devoted to that concern. We will not be concerned, then, with the question whether theistic belief makes believers feel better.

How should we understand the demand for adequate evidence? Many religious skeptics set the standard very high indeed. One very high standard demands *cognitive reproducibility*. Given this standard, adequate evidence of God's reality must be reproducible either for a single person or for a group of people. If someone asks, for instance, whether I know how to speak English, I can supply the needed evidence *by speaking English*, loud and clear, in the person's presence. In addition, I can reproduce this evidence for myself and for the person in question. I can simply speak English again and again until my interlocutor yields or departs. I have control over the production of the needed evidence. Given control over evidence, I can meet the demand of cognitive reproducibility.

Must evidence be under our control? Certainly not. Much of the original evidence in cosmology, astrophysics, and geology, among other sciences, is neither under our control nor reproducible by us, even if we can supply helpful analogies. We cannot control or reproduce, for instance, the original evidence of the big bang origin of the universe billions of years ago. We lack the power to do so; the original evidence is literally beyond our powers of actual reproduction, and we cannot change this. Still, the original evidence is real and available to us indirectly via inference. Likewise, if I whisper a secret to you, you have evidence from your experience of hearing my whisper, but you cannot thereby control or reproduce the original evidence (given that you cannot control me and, as it happens, I refuse to repeat my whisper). The original evidence in your experience of hearing is real indeed but beyond your control. We should reject, then, any requirement that evidence must be under our control or reproducible by us. As a result, we should reject any skeptical argument assuming that if evidence of God's reality is not reproducible, then it is not genuine evidence. Our receiving evidence can be free of our being able to reproduce that evidence. On reflection, it is amazing that any mature adult would think otherwise. Still, hasty generalization does its damage in this quarter, inspiring and reproducing many wayward religious skeptics.

In popular discussions of theism, some skeptics demand "proof" of God's existence, sometimes without clarification of what they mean by the overused word "proof." Let us define "proof," for the sake of intelligibility, as a deductively valid argument with true premises. Must adequate evidence of God's reality include such an argument? Certainly not. Very little of the evidence for what we know includes deductively valid argument. Most of our empirical knowledge, for instance, rests on evidence free of deductively valid arguments. Likewise, most of your knowledge about yourself and about other people does not arise from proof. Typically, proof resides in the domains of logic and mathematics, but the claim that God exists is definitely not a claim of logic or mathematics. God, by hypothesis, is a personal agent, not an axiom or a theorem; it is a serious category mistake to suppose otherwise. In addition, we lack not only proof but also adequate evidence for thinking that adequate evidence of God's existence must include proof as just defined. Let us not be hindered, then, by any skeptical demand for proof of God's existence. Instead, we will let the relevant *notion* of God guide the suitable cognitive parameters. Otherwise, we risk begging some important questions about God's reality and evidence thereof.

Evidence of God's reality, by definition, is evidence of the reality of a morally perfect agent who is worthy of worship. Where might we find such evidence? In nature? In history? In books? In ourselves? People have looked far and wide for evidence of God, even in their free time, and skeptics typically remain unconvinced. Famously, Bertrand Russell (1970) anticipated his response if after death he met God: "God, you gave us insufficient evidence." That sounds blaming, to put it mildly. Russell might have considered a bit more modesty in the presence of an all-knowing God. At any rate, we now face a question widely neglected by religious skeptics. If God would choose to give us evidence of God's reality, what parameters, or defining features, for the evidence would God observe?

It is not obvious that if God exists, God *owes* us evidence of God's reality, just as God would not be morally obligated to redeem humans. At least, it is not clear what would yield such an evidential obligation on God's part. If we assume that God would be inherently merciful even toward enemies, however, we may assume that God's character would incline (but not morally obligate) God to give us, in our desperate situation, evidence of God's reality. If we assume, accordingly, that God would choose to give us such evidence, we should ask about the parameters for this evidence.

Clearly, the evidence would have to be suitable to God's character as morally perfect and worthy of worship. If, for instance, we were to face a world of *nothing but* unrelenting pain and suffering, we would have some evidence against God's reality. We would then have some evidence against the reality of a God who truly cares for humans, and we would have no positive indication of a God who truly cares for us. The actual world, though deeply troubled and torn, is clearly not a world of nothing but unrelenting pain and suffering. It has its silver, if subtle, lining of good, even when its evil seems to have a monopoly. Consider, for instance, a mother joyously caring for her newborn child. That is a silver lining indeed, if anything is.

What would evidence suitable to God's character look like? In other words, what kind of evidence would fit with the reality of a God worthy of worship. Let us consider a more specific question: what kind of evidence would be given to us by a morally perfect God worthy of worship? The answer depends on what God would intend to do with the world, and God's intention would depend on how the world actually stands in relation to God's purposes for it. In any case, it would be God's prerogative to reveal the things of God *in God's preferred ways* (in keeping, of course, with God's character). We must beware, then, of uncritically demanding that (evidence of) God's reality must meet *our* preferred standards of evidence. Instead, our evidential demands must be attentive to what would be God's nature and resulting purposes. Russell and many other religious skeptics have overlooked this basic cognitive lesson. As we will see, it is an uncomfortable lesson indeed for such skeptics.

3. God and Judgment

Let us move further away from abstraction, so as not to languish in sterile generalities (an occupational hazard in academic, especially philosophical, discussions of "God"). The God of Jewish-Christian monotheism is widely disavowed by religious skeptics. Even so, many Jews and Christians regard this God as worthy of worship and thus as perfectly loving and inherently good. So, in the absence of a better candidate, we will give some attention to the nature of this God. This God, we are told, seeks to redeem (i.e., to reconcile to God) a world alienated from its creator and thereby gripped by moral failure and personal dying and death. The alienation of humans arises, at least in part, from their selfish willfulness, their asserting their own wills in conflict with what is, or at least would be, willed by the perfectly loving God. All human life is surrounded by this alienation and tainted by it too. We will pursue this approach to God to see if it can answer and even challenge religious skeptics.

We will not simply assume that the Jewish-Christian God exists, because that would gain nothing. Instead, we will ask what we should expect cognitively regarding God if this God exists. We can then ask if our world and our experience fit well with this expectation. We will then be able to ask where our evidence actually points, either toward God or not toward God.

Skeptics are very rarely, if ever, challenged by a case for the God of deism or minimal theism. We will move beyond minimal theism and look for the consequences for religious skepticism. Let us continue, then, if only for the sake of argument, with the story of robust monotheism found in Jewish and Christian theism. If we ignore this story for the sake of attenuated, minimal theism, we will fail to appreciate the bearing of robust theism on religious skepticism. Settling for minimal theism, philosophers often miss this opportunity, but we will seize it here. At least we will then apprehend what kind of theism is in question or, instead, is putting us in question. Such a reversal of who is judging and who has a right to judge is characteristic of robust Jewish-Christian monotheism. It takes any sophomoric easiness out of skepticism.

Humans, as a group, seek their ultimate security and contentment from things other than God, typically from things in the world that seem to offer satisfaction. The familiar list goes on and on: health, wealth, survival, education, family, reputation, physical appearance, entertainment, self-serving religion, sexuality, human friendship, and so on. In perfect love, God would place the world under judgment to try to save people from dying with their idols, their insecure replacements for God. God would try to bring people to recognize the ultimate futility of the idols offered by the world apart from God. This would be integral to the attempted divine redemption, or salvation, of humans.

The theme of divine *judgment* is Christian as well as Jewish. For instance, the apostle Paul (a Jewish Christian) echoes a theme from Ecclesiastes:

> the creation was subjected to futility, not by its own will, but by the will of the One who subjected it, in [this One's] hope that the creation itself will be liberated from its bondage to decay and brought into the glorious freedom of the children of God.
> (Romans 8:20–21; translations from the Greek New Testament are my own)

Many religious skeptics have raised doubts about God's existence on the basis of the reality of extensive pain and suffering in our world. They doubt that a perfectly loving God would allow the pain and suffering in this world. Of course, we humans are not (nor should we expect ourselves to be) in a position to explain why all the pain and suffering in this world occur or are allowed to occur. Our explanatory and cognitive resources are much too limited for the difficult task. Even so, we can consider that some pain and suffering result from the way that creation has been "subjected to futility."

The created world, according to Jewish-Christian monotheism, was made to break down, as in the case of physical entropy, in order that (according to God's hope) all observers would learn that their lasting security and contentment will not be found in any part of the created world. Lasting security and contentment must be found elsewhere, and according to the apostle Paul, "the children of God" will find it in God rather than in the created world. They will then be liberated from the idols of this world. We can thus make some sense of why a perfectly loving God would allow certain kinds of pain and suffering. God's hope that people will be liberated from deadly idols could make good use of allowing pain and suffering among us rather than protecting us from all pain and suffering. This would be part of God's redemptive judgment. God could still reserve his decisive judgment for a special redemptive situation: the innocent sacrificial death of God's unique Son, Jesus (on which see Moser 2007a, 2008, chap. 3).

The prospect of divine redemptive judgment bears importantly on our acquiring evidence of God's reality. As part of creation, humans too would be under divine judgment for their selfish, anti-God ways. So, we should expect that our coming to know God's reality would have a central place for divine judgment of us and our self-serving ways. We humans are ourselves our most common idol, even though we obviously cannot supply lasting security and contentment for ourselves. We cannot even supply lasting subsistence for ourselves. This is painfully obvious, if anything is. As a result, in redemptive love, God would subject *us* to futility owing to our pretensions of self-reliance. This futility would include our impending physical death, when we will meet our end in this world. God's hope, out of redemptive love, would be that we see the futility of our self-reliance and come to our senses, thereby turning to trust in God. Evidence of God's reality would fit with such divine hope. We will consider how.

The God of deism, the cosmic watchmaker, would perhaps settle for providing us with evidence that the God of deism exists. This God would have no message of redemptive judgment but would be content to have people acknowledge, on the basis of evidence from creation, that the creator exists. The Jewish-Christian God would not be reduced to the God of deism; the former would, in redemptive love, intervene too much for the latter. In addition, the Jewish-Christian God would not be impressed at all with belief that God exists. The Epistle of James, one of the most Jewish writings in the New Testament, makes a related point regarding mere belief that the God of Jewish-Christian monotheism exists: "Even the demons believe [that God is one], and shudder" (James 2:19). The Jewish-Christian God would seek a human response that goes beyond belief, and even knowledge, that God exists. The distinctive evidence provided by this God would contribute to that goal. We will see later what this goal would include. Philosophers and religious skeptics typically miss this crucial lesson, but we will give it full attention. Otherwise, we will fail to give robust monotheism a fair hearing. It rarely gets a fair hearing from religious skeptics or from philosophers. In the interest of such a fair hearing, we will make things uncomfortable for ourselves.

4. Spectator versus Authoritative Evidence

The Jewish-Christian God, unlike the God of deism, would not approach us as people who will fully welcome evidence of the reality of God. The evidence in question concerns a God who, out of unselfish love, would challenge our selfish, deadly ways. We would not start out as friends of this God. We rather would be at odds with this God, given our selfish ways; indeed, the notion of "enemies" of God readily comes to mind. The Jewish-Christian God would thus come to us with redemptive judgment of us and our ways for our own good. (We will not confuse such judgment with destructive *condemnation*; there is a big difference between the two.) So, this God would not come to us with *spectator evidence*, that is, evidence not demanding that its recipients yield their wills to the source of the evidence.

Instead, the God in question would come to us with *authoritative evidence*, that is, evidence demanding that we yield our wills to the source of the evidence in question. Indeed, this God would come with *perfectly* authoritative evidence: evidence demanding that we yield our wills to the perfect source of the evidence in question, that is, God. (A merely human moral leader might offer us authoritative evidence by making a demand on our wills, but this would fall short of perfectly authoritative evidence. In addition, God's authoritative status would entail *worthiness* of authority in all relevant areas.) The God in question, then, would be no friend of cognitive voyeurism regarding divine reality, given the demand that we yield our wills to God's perfect will. So, this God would be at odds with ordinary philosophical and skeptical ways of approaching the question of evidence of God's existence. This God would recognize that human inquirers suffer volitional (will-related), as well as cognitive, impediments. (For elaboration on this theme, see Moser 2002, 2008.)

Religious skeptics typically miss the main aim suitable to the Jewish-Christian God when they demand that God provide spectator evidence. They overlook that faced with our world, the morally perfect titleholder of "God" would be (*if* he chooses to save us) a God of redemption who comes to us, not with spectator evidence, but rather with perfectly authoritative evidence. Spectator evidence from God would allow God to be domesticated and taken for granted by us in our self-serving ways. Such evidence would thus risk serious harm to us and fail as a means of genuine redemption. In choosing to redeem us, the true God would be a God of perfectly authoritative evidence. So, this God would have a definite purpose beyond our knowing that God exists: the purpose of bringing us into loving and obedient fellowship with God. We should thus expect the titleholder of "God" to offer evidence of God's reality, if any is offered, that advances this redemptive purpose. Divine redemption need not be comfortable for us in its being good for us. On the contrary, we should expect it to exceed our comfort zone.

The main problem of divine redemption would be that we need to be saved from ourselves. We would need to be saved from our deadly self-reliance into obedient trust (on God's terms) of the God who could save us from our selfishness and impending personal death. (For elaboration on this twofold human predicament, in connection with evidence of God's reality, see Moser 2007b, 2008.) Unlike spectator evidence, perfectly authoritative evidence would attend to this predicament. It would thus work by *cognitive grace*, a free, unmerited gift from God, rather than by any human earning that obligates God. It would counter our powers of intellectual earning in order to deflate intellectual pride. It would thus demonstrate our weakness, our self-inadequacy, regarding finding the true God on our own. The God of perfectly authoritative evidence thus would not fit well with the god of the philosophers and the natural theologians. (On the significance of cognitive grace, see Moser 2006, 2008, chap. 2.)

We could not think or reason our way to the Jewish-Christian God by our own resources, as if we did not need a revelation from this God via perfectly authoritative evidence. The true God would be too different from us, in terms of moral character and cognitive subtlety and depth, to be at our convenient cognitive disposal. So, we must contrast (a) the attempt to argue our way to knowledge of God's reality on our own with (b) our need to receive perfectly authoritative evidence from God's free, unearned call to us to live as God's dependent children. This lesson is altogether foreign to how philosophers, including skeptics, typically think of evidence, but this does not count against its truth at all. Instead, it ultimately yields, we will see, a new challenge to religious skeptics. As I suggested, the things of God need not be comfortable for us.

God would need to supply the perfectly authoritative evidence of God's reality, because God alone would be perfectly authoritative and have the prerogative to decide, in accordance with perfect divine character, what exactly this evidence is. According to many first-century Jewish Christians, God chose to supply perfectly authoritative evidence through his divine Son, Jesus of Nazareth. This evidence, according to these Christians, was ratified by God's own Spirit, the Holy Spirit. (On the epistemological role of God's Spirit, see Moser 2003, 2008, chap. 3.) In John's Gospel, Jesus characterizes the cognitive and moral role of God's Spirit as follows:

> When [the Spirit] comes, he will convict the world of guilt regarding sin, righteousness, and judgment. . . . [W]hen . . . the Spirit of truth, comes, he will lead you into all truth. He will not speak on his own, but will speak only what he hears, and he will announce to you what is yet to come. He will bring glory to me, because he will take from me and announce this to you.
>
> (John 16:8,13–14)

God's own Spirit, according to this portrait, has the cognitive role of making things known regarding God and Jesus. Jesus is presented as God's unique revealer who calls us (a) to receive God's Spirit of redemption through trust (that is, faith) in God and (b) thereby to live as God's beloved obedient children. This theme emerges elsewhere in the New Testament, including 1 Corinthians 2:11–12 and Romans 8:14–16; compare Matthew 16:16–17. It captures what Jesus is all about and it has, as we will see, revolutionary cognitive implications. We have entered strange cognitive territory, where the true God may lurk. We do well to linger here a bit to examine the evidential situation.

God's Spirit, on the portrait under review, would noncoercively "lead" people to Jesus and his Father as their Lord and their God, and the experience of "being led" in this way would be cognitively significant. It would include the perfectly authoritative call to relinquish our own selfish willfulness for the unselfish will of the living God. This elusive call would work through conscience and would not be reducible to spectator evidence. It would come with moral challenge, even if we dislike and dismiss it. (On the role of conscience in God's call, see Forsyth 1912.) Our failure to hear this authoritative call may be the result of our not wanting to hear it on God's terms of unselfish love. We often prefer, for instance, *not* to have to forgive, to be thankful for, or to love our enemies. (Check any daily newspaper.) It seems easier, or at least more in our own interest, to suppress and ignore any call from God for us to live as obedient children of God who reflect, if imperfectly, perfect divine love. God's call of perfect love would be anything but comfortable, given our selfish ways. Still, goodness does not reduce to comfort.

In our skeptical moments, we sometimes ask: God, are you there at all? Are you truly *with us*? Instead, in redemptive love, God would ask us: Are you truly *with me* in your will, as well as in your thought? If we are not, spectator evidence of God's reality would only domesticate God's sacred reality, because it would not challenge us to submit to God as the Lord of our lives. The providing of such spectator evidence would be akin to what Jesus called "casting pearls before swine." Only harm would be done, because God would become at best a cognitive idol for us, an object of cognitive voyeurism to be used by us as *we* wish. We have enough such idols. For the sake of redemptive love, God would preserve his holy love and not trivialize it as if knowing God were an optional spectator sport. As a result, in redemptive judgment, God would hide his ways from those who are "wise and intelligent" on their own terms (cf. Matt. 11:25–27; 1 Cor. 1:19–21). He would find nothing to gain in revealing himself to prideful supposed cognitive superiors who are not volitionally ready for needed divine revelation.

Perfectly authoritative evidence, we have noted, would demand that we yield our wills to the perfect source of the evidence in question, namely, God. Such demanding would include an authoritative but noncoercive *call* to us to yield to God. It would require a personal source, an intentional agent, who has a will and a purpose. In this case, the purpose would be to have us freely yield to God's life-giving will as opposed to our own deadly selfish willfulness. So, nonpersonal evidence (such as that from mountains, sunsets, and biological complexity) cannot be perfect (or imperfect) authoritative evidence; it lacks the needed will and call from a personal agent. Accordingly, the kinds of evidence offered by familiar first-cause, design, and ontological arguments for God's existence are nonpersonal and thus not perfectly authoritative evidence. They lack a demand, a call, to yield our selfish willfulness to the unselfish will of God. They thus are spectator evidence at best, and leave us with no challenge from God. They are not the kinds of evidence a perfectly loving God of redemption would supply to humans, because they are extraneous to what would be God's redemptive purpose.

A key challenge for us from a perfectly loving God would be an authoritative call to *repent and to obey faithfully*: to turn our wills obediently toward God's unselfish, perfectly loving will that offers everlasting life with God. In receiving God's will as preeminent, we would acknowledge God as *our* God, as Lord of *our* lives. We would thereby acknowledge our status as creatures dependent on God. In that case, we *should* renounce our pretensions to be in charge of our lives, although mere knowledge that God exists would not make such renunciation automatic. My knowing that something is so, here as elsewhere, does not entail my yielding my will to another will. Authoritative evidence from God, in virtue of its including a call to yield to God, would thus differ in kind from the types of spectator evidence common to traditional natural theology and philosophy of religion. In fact, traditional natural theology and philosophy of religion have neglected authoritative evidence, including perfectly authoritative evidence, for the sake of spectator evidence. As a result, religious skeptics have not been adequately challenged. We are in the process of correcting this deficiency now.

We should oppose any view implying that one's *having conclusive evidence* of God's reality requires one's *obediently yielding* to God's call to faithful obedience. Any such view is clearly too demanding regarding one's having conclusive evidence of divine reality. One could have conclusive evidence of God's existence but resolutely hate and consistently oppose God on all fronts. In particular, one could acknowledge and receive God's call to faithful obedience and volitional fellowship, on the basis of conclusive evidence, but intentionally disobey the call. I find no convincing reason of any kind to suggest otherwise.

In contrast with authoritative evidence, spectator evidence makes it too easy for people to run away from any authoritative call from God. We can assess spectator evidence without assessing who we would be before God, that is, people under God's redemptive judgment. Spectator evidence easily allows us to ignore any divine call to us to repent of our selfish willfulness for the sake of God's perfectly loving will. It thus easily allows us to ignore what would be a redemptive God's main purpose for us: to be made new by the power of God's will as we die to our selfish willfulness and live as God's dependent children. Spectator evidence easily allows us to treat God as just another undisturbing object of our intellectual reflection. It thus allows us easily to ignore any God of redemptive judgment. It replaces any such God with a deadly idol, typically a reflection of ourselves. Our self-made gods end up looking a lot like us.

How, exactly, would God call us to repent? This is a dangerous question if it assumes that we are in a position to explain exactly how God would work in the world with regard to God's self-revelation. Clearly, given our serious cognitive limitations, we have no reason to suppose that we are in such a position. A recurring theme of Jewish-Christian theism is that we are not in such a position (see, for example, Job 38–40; John 3:7–8; 1 Cor. 2:6–16). God's ways of self-revelation would often leave us without an exact explanation of how the self-revelation arose. On reflection, this is not surprising at all. A perfectly loving redemptive God would be committed to self-revelation but not thereby to revealing an exact *explanation* of how the self-revelation arose. The former does not require the latter. God could call us to repent, for instance, and leave us in the explanatory dark regarding exactly how God calls us to repent. Explanatory "how" questions, then, can be misleading regarding God's ways, owing to a false assumption about our explanatory and cognitive resources. This lesson parallels a more familiar lesson about explanatory "why" questions regarding God's ways, particularly regarding why God would allow evil. (On the parallel lesson about evil, see Howard-Snyder 1996.)

Even so, we are not completely in the dark regarding what could be God's ways of making demands on us. We are all familiar, for instance, with moral demands found in our conscience. Some of these demands go against our own preferences; they do not arise from our individual wills or even the common will of our peer group. We see a clear example of this in the case of a lone moral reformer who, after having had his or her own will morally corrected, speaks against societal racism or some other widespread injustice. Some of the Hebrew prophets may fall into this category. Some of our own peers may too; Mother Teresa of Calcutta readily comes to mind. The moral demands found in conscience can serve as ways for God's will to be communicated to us. We must use discernment toward the various demands of conscience, however, since our conscience can be corrupted and confused. Still, the presence of bad input does not preclude the presence of good input. It would be unreasonable, even logically fallacious, to suppose otherwise.

Divine use of perfectly authoritative evidence could account for God's appearing at times to be cognitively subtle, elusive, and even hidden. (On the relevance of divine hiddenness to atheism, see Moser 2004a; cf. Moser 2002, 2008, chap. 2.) When we disregard perfectly authoritative evidence, perhaps for the sake of more comfortable spectator evidence, we make ourselves poorly positioned to receive in a salient manner what would be evidence characteristic of God's reality. We then become unsuited to receive the authoritative evidence in question, in much the way that our refusing to open our eyes would block much salient perceptual evidence from reaching us. In excluding perfectly authoritative evidence, we would risk harm, even to ourselves, because we would exclude any good, life-giving creator-creature relationship God offers us. To the extent that we block perfectly authoritative evidence of God, God would appear (at best) to be cognitively subtle, elusive, and even hidden. Is, then, the key cognitive shortcoming with *religious skeptics* rather than with God? Religious skeptics rarely, if ever, consider this question seriously. This deficiency typically stems from inadequate cognitive modesty regarding the question of God's existence. Appropriate cognitive modesty requires that we be open to what would be God's self-revelation *on God's terms*, even if God's terms take us beyond comfortable spectator evidence to perfectly authoritative evidence.

5. VOLITIONAL KNOWLEDGE OF GOD

Spectator evidence is *volitionally casual* in that it does not demand that we yield our wills to the source of such evidence. In this regard, it allows for volitional promiscuity. Spectator evidence of God would thus allow casual access to God, with no demand on our wills relative to God's will. It would thereby neglect God's status as supremely and perfectly authoritative for us in terms of the direction of our wills.

We now can ask why the human will matters at all in our receiving evidence of God's reality. The answer is found in what would be a perfectly loving God's redemptive purpose if such a God were to choose to redeem humans. This purpose would include our *volitionally knowing God as perfectly authoritative Lord*: that is, knowing God as Lord in a way that we submit, even if imperfectly, to God as the one whose will is perfectly and thus supremely authoritative. Such volitional knowing would not approach God as a self-serving idol made in our own image. Instead, it would include our submission to God as perfectly authoritative even over our own wills. As long as I would refuse to acknowledge God's will as perfectly and supremely authoritative for us, I would refuse to acknowledge God as God. In addition, as long as I would refuse to submit to God as the one whose will is perfectly authoritative, I would thereby block myself from volitionally knowing God as perfectly authoritative Lord. This would interfere both with the aforementioned divine redemptive purpose and with the receiving of any evidence of divine reality dependent on one's yielding to that purpose.

We find a suitable cognitive (as well as ethical) model in Jesus' reported response to God in the Garden of Gethsemane: "Not what I will, but what You will" (Mk. 14:36). This was no casual concession to God. Jesus was conceding to God his upcoming torturous death by Roman crucifixion. He was yielding his will, even his very life, completely to God as one whose will is perfectly and thus supremely authoritative. Such yielding of one's will to God does not entail extinguishing one's own will or being left without a will; it is rather a matter of conforming one's will to God's will, or at least allowing one's will to be conformed to God's will. If we recast the appropriation of divine evidence volitionally, on the Gethsemane model, we are left with volitional knowledge *sub specie crucis*: a manner of volitionally knowing God's reality that reflects the volitional perspective of Jesus on his way to the cross. This volitional cognitive model is hinted at in the remark attributed to Jesus in John 7:17: "If anyone wills to do God's will, he will know whether my teaching comes from God or whether I speak on my own."

Willingness to submit to God, if imperfectly, is central to volitionally knowing God as perfectly authoritative Lord. It is the avenue to knowledge of God's reality on the basis of perfectly authoritative evidence. In seeking to be known volitionally as God (rather than as an object of casual speculation or voyeurism), a perfectly loving God would tailor evidence of God's reality to the divinely desired volitional yielding of potential knowers. This would advance God's redemptive aim to transform selfish human wills without domesticating evidence of God's authoritative sacred reality. Even if volitional factors figure in knowing humans as persons, we have no basis for yielding to other humans as *perfectly* authoritative. God alone, given a perfect moral character, would merit such submission.

Volitional knowledge of God as perfectly authoritative Lord calls for a cognitive taxonomy beyond the familiar options of rationalism and empiricism. Pure rationalism about knowledge of God's reality implies that human reason is the source of knowledge of God's reality, whereas pure empiricism about knowledge of God's reality implies that human (sensory or perceptual) experience is the source of knowledge of God's reality. *Volitionalism* about knowledge of God's reality, in contrast, implies that the human will is a central human source, or avenue, of conclusive evidence and knowledge of God's reality. More accurately, it implies that the yielding of the human will to (the demand of) perfectly authoritative evidence from God is a central source, or avenue, *within humans* of proper knowledge of God. (God alone, of course, would be the *superhuman* origin of human evidence and knowledge of God's reality.) Volitionalism thus gives a role to perfectly authoritative evidence that is neglected by pure rationalism and pure empiricism. It excludes the dominance of spectator evidence found in such rationalism and empiricism.

6. Skeptical Worries and Tests

Skeptics will doubtless ask how we are to test for the reliability of perfectly authoritative evidence. The question seems plausible, but we must be cautious not to impose tests at odds conceptually with what is being tested: the reality of a perfectly loving God who would challenge us with perfectly authoritative evidence. If we aim to make a perfectly loving God jump through hoops of our own making, we are bound to be disappointed. Such a God would not play our intellectual games, given that our intellectual games (including the ways we set our cognitive standards) typically insulate us from being challenged by God.

God would not owe any human the role of a supposedly neutral judge over God, even in the cognitive domain. In addition, God would not owe humans spectator evidence of divine reality *before* he makes authoritative demands on them. Humans do indeed need evidence of who God is, but a perfectly loving God could, and would, supply all needed evidence in a context of perfectly authoritative evidence. This would be in keeping with a divine redemptive plan to transform human wills rather than to leave us as dying selfish spectators.

Religious skeptics, in agreement with many advocates of natural theology, will insist that we begin with "mere-existence arguments" concerning God. Their demand will be that we consider only spectator evidence and omit any consideration of perfectly authoritative evidence. This, however, seems misguided. In the case of a perfectly loving God, the crucial cognitive role of a perfectly authoritative and loving character must not be bracketed for the sake of mere-existence arguments. The present approach holds this cognitive role, thus preserving the explanatory, psychological, and existential richness of evidence that would be supplied by a perfectly loving God who opts for human redemption. Genuine existence evidence regarding the Jewish-Christian God would come not as a needed preliminary to, but instead directly *through*, the good news of what God has done for us and demands of us by way of redemption. The ground for this approach is straight-forward: proper conviction of God's reality would come via perfectly authoritative evidence that challenges humans to yield to the transforming power of a perfectly loving God. So, robust monotheism would begin not with mere-existence evidence but rather with perfectly authoritative evidence that purportedly calls people to submit to God as perfectly authoritative Lord. This approach will avoid the risk of being diverted to deism or mere theism. It will also avoid the implausible result that a person must be able to follow intricate arguments to receive evidence of God's reality.

Some religious skeptics will worry that perfectly authoritative evidence would not include a non-question-begging argument for God's reality. This, however, is no real problem because the reality of evidence, even evidence adequate for the justification condition for knowledge, does not depend on a non-question-begging argument or on an argument of any kind. For example, suppose that I do not have a non-question-begging argument for my belief that I am thinking now, at least relative to an extreme skeptic's thoroughgoing questions. Still, I have cognitively good evidence from my current experience, which is not an argument of any sort, that I am thinking now. (In addition, as it happens, I *am* thinking now.) The unbridled skeptical demand for "argument" of a preferred sort often blinds skeptics from seeing that "evidence" is not automatically reducible to an argument (see Moser 1989).

Whether an argument is non-question-begging may vary with the variable interrogative features of an exchange, namely, with the questions actually raised in an exchange. Evidence itself, however, is not exchange sensitive in this way. A person's *having* evidence does not entail *giving* an answer of any kind. So, we should not be troubled if we lack a non-question-begging argument relative to an extreme skeptic's questions (see Moser 2004b for problems facing extreme skep-ticism and a non-question-begging reply to such skepticism). We should rather invite skeptics to consider the kind of evidence suitable to a personal loving God who would seek redemptive transformation rather than mere reasonable belief.

Acknowledgment of a perfectly loving God with redemptive purposes can yield unsurpassed genuine explanatory value in certain areas of inquiry (for details, see Moser 2002, pp. 121–25, 2008, chap. 2). This acknowledgment, we could argue, makes the best sense of, among other things, who we are and of why we have come into existence. The cognitive reasonableness of robust theistic belief may thus be recommended as underwritten by an inference to a best genuine explanation on the basis of the whole range of our experience and other evidence. Still, the non-inferential, foundational evidence of God's reality would be irreducibly a matter of one's experiencing, via attention-attraction in conscience, what is evidently God's perfectly authoritative call to one to live in obedience to God. This experience would not be an argument of any kind, but instead would be one's experiential acquaintance with what seems to be God's authoritative call on one's life. If the best available genuine explanation of such experience is that a perfectly loving God has actually intervened in human experience, we have the resources for an argument for the cognitive reasonableness of robust theism (on which see Moser 2008, chap. 2). Still, the perfect authority would rest in God, not in our argument. Of course, not just any call would qualify as divine. If a call promotes hate, it is not from a perfectly loving God. False gods can compete with the true God, and they would be known relative to the standard of perfect unselfish love as a corrective to our natural ways. This standard will leave us with very few candidates, and perhaps only one candidate, if any. Many familiar candidates will fail at the start, but we will not digress to name names. Instead, readers can decide in their free time which popular and unpopular gods fail the test.

God could be put to the test as long as the test is fitting. Likewise, even more obviously, we humans can be put to the test too. Some immediate test questions for us humans are the following: (1) Are we *willing* to receive a perfectly loving God's challenging call to us, including a call for love and forgiveness of our enemies? (2) Are we *willing* to engage in the attentive listening and discernment integral to hearing God's challenging call? (3) Are we *willing* to be judged and then remade by the power of God's holy, unselfish love? (4) Are we *willing*, even in our own lives, to let God be God, that is, the Lord whose will is perfectly authoritative for us regarding our own attitudes, actions, and lives? If we honestly answer yes to these questions, we can fruitfully begin to seek (to "test for") God's reality. We can then sincerely ask whether there is a sacred space deep within us, beneath the noise and the chatter of this dying world. This would be a place where we could hear the very voice of God, the perfectly authoritative but "still, small voice" that evidently challenged the prophet Elijah (1 Kings 19:12), among many other prophets, and visited Jesus on many occasions. We can then pursue the attentive and willing listening that would enable us to hear God's perfectly authoritative call to us to be changed by divine power from the inside out. This call would, of course, fit with God's perfectly loving character (and so would not promote murder, hate, or even selfish anger), and it would have a perfect authority foreign to us. Its perfect authority would be palpable and salient when one's conscience is receptive.

In the end, God's own perfectly authoritative character would answer our suitable test questions, if anything would. Otherwise, we would be faced with a cognitive authority higher than God and thus a rejection of God's supreme authority, including supreme cognitive authority. God would then no longer be God. God would then be under the supposed alternative cognitive authority. My position on divine authority does not give God absolutely free cognitive rein, however, as if *whatever* God happened to will would be cognitively acceptable. The point, instead, is that God's cognitive authority would proceed by the perfect authority of God's own genuinely perfectly loving character. Evidence of God's reality would fit with this perfect authority, the authority of God's own perfect character. So, we have no cognitive analogue to Plato's *Euthyphro* problem here, where mere willing would create merit. God's perfectly loving character, rather than an arbitrary will, would have ultimate perfect authority. (The next section returns to this point.)

The plot thickens, as it typically does in matters cognitive. Humans may be largely spiritually blind and deaf relative to the impeccable standard of a perfectly loving God. So, humans may be in need of *God* to open their eyes and ears to receive adequately the authoritative evidence of God's reality. We may see vague glimmers and hear muted echoes of God's reality intruding in our awareness, but we may need God to give us new eyes to see and ears to hear aright evidence of God's reality with some transparency. We may need cognitive help *from God* in our coming to know God, and we may need to ask for such help in light of initial vague glimmers of divine reality. God would thus be indispensable as our helper even regarding our suitably receiving evidence of God's reality. It would not follow that we risk a circular argument, since we are concerned with purposively available evidence more basic than an argument (that is, evidence available in keeping with divine redemptive purposes; cf. Moser 2008). Skeptics have consistently avoided consideration of this live option, perhaps because we have here a serious cognitive blind spot among skeptics. I suspect that it is anchored in volitional leanings against divine reality that are characteristic of skeptics.

The evidential glimmers and echoes of God's reality may strike us more or less vaguely, but we would need to recruit God's help to receive the evidence aright, with spiritual eyes and ears (i.e., a new cognitive perspective) supplied by God. We would have to trust God's provision even in the case of our suitably apprehending evidence of divine reality. God would be Lord, then, even over our appropriately receiving evidence of God's reality. That is a cognitive option worthy of a skeptic's careful attention. We would thus be in a position of genuine cognitive need and dependence, even if we think otherwise. This would fit with the aim of a perfectly loving God to affirm our status as (at least cognitively) dependent creatures and to challenge our prideful pretensions, including any veiled pretensions to divinity. These pretensions of self-reliance and self-assertion emerge particularly in cognitive areas of life, where we readily take self-credit and easily overlook that a perfectly loving God would operate by grace, or unmerited gift, rather than by any human earning that obligates God. The tyranny of human earning dies hard in cognitive and other areas of human life.

7. Trust, Distrust, and Skeptics

A perfectly loving God who seeks redemption would aim to build human trust in God *on God's terms*. Could, however, the God in question *be* reliably trusted? If so, trusted with what? With satisfying our desires and delivering us from all evil now? Clearly not. Our desires are not fully satisfied, and we all face evil and its effects each and every day. In addition, we will all undergo physical death someday. What, then, could God be trusted *for*? Religious skeptics might say: *nothing*. In any case, they doubt, more or less loudly, that the God in question actually exists.

The best answer is this: God, if real, could be trusted for what he has *actually promised*. One promise from the Jewish-Christian God stands out: the promise to remain with his human children in an everlasting life of fellowship as he frees them from deadly idols by bringing them into volitional conformity with his self-giving crucified and resurrected Son, Jesus. Contrary to much popular religion, this does *not* include a promise to save God's human children from pain, suffering, tragedy, or physical death. It is rather a promise of God's abiding and transforming redemptive presence with God's people, come what may. Many people want something else and thus have no interest in any such divine promise. This could easily create a serious cognitive disconnect between these people and God. Misguided expectations could blind people from seeing (evidence of) God's reality even when it is at hand.

Skeptics will ask: why should we accept any such answer regarding God's reliability? Part of the answer has already emerged. Clearly, we cannot give spectator evidence of God to skeptics;, nor should we expect or want to be able to do so. Instead, we should consider whether perfectly authoritative evidence regarding God is actually available. Such evidence would call people to trust, and to be volitionally conformed to, a perfectly loving God, even in the face of pain, suffering, tragedy, and physical death. It would call people to trust God with regard to *his perfectly loving promises* rather than our (often confused and fleeting) desires. The perfectly authoritative evidence would come from God's authoritative call via the divine Spirit that reportedly led Jesus into his notorious trials in the wilderness, in Gethsemane, and on Calvary. So, this call is anything but a call to a casual picnic.

The question now facing skeptics is this: are they *willing* to hear an authoritative divine call and, if they experience it, to come to trust God? Or, alternatively, is their *un*willingness to do so interfering somehow with their appropriating purposively available authoritative evidence of God's reality? Have they put themselves in a cognitive position unfavorable to receiving the distinctive evidence? At a minimum, skeptics must honestly face such questions, however unfamiliar they are to their ordinary ways of thinking. The removal of cognitive blind spots among skeptics could allow for much illumination via newly appropriated available evidence.

Contrary to our familiar ways, the Jewish-Christian God would promote a grand divide between (a) what God has done for us (and is to be received as a gift by suitably grounded trust in God) and (b) what we have accomplished on our own relative to earning security with God in a way that obligates God to honor or benefit us. This is the divide between divine grace (or unmerited gift) and human earning. This divide allows that God can work through our wills and intellects, but it disallows that we "earn" our cognitive standing before God in a way that we obligate God to benefit us. In the cognitive domain, contrary to familiar philosophical thinking, a perfectly loving God would be revealed by grace rather than by human earning. The reason is straightforward: a perfectly loving God would seek to deflate human pride, boasting, and self-credit and to promote instead ultimate trust in the only one who can sustain humans in life. This would be part of God's redemptive purpose toward humans. Evidence of God's reality would be suited to this divine purpose. It would thus be perfectly authoritative evidence initiated by God (without human earning), and it would thereby call for volitional knowledge of God as perfectly authoritative Lord. This plausible consideration is rarely, if ever, considered at all by skeptics and philosophers in general. We are undoing this deficiency now.

The kind of ultimate trust promoted by a perfectly loving God would be doubly ultimate: *purposively* ultimate and *cognitively* ultimate. Purposively ultimate trust in God would not be *merely* a means to another end. One might trust God as a means to various other ends (including health, wealth, or survival), but purposively ultimate trust in God would not depend on such instrumental trust. It would be trust in God as an end in itself, for its own sacred value. Such trust would exclude trusting in God *solely* as a means to another end. Cognitively ultimate trust in God would not depend for its cognitive support (or evidence) on anything other than one's salient experience of God's perfectly authoritative, trust-building voice, or call, revealed to a person. Such trust may still require the absence of defeaters (such as equally illuminating opposing voices), but this would not be a requirement on the (positive) cognitive support for trust in God. The absence of defeaters does not amount to or entail positive cognitive support. As ultimately authoritative on all fronts, owing to the perfect authority of a divine perfectly loving character, God would be in a unique position to demand and to build cognitively ultimate trust in himself. In contrast with imperfect humans, God would not need another voice or standard to authenticate his own perfectly authoritative voice. A regress of needed authoritative voices or standards thus fails to threaten. Skeptics will find no skeptical foothold here.

Cognitively ultimate trust may be called *foundational* trust. We can ask the following question to illuminate such trust: whose voice has, and should have, primary cognitive authority for me: my voice or God's? We can put a similar question in different terms. Which personal relationship has, and should have, primary cognitive authority for me: my relationship with myself or my relationship with God? (Philosophers, including skeptics, rarely take up this question; still, the question is vitally important.) Clearly, if I do not even acknowledge the reality of God's authoritative voice, God's voice will not have primary cognitive authority for me in terms of what I *acknowledge*. The natural skeptical response is to infer that there is (at least in all likelihood) no voice of God to be heard at all. The cognitively more careful response is to ask first: am I somehow blocking myself from hearing God's perfectly authoritative voice? If I have set myself against trusting God, owing to a preference to trust *myself* instead, I will be disinclined to hear or acknowledge God's authoritative voice. I will then prefer to ignore it. Religious skeptics should examine whether they are in just that cognitive position relative to God. They must ask whether they suffer a *cognitive* deficiency owing to their implicit bias against, or explicit resistance to, God's perfect authority in the cognitive domain and elsewhere. Here, then, is an unfinished but urgent project for religious skeptics.

Can we reasonably trust religious skeptics to be sincerely open with regard to hearing and receiving evidence of God's perfectly authoritative voice? Suppose that I in particular have heard God's perfectly authoritative voice in a life-changing way that many morally and cognitively responsible people have. (We could name names here, but we will not digress.) Why, then, should I give cognitive priority to the (now-questionable) doubts about God's reality from religious skeptics? Why should I trust that skeptics are better listeners than I am for God's voice, especially given that cognitive modesty is rare among religious skeptics (evidenced by the typically uncritical ways they—Hume [1780] and Russell [1953] are familiar text-book examples—wield their own skeptical cognitive standards and demands)? At a minimum, skeptics must give us good reason to believe that their listening for God's perfectly authoritative voice is at least as reliable as the listening of careful nonskeptics. Even before that, they must give us good reason to believe that they are genuinely willing to listen for God's authoritative voice despite their skeptical tendencies. As for me, I remain doubtful on both fronts, at least until the needed evidence is in. Skeptical doubts themselves remain distinctively questionable in this connection, and I have no undefeated defeater of my experiential evidence of God's authoritative call and reality.

The authoritative call of a perfectly loving God would manifest the power of perfect self-giving love, the kind of love demonstrated by the redemptive, self-giving death of Jesus on the cross. This call would command people to turn from their selfish ways through obedient fellowship with the unselfish, perfectly loving God. Apprehending the power of God's call accurately would be to apprehend it *as the authoritative voice of God*, which requires apprehending it as authoritatively supreme over other voices and wills, including over my own voice and will. So, apprehending God's voice accurately would require my apprehending that I *should* (be willing to) yield to God's voice. If, however, I would be unwilling to yield to God's voice after having apprehended God's voice accurately, I would be left with a serious cognitive-volitional disconnect. I would then apprehend correctly that I should yield to God's authoritative voice but remain unwilling to yield. My will would then be out of line with what I had apprehended correctly regarding God's authoritative will, namely, that it was authoritatively supreme for myself and others. In that case, I might very well try to sidestep the disconnect by denying that I had actually apprehended God's voice. I would then purchase cognitive-volitional coherence at the expense of what I had actually apprehended. A skeptic in such a position would not be a reliable guide to matters concerning the reality of God's voice. My own evidence indicates that many skeptics are in exactly that unhappy position. (Again, we could name names, but we will not digress.)

Someone might propose that acknowledging God's voice as authoritative is itself an act of yielding one's will to God. This might seem to minimize the danger of the aforementioned cognitive-volitional disconnect. The problem, however, is that yielding one's will to God is *not* entailed by one's merely acknowledging God (or, God's voice) as authoritative. *Acknowledging* something regarding God does not entail, and so is not the same as, *yielding (one's will) to God* as an authoritative personal agent. So, the aforementioned cognitive-volitional disconnect is a real threat for skeptics unwilling to yield to God. A perfectly loving God would rightly avoid trivializing divine revelation in the presence of skeptics unwilling to yield to God's will, given that they are not ready for divine revelation. This fits with the injunction of the Sermon on the Mount not to cast pearls before swine, that is, not to treat divine revelation as if it were dispensable rather than utterly sacred and indispensable.

Nobody would gain, not even skeptics, if evidence of divine reality were readily at our disposal, to be used on *our* preferred terms, as if God should pander to us cognitively. A perfectly loving God would not be cognitively promiscuous, and for this we should be grateful. Given a divine choice to redeem humans, God would have the redemptive aim to transform our selfish wills into wills in agreement with the perfectly loving divine will. This aim would inform the character of genuine divine revelation for our own good, and in such divine revelation cognitive promiscuity would be out. God's redemptive aim would supply what we truly *need*, as wayward people, however much we resist it or do not want it. Indeed, it would seek to break down our selfish willfulness even in the cognitive domain, where we set up cognitive standards to serve our own purposes and thereby block any divine purposes. For our own good, divine revelation would come through perfectly authoritative evidence for the sake of volitional knowledge of God as perfectly authoritative Lord. The stretching of our cognitive comfort zone would thus be expected by God.

Proper obedient reception of authoritative evidence from God would avoid the aforementioned cognitive-volitional disconnect. In that case, God's will (promoting unselfish love in place of our selfishness) would become mine too as I yield my will to God in volitional knowledge of God as authoritative Lord. Until religious skeptics have dealt carefully and honestly with the option of perfectly authoritative evidence that goes beyond spectator evidence, we should be altogether skeptical about their religious skepticism. We should doubt that they are in a suitable position to report on the reality of God or on evidence of the reality of God. They would remain in a position akin to that of the willful child who refuses to open his eyes to apprehend the challenging evidence around him. Clearly, "out of awareness" does not entail "out of reality in the case of evidence of divine reality.

Religious skeptics typically fail to acknowledge the kind of cognitive difference that we should expect between God (if God exists) and ourselves (if we exist). In particular, they typically assume that since we humans are content with spectator evidence as a basis for ordinary knowledge, God would be too, even regarding knowledge of God. Skeptics thereby neglect cognitively important features of a perfect divine character, such as the fact that a redemptive God would seek, with perfect authority, to transform selfish human wills into unselfish wills, without pretending that humans are but innocent spectators. To the extent that skeptics neglect this, they neglect the central place of purposively available authoritative evidence and volitional knowledge regarding divine reality. Traditional philosophy, including traditional religious skepticism, is marked and hindered by this serious neglect. In identifying this cognitive blind spot, we may hope that it soon gets the attention it merits.

Skeptics will likely object as follows. If I, for instance, am willing to submit to God, as volitional knowledge requires, then I may very well be biased in favor of theism in a way that taints me cognitively. I cannot then be trusted as a reliable listener for God's voice because I am then listening in a way that makes me readily *creative* rather than just receptive. This line of objection, however natural, is too quick. Willingness to submit to God does not entail willingness, or any other tendency, to fabricate evidence of God's reality in the absence of such evidence. Consider a simple analogy. I may like the taste of bitter dark chocolate (say, with 85 percent cocoa) and willingly seek it in a candy bar, but this would not lead me to fabricate the taste if instead I tasted something else that I do not like, such as sweet milk chocolate (say, with just 30 percent cocoa). Skeptics would need to show that willingness to submit to God yields a tendency to fabricate evidence of divine reality in the absence of such evidence. This is a tall order indeed, and I see no reason to think that it will be discharged. Religious frauds, incidentally, are typically the last people to be willing to submit to God. They characteristically put themselves first, and their god becomes a means to their own ends. (Once again, we forgo naming names; see, with due caution, many of the televangelists scheduled for Sunday morning.)

Some religious skeptics share Thomas Nagel's worry that the existence of God would pose a serious "cosmic authority problem" for us, and thus, like Nagel, they hope that God does not exist. Nagel claims: "I want atheism to be true . . . . I hope there is no God! I don't want there to be a God; I don't want the universe to be like that" (1997, p. 130). Behind this strikingly bold attitude, Nagel evidently misses the tragedy of the desired situation, the tragedy of a missed opportunity of a *lastingly* good life supported by a perfectly loving God. Something has gone wrong here, and some people do not even notice this. We face yet another blind spot.

It would be a strange, pathetic God indeed who did not pose a serious cosmic authority problem for us selfish humans. It would be part of the status of being *God*, after all, that God has unique authority, or lordship, over us humans. Since we humans are not God, the true God would have perfect authority over us and, if he chose to redeem us, would thus seek to correct our profoundly selfish ways. Nagel confesses to having a fear of any religion involving God. This fear seems widespread among humans and seems to arise from human fear of losing our own supposed lordship over our lives. A philosopher might think of this as fear of losing "autonomy," whatever that slippery term connotes. Willful children are good at exhibiting this fear, and adults can be too. The fearful attitude is "It's my way or no way." This attitude runs deeper than the reach of argument, since one can hold it consistently, and tragically. It needs a perfectly authoritative, corrective word from God. Still, the proponent of such an attitude may rebuff any such word, choosing death instead. Tragically, one can consistently choose death here. The opposing arguments or evidence against choosing death may get no real foothold. Philosophers may wish otherwise, but evidence and arguments will not always prevail in this connection.

At this point, I can go no further with religious skeptics, since I (obviously) am not God. Just as I cannot control your voice, I cannot control the voice of God either. God must ultimately provide the perfectly authoritative evidence of God's reality, and that is a good thing. The big question now is: are skeptics willing to receive such evidence? Time alone will tell.

8. CONCLUSION

We have found no easily generalizable support for religious skepticism about the reality of God. Even *if* an individual were to lack adequate evidence for God's reality, this individual would have no ready way to generalize to the truth of religious skepticism for people in general. Salient evidence of God's reality possessed by nonskeptics is not challenged at all by the fact that there is an individual (or even a group) lacking such evidence. Analogously, the fact that one person lacks a religious experience does not challenge the religious experience of others. In addition, we may now ask *why* an individual lacks evidence of God's reality. Specifically, we may ask whether that person is genuinely open to perfectly authoritative evidence and volitional knowledge regarding divine reality. If the person is not, we should question whether the person is in a good cognitive position to recommend skepticism. If the person is open to perfectly authoritative evidence, we should wait to see if his days as a religious skeptic are numbered. In either case, religious skepticism poses no general or immediate threat. Proponents of rumors to the contrary now owe us a reasonable counter, or defeater, to perfectly authoritative evidence of divine reality. We are, in any case, no longer playing a spectator sport, because we are ourselves candidates for divine judgment. In the presence of the true God, all things become new, even in epistemology and philosophy.

NOTE

This chapter has benefited much from helpful comments by John Greco, numerous Loyola University of Chicago graduate students, and a number of participants in a philosophy conference at the University of Wisconsin, Madison, in the fall of 2005. I express my thanks to them.

REFERENCES

Evans, C.H., and W.R. Herzog, eds. 2002. *The Faith of Fifty Million: Baseball, Religion, and American Culture.* Louisville: Westminster.

Forsyth, Peter T. 1912. *The Principle of Authority.* London: Hodder & Stoughton.

Howard-Snyder, Daniel, ed. 1996. *The Evidential Argument from Evil.* Bloomington: Indiana University Press.

Hume, David. 1780. *Dialogues concerning Natural Religion.* Ed. N. Kemp Smith. London: Macmillan, 1947.

Moser, Paul K. 1989. *Knowledge and Evidence.* New York: Cambridge University Press.

———. 1993. *Philosophy after Objectivity.* New York: Oxford University Press.

———. 2000. "Realism, Objectivity, and Skepticism." In John Greco and Ernest Sosa, eds., *The Blackwell Guide to Epistemology*, pp. 70–91. Malden, Mass.: Blackwell.

———. 2002. "Cognitive Idolatry and Divine Hiding." In Daniel Howard-Snyder and Paul Moser, eds., *Divine Hiddenness*, pp. 120–48. New York: Cambridge University Press.

———. 2003. "Cognitive Inspiration and Knowledge of God." In Paul Copan and Paul Moser, eds., *The Rationality of Theism*, pp. 55–71. London: Routledge.

———. 2004a. "Divine Hiddenness Does Not Justify Atheism," and "Reply to Schellenberg." In M.L. Peterson and R.J. Van Arragon, eds., *Contemporary Debates in Philosophy of Religion*, pp. 42–54, 56–58. Oxford: Blackwell.

———. 2004b. "Skepticism Undone?" In John Greco, ed., *Ernest Sosa and His Critics*, pp. 135–44. Malden, Mass.: Blackwell.

———. 2006. "Reorienting Religious Epistemology: Cognitive Grace, Filial Knowledge, and Gethsemane Struggle." In James Beilby, ed., *For Faith and Clarity*, pp. 65–81. Grand Rapids: Baker.

———. 2007a. "Christianity." In Paul Copan and Chad Meister, eds., *Routledge Companion to Philosophy of Religion*, pp. 65–73. London: Routledge.

———. 2007b. "Divine Hiddenness, Death, and Meaning." In Paul Copan and Chad Meister, eds., *Philosophy of Religion: Classic and Contemporary Issues*, pp. 215–27. Oxford: Blackwell.

———. 2008. *The Elusive God: Reorienting Religious Epistemology.* New York: Cambridge University Press.

Nagel, Thomas. 1997. *The Last Word.* New York: Oxford University Press.

Russell, Bertrand. 1953. "What Is an Agnostic?" In Louis Greenspan and Stefan Andersson, eds., *Russell on Religion*, pp. 41–49. London: Routledge, 1999.

———. 1970. "The Talk of the Town." *New Yorker* (February 21, 1970), p. 29. Cited in Al Seckel, ed., *Bertrand Russell on God and Religion*, p. 11. Buffalo: Prometheus, 1986.

CHAPTER 10

....

LIVE SKEPTICAL HYPOTHESES

....

BRYAN FRANCES

1. Skeptical Threats, Real and Merely Academic

....

Those of us who take skepticism seriously typically have two relevant beliefs: (a) it is plausible (even if false) that in order to know that I have hands, I have to be able to epistemically neutralize, to some significant degree, some skeptical hypotheses, such as the brain-in-a-vat (BIV) one; and (b) it is also plausible (even if false) that I cannot so neutralize those hypotheses. There is no reason for us to think also (c) that the BIV hypothesis, for instance, is *plausible or probably true*. In order to take skepticism seriously, it is sufficient to hold (a) and (b); one need not hold (c). Indeed, philosophers who accept (a) and (b) *never* endorse (c). Show me a philosopher who suspects that he is a brain in a vat, and I will show you someone who is deranged.

That is one thing that bothers undergraduates in philosophy. They object: why on earth do some philosophers take the BIV hypothesis to pose *any* threat at all to our beliefs, given that those very same philosophers think that there is *no real* chance that the BIV hypothesis is true? Sure, the BIV hypothesis is *formally inconsistent* with my belief that I have hands, so if the former is true, then my belief is false. But so what? Why should that bare inconsistency matter so much? Is this strange attitude among philosophers the result of some logic fetish infecting the philosophical community? It is sometimes said that the skeptical hypotheses not only are inconsistent with our beliefs but also are *explanatory* of our experiences, which is supposed to make them more of a threat. But students are not fooled:

although the skeptical hypotheses may attempt to explain why our experience is as it is, it is the kind of attempt appropriate for science-fiction movies that are all special effects and virtually no plot. No one with any sense of reality will take the evil-demon hypothesis to be even tenuously explanatory.

The students would understand the fuss over the BIV hypothesis if there were some decent reason to think that the BIV hypothesis was really true. If you believe P, a contrary hypothesis Q has some reasonably good backing—perhaps endorsement by legitimate experts in the relevant field—and you are quite familiar with Q's good status, as well as the conflict between P and Q, then the Q possibility *does* seem to mount a *significant* threat to one's belief in P, where a threat is significant just in case when left unneutralized, it ruins one's chance at knowledge of P's truth. If the BIV or evil-demon hypotheses were like Q, then we would have a real threat to our belief that we have hands.

Here is an example to which I will appeal later in this chapter as well. When Jo was a teenager, she learned the theory that a huge meteorite wiped out the dinosaurs. She learned this theory in the usual way, hearing it from her parents and teachers and reading about it in books. Now pretend that at the time she was told the meteor story as a child, say, at the age of eight, the scientific community was sharply divided on the issue of what caused the demise of the dinosaurs. Although most scientists accepted the meteor hypothesis, many others subscribed to the idea that their death was caused by some enormous solar flare. A significant number of other scientists thought that it was not a solar flare or a meteor but a particularly nasty series of supervolcanos. These latter two classes of dissenters had decent evidence concerning the sun and supervolcanos that the meteor advocates took seriously. Both the solar-flare theorists and the supervolcano theorists were professors who were highly respected by the meteor theorists and at the top of their profession. Whole book series, conferences, and doctoral dissertations were devoted to these competing hypotheses. Suppose further that upon going to her university, Jo found out about the rival and highly respected hypotheses. She did not understand all the reasons why they were so well respected and endorsed, but she was well aware that they were well respected and frequently endorsed by the experts, even the best among them. Even so, she kept her meteor belief.

As it turned out, the meteor hypothesis was the right one; lucky Jo! But although some experts may have known that fact, surely Jo was in no position to know it after she found out about the eminent status of the rival hypotheses. She could do little or nothing to defeat the rival hypotheses. Even after studying the issues as an undergraduate, she could not *know* that a meteor wiped out the dinosaurs, for from the moment she first studied the dinosaurs until she graduated with a bachelor's degree in paleontology, she was perfectly aware that there were two "live" contrary hypotheses that she was in no position to rule out—and they had not been ruled out for her, either, for instance, by her teachers. And if she was aware of these alternative hypotheses, as well as their liveness and how they conflict with the meteor hypothesis, then as long as the competing hypotheses were not ruled out, she could not know that the meteor hypothesis was correct. Perhaps in order to know the meteor truth, she would not have needed to rule out the possibility that she was a brain in a vat. And perhaps someone mostly outside the scientific community and thus not exposed to the *ultimately* misleading supervolcano and solar-flare evidence could know that the meteor hypothesis is true. Still, in order for Jo to know the meteor fact, she *does* have to be able to rule out, at least to some degree, the solar-flare and supervolcano possibilities, for, unlike the crazy philosophical hypotheses, these are "real, live possibilities," *and* she is perfectly aware of their existence, live status, and inconsistency with her belief. Perhaps she does not have to completely *demolish* the supervolcano and solar-flare hypotheses in order to know that the meteor story is true, but she certainly has to knock them down a few epistemic notches.

The heart of the dinosaur argument is simple: because the supervolcano and solar-flare hypotheses are real, live possibilities inconsistent with the meteor hypothesis, Jo is *aware* of all that, she is nothing even approaching an expert or genius on these matters, and those hypotheses are not ruled out, she does not know that the meteor story is true. There are not many ideas in philosophy that cannot be coherently and cleverly challenged, but it is a brave philosopher who thinks that Jo's story is misguided. Surely, one would think, in *those* circumstances Jo's true and partially justified belief in the meteor hypothesis did not amount to knowledge.

Let us return to our students' skeptical attitude toward skepticism. If we could find some skeptical hypotheses that were false but *live* in something like the way the supervolcano and solar-flare hypotheses were, then we would think that they pose a significant threat to our beliefs that are obviously inconsistent with them: if we could not epistemically neutralize those skeptical hypotheses (whatever neutralization amounts to), then our beliefs obviously inconsistent with those false but live hypotheses would fall short of knowledge (even if they were true beliefs). At least, this lack of knowledge would follow if the people in question were well *aware* of the live status of the skeptical hypotheses, as well as the inconsistency between their beliefs and the live skeptical hypotheses. For in that case, we would have the threat to our beliefs staring us right in the face, as it were. The threat would be out in the open. Our students would understand our skeptical worries better.

Are there any such skeptical hypotheses—live hypotheses inconsistent with huge portions of our commonsensical beliefs? It is easy to adjust the BIV story so that it becomes live in another possible world. BIVs become technologically and fiscally possible; a team of mad scientists ends up ruling the world; certain top secret documents detailing plans for massive kidnapping and BIVing are discovered and leaked to the public; impenetrable 100,000-square-mile complexes of laboratories are set up in the wilds of Canada, Brazil, and elsewhere; thousands of people start mysteriously disappearing in the middle of the night to become BIVed. You can see how at least one BIV hypothesis—"I have become a BIV as the result of these crazy mad scientists"—could become something close to a real, live possibility for almost any person (not the mad scientists themselves, provided we tell the story right). Even if you are never BIVed in that world, does your true belief that you have a bicycle in your garage amount to knowledge?

The students will not be satisfied with this skepticism, not fully, anyway. For we have yet to find any real skeptical threat. No *actual* version of skepticism is on the horizon. None of our students' actual beliefs are threatened by any skeptical hypothesis. Skepticism remains merely academic and highly dubious. They are still skeptical about skepticism.

However, there are skeptical hypotheses that are actually live; others are at least very nearly actually live. In this chapter, I will list some of these hypotheses and show why they do generate a "real" skeptical threat, one quite different from the usual, merely academic threats. The skeptical theory that results I call *live skepticism*.[1]

2. The Live Skeptic's Argument

The live skeptic uses an argument just like the dinosaur one: if you believe *P*, hypothesis *H* inconsistent with *P* is a live hypothesis, and you are like Jo in being a well-informed "mere mortal" with regard to H, then you do not know *P*. Let us make the argument moderately precise.

We start with a sufficient condition for a hypothesis *H* to be a "real, live" socioepistemic possibility in our intellectual community.

1. In our intellectual community, hypothesis *H* has been through a significant (not to say exhaustive) evaluation by experts over many years.

2. It is judged actually true or about as likely as any relevant possibility by a significant number of well-informed, well-respected, and highly intelligent experts in the field(s) *H* belongs to. Also assume that there are lots of these experts, and they are not crackpots.

3. Those experts reached that favorable opinion based on *H*'s merits in a familiar, epistemically responsible way (that is, the way they reached their opinion seems as epistemically responsible as any).

4. Those experts consider that there are several decent and independent sources of evidence for *H*, so it is not the case that the only reason people pay serious attention to *H* is the presence of one weird experiment or line of reasoning.

5. Many of those experts consider *H* a "real, live possibility" (i.e., this is what they would say if you asked them).

The second task is to articulate a set of sufficient conditions for being a *well-informed mere mortal* with respect to a hypothesis *H*.

6. You know that the hypothesis *H* is inconsistent with *P* (where you believe *P*).

7. You are at least somewhat familiar with H and the issues surrounding H, including the fact that H is live in the sense of (1)–(5). (Thus [7] entails [1]–[5].) In fact, you are as aware as just about anyone of the fact that H is live.

8. Your intelligence, understanding, and knowledge are not extraordinary for people in your intellectual community with regard to H or the issues surrounding H. (So although you *may* be an expert, you are certainly no better than the other experts—in particular, the ones who insist that H is or could very well be true.)

9. If you have any reasons or evidence you can marshal for casting doubt on H, and if they were carefully considered by the members of that community— in particular, by the well-informed, well-respected, and highly intelligent experts who were thoroughly familiar with the hypothesis—they would be nearly universally and confidently rejected as clearly insufficient to rule out the hypothesis (although they may have other merits).

Roughly put, "S is *as aware as just about anyone* that X" in (7) means that X is true and S has all the usual good warrant for believing X, warrant that usually suffices for knowledge. I cannot say that it entails *knowledge* of X, however, for reasons that will become clear later. Briefly, the reason is that even though S has the usual "positive" warrant sufficient for knowledge of X, she also has some "negative" warrant that offsets or vetoes that positive warrant enough so that her belief in X no longer is, on balance, warranted or sufficient for knowledge.

The conjunction of (6) and (7) (which, as noted in [7], includes by entailment [1]–[5]) says, very roughly, "You are fully aware of what is going on with the live hypothesis, so it is a real threat to your knowledge, a threat that must be defused." The conjunction of (8) and (9) says, again roughly, "You do not have what it takes to defuse the threat."

Please note the strength of (9): it is not merely saying that you cannot convince experts that H is false. Condition (9) does not just mean that you lack reasons that would be accepted as establishing beyond serious dispute that H is false. It is saying that even the experts who *reject* H would say that your reasons for rejecting H are clearly inadequate by just about anyone's lights and not just by the lights of those who accept H. For instance, you might be a graduate student in paleontology who is aware of the rival hypotheses about the demise of the dinosaurs and who happens to believe the true meteor hypothesis. You go to see your PhD supervisor, and she asks you what you plan to say about the supervolcano hypothesis in your dissertation. You say that that theory is not very plausible, but you are happy to throw in a brief section showing why it is implausible. She *agrees with you* that the meteor hypothesis is correct, but she asks you what you plan to say against the supervolcano hypothesis. You give your spiel, and she tells you flat out that what you have said is clearly inadequate and you should either do much better with a critical section or drop it entirely and say in a footnote that you will be merely assuming the falsehood of the supervolcano theory. After all, professor so-and-so right down the hall is an advocate of the supervolcano theory, he is certainly no dope, he is not alone in his expert opinion, and you have said virtually nothing to put any pressure on his view.

The graduate student is a well-informed mere mortal, "mere mortal" for short. A child is not, because she fails to satisfy either (6) or (7). Another kind of mere mortal is an expert in the field but whose specialization lies elsewhere. Professor Smith teaches various science classes. She is perfectly aware of the supervolcano and solar-flare hypotheses but would not be able to say anything interesting against them. She has the true meteor belief, but like the graduate student, her belief is too lucky to amount to knowledge. *That* is the type of person I have in mind as a well-informed mere mortal; my hope is that conditions (6)–(9) capture the important aspects of their epistemic position. Needless to say, there could be many such individuals.

The live skeptic now makes three key claims.

The modesty principle: if S is a mere mortal with respect to live hypothesis H (so conditions (1)–(9) hold), then H is not ruled out with respect to S.

The live-hypothesis principle: if S knows that P entails $\neg H$ and is as aware as just about anyone that H is live (so H really is live), then if H is not ruled out with respect to S, S does not know P.

The liveness-mortality premise: in the actual world or an extremely realistic, very close possible world, many members of our actual intellectual community of contemporary analytic philosophers, cognitive scientists, and their advanced students are mere mortals with respect to each of the following live hypotheses (so conditions 1–9 all hold in that world):

Belief error theory: no one believes anything (endorsed to some significant degree at various times by, e.g., Patricia Churchland [1986], Paul Churchland [1989], Stephen Stich [1983], Daniel Dennett [1978], Paul Feyerabend [1963], Richard Rorty [1970], and Willard Quine [1960, 1985]).
Pain error theory: pain is only in the brain (endorsed by Russell, Broad, Ryle, David Lewis, and David Armstrong; see Hyman 2003 for references).
Color error theory: no ordinary physical objects are colored (endorsed by, e.g., Galileo, Larry Hardin, Paul Boghossian, David Velleman, Emmett Holmon, and Frank Jackson, as well as by scientists Semir Zeki, Stephen Palmer, Werner Backhaus, and Randolf Menzel; see Byrne and Hilbert 2003 for references).
Trait error theory: no one has any character traits (endorsed by Gilbert Harman [1999, 2000[and John Doris [1998, 2002]).

The live skeptic's validly inferred conclusion from these three claims is that in either this world or some very close possible worlds, many of us do not know that fire engines are red, we do not know that we sometimes have pains in our lower backs, we do not know that John Rawls was kind, and we do not even know that we *believe* any of those truths. This skeptic does not say that any of those four error theories are true; she can safely believe that they are (utterly, completely) *false*. The *error theorist* says that we do not know that fire engines are red because they are not red; the *live skeptic* says that we do not know that fire engines are red because even though our belief may well be true, it is not sufficiently warranted. Obviously, if the error theories are true, then the live skeptic's conclusion holds, assuming that knowledge requires truth. And for the very same reason, if the error theories are truth-valueless, the live skeptic still wins. So no matter what the status of the live error theories is (true, false, without truth-value), we mere mortals about those error theories do not know that anyone has any beliefs, anything is colored, and so on.

3. THE LIVENESS-MORTALITY PREMISE

Consider belief error theory, or eliminativism, as it is commonly called.[2] Eliminativism is currently a live possibility in our intellectual community (of contemporary analytic philosophers, cognitive scientists, and their advanced students). The hypothesis is a going concern among the experts. That is just a brute fact about the community of philosophers of mind and cognitive scientists. You might not like it, but that is just the way it is. The Churchlands, Feyerabend, Stich, Rorty, Quine, Dennett, and others have at various points in their exceedingly distinguished careers concluded upon careful reflection that it is very probably true or as serious a contender as any other hypothesis about folk psychology. They arrived at these views in the familiar and epistemically responsible way of looking hard at data and lines of reasoning and then thinking about them in highly intelligent, relatively unbiased and open-minded ways. These people are not dopes. And it goes without saying that no magic bullet has been found for it, and people still take it virtually as seriously as ever. What this means is that the live status of a hypothesis is a *sociological* fact, not a matter for philosophical argument.

Okay, I lied: eliminativism is not live today and was not even in the 1980s or 1990s. It has too few supporters. But if Fodor, Dretske, Burge, and a few other realists had died in 1974, the reaction to the eliminativist-leaning writings of Stich, Dennett, the Churchlands, and others had been more positive in the 1980s and 1990s, the "Who cares what common sense says?" attitude in contemporary metaphysics and other areas of philosophy was alive in the philosophy of mind . . . You get the idea. Surely, in some possible worlds practically next door to ours, eliminativism is a live hypothesis in both the cognitive science and philosophy-of-mind communities. In case you were not aware of it, color error theory is practically the dominant view among color scientists today; the same holds for error theory for pain location. And character trait error theory, although not actually live, could easily become live in the same way eliminativism could. My interest lies in the epistemic status of mere mortals in those actual or almost actual communities: what do *they* know about beliefs, colors, pain locations, or character traits? The live skeptical argument concludes that a society virtually just like ours but with sufficient philosophical confusion regarding eliminativism, for instance, could have a significant period of time (decades, even centuries) in which most philosophers and cognitive scientists knew nothing of the form "S believes P." That is shocking enough. And yet, for all we know, *our* society will soon enter into philosophical depravity and wholeheartedly vote eliminativism as the theory of cognition most likely to be true.

The live skeptic need not think that eliminativism (or the other error theories) is remotely plausible. Even Fodor could be a live skeptic. In fact, the live skeptic herself could not only *know* that eliminativism is false but *know* that she has refuted it and know that she knows that it is false—even though she claims that in her own philosophical community eliminativism is live. She could hold herself to not be a mere mortal; and she could be right about that because she really does have a refutation of eliminativism. Exactly the same holds in the more familiar dinosaur case: a paleontologist genius could *know* full well that the supervolcano hypothesis is mistaken and the meteor theory true while holding that most of her students and colleagues do not know either of those facts because of their mere mortality with respect to the live supervolcano hypothesis. Throughout this chapter, I assume with the live skeptic that the error theories are false and nowhere in the vicinity of the truth. All the live skeptic is claiming, in endorsing the liveness-mortality premise, is that there are easily possible philosophical communities in which the error theory in question is live in the sense of (1)–(5), and there are many ordinary individuals in those communities who satisfy (6)–(9)—individuals just like us philosophers in the actual world. There is no tension at all in endorsing that claim while holding that eliminativism is utterly implausible and has even been ruled out by oneself. Perhaps Kripke, Burge, and a few others have unpublished but rock-solid proofs that eliminativism is false; even the eliminativists would admit defeat if they just had a chance to see them. It does not matter in the least because those proofs are irrelevant to the epistemic status of mere mortals in communities in which those proofs do not exist or are known by just a few philosophical hermits.

I assume that the only reason to balk at the liveness-mortality premise lies in condition 9. One might think that even if eliminativism is live in the sense of (1)–(5), one could still easily rule it out by merely reflecting on the fact that one has beliefs. But (9) is just saying that virtually all experts would *judge* the evidence you can marshal for casting doubt on *H* to be clearly insufficient to rule it out. It does not say that the experts are *right* about that. Perhaps every one of us can rule out eliminativism, for instance, merely by saying to ourselves, "It sure seems to me that I believe that $2 + 2 = 4$." I will be considering and arguing against such ideas later in this chapter. But in the worlds in which eliminativism is live, philosophers sufficiently skeptical about the truth of common sense will not consider such a line of reasoning as sufficient to rule out eliminativism (so there are not too many John Searles there).

One might suspect that in the actual world, a large majority of philosophers of mind really do think that one can refute eliminativism merely by breezily reflecting on one's own beliefs. (Recall that we are assuming that eliminativism is false.) If so, then perhaps worlds that make (1)–(9) true—(9) in particular—are quite distant from actuality, contrary to the liveness-mortality premise.

I think that the objector's claim about the actual world is mistaken, but it will help the live skeptic's cause if we get clearer on just how a world could make (1)–(9) true and yet remain very similar to actuality.

A quick answer is that just as color error theory is *actually live today*, as anyone familiar with the philosophy and science of color can attest, belief error theory could have the same respected status. Both error theories are radically and comparably opposed to common sense; so that hurdle can be met. Perhaps more convincingly, one additional feature, briefly mentioned earlier, easily makes (1)–(9) true at a world: more people being skeptical about the strength of the connection between common sense and truth. As matters stands today, in the philosophy of mind and epistemology communities, there is a strong confidence that statements that are conversationally appropriate in ordinary contexts are true. Epistemologists and philosophers of mind are typically loath to claim that large parts of common sense are radically mistaken. In metaphysics and the philosophy of language and logic, however, one does not find this faith in the inference from common sense to truth. (Think of theories of vagueness, truth [the semantic paradoxes], material constitution, and identity through time—not to mention the philosophy of physics.) Indeed, it is hard to find any contemporary metaphysician who *does not* hold claims that are about as outrageous, from the perspective of common sense, as eliminativism. In my experience, those who work only in epistemology or the philosophy of mind often find this attitude highly dubious or even hard to fathom, but there are good reasons why it is prominent in other areas of philosophy.

The live skeptic needs a weak claim, one operative in her rebuttal to the objection that worlds in which (1)–(9) are true are remote from actuality: the skeptical attitude we find in contemporary metaphysics, philosophy of language, and philosophy of logic regarding even the most well entrenched and nearly universal common sense could easily permeate the philosophy of mind, while eliminativism had more expert supporters and fewer detractors.[3] I am not claiming that such an attitude movement would be correct or fully justified; I am just saying that it could easily happen. In those worlds, which I claim are highly realistic in being very similar to the current time of the actual world, eliminativism is live, and many of us are mere mortals regarding it. So we have justified the live skeptic's claim that worlds satisfying (1)–(9) are next door to actuality.

4. THE NATURE OF LIVE SKEPTICISM

In later sections, I will address some objections to the live skeptic's argument. I cannot consider more than a small fraction of all the reasonable objections (see Frances 2005a and 2005b for more thorough treatment), so your favorite might not get investigated here. And I do not treat the few I do consider as thoroughly as I should. But I hope to provide some initial reason for doubting that they succeed.

The objections will fall into two classes. First, there are reasons for thinking that we do not have to be able to rule out, in any significant sense, the error theories in order to know truths obviously inconsistent with them. For instance, relevant-alternatives and contextualist theories are important here. These objections fault the live-hypothesis principle, which says that we do need to rule out the error theories. Second, one can admit the ruling-out requirement but argue that it is actually pretty easy to do the ruling out. Reliabilism and introspective accounts figure here, among others. These objections target the modesty principle, which says that mere mortals cannot manage the ruling out.

But before we put our critical hats on, we must understand the nature of live skepticism, for it is quite different from any traditional skeptical theory. In fact, it is so strikingly different, in several ways, that to a certain extent I lose the *motivation* to find fault with the live skeptic's argument. I will list three key marks of live skepticism.

First, the live skeptic is claiming that we lose our knowledge by means of a perfectly familiar mechanism.[4] Pretend that it had been common sense for hundreds of years that whales are fish; pretend that it is also true. Then scientists came along to challenge that bit of common sense. They admit that there are many fish and many whales, but they have some impressive arguments for the shocking claim that whales are not fish—they are mammals instead. If you take a quiz listing kinds of fish and you write "whale," scientists will mark your answer as incorrect. If you say to your child, "Look at the whales, Julia; they are the biggest fish there are," they will claim that what you say is fine in some respects but really false. For the purposes of this chapter, pretend that the scientists are wrong: whales are fish. So one familiar and even highly reliable method for finding out that something is a fish—find out that it is a whale—would clearly be question begging against the group of scientists. In this scenario, if you were a mere mortal regarding the whale-fish controversy, then you would be familiar enough regarding the relevant issues that in order to know that Keiko (the whale) is a fish, you would need to have some way of neutralizing the live whales-are-not-fish hypothesis.

Consider the advocate of the pain-is-only-in-the-brain hypothesis and compare what she says with what the whales-are-not-fish advocate says (keep in mind that we are pretending that whales are fish and assuming that toes sometimes throb in pain).

- I realize that it is common sense that whales are fish.
- I grant that there are loads of fish and loads of whales, and to a certain extent there is nothing wrong with classifying whales as fish.
- But they are not fish, not really.
- Whales are actually mammals, not fish, for various technical reasons.
- There are zillions of fish to be found, but they are not to be found among the whales.

- I realize that it is common sense that toes sometimes throb with pain.
- I grant that there are loads of throbbing feelings and loads of toes, and to a certain extent there is nothing wrong with classifying some toes as throbbing.
- But they are not throbbing, not really.
- The throbbing feeling is actually in your brain, not your toe, for various technical reasons.
- There are zillions of throbbing feelings to be found, but they are not to be found among the toes.

I take it as intuitive that in the envisioned whale-fish scenario mere mortals would not know that Keiko the whale is a fish—even though they used the familiar, commonsensical, and highly reliable "If you find a whale, then you have found a fish" method to form the true belief that Keiko is a fish. By analogy, just because you (a mere mortal) have a true belief that Mary's toe is throbbing and you formed it in a common way—you saw her stub her toe and heard her curse and tell you that it was throbbing painfully—this method, as familiar, commonsensical, and reliable as it indeed is (in that world and our world), is not sufficient to make you know that Mary's toe is throbbing, not when you are a mere mortal with respect to the live pain-is-only-in-the-brain hypothesis. Again, the *reason* for the lack of knowledge is exactly the same as in the whales-are-not-fish case. The live skeptic is saying that our knowledge is sabotaged because of the operation of a perfectly familiar epistemic mechanism, the one governing the whales-fish or dinosaur cases.

Now for the second interesting feature of live septicism. Suppose once again that live skepticism is true. Suppose that tomorrow the definitive refutations of color error theory and eliminativism are published and widely digested. It is reasonable to think that we *then* know that fire engines are red and that Moore believed skepticism false, for at that point the error theories have been ruled out on our behalf. In addition, it is plausible to hold that since my father knows nothing of eliminativism, color error theory, professional philosophy, or cognitive science, *he currently* knows that fire engines are red and that my mother believes that motorcycles are a menace. It is also reasonable and consistent with the new skeptic's position to think that my father knew those facts years ago before eliminativism (and, let us pretend, color error theory) was even on the radar screen in science or philosophy. Finally, we should hold that before we were mere mortals, say, when we were children, we had loads of knowledge inconsistent with the skeptical hypotheses even if the latter were already live.

This is just to say that the reach of the epistemic threat posed by the live skeptical hypotheses is not sufficient to affect those people for whom it is not live. In a way, this makes the new skepticism modest: by saying that it rules out knowledge *only* for mere mortals, we are restricting its scope severely. In other ways, the new skepticism is now unlike anything we have ever encountered.

Here is why. Skepticism has always been considered a permanent, blanket, and highly negative condition. If you are in it, then everyone else is in it too (that is "blanket"), forever ("permanent"); and this marks a significant epistemic deficiency on our part ("highly negative"). If skepticism is right, then it must reflect an ever-lasting, perhaps absolutely necessary, failure of our cognitive systems to achieve a certain result. The idea that some kind of radical, even if restricted, skepticism could be the result of a purely accidental, contingent, and temporary confluence of chance social events affecting a fully rational, cognitively well-off individual seems absurd. And it is absurd, at least for classic versions of skepticism. But we have seen that skepticism can be thus accidentally generated. The skepticisms discussed in this chapter are relatively fleeting and are no indictment of our cognitive systems or evolutionary progress. Most surprisingly, the new skepticisms are the odd result of cognitive systems and procedures working *well*, not poorly: it is through the epistemically beneficial practices embodied in the premises of the new skeptical argument template that we have temporarily fallen into our regions of restricted skepticism. By being part of a community that pays due heed to expertly produced contrary evidence, we have temporarily robbed ourselves of large portions of knowledge, but we have done so as the result of following epistemic practices that almost always actually *buy* us knowledge. Once we understand how we got into the mess of not having knowledge of color, belief, or pain location, for instance, we see that it is not a bad thing. In fact, *we are epistemically better off than we were before.* Yesterday you knew; today you do not; but today you are smarter than you were yesterday regarding color, belief, and pain. People unacquainted with philosophy or color science or cognitive science may know more than we do, but this just shows that we need a new and improved measure of epistemic standing. Suppose I think that on balance, color error theory is very likely mistaken, and so, even in the full awareness of the live status of that theory, I continue to hold ordinary color beliefs. My mother's belief that fire engines are red is warranted enough for knowledge; mine is not because I remain a mere mortal; but in some sense I am in the superior epistemic situation with regard to the color of fire engines despite my lack of knowledge and lack of immortality vis-à-vis color error theory.

That may sound contradictory: if token belief *A* (my mother's) is better warranted than token belief *B* (mine), and *A* and *B* have the same content (e.g., that fire engines are red), then of course *A* is epistemically better than *B*. In the previous paragraph, I had the live skeptic deny this conditional, but she need not. Perhaps the *collection* of my attitudes regarding color is epistemically superior to hers, even though when it comes to the *particular* fire-engine belief her position is superior to mine. The details on how best to describe the differences in the two believers are interesting, but in any case the end result is that a typical reaction to skepticism—the kind of epistemic failure attributed to us by the skeptic just could not be built into our cognitive systems—does not touch the live skeptical theses. Similarly for the objection that runs as follows: according to the skeptic, we are cut off from reality, unable to know it, and that is just implausible. On the contrary, by becoming a mere mortal and thereby falling into the live skeptical trap, I am in a better epistemic position than I was before; skepticism is an *improvement*, something to be bragged about, not ashamed of. Falling "victim" to the live skeptical snare does not cut me off from the reality of color, belief, pain, and knowledge compared with those nonphilosophical folk who in a real sense know more than I do. Instead, I am the one better in tune with the facts; my opinions dig deeper into the nature of reality than theirs do. This is not too surprising: by knowing more about the possibilities regarding color and belief, I have a better appreciation of the "whole color thing" or the "whole story regarding cognition." The ordinary person may know that fire engines are red, while I do not, but her belief has a measure of accidentalness that mine will never have. If she had just been privy to the intelligent and sophisticated ruminations of some philosophers and scientists, then she would no longer know. It is just an accident that she does know. The nature of the accidentalness is not so great as to rob her of knowledge, or so the antiskeptic says and the live skeptic may admit, but coupled with my expanded knowledge of possibilities and evidence for and against those possibilities, it is enough to render her overall epistemic situation less secure than mine.

Furthermore, *I have all the positive warrant that she does* when it comes to our beliefs that fire engines are red. This point is so important that I will put it in a box, as if it were in a science textbook.

> The live skeptic is not denying us any
> of the warrant we think we have;
> neither is she denying its quality.

The live skeptic's crucial claim is this: the overall warrant possessed by the beliefs targeted by the live skeptical hypotheses is anemic compared with that had by our other beliefs that amount to knowledge and are not targeted by any live skeptical hypotheses.

Engage in the useful fiction that warrant comes in units (we can make the same point without the fiction). She has 1,200 positive warrant units for her fire-engine belief; I have just 800; one needs 1,000 for the true belief to be knowledge. I have had all the same fire-engine and color experiences that she has had; I have each of her 1,200 units. My only problem is that I have 400 *negative* warrant units, coming from my foray into color science and philosophy. Perhaps we need to judge the epistemic standing of beliefs with additional measures, such as with positive warrants (I have all the good reasons, reliability facts, and so on that she has) and absolute-value warrants (since the absolute value of my warrants is much greater than hers, I am much more familiar with the relevant issues regarding the content of the belief).

In any case, I am not claiming that live skepticism does not apply to people who know nothing of the error theories. I am just allowing for that relatively likely possibility. If it does apply to them, then live skepticism is even stronger, covering a much wider range of beliefs, although it still does not affect the millions of beliefs not targeted by live contrary hypotheses.

Now for the third interesting feature of live skepticism. Suppose that live skepticism is true, so you do not know that the table is brown, nor do you know that you believe that. Still, no one said that you did not *know perfectly well* that the table looks brown and is for all practical purposes brown. Further, you still know that red is darker than yellow. In addition, I still know that I act like I believe *P*, that it seems to me that I believe *P*, that I feel like I believe *P*, that it seems as though Mary believes *Q*, and so on. I also know that for all practical purposes, Moore believed skepticism false. And I know that belief and truth are required for knowledge. If that is the case, then what have we lost, really, in losing our knowledge that fire engines are red? He knows that fire engines are red; we do not; but we are familiar with much more color theory than he is, and we still know that fire engines look red and are red for all practical purposes. Now who is in the better epistemic position vis-à-vis the redness of the fire engine?

5. Do We Really Need to Rule Out the Error Theories?

Now we move on to consider objections to the live skeptic's two principles. If we answer no to this section's title question, then we are rejecting the live-hypothesis principle, which says that we mere mortals do need to rule out the error theories in order to know things obviously inconsistent with them.

The live-hypothesis principle is akin to, but much more plausible than, any of the standard epistemic closure principles. Compare what might be called simple closure with the live hypothesis principle.

> *Simple closure*: if S knows that *P* entails ¬*H*, then if *H* is not ruled out with respect to S, S does not know *P*.[5]

> *The live-hypothesis principle*: if S knows that *P* entails ¬*H* and is as aware as just about anyone that *H* is live (so *H* really is live), then if *H* is not ruled out with respect to S, S does not know *P*.

The two principles differ in two crucial ways: only the live-hypothesis principle demands that *H* be live *and* that the subject be fully aware of *H*'s live status. As we are about to see, by incorporating these conditions, the live-hypothesis principle is immune to the plausible objections raised against simple closure.

It is sometimes said that one need not, in order to know *P*, rule out (or know the falsehood of) counterpossibility *H* provided *H* is appropriately "irrelevant."[6] Maybe so, but it is hard to see how this would apply if *H* were live in the manner described earlier, you were fully aware of the liveness, and you knew full well the inconsistency of *H* and *P*. If what I have argued previously is wrong, then some hypotheses do not need to be ruled out for you in order for you to know *P* even though all the following conditions obtain:

- (i) Most people including yourself believe *P*.
- (ii) Everyone believes (correctly) the obvious fact that *H* is inconsistent with *P*.
- (iii) You have actually put together *P* and *H* and know as well as anyone that *H* is inconsistent with *P*.
- (iv) *H* is a real, live contender in your intellectual community.
- (v) You are aware that *H* is a real, live possibility actually endorsed by plenty of top experts.
- (vi) Lots of people worry about their attitude toward *P* in light of what they think about *H*.
- (vii) Even the experts who think that *H* is rubbish would pretty much laugh at any reasons you could give against *H*.

If just conditions i–iii hold, then perhaps I do not have to rule out *H* in order to know *P*. Such a situation may obtain when *P* is "I have hands" and *H* is some traditional skeptical hypothesis. We *might* (I do not know) get the same answer if just the first four conditions hold. Perhaps one could know *P* without ruling out *H* provided one believed *P* for the "right" reasons and was unaware that *H* was a live possibility endorsed by experts. But when all seven conditions hold, one cannot know *P* without being able to rule out *H*. If all seven conditions hold, then *H* needs to be ruled out because it is now a "relevant alternative" to what I believe; I am "epistemically responsible" to *H*. It seems to me that that is a reasonable constraint on relevant-alternatives theories.

Contextualists hold that different uses of "S knows P" can have different truth-values even when they concern the same person, truth, and time. The idea is that depending on the context of utterance, different levels of epistemic standing for S's belief in *P* are necessary for the truth of a use of "S knows *P*" in that context. In some contexts, for instance, when a lot is riding on whether *P* is true or S can be relied on, then S's warrant has to meet a high standard to make the knowledge attribution true. In other circumstances, when, for instance, little rides on the truth of *P*, S's warrant need meet only a low standard.

This theory schema can be filled out in many ways, depending on how one fills out "standards," what one says about which contextual factors can raise or lower standards, and what one says about how much those factors can raise or lower standards. There are many examples that support contextualism to some extent. Independently of that matter, contextualism is also thought to offer a plausible response to skepticism by making room for the claim that in discussions of skepticism, the standards can, if the conversation proceeds just right, get raised absurdly high, so when the skeptic concludes with "So we do not know anything," she speaks the truth—even though in other contexts of utterance, governed by low standards, we speak the truth when we say, "I know she hates my motorcycle." But can the theory provide a decent response to live skepticism?

Take as our example eliminativism. It is natural to say that in theoretical contexts (e.g., discussions of connectionism or Fodor's theory of content), eliminativism definitely poses a threat that can be neutralized only by some strong epistemic factors. The live skeptic seems right about knowledge attributions in those contexts. But what about the completely ordinary conversational contexts in which mere mortals discuss their alleged knowledge of a friend's beliefs? Or the color of their socks? Or whether the doctor is aware of the new pain in their grandfather's hip? Here the error theories are far from anyone's mind. So the live eliminativist hypothesis does not have to be ruled out in order for the mere mortal's "I know she thinks motorcycles are dangerous" to be true. Or so the objection to live skepticism goes.

For the sake of argument in the remainder of this subsection, I will assume that contextualism of some sort is true. The issue here is the truth-value of a *specific* kind of contextualism, one that implies that, for instance, "I know you think motorcycles are dangerous" is true when the mere mortal conversational participants are not thinking or talking about live eliminativism (that is the objection to live skepticism), even though when they discuss eliminativism or other relevant theoretical topics appropriately, then the very same knowledge sentence is false (that is the concession to live skepticism). I will include just one argument regarding this kind of contextualism.

It is plausible to think that the BIV hypothesis needs to be ruled out in order to save the truth of ordinary knowledge attributions only if it is being *discussed or thought about* appropriately. It is hard to see what else could make the BIV hypothesis a threat to one's belief that one has hands. However, that does not mean that occurrent discussion and thought are the *only* ways to make a hypothesis threatening. On the face of it, liveness conditions make a hypothesis just as much or even more of a threat than occurrent attention. We already saw this point when we were briefly discussing relevant-alternatives theories. So we cannot just say, "Well, we have already seen that skeptical hypotheses can be truth-conditionally irrelevant in some contexts; so that is what must be happening with the error theories too." Neither can we get away with "Well, we know that if one is just minimally rational, then one has neutralized the BIV hypothesis, so the same must be true for the color error theory hypothesis." The liveness conditions 1–5 and the mere mortality conditions 6 and 7 make the error theories truth-conditionally relevant as they are "highlighted" or contextually salient.

6. IS IT NOT ACTUALLY EASY TO RULE LIVE ERROR THEORIES OUT?

So perhaps we do need to be able to rule out the live error theories. Can we mere mortals do it? If we can, then the modesty principle is false because it says that we cannot.

Maybe we can neutralize eliminativism without really doing anything. To see how, suppose that philosophers and cognitive scientists proclaim that there are no feelings at all. These eliminativists about feelings argue just as the eliminativists about belief argue:

> No one has any beliefs/feelings. I realize that there are all sorts of cognitive/experiential processes or states in our heads and bodies, but none of them have what it takes to be a belief/feeling. The notion of a belief/feeling is a muddled folk notion that has been constructed in such a way that anything that is a belief/feeling must satisfy certain conditions. But in all probability nothing comes close to satisfying those conditions, which is why there are no beliefs/feelings.

I assume that eliminativism about feelings really is crazy. Even if all the philosophers of mind and cognitive scientists were screaming at my door, "No one has ever had a painful feeling! There are no feelings! No one has ever been in pain!" I would still *know* that I have had loads of painful feelings. My "access" to my painful feeling is so reliable or direct that I can epistemically neutralize, without even thinking about it, any hypothesis that says that I have no feelings. I might be wrong about the location of the feeling, but there is no way in hell that I am wrong that I have a painful feeling.

Now it might be thought that we have given the antiskeptic all she needs. Since I can know without any effort that the eliminativist about feeling is wrong, since I automatically have evidence (very broadly construed) that rules it out, similarly I can know without effort that the eliminativist about belief is wrong, since I automatically have evidence that rules it out. Perhaps this maneuver will not work for the other error theories, but it works for the most interesting one, eliminativism.

I do not think so. For one thing, I simply cannot imagine any remotely plausible reasons for thinking that no one is ever in pain. The no-pain hypothesis just could not be live in a rational community.[7]

More to the point, the notion of belief is just more theoretically loaded than that of feeling. For belief is not some subjective state like feeling. Perhaps a painful feeling just is something that seems painful, but the analogous claim for belief does not work. Sure, there is a feeling of subjective certainty toward a claim; to that extent, belief can involve something akin to sensation. I can know, no matter what the experts say, that I have a feeling of certainty that is directed toward a claim. But there is more to belief than that. Beliefs are not subjective feelings of certainty or anything else. They might include such feelings, but they are more than that. At the least, it is pretty unreasonable to reject this view about belief going beyond feeling. In fact, I do not know anyone who rejects this view. So even though I do have "subjective evidence" that neutralizes the hypothesis that I do not have any feelings of certainty or at least approval of a claim, I do not have subjective evidence that rules out eliminativism about belief. Similar points hold for pain locations, character traits, and colors. For those reasons, I do not think that the antiskeptic can reasonably hold that we all automatically, or upon easy reflection, possess warrant that is, on balance, sufficient to neutralize the error theories. We possess positive warrant that when left alone is sufficient for knowledge of facts about beliefs, but the liveness and mere mortality conditions generate enough negative warrant to sabotage that knowledge.

Maybe reliabilism will suffice to doom live skepticism. Suppose that reliability facts suffice to place a significant amount of positive epistemic warrant on our second-order, first-person beliefs. Perhaps they supply enough warrant that in ordinary circumstances, when we are not in a society fallen to serious consideration of eliminativism, true second-order, first-person beliefs are often good enough for knowledge. The live skeptic can agree with all of that. Perhaps they supply so much warrant that even in an eliminativist-live society, people can have second-order knowledge if they are quite divorced from and ignorant of both philosophy and cognitive science. Even so, eliminativism is actually live, and I am aware of it and its status. Suppose that I happen to reject the eliminativist hypothesis and so believe that I have beliefs. Still, I am no immortal regarding eliminativism. It seems that there is now a significant amount of *negative* epistemic warrant placed on my second-order, first person beliefs (this is the negative warrant revealed by the eliminativist skeptical argument). And there is enough of it to render the positive reliability-based warrant insufficient to render my second-order beliefs warranted enough for knowledge. Only an exceedingly strong form of reliabilism can back up a neutralization of the eliminativist hypothesis. Everyone has admitted that factors like the recognition of expert counteropinion, liveness, independent contrary evidence, and whatnot can defeat a reliably formed belief—even highly reliable ones.

A relevant point here is that if the degree of reliability of the belief-*producing* process has significant epistemic weight (as the reliabilist reasonably holds), then the degree of reliability of the belief-*sustaining* process also has significant epistemic weight. This is no mystery. The belief-sustaining process has to be reliable to *retain* knowledge, and in the cases described in this chapter—liveness, mere mortality—to continue to have beliefs that are known to be in contradiction with the recognizably live hypotheses is clearly *highly* unreliable. That is, the following belief-sustaining procedure—which applies to the beliefs in question—is unreliable: continue to believe that P even though a contrary hypothesis Q has become live and one is a mere mortal with respect to Q. The reliabilist might be right that the reliability of the belief-forming process is often enough to make a true belief knowledge; so when we are children those beliefs amount to knowledge. Our question has to do with the *retention* of that knowledge upon becoming aware of contrary expert evidence. The reliabilist who wants to use reliability factors to defeat the live skeptical arguments has to claim not only that the belief-producing reliability confers a significant amount of warrant, but also that, mysteriously, belief-sustaining reliability is irrelevant. Reliability of belief formation gives me 1,218 positive warrant units; standing fast with the belief that P in face of appreciated, well-respected, expert evidence produces just 200 negative warrant units; I needed just 1,000 units to have my true belief turned into knowledge. Alternatively, belief-forming reliability gives me positive warrant of sufficient quality for knowledge, and belief-sustaining unreliability amounts to no veto. Should we swallow this extremism? I certainly do not feel any temptation to do so when it comes to philosophically uninteresting examples, so I do not see why we should when it comes to philosophically interesting examples.

7. WATERING DOWN THE CONCLUSION

Suppose that despite everything I have just argued, some antiskeptical solution for ordinary, everyday contexts is right even though *perhaps* in theoretical contexts the live skeptic wins. So in ordinary-life contexts "I know my socks are blue" is true. I will make two comments in response.

I have given some pretty good arguments that in theoretical contexts—ones analytic philosophers and cognitive scientists often find themselves in—the new skeptical arguments go through. I find that skeptical result pretty amazing. If it is right, then you do not know much of anything *right now* about the color of objects around you, anyone's beliefs, anyone's character traits, or the pains in your knees. And you do not know any of that in many, many philosophical and even scientific contexts. In spite of the recent endorsement of skeptic-friendly versions of contextualism, according to which we know very little if we are discussing a classic skeptical hypothesis and argument in the right way (thereby making those hypotheses mount real epistemic threats despite being *nowhere near* live), I still find it almost unbelievable that we do not know, *right now*, simple facts about the colors of our socks, our aches and pains, or what we believe.

Finally, suppose once again that some antiskeptical solution is right; so live skepticism is defeated. Then perhaps the antiskeptic may have won a battle but lost the war. Knowledge attributions are often true (that is the won battle), but the truth conditions of those attributions are so meager that we should feel a little ashamed (that is the lost war). The *persistent* live skeptic will say that even if the relevant ordinary knowledge attributions are true, skepticism wins because the truth conditions for those knowledge claims are impoverished. It should be clear that the persistent skeptic's position is not that although "S knows P" is true, S's knowledge is not "high-standards" knowledge. *This* skeptic is not complaining that our knowledge does not fulfill some super-duper high-octane condition that only a philosopher could love. The persistent live skeptic who objects that even if the relevant knowledge attributions are often true, the knowledge states would exist but be pathetic is not whining that knowledge is not what she always fantasized it should be. She has admitted that we can have all the positive warrant we thought we had; she can even admit that we often have super-duper high-octane knowledge of contingent matters of fact. She is targeting a special set of beliefs, ones targeted by the live error theories, and making one crucial claim: the overall warrant possessed by the beliefs targeted by the live skeptical hypotheses is anemic compared with that had by our other beliefs that amount to knowledge and are not targeted by any live skeptical hypotheses. There are seven reasons—(1) through (7)—for thinking that I need some powerful epistemic factors to defuse the expertly endorsed, highly respected contrary scientific error theories plus two reasons—(8) and (9)—to think that I have no such factors; and yet you are telling me that I can know lots of things inconsistent with those error theories? This cannot be a victory the antiskeptic should celebrate. If this realism about knowledge is accurate, then it is a gaunt realism, and the live skeptic has been closer to the truth than the realist.

NOTES

1. I have introduced and evaluated live skepticism in more detail elsewhere (Frances 2005a, 2005b).

2. For my purposes, "eliminativism" indicates just the view that no one believes anything (although it is convenient to conjoin it with the thesis that knowledge requires belief). It is silent—neither pro nor con—on the status of other folk psychological concepts. Stich (1996, 16–29) offers a very helpful summary of eliminativist arguments (eleven by my count). Since the details of these positions and arguments are both distracting and irrelevant to my purposes, I will not examine them here.

3. How large does the group have to be? Surely precision is out of place here. There is a group of well-informed, mere mortal philosophers who take seriously the possibility that there are no chairs, but there are not enough of them to make it live, at least in my judgment. More to the point, that hypothesis does not even come close to meeting all five of the liveness conditions. There are deep issues involved in determining what kinds of hypotheses generate decent live skepticisms when plugged into the argument template of the previous section, none of which I can go into here. Suffice it to say that being a live hypothesis involves meeting a very demanding set of conditions. In part, I stick with hypotheses that have scientific backing because we defer to scientists more than we defer to philosophers, and this difference seems wise.

4. Here I am assuming that before we become mere mortals, say, as children, the liveness of the skeptical hypotheses does not sabotage our knowledge. I will say more on this point later in this section.

5. Of course, this principle is usually stated differently, but those differences will not matter. Minor objections to simple closure, e.g., that the subject has to "think through" the connection between the entailment and her belief in P, can be avoided by building additional conditions into the antecedent. Of course, these can be applied to the live-hypothesis principle as well.

6. I have in mind contextualist and relevant-alternatives theories, although what appears in the following discussion addresses contextualism primarily. These theories are discussed in Chapters 19 and 21 of this volume.

7. One can, of course, marshal good reasons for thinking that a certain kind of "phenomenal pain" does not exist, where a theoretically loaded reference-fixing definition of "phenomenal pain" is in play, but that is another matter entirely.

REFERENCES

Byrne, Alex, and David Hilbert. (2003). "Color Realism and Color Science." *Behavioral and Brain Sciences* 26: 3–21.

Churchland, Patricia S. (1986). *Neurophilosophy: Toward a Unified Science of the Mind-Brain.* Cambridge, MA: MIT Press.

Churchland, Paul M. (1989). *A Neurocomputational Perspective: The Nature of Mind and the Structure of Science.* Cambridge, MA: MIT Press.

Dennett, Daniel. (1978). *Brainstorms.* Cambridge, MA: MIT Press.

Doris, John. (1998). "Persons, Situations and Virtue Ethics." *Noûs* 32: 504–30.

———. (2002). *Lack of Character.* Cambridge: Cambridge University Press.

Feyerabend, Paul. (1963). "Materialism and the Mind-Body Problem." *Review of Metaphysics* 17: 49–66.

Frances, Bryan. (2005a). *Scepticism Comes Alive.* Oxford: Oxford University Press.

———. (2005b). "When a Skeptical Hypothesis Is Live." *Noûs* 39: 559–95.

Harman, Gilbert. (1999). "Moral Philosophy Meets Social Psychology: Virtue Ethics and the Fundamental Attribution Error." *Proceedings of the Aristotelian Society* 99: 315–31.

———. (2000). "The Nonexistence of Character Traits." *Proceedings of the Aristotelian Society* 100: 223–26.

Hyman, John. (2003). "Pains and Places." *Philosophy* 78: 5–24.

Quine, Willard.V.O. (1960). *Word and Object.* Cambridge, MA: MIT Press.

———. (1985). "States of Mind." *Journal of Philosophy* 82: 5–8.

Rorty, Richard. (1970). "In Defence of Eliminative Materialism." *Review of Metaphysics* 24: 112–21.

Stich, Stephen. (1983). *From Folk Psychology to Cognitive Science: The Case against Belief.* Cambridge, MA: MIT Press.

———. (1996). *Deconstructing the Mind.* New York: Oxford University Press.

PART II

RESPONSES TO SKEPTICISM

CHAPTER 11

BERKELEY'S TREATMENT OF SKEPTICISM

GEORGE PAPPAS

BERKELEY'S second book, *Principles of Human Knowledge*, published in 1710, was not particularly well received. Readers and reviewers thought that the work provided support for skepticism and even that it was an outright defense of skepticism. Since Berkeley denied the existence of material substance, he was read as denying the existence of ordinary physical objects. From there it is easy to construe Berkeley as supporting skepticism: if there are no physical objects, then of course nobody has any positive knowledge of them, either of their existence or of their nature.[1]

Berkeley was stung by this reading of *Principles*, and he resolved to set the record straight in his third book, *Three Dialogues between Hylas and Philonous*, published in 1713. One of his chief aims in this book was to show just how opposed he was to skepticism, and that none of his deeply held philosophical positions committed him to skepticism. To the contrary, Berkeley paints his position as one that defends the views of common sense. He also aims to show both that some key doctrines of his philosophical opponents, whom he generally terms "materialists," actually lead to skepticism, which Berkeley interprets as evidence against those doctrines of his opponents; and that Berkeley's own philosophy contains the resources to refute skepticism, not merely to avoid it.

1. BERKELEY'S UNDERSTANDING
OF SKEPTICISM

Berkeley's fullest discussion of skepticism comes in *Three Dialogues*.[2]
There he initially characterizes skepticism in terms of doubt:

> PHILONOUS: Pray, Hylas, what do you mean by a *sceptic?*
> HYLAS: I mean what all men mean, one that doubts of everything.
> (*Works*, vol. 2, 173; all emphases Berkeley's
> unless otherwise noted)

Berkeley, through Philonous, gets Hylas to concede that this definition is too
broad, and so Hylas offers an amended definition that Philonous finds acceptable:

> HYLAS: What think you of distrusting the senses, of denying the real
> existence of sensible things, or pretending to know nothing of them. Is not
> this sufficient to denominate a man a *sceptic?*
> PHILONOUS: Shall we therefore examine which of us it is that denies the
> reality of sensible things, or professes the greatest ignorance of them; since,
> if I take you rightly, he is to be esteemed the greatest *sceptic?*
> (Ibid.)

If we take the phrase "distrusting the senses" to mean the view that perception does
not afford knowledge of physical objects, then this exchange between Hylas and
Philonous provides three notions of skepticism that concern Berkeley:

1. We do not have perceptual knowledge of objects.
2. We do not have any knowledge of objects.
3. There are no physical objects.

Statement 3, of course, is not a skeptical doctrine per se, since it concerns
merely the existence of physical objects and is silent on any knowledge we may have
of them. Even so, (3) is important because if it is true, then so are (2) and (1), since
if there are no physical objects, then we have no positive knowledge of them.

We will see later that Berkeley does not really contend that Hylas's philosophical views entail (3). Instead, what Berkeley alleges is that, given Hylas' doctrines, we would not know that there are physical objects. This is a much different
and properly epistemic thesis.

In the preface to *Three Dialogues*, Berkeley says:

> Upon the common principles of philosophers, we are not assured of the existence
> of things from their being perceived. And we are taught to distinguish their
> real nature from that which falls under our senses. Hence arise *scepticism* and
> *paradoxes.* It is not enough that we see and feel, that we taste and smell a thing. Its
> true nature, its absolute external entity, is still concealed.
> (*Works*, vol. 2, 167)

Skepticism about the nature of objects is a quite different position from general skepticism about objects, expressed in (2). For while (2) implies skepticism as to the nature of objects, clearly the converse does not hold. One may have all manner of knowledge of objects, including that of their existence, but remain ignorant of their "inner" nature. Indeed, on one reading, that is exactly Locke's official position.

Berkeley also speaks, in the last-quoted passage, of not being "assured of the existence of things." A natural reading of the word "assured" is "certain of," and so understood, Berkeley would be alluding to a skeptical doctrine we might express as follows:

4. Our beliefs about the existence and character of objects are not certain.

In the third dialogue, after a summary statement of his own position, Philonous says:

> Away then with all that scepticism, all those ridiculous philosophical doubts. What a jest it is for a philosopher to question the existence of sensible things, till he hath it proved to him from the veracity of God: or to pretend our knowledge in this point falls short of intuition or demonstration! I might as well doubt of my own being, as of the being of those things I actually see and feel.
>
> (*Works*, vol. 2, 230)

The reference to God's veracity is plainly to Descartes, and the subsequent reference to intuition and demonstration can be read naturally as referring to Locke's account of sensitive knowledge. According to Locke, we have sensitive knowledge of objects that has some degree of certainty that falls short of the certainty that attends beliefs about immediately experienced ideas of sensation. We have intuitive and maximally certain knowledge, Locke says, of ideas only at the time we experience them, and we never have intuitive knowledge of objects. Berkeley's claim in the passage just quoted, then, is that on Locke's position we lack certain knowledge of objects, while on Berkeley's own view of the matter we have such knowledge. Skepticism of the sort expressed in (4) will be taken up in the last section of this chapter. Skepticism about the nature of objects will not be taken up because it would take us too far afield into Locke's philosophy.

2. THE COMMON PRINCIPLES OF PHILOSOPHERS

Berkeley contends that there are some common principles of philosophers, and that these principles, either individually or jointly, lead to skepticism of some form. He does not mention which philosophers he has in mind, however. It seems clear that Locke is one of Berkeley's chief targets. Locke is mentioned by name in the discussion of abstract ideas in the introduction to *Principles*, and in both *Principles* and *Three Dialogues* Berkeley singles out certain doctrines that we know were accepted by Locke. Examples include the distinction between primary and secondary qualities, the realist thesis that objects and their various qualities exist independently of perceivers and of perceptions by them, and the thesis that there are abstract ideas. It is also clear that in referring to reliance on the veracity of God to help establish that there are physical objects, as we noted earlier, Berkeley has Descartes in mind, though it remains unclear whether Descartes is thought by Berkeley to be one who accepts the common principles that Berkeley will single out for attention.

Given this uncertainty about the philosophers Berkeley refers to, we will look instead just at the common principles that Berkeley claims have skeptical consequences. It will seem, perhaps correctly, that Locke is uppermost in Berkeley's mind on these points, though no presumption of the correctness of this point will be made.

In the introduction to *Principles*, Berkeley writes:

> My purpose therefore is, to try if I can discover what those principles are, which have introduced all that doubtfulness and uncertainty, those absurdities and contradictions into the several sects of philosophy.
>
> (*Works*, vol. 2, 26)

The first principle that Berkeley claims engenders skepticism is the thesis that there are abstract ideas. He says, immediately following the passage last quoted:

> [the] unraveling this matter leads me in some measure to anticipate my design, by taking notice of what seems to have had a chief part in rendering speculation intricate and perplexed, and to have occasioned innumerable errors and difficulties in almost all parts of knowledge. And that is the opinion that the mind hath a power of framing *abstract ideas* or notions of things.
>
> (Ibid., 27)

A second principle that is held to lead to skepticism is the thesis that matter exists, or more exactly, that physical objects consist in a material substratum in which qualities inhere. One passage where this is made clear is in an exchange between Hylas and Philonous:

> HYLAS: What! Can anything be more fantastical, more repugnant to common sense, or a more manifest piece of skepticism, than to believe there is no such thing as *matter*?
> PHILONOUS: What if I should prove, that you who hold there is, are by virtue of that opinion a greater *sceptic*, and maintain more paradoxes and repugnancies to common sense, than I who believe no such thing?
>
> (*Works*, vol. 2, 172)

Lest we think that Berkeley is really only speaking of degrees of commitment to skepticism, since he does have Philonous claim that Hylas is a "greater sceptic," consider how Berkeley puts the matter a little later in the third dialogue, after Hylas has presented a concession speech in which he says that it is impossible that corporeal bodies should exist:

> PHILONOUS: You amaze me. Was ever any thing more wild and extravagant than the notions you now maintain: and is it not evident that you are led into all these extravagancies by the belief of *material substance*? It is this occasions your distinguishing between the reality and sensible appearances of things. It is to this you are indebted for being ignorant of what every body else knows perfectly well.
>
> (*Works*, vol. 2, 229)

Closely connected to the material-substance thesis is the point that objects have a real absolute existence. As Berkeley uses this term, it means that objects exist independently of all perceivers and of perceptions, or, in different terms, it is the very denial of Berkeley's own thesis that for objects and their qualities, to be is to be perceived. The connection of this thesis to skepticism, in Berkeley's eyes, is made clear in this passage from *Principles*:

> So long as we attribute a real existence to unthinking things, distinct from their being perceived, it is not only impossible for us to know with evidence the nature of any real unthinking being, but even that it exists. Hence it is, that we see philosophers distrust their senses, and doubt the existence of heaven and earth, of every thing they see or feel, or even of their own bodies.
>
> (*Works*, vol. 2, 79)

A fourth and final principle that is taken to lead to skepticism is representative realism. A representative passage that shows this, drawn from many, is *Principles* 87:

> Colour, figure, motion, extension and the like, considered only as so many *sensations* in the mind, are perfectly known, there being nothing in them which is not perceived. But if they are looked on as notes or images, referred to *things* or *archetypes* existing without the mind, then are we involved all on *scepticism*.
>
> (*Works*, vol. 2, 78)

The passages we have noted make it clear that Berkeley thinks that each of the four principles by itself leads to skepticism. In fact, it is clear from these passages that he holds that all the skeptical doctrines identified earlier, with the exception perhaps of (3), follow from each of these principles. He does not indicate what he means by the claim that these principles *lead to* skepticism, though a natural reading would be that each of these principles implies one or more skeptical doctrines, or that each of the common principles taken in conjunction with some other obvious truths implies skepticism.

3. LEADING TO SKEPTICISM

It is not difficult to see that by Berkeley's own lights, the first three of the common principles do not individually imply skepticism. In fact, it does not seem that they have that implication even taken collectively. The reason is that each of the first three common principles is compatible with direct realism about perception. On that theory, of course, physical objects and not some phenomenal intermediaries are typically immediately perceived. Berkeley himself takes the immediate perception of physical objects to be sufficient in many contexts for knowledge of those objects. Thus by Berkeley's own position, none of the first three common principles itself implies skepticism. Moreover, the same seems to hold for the three principles taken as a group, for the conjoined three principles are also perfectly compatible with direct realism.

We can reconstruct Berkeley's thought on this topic, however, as the claim that each of these three common principles, when taken together with some other obvious truths, implies skepticism. Consider first the second common principle, namely, the material-substratum thesis. If objects consist in qualities inhering in a material substratum, then Berkeley contends that those objects exist unperceived. He notes:

> But why should we trouble ourselves any farther, in discussing this material *substratum* or support of figure and motion, and other sensible qualities? Does it not suppose they have an existence without the mind? And is not this a direct repugnancy, and altogether inconceivable?
>
> (*Principles* 17, in *Works*, vol. 2, 35)

Although one might question this inference, here we are only asking how Berkeley was reasoning, not whether he was correct.[3] Berkeley also seems to have felt that the abstract-ideas thesis implies that objects exist unperceived. He says early in *Principles*:

> If we thoroughly examine this tenet, it will, perhaps, be found at bottom to depend on the doctrine of *abstract ideas*. For can there be a nicer strain of abstraction than to distinguish the existence of sensible objects from their being perceived, so as to conceive them existing unperceived?
>
> (*Principles* 5, in *Works*, vol. 2, 42)

Here the tenet Berkeley refers to is the claim that sensible objects exist unperceived. Berkeley does not further clarify what he means by "depends on," but one possible reading is that the truth of the abstract-ideas thesis is logically sufficient for the truth of the claim that objects exist unperceived.[4] If this is what Berkeley means, then his view would be that the first of the common principles considered here, namely, the thesis of abstract ideas, implies the third common principle, that objects exist unperceived, so that the principle "to be is to be perceived" as applied to sensible objects would be false.

On this reconstruction, each of the first and second common principles implies the third. By itself, as we have noted, this is not enough to get us to skepticism. However, along with many other philosophers of the period, Berkeley also assumes that the theory of ideas is correct, so that in every perceptual experience, at least one idea is immediately perceived. Then the conjunction of the thesis that objects exist unperceived and the theory of ideas would imply that some form of indirect realism would be correct as a theory of perception, and Berkeley holds that indirect realism generates skepticism.

In a nutshell, the reasoning is this: the abstract-ideas thesis and the material-substratum thesis each imply that objects exist unperceived. The latter claim, conjoined with the theory of ideas, implies indirect realism; and indirect realism leads directly to skepticism about objects.

I do not think that Berkeley holds that indirect realism alone entails skepticism. Once again, something has to be added to it to get that result. Berkeley indicates what these extra elements are in *Principles* 18–20, where he notes that if indirect realism is correct, then any perceptual knowledge we might have about objects would have to be inferential knowledge. In short, we would need to be able to derive beliefs about objects from beliefs about immediately experienced ideas. Deductive inferences would not be available here because

> what reason can induce us to believe the existence of bodies without the mind, from what we perceive, since the very patrons of matter themselves do not pretend, there is any necessary connexion between them and our ideas?
>
> (*Works*, vol. 2, 48)

If the inferences in question were inductive, they would likely be explanatory, with the supposition of unperceived objects helping explain the sorts and sequences of ideas we experience. Berkeley thinks that this sort of inductive inference will not succeed because it would require that material objects causally affect minds, which Berkeley assumes are immaterial entities. Thus the most plausible inductive inference from beliefs about ideas to beliefs about objects will not succeed, and since these inference options are exhaustive, skepticism about objects results. We thus see that none of the first three common principles identified by Berkeley implies skepticism, and neither do they do so when taken jointly. It is only with the addition of substantive further premises, most important, a statement of the theory of ideas and some claims about inferential knowledge, that skepticism would emerge as a conclusion.[5]

The fourth common principle is the representative-realist theory of perception, a species of indirect realism, and we have noted that Berkeley thinks that it, too, leads to skepticism. Again, it is not a direct entailment; some extra premises are needed. Berkeley gives them in what we can call the *conformity argument*:

> And first as to ideas or unthinking things, our knowledge of these has been very much obscured and confounded, and we have been led into very dangerous errors, by supposing a twofold existence of the objects of sense, the one *intelligible*, or in the mind, the other *real* and without the mind: whereby unthinking

things are thought to have a natural subsistence of their own, distinct from being perceived by spirits. This which, if I mistake not, has been shown to be a most groundless and absurd notion, is the very root of *skepticism*; for so long as men thought that real things subsisted without the mind, and that their knowledge was only so far forth *real* as it was conformable to *real things*, it follows, they could not be certain that they had any real knowledge at all. For how can it be known, that the things which are perceived, are conformable to those which are not perceived, or exist without the mind?

> (*Principles*, 86, in *Works*, vol 2, 76; a similar conformity argument
> appears in *Three Dialogues*, in *Works*, vol. 2, 246)

With this fourth common principle, the needed extra premises are that we have knowledge of objects, given representative realism, only if that knowledge is inferential. The needed inferences would plainly not be deductive, though Berkeley omits that point. They would succeed as inductions only if we could also establish that a conformity holds between ideas and objects, and Berkeley takes the needed conformity to be resemblance. However, we can establish this sort of resemblance only if we can compare both of the resembling items, and, given the representative-realist theory, that is something we cannot do. Hence if representative realism is correct, we end with skepticism about objects, not directly, but via the additional premises supplied with the conformity argument.[6]

4. VANQUISHING SKEPTICISM

Berkeley is not content to expose principles that give rise to skepticism. He also wants to undermine skepticism by refuting those principles. There is no reason to attribute to Berkeley what would be the quaint idea that skepticism would not arise on any other principles, of course. Berkeley was attending to the principles that, as he understood things, were operative in his own time.

Berkeley's criticisms of the four common principles are long and complex and will be presented here only in summary form. His criticisms of abstract ideas and of the process of abstraction occur mainly in the introduction to *Principles*, though he does have critical comments on abstract ideas in other writings as well, including *Three Dialogues*.[7] Berkeley distinguishes several types of abstract ideas, some of which he opposes on the grounds that they cannot be acquired. An example of this type would be the abstract idea of a color instance, say, this instance of red shade 36. The process of acquiring this idea would be that of abstracting it, or separating it, from the idea of a certain shape with which it is fused, and this is something Berkeley claims cannot be done. He holds, with others, that what cannot be separated in reality cannot be separated in thought. In reality, we cannot separate a red shade 36 instance from some shape instance. Hence we cannot have an idea of just red shade 36 because we cannot succeed in acquiring it.[8]

Other types of abstract ideas cannot be possessed because they are intrinsically impossible. An example would be the abstract idea of color, formed by attending to ideas of various colors and separating out what they have in common, namely, being colors. The resulting abstract idea of color would have to be of neither the color red, nor green, nor yellow, nor any of the other determinate colors, but would still have to be an idea of (mere) color. Berkeley takes this abstract idea to be an impossible object, something that cannot exist. The abstract idea of man is supposed to be something like that of color, a mere determinable. It is an idea

> wherein there is included colour, because there is no man but has some colour, but then it can be neither white, nor black, nor any particular colour; because there is no one particular colour wherein all men partake. So likewise there is included stature, but then it is neither tall stature nor low stature, nor yet middle stature, but something abstracted from all these.
>
> (*Works*, vol. 2, 28–29)

Berkeley claims that one cannot have an idea of this sort, any more than one can have an abstract idea of color:

> The idea of man that I frame to myself, must be either of a white, or a black, or a tawny, a straight, or a crooked, a tall, or a low, or a middle-sized man.
>
> (Ibid., 29)

Abstract ideas of color or of man are what Berkeley considers abstract general ideas, and it is their generality to which he is most opposed because that conflicts with one of his deepest principles, namely, that everything that exists is particular.

The thesis that objects exist independently of perceptions and of perceivers is criticized by Berkeley mainly in his attempts to establish the principle that for all nonperceiving things, to be is to be perceived. In the first of the *Three Dialogues*, he considers singly each of the sensible qualities and tries to show by means of familiar perceptual relativity arguments that none of those qualities exists unperceived. If successful, these arguments would not suffice to show that objects exist only when perceived, for an object might consist of more than sensible qualities. It might, for instance, consist, in part, of a material substratum in which qualities inhere. Berkeley has a battery of arguments against material substance, especially in *Three Dialogues*, where he has Hylas present a number of different ways of conceiving of matter. One of the main arguments he uses, however, is that no clear sense can be made of the inherence relation. A substratum is supposed to support and unify the qualities inherent in it. However, ordinary ways of understanding the support relation require that the supporting entity be extended, contrary to the very concept of a substratum.

The representative-realist theory of perception is criticized mainly on the grounds that it requires that some ideas resemble real qualities of bodies, and that this is impossible. Resemblance between ideas and qualities in bodies, Berkeley holds, would violate the likeness principle, according to which an idea can only be like, or resemble, another idea. Accordingly, he maintains that the representative-realist theory is simply false. His main argument against the theory is not that it leads to skepticism regarding bodies, though we have seen that he holds that. Rather, his main argument against the theory is that it requires a resemblance relation that cannot obtain.

5. REFUTING SKEPTICISM

Berkeley wants to go beyond merely undermining skepticism by refuting the common principles that give rise to it. He wants also to refute skepticism outright. The key to understanding how this will work is to explain what Berkeley says about the perception of objects.

To understand Berkeley's view, it helps to start with the view he rejects, namely, indirect realism, including the representative-realist version of that theory, which Berkeley attributes to Locke. On those theories, only sensible ideas are immediately perceived. Physical objects and the qualities of them, when perceived, are always perceived indirectly. Berkeley thinks, as we have noted, that this means that if there is to be knowledge of objects gained through perception, for both indirect realism and its representative version, this knowledge would have to be inferential. Further, for reasons already given, Berkeley thinks that the prospects for such inferences actually succeeding are worse than merely bleak. He further holds that matters are entirely different on his philosophical position because it allows for the immediate perception of objects. It is this fact that is supposed to support Berkeley's claim that on his philosophy, we have not just perceptual knowledge of objects, but immediate and noninferential knowledge of objects.

Berkeley endorses immaterialism about objects, that is, the view that objects are nothing more than bundles of sensible qualities. These qualities do not further inhere in a material substance; for Berkeley, there is no such thing, as we noted earlier. In *Principles*, Berkeley assumes without argument that each sensible quality is an idea, and that together with immaterialism, this yields the result that objects are really bundles of sensible ideas.

Berkeley may have realized that it was not enough to merely assume that sensible qualities are each ideas, for in *Three Dialogues* he spends a good bit of effort trying to establish that very point. In the first dialogue, Berkeley uses mainly perceptual relativity arguments on each of the sensible qualities and concludes in each case that the sensible quality in question is an idea that exists only when perceived (or, as he usually puts it, only in the mind). Armed with this result, together with the assumption that he has covered all the sensible qualities and the further assumption of immaterialism, Berkeley reaches the position that objects are bundles of sensible ideas.

Sensible ideas are paradigmatically entities that are immediately perceived. Berkeley thinks that physical objects are also immediately perceived. For example, he says:

> Wood, stones, fire, water, flesh, iron, and the like things, which I name and discourse of, are things that I know. And I should not have known them, but that I perceived them by my senses; and things perceived by the senses are immediately perceived.
>
> (*Works*, vol. 2, 230)

In a letter to the American philosopher Samuel Johnson, Berkeley wrote:

> I see no difficulty in conceiving a change of state, such as is vulgarly called Death, as well without as with material substance. It is sufficient for that purpose that we allow sensible bodies, i.e., such as are immediately perceived by sight and touch.
>
> (Ibid., 282)

Berkeley is in a position to maintain that objects are immediately perceived, given his bundle theory of objects and given the fact that sensible ideas are immediately perceived. Insofar as one may be said to immediately perceive an object *by* immediately perceiving some of its constituent elements, namely, the ideas that make up that object, Berkeley will be on safe ground is claiming that objects are immediately perceived.

It is no objection to this point that one never immediately perceives all the sensible ideas constituting an object. In ordinary circumstances, one virtually never perceives all of an object's parts or other elements composing that object, and we do not find this to be an impediment as far as perception goes. We still say, that is, that the object in question is perceived. When I look at the Brandenburg Gate from one side, I hardly see all of its parts, maybe not even most of them. Nonetheless, I see the Brandenburg Gate from that angle and position. A similar point holds in Berkeley's case. It is not exactly the same point, of course, because sensible ideas that make up an object are not parts of the object, but the analogy is close enough for these illustrative purposes.

If objects and their sensible qualities are immediately perceived, Berkeley says, then we also have knowledge of those objects and qualities. The last-quoted passage but one shows this clearly, assuming that we can contrapose Berkeley's phrase "I should not have known them, but that I perceived them by my senses" so that it reads "If I immediately perceive those objects, then I know those objects (have knowledge of those objects)." That Berkeley conceives of this knowledge as immediate and noninferential is indicated by two entries from the *Philosophical Commentaries*:

> We have an intuitive Knowledge of the Existence of other things besides ourselves & even praecedaneous to the Knowledge of our own Existence. in that we must have Ideas or else we cannot think.
>
> (Entry 547, in *Works*, vol. 1, 69)

Here the term "other things" may be referring solely to sensible ideas and not to objects. However, Berkeley returns to the same point at entry 563:

> I am the farthest from Scepticism of any man. I know with an intuitive knowledge the existence of other things as well as my own Soul. This is w^t Locke nor scarce any other Thinking Philosopher will pretend to.
>
> (Ibid., 70)[9]

In this second passage, Berkeley also uses the term "other things." The important point is that he contrasts his view with that of Locke. There would be no contrast if Berkeley used "other things" to refer to ideas, because Locke grants that we have intuitive knowledge of them. To make a contrast with Locke stand out, Berkeley has to mean by "other things" sensible objects and their qualities. Further, the stress he places on intuitive knowledge, as Locke conceives of this notion, clinches the point that Berkeley is claiming that we gain immediate and noninferential knowledge of objects by immediately perceiving them.

In sum, Berkeley thinks that he can plausibly maintain that physical objects and their qualities are immediately perceived. He can reach this result by means of his bundle theory of objects, the obvious truth that sensible ideas are immediately perceived, and the presumption that we can immediately perceive an object by immediately perceiving some of the elements that constitute it.[10] In turn, he holds that this immediate perception of objects suffices for us to have noninferential knowledge of objects. This amounts to Berkeley's response to the forms of skepticism cited earlier as (1) and (2). Moreover, we have knowledge of objects from having immediately perceived them only if there are, or were, objects, so Berkeley plausibly feels that he also has an effective response to skepticism in the form of (3).

6. CERTAINTY

Another form of skepticism of concern to Berkeley is the thesis that we do not have certainty in our beliefs about objects, expressed earlier as (4). Here a bit of complexity in Locke is important. Locke distinguishes between intuitive, demonstrative, and sensitive knowledge. Intuitive knowledge is had only of immediately experienced ideas and idea-pairs and of the self. Locke thinks not only that this sort of knowledge is noninferential, but also that it enjoys the highest level or degree of certainty. By contrast, sensitive knowledge is knowledge of objects, and whether or not Locke thinks that it is noninferential, it has a lesser degree of certainty than that possessed by intuitive knowledge, though it is a level of certainty that suffices to qualify sensitive knowledge as genuine knowledge and not merely well-formed belief.[11]

We have seen that Berkeley claims that on his philosophy, we have intuitive knowledge of objects and not merely of ideas. If he means by this that we have noninferential knowledge of objects, since noninferentiality is part of what Locke means by intuitive knowledge, then Berkeley would have a reasonable case based on the considerations adduced in the preceding section. But if he means to be stressing, instead, that our knowledge of objects has the highest degree of certainty that Locke claims attends intuitive knowledge, then Berkeley would be quite definitely mistaken. This highest degree of certainty, for Locke, is Cartesian and amounts to the impossibility of mistaken belief. In *Draft A* of the *Essay*, Locke speaks of certainty in terms of infallibility, or the impossibility of mistaken belief. For example, he says:

> That a man may have a certaine infallible knowledg of universal affirmative Identicall propositions (viz wherein any of his Ideas is affirmed of its self) and of all propositions depending there upon.[12]

Here Locke is speaking of single ideas presently before the mind. If one is presently immediately aware of an idea of red color, then one cannot be mistaken in believing that one is then immediately aware of red color. Locke extends the point to some pluralities of current ideas:

> That a man may have a certain infallible knowledg of universal negative propositions wherein one of his simple Ideas is denyed of an other and all subsequent propositions depending there on.
>
> (*Draft A*, 53)

Locke's examples in this sort of case include situations when one has two visual ideas, one of red and another of yellow, about which he says that "when he hath in his understanding...the Idea of yellow and Idea of red he cannot but certainly know...that the Idea of red is the Idea of red and not the Idea of yellow" (Ibid.).

Locke's comments about infallibility are stated in the form of rules, but in the remarks he makes just before the rules, he says:

> All which certainty arises only from that cleare evident distinct knowledge our understanding hath of those simple Ideas it hath received from the operations of our own minds..., which perception and knowledge of its own Ideas that are in it cannot erre about them.
>
> (Ibid., 52)

We thus see that Locke understands the notion of infallibility to mean the impossibility of mistaken belief. In turn, this notion implies that of having a probability of one.

The propositions Locke identifies as infallibly known in *Draft A* correspond to some of those propositions he says are known intuitively in the published *Essay*. There Locke repeats the claims about infallibility (E, IV, I, 4), but then adds:

> Such kind of Truths, the Mind perceives at the very first sight of the *Ideas* together, by bare *Intuition*, without the intervention of any other *Idea*; and this kind of

> Knowledge is the clearest, and most certain, that human Frailty is capable of. This
> part of Knowledge is irresistible, and like the bright Sun-shine, forces it self
> immediately to be perceived.
>
> (Essay, IV, II, 1)¹³

Locke himself never claims this level of certainty for sensitive knowledge of bodies.
If Berkeley is claiming to have this level of certainty attending beliefs about bodies,
given his own philosophy, then he is mistaken, for our beliefs about bodies, even
those immediately perceived and noninferentially known, are not such as to rule
out the logical possibility of error.

Berkeley has a weaker concept of certainty by which he seems to put great
store. To see what this is, we can consider some passages from the *Philosophical
Commentaries*. In one, Berkeley says:

> I am certain there is a God, tho I do not perceive him have no intuition of him.
> This not difficult if we rightly understand wᵗ is meant by certainty.
>
> (Philosophical Commentaries, Entry 813; Works, vol. 1, 97)

At Entry 776 Berkeley speaks of other religious statements that are "Agreeable to
my Doctrine of Certainty." And at Entry 800, Berkeley says:

> Malbranch in his Illustration differs widely from me. He doubts of the Existence of
> Bodies I doubt not in the least of this.
>
> (Ibid., 96)

Nor did Berkeley drop this line of thought in the published works. Consider these
passages from *Three Dialogues*:

> Let me be represented as one who trusts his senses, who thinks he knows the
> things he sees and feels, and entertains no doubt of their existence.
>
> (Works, vol. 2, 237)

> I do therefore assert that I am as certain as of my own being that there are bodies
> or corporeal substances (meaning the things I perceive by my senses).
>
> (Ibid., 238)

> I might as well doubt of my own being as of the being of those things I actually see
> and feel.
>
> (Ibid., p. 230)

If we read the first and third of these passages in light of the second, then Berkeley is
speaking of certain knowledge of bodies throughout. More generally, in this part of
Three Dialogues he is at pains to contrast his position with that of Hylas, presumably representing Locke and perhaps others, for whom (by Berkeley's lights, at
any rate) doubt is perfectly appropriate vis-à-vis the existence and nature of bodies.

When these passages are read in light of the reference to "my doctrine of
certainty" from the *Notebooks*, we get a different concept of certainty emerging,
and a different set of things, other than ideas, to which this second concept of
certainty applies. We can express this weaker concept of certainty as the complete

absence of doubt vis-à-vis some proposition. Armed with this concept of certainty, Berkeley would have good grounds for holding, as we have seen that he does, that we have certain knowledge of bodies and, indeed, of much else. These are among the entities to which Berkeley applies this weaker concept of certainty, and it is this weaker concept, I think, to which he is alluding when he speaks of "my doctrine of certainty."

If Berkeley is speaking of certain knowledge of bodies and using this weak concept of certainty, according to which one is certain that p just in case one believes that p and one has no doubts vis-à-vis p, then he would be on much safer ground. That is, it would be quite plausible for him to maintain, as we have seen that he does, that on his philosophy we have certain knowledge of bodies. In that sense, he could be understood as having refuted the form of skepticism initially given by (4). On the other hand, if this is what Berkeley means by certain knowledge of bodies, then he has purchased a refutation of this form of skepticism at a cost, for this sort of certainty in one's beliefs about bodies is perfectly consistent with indirect realism about perception and with the representative-realist version of indirect realism that Berkeley attributes to Locke. In that case, Berkeley would be in no position to claim that Locke's theory of perception leads to skepticism of the sort formulated in (4). That is, skepticism of the sort found in (4) would not be something one would be led to by the common principles of philosophers identified by Berkeley.

NOTES

1. On the interpretation readers gave to Berkeley's early works, see Harry Bracken, *The Early Reception of Berkeley's Immaterialism* (The Hague: Martinus Nijhoff, 1959; revised version, 1965).

2. References to Berkeley's writings throughout this chapter will be to *The Works of George Berkeley,* ed. T.E. Jessop and A.A. Luce (Edinburgh: Thomas Nelson, 1948–57). Both *Principles* and *Three Dialogues* are in volume 2.

3. On the material-substratum thesis, an object consists in the substratum plus the inhering qualities. The claim that this thesis implies that objects exist unperceived is equivalent, by contraposition, to the claim that: the statement that objects exist only if they are perceived, implies that objects are not substrata plus inherent qualities. However, it certainly seems a consistent position to hold that the object and its qualities exist if and only if perceived, but that some constituent element of the object, namely, the substratum, does not.

4. This is not the only reading, of course; Berkeley may mean to be picking out just a necessary condition, or even both necessary and sufficient conditions. For further discussion of this issue, see George Pappas, *Berkeley's Thought* (Ithaca, N.Y.: Cornell University Press, 2000), 87.

5. Berkeley's claim that if indirect realism is true, then our knowledge of objects would have to be inferential is critically examined and found wanting in George Pappas, "Ber-

keley's Assessment of Locke's Epistemology," *Philosophica* 76 (2005), 91–114. The point that the relevant inductive inferences would fail is contested by J.L. Mackie, *Problems from Locke* (Oxford: Clarendon Press, 1976), 62–71.

6. The conformity argument is further discussed in Pappas, "Berkeley's Assessment of Locke's Epistemology."

7. Criticism of abstract ideas in *Three Dialogues* is discussed in Tom Stoneham, *Berkeley's World* (Oxford: Oxford University Press, 2002), chap. 7; in connection with the *Essay towards a New Theory of Vision* in George Pappas, "Abstract Ideas and the *New Theory of Vision*," *British Journal for the History of Philosophy* 10(2002):55–71; and in connection with Berkeley's philosophy of mathematics in Douglas Jesseph, *Berkeley's Philosophy of Mathematics* (Chicago: University of Chicago Press, 1993).

8. There is disagreement over whether Berkeley was correct in understanding abstraction as separation, as opposed to selective attention. For some of the issues, see Kenneth Winkler, *Berkeley: An Interpretation* (New York: Oxford University Press, 1989), and Pappas,*Berkeley's Thought*, chap. 3.

9. The *Philosophical Commentaries* are notebooks that Berkeley kept in the months just before the publication of his first book, the *Essay towards a New Theory of Vision*, in 1709. The notebooks were first uncovered and published by A. C. Fraser in 1870.

10. To be sure, Berkeley needs a concept of immediate perception that will support this presumption. Three different attempts to get at this concept are in Georges Dicker, "Berkeley on Immediate Perception: Once More unto the Breach," *Philosophical Quarterly* 56(2006): 517–535; Stoneham, *Berkeley's World*, 89–92; and Pappas, *Berkeley's Thought*, 158–172.

11. The thesis that for Locke, sensitive knowledge is also noninferential is defended in Michael Ayers, *Locke: Epistemology and Ontology*, vol. 1 (London: Routledge, 1991), and in George Pappas, "Locke's Account of Sensitive Knowledge," in M. O'Rourke, ed., *Knowledge and Scepticism: Topics in Contemporary Philosophy* (Cambridge, Mass.: MIT Press, forthcoming).

12. John Locke, *An Early Draft of Locke's Essay*, ed. R. Aaron and J. Gibb (Oxford: Clarendon Press, 1936), p. 53. Further citations in the text are to this book.

13. John Locke, *An Essay Concerning Human Understanding*, ed. P. Nidditch (Oxford: Oxford University Press, 1975).

CHAPTER 12

KANT'S RESPONSE TO SKEPTICISM

ROBERT STERN

WITHIN much contemporary epistemology, Kant's response to skepticism has come to be epitomized by an appeal to *transcendental arguments*. This form of argument is said to provide a distinctively Kantian way of dealing with the skeptic, by showing that what the skeptic questions is in fact a condition for her being able to raise that question in the first place, if she is to have language, thoughts, or experiences at all. In this way, it is hoped, the game played by the skeptic can be turned against herself.[1] At the same time, however, this appeal to transcendental arguments is also widely felt to show what is *wrong* with Kant's response to skepticism: for, it is suggested, such arguments can only be made to work against the background of his transcendental idealism. As we shall see, what this doctrine amounts to is much disputed; but as with any form of idealism, the worry is that it means compromising the very realism and objectivity we want to defend against skepticism in the first place, so that the price for adopting this Kantian strategy appears too high—the cure of using transcendental arguments in conjunction with transcendental idealism is almost as bad as the disease.[2]

Faced with this difficulty, two kinds of response have been canvassed. On the first, it is accepted that transcendental arguments do require a commitment to the wider philosophical framework of transcendental idealism, but it is claimed that this framework can and should be defended against the suggestion that it is itself "quasi-skeptical." On the second, transcendental idealism is indeed abandoned as wrongheaded, but it is held that Kant's transcendental arguments can be made to work without it and so can be isolated from the rest of his philosophical system. In what follows (in section 1), I will run through responses of both kinds and suggest that at least one of Kant's transcendental arguments can in fact be understood in a way that involves very little appeal to the rest of the Kantian framework, whether one sees that as problematic or not.

However, I will also argue (in section 2) that this preoccupation with transcendental arguments is not the right way to get the full picture of how Kant saw the threat of skepticism, or indeed what he took skepticism to be, so that we should not consider the relation between skepticism and transcendental idealism only in these terms; we must get beyond viewing transcendental arguments as the central issue in Kant's response to skepticism if we are to properly understand what he took that response to involve and require. In coming to see what we are likely to miss if we focus only on the issue of transcendental arguments and whether or not they require transcendental idealism, we will also be brought to view the connection between Kant's response to skepticism and the rest of his philosophical project in a new light.

1. KANT, SKEPTICISM, AND TRANSCENDENTAL ARGUMENTS

As we have observed, when Kant's response to skepticism is discussed, it is commonly taken that at the center of this response is an appeal to transcendental arguments.[3] Although the exact nature of these arguments is far from unproblematic, they are widely held to have the following features: they begin from some sort of self-evident starting point concerning our nature as subjects (for example, that we have experiences of a certain kind, or have beliefs of a certain kind, or make utterances of a certain kind) that the skeptic can be expected to accept, and then proceed to show that this starting point has certain metaphysically necessary conditions, where, in establishing that these conditions obtain, the skeptic is thereby refuted. So, in the face of the skeptical suggestion that we do not know that there is an external world, or other minds, or the past, a transcendental argument might be offered to provide deductive support for these claims from certain facts about our nature as subjects, based on the premise that the former are necessary conditions for the latter, where the form of the argument is this: we have certain experiences, etc; a necessary condition for us having these experiences, etc is the truth of P; therefore P.

It is, of course, no accident that Kant has come to be associated with this kind of response to skepticism, for this may well seem to be what he is aiming at when he introduces his Refutation of Idealism in the preface of the *Critique of Pure Reason* in the following terms: "[I]t still remains a scandal to philosophy and to human reason in general that the existence of things outside us (from which we derive the whole material of knowledge, even for our inner sense) must be accepted merely on *faith,* and if anyone thinks good to doubt their existence, we are unable to counter his doubts by any satisfactory proof."[4] Kant thus appears to want the Refutation of Idealism to be taken as a proof of the existence of the external world, insofar as this is a necessary condition for "inner sense," by which the mind (*Gemüt*) "intuits itself or its inner state."[5]

However, it is widely held that this proof cannot proceed straightforwardly and can only be made to work by invoking Kant's transcendental idealism. A highly influential source of this suspicion is Barry Stroud, who in his article "Transcendental Arguments" suggested that for any claim concerning the necessary condition S, "the sceptic can always very plausibly insist that it is enough [that] we *believe* that S is true, or if it looks for all the world as if it is, but that S needn't actually be true."[6] So, in the case of the Refutation of Idealism, the concern is that no argument can be constructed to show that there must actually *be* an external world, but just that there must appear to us to be one, or that we must believe there to be one. If this is so, Stroud suggests, we have two options: on the first, we will need to bridge the gap between how things appear to us or how we believe them to be and how they are, perhaps using some sort of verificationism (where it is claimed that to believe that S, we must be able to establish the truth or falsity of that belief); on the second, we will need to close the gap altogether by denying that there can be any fundamental difference between how things appear to us or how we believe them to be and how they are, because things are themselves really appearances dependent on our conceptualization of them. The difficulty with the first option, Stroud argues, is that it renders the appeal to transcendental arguments redundant because verificationism is enough on its own to refute the skeptic. The difficulty with the second option, which is said to be Kant's, is that it requires a commitment to idealism and thus to a position that many would consider as problematic as the skepticism it is designed to refute.

It might be felt, however, that Stroud has not yet done enough to show that by virtue of adopting a transcendental argument against the skeptic, Kant is obliged to turn toward idealism, and thus that this is what the Kantian antiskeptical strategy entails,[7] for it might be argued that he has not shown why the skeptic can "very plausibly" weaken the necessary condition for experience from "there is an external world" to "there appears to us to be, or we believe there to be, an external world." In subsequent work, however, Stroud has explained further why he thinks that it is hard to resist this kind of weakening move. Although he allows that we might plausibly be able to make modal claims about "how our thinking in certain ways necessarily requires that we also think in certain other ways," he thinks that it is puzzling "how . . . truths about the world which appear to say or imply nothing about human thought or experience" (for example, that things exist outside us in space and time, or that every event has a cause) "[can] be shown to be genuinely necessary conditions of such psychological facts as that we think and experience things in certain ways, from which the proofs begin." Stroud goes on: "It would seem that we must find, and cross, a bridge of necessity from the one to the other. That would be a truly remarkable feat, and some convincing explanation would surely be needed of how the whole thing is possible."[8] Now, Stroud thinks, Kant's commitment to transcendental idealism means that he can avoid the need for any such "remarkable feat" and so can avoid the troubling demand for an explanation of how that feat can be achieved, for (on Stroud's account of Kant's position) when we claim that our experience depends on "the world" being a certain way, "[t]he world of which [this] is true is not really a world which is in every sense fully independent of all thought and experience. It is a world which, transcendentally speaking, depends on or is 'constituted' by the possibility of our thinking and experiencing things as we do"—so in this sense we are not crossing any "bridge of necessity" at all, with the "unpalatable metaphysical excesses" such adventures would require.[9] Stroud therefore concludes that "[i]dealism, or the world's dependence on the mind . . . is therefore the price one has to pay" for adopting a Kantian approach of this kind.[10]

When presented with the difficulties raised by Stroud, it may appear that those engaged in interpreting or reconstructing Kant's position are faced with a choice: either take an idealist route but try to qualify that idealism in such a way as to render it somehow unproblematic, or hold that Stroud's central worry can best be answered in a different way, by claiming that sufficient antiskeptical work can be done with a transcendental argument that merely establishes how things must appear to us, or how we must believe things to be, without needing to cross Stroud's "bridge of necessity" from his "psychological facts" to facts about a world conceived in a fully realist way. These options can be labeled the *transcendental idealist* strategy and the *modest transcendental argument* strategy.

As we have seen, perhaps the main difficulty facing the transcendental idealist strategy is the concern that this is just too great a price to pay, where the suspicion is that it involves as much uncomfortable revisionism in our beliefs about the world as does skepticism. However, many interpreters of Kant have of course argued that, properly understood, transcendental idealism is less troubling than it may at first appear, particularly when it is carefully distinguished (as Kant intended it to be) from *empirical* idealism. Thus, it can be claimed, Kant never wanted to deny that objects as we experience them in space and time are empirically real in that they exist independently of our inner mental states and can be the subjects of true and false beliefs; however, although these objects are not "in the mind," they are as they are because of how we experience them and not vice versa, and so are *transcendentally* ideal (just as one might argue that being blue is a feature of this book and that blueness is not "in the mind" or a mental image while claiming that the book's blueness depends on how it appears to me and others like me).[11]

Of course, the question of whether this is the right way to proceed in understanding Kant's transcendental idealism is a large one and cannot be considered fully here. But even if it is right, and even if it does not amount to a form of mentalistic idealism or phenomenalism (which put objects and their properties "in the mind"), it may still be felt to have troubling consequences as amounting to a form of *subjectivism*, whereby all the things we might suppose are features of reality as such, independently of us, are only features that belong to reality *as we see it*, not as it is in itself, regardless of the human perspective. Thus, although some will accept that Kant's position might allow us to hold to claims about knowledge and truth from within our perspective, they may nonetheless feel that Kant is wrong to treat all features of reality as we experience it as merely perspectival in this way; and others will be concerned that this position makes it impossible for us to claim knowledge of reality as it is "in itself" or absolutely, and so it involves a significant concession to skepticism—or perhaps even to be dubiously coherent as a result, for how could we know that everything we have cognitive access to is true of the world only insofar as it appears to us unless we had *some* knowledge of the world as it is in itself, on the basis of which to give content to this contrast?

Faced with these difficulties, it has been suggested that a different way of handling transcendental arguments is called for, which, rather than trying to respond to Stroud's concerns by using transcendental idealism, does not attempt to cross his "bridge of necessity" at all; instead, it allows that the only necessary conditions we can establish concern how we must think or how things must appear to us, thus avoiding Stroud's call for an explanation of how we can get from the "psychological" to the "nonpsychological" by remaining within the former and eschewing claims about the latter.

It might reasonably be wondered how this so-called modest approach to transcendental arguments could have any bite against skepticism: if the transcendental argument is just making some claim about how the world must appear to us, or what concepts we must use in thinking about it, how could that possibly trouble the skeptic, who presumably is challenging our right to make claims about how things actually are independently of how things appear to us to be or how we think of them? However, perhaps surprisingly, varieties of modest transcendental arguments of this kind have been developed. One such variety argues that transcendental arguments of this modest kind can be used to establish that some of our beliefs are invulnerable because they are necessary for us to have thoughts or experiences at all. The fact of this invulnerability is then variously claimed to render skeptical doubt unintelligible or, if not unintelligible, at least pointless; or these arguments may perhaps provide a reassurance of some other kind.[12] Another sort of approach holds that if we think of the skeptic as challenging the *justification* of our beliefs, and if by justification we mean an ability to show that our normal standards of evidence are satisfied, then a modest transcendental argument can help establish this, for while, in the case of the problem of the external world, the justificatory skeptic characteristically argues that our belief in the external world lacks proper inferential support (for example, as either a causal inference or an inference to the best explanation), the modest transcendental argument might then be used to show that it is necessary for us to have experience as of a world outside us in space and time, so that no such problematic inference is required; rather, the belief in the external world is shown to conform to our perceptual experience and so does not stand in need of any such inference in order to be justified.[13]

It might be wondered, however, how far such modest transcendental arguments can lay any claim to be properly Kantian, and how far they are merely possible "reconstructions." It is clear that some proponents of these arguments, such as Strawson, see themselves as leaving Kant behind in taking up this approach. Strawson's position is in the end more Humean than Kantian,[14] where the suggestion is that because the transcendental argument shows that we will find it impossible to give up certain beliefs insofar as they are necessary conditions for our believing anything at all, this is sufficient in itself to render skepticism about such beliefs "idle" and thus something we can legitimately ignore. It is possible to claim, however, that a closer connection to Kant can be maintained than this even while adopting a modest transcendental argument strategy, for it is arguable that it is just this kind of modesty that lies behind Kant's transcendental idealism, rather than the subjectivist turn discussed earlier. On this account, rather than seeing transcendental idealism as making a claim about the status of things in the empirical world (as being dependent on our perspective on it for their existence), we should see it as making a more *epistemological* claim, namely, that our belief in the existence of a causally ordered world outside us in space and time is a well-grounded epistemic position, but it does not provide us with a full knowledge of reality, which has a nature we are unable to grasp, given the way in which our cognitive capacities operate; so the modest transcendental argument is designed to support the view that those cognitive capacities are working perfectly well within those limits, while the position is transcendental idealist in insisting that those limits nonetheless be respected and observed.

However, even if some interpretive issues can be settled in this way, there are those who may still feel that this does not answer the *philosophical* worry, that a more ambitious approach is required in employing transcendental arguments if skepticism is to be properly seen off, and they may be emboldened in this feeling by believing that we have been too quick in going along with the concerns Stroud raises. As we have seen, at the center of those concerns is the worry that if transcendental arguments are conceived of in an ambitious manner, they involve "a truly remarkable feat," namely, that we cross "a bridge of necessity" from "psychological facts as that we think and experience things in certain ways" to "truths about the world which appear to say or imply nothing about human thought and experience." Stroud is prepared to allow (and indeed exploits our capacity himself in his own arguments against the skeptic) "that we can come to see how our thinking in certain ways necessarily requires that we also think in certain other ways, and so perhaps in certain other ways as well, and we can appreciate how rich and complicated the relations between those ways of thinking must be,"[15] but he believes that anything more than this that asserts that "non-psychological facts" about the world outside us constitute necessary conditions for our thinking is problematic. However, it might be objected, if this is Stroud's reason for rejecting ambitious transcendental arguments (which make claims about the world having to be certain ways to make certain facts about us possible) and adopting more modest ones (which make claims only about how we think about or experience the world), it is less than compelling, for why should it somehow be easier to make modal claims involving the latter than the former? Why is it less problematic to establish that "our thinking in certain ways necessarily requires that we also think in certain other ways" than that our thinking in certain ways necessarily requires that the world *be* certain ways? Why are such "bridges" or modal connections any easier to make "within thought" than between how we think and how the world must be to make that thought possible? Unless Stroud can offer us some principled reason for thinking that it is somehow less problematic to make these transcendental claims in the former case than the latter, he must either reject both (and so abandon his own project of establishing that some of our beliefs are invulnerable in certain ways because they are necessary for us to have beliefs at all) or allow that ambitious transcendental arguments are just as feasible as his more modest ones.[16]

Nonetheless, whatever the philosophical issues this raises, it might be said that Stroud at least appears to reflect a genuinely Kantian worry here, and that this worry is arguably the source for the "neglected alternative" that Kant has frequently been accused of missing in this area.[17] The idea behind this criticism is roughly this: Kant can be credited for seeing that we may need certain conditions to be satisfied in order for experience to be possible for us, but Kant wrongly took it that what fulfills those conditions cannot be the world as it is in itself, but only the world as it appears to us. Kant fell into this error, it is argued, because he believed that to go further is to hold that a world over which we have no control is nonetheless set up in such as way as to meet the conditions necessary to make our experience possible; but then such a fact demands an explanation of the sort provided by a belief in a benign God or a preestablished harmony between us and the world. But Kant, who rejected any such metaphysical Panglossianism as fanciful, may then be said to agree with Stroud that we should confine our claims about the conditions of experience to claims about a world we have constructed because this makes it less mysterious why that world meets our conditions for experience, for that it does so is in effect down to how we have constructed it in the first place rather than some "third thing," such as a benign God.

Perhaps, then, something like this view might make Kant agree with Stroud, that ambitious transcendental arguments are more problematic than those of other kinds, because there is something less mysterious in claiming that the conditions of experience are met by facts about us (as on 'modest' transcendental arguments) or facts about things somehow dependent on us (as when these arguments involve some form of idealism), than by a world independent of us—for why should that world do us any "'favours'" in this way? However, if this was Kant's concern, how right was he to be moved by it? It has been argued that after Darwin, we can see that Kant was wrong, for that the world in itself should meet our conditions for experience or knowledge is no more mysterious than that the world should contain air that meets the conditions required for our respiratory apparatus, or that the way things reflect light meets the conditions required for our vision. In a sense, it can be suggested, Kant made the situation look more mysterious than it is by getting the order of explanation the wrong way around: we are only here at all because the limitations on our various capacities nonetheless fit the prevailing conditions, whereas Kant wanted an account of why the prevailing conditions fit our limited capacities. Of course, even after Darwin, it may still be felt that this sort of evolutionary explanation is inadequate, and that much still remains to be accounted for, while the Kantian can hardly be expected to endorse an account that is purely naturalistic in this way; but it can also be argued, nonetheless, that once we address Kant's concerns along these lines, we may remove a good deal of heat from his worries.

In the face of these objections to Stroud's influential concerns over transcendental arguments, which seemed to require us to turn toward transcendental idealism or a more modest approach, we might then feel that we should go back to a more straightforward understanding of these arguments, which are "ambitious" in attempting to establish something about the world as a necessary condition for certain facts about us. Just as with the other approaches, there is some warrant for this approach in Kant's own work, most notably in the Refutation of Idealism. The refutation has always been something of a puzzle for commentators where it appears to offer a "direct" response to the skeptic (or "problematic idealist")[18] by presenting a proof of "the existence of objects in space outside me" based on the claim that the determination of our existence in time "is possible only through a *thing* outside me and not through the mere *representation* of a thing outside me."[19] Even if this conclusion does not stand in tension with Kant's own transcendental idealism (which *itself* talks of empirical objects as "representations" in some sense),[20] it at the very least is an argument that is presented without any appeal to Kant's transcendental machinery.[21] It is sometimes suggested that the reason the Refutation is anomalous in this way is that it was added to the second edition of the *Critique* because Kant had been stung by accusations of skepticism and idealism made against the first edition and, in his concerns to overturn those accusations, came to present a more "ambitious" style of transcendental argument than any he had previously entertained.

On an account of the transcendental argument of this kind, one way to read the Refutation of Idealism would be as follows:

1. You are aware of your mental states (thoughts and sensations) as having a temporal order (e.g., that the sensation of pain you are having now was preceded in time by a feeling of pleasure).
2. To be aware of your mental states as having a temporal order, you must be aware of something that existed from the time of your previous mental state to the present.
3. For that awareness of permanence to be possible, it is not sufficient to have awareness of your self (because no permanent self is revealed to us in inner sense, as Hume argued)[22] or to have impressions or representations (because these impressions have a "perishing existence," as Hume also argued).[23]
4. Therefore, the "permanent" of which you are aware must be something that is neither you qua subject nor your subjective impressions but must be something distinct from both of these, that is, an object outside you in the external world.

5. Therefore, your awareness of the external world cannot come from a prior awareness of your subjective impressions because the latter awareness is not possible without the former, and so awareness of the external world cannot be based on the imagination but rather comes from generally veridical experiences.

Of course, this argument is far from unproblematic and can be challenged at a number of points, and it is possible that when it is so challenged, some resort to a form of transcendental idealism may be required.[24] Nonetheless, at least on the face of it, it looks as if we have here a Kantian reply to skepticism that someone who sees herself as a realist could accept and use.

It seems, therefore, that by taking transcendental arguments to be the core of Kant's response to skepticism, we could understand that response in a way that turns out to involve little of the rest of the Kantian framework because nothing here commits us to the use of transcendental idealism, in whatever way one understands that position.

2. KANT, SKEPTICISM, AND THE CRITICAL PHILOSOPHY

I do not think that it is sufficient to leave things at this point, however, because by following most of the recent literature in focusing on the issue of Kant's relation to skepticism merely through the question of transcendental arguments, we have left out the context of much of Kant's engagement with the skeptic; as a result, we are in danger of missing a properly Kantian perspective on what skepticism is, and what a genuine reply to it must involve. Once this context is brought in, I will now suggest, we can see more clearly why it is more difficult than it just appeared to isolate that reply from the rest of Kant's philosophical framework.

The first point to emphasize is that from the perspective of contemporary debates on these questions, Kant has a conception of "the skeptic" that is closer to the ancient tradition than to our own.[25] For our purposes here, this difference may be very roughly characterized as follows. On the modern conception, the skeptic is someone who holds and sets out to demonstrate that our beliefs are insufficiently protected from error, and that as a result, we cannot claim to have knowledge or even rational justification. On the ancient conception, by contrast, the skeptic is someone who holds that for some or all of the issues we set out to investigate, equally strong arguments can be found to support different views of the subject in question, so that on such issues we should suspend judgment for now or perhaps avoid persisting in our inquiries altogether in order to avoid endless and vexatious disputes and instead to attain *ataraxia*, or tranquility, as the better form of life. The natural target of the ancient skeptic, therefore, is the *dogmatist*, who thinks that he has arrived at the truth on some matter and so has no need to suspend judgment because attaining the truth will bring consensus and hence tranquility; but for the skeptic, it is naïve to think that this point has been or even can be reached, and the only stability the dogmatist achieves is the fragile one of failing to properly recognize the counterarguments to his position.[26] To succeed against the dogmatist, therefore, the skeptic must persuade him that he is premature in thinking that a position on some issue has been decisively established because whatever position the dogmatist has (or perhaps can ever) come up with faces an equally strong opposing position on that issue, and no decisive judgment can be made between these positions; it is therefore best for the dogmatist to become a skeptic and suspend judgment on this question, maybe even give up inquiring further into it altogether, if he hopes to attain tranquility. In modern debates, by contrast, the skeptic is not seen as advocating a picture of the good life, and the success of the skeptic is not judged on whether he shows that the goal of tranquility can only be achieved by suspending judgment rather than by having reached an indisputable view. Rather, the issues raised by modern skepticism concern how far we can show that our beliefs and the methods we use to form them are sufficiently errorproof to sustain the epistemic weight we put upon them.

If we take the Refutation of Idealism as our starting point, it is natural to assume that Kant views skepticism in the modern manner, for the position he is concerned to refute asserts "our incapacity to prove, through immediate experience, any existence except our own,"[27] where it is held that this lack of proof undermines any certainty we might have regarding the reality of the world outside us and should thus incline us to doubt rather than belief on this matter. Moreover, as we have seen, Kant's response to this position may be taken in a thoroughly modern light: that is, he attempts to provide just the proof that the "problematic idealist" says is lacking, and so to shore up our belief in the external world in the face of these skeptical doubts.

However, Kant's concern with skepticism can also be put in a broader context than this, and once it is, it appears that it is ancient rather than modern skepticism that is his model. This broader context provides the starting point of the *Critique*, namely, the problematic status of metaphysics. Kant sees the difficulties of metaphysics in terms of the classical dispute between dogmatism, on the one hand, and skepticism, on the other, where what is at issue is which of these approaches can bring us peace with respect to metaphysical questions. Thus the dogmatist thinks that he can settle various metaphysical disputes by arguing for a position that is true and will therefore command consensus, but the skeptic argues that contrary views are also available, so that faced with *isostheneia*, or "equal force on both sides," the only rational course is to suspend judgment—and if this problem persists, perhaps also abandon further inquiry altogether.[28] Kant agrees with the skeptic that under the rule of the dogmatists, the "empire" of metaphysics "gradually through internal wars gave way to complete anarchy,"[29] so that it is now a "battle-field of . . . endless controversies,"[30] but he nonetheless thinks that the way to break the dogmatists' hold over metaphysics is not to side with the skeptic, because the skeptic cannot prevent the dogmatist regaining his confidence, and thus the battles breaking out again. Thus, Kant argues, it is rather only by becoming a *critical philosopher* that the tranquility the skeptic is looking for can be attained, so that in the end the latter must give way to the former.

Kant's argument with the skeptic here can be considered in more detail by looking at his treatment of Hume. Just as Kant begins the first *Critique* by reflecting gloomily on the "battle-field" of metaphysics, so Hume begins his *Treatise* by commenting on the unsatisfactory state of the subject, emphasizing the seemingly endless arguments to be found on all sides:

> There is nothing which is not the subject of debate, and in which men of learning are not of contrary opinions. The most trivial questions escapes not our controversy, and in the most momentous we are not able to give any certain decision. Disputes are multiplied, as if every thing was uncertain; and these disputes are managed with the greatest warmth, as if every thing was certain. Amidst all this bustle 'tis not reason, which carries the prize, but eloquence, and no man needs ever despair of gaining proselytes to the most extravagant hypothesis, who has art enough to represent it in any favourable colours. The victory is not gained by the men at arms, who manage the pike and the sword; but by the trumpeters, drummers, and musicians of the army.
>
> From hence in my opinion arises that common prejudice against metaphysical reasonings of all kinds, even amongst those, who profess themselves scholars, and have a just value for every other part of literature.[31]

Kant takes Hume's response to this situation to be a skeptical one, namely, that the endless disputes show that we must think again about what metaphysical inquiry can hope to achieve, and we must refuse to commit ourselves on such matters, turning instead to more modest investigations where the possibility of consensus is more real. The question for Kant, however, is whether Hume can do enough to persuade the dogmatist to join him and to give up his pursuit of metaphysical truth. Kant argues that Hume cannot succeed because he is not a properly critical philosopher.

The problem Hume faces, according to Kant, is that (as Kant sees it) Hume is obliged to be too radical in his attempt to bring "peace" to metaphysics, radical in a way that undermines his efforts to persuade the dogmatist that he would do best to withdraw from the fray because the fight cannot be won. This is because, Kant thinks, the principles on which the dogmatic metaphysician bases his claims are ones that have a good deal of plausibility, so that in rejecting these arguments, Hume is forced to question what look like well-grounded principles of ordinary thinking.[32] Kant therefore holds that we end up on the "battle-field" of metaphysics by beginning "with principles which [reason] has no option save to employ in the course of experience, and which this experience at the same time abundantly justifies it in using." However,

> Rising with their aid (since it is determined to this also by its own nature) to ever higher, ever more remote, conditions, it soon becomes aware that in this way— the questions never ceasing—its work must always remain incomplete; and it

therefore finds itself compelled to resort to principles which overstep all possible empirical employment, and which yet seem so unobjectionable that even ordinary consciousness readily accepts them. But by this procedure human reason precipitates itself into darkness and contradictions; and while it may indeed conjecture that these must be in some way due to concealed errors, it is not in a position to be able to detect them. For since the principles of which it is making use transcend the limits of experience, they are no longer subject to any empirical test.[33]

The principle of causality (that every event has a cause that brings it about necessarily) is a case in point here: Kant believes that this is a principle that we have "no options save to employ in the course of experience," and that seems "unobjectionable" to "ordinary consciousness," which cannot conceive of an event happening without a cause and that event following from the cause merely by accident, in a way that is not governed by any law. However, using this principle, the philosopher can find himself drawn into the "battle-field" of metaphysics, concerning such issues as the existence of God, for example,[34] in a way that then gives rise to familiar controversies. The skeptical response is to say that we should withhold assent on such metaphysical matters and consider our inquiry futile; but, the dogmatist can ask, if we are here using principles (like the principle of causality) that are indeed "unobjectionable" to "ordinary consciousness," why should we accept that no consensus is possible, and that no single view on such matters can be attained?

As Kant sees it, Hume's response to this challenge to the skeptic is a very radical one, namely, to question whether "ordinary consciousness" is *right* to view a principle like causality as "unobjectionable" in this way, as a way of preventing the dogmatic metaphysician from licensing his speculations by appeal to the apparently unproblematic nature of the principles it is using—for Hume, even our "ordinary consciousness" has gone astray on this matter. Hume thus opts for a mitigated skepticism which holds that there is no way to justify principles like that of causality, even though ordinary life and human nature in fact do not permit us to reject them completely and give them up entirely. Hume thinks he can thereby allow us to adopt the causal principle for practical purposes, but in a way that blocks its use in metaphysics,[35] where, as Richard Popkin has put it, "Nature leads us to this suspensive attitude when the dogmatist's arguments go too far away from the affairs of common life. On the other hand, nature does not lead us to a suspensive attitude on many unfounded beliefs about the common affairs of mankind."[36]

Kant therefore views Hume as a skeptic in a classical as well as modern sense, who aimed at tranquility by trying to prevent us becoming mired in the "battle-field" of metaphysics, where only the dogmatist could naïvely think our disputes might be brought to a satisfactory conclusion; by getting us to accept that further inquiry here is misguided, Hume, like the classical skeptic, hoped to bring us peace.[37] However, Kant takes Hume's strategy to be fatally flawed: for Kant thinks he can show (in the Second Analogy and elsewhere) that the principle of causality is not to be found wanting in the way Hume claims, and the same is true of other principles of "ordinary consciousness" (such as the principle of permanence: "in all change of appearances substance is permanent; its quantum in nature is neither increased nor diminished")[38] which the metaphysician makes use of. As a result, Kant believes, as long as the dogmatist feels that his inquiry is based on sound principles of "ordinary consciousness," he will be not be persuaded to adopt any sort of "suspensive attitude" in metaphysics any more than in ordinary life, and will continue with his inquiries unchecked. In view of what Kant saw as Hume's misguided challenge to the principle of causality and his attempt to reject it altogether,[39] he therefore warns that Hume's attempt to bring an end to the speculations of metaphysics will inevitably be undermined, and the dogmatist will come to feel that he is back in business:

> Thus the fate that waits upon all scepticism likewise befalls Hume, namely, that his own sceptical teaching comes to be doubted, as being based only on facts [*facta*] which are contingent, not on principles which can constrain to a necessary renunciation of all right to dogmatic assertions.... Accordingly that peculiarly characteristic ardour with which reason insists upon giving full rein to itself, has not in the least been disturbed but only temporarily impeded. It does not feel that it has been shut out from the field in which it is wont to disport itself; and so, in spite of its being thwarted in this and that direction, it cannot be made entirely to desist from these ventures. On the contrary, the attacks lead only to counter-preparations, and make us the more obstinate in insisting upon our own views.[40]

Instead of bringing the combatants to their senses, Kant holds, Hume's approach leaves them free to carry on much as they did before.

Kant argues, therefore, that by considering Hume's skeptical strategy and the way that in fact it allows metaphysical hostilities to continue, we can see that although "the skeptical method of escaping the troublesome affairs of reason appears to be, as it were, a shortcut by which we can arrive at a permanent peace in philosophy,"[41] this is nonetheless a shortcut that cannot really be made to work or get us where we want to go. Rather, Kant claims, we need to take the "long road" of critical philosophy if we really want to achieve the tranquility that the skeptic desires.[42] How is this so?

The key to Kant's strategy is to offer a way of allowing "ordinary consciousness" to hang on to principles such as the principle of causality and the principle of permanence (contra Hume), but to argue that these principles are only valid for objects as they appear to us within experience and so cannot be employed within any metaphysical speculations, which concern objects that lie outside our experience (such as God); the dogmatist is therefore not entitled to appeal to these principles as a way of arguing for the possibility of progress in his metaphysical speculations. Where the critical philosopher differs from the skeptic, then, is that although both hold that the dogmatist has little hope of succeeding in his inquiries, the critical philosopher shows the dogmatist exactly where he has gone wrong and offers him a principled argument that shows not just why his inquiries have failed up to now, but why they will always fail, and the critical philosopher does this in a way that nonetheless respects our "everyday" commitment to principles like the principle of causality within the bounds of experience. As Kant puts it, therefore, where the skeptic merely *censors* human reason and its attempt to conduct metaphysical inquiries, the critical philosopher sets it within well-defined *limits* in a way that (Kant thinks) will finally bring us the kind of lasting peace the skeptic was after but could not attain:

> All sceptical polemic should properly be directed only against the dogmatist who, without any misgivings as to his fundamental objective principles, that is, without criticism, proceeds complacently upon his adopted path; it should be designed simply to put him out of countenance and thus to bring him to self-knowledge. In itself, however, this polemic is of no avail whatsoever in enabling us to decide what it is that we can and what it is that we cannot know. All unsuccessful dogmatic attempts of reason are facts [*facta*], and it is always of advantage to submit them to the censorship of the sceptic. But this can decide nothing regarding those expectations of reason which lead it to hope for better success in its future attempts, and to build claims on this foundation; and consequently no mere censorship can put an end to the dispute regarding the rights of reason.[43]

What is needed, therefore,

> is not the censorship but the *criticism* of reason, whereby not its present *bounds* but its determinate [and necessary] *limits*, not its ignorance on this or that point but its ignorance in regard to all possible questions of a certain kind, are demonstrated from principles, and not merely arrived at by way of conjecture. Scepticism is thus a resting-place for human reason, where it can reflect upon its dogmatic wanderings and make survey of the region in which it finds itself, so that for the future it may be able to choose its path with more certainty. But it is no dwelling-place for permanent settlement. Such can be obtained only through perfect certainty in our knowledge, alike of the objects themselves and of the limits within which all our knowledge of objects is enclosed.[44]

Ultimately, therefore, Kant's response to skeptics like Hume is to argue that they must let themselves be co-opted into Kant's critical program for philosophy, which will allow a genuine peace for metaphysics to be achieved. And this enables Kant to say that while critical philosophy incorporates something of the skeptical method, it avoids succumbing to skepticism proper, by offering a way out of the toils of metaphysics while keeping our ordinary knowledge claims in place.[45]

If the Kantian response to skepticism is seen in this way, it is clearly much harder than it seemed previously to divorce that response from the rest of Kant's philosophical framework because it requires an understanding of how his critical philosophy was meant to operate, and in particular of his account of how "ordinary consciousness" can know synthetic a priori principles like that of causality, but without such principles becoming applicable beyond experience. Kant's position is that unless we abide by the latter constraint, we cannot avoid the oscillation between dogmatism and skepticism, but to explain why this constraint obtains, we need to accept that a principle like the principle of causality applies necessarily to the world as we experience it but not beyond, because this is how that world is structured by us, whereas the world beyond experience conforms to no such constraint. This, of course, takes us to the heart of Kant's "Copernican revolution" in philosophy and his transcendental turn.

We also now have a different way of considering the *adequacy* of Kant's response to skepticism, which is not just to ask whether (say) the Refutation of Idealism proves what the external-world skeptic says should be doubted, but whether Kant can achieve what he said Hume could not: namely, giving us a way of thinking about principles like those of causality that will satisfy "ordinary consciousness" on the one hand, without giving the dogmatic metaphysician grounds for encouragement on the other. For this is the central advantage that Kant claims for his critical philosophy over Hume's skeptical one. Just as Kant thought that Hume ultimately failed to bring peace to the battlegrounds of metaphysics, because he had not properly handled the fundamental principles we use to get metaphysical speculation started, the question here then is whether Kant does any better with his critical project. And we might also ask, conversely, whether Kant is fair to Hume in the way he characterizes Hume's approach and the differences he asserts for his own, as well as asking whether he is right to say that the Humean approach cannot succeed in bringing about the tranquility in metaphysics that they both desired.[46]

We cannot attempt to follow Kant any further here. But it does seem that we have shown that unless we accept that there is more to Kant's engagement with skepticism than is commonly assumed, we will miss how far that engagement takes us into his critical philosophy in a way that remains to be taken up by those interested in the problem of skepticism, notwithstanding Kant's already-considerable influence in this field.

NOTES

I am grateful to David Bell, John Greco, Kristina Mussgnug Barratt, and Ken Westphal for helpful comments on earlier drafts of this paper.

1. Cf. Immanuel Kant, *Critique of Pure Reason* (hereafter *CPR*) trans. Norman Kemp Smith (London: Macmillan, 1933), B276. References to the *CPR* will be given in the standard form, relating to the pagination of the A (first) and B (second) editions. References to works of Kant other than the *CPR* will be to volume and page number of the Akademie edition (*Kants gessamelte Schriften*, ed. Deutsche [formerly Königliche Preussisch] Akademie der Wissenschaften, 29 vols. [Berlin: Walter de Gruyter, 1902–]), together with a reference to a standard English translation.

2. For some prominent discussions, see Henry Allison, *Kant's Transcendental Idealism* (New Haven, CT: Yale University Press, 1983); Graham Bird, "Kant's Transcendental Idealism," in Godfrey Vesey (ed.), *Idealism Past and Present* (Cambridge: Cambridge University Press, 1982); Arthur Collins, *Possible Experience: Understanding Kant's "Critique of Pure Reason"* (Berkeley: University of California Press, 1999); Paul Guyer, *Kant and the*

Claims of Knowledge (Cambridge: Cambridge University Press, 1987); Rae Langton, *Kantian Humility: Our Ignorance of Things in Themselves* (Oxford: Oxford University Press, 1998); James Van Cleve, *Problems from Kant* (Oxford: Oxford University Press, 1999); Kenneth R. Westphal, *Kant's Transcendental Proof of Realism* (Cambridge: Cambridge University Press, 2004); Graham Bird, *The Revolutionary Kant: A Commentary on the "Critique of Pure Reason"* (La Salle: Open Court, 2006).

3. For a bibliography of works on transcendental arguments, see Robert Stern (ed), *Transcendental Arguments: Problems and Prospects* (Oxford: Oxford University Press, 1999), pp. 307–22. For some more recent contributions that discuss the role of transcendental arguments in Kant's thought, see Sami Pihlström, *Naturalizing the Transcendental* (Amherst: Humanity Books, 2003); Mark Sacks, *Objectivity and Insight* (Oxford: Oxford University Press, 2000); and Wesphal, *Kant's Transcendental Proof of Realism*.

4. *CPR* Bxxxix n.

5. *CPR* A22/B37.

6. Barry Stroud, "Transcendental Arguments," reprinted in his *Understanding Human Knowledge* (Oxford: Oxford University Press, 2000), p. 24.

7. In fairness to Stroud, it should be noted that this is not a point he seeks to make in relation to Kant in "Transcendental Arguments," where his focus is more on contemporary attempts to adopt the Kantian approach, particularly by Strawson and Shoemaker. But cf. Barry Stroud, "The Allure of Idealism," in *Understanding Human Knowledge*, pp. 87–88: "Kant begins by 'deducing' what our concepts or categories are or must be and exploring the conditions of our thinking in those ways. He finds that they are conditions of our thinking of anything at all. Now how could such an investigation of how we think, or of how it is possible for us to think at all, reveal to us . . . 'what it is to be *X*', as opposed to what it is to think about *X*, or what makes it possible (and perhaps also necessary) for us to think about *X*? . . . It does so by showing that what makes it possible for us to think about or perceive objects at all makes it true that there are objects of the sorts we think about and perceive. There being such objects is a condition of our being able to think about or perceive any objects at all. The short answer to how that is established is to say that the objects we think about or perceive are in some way dependent on our faculty of thinking or perceiving."

8. Barry Stroud, "Kantian Argument, Conceptual Capacities, and Invulnerability," in *Understanding Human Knowledge*, pp. 158–59. Cf. also Stroud, "The Goal of Transcendental Arguments," in *Understanding Human Knowledge*, p. 212: "All this would be so on the assumption that transcendental arguments deduce the truth of certain conclusions about the world from our thinking or experiencing things in certain ways. That strong condition of success is what I continue to see as the stumbling-block for such ambitious transcendental arguments. Can we ever really reach such conclusions from such beginnings? . . . [The most troubling danger is] that of not being able to reach substantive, non-psychological truths from premises only about our thinking or experiencing things in certain ways."

9. Stroud, "Kantian Argument, Conceptual Capacities, and Invulnerability," p. 159.

10. Ibid. Cf. also ibid., pp. 162–63: "Without questioning the demonstrated connections *within* our thought, we might agree that thought of an independent world, for example, ultimately requires that we possess an elaborate conception of particular objects which endure and are reidentifiable in a single spatio-temporal system. That is still only about how we do or must think. But why, we will ask, does our possession of such a conception, our *thinking* of and *believing* in such objects, also require that there actually *be*

such objects, or even that we can know or have good reason to think that there are? We know why Kant thought there had to be. But if we do not go in for transcendental idealism, why would the existence or even the knowability of such objects be derivable from our thinking in certain ways? Would not the most that we can see to be necessarily connected with our thinking in a certain way be only our having to *think* or *believe* that certain other things are true, and not the actual truth of those other things as well?"

11. Cf. Immanuel Kant, *Prolegomena to Any Future Metaphysics*, 4: 289; translated by Gary Hatfield (Cambridge: Cambridge University Press, 1997), p. 41: "as little as someone can be called an idealist because he wants to admit colors as properties that attach not to the object in itself, but only to the sense of vision as modifications, just as little can my system be called idealist simply because I find that even more of, *nay, all of the properties that make up the intuition of a body* belong merely to its appearance: for the existence of the thing that appears is not thereby nullified, as with real idealism, but it is only shown that through the senses we cannot cognize it at all as it is in itself."

12. Cf. P.F. Strawson, *Skepticism and Naturalism: Some Varieties* (London: Methuen, 1985); Barry Stroud, "The Goal of Transcendental Arguments," reprinted in his *Understanding Human Knowledge* (Oxford: Oxford University Press, 2000), pp. 203–23.

13. For further discussion of some of these positions and the issues they raise, see my *Transcendental Arguments and Scepticism: Answering the Question of Justification* (Oxford: Oxford University Press, 2000).

14. Cf. Strawson, *Skepticism and Naturalism*, pp. 10–14.

15. Ibid., pp. 158–59.

16. For further discussion of this worry, and how a less Stroudian argument can be given in favor of the modest approach, see my "Transcendental Arguments: A Plea for Modesty," *Grazer Philosophische Studien* 74 (2007), pp. 143–61; reprinted in Christian Beyer and Alex Burri (eds.), *Philosophical Knowledge: Its Possibility and Scope* (Amsterdam and New York: Rodopi, 2007), pp. 143–61.

17. Cf. Ross Harrison, "Transcendental Arguments and Idealism," in Godfrey Vesey (ed.), *Idealism Past and Present* (Cambridge: Cambridge University Press, 1982), pp. 211–24.

18. It is, I think, rarely noted as significant that Kant himself does not call the position he is attacking in the refutation "scepticism," but "problematic idealism." That he does not call it "scepticism" may have the straightforward explanation that his target here is Descartes, and he would not have wanted to label Descartes a skeptic because, of course, Descartes' position is intended to be *anti* skeptical. But in the light of my discussion in the next section, it may also be that in Kant's terms, to be someone who simply doubts the existence of the external world is just to be a modern skeptic and so not really a proper skeptic at all, but only a "problematic idealist."

19. *CPR* B275.

20. Cf. *CPR* A30/B45: "The transcendental concept of appearances in space, on the other hand, is a critical reminder that nothing intuited in space is a thing in itself, that space is not a form inhering in things in themselves as their intrinsic property, that objects in themselves are quite unknown to us, and that what we call outer objects are nothing but mere representations of our sensibility, the form of which is space."

21. This is brought out very clearly by David Bell in his "Transcendental Arguments and Non-naturalistic Anti-realism," in Robert Stern (ed.), *Transcendental Arguments: Problems and Prospects* (Oxford: Oxford University Press, 1999).

22. David Hume, *A Treatise of Human Nature*, edited by L.A. Selby-Bigge and P. H. Nidditch, 2nd ed. (Oxford: Oxford University Press, 1978), bk. 1, pt. 4, sec. 6, p. 252.

23. Ibid., bk.1, pt.4, sec. 2, p. 194.

24. Most obviously, perhaps, the Humean assumptions in premise 3 might be questioned, both as regards the possibility of intuiting an abiding self, and as regards adopting a less atomistic view of our representational states.

25. For a discussion of Kant's understanding of ancient skepticism and its contemporary context, see Giorgio Tonelli, "Kant und die antiken Skeptiker," in *Studien zu Kants philosophischer Entwicklung*, ed. Heinz Heimsoeth, Dieter Henrich, and Giorgio Tonelli (Hildesheim: Georg Olms, 1967), pp. 93–123. For an extensive discussion by Kant himself, see *The Blomberg Logic* (lectures from c. 1770), 24: 207–18; in Immanuel Kant, *Lectures on Logic*, translated by J. Michael Young (Cambridge: Cambridge University Press, 1992), pp. 163–73.

26. It is a matter of great dispute in the understanding of ancient skepticism, whether the ordinary person counts as a dogmatist and hence a target for the skeptic in this way, or just the philosopher; it is therefore a matter of disagreement how far and in what way the skeptical suspension of belief was meant to extend—to our ordinary beliefs, or just to our philosophical ones? On this issue, see M.F. Burnyeat, "Can the Skeptic Live his Skepticism?" in Myles Burnyeat (ed.), *The Skeptical Tradition* (Berkeley: University of California Press, 1983), pp. 117–148 and Michael Frede, "The Skeptic's Beliefs," reprinted in his *Essays in Ancient Philosophy* (Oxford: Oxford University Press, 1987), pp. 179–200. For a helpful general overview of ancient skepticism, see David Sedley, "The Motivation of Greek Skepticism," in Burnyeat, *The Skeptical Tradition*, pp. 9–30.

27. *CPR* B275.

28. Cf. Immanuel Kant, *Metaphysik Vigilantius* [1794–1795], Akademie edition, Deutsche Akademie der Wissenschaften (Berlin: Walter de Gruyter, 1902-) (hereafter *AK*), 29: 957–58, translated by Karl Ameriks and Steve Naragon, in *Lectures on Metaphysics* (Cambridge: Cambridge University Press, 1997), p. 429: "All judgments and every whole system were accepted [in metaphysics], if one only remained consistent and did not contradict oneself. But there arose a dispute of the philosophers among themselves over the propositions maintained as conclusions of their systems, in that one group believed that they were grounded, and the other group that they were just as clearly refuted, and showed that the opposite could be grounded just as clearly.... Thus as soon as the contradiction and the existence of the wholly conflicting propositions was quite clear, there arose that *party* [i.e., the skeptics] which doubted the certainty of either; this party took the opportunity thereby to declare all truths of reason as uncertain, and accepted the principle that we lack certainty in all our cognitions; it even contradicted itself, and admitted that even the question whether everything is uncertain is itself uncertain. Now this killed all progress of the investigation because dogmatism was overthrown and skepticism affirmed no principles <*principium*> from which one could proceed. The interest of human beings suffered under this, and neither of the opposites <*opposita*> served any use."

29. *CPR* Aix (translation modified).

30. *CPR* Aviii. Cf. also Immanuel Kant, *Prolegomena to Any Future Metaphysics*, Ak 4: 255–57, translated by Gary Hatfield (Cambridge: Cambridge University Press, 1997), pp. 5–7, and Ak 4: 271, trans. Hatfield, pp. 24–5: "[O] ne metaphysics has always contradicted the other, either in regard to the assertions themselves or their proofs, and thereby metaphysics has itself destroyed its claim to lasting approbation. The very attempts to bring such a science into existence were without doubt the original cause of the skepticism that arose so early, a mode of thinking in which reason moves against itself with such violence that it never could have arisen except in complete despair as regards satisfaction of reason's most important aims." And also *Metaphysik Mrongovius* (lecture notes from 1782–1783), 29: 779, trans Karl Ameriks and Steve Naragon, in Kant, *Lectures on Metaphysics*, p. 134: "The whole

of metaphysics is nothing other than a chain of built-up and overthrown systems. No book has yet appeared where there is something permanent. It is not a science which has the fate to be permanent."

31. Hume goes on in this passage to make clear that this problem can be attributed not just to metaphysics 'proper' (as a 'particular branch of science') but to 'every kind of argument, which is any way abstruse', where Hume shows no sympathy with this kind of 'most determined scepticism' and 'indolence' (partly, of course, because he acknowledges, the *Treatise* itself may be counted as 'abstruse'). But that Hume shared these skeptical misgivings regarding metaphysics 'proper' is made clear by Philo in the *Dialogues Concerning Natural Religion*, particularly at the beginning and end of Part VIII, which concludes in a way that may be taken to be an expression of Hume's own view: 'All religious system, it is confessed, are subject to great and insuperable difficulties. Each disputant triumphs in his turn, while he carries on an offensive war, and exposes the absurdities, barbarities, and pernicious tenets of his antagonist. But all of them, on the whole, prepare a complete triumph for the *sceptic*, who tells them that no system ought ever to be embraced with regard to such subjects; for this plain reason, that no absurdity ought ever to be assented to with regard to any subject. A total suspense of judgment is here our only reasonable resource'.

32. Cf. Kant, *Blomberg Logic*, 24: 217; translated by Young, p. 172: "In most recent times, *David Hume* is especially known as a *scepticus* who had an overwhelming, indeed, a somewhat extravagant inclination to doubt. . . . In [his] writings is to be found a gentle, calm, unprejudiced examination. In them he considers, namely, first of all one side of thing; he searches for all possible grounds for it, and expounds them in the best oratorical style. Then he takes up the other side, presents it for examination, as it were, completely without partisanship, expounds again all the opposing grounds with just the same eloquence, but at the end and in conclusion he appears in his true form as a real skeptic[;] he complains about the uncertainty of all our cognition whatsoever, shows how little these can be trusted, and finally he doubts instead of inferring and settling which of the two cognitions is true and which false. He would, however, certainly be one of the best authors, and one of those most worthy of being read, if only he did not have the preponderant inclination to doubt everything, but instead wanted to seek to attain a true certainty by means of the examination and investigation of cognitions." Cf. also Kant, *Prolegomena*, 4: 258 note; translated Hatfield p. 8: "The acute man [i.e. Hume] was, however, looking only to the negative benefit that curbing the excessive claims of speculative reason would have, in completely abolishing so many endless and continual conflicts that perplex the human species; he meanwhile lost sight of the positive harm that results if reason is deprived of the most important vistas, from which alone it can stake out for the will the highest goal of all the will's endeavours."

33. *CPR* Avii–viii.

34. Cf. *CPR* A609-10/B637-38.

35. Cf. David Hume, *An Enquiry Concerning Human Understanding*, in *Enquiries Concerning Human Understanding and Concerning the Principles of Morals*, ed. L. A. Selby-Bigge, 3rd ed. revised P.H. Nidditch (Oxford: Oxford University Press, 1975), Section XII, Part III, pp. 161–62: "There is, indeed, a more *mitigated* scepticism or *academical* philosophy, which may be both durable and useful, and which may, in part, be the result of this Pyrrhonism, or *excessive* scepticism, when its undistinguished doubts are, in some measure, corrected by common sense and reflection. The greater part of manking are naturally apt to be affirmative and dogmatical in their opinions; and while they see objects only on one side, and have no idea of any counterpoising argument, they throw themselves pre-

cipitately into the principles, to which they are inclined; nor have they any indulgence for those who entertain opposite sentiments. To hesitate or balance perplexes their understanding, checks their passion, and suspends their action. They are, therefore, impatient till they escape from a state, which to them is so uneasy: and they think, that they can never remove themselves far enough from it, by the violence of their affirmations and obstinacy of their belief. But could such dogmatical reasoners become sensible of the strange infirmities of human understanding, even in its most perfect state, and when most accurate and cautious in its determinations; such a reflection would naturally inspire them with more modesty and reserve, and diminish their fond opinion of themselves, and their prejudice against antagonists." And cf. Hume, *An Enquiry Concerning Human Understanding*, Section XII, Part III, p. 162, where Hume argues that once we see how even our ordinary inductive beliefs (for example) are problematic, we will not be tempted into anything as ambitious as metaphysics: "While we cannot give a satisfactory reason, why we believe, after a thousand experiments, that a stone will fall, or fire burn; can we ever satisfy ourselves concerning any determination, which we may form, with regard to the origin of worlds, and the situation of nature, from, and to eternity?" This is in support of his earlier hope that "could such dogmatical reasoners [in metaphysics] become sensible of the strange infirmities of human understanding, *even in its most perfect state* [i.e. in ordinary life], *and when most accurate and cautious in its determinations*; such a reflection would naturally inspire them with more modesty and reserve, and diminish their fond opinion of themselves, and their prejudice against antagonists [in their metaphysical speculations]" (ibid., p. 161, my emphasis).

36. Richard H. Popkin, "David Hume: His Pyrrhonism and his Critique of Pyrrhonism," in V.C. Chappell (ed)., *Hume* (London: Macmillan, 1966), p. 91.

37. My position is therefore different from the more standard view, defended recently by Paul Guyer, which tends to distinguish between Kant's treatment of Humean scepticism on the one hand (in the Transcendental Analytic section of the *Critique*) and Pyrrhonian scepticism on the other (in the Transcendental Dialectic): see Paul Guyer, "Kant on Common Sense and Scepticism," *Kantian Review*, 7 (2003), pp. 1–37. For a more detailed critique of Guyer's view, see my "Metaphysical Dogmatism, Humean Scepticism, Kantian Critique," *Kantian Review*, 11 (2006), pp. 102–16.

38. Kant, *Critique of Pure Reason*, B224.

39. Cf. Kant, *Critique of Pure Reason*, A765–67/B793–95.

40. *CPR* B224.

41. *CPR* A765-67/B793-95.

42. *CPR* A767–68/B795–96. Cf. also B127–28, where Kant argues that Hume's radically empiricist treatment of concepts like causality was designed to put a break on Locke's attempts "to obtain knowledge which far transcends all limits of experience" in a way that meant Locke "opened a wide door to *enthusiasm*—for if reason once be allowed such rights, it will no longer allow itself to be kept within bounds by vaguely defined recommendations of moderation." In the face of this "enthusiasm," therefore, Kant thinks that Hume "argued quite consistently [in declaring that it] is impossible . . . with these concepts and the principles to which they give rise, to pass beyond the limits of experience," based on the premise that they are derived "from experience, namely, from a subjective necessity (that is, from *custom*), which arises from repeated association in experience, and which comes mistakenly to be regarded as objective." However, Kant thinks that as a result Hume "gave himself over entirely to *scepticism*, having, as he believed, discovered that what had hitherto been regarded as reason was but an all-prevalent illusion infecting our faculty of knowledge." As a result, Kant says here of his own project, "We now propose to make trial

whether it be not possible to find for human reason safe conduct between these two rocks [namely, of Lockean 'enthusiasm' and Hume an skepticism], assigning to her determinate limits, and yet keeping open for her the whole field of her appropriate activities."

43. *CPR* A757/B785.

44. Cf. also Kant, *Prolegomena Ak* 4: 262, trans. Hatfield, p. 12: "[Hume] deposited his ship on the beach (of skepticism) for safekeeping, where it could then lie and rot, whereas it is important to me to give it a pilot, who, provided with complete sea-charts and a compass, might safely navigate the ship wherever seems good to him, following sound principles of the helmsman's art drawn from a knowledge of the globe"; and ibid. *Ak* 4: 351, trans. Hatfield, p. 105: "Skepticism originally arose from metaphysics and its unpoliced dialectic. At first this scepticism wanted, solely for the benefit of the use of reason in experience, to portray everything that surpassed this use as empty and deceitful; but gradually, as it came to be noticed that it was the very same *a priori* principles which are employed in experience that, unnoticed, led further than experience reaches—and did so, it seemed, with the very same right—even the principles of experience began to be doubted [cf. Hume]. There was no trouble with this, for sound common sense will always assert its rights in this domain; there did arise, however a special confusion in science, which cannot determine how far (and why only that far and not further) reason is to be trusted, and this confusion can be remedied and all future relapses prevented only through a formal determination, derived from principles, of the boundaries for the use of our reason [cf. Kant]."

45. Cf. Kant, *CPR* A423–24/B451–52: "This method of watching, or rather provoking, a conflict of assertions, not for the purpose of deciding in favour of one or other side, but of investigating whether the object of controversy is not perhaps a deceptive appearance which each vainly strives to grasp, and in regard to which, even if there were no opposition to be overcome, neither can arrive at any result,—this procedure, I say, may be entitled the *sceptical method*. It is altogether different from *scepticism*—a principle of technical and scientific ignorance, which undermines the foundations of all knowledge, and strives in all possible ways to destroy its reliability and steadfastness." Cf. also Immanuel Kant, *Dohna-Wundlackhen Logic* (lectures from c. 1790), 24: 245; translated by J. Michael Young, in Kant, *Lectures on Logic*, p. 480: "Criticism is the middle way between dogmatism and skepticism, [as] the principle of a rightful trust in one's use of reason"; and also *The Jäsche Logic*, 24: 83–84; translated by J. Michael Young, in Kant, *Lectures on Logic*, p. 585.

46. For a helpful introduction to some of these issues, see H. O. Mounce, *Hume's Naturalism* (London: Routledge, 1999).

CHAPTER 13

REID'S RESPONSE TO THE SKEPTIC

JAMES VAN CLEVE

REID is renowned for his response to the skeptic. If ridicule is a response, he certainly has one.[1] But does he have a *refutation* of skepticism, or anything to offer by way of undercutting it? To answer that question, I discuss here the potential bearing against skepticism of four Reidian motifs—direct realism, nativism, naturalism, and externalism.

Skepticisms may be distinguished by asking two questions. First, what epistemic commodity does the skeptic deny us: certainty, knowledge, justification adequate for knowledge, or even any degree of justification at all? Second, in what sphere of belief is the commodity denied us: beliefs about the external world, the past, the minds of others, the truths of reason, or perhaps all beliefs whatsoever? I shall focus here mainly on skepticism that denies that we have knowledge or adequately justified belief concerning objects in the external world. This is Reid's main focus, though he also discusses skepticism in other domains or says things about one that carry over to others.

1. DIRECT REALISM

A major source of skepticism about the external world in the opinion of Reid and many other philosophers is what Reid calls the theory of ideas—the view that the direct or immediate objects of perceptual acquaintance are not objects in the external world but only ideas, images, or representations in the perceiver's own mind. If I do not see the tree in my back yard, but only an image of it, how can I know that the tree is anything like my image? More radically still, how can I know that the tree (or any external object) is there at all? I would evidently have to know this by some kind of inference, but the inference is notoriously problematic. As Hume argues, the inference would presumably go from the idea as effect to the object as cause. But if Hume's philosophy is correct, we have reason to believe in a causal connection between X s and Y s only if we have experienced X s conjoined with Y s in the past, and if the theory of ideas is correct, we have *never* experienced any of the Y s—any objects other than our ideas.[2] We are therefore in no position to make any causal inferences to external objects, and we are trapped behind the veil of ideas.

The theory of ideas is the main impetus for skepticism that exercises Reid, and he devotes a great deal of his philosophy to exorcising the theory. He points out the absurd consequences of the theory, notes that it has scarcely any explanatory value, and criticizes the arguments for embracing it. In its place, he seeks to uphold direct realism—the view that physical objects exist and are independent of the mind (realism), and that we perceive the objects themselves rather than any mental intermediaries (directness).

I have expounded Reid's critique of the theory of ideas and the positive features of his direct realism elsewhere,[3] and I shall not do so again here. In this section, I shall discuss the following pair of questions instead: Does the theory of ideas inevitably lead to skepticism? Conversely, may we avoid skepticism by rejecting ideas and embracing direct realism?

Reid thought that the answer to both questions is yes—that the theory of ideas and skepticism stand or fall together. Here are three passages in which he affirms that the theory of ideas is sufficient to engender skepticism:

> The theory of ideas has scepticism "inlaid in it, and reared along with it."
>
> (*IHM* 1.7: 23)

> The natural issue of [the ideal system] is scepticism with regard to every thing except the existence of our ideas, and of their necessary relations which appear upon comparing them.
>
> (*IHM* 7: 212)

> But that which chiefly led Descartes to think that he ought not to trust to his senses without proof of their veracity, was, that he took it for granted, as all Philosophers had done before him, that he did not perceive external objects themselves, but certain images of them in his own mind, called ideas. He was certain by consciousness, that he had the ideas of sun and moon, earth and sea; but how could he be assured that there really existed external objects like to these ideas?
>
> (*EIP* 2.8: 116; see also *IHM* 2.3: 28, *IHM* 7: 210, *EIP* 2.14: 186, *EIP* 3.7: 289, *EIP* 6.3: 446 and 450)

And here are two passages in which he implies that the theory of ideas is necessary for engendering skepticism:

The sceptical system "leans with its whole weight" upon the theory of ideas.

(*IHM* Dedication: 4)

All the arguments urged by Berkeley and Hume against the existence of a material world are grounded upon this principle, That we do not perceive external objects themselves, but certain images or ideas in our own minds.

(*EIP* 6.5: 478)

Is direct realism really sufficient for escaping skepticism? It is by no means obvious that the answer is yes. Here is one reason for thinking not: directly seeing (or otherwise perceiving) something that is in fact a *K* is not sufficient for knowing that there is a *K* there to be seen. This is immediately clear as soon as we allow *K* to stand for a kind of thing that is somewhat esoteric. For example, I may be seeing what is in fact a carburetor without knowing that it is a carburetor than I am seeing.

Even if we restrict the permissible values of *K* to some narrowly demarcated range of easily recognizable kinds of things, such as hands or red triangles, it is not clear that directly seeing a *K* is sufficient for knowing that a *K* is there. Direct realism by itself does not give us sufficient resources for answering skeptical arguments of the following recently much-discussed pattern:

1. I know that there is a hand in front of me only if know that there is no Cartesian demon or Matrix manipulator making me believe erroneously that there is a hand in front of me.[4]
2. I do not know that there is no such demon or manipulator.
3. Therefore, I do not know that there is a hand in front of me.

The premises of this argument are compatible with direct realism. Let me perceive a hand as directly as you please; I still do not thereby have knowledge of the absence of demons and manipulators.

So direct realism is not sufficient for avoiding skepticism. Is it necessary? This, too, can be questioned. There are at least three types of thinkers who aspire to be antiskeptical without embracing direct realism: phenomenalists, advocates of inference to the best explanation, and proponents of sui generis epistemic principles.

Phenomenalists renounce realism but keep directness. For a phenomenalist like Berkeley, a table or a cherry is a congeries of ideas, so in perceiving an idea, I am ipso facto aware of something that is (or may be) part of a physical thing. For latter-day phenomenalists like A.J. Ayer or C.I. Lewis, any statement about a table is logically equivalent to a complicated statement about what sense data are being sensed or would be sensed under certain conditions, so in sensing a sense datum, one can know that part of the logical content of the table statement is true. I shall not discuss here whether phenomenalism has any chance of being true. Suffice it to say that as an epistemological strategy, phenomenalism still has significant gaps to deal with. How do I know, on a given occasion of perceiving a table-shaped expanse of brown, that all the other sense data (of differently shaped expanses from other viewpoints, rapping sounds if I strike with my knuckles, and so on) are in the offing that would have to be in the offing if my expanse is really part of a table?

Partisans of the second strategy, inference to the best explanation, retain realism while abandoning directness, maintaining that we can secure knowledge of the external world even if ideas are all we perceive. They maintain that Hume's strictures on causal inference, which permit us to infer the existence of things only of kinds that have previously come within the scope of direct observation, are too narrow. We can postulate a world of objects that is in some way isomorphic to our ideas, and if this postulate is the best explanation of our ideas (best because simplest, perhaps), we are adequately justified in believing it (even if we cannot know for certain that it is true). Skepticism of all but the first degree (which denies us *certainty* concerning the external world) is avoided. This sort of antiskeptical strategy has been defended in recent epistemology by Jonathan Vogel and Laurence BonJour, among others.[5]

Inference to the best explanation is not a strategy that would have appealed to Reid. In his discussion of proper philosophical method, Reid inveighs against the acceptance of hypotheses. By a hypothesis he means a proposition whose only recommendation to our belief is that it would, if true, explain other things that we know to be true, but whose truth is not open to verification by any more direct method. An example is the Indian philosopher's hypothesis of a great elephant supporting the earth on its back, offered to explain why the earth does not hurtle downward—"His elephant was a hypothesis, and our hypotheses are elephants" (*IHM* 6.19: 163). By what Reid takes to be proper Newtonian method, a hypothesis is legitimately invoked to explain phenomena only when it is supported by induction from the phenomena themselves—either the phenomena to be explained or other related phenomena. Hypotheses that transcend the phenomena altogether—and if the theory of ideas is true, that includes even humdrum hypotheses about tables and chairs—are to be abjured (*EIP* 1.3: 47–52).

The third way of circumventing skepticism without essential reliance on direct realism ironically has precedent in Reid's own philosophy. I have in mind epistemologies, such as Chisholm's, that lay down epistemic principles whereby beliefs in certain sorts of propositions are justified by certain sorts of experiences or in certain sorts of conditions. For example, one of Chisholm's principles is the following:

> For any subject S, if S believes, without ground for doubt, that he is perceiving something to be *F*, then it is beyond reasonable doubt for S that he perceives something to be *F* [and thus that there is something *F*].[6]

Reid lays down similar-sounding principles that will be discussed further in section 4. It is, of course, a question of some moment what justifies such principles themselves. Promulgating them may simply invite the charge that one is begging the question against the skeptic. Be that as it may, my point for now is just that the legitimacy of such principles governing some domain need not be tied (or so it may be argued) to direct realism about that domain.

To illustrate, here is a principle that Reid himself lays down as an epistemic principle pertaining to our justification for believing in other minds:

> Another first principle I take to be, That certain features of the countenance,
> sounds of the voice, and gestures of the body, indicate certain thoughts and dis-
> positions of mind.
>
> (EIP 6.5: 484)

Reid does not believe that anything like direct realism is true about the minds of
other people. He does not believe that we have any access to the mental states of
others not mediated by their faces, words, and gestures. If it is nonetheless permissible to lay down the principle just stated, why should it not also be permissible
for an indirect realist, who believes that our access to the physical world is mediated by our own ideas, to lay down a parallel principle such as the following?

> Another first principle I take to be, that certain ideas and images presented to the
> senses, indicate certain objects and happenings external to the mind.

I do not say that there is no good answer to this question, but until we have one, we
may not assume that indirect realism inevitably engenders skepticism.[7]

I myself think that the fight for direct realism is a fight worth fighting, and I am
grateful to Reid for his contributions to the campaign. However, I do not see the
avoidance of skepticism as the main thing at stake. When I look upon the sky at
sunset, I like to believe that the colors and forms I see are there on the horizon,
not simply splashed across some screen inside my mind. This is not merely because I desire to *know* what my environment is like. Even if God were to assure
me that there is a systematic correspondence between what I see and what is there,
my pleasure in the experience would be diminished by the thought that the
beauties I see are only in me.[8]

2. NATIVISM

In *Essays on the Intellectual Powers of Man*, Reid portrays the theory of ideas as
engendering epistemological skepticism, as we have just discussed. In *An Inquiry
into the Human Mind*, he portrays the theory of ideas as engendering a different
kind of skepticism that we might call semantic skepticism as opposed to epistemological skepticism, or skepticism about understanding as opposed to skepticism
about knowledge. Insofar as we cannot know what we cannot understand, semantic skepticism entails epistemological skepticism, but the converse entailment
does not hold.

The main tenets of semantic skepticism are contained in the following syllogism, which Reid attributes to Berkeley and Hume:

1. We can have no conception of any thing but what resembles some sensation
   or idea in our minds.

2. The sensations and ideas in our minds can resemble nothing but the sensations and ideas in other minds.

3. Therefore, we can have no conception of an inanimate substance, such as matter is conceived to be, or of any of its qualities.[9]

If this argument were correct in both its premises, it would follow that we cannot even *conceive* of a world beyond our sensations, let alone have knowledge of it. Reid thinks that the second premise is correct, and he credits Berkeley with having established it. But he thinks that the first premise—which states in Reid's language Hume's principle that all our ideas are copied from precedent impressions—is demonstrably false.

To combat the Humean premise, Reid offers a thought experiment he calls his *experimentum crucis*.[10] He cites two conceptions that he thinks everyone will agree we genuinely possess, but that lack a proper Humean birthright in our sensations. One is the conception of hardness, the other that of extension. He introduces the experiment concerning extension in the following words:

> To put this matter in another light, it may be proper to try, whether from sensation alone we can collect any notion of extension, figure, motion, and space.
>
> (*IHM* 6.6: 65)

He then asks us to consider a blind man deprived of all the notions he formerly had through touch and in need of acquiring them anew. Could he do it just by attending to his sensations and exercising his powers of reasoning upon them? Reid's answer is no. He asks us to imagine the subject being given a progressively richer array of sensations, beginning with the prick of a pin and moving on to the pressure of a blunt object against his arm, the dragging of a fingertip along his face, and the sensations accompanying the moving of his limbs with and without resistance. He asks at each stage whether any of the sensations would convey to the blind man the notion of extension if he had lacked it before, and his answer is no. So the conception of extension is not derivable from tactile sensations. But all of us, including the blind, do somehow have it. Reid's conclusion is that our conception of extension must be innate—not in the sense that we have it from birth, but in the sense that we form it as a hardwired response to certain sensations from which it could never have been derived by any process of abstraction or ratiocination.[11]

Once he has established that we have some conceptions not derived from our sensations, Reid thinks that the way is open for admitting that we have others too. Among them are the notion of a *self*, considered as a "haver" of sensations rather than a bundle of them; the idea of *power*, considered as causal efficacy in a sense going beyond constant conjunction; and the notion of *body*, considered as something outside us in space neither resembling nor depending on any operations of the mind. Thus does Reid counter the argument for skepticism about understanding stemming from Berkeley and Hume.

Reid's reply to Berkeley and Hume has an echo in our own time in the response of Edward Craig to the positivist semantics of Schlick and Dummett.[12]

According to Schlick, if a term is not definable by means of terms whose meaning can be conveyed ostensively—by displaying their referents within the content of our sensory experience—we cannot understand it. According to Dummett, if a sentence does not express a verifiable state of affairs—one lying wholly within the scope of what one can observe—its meaning can never be learned, and even if it could be learned, teacher and learner could never know that they were using their terms with the same meaning. Schlick and Dummett can be seen as offering "linguisticized" versions of Hume, transmuting what he says about the provenance of concepts into doctrines about the understanding of language.

Craig seeks to get around such positivist strictures on the limits of understanding by invoking something strikingly similar to Reid's nativism. Here are Craig's proposals:

> Suppose for a moment that there are some human beliefs not equivalent in content to any construction out of observables or what is experienceable. Then these beliefs may enter into the process of language learning, for all that has yet been shown to the contrary. For the learner might, when faced with the ostended object, form beliefs about it beyond what he experienced or observed; why should he not then take the words he hears to be the expression of that belief, and so come to ascribe to them a meaning not admissible according to Schlick's semantic theory?[13]

> Suppose that all human beings, when faced with certain sense data, naturally form beliefs which go beyond sense data, in the sense of not being reducible to complex beliefs about them. Then our learner will come to hold such beliefs. In accordance with the hypothesis [that learners attribute to others in the same circumstances the beliefs they form themselves], he will impute similar beliefs to his teachers, and they to him, and both sides will be right, even though the states of belief, about which the assumption is confidently made, are unobservable to anyone but their subject.[14]

These suggestions have a remarkably Reidian ring. Craig's first supposition is that humans are so constituted as to form certain conceptions and beliefs in response to sensory data that go beyond anything simply to be found in the data themselves. That is exactly what Reid says about the concept of body in relation to tactile sensation. Craig's second supposition is that human beings take others to form the same beliefs as themselves under the same circumstances. Though not explicit in Reid, that is certainly Reidian in spirit. Combining the two suppositions, Craig concludes that there is no reason why human beings should not come to understand language describing matters going beyond the sensory given and, moreover, to understand it in the same way as their fellows.[15]

Reid's nativism can thus serve as an antidote to certain forms of skepticism about understanding. However, as noted earlier, although semantic skepticism entails epistemological skepticism, the latter type of skepticism does not depend on the former. Epistemological skepticism, which is our main topic in this chapter, remains to be reckoned with.[16]

3. NATURALISM

Reid tells us again and again that we cannot help believing in the existence of external bodies when we have perceptual experiences of them. Here are two representative passages:

> Even those philosophers who have disowned the authority of our notions of an external material world, confess, that they find themselves under a necessity of submitting to their power.
> Methinks, therefore, it were better to make a virtue of necessity; and since we cannot get rid of the vulgar notion and belief of an external world, to reconcile our reason to it as well as we can.
>
> (IHM 5.7: 68)

> My belief is carried along by perception, as irresistibly as my body by the earth. And the greatest sceptic will find himself to be in the same condition.
>
> (IHM 6.20: 169)

Is there any leverage to be gotten here against the external-world skeptic? Yes, say those philosophers who promote what they call *naturalism*. A recent book devoted to this topic begins thus:

> Historically, one of the ways in which people have attempted to counter scepticism has been by appeal to . . . "the natural"—to how we are constituted, to what we, as human beings, are and do in the arena of believing.[17]

P.F. Strawson has championed the naturalist attitude in his book *Skepticism and Naturalism*.[18] Strawson says that according to the naturalist position, "whatever arguments may be produced on one side or the other of the question, we simply *cannot help* believing in the existence of body."[19] Skeptical arguments are therefore to be *neglected*: "neglected because they are *idle*; powerless against the force of nature, of our naturally implanted disposition to belief."[20]

Ironically, Strawson finds that a leading exponent of the naturalist attitude is the great skeptic Hume himself.[21] Here are some relevant quotations from Hume:

> Nature, by an absolute and uncontrollable necessity has determin'd us to judge as well as to breathe and feel.[22]

> Nature has not left this [whether to believe in body] to [our] choice, and has doubtless esteem'd it an affair of too great importance to be trusted to our uncertain reasonings and speculations.[23]

Other commentators have also pointed out that Hume is no less aware than Reid of the fact that we cannot help believing as we do.[24]

But what exactly is the antiskeptical significance of the fact that we cannot help believing as we do? If skepticism is the position that we have no knowledge or adequately justified belief in the existence of bodies, I cannot see that it has any.

And I think that it is possible that Hume would agree. In the following passage, Hume is speaking of induction, but his point is equally applicable to our beliefs about the material world:

> My practice, you say, refutes my doubts. But you mistake the purport of my question. As an agent, I am quite satisfied in the point; but as a philosopher, who has some share of curiosity, I will not say skepticism, I want to learn the foundation of this inference.[25]

A philosopher who believes in material things as irresistibly as the next person may nonetheless be curious about whether and how such beliefs have justification or constitute knowledge, and he may even conclude that they do not.

I therefore find neither in Reid the naturalist nor in Hume the naturalist anything to counter Hume the skeptic. Naturalism as so far delineated is an antidote to skepticism only in the sense that it saves us from unbelief. It does nothing to show that our beliefs are justified or that they constitute knowledge.[26]

Naturalism may be pushed further, however, for there is another way in which the fact that we cannot help believing certain things might be exploited against the skeptic. If in circumstances C we cannot help believing proposition P, then in C we have evidence for P, it might be urged, *because that is what having evidence is.* Evidence is simply whatever forces our assent, so if our sensory experiences make us believe in bodies, we thereby have evidence for that belief.

We can find a hint or two of such a position in Reid. He writes:

> We give the name of evidence to whatever is a ground of belief. . . . I confess that, although I have, as I think, a distinct notion of the different kinds of evidence above mentioned [of sense, memory, consciousness, testimony, axioms, and reasoning] . . . yet I am not able to find any common nature to which they may all be reduced. They seem to me to agree only in this, that they are all fitted by Nature to produce belief in the human mind.
>
> (*EIP* 2.20: 228–29)

Alston cites this passage as raising the possibility that Reid meant to offer a purely psychologistic characterization of evidence.[27]

A conception of evidence as what forces belief might be motivated by the following question: if God wanted to make something maximally evident to you, what would he do? Would he surround the proposition with a special kind of glow? Or would he simply make you believe it willy-nilly? It might seem that he could scarcely do better than the latter, suggesting that the latter is all that evidence is.[28]

When all is said and done, however, I do not believe that Reid wishes to define evidence as what forces belief. Perhaps there is normally an alignment between what is evident and what we must believe, but it is not a matter of definition, as may be brought out by asking a *Euthyphro* question: are things evident because we are forced to believe them, or are we forced to believe them because they are evident? I think that Reid would endorse the latter alternative, which implies the falsity of the former.[29]

One reason to think that Reid would not define evidence as what forces assent is afforded by the following passage:

This, however, is certain, that such is the constitution of the human mind, that evidence discerned by us, forces a corresponding degree of assent. And a man who perfectly understood a just syllogism, without believing that the conclusion follows from the premises, would be a greater monster than a man born without hands or feet.

(EIP 6.5: 481)

Here it is the natural constitution of our minds that is responsible for evidence forcing our assent, not the definition of evidence. Moreover, if evidence were *defined* as what compels assent, a man who refused to accept an evident syllogism would not be a monster, as Reid says he is, but an impossibility.

Another reason not to define evident beliefs as forced beliefs emerges when we consider the analog of an argument Reid gives about moral principles. In his discussion of morals, Reid considers the view that right and wrong are simply matters of agreeing or disagreeing with our moral sense. He argues against the view as follows (*EIP* 6.6: 494–95; see also *EIP* 7.2):

1. If right and wrong were defined as agreeing or not with our moral sense, then moral principles—principles specifying which types of action are right and which wrong—would be contingent.
2. But in fact moral principles are necessary truths.
3. Therefore, right and wrong are not defined as agreeing or not with our moral sense.

The analogous argument in epistemology would run thus:

1. If being evident were just a matter of forcing our assent, then epistemic principles—principles specifying which types of belief are evident—would be contingent.
2. But in fact epistemic principles are necessary truths.
3. Therefore, being evident is not just a matter of forcing our assent.

Whether Reid would actually give this argument depends on whether he agrees with the premise that epistemic principles are necessary. Epistemic principles will be discussed at greater length in the next section, where I shall point out some evidence that Reid does indeed regard them as necessary.

I end this section with another parallel between Reid and Hume. In Hume, too, we occasionally find reason to think that he identifies the evident with what must be believed. As is well known, he defines belief in terms of the force and vivacity of ideas, but he also defines evidence in the same way.[30] He also treats it as an objection to his philosophy that "the evidence of ancient history will decay on my system, yet posteriority will believe in Caesar"—as though there must be evidence where there is belief. On the other hand, in his essay on miracles, Hume says, "A wise man, therefore, proportions his belief to the evidence."[31] If strength of evidence were simply to be equated with strength of belief, wisdom would be the lot of every man, and there would have been no need for Hume to compose his "everlasting check to all kinds of superstitious delusion."

4. EXTERNALISM

The last antiskeptical motif I wish to discuss is *externalism*. The name, being of recent provenance, is not to be found in Reid, but the doctrine arguably is. Externalism is so called because it holds that there are important knowledge-making factors that obtain (or may obtain) outside the subject's knowledge—they do their work of conferring or enabling knowledge regardless of whether the subject knows anything about their existence or their knowledge-making power. In this section, I sketch three interpretations of Reid's epistemology, two of which take him to be an externalist, and I show that externalism undercuts a powerful argument for skepticism. I begin by setting out the argument for skepticism, which is sometimes called "the problem of the criterion."[32] The argument requires only two premises. The first premise endorses a requirement on knowledge accepted by many thinkers and articulated by Stewart Cohen as follows:

> (KR) A potential knowledge source *K* can yield knowledge for a subject *S* only if *S* knows *K* is reliable.[33]

KR is short for "knowledge of reliability." What the principle says is that no alleged source of knowledge, such as perception, memory, or reason, yields knowledge for a person unless the person knows that the source is reliable in the sense of producing true beliefs all or most of the time. In short, knowledge of the reliability of *K* is a necessary condition for having any knowledge by means of *K*. Moreover, in the version of the premise I shall use here, it is an *antecedent* condition of knowledge—one cannot know anything through *K* unless one *first* knows that *K* is reliable.

The second premise is that knowledge of the reliability of a source can come about in one way only, namely, by inference from premises obtained from that very source. For example, to know that perception is reliable, I would have to tote up a wide range of instances in which I believed things on the strength of perception (that here is a hand, there is a goat, and so on), note that the vast majority of things I believed in these various instances were true, and conclude by induction that perception is reliable. Such arguments are sometimes called track-record arguments.[34] A key feature of a track-record argument for the reliability of a source of knowledge is apparently this: to establish that its premises are true, one must rely on the very source on behalf of which the argument is being given. For example, to verify that most of my perceptual beliefs have been true—that there really were hands or goats and so forth on the occasions when I thought I saw or felt them—I would need recourse to further exercises of perception.[35] So it appears that the reliability of a source (at least if it is a fundamental source, that is, a way of knowing about its domain on which all other ways of knowing about that domain depend) can be vouchsafed only by using deliverances of that very source.

If we put these two points together, we find ourselves in the following skeptical predicament:

1. We can know that a deliverance of *K* is true only if we first know that *K* is reliable.

2. We can know that *K* is reliable only if we first know, concerning certain of its deliverances, that they are true.

If (1) and (2) are both true, skepticism is the inevitable consequence. Clearly, if we cannot know either of two things without knowing the other *first*, we cannot know either of them at all. It thus follows from (1) and (2) that we cannot know that any source is reliable or that any single deliverance of any source is true. And if we cannot know that any deliverance of any source is true, we cannot know anything at all.

How are we to avoid this sweeping skeptical result? Plainly, we must deny either (1) or (2). Under the first of the interpretations of Reid I discuss here, he denies (2); under the other two, he denies (1).

To deny (2) is to deny that knowledge of the reliability of a source must be derived by inference from deliverances of that very source. But if knowledge of *K*'s reliability is not derived from knowledge of its own particular deliverances, from what other knowledge *could* it be derived? One answer is: from *no* other knowledge. Knowledge of the reliability of our faculties is epistemically basic, not derived from anything else.

It can easily appear that Reid himself takes this line. In essay 6, chapter 5, of *Essays on the Intellectual Powers of Man*, he presents us with a list of "First Principles of Contingent Truths." Some of these principles are purely or primarily metaphysical; for example, principle 2 tells us that thoughts require a thinker. But others are plainly intended to have epistemological significance, proclaiming the trustworthiness of consciousness or introspection (principle 1), memory (principle 3), perception (principle 5), our faculties in general (principle 7), our beliefs concerning the minds of others (principles 8 and 9), testimony (principle 10), and induction (principle 12). I list here as specimens principles 1, 3, and 5:

> First, then, I hold, as a first principle, the existence of every thing of which I am conscious. [By "consciousness" Reid means that by which we have knowledge of the operations of our own minds; it is roughly synonymous with "introspection."]
>
> (*EIP* 6.5: 470)

> Another first principle I take to be, that those things did really happen which I distinctly remember.
>
> (*EIP* 6.5: 474)

> Another first principle is, that those things do really exist which we distinctly perceive by our senses, and are what we perceive them to be.
>
> (*EIP* 6.5: 476)

What is a first principle? As the name implies, it is a principle that comes first in all reasoning or inquiry; that is, it is a principle on which we base other beliefs, but which is based on nothing in turn. In company with tradition going back to Aristotle, Reid thinks that a principle is fit to play this role only if it is self-evident:

It is demonstrable, and was long ago demonstrated by Aristotle, that every proposition to which we give a rational assent, must either have its evidence in itself, or derive it from some antecedent proposition. And the same thing may be said of the antecedent proposition. As, therefore, we cannot go back to antecedent propositions without end, the evidence must at last rest upon propositions, one or more, which have their evidence in themselves, that is, upon first principles.

(*EIP* 6.7: 522)

Reid affirms the self-evidence of first principles in many other passages as well, including this one:

There is no searching for evidence; no weighing of arguments; the proposition is not deduced or inferred from another; it has the light of truth in itself, and has no occasion to borrow it from another. Propositions of the last kind, when they are used in matters of science, have commonly been called *axioms*; and on whatever occasion they are used, are called *first principles, principles of common sense, common notions, self-evident truths.*

(*EIP* 6.4: 452; paragraph break omitted)

So the central trait of first principles is their self-evidence. Reid does not necessarily mean by this that they are evident simply upon being understood, but that they are evident without need of deriving their evidence from that of any other propositions.[36]

In advancing his list of first principles, then, Reid appears to hold that we know that our faculties are reliable simply because it is immediately evident that they are. It is a self-evident first principle that consciousness is reliable; it is likewise a self-evident first principle that perception is reliable; and so on for all our other faculties. If this is right, we have a way of breaking the skeptical impasse set up by propositions 1 and 2. We can accept the condition that KR lays down for all knowledge, but we can affirm that this condition is thankfully met owing to the first principles of human knowledge. This interpretation of Reid's position has been forcefully advocated by Keith Lehrer.[37]

Many of Reid's readers have found it difficult to go along with the contention that it is self-evident that our faculties are reliable, and I am among them.[38] Principles affirming the reliability of our faculties are both *contingent* and *general*. For me, it is hard to see how a principle combining these features can be self-evident. There are, of course, some contingent truths that I find self-evident (for example, that I exist), and there are also many general truths that I find self-evident (for example, that all radii of a circle are equal). But it is hard for me to accept as self-evident any truths that are *both* contingent and general. So I find it hard to accept the position of Lehrer's Reid, and I therefore turn to the other interpretations of his epistemology.

In the remaining interpretations, Reid breaks the skeptical impasse by denying premise 1 rather than premise 2. The interpretations are both externalist in the sense I have indicated earlier: they have Reid affirming that there are knowledge-making factors that are sufficient for knowledge even if they are not themselves known. In particular, they have him affirming that there are sources that give subjects knowledge even if the subjects do not know that the sources are reliable. Externalism in this sense is the express denial of the KR requirement in premise 1 of the skeptical argument.

The best known variety of externalism on the contemporary scene is Goldman-style reliabilism—the view that a necessary and sufficient condition for a belief's being justified (and so potentially a piece of knowledge) is its having been produced by a reliable process or (in language closer to Reid's) its having issued from a reliable source or faculty.[39] For a reliabilist, in order for a belief to be justified, it is not necessary that the subject *know* that the process that produced the belief is reliable; it suffices that the process *be* reliable. So the KR requirement is rejected.

An interpretation of Reid as a reliabilist has been advanced by Philip de Bary.[40] According to de Bary, when Reid draws up his list of first principles, he is in the first instance simply formulating psychological laws about human belief formation—laws specifying what sorts of things people instinctively and inevitably believe in various circumstances. When I have a perception of a tree or a star, I automatically believe that one is there; when I remember walking on the beach yesterday, I believe that I did so; and so on. On a naturalist interpretation of Reid, that would perhaps be the end of the matter. But according to de Bary, if Reid went no further than this, his list of first principles would "lack any epistemological bite."[41] Reid does go further, says de Bary, embedding his principles in a framework of reliabilism. Reid believes that "the instinctive beliefs of healthy people ... tend towards the truth," and that such a tendency is sufficient (given a reliabilist view such as that previously sketched) for their being justified and amounting to knowledge when true.[42] So the various classes of belief marked out in Reid's list of first principles are not only psychologically immediate but epistemically justified. When they are true, they qualify as knowledge, and this is so regardless of whether the believer knows anything about the reliability of his own cognitive mechanisms. As advertised, the KR requirement and its attendant skepticism are rejected.

I turn now to the third interpretation of Reid. To make room for it, we must note that reliabilism is not the only variety of externalism. There are nonreliabilist views, including even views often considered to be paradigms of internalism, that are externalist in the sense I have defined earlier. A case in point is Chisholm:

> [T]he concept of epistemic justification is ... *internal* ... in that one can find out directly, by *reflection*, what one is justified in believing at any time.[43]

That sentence makes Chisholm an internalist in one sense of the term.[44] At the same time, however, it arguably makes him an externalist in the sense that is important here. "What one is justified in believing" is a function of two things, certain justifying states and the relations whereby they confer justification on what they justify. To know by reflection that one is justified in believing *p*, one must therefore know by reflection, with respect to some factor *f*, (1) that *f* obtains and (2) that *f* confers justification on belief in *p*. Knowing (2) by reflection arguably implies that justifying factors do their work even if they are not reliably connected with the truth of what they justify, since reliability relations do not seem to be the sort of thing that can be known to obtain simply by reflection. So for Chisholm, justifying factors need not be reliably connected with what they justify.[45] A fortiori, justifying factors need not be *known* to be reliably connected with what they justify. And that means that Chisholm is an externalist in the sense that matters here: there are sources of justification or knowledge that deliver their goods even if the subject does not know that they are reliable.

In the third interpretation of Reid I am going to sketch, he is an externalist but not necessarily a reliabilist. The entering wedge for my interpretation is provided by a little-noted scope ambiguity in the wording of principle 1 and some of the other principles. Here is how Reid formulates principle 1:

> First, then, I hold, as a first principle, the existence of every thing of which I am conscious.
>
> (EIP 6.5: 470)

Before going further, I propose that we systematically transmute Reid's talk of existence into talk of truth. Thus when he says, "If I am conscious of a certain thought, it exists," I shall say, "If I am conscious that I am thinking thus and so, then I *am* thinking thus and so." That will facilitate the symbolization I am about to use without distorting Reid's views.

The ambiguity to which I wish to call attention may now be brought out by the following two ways of symbolizing principle 1 (where "Cp" is short for "I am conscious that p"):

1A. It is a first principle that $(p)(Cp \rightarrow p)$.
1B. $(p)(Cp \rightarrow$ it is a first principle that $p)$.

What is a first principle according to (1A) is a *single general* principle—a principle affirming that anything I am conscious of as being the case is indeed the case. In effect, (1A) says that it is self-evident that consciousness is a reliable faculty. By contrast, what are first principles according to (1B) are *many particular* propositions—all the particular deliverances of consciousness, such as "I now have a headache" or "I am thinking of my mother."

I believe that the same ambiguity characterizes Reid's other epistemological principles as well. The principle about perception, for example, with "Pp" abbreviating "I perceive that p," could be understood in either of the following ways:

5A. It is a first principle that $(p)(Pp \rightarrow p)$.
5B. $(p)(Pp \rightarrow$ it is a first principle that $p)$.[46]

As before, we get either a single first principle affirming that perception is a reliable faculty or a multitude of first principles, each of them a particular deliverance of perception such as "there is a tree over there."

If the A reading of the various principles is correct, Reid is claiming it to be self-evident that introspection, perception, memory, and the like are reliable faculties—as in the Lehrer interpretation discussed earlier. I balked at this reading on the ground that contingent general principles cannot easily be regarded as self-evident. If the B reading is correct, Reid is claiming self-evidence only for various particular propositions—particular deliverances *of* our faculties rather than general principles *about* our faculties.

Which reading did Reid intend? My own view (for which I have argued at length elsewhere) is that although Reid himself probably was not entirely clear about the difference between the A and the B styles, he says many things that favor a reading of his epistemological principles in the B style.[47] I shall not rehearse all my arguments here. I shall simply note that the B reading fits well with the fact that in many places, Reid clearly does regard the particular deliverances of our faculties as first principles. Here is one such passage, which immediately follows a sentence in which he has offered "my perception of the tree" as an example of a perception:

> All reasoning is from principles. The first principles of mathematical reasoning are mathematical axioms and definitions; and the first principles of all our reasoning about existences, are our perceptions.
>
> (*IHM* 6.20: 172)

If the B-style or particularist reading of Reid's principles is correct, two things follow. First, Reid is a broad or nonclassical foundationalist. He thinks that the range of self-evident or basic propositions extends considerably beyond the classical Cartesian basis, including not just deliverances of consciousness and simple necessary truths but also propositions about the physical world and the past. Second, and more important for present purposes, he is again an externalist, though not necessarily a reliabilist. He holds that the mere fact that a proposition is a deliverance of perception, memory, or consciousness suffices to make that proposition evident. In order to know that there is a tree in front of one, for example, one need only have a perception as of a tree being there. Nothing else is necessary. In particular, it is not necessary that the subject know anything about the reliability of sense perception. He need take no thought of that. For Reid under this externalist reading of him, consciousness, memory, and perception are knowledge-conferring (or at least evidence-conferring) factors that do their job regardless of whether the subject knows anything about their reliability. So once again, the KR requirement that forms one half of the skeptical predicament is rejected.

I must acknowledge as a stumbling block for my interpretation that there are one or two passages in which Reid seems to endorse the KR requirement after all. Here is the principal one:

> If any truth can be said to be prior to all others in the order of nature, this [that our natural faculties are not fallacious] seems to have the best claim; because in every instance of assent, whether upon intuitive, demonstrative, or probable evidence, the truth of our faculties is taken for granted, and is, as it were, one of the premises on which our assent is grounded.
>
> (*EIP* 6.5: 481)

I think that he should not have said that. If Reid is really saying here that the reliability of our faculties is a premise needed to support anything else we claim to know, he is contradicting his frequent insistence that perceptual beliefs, memorial beliefs, and many of our other beliefs are first principles. For this reason, Noah Lemos regards this passage (along with related passages in which Reid criticizes Descartes for trying to prove the veracity of his faculties) as constituting "Reid's wrong turn."[48]

The antiskeptical strategy I am attributing to Reid has much in common with the antiskeptical position James Pryor calls *dogmatism* (with no pejorative intent).[49] Dogmatism is the position that there are certain things you can know without any proof, such as G.E. Moore's proposition "Here is a hand." You can know such things without proof because "whenever you have an experience as of *p*'s being the case, you thereby have immediate *prima facie* justification for believing *p*."[50] Such justification can be defeated, but in normal circumstances it gives you knowledge. Dogmatism has antiskeptical import, according to Pryor, because it implies the falsity of a premise that figures in many skeptical arguments: that you cannot know *p* on the strength of your experience unless you have antecedent knowledge that things are not going bad somehow—for example, that your experience is being manipulated by a Cartesian demon. Dogmatism has additional antiskeptical import, according to me, because it implies the falsity of KR: if perceptual experience by itself can give you knowledge of *p*, then, contrary to KR, you do not need to know first that perceptual experience is a reliable source.

The basis for externalism I have identified in Reid is the particularist reading of his principles, under which the particular deliverances of our faculties are immediately evident. This reading is compatible with reliabilism but does not imply it. It is compatible with reliabilism because a reliabilist can admit that there are self-evident or immediately justified particular beliefs. If the belief "There is a tree over there" is both psychologically immediate (not inferred from other beliefs) and reliably formed, it will count as immediately justified for a reliabilist. But the particularist reading does not imply reliabilism, since it need not be held in conjunction with the view that being reliably formed is either necessary or sufficient for being justified. It could be joined instead with the view that being justified is a sui generis normative status not logically tied to reliability, as in the view of Chisholm discussed earlier.[51] There is a hint of this position in Reid's remark that he can find no common denominator to evident beliefs except that they are "fitted" to produce belief. If "fitted" is a normative term, Reid's epistemology would be more like Chisholm's normativist externalism than Goldman's reliabilist externalism.

The question whether Reid's externalism is of the reliabilist or the normativist variety connects with a question I raised but did not answer in section 3. That question concerned the modal status of epistemic principles, or principles specifying which types of beliefs are justified. Is it plausible to regard such principles as necessary? For a reliabilist, the answer would be no. Epistemic principles would imply reliability principles, principles affirming that beliefs formed in specified ways are always or usually true, and such principles are contingent. On the other hand, if Reid is a normativist, the answer could conceivably be yes. Epistemic principles could have the same necessity Reid attributes to principles saying that this or that type of action is right.[52]

The last matter to be discussed in this section is how we could ever know that our faculties are reliable if (as I have maintained) it is not self-evident that they are. Would it not have to be by a track-record argument? And would we not need to use the faculties in question to establish the premises of that argument? Is not the entire procedure therefore deplorably circular?

My answers to these questions are yes, yes, and no. I do not envision any alternative to track-record arguments for establishing the reliability of our faculties, and such arguments do indeed use the faculties on whose behalf they are employed. They are therefore admittedly circular in one sense of the term: they use premises generated by perception to argue that perception is reliable, premises generated by memory to establish that memory is reliable, and so on. But the form of circularity involved here is not the bad kind of circularity. The bad kind of circularity, the kind that would prevent an argument from being a means whereby you could come to know that its conclusion is true, is present when the following holds: you could come to know that the premises are true only if you already knew that the conclusion is true. But on externalist principles, that last statement is false. When we reject the KR requirement, we allow that one can come to know that various deliverances of our faculties are true without any antecedent knowledge that our faculties are reliable. In short, if knowledge of reliability is not necessary in the beginning, it is possible at the end. Such, in my opinion, is a further advantage of externalist interpretations of Reid.[53]

To summarize this section, we began by noting two premises that imply a sweeping skepticism, the KR requirement of (1) and the contention of (2) that a source can be known to be reliable only through its own deliverances. We then considered three interpretations of Reid's system of first principles. Under Lehrer's interpretation, Reid would evade the argument by denying (2), and under the two externalist interpretations (one reliabilist, the other normativist), he would evade it by denying (1). I have favored the third interpretation, but each of them would give Reid a response to the skeptic.[54]

5. Conclusion

We have discussed four themes in Reid. *Direct realism* is touted by many of its proponents, including Reid, as a way of undercutting skepticism about the external world, but is not by itself sufficient. What is really needed is for beliefs about the external world to be epistemically basic, which requires epistemological doctrine that goes beyond direct realism. *Nativism* can be used to dispel one kind of skepticism, semantic skepticism or skepticism about understanding, but it leaves epistemological skepticism standing. *Naturalism* also leaves epistemological skepticism standing, however much it bowls over skeptics themselves by making them believe the things they profess not to know. Finally, *externalism* has the most antiskeptical force of all, since it undercuts the powerful argument for skepticism based on the KR requirement.

But can the skeptic's position itself, as distinct from any of the arguments for it, be refuted? Let us heed some of Reid's remarks on this topic.

> But are we to admit nothing but what can be proved by reasoning? Then we must be sceptics indeed, and believe nothing at all. The author of the *Treatise of human nature* appears to me to be but a half-sceptic . . . and yields himself a captive to the most common of all vulgar prejudices, I mean the belief of the existence of his own impressions and ideas. . . . I affirm, that the belief of the existence of impressions and ideas, is as little supported by reason, as that of the existence of minds and bodies. . . . A thorough and consistent sceptic will never, therefore, yield this point [that not even the existence of ideas and impressions merits credence]; and while he holds it, you can never oblige him to yield any thing else. To such a sceptic, I have nothing to say; but of the semi-sceptics, I should beg to know, why they believe the existence of their impressions and ideas.
>
> (*IHM* 5.7: 71)

> Reason, says the sceptic, is the only judge of truth, and you ought to throw off every opinion and every belief that is not grounded on reason. Why, Sir, should I believe the faculty of reason more than that of perception; they came both out of the same shop, and were made by the same artist; and if he puts one piece of false ware into my hands, what should hinder him from putting another?
>
> (*IHM* 6.20: 169)

> Thus the faculties of consciousness, of memory, of external sense, and of reason, are all equally the gifts of Nature. No good reason can be assigned for receiving the testimony of one of them, which is not of equal force with regard to the others. The greatest Sceptics admit the testimony of consciousness, and allow, that what it testifies is to be held as a first principle. If therefore they reject the immediate testimony of sense, or of memory, they are guilty of an inconsistency.
>
> (*EIP* 6.4: 463)

> If a Sceptic should build his scepticism upon this foundation, that all our reasoning and judging powers are fallacious in their nature, or should resolve at least to with-hold assent until it be proved that they are not; it would be impossible by argument to beat him out of this strong-hold, and he must even be left to enjoy his scepticism.
>
> (*EIP* 6.5: 480)

In these passages, Reid distinguishes two kinds of skeptics. *Semiskeptics*, such as Reid took Descartes and Hume to be, trust the deliverances of one or two of our faculties, reasoning and perhaps also consciousness, but refuse to admit anything that is not provable by reasoning from the deliverances of consciousness. *Total skeptics* refuse to trust even the deliverances of consciousness and reasoning. Reid concedes that total skeptics cannot be refuted; before them we must be silent. But semiskeptics can be charged with inconsistency, or at least arbitrariness. They trust some faculties but not others, with no real reason for doing so.[55]

To what Reid has said, I shall add just one observation. He says that we cannot refute the thoroughgoing skeptic, that is, prove that he is wrong using premises that he would accept. We cannot *show* that he is wrong. But can we nonetheless *know* that he is wrong? If Reid's externalist epistemology is correct, we can at any rate know many of the things the skeptic says we cannot know—we can know things our knowing of which implies that the skeptic is wrong.[56]

NOTES

1. For example, Reid says that the upshot of believing the skeptic's injunction not to believe my senses would be this: "I break my nose against a post that comes in my way; I step into a dirty kennel; and, after twenty such wise and rational actions, I am taken up and clapt into a mad-house" (*IHM* 6.20: 170). Reid even endorses ridicule as "the proper method of refuting an absurdity" (*EIP* 6.6: 507). He notes that "to discountenance absurdity, Nature hath given us a particular emotion, to wit, that of ridicule, which seems intended for this very purpose of putting out of countenance what is absurd, either in opinion or practice" (*EIP* 6.4: 462).

"*IHM* 6.20: 170" refers to chapter 6, section 20, p. 170 of Thomas Reid's *An Inquiry into the Human Mind*, edited by Derek R. Brookes (Edinburgh: Edinburgh University Press, 1997), first published in 1764."*EIP* 6.6: 507" refers to essay 6, chapter 6, p. 507 of Reid's *Essays on the Intellectual Powers of Man*, edited by Derek R. Brookes (University Park: Pennsylvania State University Press, 2002), first published in 1785. References to these works will henceforth be given in the text.

2. David Hume, *An Enquiry Concerning Human Understanding*, sec. 12; p. 105 in the edition edited by Eric Steinberg (Indianapolis: Hackett, 1977). For a similar argument, compare the Fourth Paralogism in Kant's *Critique of Pure Reason*, A366–67.

3. James Van Cleve, "Reid's Theory of Perception," in *The Cambridge Companion to Reid*, edited by Rene van Woudenberg and Terence Cuneo (Cambridge: Cambridge University Press, 2004), pp. 101–33.

4. This premise can be derived from the principle that knowledge is closed under known implication together with the assumption that I do know such obvious implications as that from "there is a hand in front of me" to "I do not erroneously believe that there is a hand in front of me."

5. Jonathan Vogel, "Cartesian Skepticism and Inference to the Best Explanation," *Journal of Philosophy*, 87 (1990): 658–66; Laurence BonJour, *Epistemology: Classical Problems and Contemporary Responses* (Lanham, MD: Rowman and Littlefield, 2002), chap. 7. BonJour is explicitly an indirect realist; I am not sure about Vogel, but direct realism forms no part of his antiskeptical strategy.

6. Roderick M. Chisholm, *Theory of Knowledge*, 2nd ed. (Englewood Cliffs, N.J.: Prentice-Hall, 1977), p. 76. By "believing that one perceives," Chisholm may be referring not to an act of believing about a perceiving but to *ostensible* perceiving—a state just like perceiving, but not necessarily veridical.

7. As John Greco points out, Reid notes that the ancient Greek philosophers believed in a materialized version of the theory of ideas but were not skeptics (*IHM* 7: 210). This is either a tacit admission on Reid's part that the theory of ideas alone does not entail

skepticism or a tacit charge by him that the ancients were inconsistent. See John Greco, "Reid's Reply to the Skeptic," in *The Cambridge Companion to Reid* (see note 3), pp. 134–55, at p. 151. In his "Reid's Critique of Berkeley and Hume: What's the Big Idea?" *Philosophy and Phenomenological Research* 55 (1995): 279–96, Greco also suggests that one who adheres to the theory of ideas could still hold a theory of evidence that provides for non-inferential knowledge of external things.

8. I have always been in sympathy with the sentiments expressed in the long speech by Philonous at the beginning of the second of Berkeley's *Three Dialogues between Hylas and Philonous*, in which Philonous castigates those thinkers who would reduce the glories of creation to a "false imaginary glare." Contrast Alfred North Whitehead: "The poets are entirely mistaken. They should address their lyrics to themselves, and should turn them into odes of self-congratulation on the excellency of the human mind. Nature is a dull affair, soundless, scentless, colourless; merely the hurrying of material, endlessly, meaninglessly" (*Science and the Modern World*[New York: Macmillan, 1925], p. 80).

9. The conclusion and both premises may be found, in these words, among lines 4–12 of *IHM* 5.8: 75. The argument is reprised at *IHM* 7: 212, where Reid states the conclusion thus: bodies are either reducible to ideas, in which case they have no existence outside the mind, or not reducible to ideas, in which case "they are words without any meaning." Hence my label "semantic skepticism."

10. *IHM* 5.6 and 5.7; the term *experimentum crucis* occurs on p. 70.

11. For discussion of the senses in which various furnishings of the mind are and are not innate for Reid, see Lorne Falkenstein, "Nativism and the Nature of Thought in Reid's Account of Our Knowledge of the External World," in *The Cambridge Companion to Reid* (see note 3), pp. 156–79. For further discussion of Reid's *experimentum crucis* and possible criticisms of it, see James Van Cleve, "Touch, Sound, and Things without the Mind," *Metaphilosophy* 37 (2006): 162–182.

12. Edward Craig, "Meaning, Use, and Privacy," *Mind* 91 (1982): 541–64.

13. Ibid., p. 543.

14. Ibid., p. 557.

15. But can we *know* that we understand language in the same way as our fellows? To secure that result, we probably need to supplement Craig's proposals with an externalist theory of knowledge, such as I discuss in section 4.

16. The distinction between semantic and epistemological skepticism is sometimes missed. For example, Michael Morgan says that making an idea innate protects it from skepticism, and that "[t]o the extent we can show that an idea is innate, we can trust it" (Michael Morgan, *Molyneux's Question* [Cambridge: Cambridge University Pres, 1977], pp. 111 and 125). I say to the contrary that if to "trust" a concept means to believe justifiably that it is instantiated in the world, nativism does nothing to make our concepts more trustworthy.

17. M. Jamie Ferreira, *Scepticism and Reasonable Doubt: The British Naturalist Tradition in Wilkins, Hume, Reid, and Newman* (Oxford: Clarendon Press, 1986), p. vii. In a similar vein, Derek R. Brookes says by way of introducing Reid's *Inquiry* that skepticism is untenable because "the operation of mind by which we form beliefs is largely involuntary and irresistible, much like breathing or swallowing" (*IHM*: xiii).

18. P.F. Straws on, *Skepticism and Naturalism: Some Varieties* (New York: Columbia University Press, 1985), esp. chap. 1.

19. Ibid., p. 10.

20. Ibid., p. 13.

21. Strawson's other main model of the naturalist attitude is the Wittgenstein of *On Certainty* (Oxford: Blackwell, 1969). For an interpretation of Reid that highlights his similarities to Wittgenstein, see Nicholas Wolterstorff, "Reid on Common Sense, with Wittgenstein's Assistance," *American Catholic Philosophical Quarterly*, 74 (2000), 491–517, or his book *Thomas Reid and the Story of Epistemology* (Cambridge: Cambridge University Press, 2001).

22. David Hume, *A Treatise of Human Nature*, 2nd ed., edited by L.A. Selby-Bigge and revised by P.H. Nidditch (Oxford: Clarendon Press, 1978), I.iv.1; p. 183.

23. Ibid., I.iv.2; p. 187.

24. This is the theme of Louis Loeb's Romanell Lecture, "The Naturalisms of Reid and Hume," given at the 2007 meeting of the American Philosophical Association. It was also noted in 1812 by Thomas Brown, who thought that the difference between Reid and Hume was merely one of emphasis: "Reid bawled out, We must believe an outward world; but added in a whisper, We can give no reason for our belief. Hume cries out, We can give no reason for such a notion; and whispers, I own we cannot get rid of it" (quoted in Galen Strawson, "What's So Good about Reid?" *London Review of Books*, February 22, 1990, 14–16, at p. 15.).

25. Hume, *Enquiry*, sec. 4, pt. 2; p. 24 in the Steinberg edition.

26. Compare Noah Lemos, *Common Sense: A Contemporary Defense* (Cambridge: Cambridge University Press, 2004), p. 21: "If the only thing to be said in favor of our common sense beliefs is that they are irresistible, why should we not view them the way we view bad habits, such as smoking or overeating, that we continue to engage in even when reason convinces us that they should be given up?" Perhaps one could resist the suggestion that we *ought* to give up our commonsense beliefs by invoking the principle that *ought* implies *can*. Nonetheless, the question would remain why irresistible beliefs are justified beliefs in the sense that is relevant to knowledge.

27. William P. Alston, "Thomas Reid on Epistemic Principles," *History of Philosophy Quarterly* 2 (1985): 435–52, at p. 438.

28. A notion of evidence along these lines is discussed by Alvin Plantinga under the name "impulsional evidence"—a strong inclination to believe something, along with a perception of the attractiveness or inevitability of believing it in the circumstances. He does not, however, regard impulsional evidence as sufficient for warrant or justification. See his *Warrant and Proper Function* (New York: Oxford University Press, 1993), pp. 192–93.

29. As in Socrates' original question, "because" is not univocal in the two alternatives. In the first alternative (things are evident because we are forced to believe them), the "because" is constitutional; in the second (we are forced to believe them because they are evident), the "because" is causal. The equivocation does not harm the argument, though, because nothing can cause what it is constituted by.

30. Hume, *Treatise*, p. 154.

31. Hume, *Enquiry*, sec.11, p. 73.

32. For a presentation of the argument somewhat different from mine, see Michael Huemer, *Skepticism and the Veil of Perception* (Lanham, MD: Rowman and Littlefield, 2001), pp. 11–13.

33. Stewart Cohen, "Basic Knowledge and the Problem of Easy Knowledge," *Philosophy and Phenomenological Research* 65 (2002): 309–29. Cohen thinks that KR is required to keep knowledge from being too easy. I think that it threatens to make knowledge impossible; see James Van Cleve, "Is Knowledge Easy—or Impossible? Externalism as the Only Alternative to Skepticism," in *The Skeptics: Contemporary Essays*, edited by Stephen Luper (Aldershot, UK: Ashgate Publishing Company, 2003), pp. 45–59.

34. William P. Alston, "Epistemic Circularity," *Philosophy and Phenomenological Research* 47 (1986): 1–30, at p. 9.

35. It might be thought that I could rely in some cases on means of knowing other than perception, such as the testimony of witnesses or the information provided by surveillance cameras. But I would still be relying on perception to know what the witnesses were saying or what the cameras were showing, and I would also arguably be relying on my own previous perceptions to know that witnesses and cameras generally do not lie. So there is no escaping reliance on perception to ascertain the veracity of perception.

36. Perhaps a better term would be "immediately evident" or "immediately justified." For further clarification of this status, including a list of seven things that it is *not*, see James Pryor, "The Skeptic and the Dogmatist," *Nous* 34 (2000): 517–49, especially pp. 532–36.

37. Keith Lehrer, *Thomas Reid* (London: Routledge, 1989), and "Chisholm, Reid, and the Problem of the Epistemic Surd," *Philosophical Studies* 60 (1990): 39–45. I have discussed Lehrer's interpretation of Reid at length in James Van Cleve, "Lehrer, Reid, and the First of All Principles," in *The Epistemology of Keith Lehrer*, edited by Erik Olsson (Dordrecht, Holland: Kluwer Academic Publishers, 2003), pp. 155–72.

38. So, too, is Alston: "Any tendency to suppose [a principle affirming the reliability of sense perception] to be self-evident can be put down to a confusion between self-evidence and being strongly inclined to accept the proposition without question" ("Epistemic Circularity," p. 4).

39. A paradigmatic exposition of reliabilism is Alvin Goldman, "What Is Justified Belief?" in *Justification and Knowledge*, edited by George S. Pappas (Dordrecht: Reidel, 1979), pp. 1–23.

40. Philip de Bary, *Thomas Reid and Scepticism: His Reliabilist Response* (London: Routledge, 2002). A reliability theory is also attributed to Reid by Alston in "Thomas Reid on Epistemic Principles," cited in note 27. Plantinga attributes to Reid something like his own "proper function" theory, which I consider to be a cousin of reliabilism; see, for example, *Warrant and Proper Function*, p. 50.

41. De Bary, *Thomas Reid and Scepticism*, p. 65.

42. Ibid., p. 83.

43. Roderick M. Chisholm, *Theory of Knowledge*, 3rd ed. (Englewood Cliffs, NJ: Prentice-Hall, 1989), p. 7. Compare p. 76: "The internalist assumes that, merely by reflecting upon his own conscious state, he can . . . find out, with respect to any possible belief he has, whether he is *justified* in having that belief."

44. For a taxonomy of internalisms and externalisms, see Van Cleve, "Is Knowledge Easy—or Impossible?" pp. 45–46.

45. We find confirmation in Chisholm, *Theory of Knowledge*, p. 76: "According to the traditional conception of 'internal' epistemic justification, there is no *logical* connection between epistemic justification and truth."

46. It is true that Reid's formulation of principle 5 as quoted earlier strongly suggests (5A) and leaves little room for (5B). However, his formulation of the principle in other places shares the same ambiguity I have noted in principle 1. At *IHM* 7: 210, he says that the way to avoid skepticism is "to admit the existence of what we see and feel as a first principle, as well as the existence of things whereof we are conscious." At *EIP* 2.5: 100, he says, "[T]he constitution of our power of perception determines us to hold the existence of what we distinctly perceive as a first principle, from which other truths may be deduced."

47. James Van Cleve, "Reid on the First Principles of Contingent Truths," *Reid Studies* 3 (1999): 3–30. In this article, I connect the A–B difference with the following interpretive issue: are Reid's epistemological principles meant to be principles of truth or principles of

evidence? On the A reading, they are principles of truth, proclaiming the reliability of our faculties. On the B reading, they are principles of evidence, despite not overtly containing the *term* "evidence." They are principles attributing first-principle status to the propositions in various classes (the deliverances of perception, memory, and so on), and this status is to be explicated in terms of self-evidence.

48. Lemos, *Common Sense*, chap. 4.

49. Pryor, "Skeptic and the Dogmatist."

50. Ibid., p. 532.

51. And in the view of Pryor as well: "perceptual justification would be in place no matter how reliable our experiences were" (ibid., p. 536).

52. It does not decide against this possibility that Reid presents his epistemic principles under the heading "First Principles of Contingent Truths." They are so called because they are principles that make knowledge of contingent truths possible, regardless of their own modal status.

53. I have defended track-record arguments against the charge of vitiating circularity at greater length in Van Cleve, "Reid on First Principles," and have argued there that Reid might countenance such arguments, despite some remarks in which he criticizes Descartes for employing them.

54. There are two other ways of circumventing the (1)–(2) argument that I do not discuss here because they are not to be found in Reid. One way involves a sort of coherentism and is advocated by Cohen. Cohen accepts that knowledge of the reliability of a source and knowledge of the truth of its particular deliverances *require* each other, but denies that either must be *prior* to the other. Rather, they develop together—light dawns simultaneously over the whole. The other way involves Sosa's distinction between animal knowledge (which is not subject to a KR requirement) and reflective knowledge (which is). For further discussion of each of these strategies, see Van Cleve, "Is Knowledge Easy—or Impossible?"

55. See Greco, "Reid's Reply to the Skeptic," pp. 151–55, for more on this point.

56. Which is not yet to say that we know that the skeptic is wrong; for that, we would have to know that we know the things that we do. We would need second-order knowledge, which I have not discussed in this chapter.

CHAPTER 14

PEIRCE AND SKEPTICISM

CHRISTOPHER HOOKWAY

1. SKEPTICISM

There are different ways of formulating the problems of skepticism.[1] The one I shall employ (at least in the earlier sections of this chapter) captures the core ideas behind Pyrrhonian and Cartesian skepticism and is particularly well suited to grasping what is distinctive about Peirce's views.[2] We can set it up in terms of a dialogue involving two characters that I shall call *believer* and *challenger*. (These roles may often be filled by the same person.) The dialogue begins when believer is identified as believing some proposition; challenger then issues the primary challenge, requiring believer to demonstrate that she is entitled to accept the proposition in question. This challenge can take a number of different forms:

What reasons have you (have I) to believe that proposition?
How do you (I) know that the proposition is true?
Why are you (am I) justified in believing that proposition?
Why are you (am I) entitled to believe that proposition?

It is a presumption of the conversation that unless believer can respond to this primary challenge, her epistemic position is unsound: she is not entitled to hold to the belief in question. Moreover, for any proposition that is believed, the primary challenge can legitimately be issued, and believer must respond to it.

Once our protagonists are involved in this dialogue, the route to skepticism exploits the apparent fact that whatever answer believer provides can be shown to be incomplete or otherwise unsatisfactory. If believer invokes other beliefs in order to provide reasons for the belief, challenger can respond by issuing a version of the primary challenge directed at them in turn. Or challenger can point out that the reasons provided are insufficient to render the belief legitimate. We can illustrate this by appeal to J.L. Austin's well-worn example from his essay "Other Minds" (in Austin 1961). Suppose I believe that the bird in the garden is a goldfinch. When asked how I know ("How can I tell that it is a goldfinch?"), I may respond, "By its red head." Challenger may then issue a further primary challenge:how do I know that goldfinches have red heads? How do I know that the bird in the garden has a red head? Alternatively, she may question the adequacy of my reason: have I eliminated the possibility that it is a woodpecker, since they can have red heads too? And the most powerful challenges in her arsenal will appeal to familiar unverifiable alternatives: can I rule out such possibilities as that I am dreaming that there is a bird with a red head or that I am deceived by wicked scientists using a computer wired into my disembodied envatted brain?

One common style of response to skepticism questions the legitimacy of the challenges that are used to impugn the legitimacy of our beliefs. Peirce's response is of this kind. However, we should bear in mind that such responses can have a number of different immediate targets. One strategy rejects the idea that it always makes sense to ask the questions that express the primary challenge; it denies that we can always appropriately ask how someone knows some proposition, or why that person is right to believe it. Another focuses on the ways in which skeptical challenges are used to question the sufficiency of the reasons we offer when we respond to a primary challenge. Some skeptical challenges question our reasons for belief simply by identifying logically possible situations in which the reason would obtain and the proposition for which it is a reason would be false. Others posit situations that are unverifiable or undetectable—for example, the possibility that we are deceived by an evil demon. This antiskeptical strategy allows that we need reasons for our beliefs but denies that *these* possibilities present challenges to our reasons. As we shall see later, Peirce adopts the first of these strategies: unless we have reason to doubt one of our beliefs, we may not need a reason to believe it.

Peirce's defense of this position depends upon his views about reasons for doubt. Before we turn to this in section 3, there is a preliminary issue to be discussed. As I have indicated, skeptical challenges feed on the ways in which we are fallible in our beliefs. Since Peirce claimed to be a "contrite fallibilist," his work raises some important issues about how that position can be reconciled with a rejection of skepticism. Section 2 considers how we should understand fallibilism and examines how we should understand Hilary Putnam's claim that the combination of fallibilism with antiskepticism was one of the defining marks of American pragmatism. Section 3 explores some of Peirce's views about *doubt*, trying to understand how he can dismiss philosophers' doubts as "unreal" and as "paper" (or "pretend") doubts. This leads to the identification of some views about reasons for belief and doubt that are relevant to sustaining the combination of views discussed in section 2. We then turn to his identification of some philosophical errors about how to think about *reality* that are likely to make the skeptical dialogue unavoidable. As we see in section 4, Peirce wants to avoid "nominalism" and embrace "realism" and holds that doing so enables us to resist skepticism (as well as many other philosophical errors). In the closing section, we consider how skepticism may emerge once again in the light of Peirce's fallibilist, pragmaticist realism,[3] and we assess, in general terms, how he responds to this revised version.

2. SKEPTICISM AND FALLIBILISM

Hilary Putnam once suggested that "it is perhaps *the* unique insight of American pragmatism" that someone "can be both fallibilistic and antiskeptical" (Putnam 1994: 152). When one thinks about it, combining fallibilism with antiskepticism should not be difficult. As C.F. Delaney has put it, skepticism is an "attitude of cognitive despair," while "fallibilism seems to be perfectly compatible with robust cognitive hope" (1993: 111). However, as we have seen, there are familiar philosophical moves that appear to undermine such optimism; Descartes, for one, seems to have thought that the possibility that one of our beliefs might turn out to be mistaken somehow undermines the legitimacy of our holding to them (see Smyth 1997: 227).

In this section, I shall examine how Peirce articulated and defended this "unique insight." Skepticism occasions despair by suggesting that all our beliefs are illegitimate, and that we can be given sufficient reason to doubt each proposition that we currently believe. Even if we *cannot* doubt all these propositions, the standards of epistemic evaluation that we (do or should) take for granted decree that we *ought* to do so.

Fallibilism is more difficult to define. We can start from the observation that we have many beliefs that we actively regard as fallible, and we can understood how these beliefs are acquired in ways that are compatible with their being false. We rely on someone's testimony, and that person turns out to be insincere or mistaken; we base our beliefs upon evidence while aware that more evidence may show that we were mistaken; we know that we often form beliefs upon the basis of reasons while unaware of potential defeaters. In such cases, we can follow Delaney in describing fallibilism as a distinctive "attitude of mind" (1993: 110): we recognize that a well-supported belief may yet turn out to be false; we cannot insulate ourselves from all possibility of error. Such observations suggest that we often take ourselves to be right to believe propositions when we recognize that there is a real, albeit slight, possibility of error. But fallibilism is a bolder claim that this. In 1910, Peirce expressed his fallibilism thus:"I will not, therefore, admit that we know anything whatever with *absolute certainty*" (CP 7.108).[4] Putnam has characterized fallibilism as holding that "there is never a metaphysical guarantee to be had that such-and-such a belief will never need revision" (1994: 152). The talk of "absolute certainty" and "metaphysical guarantee" is supposed to extend our sense of fallibility beyond the familiar cases to cover all our beliefs, including examples where we feel wholly certain of propositions and cannot readily imagine any circumstances in which we might come to abandon our acceptance of them. How is this supposed to work?

When we describe a judgment or belief as "infallible," we identify it as belonging to an epistemic kind of which, of necessity, all members are true. If direct reports of sense data are infallible, then necessarily, all direct reports of sense data are true; if reports of one's sensations are infallible, then all such reports are true; if intuitions of the rational structure of reality are infallible, then all such intuitions are correct. This assignment to a kind identifies a metaphysical feature of the judgment or belief that guarantees its truth. (This must be a nontrivial matter; we do not show that a judgment is infallible by assigning it to the class of "veridical judgments," for example.) If this is how we understand infallibility, then we can show that a judgment is *fallible* by demonstrating that there is no such kind to which it belongs. And this suffices to show that it is not infallible even if we feel totally certain of it and cannot conceive of what might lead us to revise our judgment. I suggest that Putnam's talk of "metaphysical guarantees" and Peirce's appeal to "absolute certainty" should be understood in terms of this understanding of fallibility: nothing is absolutely certain because no judgment belongs to an epistemic kind that rules out the possibility of error.[5]

This characterization of infallibility may face problems: there may be judgments of which we do not feel confident yet which, for all that, possess features that guarantee their truth.[6] Suppose that we adopt a disjunctivist account of perception: perceptual judgments are factive, so all perceptual judgments, of necessity, are true. Yet we may be unconfident of our judgment because we are unsure whether it is a judgment of perception or, perhaps, a state of a different kind, a report of illusion or hallucination, for example. There are two ways to deal with such examples. We might revise the characterization of infallibility to require that the belief *detectably* possesses features that guarantee its truth. Alternatively, we might accept that fallibilism does not extend to all our judgments, recognizing the infallibility of perceptual ones while also insisting that our beliefs *about* whether a given judgment is a perceptual judgment are fallible. I shall not discuss this further here.

Support for this way of understanding Peirce's position can be found in his explanation of why his fallibilism extends to the claim that twice two is four (*CP* 7.108, 1910). He acknowledges that he feels "not the slightest real doubt of it" (*CP* 7.109), and, indeed, "that it would be difficult to imagine a greater folly than to attach any serious importance" to the rather strained reasons for doubting it that he manages to dredge up (*CP* 7.108). He begins by noting that even "computers" occasionally make errors in simple multiplications, which he takes to establish that doing a calculation just once does not provide an absolute guarantee that no error has been made: that a belief is the result of simple multiplication does not guarantee its truth. Perhaps repetition of the calculation, possibly by different people, enables us to progress from a conclusion that we feel very certain of, one that we cannot imagine we could be in error about, to one that is absolutely certain. Since it would be absurd to see just one calculation as enabling us to cross this meta-physical boundary, the safest recourse is to acknowledge that we are often ex-tremely certain of the results of calculations but conclude that"man is incapable of absolute certainty" (*CP* 7.108). This rests on the assumption that if there is a real distinction between fallible and "absolutely infallible" beliefs, it needs to be a sharp one: there cannot be borderline cases between the fallible and the *absolutely* in-fallible; and Peirce agrees with Quine that philosophy cannot provide a sharp boundary of this kind. He denies that we can be "absolutely certain" that twice two is four, and this denial is grounded on the demonstration that we cannot identify a sharply demarcated class to which this judgment belongs and which guarantees its truth. I suspect that something similar is going on in the closing section of Quine's "Two Dogmas of Empiricism" (1980: 42-46): once the analytic/synthetic distinc-tion and a reductionist verificationism are abandoned, we have to recognize that even if we cannot conceive how we could be brought to question them (or to see them as anything other than certain), we have no way of proving that (no meta-physical guarantee that) they are absolutely infallible. And it can support this that we know that (very rarely) what has seemed to be wholly certain has been aban-doned.

Although Peirce and Putnam endorse fallibilism as a thesis about *all* our beliefs, it may not matter if this strong version of fallibilism can be sustained. It is enough that there are very many beliefs that we take to be legitimate and that are manifestly fallible. The challenge remains of showing that skeptical challenges do not demonstrate that our hold on *these* is illegitimate.

3. REASONS FOR BELIEF AND REASONS FOR DOUBT

In defending the claim that the pragmatists were antiskeptics, Putnam invoked the fact that they held that "*doubt* requires justification just as much as belief" (1994: 152). Indeed, most epistemologists who refer to Peirce's writings focus on passages critical of Cartesian approaches to the theory of knowledge in which he insists that the sorts of skeptical challenge associated with such approaches can be safely ignored. He thinks that there is something absurd and even intellectually dishonest about taking skeptical challenges seriously. These views on doubt and Cartesian strategies in epistemology are found in some rather brief passages in two of his best known relatively early articles.[7]

The first of these two passages is in "Some Consequences of Four Incapacities," which appeared in the *Journal of Speculative Philosophy* in 1868. His aim is to challenge a philosophical picture that he calls "the Spirit of Cartesianism." It marked a radical break with the spirit of Scholasticism; and modern logic and science require a perspective that is, in many ways, closer to Scholasticism.

The first of his four "marks of Cartesianism" is the following:

> [Cartesianism] teaches that philosophy must begin with universal doubt; whereas scholasticism had never questioned fundamentals.
>
> (*EP* 1: 28)

Nine years later, in "The Fixation of Belief," considering what norms we should accept for the conduct of inquiry, he identifies a similar target:

> Some philosophers have imagined that to start an inquiry it was only necessary to utter a question or set it down on paper, and have even recommended us to begin our studies with questioning everything!
>
> (*EP* 1: 115)

His response to this suggestion is consistent. In the earlier discussion, he tells us that "we cannot begin with universal doubt." Inquiry must "begin with all the prejudices which we actually have when we enter upon the study of philosophy." Indeed, these prejudices are things that "it does not occur to us can be questioned," and, for this reason, they "cannot be dispelled by a maxim" (*EP* 1: 28–29). In the later discussion, he warns his readers that"the mere putting of a proposition into the interrogative form does not stimulate the mind to any struggle after belief"(*EP* 1: 115). Doubt that derives from the "Cartesian maxim" is of no epistemic value. In each passage, he concludes with a call to arms:

> Let us not pretend to doubt in philosophy what we do not doubt in our hearts.
>
> (1868; *EP* 1: 29)

> There must be real and living doubt, and without this all discussion is idle.
>
> (1877; *EP* 1: 115)

We should be careful in interpreting these passages. What is the method of doubt? In the *Meditations*, Descartes undertook to examine all his beliefs and reject all those for which there was any ground of doubt. Effectively this means that for each belief (or, more strictly, for each class of beliefs) he issues the primary challenge, demanding to know what reason there is to believe the proposition in question and, in addition, whether there is any reason to doubt it. Then, if the evidence for the belief is anything less than conclusive, the belief is to be (or should be) abandoned (Descartes 1984: 9–12). The primary challenge must be presented in a way that treats it as an open question whether there is sufficient reason to believe the proposition. And Peirce seems to think that this is impossible.[8]

It will help if we consider an example. I believe that I was born in Southeast England, in Kent. Suppose that in Cartesian spirit, I reflect on my belief to determine whether I am right to believe it. Let us suppose that I cannot find my birth certificate or any other documentary evidence that might settle the matter. One thing that can occur is that I encounter genuine reason to doubt this memory:

perhaps I find evidence that my parents were living abroad around the time that I was born, or perhaps my relations become very evasive when I ask about my place of birth. In that case, I acquire a positive reason to doubt what I previously believed; it is intelligible that it would shake my habitual confidence about my birthplace and produce what Peirce would call a "living doubt." Another possibility is that I simply find no positive reason to believe that I was born in Kent: I have been certain of this for a long time; I have no positive reason to doubt it; but I can summon up no positive reason to believe it either. I suspect that many of my beliefs are like this. The method of doubt would require me to abandon this belief and to suspend judgment about where I was born solely because I cannot now find a positive reason in its favor. Peirce thinks that in practice, I do not come to doubt propositions in these circumstances, and, indeed, that I cannot do so. If I were to start inquiring into the matter, my residual certainty that I was born in Kent would actually distort the inquiry, making me insensitive to how paltry my evidence is. And this is not irrational.

Descartes may agree that it is not irrational to hold to everyday beliefs in these sorts of cases. The method of doubt is adopted in special circumstances as part of a strategy that will enable us to make progress in the sciences, to obtain accurate knowledge of an independent reality. The special circumstances include the fact that at the time at which Descartes wrote, there was much controversy about the fundamental principles of science and about the criterion of truth in the sciences. The early seventeenth century witnessed a "*crise pyrrhonienne*" (Popk in 1979: 108–109). We must now examine how Peirce was able to reject this method of doubt and repudiate Descartes' views about when we are warranted in coming to doubt what we currently believe.

In order to understand these Peircean views about when doubt is warranted, it is helpful to begin by considering the views of Isaac Levi, a philosopher whose work in epistemology is marked by his reading of Peirce. In a 1998 article, Levi emphasized that traditional foundationalist epistemology has had two distinctive features. The first of these concerns the structure of justification: there must be "foundational premises and principles of reasoning that are self-certifying on the basis of which the merits of other beliefs and principles may be derived." All antifoundationalists reject this, but pragmatists additionally reject a more fundamental claim: the view, at first sight a platitude, that rationally requires that all our current beliefs should be justified. Levi takes this to entail that belief is illegitimate if the believer does not possess reasons or justifications that can be used to support it. He comments:

> Pragmatists do not think that the project of justifying current beliefs is implementable. In this respect they are skeptics. Such skepticism does not imply that because agent X at time *t* cannot justify his current beliefs, he should cease having them. Scepticism about reasons does not imply scepticism about belief.
>
> (Levi 1998: 177)

The fact that we cannot provide rational support for most of our beliefs—such as those mentioned in my example—does not show that we are wrong to hold them. Peirce, Levi tells us, "was a fan of the principle of doxastic inertia according to which there is no need to justify current beliefs, only changes in belief" (Levi 1998: 179). This is initially offered as a description of our practice with epistemic norms. But Levi is quick to point out the corollary that "the burden is on the sceptic why I should cease being certain about many current [beliefs] just because there is a logical possibility that they are mistaken" (Levi 1998: 178). "Real doubts" are based on real possibilities of error.[9] "The inquirer's current state of full [i.e., certain] belief is the standard by which she currently judges truth," and it also sets her "*standard for serious possibility*" (Levi 1998: 179).[10]

In a manuscript from around 1906, Peirce endorses this position. Belief does not always require a reason: "If you absolutely cannot doubt a proposition— cannot bring yourself, upon deliberation, to entertain the least suspicion of the truth of it, it is plain that there is no room to desire anything more" (*CP* 6.498).[11] He continues, "What one does not doubt cannot be rendered more satisfactory than it already is."[12] And the pragmatist knows that "doubt is an art which has to be acquired with difficulty" (ibid.).

The assumption here about when we need epistemic reasons is an important one, although Levi's suggestion that we only need reasons for "changes of belief" may overstate the case. It is important to keep in mind that the Cartesian "method of doubt" is concerned with whether we have reasons to change our epistemic stance toward some proposition: if it is possible to doubt the proposition, then we ought to abandon our belief and replace it by an agnostic attitude toward that proposition, perhaps involving motivation to settle the matter one way or the other. Both Peirce and Levi deny that recognition that there is a *logical* possibility of error is sufficient to count as a reason for doubt. Once it is established that there is a prima facie reason for doubting the proposition, then a reason for belief may be required even if there is no change of belief: in order to resist the doubt, we need reason to eliminate the possibility of error that it proposes. And, of course, reasons for belief are (always?) required when we move from an agnostic stance toward a proposition to one of belief. In other cases, it may be important to keep track of the reasons that have persuaded us of the truth of some proposition because we are aware that we may be proved wrong about the reason and want to be in a position, if that occurs, to revise our attitude toward the proposition. There are also some cases where the lack of a reason to believe a proposition *can* provide a reason to doubt it—and there are interesting questions about how these cases are distinguished from the others. There are cases where this might have a moral grounding: certainty that a friend is disloyal or a partner is unfaithful needs to be supported by reasons. Other cases arise with scientific views that others might reject, for example, or with cases where there is general recognition that mistakes are likely to occur. The important point is that it is primarily changes in cognitive stance (or retention of a cognitive stance in circumstances where a change was in the cards) that require a reason, and there must always be a special reason in other cases why reasons are required for belief to be legitimate.

This provides a description of our practice: we do not think that belief always requires reasons or "justification." Its antiskeptical force is important. First, the fact that we cannot provide a solid justification for one of our certain beliefs does not provide us with any reason to doubt it. The skeptical challenge to it can be resisted. Second, as Olsson (2005: 188; cf. Levi 1991: 58) reminds us, this allows for a quick dismissal of the skeptical possibilities exploited in modern skeptical arguments. The certainties that stand in no need of further justification will include the fact that I am not the victim of a *malin génie* or a disembodied brain in a vat of chemicals.[13] It is another corollary of this position that it helps us see how fallibilism can be undisturbing. Our fallibility extends to these propositions of which we are certain, even after careful deliberation. We are confident that few of these certainties will be shaken, but we allow (as an abstract possibility) that any of them might. Since our certainty does not depend upon reasons, it is not shaken by this abstract acknowledgment of fallibility. The fact that we cannot rule out the possibility that we will come to have a reason to doubt some proposition is not itself a reason to doubt the proposition.

But, as Levi points out, all this does for epistemology is to shift the burden of proof: good reasons are required before we adopt the epistemic standards that lead to the method of doubt. Descartes himself did not hold that the method of doubt was implicit in our ordinary epistemic practices; he thought that there were positive reasons for adopting this strategy. And Peirce too held that it might be rational to do so, given either a distinctive set of metaphysical and epistemological views or some views about the real possibilities for the progress of inquiry. The next two sections consider these two possibilities in turn.

4. NOMINALISM AND TWO CONCEPTIONS OF REALITY

The previous section suggested that the Cartesian method of doubt, which can be used to mount some strong skeptical challenges, is not obviously compelling. Our normal practice of epistemic evaluation does not require us to have sufficient reasons for *all* our (legitimate) beliefs. Reasons come into their own when we consider changing our system of epistemic stances. But, as we noted, this is not sufficient to dismiss these challenges: even if the method of doubt is not a natural outgrowth of our ordinary habits of reflection, it is still conceivable that the method is one that we *ought* to use in place of our customary practices, at least in some circumstances. At best, Peirce's views about doubt establish that the burden of proof lies with someone who wishes to adopt methods that are in harmony with the method of doubt: they must persuade us to change our habits of epistemic evaluation. This would have come as no surprise to Descartes.

In his earlier writings, Peirce identified a pair of closely related views that were conducive to adoption of the method of doubt. One of these was a view about the structure of cognition and justification; the other involved adoption of a distinctive view of *reality*. Each, he thought, was a consequence of nominalism, a philosophical vice that he uncovered in the work of almost all his predecessors, from Plato to Kant and Hegel. The view of cognition was a kind of foundationalism; the view of reality allowed for the existence of a potentially unbridgeable gap between the real and the knowable. Peirce, always ready to insist upon his extreme realism, criticized these ideas about the structure of cognition in some articles published in the late 1860s. During the 1870s, he set about clarifying the concept of *reality*, defending what he called a "realist" conception that, he thought, kept Cartesian challenges at bay.

As this terminology suggests, Peirce's "realism" contrasts with "nominalism"; he thought that pragmatism was unavoidably committed to a non-Humean view of laws and "generals," and in his later work, he emphasized that generality, causal interactions, and law-governed patterns were present in perceptual experience. But he also embraced quite a robust realism about external things. We get the flavor of his realism in the 1870s when we identify a commonsense assumption that, in "The Fixation of Belief" (1877), he seemed to think was required if we are to make sense of the possibility of *doubt* and also to make sense of there being a question of which methods of inquiry we *ought* to adopt:

> There are real things, whose characters are entirely independent of our opinions about them; those realities affect our senses according to regular laws, and, though our sensations are as different as our relations to the objects, yet, by taking account of the laws of perception, we can ascertain by reasoning how things really are, and any man, if he have sufficient experience and reason enough about it, will be led to the one true conclusion.

> (*EP* 1: 120)

We will only understand this when we know what it means to describe something as "real." The nominalist conception seems to be designed to capture this perspective but does not do so. Peirce's own realist conception is designed to clarify this assumption.

In "Questions Concerning Certain Faculties Claimed for Man" (1868), Peirce attacks the idea that cognition involves having "intuitions," a word he presumably takes from Kant.[14] Sometimes he characterizes cognitions in terms of a foundationalist account of knowledge. An intuition is "nearly the same as 'premiss not itself a conclusion.'" This has to be qualified only because terms like "conclusion" and "premiss" apply only to "judgments," while an intuition can be "any kind of cognition whatever." This is intended to allow for the possibility that a sensory experience may be an intuition. The official definition of intuition is "a cognition not determined by a previous cognition of the same object, and therefore so determined by something out of consciousness." Peirce allows that "cognitions not judgments may be determined by previous cognitions; and a cognition not so determined, and therefore determined directly by the transcendental object, is to be termed an intuition" (*CP* 5.213). The insistence that intuitions may be (always are?) cognitions that are not judgments is required to capture the nominalist character of this view: the cognitions solely determined by the transcendental object are taken to be wholly singular representations, not involving any predication.

Three years later, in a review of a new edition of Berkeley's philosophical writings, Peirce formulates this perception as an account of reality. Having noted that "objects are divided into figments, dreams, etc., on the one hand, and realities on the other," he states that the "latter are those which have an existence independent of your mind or mine or that of any number of persons." He then offers a simple "definition" of reality: "The real is that which is not whatever we happen to think it, but is unaffected by what we may think of it" (*CP* 8.12). The nominalist conception tries to further clarify this idea of mind independence by exploiting the idea that our thoughts are caused by our sensations and these sensations by some thing out of the mind: "This thing out of mind, which directly influences sensation, and, through sensation, thought, because it is out of the mind, is independent of how we think it, and is, in short, the real" (*CP* 8.12). We know about external things through the mediation of what seem to be intuitions, singular representations ("sensations") that are determined by ("directly influenced by") the transcendental object and provide the sole basis for our thoughts.

If this is the correct way to think about reality and experience, then it may be possible to make a case for adopting Cartesian epistemological strategies. This view assigns a fundamental role to intuitions: they are our point of contact with (and only source of information about) reality. (1) The method of doubt can then be seen as a device for identifying what is really given to us in intuition; it helps us free ourselves from those aspects of our perceptual beliefs that are determined by background substantive assumptions rather than being determined by the transcendental object. (2) It also supports an individualist approach to epistemic evaluation. Although we *can* use the testimony of others as a source of corrective information, this function is mediated through the intuitions that are determined in *us* by the utterances and other behavior of our fellows. (3) It supports the possibility that once error enters our system of belief, we cannot be confident that further inquiry will enable us to correct it. As Descartes put it, once one bad apple enters our corpus of opinions, it is likely to infect the others; our only source of confidence in our ability to acquire knowledge of reality is to prevent error ever entering the corpus. (4) Our confidence in our knowledge has to depend upon assumptions that are inexplicable and unknowable on ordinary empirical grounds. Thus Descartes needs belief in God (an "absolutely inexplicable, unanalyzable ultimate") to assure us that the processes by which our intuitions are determined by the transcendental object are reliable (see *EP* 1: 28–29).

If he has to sustain his antiskeptical confidence and also reconcile it with fallibilism, Peirce thinks that he needs to reject this nominalist vision. In "Some Consequences of Four Incapacities," he tells us:

Philosophy ought to imitate the successful sciences in its methods, so far as to proceed only from tangible premises which can be subjected to careful scrutiny, and to trust rather to the multitude and variety of its arguments than to the conclusiveness of any one. Its reasoning should not form a chain which is no stronger than its weakest link, but a cable whose fibres may be ever so slender, provided they are sufficiently numerous and intimately connected.

(*EP* 1: 29)

If our knowledge is based upon intuitions, we might suppose, we have no alternative but to view our reasoning as a chain, which is no stronger than its weakest link.

Peirce considers several ways of arguing for the claim that we rely upon intuitions for our knowledge. In 1868, he evaluates the suggestion that it is evident to introspection that there are intuitions, and he considers the argument that they are required to block a potential regress of justification and cognition. In "Questions Concerning Certain Faculties Claimed for Man," he responds to this in the course of a complex argument. He appeals to a variety of facts about our unreliability in describing our own psychological states in order to argue that not only can we not tell "intuitively" whether a state is an intuition, but also we lack an introspective ability to examine our cognitions and see what they are determined by. We can establish that we have intuitions only as the conclusion of an explanatory inference; and all the evidence shows that our cognitions are all partly determined by other cognitions of the same object. Once we recognize that not all cognitions are judgments, the supposed regress ceases to be a cause for concern: Peirce is happy to see sensory experience as a continuous process and to deny that the experience of a particular object must have a fixed first point. I am not exploring the details of these arguments here; it would take too much space, and the interest of the strategy does not stand or fall with the details of its execution in Peirce's writings.[15]

The other argument for the Cartesian picture of cognition that Peirce considers depends upon the analysis of reality. We need to understand what the mind independence of real things consists in, and if the nominalist conception of reality is the best clarification of this, then there may be another route into the doctrine of intuitions. But after describing the nominalist conception of reality, Peirce offers an alternative, which he describes as "less familiar" but also as "even more natural and obvious" (*CP* 8.12). He also describes it as "a highly practical and common-sense position" (*CP* 8.16). The underlying idea is that "human opinion universally tends in the long run to a definite form, which is the truth" (8.12):

The arbitrary will or other individual peculiarities of a sufficiently large number of minds may postpone the general agreement in that opinion indefinitely; but it cannot affect what the character of that opinion shall be when it is reached. This final opinion, then, is independent, not indeed of thought in general, but of all that is arbitrary and individual in thought; is quite independent of how you, or I, or any number of men think.

(*CP* 8.12)[16]

This is supposed to be enough to make sense of the mind independence of reality. This picture is thus meant to provide for the thought that although "all human thought and opinion contains . . . an element of error," further inquiry and investigation will enable us to remove errors and improve our cognitive position.[17] It is easy to see that this conception of reality need provide no obstacle to combining fallibilism and antiskepticism. Indeed, it seems to be a positive mark of realism that there is no gap between what is real and what, in principle, can be known. However, although the strategy adopted in these early writings may enable us to see that the Cartesian cannot discharge the burden of showing that a lack of reason for a proposition provides us with a reason to doubt that proposition, there is still work to be done before we stop worrying about skepticism.

5. EXPERIENCE AND EXTERNAL WORLD

The story we have examined so far may suggest that Peirce is stuck in a familiar dialectic. The characterization of his realism that we took from "The Fixation of Belief" had an empiricist flavor: we can obtain stable knowledge of reality by exploiting the ways in which external things affect our senses. Indeed, it is through the senses that we encounter the external world. The nominalist conception of reality incorporated that idea: sensory intuitions serve as intermediaries between external things and our thoughts about them. But the nominalist conception was neither true to our experience nor satisfactory as a basis for explaining how our beliefs are legitimately held. When we turn to the realist conception, which appears to explain reality in terms of a fated consensus about a body of coherent opinions, we face the questions of how we should explain the fundamental role of perception in the fixation of belief and also how experience can be understood as an encounter with an external world. Part of this explanation will consist of an account of the role of, for example, inductive and experimental reasoning in enabling us to revise and correct our beliefs en route to the truth. In this section, I want to consider another distinctively pragmatist theme, the account of perception that Peirce began to develop after 1880.

The problem we have just raised has two aspects. First, there is the idea that we *encounter* the external world through perceptual experience: there is a kind of *directness* in our perceptual contact with things. Second, the testing of empirical beliefs and theories depends upon experiment and observation. If we do arrive at the truth through inquiry, this depends fundamentally on our having perceptual experiences of things. The nominalist conception of reality builds these features into cognition from the beginning by claiming that the first premises from which all our beliefs should be derived are descriptions of our sensory experience. The realist conception does not give this role to perception. Can it give perception a fundamental role at all?

Let us begin with the dimension of *encounter* or *directness*. It is because we experience objects that we are able to refer to them, to think about them, or to talk about them. One aspect of *encountering things* seems to be a sort of direct reference to them. When I observe the book on my desk, I can pick it out through a demonstrative or indexical sign; I report what I see by saying or thinking, "*That* is a yellow book." Indeed, I encounter the object directly even if the perceptual judgment I form is false. For example, the thing I take to be a yellow book may be a box painted to look like a book. I make fallible judgments that involve direct reference to external things. On the nominalist view, reference to external things is likely to be *indirect*: the book should be referred to as the "object out of mind" that caused this sensation or experience. I should think of external things as the causes of the sensations that are the things I really encounter.

In two ways, the content of experience is richer than it is taken to be in the sort of traditional empiricism allied to what Peirce calls the nominalist conception of reality. The first, which we have just considered, is that we experience things as external, as available for direct reference. Second, in experiencing things, we bring concepts to bear, experiencing things as behaving in patterned and law-governed ways. In a lecture from 1903, Peirce appeals to ambiguous figures such as the Schroeder stair to show that general concepts are present in perceptual experiences as much as they are in reflective and conscious reasoning. Walking in the country in the late evening, I make the perceptual report that "that sheep is lying on the ground." The object is picked out demonstratively, and how it looks reflects the concepts that are brought to bear. In view of the links between these concepts and others, I expect my experience to develop in predictable ways—for example, I expect the sheep to get up and move away under appropriate circumstances, and I expect distinctive tactile experiences if I move up close to it. When it does not behave as expected, I can revise my judgment: that object, which I took to be a sheep on the basis of how it looked, turns out to be a bush. I revise my judgment by interacting with the thing that I saw, and I learn what the thing I saw *really* was by interacting with it and collecting more information about it. We can thus combine the thesis that we directly perceive external things with the claim that what these things *really* are is to be clarified through further inquiry. This view accords with the realist conception of reality.

In a discussion of facts from the mid-1890s, Peirce claims that our knowledge of facts depends upon their "resisting us." He continues:

> A man may walk down Wall Street debating within himself the existence of an external world; but if in his brown study he jostles up against somebody who angrily draws off and knocks him down, the sceptic is unlikely to carry his scepticism so far as to doubt whether anything beside the ego was concerned in that phenomenon. The resistance shows him that something independent of him is there.

(CP 1.431)

This passage describes some aspects of the "outward clash of experience," features that are evidently relevant to skepticism about external things. As we have just seen, experience does not simply provide neutral or subjective sense data that can serve as evidence for the existence of external things. Rather, it presents something as *other* or as external: something "beside the ego" is contained in the perceptual phenomenon. It is not merely that I cannot prevent a judgment about external things arising, one that is not open to critical self-control as it is formed; it is the experience of encountering something external that is distinctive in the perceptual encounter. We directly perceive external things, albeit fallibly.[18]

Perceptual judgments anchor our beliefs in two distinct ways. First, the primary form of reference to external things is through the use of demonstrative signs in perceptual judgments: that is how we encounter external things, and it is the source of our sense that we are part of a world of objects with which we can interact and of which we can obtain knowledge. Second, perception provides premises for our reasoning. Perceptual judgments force themselves upon us: we find them irresistible and do not accept them on the basis of conscious *reasons*. When we accept perceptual judgments, we see no need to raise the primary challenge and ask what reason we have to accept them. Peirce sometimes describes them as (at the time they are made) "acritical." But it is compatible with this that subsequently, we can have reason to doubt them. We recognize that they are not to be taken at face value, and in revising them, we are guided by our background knowledge: we can understand how a bush on a hillside in murky light can appear to be a sleeping sheep.[19]

6. AVOIDING DESPAIR IN THE FACE OF THE FUTURE

Several of the pragmatist ideas that I have discussed will remind readers of themes from the later Wittgenstein. The claims about perception mentioned in section 5 resemble views from part 2 of the *Philosophical Investigations*(1953), and Peirce's theses about reasons for belief and reasons for doubt have much in common with claims to be found in *On Certainty* (1969).[20] I do not intend to make a detailed comparison here, but I shall draw attention to some pertinent differences in order to identify yet another pragmatist theme in thinking about these issues.

It is common ground that the legitimacy of most of our current beliefs should not be threatened by skeptical challenges. It is also agreed that for many of our certainties, we can offer no reasons and do not need to do so unless some reasonable doubt is raised about them. Doubts need a reason, and reasons for doubt are harder to come by than many epistemologists have supposed. One difference, noted by Tiercelin (2005: 64–69), is that in effect, Wittgenstein stops at this, and for that reason, it is easy to follow Robert Fogelin in seeing his work as capturing what is living in Pyrrhonian skepticism. Peirce does not stop at this point. First, a representative figure of the nineteenth century, he aspired to embed his discussion in an ambitious philosophical architectonic that included a system (empirically grounded) of metaphysics. This is linked to the fact that unlike Wittgenstein, he had a strong need to vindicate realism. I do not propose to discuss this here, although I shall consider one of the strategic moves that led him in this direction. Second, as the realist conception of reality indicates, Peirce views inquirers as occupying a position in history. We need to be confident not only of our current certainties but also of our ability, as time goes by, to identify and correct errors and to find the right answers to our questions and solutions to our problems. We need to be confident that we are indeed fated to arrive at the truth, so long as we manage our inquiries to the best of our ability. This concern is absent from *On Certainty*.

In many cases, this presents no problem. For example, I am certain of the short-term reliability of induction and testimony, I have no reason to doubt that I am poor at assessing the reliability of doubts in ordinary cases, and I know that in may circumstances, I am good at solving problems and answering questions. Unless there is a good reason to doubt one of these certainties, then there is nothing illegitimate in my relying on these methods and capacities in managing my beliefs and inquiries. The strategy described in section 3 can be used to address these issues too.

But it is not clear that we can always sustain our confidence that we can obtain knowledge of reality in this way. Particularly in the more theoretical reaches of the sciences, and perhaps in connection with ethical propositions, there are too many contingencies that can get in the way of our progress toward the "fated consensus." Think, first, of some of the capacities we need to carry out inquiries successfully. For example, we must be able to analyze and describe problems and questions clearly, evaluate what sorts of considerations are relevant to the issue, think up solutions that we find plausible, evaluate and try to answer subordinate questions, and reflect on the ways in which sociohistorical considerations can distort our (and other people's) thoughts about the matter.[21] The capacities we have will be determined in large part by training and education and by experience that need not be directly applicable to the new problems we face. Particularly when we are dealing with difficult and novel kinds of issues, it is hard to see that we will be certain that we possess all the capacities that are required for making a serious contribution to solving our problem. And in that case, it is hard to see that the strategies described in section 3 will fit the bill.

In that case, another pragmatist strategy enters the frame. In later work, Peirce appears to allow that our confident participation in inquiry does not always require confident certainty that we have the abilities required to advance toward the fated consensus. It may be enough that we rationally *hope* that we can do so. We hope that the problem can be solved, and that we possess the capacities required for solving it. We hope that our sense of plausibility (for example) will lead us to favor the right sorts of hypotheses. This offers a way of recognizing the unanswerability of challenges that might lead to skepticism, but disarming their tendency to lead us to doubt our ability to participate.

7. CONCLUSION

This chapter has offered an account of the most important themes in Peirce's pragmaticist response to skepticism. These include the following:

- The attempt to combine an antiskeptical stance with a thoroughgoing fallibilism (section 2).
- Some distinctive views about when we need reasons for our beliefs and about the nature and importance of reasons for doubt. It is a mark of the pragmatist outlook that reasons for doubt (and for changes in belief) are much more important than reasons for our other beliefs (section 3).
- A rejection of a foundationalist account of justification, together with the rejection of some metaphysical pictures that would lead us to think that such an account of justification was required (section 4).
- A defense of a much richer account of the content of experience than classical empiricists have favored and of a nonempiricist epistemology that gives a fundamental role to experience (section 5).
- A role for regulative ideas, or rational hopes, in sustaining our confidence that we are able to contribute to inquiry effectively (section 6).

Although I have discussed these ideas as they are expressed in Peirce's work, I think that variations upon them are to be found in all the classical pragmatists.

NOTES

1. Erik J. Olsson offers a "reconstruction" of Peirce's antiskeptical strategy that is not directed at the sort of doubt-based skepticism I am considering but at more modern skeptical positions that exploit a closure principle to show that I cannot know that I have a hand, for example, unless I can know that I am not a brain in a vat (Olsson 2005: 187–90).

2. Where possible, references to Peirce's writings are given to *The Essential Peirce* (Peirce 1992, 1998). In some cases, I have used *Collected Papers of Charles S. Peirce* (Peirce 1931–58). For each of these sources, I employ standard scholarly methods of reference. For example, "*EP* 1: 17" refers to page 17 of volume 1 of *The Essential Peirce*; and "*CP* 5.18" refers to paragraph 18 of volume 5 of *The Collected Papers*.

3. "Pragmaticism" is the word that Peirce introduced in 1905 to distinguish his nuanced position from other views falling under the general characterization "pragmatism."

4. He makes similar remarks elsewhere. "There are three things to which we can never hope to attain by reasoning: namely absolute certainty, absolute exactitude, absolute universality" (*CP* 1.141, 1897). It is hard to say what expressions like "metaphysical guarantee" and "absolute certainty" mean, but I take it that talk of the "metaphysical" and the "absolute" go together.

5. This way of understanding fallibilism is useful for understanding the later sections of Quine's "Two Dogmas of Empiricism" (1980). There are also points of similarity with

Michael Williams's views about the role of what he calls "epistemological realism" in generating scepticism (Williams 1991: 108–113). This view holds that, in evaluating our beliefs, we think of them as belonging to broad natural kinds, our justification in holding a belief depending upon the reliability of beliefs that depend upon those kinds. In each case, the views lead to the contextualist claim that epistemic evaluation occurs within a context, where much is taken to stand firm and to require no reflective defense. Two differences are that, where Williams is concerned with the role of what we might call "explanatory kinds" of beliefs, Peirce discusses whether there are sharply demarcated classes of beliefs; and where Williams is concerned with identifying the errors that make skepticism seem unavoidable, Peirce's aim is to make a case for an extreme form of fallibilism.

6. I am grateful to Alan Millar and Duncan Pritchard for helpful discussions of this.

7. In a draft of a logic text written in 1893, Peirce observes that "Descartes marks the period when Philosophy put off childish things and began to be a conceited young man" (CP 4.71). The child treats tradition as infallible, the mature thinker treats it as a valuable albeit fallible resource; and the philosophical adolescent undertakes to abandon it.

8. Peirce has other objections to the method of doubt too (see Feibleman 1946: 70–71). One of these is that Descartes never extends his doubt to his assurance that he doubts some proposition (see, for example, CP 5.382n). He is satisfied that if he deliberately includes the proposition in a conscious list of doubted ones, then it is really doubted. Peirce suspects that the proposition will usually remain active in a habitual, unconscious way, influencing how we act and how we adjust our other beliefs. The unconscious operation of our beliefs will then interfere with our attempts to evaluate the proposition that we "pretend" to doubt.

9. This combination of views reconciles antiskepticism with fallibilism. A real doubt of a belief must rest on the recognition of a real possibility that the belief may turn out to be mistaken. If we have no information that will provide a real doubt of some proposition, then we are entitled to continue in our acceptance of it. But the lack of reason to doubt a proposition is compatible with belief in it being fallible.

10. It is worth noting a similar asymmetry between the legitimacy of belief and doubt in Olsson's writings on coherentism. Having spent most of his book arguing that the fact that our beliefs are coherent does not provide us with a reason for accepting them, he does allow (in the Peircean final section) that incoherence among our beliefs does provide a reason for doubt (Olsson 2005: 190–93).

11. To avoid confusion, I take it that the claim that I "absolutely cannot doubt" something in this passage should be compatible with the fallibilistic claim (see section 2) that it is not "absolutely certain."

12. Other remarks in this passage show how far Peirce had been influenced by the commonsense tradition in philosophy. On most "ordinary mattes of everybody's life," we observe that what we find indubitable coincides with what "no well matured man doubts." Such certainties are often instinctive, although the things we find indubitable mutate over our lifetimes.

13. This is a legitimate use of the Peircean strategy and may be a sufficient response to these possibilities. We should note, however, that Peirce's pragmatist maxim might also be employed to show that these possibilities are empty or unintelligible because their realization would make no (practical) difference to our experience. I suspect that the move considered in the text is the more fundamental one: if we did not have this reason to discount such possibilities, then we might have reason to doubt the pragmatist maxim. (For an examination of the pragmatist maxim, see Hookway 2004a.)

14. There is at least one respect in which Peirce's account of intuitions differs from Kant's. In *The Critique of Pure Reason*, space and time are introduced as the forms of intuition rather than as general categories of the understanding. From his earliest writings, Peirce explained our understanding of space and time as involving the mastery of general spatial and temporal concepts, subject to his system of categories, and denied that there were any a priori structures other than those provided by his system of categories.

15. There is another theme, one that anticipates the pragmatist maxim for clarifying ideas from ten years later. Peirce undertakes to show that we can have no conception of something that is "incognizable." Since the nominalist conception, according to Peirce, requires the incognizable idea of a transcendental object, this may offer a direct argument against nominalism. It also provides a reason to reject the idea that we can understand the more extreme skeptical possibilities.

16. Contra Bernard Williams and Hilary Putnam, this explanation of truth and reality in terms of the convergence of opinion does not involve any sort of commitment to there being what is sometimes called an "absolute conception of reality." Indeed, Peirce takes it to be a merit of his view that it enables him to acknowledge the reality of secondary qualities and artefact kinds. See Hookway 2004b.

17. Some readers may be puzzled at this conception of reality being called "realist," since it does not appear to allow for any gap between what is real and what is knowable. It may help to think of Peirce's position as a generalization of the view that Kreisel expressed about Platonism versus constructivism in mathematics: "the problem is not the existence of mathematical objects but the objectivity of mathematical statements" (Kreisel 1958). (There is a mystery about this view of Kreisel's. It is often referred to, for example, by Dummett and Crispin Wright, and is always accompanied by a reference to this article, but I have been unable to find the quoted passage there.) The realities are captured through objective statements; and the identity of the propositions on which we converge does not depend upon the will or feelings of ourselves or our fellows. The convergence is unforced, "fated," or "destined."

18. This duality of ego and object within perceptual experience is a manifestation of what Peirce calls "second ness" (see, for example *CP* 1.24).

19. For further discussion of these issues, see Hookway 1985, chap.5, and 2000, chap.4.

20. There is an extensive and interesting discussion of what she sees as Peirce's and Wittgenstein's related but distinct "pragmatist strategies" for dealing with skeptical doubts in chapter 3 of Tiercelin 2005.

21. Some of these intellectual virtues are suggested by Westphal's characterization of "mature judgment (2004: 47–50)." He is discussing Hegel's epistemology, but since he reads Hegel as a somewhat Peircean pragmatist, what he says is relevant here too.

REFERENCES

Austin, J.L. 1961. *Philosophical Papers*. Oxford: Oxford University Press.

Descartes, René. 1984. *The Philosophical Writings of Descartes* vol. II. Translated by J. Cottingham, R. Stoothoff, and D. Murdoch. Cambridge: Cambridge University Press.

Feibleman, James K. 1946. *An Introduction to Peirce's Philosophy*. Reprinted 1971. Cambridge, MA: MIT Press.

Haack, Susan. 1983. "Descartes, Peirce and the Cognitive Community." In E. Freeman (ed.), *The Relevance of Charles Peirce*. La Salle, IL: Monist Library of Philosophy, 238–63.

Hookway, Christopher. 1985. *Peirce*. London: Routledge and Kegan Paul.

———. 2000. *Truth, Rationality, and Pragmatism: Themes from Peirce*. Oxford: Clarendon Press.

———. 2004a. "The Principle of Pragmatism: Peirce's Formulations and Examples." *Midwest Studies in Philosophy* 28: 119–36.

———. 2004b. "Truth, Reality, and Convergence." In C.J. Misak (ed.), *The Cambridge Companion to Peirce*. Cambridge: Cambridge University Press, 127–49.

Kreisel, Georg. 1958 "Wittgenstein's *Remarks on the Foundations of Mathematics*." *British Journal of the Philosophy of Science* 9: 135–58

Levi, Isaac. 1991. *The Fixation of Belief and Its Undoing*. Cambridge: Cambridge University Press.

———. 1998. "Pragmatism and Change of View." In C.J. Misak (ed.), *Pragmatism. Canadian Journal of Philosophy*, supplementary volume 24: 177–201.

Olsson, Erik. 2005. *Against Coherentism*. Oxford: Clarendon Press.

Peirce, Charles S. 1931–58. *Collected Papers*. Edited by C. Hartshorne and P. Weiss (vols. 1–6) and by A. Burks (vols. 7–8). Cambridge, MA: Harvard University Press. (References are to *CP* by volume and paragraph number.)

———. 1992, 1998. *The Essential Peirce*. Edited by N. Houser and C. Kloesel (vol. 1) and by the Peirce Edition Project (vol. 2). Bloomington: Indiana University Press. (References are to *EP* by volume and page.)

Popkin, Richard H. 1979. *The History of Scepticism from Erasmus to Spinoza*. Berkeley: University of California Press.

Putnam, Hilary. 1994. *Words and Life*. Cambridge, MA: Harvard University Press.

Quine, W.v.O, 1980. "Two Dogmas of Empiricism" in W.v.O. Quine, *From a Logical Point of View: Nine Logico-Philosophical Essays*. Cambridge, MA: Harvard University Press, esp. pp. 42–46.

Skagestad, P. 1981. *The Road of Inquiry: Charles S. Peirce's Pragmatic Realism*. New York: Columbia University Press.

Smyth, Richard A. 1997. *Reading Peirce Reading*. Lanham, MD: Row man and Littlefield.

Tiercelin, Claudine. 2005. *Le Doute en Question*. Paris: Éditions de L'Éclat. Westphal, Kenneth. 2004. *Hegel's Epistemology*. Indianapolis, IN: Hackett.

Williams, Michael. 1991. *Unnatural Doubts*. Oxford: Blackwell.

Wittgenstein, Ludwig, 1953. *Philosophical Investigations*, Edited by G.E.M. Anscombe and R. Rhees. Oxford: Blackwell.

———. 1969. *On Certainty*. Edited by G.E.M. Anscombe and H. von Wright. Oxford: Blackwell.

CHAPTER 15

....

MOORE AND SKEPTICISM

....

NOAH LEMOS

1. SOME MAIN MOOREAN THEMES

....

G. E. Moore wrestled with issues of knowledge and skepticism throughout his career, examining and responding in several influential essays to various skeptical arguments. Moore is among the most prominent members of the commonsense tradition in philosophy, a tradition that includes the eighteenth-century Scottish philosopher Thomas Reid and the twentieth-century philosopher Roderick Chisholm. It is characteristic of "commonsensism" to hold that we do in fact know many of the things that we ordinarily take ourselves to know, and that our philosophical views should be adequate to the fact that we know them. Thomas Reid, for example, understood Hume's empiricism to imply that we have no knowledge of the material world, no knowledge of the future, the past, or other minds, and no knowledge of ourselves as continuing subjects of experience. Reid took Hume to show that the wages of empiricism are a rather thoroughgoing skepticism. Reid writes:

> A traveller of good judgment may mistake his way, and be unawares led into a wrong track; and while the road is fair before him, he may go on without suspicion and be followed by others; but, when it ends in a coal pit, it requires no great judgment to know he hath gone wrong, nor perhaps to find out what misled him.[1]

Reid held that since we do know many of the things that empiricism would rule out, so much the worse for empiricism. We find Chisholm taking a similar stance: "We reject the sceptical view according to which there is no reason to believe the premises of an inductive argument ever confer evidence upon the conclusion. If the skeptical view were true, then we would know next to nothing about the world around us."[2] Chisholm holds that since we do know a lot about the world around us, so much the worse for skepticism about induction.

We find a similar theme throughout Moore's writings. In his 1919 essay "Some Judgments of Perception," Moore begins by considering some views about perception and the possibility of perceptual knowledge. He rejects certain philosophical views because they imply that we cannot know various facts about the external world:

> But it seems to me a sufficient refutation of such views as these, simply to point to cases in which we do know such things. This, after all, you know, really is a finger: there is no doubt about it: I know it, and you all know it. And I think we may safely challenge any philosopher to bring forward any argument in favour either of the proposition that we do not know it, or of the proposition that it is not true, which does not at some point rest upon some premiss which is, beyond comparison, less certain, than is the proposition which it is designed to attack.[3]

In this passage, Moore makes two points. First, he claims that since we do know various facts about the external world, such as "this is a finger," it follows that any philosophical view or argument that implies that we do not must be mistaken. Any philosophical argument that implies that we do not know such things must either have a false premise or be invalid. Second, Moore claims that any philosophical argument that concludes that we do not know such things rests, at some point, upon some premise that it is less reasonable to believe than the proposition it is designed to attack. So Moore would say that the proposition that I know that this is a finger is more reasonable to believe than one or more of the premises or assumptions in any skeptical argument that denies it.

Over twenty years later, Moore takes a similar stand. He claims that Bertrand Russell's skeptical view rests on premises or assumptions that are less certain than the proposition it is designed to attack. Russell held that we did not and could not have certain knowledge of such things as "this is a pencil" or "that person is conscious." Russell held that such propositions could be at most probable for us. After a long examination of Russell's view, Moore writes:

> Russell's view that I do not know for certain that this is a pencil or that you are conscious rests, if I am right, on no less than four distinct assumptions: (1) That I do not know these things immediately; (2) That they don't follow from any thing or things that I do know immediately; (3) That, *if* (1) and (2) are true, my belief in or knowledge of them must be "based on an analogical or inductive argument"; and (4) That what is so based cannot be *certain knowledge*. And what I can't help asking myself is this: Is it, in fact, as certain that all these four assumptions are true, as that I *do* know that this is a pencil and you are conscious? I cannot help answering: It seems to be *more* certain that I *do* know that this is a pencil and that you are conscious, than that any single one of these four assumptions are true, let alone all four. . . . I agree with Russell that (1), (2), and (3) *are* true; yet of no one even of these three do I feel as certain that this is a pencil. Nay more: I do not think it is *rational* to be as certain of any one of these four propositions, as of the proposition that I do know that this is a pencil.[4]

Here Moore says that he agrees with Russell that he does not know that this is a pencil immediately. He tentatively endorses Russell's view that such knowledge must be based on some analogical or inductive argument. Still, Moore insists that it is not as rational to be as certain of any of Russell's four assumptions as it is of the proposition that he does know that this is a pencil.

As we have seen, Moore claims that he knows various things about the external world and the mental states of others, and that it is more rational for him to believe these propositions than various premises in skeptical arguments. In "A Defence of Common Sense," he lists a variety of propositions that he claims to know with certainty to be true.[5] Among these are propositions about external objects, the past, and the mental states of others. He claims, for example, to know that the earth existed for many years before he was born and that since he was born he has been either in contact with, or not far from, the surface of the earth. He also claims that almost everyone knows similar sorts of propositions to be true.

But *how* does he know them? What makes it rational for him to believe such things? Moore does not give us anything like a completely satisfactory answer to these questions. He does not give us a well-developed epistemological theory about what makes a belief rational or an instance of knowledge. Indeed, Moore's views about how we know various things about the external world appear to have changed over his career. We have already seen, for example, that Moore tentatively endorses Russell's view that we do not know immediately that this is a pencil, and that such knowledge is based on an analogical or inductive inference. Yet earlier in his career, Moore held a very different view:

> Obviously, I cannot know *that* I know that the pencil exists, unless I do know that the pencil exists; and it might, therefore, be thought that the first proposition can only be mediately known—known *merely* because the second is known.
> But it is, I think, necessary to make a distinction. From the mere fact that I should not know the first, *unless* I knew the second, it does not follow that I know the first *merely* because I know the second. And, in fact, I think I do know *both* of them immediately.[6]

Here Moore says that he knows immediately *both* that the pencil exists and the epistemic proposition that he *knows* that the pencil exists. He denies implicitly that his knowledge that the pencil exists must be based on analogical or inductive arguments. In any case, while Moore seems to have held different views about *how* he knows various facts about the external world, he insists that he does know them.

Indeed, Moore held that in order to know some things, it is not necessary to know how one knows them, and it is not necessary to know what one's evidence is. In "A Defence of Common Sense," Moore writes:

> If, for instance, I do know that the earth had existed for many years before I was born, I certainly know this because I have known other things in the past which were evidence for it. And I certainly do not know exactly what the evidence was. Yet all this seems to me to be no good reason for doubting that I do know it. We are all, I think, in this strange position that we do know many things,

with regard to which, we know further that we must have had evidence for them, and yet we do not know how we know them, i.e. we do not know what the evidence was.[7]

Moore claims that we know some things because we know other things that are evidence for them. But in at least some cases of this kind, Moore denies that we must know what the evidence is. We can know some things without knowing how we know them. Perhaps Moore would say something similar concerning rational belief, namely, that in order to have a rational belief, one need not be able to say what makes it rational or what one's evidence for that belief is. Again, Moore claims in his "Proof of an External World" that he has "conclusive evidence" that he is awake and not dreaming:

> I have, no doubt, conclusive reasons for asserting that I am not now dream-ing; I have conclusive evidence that I am awake: but that is a very different thing from being able to prove it. I could not tell you what all my evidence is; and I should require to do this at least, in order to give you a proof.[8]

Though Moore claims to have conclusive evidence, evidence strong enough to conclude that he is awake and not dreaming, he cannot say what it all is.

Moore also denies that knowledge of the external world always requires proof. He denies, for example, that his knowledge that this is a pencil must be based on a proof that the pencil exists. As we have seen, he claims to know that proposition immediately, and he thus implies that he knows it without proof. Similarly, in his "Proof of an External World," he insists that he knows that he has hands and that he is awake even though he cannot prove such things.

So if we ask how we know various facts about the external world, Moore does not have a well-developed epistemological theory. But it hardly follows that he has nothing relevant or important to say. He tells us that to know some external facts, one need not know what one's evidence is, one need not be able to prove them, and one need not know how one knows them. Furthermore, he would tell us that one need not have a well-developed epistemological theory about how one knows some external facts or epistemic facts in order to know them. In order to know some external and epistemic facts, one need not be an epistemologist.

2. RELEVANTISM, CONTEXTUALISM, AND MOORE'S RESPONSE

Let us consider Moore's response to one form of skeptical argument and contrast it with two alternative approaches, relevantism and contextualism. In his 1941 Ho-wison Lecture, "Certainty," Moore considers the following skeptical argument:

The Argument from Ignorance

1. If I don't know that I'm not dreaming, then I don't know that I am standing up.
2. I don't know that I'm not dreaming.

Therefore,

3. I don't know that I am standing up.[9]

Moore agrees with the skeptic that (1) is true. But why does he accept (1)? Perhaps he accepts (1) because he accepts a principle of exclusion such as the following:

(PE) One knows that *p* only if one can rule out (know to be false) any proposition, *q*, one knows to be incompatible with one's knowing that *p*.

Since my dreaming would be incompatible with my knowing that I was standing, PE requires that I be able to rule out that I am dreaming. It requires that I know that I am not dreaming. In any case, Moore agrees with (1), but he points out that it "cuts both ways." One can also argue as follows:

Moore's Counterargument

1. If I don't know that I'm not dreaming, then I don't know that I am standing up.
~3. I do know that I am standing up.

Therefore,

~2. I know that I am not dreaming.

Here Moore stands the skeptic's argument on its head, taking the negation of the skeptic's conclusion for his second premise. Moore writes, "The one argument is just as good as the other, unless my opponent can give better reasons for asserting that I don't know that I'm not dreaming, than I can give for asserting that I do know that I am standing up."[10] Moore suggests that his counterargument is just as good as the skeptic's argument. But given Moore's other views, we may take him to hold that his counterargument is not merely just as good as the skeptic's argument but is better. Perhaps he would say, as he did in "Proof of an External World," that he has conclusive evidence that he is awake, and, therefore, that (2) is false. Perhaps he would say that it is better because the skeptic's argument rests at some point on some premise that it is less reasonable to believe than the proposition "I know that I am standing up." Perhaps Moore would say that it is more reasonable for us to believe (~3) than either (1) or (2) in the skeptic's argument. Perhaps he would say that it is more reasonable to believe (~3) than some assumption on which those premises depend, including perhaps PE.

In contrast with Moore, many philosophers are less confident about our ability to know that skeptical hypotheses are false. Many philosophers hold that we are not able to rule out skeptical hypotheses such as dreaming and demonic deception. Unlike Moore, relevantists hold that we *cannot* rule out various skeptical hypotheses such as dreaming and demonic deception, but they hold that knowledge does not require that we be able to rule out such possibilities. The relevantist holds that knowledge requires only that one be able to rule out *relevant* alternatives. So, for example, in order for me to know that I am standing up, I need to rule out that I am lying down or seated, but I do not need to rule out other possibilities such as that I am dreaming or that I am a legless envatted brain being deceived into believing that I am standing. Such possibilities are not relevant to my knowing that I am standing. I can thus know that I am standing without knowing that I am not a legless brain in a vat. The relevantist, then, rejects PE in favor of something like the following:

> (PE') One knows that *p* only if one can rule out (know to be false) any proposition *q* that is *relevant* to one's knowing *p* and that one knows to be incompatible with one's knowing that *p*.

The relevantist denies premise 1 in the argument from ignorance, a premise accepted by *both* Moore and the skeptic. The relevantist holds that since (1) is false, both the skeptic's argument and Moore's reply are unsound.

Of course, one central problem for the relevantist is what counts as a relevant alternative. Why is the possibility that one is seated a relevant alternative but not that one is dreaming or an envatted brain? Moreover, according to the relevantist, it is possible for one to know *both* (a) that I am standing *and* (b) that if I am standing, then I am not a legless envatted brain being deceived into believing that I am standing *without* knowing (c) that I am not a legless envatted brain being deceived into believing that I am standing. But how plausible is that? How could I know both (a) and (b) without knowing (c)? Indeed, the relevantist seems to allow that it is possible to know (a) and (b) without knowing (c) even when (c) is truly believed and believed on the basis of (a) and (b). To many, however, this seems an unacceptable consequence.

The contextualist holds that the standards for applying the word "know" vary from one context to another. In some contexts, the standards for "know" are fairly low and easily met. In those cases, what we express by saying "S knows that *p*" is likely to be true. In other contexts, the standards for "know" are very high. In those cases, they are very hard, if not impossible, to meet, and what we express by "S knows that *p*" is not likely to be true. So in contexts where standards for knowledge are low and easily met, attributions of knowledge will often be true, and in contexts where standards for knowledge are high, attributions of knowledge will be typically, if not always, false.

Some contextualists think of lower and higher standards in terms of ruling out alternatives. Where the standards are low, we do not have to rule out as much as in the way of alternatives as we do when standards are high.[11] For example, suppose that someone asks me if I know whether Chris is in the room. I might say, "Sure, I know he's here. I can see him." Given our ordinary low standards of knowledge, I need only rule out some fairly simple alternatives. I just need to rule out, for example, that the person I am seeing is Tom or Harry. Since I can rule out such alternatives, I know that Chris is here. But now suppose someone raises the possibility that I am being deceived by a Cartesian demon or that I am dreaming. According to the contextualist, when someone introduces such skeptical scenarios, the standards for knowledge are raised. In these contexts where skeptical scenarios are in play, the standards are higher. In these contexts, I need to be able to rule out skeptical scenarios such as dreaming and demonic deception. But, according to the contextualist, that is not something I can do. I cannot know that I am not demonically deceived. So, according to these higher standards, I do *not* know that Chris is in the room.

According to the contextualist, Moore's counterargument fails because in the context where one would assert the premises of that argument, skeptical scenarios are in play and we are using higher standards of knowledge. Given those higher standards, Moore must rule out skeptical scenarios such as dreaming and demonic deception. But, according to the contextualist, since Moore cannot rule them out, (~3) turns out to be false. So Moore's counterargument is unsound.

Does this mean that skepticism is true? According to the contextualist, the answer is no. In ordinary contexts, where skeptical scenarios are not being entertained, I *do* know that I am standing. According to the contextualist, the skeptic is mistaken in claiming that no one ever knows anything about the external world. In ordinary contexts, we have lots of knowledge about the external world. In ordinary contexts, where standards are low and we do not need to rule out much in the way of alternatives,[12] I can know, for example, that I am standing.

Contextualists claim that their theory actually explains our reactions to various claims about knowledge. In ordinary contexts, we are quite willing to say that we and others know a lot about the external world. However, many people become very reluctant to claim that they or others have such knowledge once skeptical scenarios are introduced. This often happens in epistemology classes when skeptical hypotheses are first encountered. According to contextualists, these different attitudes are explained by the fact that in ordinary cases, standards are low and easily met. When skeptical scenarios are introduced, standards are raised and not met.

In spite of its appeal, contextualism faces a variety of objections. Many philosophers, including Mooreans and relevantists, believe that they *do* know various things about the external world *even* when skeptical scenarios are introduced. Mooreans hold that they do know various things about the external world when skeptical alternatives are raised, but so too do relevantists, since they deny that the skeptical alternatives are *relevant*. These philosophers would hold that contextualists concede too much to the skeptic in holding that we do not have knowledge about the external world in those contexts. Moreover, many philosophers think that there are problems with skeptical arguments. They believe that there are plausible responses to these arguments. Both Mooreans and relevantists, for example, believe that they have plausible responses to the argument from ignorance. But if contextualism is correct, then the argument from ignorance actually succeeds. Contextualism does not offer a way of refuting the argument from ignorance. On the contrary, it endorses it. Again, to many philosophers, this seems to concede too much to the skeptic. Moreover, many philosophers would suggest that there are other ways of explaining the allure of the skeptical argument without actually endorsing it. It might be that some people find the premises of the skeptical argument plausible because they find plausible certain *mistaken* views about what knowledge requires.[13]

3. SOME OBJECTIONS TO MOORE'S RESPONSE

Moore's views have faced a variety of objections. Sometimes Moore is criticized for appealing to commonsense beliefs, such as "I know that I have hands" and "I know that I am standing." Consider the following criticism:

> Intuitive and common-sense judgments can be false, as a little reflection illustrates. Such judgments, furthermore, seem not always to be supported by the best available evidence. Consider, for instance, how various judgments of "common sense" are at odds with our best available evidence from the sciences or even from ordinary perception.[14]

In response, however, Moore does not endorse everything that might rightly be called a commonsense belief. In "A Defence of Common Sense," he is quite clear on this point:

> The phrases "Common Sense view of the world" or "Common Sense beliefs" (as used by philosophers) are, of course, extraordinarily vague; and for all I know, there may be many propositions which may be properly called features in "the Common Sense view of the world" or "Common Sense beliefs", which are not true, and which deserve to be mentioned with the contempt with which some philosophers speak of "Common Sense beliefs."[15]

Moore does not claim that all commonsense beliefs are true or justified. Moreover, he does not claim that any belief is justified *because* it is a commonsense belief. He does not claim that the propositions (a) "I have hands" or (b) "I know that I have hands" are justified for him *because* they are commonsense beliefs. More important, even if there are good reasons for rejecting *some* commonsense beliefs because they are "not supported by the best available evidence" or are at odds with "our best available evidence from the sciences" or even "from ordinary perception," there is no reason whatsoever to reject Moore's claims "I know that I have hands" or "I know that I am standing" on such grounds. The particular claims to which Moore appeals do not suffer from those defects. Perhaps some commonsense beliefs are epistemically shoddy, but there is no reason to think that that is true of the particular commonsense beliefs to which Moore appeals.

Critics often reject Moore's knowledge claims because he has not satisfied what they regard as a necessary condition of knowledge. They object, for example, that Moore has not proved that *p* or that he has not provided the appropriate analogical or inductive argument for *p*. Typically, Moore's response is that since he *does* know the proposition in question, the critic is wrong about what knowledge requires. As we have seen, Moore claims in "Proof of an External World" that he knows that he has hands even though he cannot prove it. And we have seen that Moore, in some places at least, denies the Russellian view that knowledge of the external world must be based on analogical or inductive inference. Indeed, Moore might ask whether the Russellian view is compatible with the fact that almost everyone knows various facts about the external world. Is it really plausible to think that the widespread knowledge of such external facts is based on such an inference? Is it plausible to think that the knowledge of the external world we find in children and animals is based on such an inference?

Sometimes Moore's knowledge claims are rejected on the ground that he has not *shown* that various skeptical hypotheses are false. Consider the following passages by Keith Lehrer:

> Thus, before skepticism can be rejected as unjustified, some argument must be given to show that the infamous hypotheses employed by the skeptics are incorrect and the beliefs of common sense have the truth on their side. If this is not done, then the beliefs of common sense are not completely justified because conflicting skeptical hypotheses have not been shown to be unjustified. From this premiss it follows in a single step that we do not know these beliefs to be true because they are not completely justified.[16]

> To meet the agnoiological challenge of skepticism, we must provide some argument to show that the skeptical hypothesis is false and the beliefs of common sense are correct. And this leads to a second equally inescapable conclusion. The challenge cannot be met.[17]

In his response to the argument from ignorance, Moore holds that to know some things, we must be able to rule out various skeptical hypotheses. He accepts that he knows that he is standing only if he knows that he is not dreaming. Again, perhaps Moore accepts this because he accepts PE. But Lehrer suggests that knowledge requires more. Here the suggestion is that in order to know that *p* (where *p* is the object of some commonsense belief), one must do *two* things. First, one must *show* that *p* is true. Second, one must *show* that skeptical hypotheses incompatible with *p* are false. So, instead of PE, we have the following:

(PE″) One knows that *p* only if one can show that *p* is true and one can show to be false any proposition *q* one knows to be incompatible with one's knowing that *p*.

But why should we accept this stronger view? First, why would a belief that *p* amount to knowledge only if one could *show* that it is correct? Such a view rules out the possibility of immediate knowledge. Moreover, would it not be enough that one had evidence for p? Why, in addition to having evidence for p or being justified in believing that p, would one also need to show that p is true? Second, why think that knowledge requires that one *show* that the skeptical alternatives are false? Again, would it not be sufficient for one to know that they are?

Barry Stroud also objects to Moore's response to the argument from ignorance. Stroud asks us to consider the following sort of case. A master detective and his apprentice have been summoned to investigate the murder of a young duke during a weekend party at the duke's country home.

> [The apprentice] gets from the duke's secretary a list of all those who were in the house at the time and with careful research shows conclusively and, let us suppose, correctly that the only one on the list who could have done it is the butler. He then announces to the detective that he now knows that the butler did it."No," the master replies, "that list was simply given to you by the secretary; it could be that someone whose name was not on the list was in the house at the time and committed the murder. We still don't know who did it."[18]

Stroud says that the master detective has raised a successful objection to the apprentice's claim to know. If the apprentice has not checked the completeness of the list, then he does not yet know who committed the murder. But now suppose that the apprentice tries to respond to the master's challenge in the following way:

The Apprentice's Counterargument

  1'. If I do not know that the list is complete, then I do not know that the butler did it.
  2'. But I do know that the butler did it.

Therefore,

  3'. I know that the list is complete.

Clearly, the apprentice's counterargument parallels in form Moore's response to the argument from ignorance. But the apprentice's counterargument is unsatisfactory. He does not know that the butler did it. Premise 2' in his argument is false. Stroud writes:

> If the apprentice did not even check the list, then for all he knows there could have been people in the house whose names are not on the list; he has to show how he knows that that possibility does not obtain. In the same way Moore would have to show how he knows that the dream-possibility does not obtain in his case. He cannot simply deflate the objection by reversing the philosopher's argument in the way he does.[19]

According to Stroud, the apprentice's counterargument fails because he does not know that the butler did it. Premise 2' is false. According to Stroud, in order for the apprentice to know that the butler did it, he must show *how* he knows that there were no other people in the house. He must show how he knows that that possibility does not obtain. Similarly, according to Stroud, Moore's counterargument fails. In order for Moore to know that he is standing up, he must show *how* he knows that the dream possibility does not obtain. If he cannot show how he knows that the dream possibility does not obtain, then he does not know that he is standing up, and premise 2 in Moore's counterargument is false.

But again, why would Moore have to show how he knows that the dream possibility does not obtain? This requirement does not follow from PE. All that PE requires is that Moore be able to rule out the dream possibility, to know that it is false, and Moore holds that he has conclusive evidence that he is not dreaming. PE simply requires that Moore know that he is not dreaming. It does not require that he show or explain how he knows it. But what is more, PE does not require that in order for Moore to know that he is standing, he must *first* show that he is not dreaming. It does not require that he must first eliminate *that* possibility before he can know that he is standing. Perhaps Stroud is appealing to some principle of exclusion other than PE, but it is not at all clear what that principle is or why we should accept it.

Is Moore's counterargument really no better than that of the apprentice? The apprentice's argument strikes us as unsound. In the example, it seems clear that the apprentice's knowledge that the butler did it must be *based* on his knowing that the list is complete. If we assume that he has not checked whether the list is complete and does not know that the list is complete, then the second premise of his argument is false. It is false that he knows that the butler did it. Moore's response *would* be just as poor *if* the second premise of his argument were false, if he did not know that he was standing. But unless we have some reason for thinking that Moore's premise is false, we have no reason for thinking that his response is as bad as that of the apprentice.

4. MOORE DEFENDED

In his defense of Moore, William Lycan claims that all skeptical arguments rest on some abstract metaphysical or epistemological principle that is doubtful:

> Just as there is no such thing as an idealist argument that does not appeal to some metaphysical or epistemological principle that is simply assumed without defense, there is no such thing as a skeptical argument that does not do the same thing. Which is to say that *there is no good reason to accept the argument*; the unargued principle is only philosophy stuff. Even if the principle does seem true to us when we first consider it—at the particular temporal and geographical point in history, and well cosseted amid the philosophical community we happen to inhabit and its defining fads—there is no rational ground for pledging allegiance to it *in preference to* a plain truth of common sense.[20]

Lycan claims, "No *purely philosophical* premise can ever (legitimately) have as strong a claim to our allegiance as can a humble common-sense proposition such as Moore's autobiographical ones."[21] And again, "A metaphysician who claims to 'just know' that such an abstract premise is true ('This is a deep intuition') cannot be taken very seriously."[22]

Lycan holds that all skeptical arguments rest at some point on some purely philosophical premise for which no argument is given, and that such a principle will be less reasonable to believe than the Moorean claim. So consider again the argument from ignorance. In particular, consider the first premise:

1. If I don't know that I'm not dreaming, then I don't know that I am standing up.

Why should we think that (1) is true? What supports that premise? Perhaps the skeptic will support (1) by appealing to some principle of exclusion, such as one of the following:

(PE) One knows that p only if one can rule out (know to be false) any proposition q one knows to be incompatible with one's knowing that p.

(PE′) One knows that p only if one can rule out (know to be false) any proposition q that is *relevant* to one's knowing p and that one knows to be incompatible with one's knowing that p.

(PE″) One knows that p only if one can show that p is true and one can show to be false any proposition q one knows to be incompatible with one's knowing that p.

(PE‴) One knows that p only if one can rule out (know to be false) any proposition q one knows to be incompatible with p.

Following Lycan, we might ask whether any of these exclusion principles is as reasonable to believe as "I know that I have hands" or "I know that this is a pencil" or "I know that I am standing." Surely, says Lycan, the answer is no.

Something similar might be said concerning the second premise of the argument from ignorance:

2. I don't know that I'm not dreaming.

How might the skeptic support (2)? Skeptics have sometimes appealed to principles such as the following:

(E1) One knows that p only if one's evidence for p logically implies that p is true.

(E2) If A's evidence for p is no better than B's evidence for q and A does not know p, then B does not know q.

(E3) One knows that p only if one's belief that p is sensitive. (One's belief that p is sensitive just in case if p were false, one would not believe that p.)

Again, Lycan would ask if any of these principles is as reasonable as "I know that I have hands" or "I know that this is a finger." Surely, Lycan would say, the answer is no.

But *why* is it more reasonable to believe Moore's humble epistemic claims than the principles underlying the skeptical arguments? According to Lycan, it is because the philosophical principles rest on intuitions that have no epistemic weight, that are only "philosophy stuff." But as an answer to the question and as a defense of Moore, it is not clear that this reply is satisfactory. First, it seems that Moore himself probably accepted some sort of exclusion principle as his basis for accepting (1). Most likely, Moore would have accepted PE. Moore himself would not reject all intuitions of philosophical principles as epistemically worthless. Second, to some it will seem that Lycan has overstated his case against purely philosophical propositions. As Earl Conee points out, some purely philosophical propositions seem every bit as reasonable to believe as any in the Moorean camp, for example, that one knows that *p* only if *p* is true.[23] Conee plausibly suggests that the degree of epistemic justification that attaches to one's intuitions might vary in degree from the certain to the worthless. Moore need not hold that no philosophical principle is as reasonable as his commonsense epistemic claims. He need only hold that his humble commonsense beliefs are more reasonable than *some* of the philosophical principles underlying the skeptical arguments.

So, again, we might wonder why the Moorean knowledge claims are more reasonable than the philosophical principles. Moore might note that although it would be desirable to have an explanation for their greater reasonableness, we need not have such an explanation in order for them to *be* more reasonable or for us to *know* that they are. A satisfactory epistemological account of what makes beliefs of one sort more reasonable than another is not necessary in order for us to know, in some cases, that they are more reasonable. Still, it is open to Moore or his defenders to appeal to a familiar array of epistemic views in order to explain the greater reasonableness of his commonsense epistemic claims over the competing philosophical principles. He might hold, for example, that we are more reliable about the former, that our belief in the former issues from a more virtuous intellectual faculty, or that the former cohere better with the rest of our beliefs. He might point to such factors or to a combination of them to explain why his commonsense epistemic claims are more reasonable.

Consider, for example, which coheres better with one's total body of beliefs: the proposition that I know that I have hands or some philosophical principle such as PE" or E2. One's total body of beliefs will include such things as that I have hands, almost all human beings have hands, I am very good at identifying hands and other human appendages, almost everyone knows that he and others have hands, I see that I have hands, perception under the present conditions is highly reliable, and I and others know a great many things about the world around us. If we wonder which coheres better with our total body of beliefs, can there be any serious doubt that it would be the Moorean epistemic claims rather than the premises of the skeptical argument and the philosophical principles that underlie them?

Of course, it might be held that reasonable belief requires more than coherence. Perhaps it will be urged that the reliability of the source of belief is also relevant to the reasonableness of belief. But even if this is so, is there any good reason to think that the Moorean knowledge claims would fare worse in that respect than the philosophical principles? Indeed, Moore might plausibly hold that we are far more reliable about whether we know humble epistemic propositions such as "I know that this is a finger" than about abstract philosophical principles such as the various formulations of principles of exclusion or E1–E3. In any event, the reasonableness of one's believing a proposition would seem to depend, at least in part, on the extent to which the proposition cohered with one's total body of beliefs. So even if one held that coherence was not the *only* relevant factor in assessing a belief's reasonableness, it seems that it is *a* factor, and one that the Moorean epistemic claims enjoy to a much greater extent than the premises of the skeptical argument and the philosophical principles that underlie them.

It might be objected that since Moore claims that he knows various epistemic propositions immediately, he cannot, therefore, appeal to considerations of coherence in order to explain why his epistemic claims are more reasonable than the skeptic's philosophical principles. In response, however, we should note that even if one knows some proposition *p* immediately, it does not follow that it is not also reasonable to believe *p* in virtue of the fact that *p* coheres with other things one believes. Moore might thus hold both that he knows some epistemic propositions immediately and that they are reasonable to believe in virtue of coherence. Of course, Moore might also simply give up the view that the epistemic propositions are known immediately. Moore's views about what he knows immediately appear to have changed over the course of his career. Whatever the correct philosophical explanation might be, Moore would insist that it is more reasonable for him to believe his humble epistemic claims than some of the premises or assumptions underlying skeptical arguments.

5. FURTHER OBJECTIONS

Still, many philosophers would find Moore's insistence that it is more reasonable to believe his humble epistemic claims unreasonable or unjustified. One line of objection begins with the plausible view that that the properties "being justified" and "being an instance of knowledge" are evaluative properties, and like other evaluative properties, they *supervene* on descriptive properties. According to this view, just as the rightness of an action supervenes on some of its descriptive features, for example, maximizing the balance of pleasure over pain or not treating any human as a mere means, so, too, a belief has the property of being justified or being an instance of knowledge in virtue of some of its descriptive properties. But what must one know about a belief in order to know that it has such an epistemically evaluative property? Consider the following suggestion by William Alston:

> [I]n taking a belief to be justified, we are evaluating it in a certain way. And, like any evaluative property, epistemic justification is a supervenient property, the application of which is based on more fundamental properties ... Hence, in order for me to be justified in believing that S's belief that p is justified, I must be justified in certain other beliefs, viz., that S's *belief that p* possesses a certain property Q, and that Q renders its possessor justified. (Another way of formulating this last belief is: a belief that there is a valid epistemic principle to the effect that any belief that has Q is justified.)[24]

Alston suggests that in order to be justified in believing that some particular belief is justified, one must be justified in believing some general epistemic principle. He supports this view by appealing to the supervenient character of epistemic properties.

Reflection on the preceding passage suggests the following principle:

> (S) One is justified in believing that x has F (where F is an evaluative property) only if one is justified in believing both (a) that x has some nonevaluative property Q and (b) a general principle to the effect that whatever has Q has F.

According to S, one is justified in a particular attribution of an evaluative property only if one is justified in believing some general evaluative principle. If S is true, then Moore is justified in believing his particular epistemic claims only if he is justified in believing the relevant general principle. But, the objection goes, since Moore is not justified in believing the relevant general principle, he is not justified in believing his particular epistemic claims.

But is S true? Many critics would say no. First, we should be careful not to confuse claims about exemplification with claims about application. In assuming that evaluative properties are supervenient, we assume that a thing has an evaluative property in virtue of its *exemplifying* some descriptive properties. But from this it does not follow that the *application* or attribution of evaluative properties must be based on a justified belief that a thing has those properties or justified belief in a general evaluative principle. So S does not follow from the mere fact that evaluative properties are supervenient.

Second, it seems plausible that there are justified attributions of supervenient properties that do not depend on justified belief in general principles. Many philosophers hold, for example, that mental properties supervene on physical properties. They hold that that being in pain or thinking about Boston supervenes on various physical properties, for example, physical properties of one's brain. But does our knowledge that we are in pain depend on our knowing some other propositions such as (a) "I have F" and (b) "whatever has F is in pain"? Surely I can know that I am in pain without knowing on what physical properties pain supervenes. I can know that I am in pain without knowing some general principle about the connection between being in a certain physical state and being in pain. If this is right, then justified attributions of supervenient properties need not meet the requirements we find in S. The supervenient character of epistemic properties would seem to pose no problem for Moore's view.

Finally, let us consider one further objection raised by Laurence BonJour:

> [T]o accept commonsense convictions as more or less beyond serious question, as Moore and other particularists seem in effect to do, does appear to rule out illegitimately even the possibility that skepticism might in fact be true, that common sense might be mistaken. And, equally important, if this solution were accepted at face value, it would have the effect of stifling or short-circuiting epistemological inquiry at least as effectively as would simply acquiescing to skepticism.[25]

Does the Moorean response to skepticism stifle epistemological inquiry? That depends on what one takes to be involved in epistemological inquiry. It does not seem to stifle the search for criteria of knowledge and justification. On the contrary, commonsense philosophers may take the search for such criteria to be among the principle aims of epistemology. This was the approach taken by Moore's commonsense heir, Roderick Chisholm. Even if we assume that we do know various things about the world around us, we might wonder how we know them. We still might seek philosophical answers to that question.

Furthermore, even if we embrace the Moorean response to skepticism, we need not ignore skeptical arguments or consider them idle. One could agree with Moore and yet take skeptical arguments seriously, attempting to identify what plausible, but mistaken, assumptions yield skeptical conclusions.

BonJour also objects that the Moorean view appears to rule out illegitimately the possibility that skepticism is true. But here we should be careful. Does it rule out the possibility that skepticism is true? Not if the relevant sense of possibility is that of "logical possibility." Moore would grant that it is logically possible that skepticism is true. It is logically possible that we know next to nothing about the world around us and logically possible that we are deceived by evil demons or dream experiences. Still, Moore would deny that skepticism is "epistemically possible" in the sense that, given what we know, it is reasonable to believe that skepticism is true. Since we do know much about the external world, it is not reasonable to accept skepticism about the external world. But he would deny that this is to rule out skepticism illegitimately.

NOTES

1. Thomas Reid, *Inquiry and Essays*, edited by Ronald E. Beanblossom and Keith Lehrer (Indianapolis: Hackett, 1983), p. 11.

2. Roderick M. Chisholm, "On the Nature of Empirical Evidence," in *Empirical Knowledge*, edited by Roderick M. Chisholm and Robert J. Swartz (Englewood Cliffs, N.J.: Prentice-Hall, 1973), p. 232.

3. G. E. Moore, "Some Judgments of Perception," in *Philosophical Studies* (London: Routledge and Kegan Paul, 1960), p. 228.

4. G. E. Moore, "Four Forms of Skepticism," in *Philosophical Papers* (London: George Allen and Unwin, 1959),p. 226.

5. G. E. Moore, "A Defence of Common Sense," in *Philosophical Papers*, pp. 33–34.

6. G. E. Moore, "Hume's Philosophy Examined," in *Some Main Problems of Philosophy* (New York: Macmillan, 1953), p. 142.

7. Moore, "Defence of Common Sense," p. 45.

8. G. E. Moore, "Proof of an External World," in *Philosophical Papers*, p. 149.

9. G. E. Moore, "Certainty," in *Philosophical Papers*, pp. 246–47.

10. Ibid., p. 247.

11. This is *one* way of understanding the notion of lower standards. David Lewis, for example, writes, "S knows that P iff S's evidence eliminates every possibility in which not-P—Psst!—except for those possibilities that we are properly ignoring." See his "Elusive Knowledge," *Australasian Journal of Philosophy* 74 (1996): 561. Lewis's view seems to be that there are some skeptical possibilities that we cannot rule out, but that are properly ignored in ordinary low-standard contexts. Alternatively, one could hold that when standards are low, alternatives are *easier* to rule out. On this understanding of lower standards, it takes less to rule out skeptical alternatives. According to this view, when standards are low enough, we can rule out skeptical hypotheses. This seems to be the view that Keith DeRose takes in "Solving the Skeptical Problem." DeRose writes, "Thus, on our solution, we do know, for instance, that we're not BIVs, according to ordinary low standards for knowledge." Still, while allowing that we can know that we are not BIVs when standards are low, standards tend to get raised in the face of skeptical challenges, with the result that claims to know that skeptical alternatives do not obtain turn out to be false."But though [I do not know that I am not a BIV] is false when evaluated according to those ordinary low standards, we're able to explain its plausibility, as we've seen, by means of the fact that the high standards that an assertion or denial of it puts into play. Since attempts to assert [I do not know that I am a BIV] are bound to result in truth, and attempts to deny it are destined to produce falsehood, it's no surprise that we find it so plausible." *Philosophical Review* 104 (1995): 39–40. Given that contextualists accept deductive closure, it seems that the view that skeptical possibilities are *easier* to rule out when standards are low would be preferable, but that is not a matter I shall take up here.

12. Or, alternatively, where skeptical possibilities are easier to rule out.

13. Cf. Ernest Sosa, "How to Defeat Opposition to Moore," *Philosophical Perspectives* 13 (1999): 141–53.

14. Paul Moser, "Epistemological Fission," *Monist* 81 (1998): 364.

15. Moore, "Defence of Common Sense," p. 45.

16. Keith Lehrer, "Why Not Scepticism?" in *Essays on Knowledge and Justification*, edited by George S. Pappas and Marshall Swain (Ithaca, NY: Cornell University Press, 1978), pp. 358–59.

17. Ibid., p. 361.

18. Barry Stroud, *The Significance of Philosophical Scepticism* (Oxford: Clarendon Press, 1984), p. 108.

19. Ibid., pp. 121–22.

20. William Lycan, "Moore against the New Skeptics," *Philosophical Studies* 103 (2001): 41.

21. Ibid.

22. Ibid., p. 40.

23. Earl Conee, "Comments on Bill Lycan's 'Moore against the New Skeptics,'" *Philosophical Studies* 103 (2001): 56.

24. William Alston, "Two Types of Foundationalism," *Journal of Philosophy* 73 (April 1976): 170; cf. Alston, "Some Remarks on Chisholm's Epistemology," *Nous* 14 (November 1980): 579.

25. Laurence BonJour, *Epistemology* (Lanham, MD: Row man and Littlefield, 2002), p. 265.

CHAPTER 16

....

AUSTIN'S WAY WITH
SKEPTICISM

....

MARK KAPLAN

I

....

There is no more famous argument for skepticism than the dream argument—the argument in which Descartes argues that because "there are never any sure signs by means of which being awake can be distinguished from being asleep,"[1] he cannot claim to know even so modest a proposition about the world around him as the one that he is holding a piece of paper in his hand. But the argument is a puzzling one. After all, it does not follow from there being no sure signs by means of which being awake can be distinguished from being asleep that Descartes does not know he is holding a piece of paper in his hand. So by what right can he draw the conclusion he does?

Here is an answer, due in its essential outlines to Barry Stroud.[2] Knowledge is subject to something like the following requirement: a person counts as knowing that P only if, for every coherent hypothesis Q she recognizes as being incompatible with her knowing that P, she can say how she knows that not Q—she can rule out the hypothesis that Q. Descartes rightly recognizes that the hypothesis that he is having a vivid dream is coherent. He also rightly recognizes that it is incompatible with his knowing that he is holding a piece of paper in his hand; that is, he recognizes that if he is dreaming, then (even if he really is holding the paper in his hand) his belief that he is holding the paper in his hand is, as Stroud puts it (15), "no more than a coincidence and not knowledge." And so he quite properly concludes, by implicit appeal to the aforementioned requirement, that it is necessary, if he is to count as knowing that he is holding a piece of paper in his hand, that he be able to say how he knows that he is not dreaming—that he be able to rule out the hypothesis that he is dreaming.

But how can he do that? How can he ever say anything by way of saying how he knows that he is not dreaming? How can anything he might be tempted to say he has done to show that he is not dreaming (or that has happened to him and so shows that he is not dreaming) count in favor of the hypothesis that he is not dreaming unless he is already satisfied that he has actually *done* that thing (that that thing has actually *happened* to him), and he has not merely *dreamed* that he has done it (not merely *dreamed* that it has happened)? Recognizing, again correctly, that he has no satisfactory answers to these questions, Descartes realizes that he cannot rule out the hypothesis that he is dreaming. So he concludes that he cannot count as knowing that he is holding a piece of paper in his hand.

How does one go about evaluating an argument of this sort? How does one decide whether its dire conclusion about the extent of our knowledge is correct?

To J. L. Austin, the answers to these questions were clear. Austin, a force in Oxford for the fifteen years after the end of the Second World War, was the leading exponent of what was called "ordinary language philosophy." His view was that the way to test a philosophical argument about the nature and extent of, say, knowledge, was to assess how faithful that argument is to our ordinary practices: to what we say and do, and think right to say and do, in ordinary life. By this test, Descartes' argument seems open to a pretty obvious and devastating critique, for, so reconstructed, the argument depends on a view of when to attribute knowledge to a person that is wildly at odds with our actual practice of knowledge attribution.

Imagine that you are in an unfamiliar city when you open up a nasty gash on your arm. It is bleeding—and obviously bleeding—quite profusely. You ask the next person you see if he knows where the nearest hospital is. He apologizes and says that he does not. Suppose that you later learn the following. The man you asked, in fact, had long worked as—and was currently still employed as—a nurse in what was clearly the nearest hospital. He resisted the temptation to answer your question in the affirmative only because he thought—on the basis of nothing more than Descartes offers us in the argument given earlier—that if he were challenged to say how he knew that he was not dreaming, he could not meet that challenge. Following the argument's lead, he reasoned that if he could not meet that challenge, then he did not count as knowing what he had been tempted to tell you he knew, namely, that the nearest hospital (the hospital in which, in fact, he worked) was two blocks due east, on the southwest corner. I think that there is no question but that you would—that we all would—find his reasoning, and the behavior it rationalized, entirely outrageous.

It is not hard to see why. As Austin argues in his 1946 article "Other Minds,"[3] attention to our everyday practice of making and challenging knowledge claims makes it clear that it is a practice in which there is a substantial constraint on what counts as a legitimate challenge to a person's claim to knowledge. To come up with a legitimate challenge, it will not do to pick just any coherent hypothesis Q incompatible with the person's knowing what she claims to know and challenge her claim to knowledge on the grounds that she has not (yet) said how she knows that Q is not true. If a person claims to know, from its red head, that the bird in her backyard is a goldfinch, it may be entirely legitimate to say:

> "To be a goldfinch, besides having a red head it must also have the characteristic eye-markings": or "How do you know it isn't a woodpecker? Woodpeckers have red heads too."
>
> (Austin 1946, p. 84)

The person must do enough to show that the bird really was a goldfinch (and, if applicable, that she was in a position—she was well enough situated and well enough informed about matters avian—to tell it was a goldfinch). But, Austin notes, there are limits to how much a person must do:

> Enough is enough: it doesn't mean everything. Enough means enough to show that (within reason, and for the present intents and purposes) it "can't" be anything else, there is no room for an alternative, competing, description of it. It does not mean, for example, enough to show it isn't a *stuffed* goldfinch.
>
> (Ibid.)

That is not to say that it is *never* in order to demand that the person do enough to show that it is not a stuffed goldfinch. We can surely imagine circumstances (we are in an aviary that has both stuffed birds and live ones) in which that demand would be very much in order. But Austin's thought is that we have an idea (rough, to be sure) of what normally counts as enough to establish the propriety of a knowledge claim of a particular sort (where both the content of the claim and the circumstances in which it is made contribute to determining that the claim is of that sort). And it is only in special cases, cases in which we have a special reason to suppose that something is amiss, that we can demand that more be done than normally counts as enough. As Austin puts it (writing here about what we can claim to know about other people's emotions):

> These special cases where doubts arise and require resolving, are contrasted with the normal cases which hold the field *unless* there is some special suggestion that deceit &c., is involved.
>
> (Ibid, p. 113)

And what makes a case special? Austin never explicitly says, but the following passage suggests a proposal. He is here writing about the notion that when you know, you cannot be wrong. His view, he tells us, is that this makes

> perfectly good sense. You are prohibited from saying "I know it is so, but I may be wrong", just as you are prohibited from saying "I promise I will, but I may fail". If you are aware you may be mistaken, you ought not say you know, just as, if you are aware you may break your word, you have no business to promise. But of course, being aware that you may be mistaken doesn't mean merely being aware that you are a fallible human being: it means that you have some concrete reason to suppose that you may be mistaken in this case. Just as "but I may fail" does not mean merely "but I am a weak human being" (in which case it would be no more

exciting than adding D.V."): it means that there is some concrete reason for me to suppose that I shall break my word. It is naturally *always* possible ("humanly" possible) that I may be mistaken or may break my word, but that by itself is no bar against using the expressions "I know" and "I promise" as we do in fact use them.

(Ibid., p. 98)

Here Austin seems to be telling us that we always have some reason to suppose that our claims to knowledge are mistaken: we are fallible beings.[4] But that is no bar to our using "know" as we do. Only when we have special reason to think that we are mistaken—that is, a reason we do not always have—can we legitimately say that we may be mistaken and, hence, cannot count as knowing.[5]

This suggests the following proposal. We will credit a person's claim to know that *P* when we are satisfied that she has done what counts as enough in a normal case to prove that *P*, where doing enough does not require doing everything. Only when we have some special reason to suppose that things have gone amiss will we think it legitimate to demand that she do more than what counts as enough in a normal case. And what makes something a special reason to suppose that things have gone amiss? Austin's modest answer seems to be this: it is a reason that is not present in the normal cases—the cases in which it is not legitimate to demand, of some way of things' going amiss, that the claimant to knowledge do enough to show that things have not gone amiss in that way.

This proposal makes perfect sense of the fact that we find the nurse's response to your request for directions as outrageous as we do. After all, our normal practice is to credit a person with knowledge of where she works, where she lives, and the like. We do not normally demand, with respect to some illusion, that before we credit her with such knowledge, she be able to do something to show that she has not been the victim of this illusion. We regard such a demand as legitimate only when there is a special reason to think that she is a victim of illusion—only when there is a reason that is not present in the normal cases in which people claim such knowledge, the cases in which no such demand is in order. But Descartes' argument patently affords us no such reason. The reason to which Descartes appeals—the fact that we have vivid dreams[6]—is present and, indeed, fully in our possession in the normal cases. It is a reason present and fully in our possession as we happily, appropriately, and without any fuss credit ourselves and others with knowledge of where we/they work, of where we/they live, and the like. The outrage is that the nurse supposes otherwise. He behaves as if the fact to which Descartes appeals affords him a special reason to think that he is a victim of illusion. That he should do this in the face of the obvious fact that it affords him no such thing is what makes his reasoning, and the behavior it rationalizes, so outrageous.

II

The foregoing is, of course, an obvious exercise in anachronism: the reconstruction of Descartes' argument to which I have offered Austin's response was first published over twenty years after Austin's death. But it is also a less obvious exercise in anachronism. For all the influence Austin had in the middle years of the last century, his work in epistemology now falls well outside the mainstream of the field. His epistemological writings—"Other Minds" and G. J. Warnock's reconstruction of Austin's lectures on epistemology, posthumously published in 1962 as *Sense and Sensibilia*[7]—are virtually invisible in anthologies of epistemology and barely cited at all in monographs on the subject. The thought that Austin might have a telling response to a contemporary skeptical argument is a distinctly old-fashioned one.[8]

I think that there are reasons for this—reasons that have to do with how Austin's method is misunderstood, and the shortcomings it is therefore thought to suffer. I also think that Austin is responsible in part for the misunderstanding: he did less than he might have to explain why he thought that his method of evaluating epistemological arguments and theses has the power he clearly thought it has. My purpose here will be to try to offer the needed explanation. I will try to explain, with respect to the skeptical argument with which this chapter began, why Austin's method of attack—he undertakes to show how the argument breaks faith with the way we evaluate (and think it right to evaluate) claims to knowledge in ordinary life—has force.

It is not that Austin had nothing to say about other skeptical tropes, or even nothing more to say about this skeptical trope. He had plenty to say. Most of it was, in my view, right on target—it gets our ordinary practice just right. Some, in my opinion, does not. But getting out the full story of what Austin said, why he said it, and whether it succeeded in hitting its target—a worthy enterprise, in my view—is not my purpose here. My purpose is a polemical one: to make the case that whatever the accuracy of the things he had to say about our ordinary practices, his critical method—his demand that statements of epistemological doctrine faithfully reflect what we say and do (and think right to say and do) in ordinary life—has integrity.

I propose, therefore, to let the response I have had him offer to the skeptical argument that began this chapter—a response in which, I believe, Austin does get our ordinary practice just right—serve as a test case. If his method fails to pass muster in this case, it will not do any better in any other. If the method is vindicated in this case, then we can, at our leisure, go on to see what Austin has to say elsewhere and how apt it is. Indeed, if the method is vindicated, we can do better than that. We can rescue the current exercise from anachronism; we can resolve henceforth to do epistemology Austin's way.

III

The best way to see the force of Austin's method is, I think, to see how well it handles criticism. It seems to me that there can be no better place to start, in the case at hand, than by looking more closely at Austin's distinction between those hypotheses that need and those that do not need to be ruled out in order for a claim to knowledge to be credited in a given case. It is this distinction that is meant to give the lie to what we can call the *Cartesian requirement*: the requirement that one have ruled out every hypothesis *Q* one recognizes to be incompatible with one's knowing *P* before one can count oneself as knowing *P*. The distinction is critical to Austin's attempt to expose the infidelity of the Cartesian requirement to our ordinary practices.

But the distinction will strike many as being very oddly drawn. For anti-skeptical purposes, the distinction marks off things in the right way. But nothing is offered by way of explanation of why they deserve to be so marked. Instead, Austin's account uses facts about what we are and are not required to do in ordinary life to explain why we do not have to rule out the possibility that we are dreaming. It does nothing to explain why it is appropriate that the requirements in ordinary life should be as they are. It does not prevent some such explanation, but it does not provide one, and Austin is apparently insouciant about the absence of one.

To that extent, Austin's account of where the skeptical argument goes wrong may seem quite unsatisfying. The thought is this: No one—the skeptic least of all—denies that our ordinary practice is not a skeptical one. The worry the skeptic means to be raising is that our ordinary practice, precisely because it has the nonskeptical character it has, lacks integrity. The problem with (what I have described as) Austin's response to the argument with which we began is that the response does nothing to address the worry that there really is nothing that distinguishes, in a given case, what needs ruling out from what does not, apart from ordinary practice's requiring the one to be ruled out and the other not. If this is so, then Austin's response to the argument with which this essay began (what I will henceforth, for convenience, call *the dream argument*)[9] does nothing to dispel the real worry that this argument was meant to raise.

It is worth noting, however, that if this *is* the worry that the argument is meant to raise, then the argument's pretensions are rather different than one would have supposed. It *seemed* that the point of the argument was (a) to display a set of claims about the extent and nature of our knowledge to which we recognize ourselves to be committed and (b) to show that these claims jointly lead to disaster. Austin's response shows that the argument, at least to this extent, fails to accomplish the first of its two objectives: a crucial premise of the argument—the Cartesian requirement—does not seem to be among our commitments, if ordinary practice is any guide.[10] Now, it is being complained, this alone will not suffice to do the argument in. It is incumbent on Austin to establish the integrity of the practice by appeal to whose propriety he has seen fit to reject the Cartesian requirement. If

Austin wants to say that a person does not have to rule out every hypothesis she recognizes to be incompatible with her knowing *P* in order to count as knowing *P*, he owes us an account that will explain what difference there is between the hypotheses a person does have to rule out in order to know that *P* and those she does not, and where that difference is not to be explained by appeal to our ordinary practice.

But why think that Austin owes us anything of the sort? What else is there supposed to be, among our commitments about the extent and nature of our knowledge, that Austin's response to the skeptical argument violates?

It cannot be the requirement that there be a way to distinguish what we know from what we do not know that makes no appeal to our ordinary practices, for Austin's account does not, in fact, make any essential appeal to ordinary practice. True, in its most general expression, it makes appeal to what is ordinarily required—to the standards of proof in normal cases. But these standards can be cashed out without any such appeals by stating, proposition by proposition and circumstance by circumstance, what would need to be done to establish the propriety of claiming to know this proposition in that circumstance. I do not mean to suggest that this is a straightforward task, or a task one wants really to accomplish. The point is that in particular cases, one can say tolerably well (as Austin does in the goldfinch case) what does and what does not need ruling out before a knowledge claim can be credited. No mention of ordinary practice is required.

Perhaps the thought, then, is that we are committed to there being, in principle, something more than a mere case-by-case account of what needs ruling out. There needs to be a relatively simple, general account that will tell us by virtue of what something needs (or does not need) to be ruled out in a given case—or, more ambitiously, that would state features by attention to which alone we could tell when something is, and when it is not, to be ruled out if a claim to know is to be credited.

But why should we think that there needs to be such an account? Why cannot knowing a proposition be like being out in baseball? Baseball provides us with a rulebook that offers us a case-by-case account of the circumstances under which a player is out, but it offers us no simple account—and appears not amenable to the provision of such an account—of what it is that hitting an infield fly and having exactly three (as opposed to two) strikes have in common that makes each sufficient to make a batter out. There is no simple account of the desiderata baseball is meant to satisfy that rationalizes baseball's counting a batter out in just the circumstances the rules of baseball say that a batter is out. Still, whatever we think of the game of baseball, none of us would be inclined to question its integrity—and the propriety of the verdicts umpires make on the field of play—for *this* reason. Why, then, should we think that the integrity of knowledge attribution—and of our verdicts as to who knows what—depends on there being a simple account that says in virtue of what something needs ruling out for a person to have knowledge?

Perhaps it is because we need some way to explain what is going on when worries are raised as to whether we ought to be ruling out more than is ordinarily ruled out. But do we? There is no question that our practices undergo criticism and change. Does this fact mean that there must be some relatively simple and general set of desiderata that, in every instance, the practice being criticized or changed has been shown not to satisfy? Think again about baseball. Consider the controversy over the propriety of the designated hitter. Those who would abolish the designated hitter make appeals to tradition, to baseball's being a game of strategy. On the other side, partisans of the designated hitter make appeal to the good of seeing first-class hitters at the plate instead of the completely inept hitters pitchers typically are. There are things we can and do say about what makes baseball good and what things we want from it. It is by appeal to those that we criticize it and urge change. But, again, there is nothing in this to suggest that there is—nothing in this that requires there to be—some simple, general set of desiderata by sole reference to which the exact set of rules under which baseball operates can be rationalized, and no other.

There is no reason to think that things are—or need to be—different in the case of knowledge attribution. There, too, we sometimes criticize (invariably local aspects of) our practice of knowledge attribution by appeal to aims we can articulate: reducing fallibility, avoiding undue skepticism, and the like.[11] There is no need, in order for criticism to gain traction, that there be a particularly simple, general set of desiderata by appeal to which the entire practice—this practice and no other—can be rationalized.

Of course, if there is no general set of desiderata by appeal to which knowledge attribution can be rationalized, we cannot expect always to be able to say something that will satisfy someone who is genuinely puzzled about why one hypothesis should require ruling out but not another. We certainly cannot expect to be able to say something that would satisfy a being from outer space who was genuinely puzzled about why I need to rule out the bird's being a red woodpecker but not its being a stuffed goldfinch. It is not as if hoaxes are never perpetrated; it is not as if fakes are never passed off as the real thing. Why do I have to rule out the hypothesis that it is a woodpecker but not the hypothesis that it is a fake, the product of some such hoax?[12]

But is that so disturbing? We have no less available to say to the being from outer space than we have available to say to children (beings from an inner space), who are also sometimes unable to tell when it is appropriate to stop saying, "How do you know that?" (just as they are sometimes unable to tell when it is appropriate to stop asking, "Why?"). Getting the hang of practices (as anyone who goes to live in a foreign land will attest) requires socialization and acculturation. So it is with the practice of knowledge attribution. The practice of knowledge attribution is, like other practices, something that needs to be learned. Happily, it is also, like other practices (both good ones and bad ones), learnable.

But then perhaps all these considerations have merely danced around the real worry about Austin's account. The worry is that it is simply not enough just to describe what it takes to, say, properly challenge a knowledge claim; Austin needs to say why this, and only this, *should* be required. To recapitulate the initial complaint: Austin's account does nothing to explain why it is appropriate that the requirements in ordinary life—the requirements that, to judge by what we say and do and think right to say and do, we think are correct—should be as they are.

But this is not quite true, as the following passage from "A Plea for Excuses"[13] reveals:

> Certainly ordinary language has no claim to be the last word, if there is such a thing. It embodies, indeed, something better than the metaphysics of the Stone Age, namely, as was said, the inherited experience and acumen of many generations of men. But then, that acumen has been concentrated primarily on the practical business of life. If a distinction works well for practical purposes in ordinary life (no mean feat, for even ordinary life is full of hard cases), then there is sure to be something in it, it will not mark nothing: yet this is likely enough not to be the best way of arranging things if our interests are more extensive or intellectual than the ordinary. And again, that experience has been derived only from the sources available to ordinary men throughout most of civilized history: it has not been fed from the resources of the microscope and its successors. And it must be added too, that superstition and error and fantasy of all kinds do become incorporated in ordinary language and even sometimes stand up to the survival test (only, when they do, why should we not detect it?). Certainly, then, ordinary language is *not* the last word: in principle it can everywhere be supplemented and improved upon and superseded. Only remember, it *is* the *first* word.
>
> (Austin 1956/57, p. 185; emphases in the original)

Austin's attitude is a pragmatic one. Why does he think that it is appropriate that the requirements in ordinary life should be as they are? Because they work well for our practical purposes. For all that, Austin is prepared to concede that our ordinary practices are fallible ("superstition and error and fantasy of all kinds do become incorporated in ordinary language and even sometimes stand up to the survival test") and are capable of being improved ("ordinary language is *not* the last word: in principle it can everywhere be supplemented and improved upon and superseded"). But, sensibly enough, he demands that any proposal for change—any proposal that our practice be supplemented, improved upon, or superseded in some way—offer some grounds for supposing that making the change proposed will actually leave us better off in the pursuit of those purposes. To paraphrase Austin, our ordinary practices are not the last word, but they are the first.[14]

Austin does not offer anything like a full account of what our practice of knowledge attribution does for us—and thus no full account of what it would be for a practice of knowledge attribution to work well for our purposes, practical or otherwise. But it is possible to construct, from the little he does say about the matter, the outlines of an account.

We do a brisk trade in frank avowals of knowledge—avowals through which we give our word, and take others' word, that things are thus and so. (We are not always inclined to be frank. Sometimes we want to conceal what we know because we are afraid of what the person to whom we give our word will do as a consequence.) That frank knowledge avowals have this character of giving one's word goes hand in hand with the following fact: one cannot (without opening one's position to criticism) regard oneself (or, indeed, anyone else) as knowing that P in a given circumstance yet be unwilling to act on P in that circumstance.[15] (This is why, when the consequences of being mistaken that P turn out to be much direr than one thought, one will often withdraw one's claim to know that P.) It would be monstrous to give someone your word that P, thereby inducing her to act on P, when you are not prepared to act on P yourself.

It is, of course, a consequential matter to undertake a willingness to act on P. One has to worry about the prospect of acting on P and P's being false. If acting on P involves giving one's word that P, one worries about the prospect that one's word will be taken but P will turn out to be false. (There are, of course, other worries one can have, worries about the recipient of one's word—whether she will act responsibly on P—but these worries are precisely the sort of worries that lead one to suspend one's trade in frank knowledge avowals, that is, precisely the sort of worries that make one want to conceal what one knows.) This raises the question of the propriety of regarding oneself—of one's entitlement to regard oneself—as knowing that P and so entitled to act on P. There are at least two competing desiderata that enter into the decision. One is that due precaution against error be taken. The other is that one be able to enjoy the benefit of having an established (though, of course, revisable) policy on how to act in cases in which one's decision problems are ones in which the truth-value of P is important. From the satisfaction of this second desideratum comes a further benefit: the benefit of shared expertise that a substantial trade in knowledge avowal affords. Our practice can be said to work well in the sense that it negotiates well the judicious satisfaction of these two desiderata.[16]

There is nothing here to impeach the project of trying to come up with a simple, general account of when a hypothesis does and when it does not need ruling out if a claim to knowledge is to be credited.[17] But, of course, what is under discussion is not a proposal to look for such an explanation. What is under discussion is, rather, the charge that absent such an explanation, our ordinary practice lacks integrity. It is the charge that absent such an explanation, Austin has (in his description of how knowledge claims are properly evaluated) no adequate response to Stroud's skeptical argument. What is under discussion is (by Austin's lights) a proposal to abandon our ordinary practice of knowledge attribution in favor of the skeptic's alternative precisely because (unlike the skeptic) we do not (or, at least, do not yet) have any simple, general account of when a hypothesis does and when it does not need ruling out for a claim to knowledge to be credited.

This is hardly an attractive proposal. Granted, as far as we know, there is nothing neat or tidy about the workings of ordinary practice; we know of no simple formula that encapsulates it; to our knowledge, the distinctions it draws cannot be rationalized by appeal to some discrete set of criteria. Granted, the skeptical practice the proposal urges upon us is, in contrast, very neatly and very tidily encapsulated by the Cartesian requirement. Granted, neatness is a virtue. Still, for all that, our ordinary practice of knowledge attribution works fine in practice (as Austin reminds us). This being so, one would need to be positively obsessed (neurotically obsessed, one might well argue) with neatness to think the mere fact that ordinary practice is messy a sufficient reason to give up that practice in favor of the neat but—with respect to the second of the two desiderata satisfied by our current practice—hopelessly inadequate alternative.

IV

It is precisely at this point, I think, that many readers will have made up their minds (if their minds had not been made up already) that Austin has handsomely earned his exile from the mainstream of epistemology. Why, they will wonder, would Austin think that the point of the dream argument is to reform ordinary practice? Why would he think that the dream argument is in any way undermined— why would he think that it *could* be undermined—by facts about how well our practice of knowledge attribution works for our purposes in ordinary life? The champion of the dream argument can grant everything Austin wants to say about the operation of ordinary practice—everything Austin wants to say about what is and what is not appropriate to say and do in ordinary life, everything he wants to say about how our purposes in ordinary life are served by engaging in our current practice of knowledge attribution. After all, it is one thing to describe the conditions under which it is *appropriate in ordinary life* to say that a person knows that P. It is another to describe the conditions under which it is *true* to say that a person knows that P. That is, it is entirely compatible with Austin's account of when it is appropriate in ordinary life to say that a person knows that P that the truth conditions for knowledge attributions are rather different—and, indeed, more stringent.

In fact, it may seem that there is bound to be a divergence between what it is appropriate to say and what it is true to say in these matters. As the discussion toward the end of the last section made clear, our ordinary practice of knowledge attribution is shaped by practical exigency. It is useful to adopt a policy to act on P. It is beneficial from a practical point of view that there should be a substantial trade in knowledge avowals. But insofar as this is so, it is tempting to conclude that it is, at least partly, a concern about the prudential consequences of our behavior—not simply about whether we would be speaking truly in so behaving—that is weighing with us as we decide, in ordinary life, whether to credit (or whether to make) a claim to knowledge. It appears to be just such a concern that makes us think it so outrageous that the nurse should have refused to credit himself with knowledge of where the nearest hospital was.

The thought would be that if we are concerned (which, as philosophers, we must be) with what it is *true* to say in a given case—if we are concerned with what it is true to say about the extent and nature of our knowledge—we must set aside the exigencies of ordinary life that so influence what it is appropriate to say. We must consider the matter from a detached perspective. But when one appreciates that this is the nature of our charge as philosophers, it is hard to see how Austin's appeal to how well our ordinary practice of knowledge attribution works can have any probative weight.

For what is at issue here is not, say, whether it was appropriate for the nurse to have said that he did not know where the nearest hospital was. Both the champions and the critics of the dream argument will be happy to grant that it was entirely inappropriate for him to have said what he did in the circumstances he was in. They will be happy to concede that the fact (if it is a fact—not all critics of the dream argument will think that it is) that the nurse could not rule out the hypothesis that he was dreaming in no way rendered appropriate his having used "know" in the way he did. What is at issue is whether, in saying that he did not know where the nearest hospital was, the nurse said something *true*. The point of the dream argument is to show that however inappropriate it was for the nurse to have said that he did not know where the nearest hospital was, what he thereby said was true—and it was true precisely because he could not rule out the hypothesis that he was dreaming.

This line of criticism appears fully developed in the second chapter of Stroud (1984), but it finds its roots much earlier. The initial observation, that what it is appropriate to say in ordinary life does not coincide with what it is true to say, comes some twenty-three years earlier in Paul Grice's influential 1961 attack on Austin, "The Causal Theory of Perception."[18] And the idea that Austin insufficiently appreciated the availability of a detached, philosophical perspective from which one might appraise the propriety of our ordinary practices (without meaning thereby to suggest any change in those practices) is also present in Roderick Chisholm's 1964 review of Austin's *Philosophical Papers*[19] and in work from 1965 and 1979 by Stanley Cavell.[20] Cavell puts the point this way:

> Any criticism of the classical investigations of knowledge, entered from an attention to what is ordinarily said when, must account for the fact that traditional philosophers, masters of at least the language they write, have accepted a question requiring an answer which under other circumstances, *they* (as well as the "ordinary man") would have rejected as absurd.
>
> (Cavell 1979, p. 57)

This line of criticism appears, however, to have come too late for Austin to have penned a response.[21] We will find in his writings no worked-out account of the sort that Cavell demands. All the same, I submit that there is an account available. By looking carefully at this line of criticism, we can begin to see why Austin found—and why he was right to find—his appeal to ordinary practice so telling.

V

There is no need to contest Grice's famous observations. The distinction between a knowledge (ignorance) attribution's being *appropriate* in a given circumstance and its being *true* in that circumstance is a real one and is readily acknowledged in ordinary practice. Sometimes, for example, kindness or politeness renders it appropriate to make knowledge (ignorance) attributions that are false, and that we know to be false even as we are making them. It is entirely appropriate (because it is kind) to say to someone, "Oh, I know you will do perfectly well," even when one has serious doubts that she will prevail. It is entirely appropriate (because it is polite) to feign ignorance of *P* so as not to deflate someone who takes himself to have newly observed that *P*.

Were there no option—once Austin has demanded that an epistemology be faithful to what we say and do and think right to say and do—except that Austin require an epistemology to regard these knowledge (ignorance) attributions as true, then Austin's approach would surely be worthy of dismissal. But, of course, there is another option readily available. The offending cases—the cases that no one can possibly want an epistemology to capture—are cases in which we dissemble. They are cases in which our knowledge (ignorance) attributions are, for reason of kindness or politeness, not frank. We need only say (on Austin's behalf) that it is only to what we say and do and think right to say and do by way of *frank* knowledge (and ignorance) attributions that an epistemology must be faithful. Grice's observations are thereby accommodated and disarmed.

But Austin is not yet out of the woods. After all, one way to think of the point of the dream argument is that it is to get us to see that ordinary cases of frank knowledge attribution—such as the cases in which I claim to know where I work and live and the like—are really of a kind with cases in which, out of politeness or kindness, we say things we recognize to be false. The argument is meant to get us to see that it is entirely appropriate to say what we do. To say such things in such circumstances is to do what is done. But, for all that, what we therein say is false. For all their frankness, the attributions are false.

The thought would be that the dream argument gets us into a position to see that our ordinary frank knowledge attributions—our ordinary frank claims to knowledge—are false by getting us to realize the role practical exigency plays in our ordinary practice of knowledge attribution. By raising so unfamiliar (and so unanswerable) a challenge to a knowledge claim, the argument gets us to appreciate how our ordinary practice of knowledge attribution is colored by prudential concerns, such as concerns about how best to organize our practical affairs and about communicating with and helping others. We come to see that if we were unfettered by these practical concerns, our practice would be different—indeed, it would conform precisely to the skeptic's conception of the nature of our knowledge (that the Cartesian requirement holds) and of the extent of our knowledge (that we know nothing about the world around us).[22]

But it is hard to understand how, by this means, the dream argument can possibly get us to see that our ordinary knowledge attributions are false. Granted, practical exigency shapes our practice. Suppose we grant further that absent the desideratum that we get to enjoy the practical benefits that come with our willingness to credit a substantial body of knowledge claims, our practice (which, arguably, would then be animated solely by the desideratum that we avoid attributing knowledge of any proposition that turns out to be false) would go a skeptical way.[23] Let us even grant that the dream argument somehow puts us in touch with the foregoing by bringing to our attention that absent that desideratum, even the barest possibility of error (e.g., the possibility that we are dreaming) suffices to invalidate a claim to knowledge.[24] Why think that this goes any distance at all toward showing that our ordinary knowledge attributions are false?

Notice that our practice of knowledge attribution is not unique in being shaped by practical exigency. Our practice of "doctor" attribution is likewise shaped. We could, after all, reserve the epithet "doctor" for someone who can diagnose and cure any ailment in less than thirty minutes.[25] Why do we not do this? It is not because it is an unappealing criterion. On the contrary, anyone who has a loved one who is seriously ill will feel very poignantly how wonderful it would be if we did not have to settle for doctors as we use "doctor"—how wonderful it would be if we had, for our loved one, someone who could diagnose and cure his or her ailment in under thirty minutes. Yet the realization that we could reserve the term "doctor" for someone able to diagnose and cure any disease in under half an hour—the realization of how inadequate what we call "doctors" are in comparison with a person who meets this more stringent qualification—in no way makes us feel that our ordinary use of "doctor" is deficient. It in no way makes us feel that the person we go to when we are ill is not *really* a doctor—that our practice of "doctor" attribution, though convenient (it allows us to regard ourselves as *having* doctors), is completely in error. It in no way makes us feel that if we want a doctor, then, strictly speaking, we should settle for no care less accomplished than that supplied by someone who meets the more stringent qualifications.

Why are we supposed to think that "know" ought to be treated any differently? Yes, the dream argument may cause us to reflect (if we had not had occasion to do so before) on the fact that we could require someone to meet a much higher standard than we ordinarily do before we will credit her with knowledge. Yes, the argument may cause us to reflect on how second-rate what we ordinarily call "knowledge" is in comparison with something that meets this higher standard. But there is nothing in these admissions—that knowledge attribution in ordinary life is shaped to some degree by prudential and other practical concerns—that in any way suggests that our ordinary frank knowledge attributions are not true, any more than the admission that our ordinary practice of "doctor" attribution is likewise shaped suggests that our "doctor" attributions are not true.

In the latter case, we are inclined to think that it is entirely appropriate that the following two competing desiderata—on the one hand, that we want doctors to be able immediately to diagnose and cure whatever ailments come their way; and, on the other hand, that we want the standards for the certification of doctors to be such that a substantial number of people are capable of satisfying them (and so we can *have* doctors)—should play a role in deciding who should qualify as a doctor. There is no reason why we should think that comparable desiderata—on the one hand, that we want knowledge of a proposition never to be attributed to a person if the proposition is false; and, on the other, that we want it to be the case that a substantial body of knowledge be attributable to persons—cannot likewise play a role in deciding what should qualify as knowledge.

VI

Of course, the most the foregoing shows is that the mere observation that our ordinary practice of knowledge attribution is colored by practical concerns does not of itself show that the practice is largely in error. We have so far seen no reason why some other consideration might not do the job. In particular, we have not so far seen why we cannot, upon appreciating the force of the dream argument, conclude that appropriate though it is in ordinary life to make the frank knowledge claims we do, these claims are false—and they are false precisely because the Cartesian requirement *is* a requirement on knowledge, and we cannot rule out the hypothesis that we are dreaming.

Yet Austin seems to think that we can do no such thing. He seems to think that once we conclude that we know a great deal less than we had thought, we are committed to altering our ordinary practice of knowledge attribution to suit. Why else would he think that the facts on which he dwells—facts about what it is appropriate frankly to say one knows in ordinary life—are so decisive in determining the propriety of what our epistemology says we know? Why else would he think (as I have suggested he would) that it counts decisively against the skeptic's standards for knowledge that these standards, if adopted in ordinary life, would be immensely inferior to the ordinary ones we have in place?

To appreciate (what I think was) Austin's line of thought here, let us for the sake of argument take the skeptic's part. Suppose that we agree that it is perfectly open to the skeptic to adopt the position that, while perfectly appropriate for its purposes, our ordinary practice of frank knowledge attribution is systematically mistaken. Suppose that we agree that the fact that it is ordinarily appropriate to behave in nonskeptical ways is simply not probative of whether skepticism is true. Finally, suppose that we agree that evidence of what it is appropriate and inappropriate to say and do is simply not the sort of thing to look at to tell whether skepticism is correct—and it is Austin's error to have supposed otherwise. What exactly is left for us to look at to decide whether skepticism (or some premise deployed in a skeptical argument) is true? How can we decide whether skepticism—or, for that matter, any other epistemological thesis—is true? If it is no part of the burden of an account of true knowledge attribution that it faithfully capture—that is, render largely veridical—the frank knowledge attributions that are appropriate in everyday life, what *is* supposed to constrain such a theory? To what does it have to be true?

The tempting answer is that we have a concept of knowledge, and that it is fidelity to that concept to which a proper theory of knowledge aspires. But what is supposed to convince us that a given epistemological thesis really is faithful to our concept of knowledge? We cannot examine the way the thesis tallies with what we are ordinarily inclined to say (by way of frank assertion) using the word "know," for we would then be testing the thesis as if it meant simply to codify appropriate (and frank) ordinary usage—just the sort of test that (according to the line of thought under discussion) is entirely inappropriate to apply to a proper theory of knowledge. We have to look beyond what it is ordinarily appropriate to say.

But where are we supposed to look? The only source of pretheoretical judgments concerning knowledge any of us *has* is reflection upon what she ordinarily says and does when she engages in inquiry, argument, and criticism. Our practice of inquiry, in contexts both ordinary and disciplinary, is all we have to look to in order to arrive at and test our respective conceptions of knowledge. Once we turn our back on the guidance offered us by our ordinary canons of inquiry and criticism, we have no source of pretheoretical judgment at all.

To be sure, we can direct our attention to *aspects* of our ordinary practice that will offer support for an epistemological thesis. Indeed, the dream argument does just that. It exploits the fact that in ordinary life, explaining how you know that *P* does often require ruling out (at least some of the) hypotheses you recognize to be incompatible with your knowing that *P*.[26] The argument also exploits the fact that we find circular arguments unconvincing in ordinary life. Recall the reason offered for thinking that Descartes cannot count anything he is tempted to think he did (or happened to him) as counting in favor of the hypothesis that he was not dreaming: it would require him already to have established that he really *did* the thing (the thing really happened to him) and did not merely dream he did it (dream it happened).

The trouble is that it is an elementary rule of sound inquiry that one must evaluate the adequacy of a theory not just on such evidence as one can find in its favor, but on *all* the available evidence. And, as Austin reminds us, when one looks at all the evidence—when, instead of picking just those aspects of our ordinary practice that conform to the skeptical conclusion, one looks at our ordinary practice in its entirety—one sees that the evidence does not support the Cartesian requirement or the skeptical thesis that the dream argument would have us adopt. One sees that we perfectly happily and appropriately credit knowledge claims in ordinary life without demanding that the claimant (or person to whom we are attributing the knowledge in question) be able to rule out every far-flung hypothesis we recognize to be incompatible with the truth of her claim to knowledge (the claim to knowledge we are making on her behalf).

Is it open to the purveyor of the dream argument to maintain that these additional bits of evidence to which Austin draws our attention are less salient to evaluating the propriety of a theory of knowledge than the ones upon which the dream argument rests? One would hope not. For once we grant the purveyor of the dream argument the freedom to pick and choose what aspects of our ordinary practice are to be considered salient to assessing the propriety of his argument, we have to grant the same freedom to everyone else—including the philosophers who take as salient some of the aspects of our ordinary practice (for example, the aspects to which Austin draws our attention) over which the argument runs roughshod. But then, with everyone free to pick and choose in this way, the enterprise of determining, from a philosopher's viewpoint, what we know and by virtue of what we know it degenerates into a game in which almost every move is legal and each participant plays according to her own fancy.

As his writings make clear, Austin felt that this sort of degeneration is inevitable once epistemology abandons fidelity to what it is appropriate frankly to say in ordinary life. He recognized that what it is appropriate frankly to say in ordinary life is the only thing available for an epistemology to be true to, and he recognized that an epistemological theory (like any other) must be held accountable to *all* the evidence: that is, to the story of our practice—of what it is appropriate to say and when—in all its richness.[27] This explains why he devoted (and why he was right to devote) so much effort to describing our ordinary practice and why he attached (and was right to attach) such philosophical importance to the result. And it is the failure of the traditional philosophers of whom Cavell writes to recognize this—the fact that they labor under the illusion that an epistemology can enjoy intellectual integrity even as it proceeds unconstrained by consideration of how its doctrines would fare if implemented in ordinary practice—that explains why they, "masters of at least the language they write, have accepted a question requiring an answer which under other circumstances, *they* (as well as the 'ordinary man') would have rejected as absurd."

Note, however, that the fact that an epistemology needs (if it is to enjoy intellectual integrity) to be constrained in this way does not mean that epistemology must be fundamentally conservative. As we have already seen, Austin conceded that the way ordinary language arranges matters "is likely enough to be not the best way of arranging things if our interests are more extensive or intellectual than the ordinary." His view, recall, was that "ordinary language is *not* the last word: in principle it can everywhere be supplemented and improved upon and superseded. Only remember, it *is* the *first* word." That is to say that Austin was (rightly) open to the possibility that sophisticated reflection on matters—even sophisticated *philosophical* reflection on matters—might lead us to the conclusion that our ordinary practices needed changing. What he was *not* open to—and hence his admonition that we remember that ordinary language *is* the *first* word—is the idea that our epistemology need not take on our ordinary practices. What he was not open to is the idea—expressed very clearly in the line of thought under discussion—that our epistemological research might proceed with indifference to how its results tally with ordinary practice.

Austin's requirement that epistemology be faithful to what it is appropriate in ordinary life frankly to say that people know—a requirement that, as I have just argued, we can violate only at the cost of undermining the integrity of epistemology—is thus more subtle than one might have thought. It does not demand that epistemology bend slavishly to the contours of ordinary practice. What it requires, rather, is that our philosophical assessment of our epistemic condition coincide with our ordinary assessment of that condition. Thus, when we find our epistemological inquiries leading us to views at odds with our ordinary practices, we have only two choices. We can either reconsider the path on which those inquiries have led us or change our ordinary practices to conform to our epistemological views. The position the skeptic wants to occupy—he wants to leave our ordinary practices as they are yet conclude that they are nonetheless unsatisfactory from a philosophical point of view—is unavailable. It is the unavailability of this position that makes it perfectly appropriate to assail the skeptic's dire verdict about the extent of our knowledge on the grounds that it would have us adopt a practice in ordinary life that is far inferior to the one in which we engage at present. It is the only way to take the skeptic's dire verdict if his epistemological endeavor is to be credited with intellectual integrity.

VII

I recognize that it seems extremely odd to suppose that a philosophical doctrine as venerable as skepticism—and an argument for skepticism as venerable as the dream argument—could be brought down by the mere observation that the doctrine and one of the critical premises on which the argument for the doctrine relies do not comport well with what we frankly say (and think right to say) by way of attributing knowledge in ordinary life. It seems too short a way to deal with so important a philosophical doctrine, too philistine a way to deal with so disturbing a philosophical argument.

In a sense, I agree with the sentiment. That is why I have labored to say why Austin's form of criticism carries the weight he very clearly thought it did. My hope is that in so doing, I have managed to dispel any sense that Austin's is a form of criticism that is cheap and thin. My brief has been that one does not have to look too far to find (and so it is not too much of a stretch to suppose that Austin himself saw well enough) a deep philosophical motivation for pursuing this form of criticism. The motivation arises from an appreciation of the methodological constraints under which epistemology must operate if it is to be a discipline we can credit with intellectual integrity. These methodological constraints dim the prospects for a skeptical epistemology. They require that our epistemology espouse no skeptical doctrine we are not prepared to apply in ordinary life.[28]

But it is important to note that the constraints dim these prospects only by way of redistributing light elsewhere. What they illuminate is the prospect for an epistemology that seeks insight into our ordinary practices—whether to explain how they work or to explain why they should be reformed. It is an epistemology that engages ordinary practices instead of pretending that it can insulate its results from disconfirmation by ordinary practice. What is thus illuminated, I like to think, is the prospect for doing epistemology Austin's way.[29]

NOTES

1. Descartes 1984–85, vol. 2, p. 13.
2. Stroud 1984, chap. 1.
3. Austin 1946. Page references are to Austin 1979.
4. I say that he *seems* to be saying that we always have a reason to think that we are mistaken (we are fallible beings) because he does not actually say that. Rather, he says that it is always possible that we are mistaken. That is not the same thing. But there is this much in favor of reading Austin here as I do. Were it Austin's view that our human fallibility is no reason whatsoever to suppose that we are mistaken in any particular case, one would not expect him to write that merely being aware that you are a fallible human being does not provide any *concrete reason* to suppose that you may be mistaken in this case; one would expect him to write that it provides *no reason whatsoever* to suppose that you may be mistaken in this case. That he makes (what would appear to be) the weaker claim would seem to indicate that he is willing to concede that our fallibility *is* a reason to suppose that we are mistaken in this case—just not a *concrete* or *special* reason, not the sort of reason it would have to be to be a bar to saying that (or, to its being the case that) we know in this case.
5. I offer an extended critical discussion of this passage in Kaplan 2006b.
6. Or, to take the more modest tack Stroud prefers, the fact that it is at least possible to have a vivid dream. As Stroud puts it (1984, p. 18), "[A]nything that can be going on or that one can experience in one's waking life can also be dreamt about."
7. Austin 1962.
8. Though, to his credit, not too old-fashioned for Stroud. Stroud anticipates that Austin would have the very objection to his (Stroud's) argument I have placed in Austin's mouth, and he devotes an entire chapter of his 1984 book to a response. I discuss Stroud's response at length in Kaplan 2000.
9. I say "for convenience" because there are other ways to make out how Descartes' enthymematic argument might go.
10. It might be wondered what Austin would make of the more pared-down version of the dream argument that has more recently gained interest, a version that dispenses

with the Cartesian requirement in favor of a more modest premise: If Descartes does not know that he is not dreaming, then he does not know that he has a piece of paper in his hand. I offer an answer in Kaplan forthcoming.

11. Descartes himself advertised his own new standard for knowledge attribution on the grounds that it would reduce the dubiety of knowledge attributions without unduly skeptical consequence. Elaborating on rule 2 in his *Rules for the Direction of the Mind*, Descartes writes (Descartes 1984–85, vol. 2, pp. 11–12):

> [W]e reject all such merely probable cognition and resolve to believe only what is completely known and incapable of being doubted. Men of learning are perhaps convinced that there is very little indubitable knowledge, since, owing to a common human failing, they have disdained to reflect upon such indubitable truths, taking them to be too easy and obvious to everyone. But there are, I insist, a lot more of these truths than such people think—truths which suffice for the sure demonstration of countless propositions which so far they have managed to treat as no more than probable.

12. I am indebted to Adam Leite and David Finkelstein for pressing this worry upon me.

13. Austin 1956–57. Page references are to Austin 1979.

14. In this respect (as in a number of others), Austin's attitude toward our ordinary practice of knowledge attribution is very similar to Nelson Goodman's attitude toward our inductive practice. Neither author sees any legitimate call to establish the propriety of the practice with which he is concerned. Each thinks that the philosophical challenge is to characterize as best one can what distinguishes good practices from bad. And each is happy to deploy facts about what we do and think right to do to draw that distinction. Recall that according to Goodman, what makes "green" projectible and "grue" not comes down to nothing more than our having happily projected "green" in the past. (After all, "green" projections cannot be claimed to have been anymore successful than "grue" projections would have been had we projected "grue" rather than "green" in the past.) See Goodman 1955, chaps. 3 and 4.

15. It should be noted that the willingness to act on *P* that is associated in this way with regarding oneself (or someone else) as knowing that *P* has to be considered to be circumscribed. It is, for example, no part of regarding oneself as knowing that *P* that one be unwilling to give a hearing to putative evidence that *P* is false. For a more detailed working out (and defense) of the picture sketched in this paragraph and the one that follows, see Kaplan 2006a and forthcoming.

16. How much of this is in Austin? The idea that in saying we know that *P*, we give our word that *P*, is one he gives great prominence:

> When I say "I know", I *give others my word*: I *give others my authority for saying* that "S is P".
>
> (1979: p. 99; Austin's emphasis)

The next idea, that knowing that *P* involves an entitlement to act on *P*, is not as explicit, but it is not far from the surface. Austin clearly holds that one has to earn one's right to say "I know." If, in the goldfinch case, I cannot answer your challenge to say that I know the bird is not a woodpecker, then (says Austin)

> you would be more inclined to say right out "Then you don't know". Because it doesn't prove it, it's not enough to prove it.
>
> (Ibid., p. 84)

Also:

> Whenever I say I know, I am always liable to be taken to claim that, in a certain
> sense appropriate to the kind of statement (and to present intents and purposes),
> I am able to prove it.
>
> (Ibid., p. 85)

And:

> If you say you *know* something, the most immediate challenge takes the form of
> asking "Are you in a position to know?": that is, you must undertake to show, not
> merely that you are sure of it, but that it is within your cognizance.
>
> (Ibid., p. 100)

In the second-to-last passage, as in the passage we saw earlier, in which he describes what it
takes to prove that the bird is a goldfinch as "doing enough to show that (within reason,
and for the present intents and purposes) it 'can't' be anything else," there is at least a
suggestion that among the present intents and purposes might be practical ones—thus that
doing enough to prove that *P* (and thus to be entitled to say "I know that *P*") involves
doing enough to be entitled to act on *P*. That deciding that one knows is consequential in
this way is also suggested when he writes:

> The right to say "I know" is transmissible, in the way that other authority is
> transmissible. Hence, if I say it lightly, I may be *responsible* for getting *you* into
> trouble.
>
> (Ibid., p. 100)

It is hard to see how Austin could think that the right to say "I know" can get you into
trouble (once transmitted from me to you) unless it involves the right to act on *P*.

What of the story of the two considerations that go into deciding whether we say that
we know? This is very much alive in the following passage about knowing at second
hand (as it is throughout the section of "Other Minds" titled "If you know you can't be
wrong"):

> Naturally we are judicious: we don't say we know (at second hand) if there is any
> special reason to doubt the testimony: but there has to be *some* reason. It is
> fundamental in talking (as in other matters) that we are entitled to trust others,
> except insofar as there is some concrete reason to distrust them.
>
> (Ibid., p. 82)

Austin here deploys the distinction between special (here, "concrete") reasons and the rest
to explain how our practice strikes just the right balance between our two desiderata: that
we avoid error, on the one hand, and that we benefit from the exchange of expertise, on the
other (a benefit that, as I noted earlier, accrues from our willingness, for a broad range of
propositions, to act on them).

What, I think, is least evident in Austin is the role I have attached to *frank* avowals of
knowledge—that is, avowals of knowledge that express what one regards oneself as
knowing. Austin clearly writes, three passages back, as if he thinks that before saying "I
know that *P*" and thereby giving others my authority for saying that *P*, I ought to worry
about whether I myself have the authority to say that *P*. But he would doubtless object to
describing this worry as a worry about whether to regard myself as knowing that *P*—and

more strenuously to describing the worry as a worry about whether I *do* know that *P*. Austin notoriously held that "I know" is a performative in the way "I promise" is: saying it makes it so. It is not a descriptive phrase, and so there is no finding out whether its description is correct. This is one of the places in which, it seems to me, Austin simply gets ordinary practice wrong. His heroic attempt (Ibid., pp. 101–3) to answer the objection that comes immediately to mind—that "I know" cannot be a performative, because when, in ordinary life, one finds out that the proposition one claimed to know is false, one concludes that one did not know after all—is entirely unconvincing. (But it is worth noting that this failed attempt is not an attempt to deny the aforementioned fact about what we do in ordinary life, but only an attempt to understand promising in such a way that a corresponding fact holds with respect it.) Fortunately, this misstep on his part is isolable without cost from the rest of his discussion.

17. Although Austin might well have abjured this project on other grounds—grounds having to do with his conviction (ill advised, as I suggested at the end of note 16) that the performative character of "I know" makes it impossible to offer a description of the conditions under which the quoted expression is true.

18. Grice 1961. Stroud acknowledges Grice's influence. See Stroud 1984, pp. 75–76n.

19. Chisholm 1964, p. 1.

20. Cavell 1965, pp. 216–17; 1979, p. 57. For later expressions of this idea, see McGinn 1989, p. 62; Williams 1991, pp. 147–48.

21. Austin died in 1960.

22. So, in stressing the practical import of knowledge attributions in everyday life, Austin (on this view) ends up issuing the very concession that the dream argument means to elicit.

23. This is a nonnegligible thing to grant. It is arguable that but for the role practical exigency plays in shaping our ordinary practice of knowledge attribution, our practice would go a *less* skeptical way than it does in fact. After all, we tend to think that when nothing of practical consequence turns on a person's verdict about whether *P* is true, she is apt to be less concerned to avoid error. Thus we say such things as "Easy for him to say; he's not on the hot seat the way I am!" "Actions speak louder than words," "Sure he talks the talk, but does he walk the walk?" "That's just idle talk," and "Sure he *says* so, but is he prepared to put his money where his mouth is?"

24. I am indebted to John McDowell for correspondence in which he expressed the point in this way.

25. Here I borrow an example and a line of argument due to Paul Edwards (Edwards 1949, pp. 145–46). It is a line of argument of which, I should note, Stroud is very much aware (but whose force, I think, he fails sufficiently to appreciate). See Stroud 1984, pp. 40–41.

26. Indeed, it is by appeal to rulings out that are sanctioned by ordinary practice that Stroud seeks to motivate the Cartesian requirement. See Stroud 1984, pp. 24–30. For a critical appraisal of Stroud's appeals to other aspects of ordinary practice in support of the skeptic's cause (and, in particular, his appeal to the plane-spotter analogy), see Kaplan 2000.

27. See, for example, Austin 1962, p. 3, where he decries the tendency in philosophy (or, at least, the philosophy of his day) toward "an obsession with a few (and nearly always the same) half-studied 'facts' "—a tendency toward "over-simplification, schematization, and constant obsessive repetition of the same small range of jejune 'examples.' "

28. As a consequence, these methodological constraints do not cut against a skepticism that is meant (as the ancient skepticisms were) to be lived. (Nor do the constraints

have, of themselves, any critical bite against deviant practices of knowledge attribution [such as those espoused by some antiscientific religious sects], so long as their advocates are happy to live the practices in question.) Hence my claim that the constraints dim, rather than darken entirely, the prospects for a skeptical epistemology.

29. This chapter consists, in part, of a bringing together of ideas I have published elsewhere by way of making out a sustained case for the integrity of Austin's approach to epistemology. In particular, section I borrows heavily from Kaplan 2000, and a large part of section VI is lifted (albeit with some changes) from Kaplan 2006b. I am indebted to John Greco, David Finkelstein, Adam Leite, John McDowell, Ram Neta, and Joan Weiner for extremely helpful conversations about the doctrines herein espoused.

REFERENCES

Austin, John L. (1946). "Other Minds." *Proceedings of the Aristotelian Society*, supplementary volume 20: 148–87. Reprinted in Austin 1979, pp. 76–116.

———. (1956–57). "A Plea for Excuses." *Proceedings of the Aristotelian Society* 57: 1–30. Reprinted in Austin 1979, pp.175–204.

———. (1962). *Sense and Sensibilia*. Ed. G. J. Warnock. Oxford: Oxford University Press.

———. (1979). *Philosophical Papers*. Ed. J. O. Urmson and G. J. Warnock. 3rd ed. Oxford: Oxford University Press.

Cavell, Stanley. (1965). "Austin at Criticism." *Philosophical Review* 74: 204–19. Reprinted in Stanley Cavell, *Must We Mean What We Say?* Cambridge: Cambridge University Press, 1976, pp. 97–144.

———. (1979). *The Claim of Reason: Wittgenstein, Skepticism, Morality, and Tragedy*. Oxford: Oxford University Press.

Chisholm, Roderick M. (1964). "Austin's *Philosophical Papers*." *Mind*, n.s., 73: 1–26.

Descartes, René. (1984–85). *The Philosophical Writings of Descartes*. Ed. John Cottingham, Robert Stoothoff, and Dugald Murdoch. 2 vols. Cambridge: Cambridge University Press.

Edwards, Paul. (1949). "Bertrand Russell's Doubts about Induction." *Mind* 58: 141–63.

Goodman, Nelson. (1955). *Fact, Fiction, and Forecast*. Indianapolis: Bobbs-Merrill Company.

Grice, H. Paul. (1961). "The Causal Theory of Perception." *Proceedings of the Aristotelian Society*, supplementary volume 35: 121–52. Reprinted in H. Paul Grice, *Studies in the Way of Words*. Cambridge, MA: Harvard University Press, 1991, pp. 224–47.

Kaplan, Mark. (2000). "To What Must an Epistemology Be True?" *Philosophy and Phenomenological Research* 61: 279–304.

———. (2006a). "Deciding What You Know." In *Knowledge and Inquiry: Essays on the Pragmatism of Isaac Levi*, ed. Erik J. Olsson. Cambridge: Cambridge University Press, pp. 225–40.

———. (2006b). "If You Know You Can't Be Wrong." In *Epistemology Futures*, ed. Stephen Hetherington. Oxford: Oxford University Press, pp. 180–98.

———. (Forthcoming). "Tales of the Unknown." In *New Essays on the Philosophy of J. L. Austin*, ed. Richard Sørli and Martin Gustafsson. Oxford: Oxford University Press.

McGinn, Marie. (1989). *Sense and Certainty: A Dissolution of Scepticism*. Oxford: Blackwell Publishers.

Stroud, Barry. (1984). *The Significance of Philosophical Scepticism*. Oxford: Clarendon Press.

Williams, Michael. (1991). *Unnatural Doubts: Epistemological Realism and the Basis of Scepticism*. Oxford: Blackwell Publishers.

CHAPTER 17

WITTGENSTEIN ON CERTAINTY

MARIE MCGINN

WITTGENSTEIN'S philosophical purpose vis-à-vis the skeptic in *On Certainty* is a matter for dispute. He has variously been held to refute skepticism by showing that it is self-defeating;[1] to reveal the truth in skepticism and to offer an accommodation with it;[2] and to diagnose the misconceptions that underlie skeptical doubt, which does not itself constitute a refutation of skepticism but opens the way to our liberating ourselves from its philosophical grip.[3] These three approaches to interpreting the remarks collected in *On Certainty* do not, I am sure, amount to an exhaustive classification of the interpretations put forward in the secondary literature. However, they do at least represent three importantly distinct ways of responding to skepticism that have been attributed to Wittgenstein, and this invites the question whether, on any of these interpretations, Wittgenstein's notes contain the makings of a philosophically satisfactory response to philosophical skepticism.

It may seem prima facie that the interpretation that offers the best hope of a philosophically satisfactory response to skepticism is one that holds that Wittgenstein's remarks contain a demonstration that skepticism is self-refuting. This approach promises to show that there simply is no intelligible doubt that needs to be removed before our ordinary knowledge claims can count as legitimate. Avrum Stroll defends an interpretation along these lines. He argues that Wittgenstein's remarks present a nonconventional and unique form of foundationalism. The idea is that the foundations of human knowledge do not themselves belong to the category of things that are known. The propositions that belong to the foundation are called "hinge propositions" and are exempt from epistemic evaluation. Our attitude toward what lies at the foundation of knowledge is a form of nonepistemic certainty, a form of sureness that, Stroll claims, is not the product of ratiocination but "is something primitive, instinctual, or animal," a way of acting that "derives from rote training in communal practices" (Stroll, 1994, p.157). By means of training in communal practices, we inherit a picture of the world that is expressed not merely in how we think about the world but in how we live and act; our picture of the world constitutes the framework within which all ordinary doubt and inquiry, all ordinary confirmation and disconfirmation of belief, take place. It is this description of the structure of our ordinary practice, according to Stroll, that provides the basis for Wittgenstein's refutation of skepticism.

On this account, Wittgenstein holds that the hinge propositions that form the framework of our practice lie outside the route taken by inquiry. They "stand fast for us," and that means that within the practice in which we have been trained, the question of truth or falsity does not arise for them. Stroll allows, however, that a skeptic might concede that Wittgenstein's description of our attitude to the commonsense framework within which the justification of knowledge claims ordinarily takes place is quite correct: ordinarily we are certain concerning the propositions of the frame and would normally disregard any serious attempt to doubt them. But the skeptic is not concerned with the questions whether we are *certain* that the world exists, that it has existed for a long time past, that there are other human beings who think and feel as we do, and the like. He is concerned with whether we *know* these things, and that we know does not, as Wittgenstein observes, follow from the fact that we are certain. It is at this point, on Stroll's interpretation, that the real refutation of skepticism begins. According to Stroll, Wittgenstein argues that by trying to raise a doubt about the propositions of the frame, the skeptic is employing expressions that belong to our language game and at the same time attempting to doubt the presuppositions on which the existence of the language game depends: "The skeptic is thus engaged in an activity that is sensible only if he rejects the conditions that make that activity sensible" (Stroll, 1994, p.162). If the expressions that the skeptic uses to express his doubt belong to our language game, then the skeptic, by engaging in the game, is committed to treating as certain the very things that he attempts to doubt. Skepticism is not, therefore, a coherent position; it is inherently unintelligible, and no counterargument to it needs to be mounted.

Does this provide a satisfactory response to the skeptic? Let us assume that Stroll is correct in holding, and in holding that Wittgenstein holds, that skeptical doubt has no place in our ordinary language game of doubt and inquiry. Let us accept also that if we put the presuppositions that constitute the framework of our ordinary practice in doubt, all possibility of confirming or disconfirming beliefs breaks down, and our capacity to engage in the language game is put under threat. The question is what follows from this. Does it follow that the doubt that the skeptic raises about the propositions of the framework is senseless?[4] Against that, we might point out that the skeptical conclusion arises when our everyday practice of investigating whether a claim to know rests on unwarranted presuppositions is directed at our practice of claiming to know about the world as a whole. Such a process of reflection need not question the fact, or the role, of our certainty concerning these presuppositions in the inquiries we ordinarily undertake; the skeptic can even concede that as far as our ordinary lives go, there is no alternative to it. What the skeptic draws our attention to is the utter groundlessness of our certainty. He may concede that we cannot dispense with these groundless beliefs and still take part in our practice, but he holds that we cannot, from a position of philosophical reflection, regard what is achieved within the context of these groundless presuppositions as knowledge. The kind of nonepistemic or instinctual certainty that Stroll claims makes us immune to skeptical doubt appears, from the perspective of philosophical reflection, actually to invite the conclusion that the foundation of our language game is, epistemically speaking, insecure; our language game appears to rest upon a leap in the dark that we all quite naturally make, but that cannot properly constitute a framework for the achievement of knowledge.[5]

Crispin Wright also claims (tentatively) that *On Certainty* "gesture[s] at a principled and stable response to . . . scepticism about our knowledge of the material world" (Wright, 2004, p.22). Wright, like Stroll, begins with Wittgenstein's distinction between knowledge properly so recognized—what Wright calls "a state of cognitive achievement, based on completed enquiry" (Wright, 2004, p.31)—and certainties or propositions that "stand fast for us." These framework or hinge propositions, Wright suggests, play a regulative or presuppositional role in our language game of gathering and assessing evidence; they "play a pivotal role in our *methodology* of empirical investigation and thereby contribute to the background necessary to make cognitive achievement possible" (Wright, 2004, p.32). A proposition that, in a particular context, belongs to the presuppositional framework of inquiry functions as a norm of description; its certainty is something against which evidence is assessed. To doubt these propositions would not only bring down whole systems of beliefs but would also threaten the methods by which we assess evidence and appraise beliefs. What distinguishes Wright's interpretation of the key ideas of *On Certainty* from Stroll's is that he does not attempt to use these reflections as the basis for an outright refutation of skepticism. Indeed, as Wright sees it, Wittgenstein's reflections effectively take the skeptic's point, for he has conceded that what we ordinarily count as knowledge depends upon essential, groundless assumptions that we have no positive reason to affirm are true. On Wright's reading, what Wittgenstein sets out to show in *On Certainty* is that the groundlessness of the framework of what we ordinarily regard as cognitive achievement does not have the skeptical consequences that it has been thought to have.

Wright believes that there is only limited mileage in the idea that the norms that define a practice cannot, as norms, be considered correct or incorrect. He argues that the fact that empirical inquiry is directed at the discovery of truths means that the question whether the norms that define our practice are such as to achieve its overall point must make sense.[6] He writes:

It will therefore seem as though there has to be a good question whether and with what right we suppose that the rules we actually rely on in empirical enquiry are conducive to the divination of what is true and the avoidance of what is false.

(Wright, 2004, p.43)

He goes on:

To allow that "The earth has existed for many years past" serves as a rule of evidence—plays a role in determining our conception of the significance of presently available states and processes—is not even superficially in tension with thinking of it as a substantial proposition, apt to be true or false. It goes without saying that our conception of the significance of items of evidence we gather will depend on what kind of world we take ourselves to be living in. That in no way banishes the spectre of profound and sweeping error in the latter regard.

(Wright, 2004, p.47)

Wright recognizes that these ideas may appear to be at odds with the later Wittgenstein's view that the rules of our language game do not have to answer to anything external to it. However, he believes not only that there is very little prospect of establishing the thesis that the propositions of the frame are not genuinely factual, but also that this idea is "much less obtrusive in *On Certainty*" (Wright, 2004, p.45) than in the *Investigations,* and that it does not play a central role in Wittgenstein's response to skepticism. Wright does not, therefore, want to see Wittgenstein's key idea as one that challenges the intelligibility of skepticism, but as one that makes "a 'liveable' accommodation with it" (Wright, 2004, p.47).

Wright believes that we should think of the propositions of the frame as "collateral information," the assumption of which provides us, on a given occasion, with a warrant either for the direct assertion of a particular proposition or for the inferring of a particular proposition from defeasible evidence. Thus, even in the case of a noninferential warrant for a proposition, there will always be presuppositions—concerning the proper functioning of the relevant cognitive capacities, the suitability of the occasion for their effective functioning, and my understanding of the concepts involved in the formulation of the relevant proposition—on which our possession of the warrant rests. The problem with Moore's reply to the skeptic is that he attempts to use the warrant for a particular proposition ("This is a hand") as a premise from which he infers a proposition of the frame ("There is a material world") when the warrant for the premise consists in defeasible evidence that provides a warrant only if the proposition of the frame is presupposed as collateral information. It is clearly the case, Wright argues, that a warrant does not transmit from a premise "to a validly inferred conclusion in cases where the very possession of the warrant for the premise in the first place depends on a prior warrant for the conclusion" (Wright, 2004, p.48).[7]

However, Wright believes that once we realize that *any* warrant for a proposition is *necessarily* achieved courtesy of some specific set of presuppositions for which we have no earned warrant, we can also recognize that our ordinary concept of an acquired warrant cannot require that we achieve an earned warrant for every presupposition; the requirement is essentially incoherent. Wright concludes:

> The general source of the limitations on warrant transmission . . . is thus a consideration about the essential limitations of any particular cognitive achievement: wherever I achieve warrant for a proposition, I do so courtesy of specific presuppositions—about my own powers, and the prevailing circumstances, and my understanding of the issues involved—for which I will have no specific, earned warrant. This is a necessary truth.
>
> (Wright, 2004, p.48)

We are thus led to accept "each and every cognitive project as irreducibly involving elements of adventure—I *take a risk* on the reliability of my senses, the amenability of the circumstances, etc" (Wright, 2004, p.49). Thus our response to the essential limitations on cognitive achievement that skeptical doubt exposes is not to conclude "that the acquisition of genuine warrant is impossible, but rather that since warrant is acquired wherever investigation is undertaken in an epistemically responsible manner, epistemic responsibility cannot, *per impossible*, involve an investigation of every presupposition whose falsity would defeat the claim to have acquired the warrant" (Wright, 2004, p.50). Our ordinary concept of warrant essentially requires only that we acquire a warrant for presuppositions concerning which there is some specific reason to doubt, and not, incoherently, that every presupposition be investigated.

How satisfactory is this as a response to philosophical skepticism? Do the ideas that Wright finds in *On Certainty* provide us with a reflective understanding of ourselves that succeeds in making the idea that we have knowledge of the objective world intelligible? In some respects, the structure of Wright's interpretation of the central argument of *On Certainty* mirrors that of his interpretation of Wittgenstein's remarks on rule following.[8] In each case, he holds that Wittgenstein's reflections begin with an acceptance that a certain intuitive understanding of what is involved in something—in our meaning something by a word or in our possessing knowledge of the world, respectively—is unsustainable in the face of skeptical attack. Thus our idea that in understanding an expression we grasp a pattern of use that extends to new cases independently of our ratification is, on Wright's reading of Wittgenstein, shown to be empty. This is held to follow from the fact that the idea of something in an individual speaker's mind that could in itself determine what counts as a correct application of a sign in future cases can be shown to be unintelligible. Similarly, our idea that our ordinary methods for investigating how things are in the world may, in suitable circumstances, yield unequivocal knowledge of what is objectively the case is, on Wright's reading of Wittgenstein, shown to be empty. All inquiry rests upon ungrounded, substantial presuppositions for which we lack an epistemic warrant, and which could, as far as available evidence is concerned, turn out to be false.

In each of these cases, Wright holds, Wittgenstein accepts that our intuitive understanding of meaning and knowledge would require us to make intelligible, respectively, the idea of an interpretation that cannot be interpreted and the idea of an inquiry in which nothing is taken for granted and we commit ourselves only to propositions for which a warrant has been earned through a specific, completed investigation. If we assume that meaning or cognitive achievement require our making each of these ideas intelligible, then we are doomed, in each case, to a paralyzing skepticism. The only way out of the skeptical bind, Wright believes, is to show that we can construct a satisfactory conception of meaning or cognitive achievement from the materials that are left to us after the impact of the skeptical argument; we must, in a word, revise our understanding of what meaning and cognitive achievement amount to. Thus we must construct an account of what meaning and cognitive achievement consist in from a perspective in which we have conceded, respectively, that there is no such thing as my keeping faith with what I mean by a word and no such thing as having unequivocally established that a particular fact obtains.

I want both to argue that the account of cognitive achievement that Wright attributes to Wittgenstein does not amount to an intelligible conception of us as knowing about the world and to question whether his account of the central insight of *On Certainty* is correct. The upshot of Wright's interpretation of Wittgenstein's alleged rejection of the idea that grasp of meaning can be conceived as grasp of a ratification-independent pattern of use is that there is nothing, in the individual case, that grounds the distinction between actually conforming to what one means by a word and merely having the impression of conforming to it. If we consider an individual in isolation, then all we can do is describe assenting and dissenting behavior, with no idea that particular occasions of assent and dissent either succeed or fail to keep faith with what the individual means by a word. Wright allows that this means that nothing normative—and thus nothing that would count as meaning—is yet in view. Normativity (and hence meaning) requires the distinction between "right" and "seems right," and this only comes into view, Wright argues, against the background of a community practice: community assent is what provides the objectivity required to transform one's blind response to particular cases into something that can be assessed for correctness or incorrectness. The normative status of concepts is secured, on this view, by patterns of community use that are not understood to be dictated independently of actual ratification.

It is not at all clear that this succeeds in making a normative notion of meaning intelligible, for it is quite unclear how merely aggregating responses that individually fail to be instances of following a norm could transform these responses into ones that can be normatively described and assessed. All we have here is a combination of nonnormative regularities that happen to match one another; any idea that the shared responses of the community are correct is empty if we cannot see those shared responses as the result of individual speakers following shared norms for the use of expressions. The normative notion of objective correctness cannot, in other words, be separated out from what Wright sees as the problematic idea that the pattern of application of a given concept is determined by the meaning of the relevant expression independently of our ratification of it. Given Wittgenstein's commitment to the idea that "philosophy leaves everything as it is," this appears to leave us with no option but to look for an interpretation of the remarks on rule following that succeeds in making sense of this idea and thus in dissociating the idea of ratification independence from the empty picture of a rule which "traces the lines along which it is to be followed through the whole of space" (Wittgenstein, *Philosophical Investigations* [hereafter *PI*] 219 [please note: all subsequent numerical references are to paragraph numbers.]).

An analogous difficulty affects Wright's concession, on Wittgenstein's behalf, to epistemological skepticism. Effectively, he allows that the skeptical argument reveals that our ordinary understanding of ourselves as being in a position to achieve unequivocal knowledge of the objective world is unsustainable. What we ordinarily regard as unassailable knowledge of how things are is revealed to depend upon a framework of presuppositions for which we lack a positive epistemic warrant, and which could, as far as the available evidence goes, be false. Wright then argues that Wittgenstein saves us from the outright skeptical consequences of these reflections by showing that since any inquiry is necessarily grounded in groundless presuppositions, cognitive achievement "must be reckoned to take place *within such limits*" (Wright, 2004, p.50, emphasis in original). This is to concede that even our very best cognitive position is always one in which the proposition that there is a material world that is more or less as our senses represent it to be has the status of collateral information: its truth is presupposed but has not been—and in this case, Wright concedes, *could* not be—established. On this understanding, a brain in a vat could, as far as the available evidence goes, be in the same position as an embodied, perceiving subject and could also possess the same pragmatic warrant for the presupposition that there is a material world broadly in keeping with the way in which sense experience represents it. However, it is clear that any cognitive achievement that such a creature took itself to accomplish within the framework of this presupposition would not amount to knowledge. Whether what is achieved within the framework of the presupposition amounts to knowledge must, on Wright's account, depend on something wholly outside the ken of the cognitive subject, namely, the truth of the proposition that any cognitive subject is obliged to presuppose, that there is a material world and that his senses reliably inform him of it.

Thus, if we are not brains in a vat but embodied human subjects, this has no impact on how matters are constituted, cognitively speaking, from within; our cognitive achievement is still based on evidence that could also be available in circumstances of total illusion, and on a presupposition of collateral information for which we have no positive epistemic warrant, and which may, as far as available evidence is concerned, be false. It is a matter of pure luck that in this case, our presupposition happens to be true, and our moves from experiential evidence to statements about the objective world result in true judgments. Thus the difference between genuine cognitive achievement and the mere appearance of it lies in a factor completely external to the reach of our cognitive powers, namely, the objective truth of propositions whose truth we are obliged to presuppose. It is quite unclear that this provides us with a form of self-understanding that succeeds in making the idea that we know about the objective world intelligible; the in-eliminable element of sheer luck on which the match between our true beliefs and the objective world depends would appear to place those true beliefs firmly in the category of mere opinion rather than genuine knowledge.[10] It seems, therefore, that the notion that we have knowledge of the objective world cannot be separated out from what Wright sees as the problematic idea that in appropriate circum-stances, we may succeed in establishing—rather than establishing modulo the truth of a presupposition whose truth *cannot* be established—that something is objec-tively thus and so. Once again, given Wittgenstein's commitment to the idea that "philosophy leaves everything as it is," this leaves us with no option but to look for an interpretation of Wittgenstein's remarks in *On Certainty* that succeeds in making sense of this idea and thus in dissociating it from the view that we would have had to remove skeptical doubt before we could count as unequivocally having knowledge of how things objectively are.

This brings us to the third interpretive approach I identified at the start: the idea that Wittgenstein diagnoses the misconceptions that underlie skeptical doubt in a way that does not itself constitute a refutation of skepticism but opens the way to our liberating ourselves from its philosophical grip. It is a version of this interpretive approach that I want to defend in the remainder of this chapter. The idea is that the problem of external-world skepticism should become obsolete through our coming to a form of self-understanding on which we see how "it might," as John McDowell puts it, "be intellectually respectable to ignore [the question of skepticism]" (McDowell, 1994, p.113). On this reading, it is not merely that we *do not* doubt the judgments that the skeptic doubts, but that any residual sense that we *ought* to doubt them—or that we ought to have removed the skeptic's doubt before we can count as achieving unequivocal knowledge of the world—evaporates. This therapeutic ap-proach to the skeptical problem sets out to achieve a form of self-understanding on which the skeptical question no longer threatens to undermine our ordinary, commonsense conception of ourselves as knowing about the world. To achieve this form of self-understanding would be to show that there is nothing in our ordinary practice that makes it susceptible to destruction by skepticism from within; it is only a false understanding—a philosophical misconception—that makes it *appear* that this is so. The aim is to achieve a reflective understanding of our ordinary practice that does not put its status in question, that is, that shows, from a position of reflection, that the doubts of the skeptic are ones that we may properly ignore. Thus the absence of justification for the propositions that form the framework of our practice of inquiry no longer appears, even from a position of reflection, as an omission that puts our capacity to achieve knowledge of the world in question. This form of therapeutic reading aims to provide what McDowell calls "a comfortable retaining" of our commonsense understanding of ourselves as possessing knowledge of the objective world; that is, it aims to achieve a reflective understanding of our ordinary practice that is neither dogmatic nor skeptical.

The therapeutic response I want to defend depends upon separating out two strands in Wittgenstein's reflections: one that is concerned with the concept of empirical judgment and one that is concerned with the concept of knowledge. Clearly, the first of these investigations is, as John McDowell points out (for example, McDowell, 1994, p.6), the more basic, for we would not be in a position to understand ourselves as having knowledge of the world if we were not first of all in a position to understand ourselves as expressing thoughts about it. Concerning our concept of knowledge, Wittgenstein wants to show that we misunderstand it if we think of knowledge as a mental state that "guarantees what is known, guarantees it as a fact" (Wittgenstein, *On Certainty* [hereafter *OC*] 12). To think of knowledge as a mental state is, he suggests, to be tempted by the idea that whether we know something must be something that can be decided purely subjectively. If we think of the concept of knowledge in these terms, we will inevitably be led to connect knowledge with a state of "transcendent certainty." This may lead us to restrict knowledge to facts about the subjective realm or to facts about how things subjectively seem; the idea that a subject is ever in a position to affirm that he knows an objective fact comes under threat. On this understanding, we would never be in a position to say more than "I am firmly persuaded that such and such is the case" or "I have a justified belief that such and such is the case"; the concept of knowledge in connection with objective states of affairs would be unusable. It is in part, Wittgenstein observes, because Moore's assurances suggest that he shares the conception of knowledge as a peculiar mental state with the skeptic that his response to the skeptic's doubt strikes us as ineffective: "When one hears Moore say 'I *know* that that's a tree', one suddenly understands those who think that that has by no means been settled. The matter strikes one all at once as being unclear and blurred. It is as if Moore had put it in the wrong light" (*OC* 481). How can Moore's sincere expression of his own mental state of being certain that something is the case guarantee that he knows it as a fact? It seems suddenly as if the question whether one knows any objective fact is essentially indeterminate.

Wittgenstein's investigation of the concept of knowledge is an attempt to show that it is a mistake to think that we must either get hold of the mental state that would guarantee its own factiveness or learn to make "a 'liveable' accommodation" with apparent skeptical consequences of accepting that there is no such state. Thus he tries to dissociate the concept of knowledge from the class of epistemic concepts that describe mental states, such as believing, being certain, and doubting. He tries to show that the word "know" is used in a quite different way, one that has no connection with a false ideal of "transcendent certainty." Thus the use of "I know" is connected with the idea of our having undertaken an appropriate investigation and of our being in a position to provide adequate grounds for a proposition, or with the idea of our having studied and mastered the relevant area of human knowledge, or with our having heard it from a reliable source, and the like. On Wright's interpretation, this move is seen as part of an overall accommodation with skepticism, that is, with the idea that we are never in a position unequivocally to establish that we know an objective fact, and that all claims to know are made within a framework of substantial presuppositions. To see why this is not the case, we need to look at what I suggested earlier is the more fundamental investigation, namely, the investigation of the concept of empirical judgment.

The idea is that Wittgenstein's investigation of the concept of empirical judgment is intended to show that the system of judgments that form the background to our ordinary, empirical inquiries, in which we understand ourselves to achieve knowledge of what is objectively the case, is not properly understood as a system of mere suppositions. On Wright's interpretation, our accepting this system of judgments is a matter of our taking on a set of presuppositions, including the presupposition that the conditions conducive to our arriving at the truth obtain, a presupposition that on Wright's account, even if it is not (or cannot be) doubted, is one that could conceivably be false. I have argued that if we do see things in the way that Wright's interpretation recommends, then we cannot intelligibly see the outcome of our ordinary inquiries as amounting to knowledge. The idea of a therapeutic interpretation is that Wittgenstein tries to show that the system of judgments that ordinarily form the background to empirical inquiry have a status such that the question of the truth or falsity of these judgments does not arise, and that the truth of these judgments cannot therefore be said to be "assumed." The claim is that this is quite different from either proving to the satisfaction of the skeptic that these judgments are certainly correct or conceding that each of us must be (subjectively) certain of them, even though they could, in some sense, be objectively false. It holds out the promise of providing an understanding of our ordinary practice on which it no longer feels, even from our position of reflection, that we would have to have answered skeptical doubt in order to be in a position to take ourselves as arriving, through the appropriate methods of investigation, at genuine knowledge of the objective world.

The fundamental problem with the two previous interpretations of Wittgenstein's response to skepticism is that they see it as focusing directly on the traditional skeptical problem, that is, directly on the issue of our *entitlement*, in the face of skeptical doubt, to our certainty concerning the propositions that form the framework of all ordinary justification of claims to know objective facts. Both interpretations see Wittgenstein as offering some account of our certainty concerning these propositions on which our lack of a positive epistemic warrant for them has no tendency to make our certainty concerning them look irrational or inappropriate. Rather, our certainty concerning these groundless presuppositions is shown, in one way or another, to be obligatory or constitutive of our practice; the only difference between the two interpretations is whether the constitutive role of certainty concerning the propositions of the frame is seen as providing the basis for an outright refutation of skepticism or as a means to making a livable accommodation with it. The difficulty, in either case, is that this is not the sort of reassurance we were seeking, for it does nothing to make the idea that we have *knowledge* of the objective world intelligible. Being shown that within our ordinary practice, we *cannot* doubt or are in some sense justified in not doubting the propositions the skeptic doubts is not the same as being shown that the skeptic's doubt does not threaten our ability to understand ourselves as knowing about the world. Thus the skeptical problem has a way of returning to undermine any respite that these responses might initially seem to provide, for even if they succeed in showing that skeptical doubt is essentially or justifiably excluded from our ordinary practice, they cannot put an end to our anxiety that our whole system of beliefs might rest upon an illusion.

The crucial idea of the interpretation I am now presenting is that it is Wittgenstein's investigation of the concept of empirical judgment that does the work of showing that the idea that our whole system of belief might rest on an illusion is itself an illusion. For what is presupposed in this idea is that the capacity to express empirical judgments—thoughts about the world—is one that can be made sense of independently of the idea that the *objective world* is precisely what is characterized in the system of judgments that, in learning to judge, we come to acknowledge. The idea that ultimately underlies our susceptibility to skeptical doubt is the idea that we can make sense of the concept of empirical judgment in a way that leaves room for the question whether the system of judgments we ordinarily accept as true matches or fails to match the world as it is in itself, that is, for "a further doubt *behind*" ordinary doubt. "That this is an *illusion*," Wittgenstein suggests, "has to be shown in a different way" (*OC* 19). That is, it is not a matter of removing a doubt by showing that we know something or by showing that a reasonable man does not, or cannot, doubt it. Rather, it is a matter of our becoming clear about something, so that there no longer appears to be a doubt that ought to be removed before our language game can be taken to be in touch with reality.

It is, I want to argue, Wittgenstein's reflections on our concept of empirical judgment that are his attempt to become clear about why the idea of "a further doubt *behind*" ordinary doubt is an illusion. Once this illusion is exposed for what it is, it will no longer appear to be the case that our empirical inquiries rest on presuppositions that amount to a collective subjective certainty that a large number of assumptions or hypotheses are correct, and thus that we can never be in a position of having established that something is objectively the case. It will no longer seem to be the case that we must either rely on our subjective certainty concerning groundless assumptions in order to bridge the gap between mind and world or succumb to skeptical paralysis. We will be in a position to make the idea of objective knowledge intelligible insofar as we come to recognize that the concept of the capacity to express empirical judgments is inseparable from the idea that what come into view with our acquisition of language are certain *facts* for which the idea of a mistake does not arise. There is no suggestion that this puts us in a position to refute—or even silence—the skeptic's doubt, but only that it provides us with an understanding of our practice of expressing thoughts about the world on which it no longer seems as if we ought, even ideally, to have answered these doubts in order to be in a position to make the relevant judgments.[11] It is no longer the case, therefore, that our reflective understanding of our ordinary practice suggests that, strictly speaking, we are essentially relying on groundless presuppositions or mere subjective certainties when we say how things are objectively. We see that being able to *say* what the world is like is not always a matter of *knowing* what it is like and thus not always a matter of being able to say how we know or of being able to justify our description.

On this reading, the theme of the strand of *On Certainty* that focuses on the concept of judgment rather than on the concept of knowledge is that we come to see that our capacity to express empirical judgments about the world is based on our initiation into the practice of expressing judgments, which brings into view a large number of facts. Acknowledging these facts is essential to our acquiring a grasp of the meaning of the expressions of the language in which empirical judgments are expressed: "If you are not certain of any fact, you cannot be certain of the meaning of your words either" (*OC* 114).[12] To master the language in which we express judgments is to master its application, and that means, for example, learning, on suitable occasions, that "This is your hand," "This is a table," "This is red," and the like. Acknowledging certain facts—recognizing objects with certainty—is the beginning of our language game, the beginning of all operating with thought. The empirical propositions that we accept as a matter of course in learning the use of the expressions of our language "do not serve as foundations in the same way as hypotheses which, if they turn out to be false are replaced by others" (*OC* 402). Nor is it the case that "one [is] trying to express even the greatest subjective certainty"; it is "rather that certain propositions seem to underlie all questions and all thinking" (*OC* 415). The idea of thoughts that are about reality but may fail to be in touch with reality—of concepts that are not, via their application in judgment, essentially already in contact with reality—is not an idea of contentful thought, that is, of thought, at all. Questions of correctness or incorrectness, of justification or evidence, have no application when it comes to the empirical propositions that serve to fix the meaning of the expressions of our language; in these cases, it is merely a matter of the teacher's *saying* (authoritatively) that *this* is a hand, *this* is a table, and the like. Questions of correctness or incorrectness apply to judgments that are intelligibly empirical—that is, about the world—only against the background of a vast range of facts that come into view with our acquisition of language.[13]

Thus we come to see that the very idea of our having the ability to express thoughts that can be compared with reality for truth or falsity, that is, whose truth or falsity can be a topic for investigation, depends on our being in possession of a system of interrelated concepts whose empirical content is ultimately fixed through the application of concepts in observational judgments. These observational judgments describe facts that we understand ourselves as in a position to apprehend simply in virtue of our mastery of the relevant concepts; the availability of these facts and our capacity to judge do not come apart.[14] What we come to see is that our conception of the world is not a conception of something set over and against our system of empirical judgments, which our system of judgments as a whole might match or fail to match, but of something that comes into view, in part at least, with our acquisition of language; it comes into view in the form of the facts that we are brought to acknowledge in learning our language. Our idea of a capacity for empirical judgment is inseparable from the idea that in learning to judge, we are acknowledging particular facts that are understood to be, in part at least, constitutive of the world; recognition of these facts is seen to be based not on evidence but on the ability to describe the world in concepts; our idea that we have thoughts about the world is inseparable from the idea that we are in a position to describe certain facts simply in virtue of our possession of the relevant conceptual abilities. Thus we come to see that the facts that constitute the objective world include not only things that we have come to know on the basis of specific investigations that have put us in a privileged position in respect of them, but also things that we are in a position *authoritatively* to describe in virtue of having acquired the relevant conceptual abilities. Thus in suitable circumstances, I am in a position to say, "You may take it from me: this is a hand." In these circumstances the question, "How do you know?" in its epistemological sense, is not applicable; if someone raises the question, "How do you know?" I can take it in a non-epistemological way, on which it is enough for me to reply, "I have learned English." We see that not all facts—all true judgments—are established by means of an inquiry that puts us in a privileged position of having established that something is the case. A vast number of facts are available to anyone who has learned language and is suitably placed to apprehend them.

On Wright's interpretation, it was claimed that Wittgenstein concedes that the acknowledgment that a particular proposition is true always depends upon the groundless presupposition of the truth of a general proposition that states that conditions are such that our methods for arriving at empirical judgments are "conducive to the divination of what is true and the avoidance of what is false" (Wright, 2004, p.43). The idea is that it is impossible to possess a warrant for the assertion of a particular proposition without relying on "collateral information" concerning the proper functioning of the relevant cognitive capacities, the suitability of the occasion for their effective functioning, and my understanding of the concepts involved in the formulation of the relevant proposition. However, Wittgenstein's remarks suggest that he does not accept this general conception of the relation between particular judgments and general propositions. First of all, his remarks on "There are physical objects" suggest that he does not take this sentence to express a general, empirical proposition at all. It does not express an empirical proposition because " 'physical object' is a logical concept (Like colour, quantity, ...)" (*OC*36): it describes the use of a class of expressions and does not ascribe a property to an object. In this case, there is no general proposition of the form "There are physical objects" that could be presupposed in my affirming the particular proposition "This is my hand." Particular judgments are the foundation of all operating with words, and on suitable occasions, they are authoritatively made; the idea that particular judgments rest upon general presuppositions rests upon the misconception that all particular judgments are knowledge claims based on evidence.

In the case of propositions such as "The world has existed for a long time past," Wittgenstein seems equally unwilling to allow that affirming particular propositions about the past rests on, or presupposes, the truth of the general claim. In acquiring the capacity to express empirical judgments in language, a child learns to believe a host of things about the past, for example, that his parents were born in such and such a place at such and such a time, that someone climbed a mountain many years ago, that there used to be a castle on this site, and that particular historical events occurred. A child never learns that the world has existed for a long time past, nor, Wittgenstein suggests, is it a presupposition of what he does learn. Rather, it is "a consequence" of what he learns in the sense that it is part of the worldview that is taken in with what is learned. Thus a whole system of propositions is "made plausible," "a system in which consequences and premises give one another *mutual* support" (*OC* 142). There is no suggestion that the worldview we acquire in acquiring our language is certainly correct, that is, that it matches something outside itself, but rather that it characterizes the way we judge, the nature of empirical judgment. The stability and universality of the system of judgments we acquire is essential to our grip on what our words mean, or on what we mean when we ask such questions as "Was there ever a human dwelling on this site?" or "In what country were you born?" The world-picture "is the substratum of all my enquiring and asserting" (*OC* 162); it characterizes the world that is brought into view by means of language.

The question is what sort of response to skepticism these reflections on the idea of empirical judgment are intended to afford us. It is clear that Wittgenstein believes that the use of the word "know" is not appropriate in the case of our relation to those facts that are, on a particular occasion, available to anyone with mastery of the appropriate concepts. They are what come into view simply in virtue of our acquiring the capacity to judge, and the concepts of evidence, justification, doubt, grounds, and the like do not apply. Thus what we see as a result of Wittgenstein's reflections is that these facts have not been established on the basis of an investigation and that our relation to them is such that the question of our justification for affirming them is not one that arises or that we *ought* to have addressed: "To use a word without a justification does not mean to use it without right" (*PI* 289). Our relation to these facts does not, of course, put us in a position to prove anything or to answer the doubt of the skeptic, but clarifying the nature of this relation provides a form of self-understanding on which our lack of justification for accepting them as facts does not appear, even from a position of reflection, as an omission; we no longer feel that, strictly speaking, there is a doubt that *ought* to be removed *before* the judgment that these facts obtain is made.

Thus we see the connection between our being in a position to raise an empirical question whether something is objectively the case and our having the world in view as what is described in the judgments that we are in a position to affirm in virtue of mastering our mother tongue. The ordinary certainties that lie at the root of our practice of expressing empirical judgments are not, on this interpretation, regarded as a matter of mere presupposition or hypothesis; we have come to see that the propositions of which we are all certain in virtue of our mastery of language constitute a system of objective judgments that we all acknowledge in virtue of having undergone the appropriate training in the use of expressions. On this interpretation, the certainty is nonepistemic in the sense that it is presupposed by, and lies apart from, the path of empirical inquiry, but this is not to say that it is merely subjective, or that the truth of the judgments it concerns is something that has still to be settled. It is against the background of this system of judgments, now recognized as something that is, for us, entirely solid, that particular empirical questions are investigated. Whether the answer to such a question is yes or no is something that we establish by means of the appropriate form of investigation, at the end of which we are, if procedures have been correctly followed, in a position of possessing an earned warrant for a claim to know how things stand. Like all such claims, it may be subjected to further critical inquiry, but it will also often be the case that the claim is absorbed into the body of knowledge of the world that we as a community share and rely upon. There is, I want to suggest, nothing in the understanding of our practice that I have just presented that has a tendency to undermine our ordinary sense that what is thereby achieved intelligibly counts as knowledge of the (familiar) objective world.

Earlier I described the aim of a therapeutic response to skepticism as the attempt to achieve a comfortable retaining of our commonsense understanding of ourselves as possessing knowledge of the objective world, that is, one that is neither dogmatic nor skeptical. What is required of such a response is that it should not appear either to beg the question against the skeptic or to concede that our system of beliefs might rest on an illusion. It must seem neither that we have assumed something that, strictly speaking, stands in need of justification nor that we have conceded that we cannot justify something that, strictly speaking, we ought to. I argued that both the previous interpretations fail in this task insofar as they focus on our right to our certainty concerning framework judgments without showing why our certainty is not a leap in the dark that, even if by a stroke of luck it is correct, undermines our ability to think of ourselves as achieving knowledge of the objective world. It is not enough, I suggested, to show that our certainty concerning the judgments that we acquire in acquiring language is constitutive of our practice if this leaves us open to the thought that the groundlessness of this obligatory certainty makes it a mere matter of presupposition and thus an inappropriate foundation for knowledge. We must not feel, from a position of reflection, that our certainty might, despite being essential to our practice, be misplaced, that is, that the correctness or incorrectness of our world-picture depends ultimately upon a matter of luck.

The idea of the therapeutic interpretation is that Wittgenstein's first concern is not to defend our entitlement to our ordinary certainty in the face of skeptical doubt, but to clarify what is involved in the idea of our possessing a capacity for empirical judgment. On this interpretation, he does not attempt to answer the skeptic's doubts directly but is primarily concerned to make our practice of expressing thoughts about the world perspicuous. What we come to see is that our practice of employing empirical concepts in judgments depends upon our recognizing that anyone who is master of those concepts has the capacity authoritatively to describe certain facts. Thus we come to see why the question of justification does not arise for those judgments that we all affirm in virtue of our shared mastery of our conceptual techniques. In affirming these judgments, we are not yet in a position of claiming to know anything or in a position of having either assumed or established that something is the case, but merely in a position of exercising our mastery of our techniques for describing the world in propositions; knowing, and the practice of providing appropriate warrants for claims about the world that not everyone accepts as a matter of course, comes later. The idea is that this self-understanding is one on which it no longer appears that we are being asked to surmise or assume something in order for inquiry to get off the ground.

The self-understanding of what is involved in our capacity to express thoughts about the world that, on this interpretation, Wittgenstein provides does not have the tendency to make us feel that we ought, strictly speaking, to have justified the judgments that stand fast for us if they are to serve as a foundation for knowledge. Recognizing our right to affirm the truth of these judgments is essentially accepting that from the perspective of our ordinary language game, these judgments do not fall short of the facts: these are facts that come into view with the mastery of our language. What we see is that the idea that we *ought* to have justified them is based on a misconception of our relation to these judgments (to the facts) and ultimately on a false picture of empirical judgment as having a content that is completely independent of the actual application of our system of concepts in particular judgments. Thus we have achieved a form of self-understanding on which, even on reflection, our ordinary practice does not have a tendency to destroy itself from within by making us feel that we have necessarily failed to do something we should do but cannot. The question whether we ought to have such a practice—a practice of employing expressions in empirical judgment—is not one that has any clear sense; it is equivalent to asking whether we ought to speak a language, or whether our words ought to mean what they do mean. What we see now is that luck comes in, insofar as it does come in, not in relation to the question whether the judgments that form the framework of our practice are correct, but in relation to the fact that all of us can be brought, by means of our training, to a shared mastery of the rules for the use of expressions, on which our capacity to express empirical judgments depends. This shared mastery is exhibited in our acknowledging the whole system of judgments in which the use of the expressions of our language is made manifest. Nothing has been proved to be correct by means of these reflections, but neither is it the case that we are left with a sense that the question of correctness or incorrectness cannot be settled. Rather, the idea of proving our system of judgments to be correct is seen to depend on the idea of a gap between empirical judgment and the world, which has not been allowed to open. The understanding of our ordinary practice that emerges frees us from the grip of skepticism, not because it entails that skeptical doubts *cannot* be expressed, but because it shows why our ordinary indifference to skeptical doubt is not the result of hastiness or superficiality but an implicit acknowledgment of our right to make certain judgments in virtue of our knowledge of our language.[15]

NOTES

....

1. See, for example, Stroll, 1994; Wright, 1985, 1991; Strawson, 1985; Putnam, 1981, 1992; and Moyal-Sharrock, 2004.

2. See, for example, Wright, 2004; Williams, 1991;and Kober, 1996.

3. See, for example, McGinn, 1989; Conant, 1998;and Williams, 2004. In the latter essay, Williams assimilates my reading of *On Certainty* (McGinn, 1989) to that of Stroll and others who claim that the argument of *On Certainty* refutes skepticism by showing that the skeptic's doubts make no sense. Williams calls this reading "the Framework Reading." I want to claim that my reading is distinct from the Framework Reading and that it is in line with an understanding of Wittgenstein's method as therapeutic. The current chapter is intended to make the distinction between the Framework Reading and the Therapeutic Reading clear. Conant's version of the Therapeutic Reading is distinctive (and distinct from the one I give here) in holding that Wittgenstein's remarks are exclusively concerned with exposing philosophical nonsense (the skeptic's doubts and Moore's knowledge claims) as nonsense.

4. There are, of course, remarks in *On Certainty* in which Wittgenstein does raise the question whether we understand the skeptic's doubts. For example:

> There are cases such that, if someone gives signs of doubt where we do not doubt, we cannot confidently understand his signs as signs of doubt.
>
> (*OC* 154)

> This doubt isn't one of the doubts in our game. (But not as if we *chose* this game.)
>
> (*OC* 317)

> Doubting and non-doubting behaviour. There is the first only if there is the second.
>
> (*OC* 354)

However, the question is whether Wittgenstein intends these remarks to serve as part of a refutation of skepticism. Trying to show that it is not clear that we understand the skeptic's doubt need not be taken as the basis of a dogmatic claim that the skeptic's doubt is nonsense, or that it is necessarily self-subverting.

5. Michael Williams makes a similar objection to what he calls the Framework Reading: "it makes Wittgenstein's response to skepticism too direct. As a result, it loses sight of an essential point: that comments on the logic of ordinary doubting and knowledge claiming will cut no ice if we are in the grip of the illusion that there is a special kind of philosophical doubt, purporting to call epistemic ordinary practices into question" (Williams, 2004, p.83). Duncan Pritchard argues that the Framework Reading becomes a more powerful response to skepticism if it is combined with an externalist epistemology; he also argues that there is some evidence that Wittgenstein himself has externalist intuitions (Pritchard, 2001).

6. This represents a modification of the view Wright argued for in Wright, 1985 and 1991. In Wright, 1985, he is inclined to argue that Wittgenstein's recognition that framework propositions have the status of "rules of procedure" entails that they do not have the status of propositions that are apt to be assessed for truth or falsity. The "non-factuality" of the propositions of the frame ("hinge propositions" in Wright's terminology) "implies an immunity to one kind of criticism: that which emphasises lack of epistemic pedigree"

(Wright, 1985, p.467); our beliefs in framework propositions have a status that "utterly absolves them from the shackles of evidential constraints," and "it is seriously unclear what it could be to suspend these beliefs, or hold others contrary to them" (Wright, 1985, p.467–68). In Wright, 1991, he argues that skepticism based on the dreaming hypothesis is self-subverting and can therefore be discounted.

7. Wright is careful to distinguish the claim that a warrant does not transmit from Moore's premise to the conclusion of his argument from a denial of closure. Knowledge does indeed transfer across known entailment: if Moore knows his premise, then he knows that there is a material world. However, Moore's warrant for affirming the premise (the evidence of his senses) does not provide a warrant for the denial of the skeptical hypothesis that there is no material world *unless* the falsity of the hypothesis is pre-supposed. Whatever warrant Moore has for the premise of his proof does not, therefore, transmit to the conclusion: it cannot give a rational agent a reason to accept that there is a material world.

8. See, for example, Wright, 1980.

9. For an interpretation of Wittgenstein's remarks on rule following along these lines, see McDowell, 1984.

10. Wright's conception of knowledge is an instance of what McDowell calls "the hybrid conception." McDowell argues that the element of luck implicit in the hybrid conception means that this conception cannot provide a satisfactory conception of knowledge (see McDowell, 1995).

11. That is, there is nothing in the understanding we achieve that puts us in a position, faced with a determined skeptic, to provide a proof of the relevant judgments. Rather, we achieve an understanding of our relation to these judgments on which the ordinary ab-sence of any question of proof does not only not appear to be an omission, but it no longer seems to be the case that, in the absence of proof, all that these judgments can amount to is a set of presuppositions.

12. Other remarks in which Wittgenstein draws attention to the connection between our acquiring the capacity to express judgments and our acknowledging certain facts (rather than accepting hypotheses) include the following:

> [The] situation is . . . not the same for a proposition like "At this distance from the sun there is a planet" and "Here is a hand" (namely my own hand). The second can't be called a hypothesis.
>
> (*OC* 52)

> A meaning of a word is a kind of employment of it.
> For it is what we learn when the word is incorporated into our language.
>
> (*OC* 61)

> The *truth* of my statements is the test of my *understanding* of these statements.
> That is to say: if I make certain false statements, it becomes uncertain whether I understand them.
>
> (*OC* 80–81)

> From a child up I learned to judge like this. *This is* judging.
> This is how I learned to judge; *this* I got to know *as* judgement.
>
> (*OC* 128–29)

> Not only rules, but also examples are needed for establishing a practice.
>
> (*OC* 139)

As children we learn facts.

(*OC* 159)

[W]e are interested in the fact that about certain empirical propositions no doubt can exist if making judgements is to be possible at all.

(*OC* 308)

We teach a child "that is your hand", not "that is perhaps (or "probably") your hand". That is how a child learns the innumerable language-games that are concerned with his hand.

(*OC* 374)

Knowledge is in the end based on acknowledgement.

(*OC* 378)

But why *am* I so certain that this is my hand? Doesn't the whole language-game rest on this kind of certainty?
Or: isn't this "certainty" (already) presupposed in the language-game? Namely by virtue of the fact that one is not playing the game, or playing it wrong, if one does not recognize objects with certainty.

(*OC* 446)

We say: if a child has mastered language—and hence its application—it must know the meaning of words. It must, for example, be able to attach the name of its colour to a white, black, red or blue object without the occurrence of any doubt. And indeed no one misses doubt here; no one is surprised that we do not merely *surmise* the meaning of our words.

(*OC* 522–23)

It is simply the normal case, to be incapable of mistake about the designation of certain things in one's mother tongue.
"I can't be making a mistake about it" simply characterizes one kind of assertion.

(*OC* 630–31)

13. This should not be taken to imply that we are infallible in our identification of objects. Rather, what the investigation of the concept of judgment makes clear is that it makes no sense to say that we may be wrong on every occasion on which a word is applied, or that we are never in a position to show someone how the words of our language are used.

14. This observation is not, however, the basis of a claim, characteristic of the Framework Reading, that skepticism is essentially self-subverting in the sense that it tries to doubt the very propositions that are the condition of the doubt's having a sense. It is rather that we have arrived at a way of looking at things on which the gap between empirical judgment and the world, which skepticism essentially exploits, does not open up; we are no longer left with a picture on which, having acquired the ability to judge, we still need to establish that our judgments connect with reality. The point is not that the propositions the skeptic doubts have no sense unless he accepts that those judgments are beyond doubt, but that the fact that these judgments are not doubted no longer appears to depend on our groundlessly accepting an antiskeptical hypothesis concerning our relation to the world. The absence of doubt is no longer seen as an expression of credulity (leaving a gap needing to be bridged), but as an expression of our mastery of our linguistic techniques; we

come to see why the skeptic's doubts may properly be ignored (why there is no gap to bridge).

15. I would like to thank Martin Smith, University of St. Andrews, for very helpful comments on an earlier draft of this chapter.

REFERENCES

Conant, J. 1998. "Wittgenstein on Meaning and Use." *Philosophical Investigations* 21:222–50.

Kober, M. 1996. "Certainties of a World-Picture: The Epistemological Investigations of *On Certainty*." In *The Cambridge Companion to Wittgenstein*, ed. H. Sluga and D. Stern, pp.411–41. Cambridge: Cambridge University Press.

McDowell, J. 1984. "Wittgenstein on Rule-Following." *Synthese* 58:325–363.

———. 1994. *Mind and World*. Cambridge, Mass: Harvard University Press.

———. 1995. "Knowledge and the Internal." *Philosophy and Phenomenological Research* 55:877–93.

McGinn, M. 1989. *Sense and Certainty: The Dissolution of Scepticism*. Oxford: Blackwell.

McManus, D., ed. 2004. *Wittgenstein and Scepticism*. London: Routledge.

Moyal-Sharrock, D. 2004. *Understanding Wittgenstein's "On Certainty."* New York: Palgrave Macmillan.

Moyal-Sharrock, D., and W.H. Brenner. 2007. *Readings of Wittgenstein's "On Certainty."* New York: Palgrave Macmillan.

Pritchard, D. 2001. "Radical Scepticism, Epistemological Externalism, and 'Hinge' Propositions." *Wittgenstein-Studien*, pp.81–105.

Putnam, H. 1981. *Reason, Truth and History*. Cambridge: Cambridge University Press.

———. 1992. *Renewing Philosophy*. Cambridge, Mass: Harvard University Press

Rhees, R. 2005. *Wittgenstein's "On Certainty,"* ed. D.Z. Phillips. Oxford: Blackwell.

Strawson, P. F. 1985. *Skepticism and Naturalism: Some Varieties*. London: Methuen.

Stroll, A. 1994. *Moore and Wittgenstein on Certainty*. Oxford: Oxford University Press.

Williams, M. 1991. *Unnatural Doubts: Epistemological Realism and the Basis of Scepticism*. Oxford: Blackwell.

———. 2004. "Wittgenstein's Refutation of Idealism." In McManus, 2004, pp. 76–96.

Wright, C. 1980. *Wittgenstein on the Foundation of Mathematics*. London: Duckworth.

———. 1985. "Facts and Certainty." *Proceedings of the British Academy* 71:429–472.

———. 1991. "Scepticism and Dreaming: Imploding the Demon." *Mind* 397: 87–115.

———. 1998. *Philosophical Investigations*, trans. G.E.M. Anscombe. Oxford: Blackwell.

———. 2004. "Wittgenstein's Certainties." In McManus, 2004, pp. 22–55.

Wittgenstein, L. 1977. *On Certainty*, trans. D. Paul and G.E.M. Anscombe. Oxford: Blackwell.

CHAPTER 18

....

THE RELATIVIST
RESPONSE TO RADICAL
SKEPTICISM

....

PETER J. GRAHAM

Do you believe that intelligent life exists on Jupiter, hiding deep within its stormy eye? If you do, then your belief is not supported by much evidence, if any at all. You are probably just making it up. On the other hand, take your belief that you are reading this book. That belief is clearly justified. Indeed, it is so well supported that we do not even usually consider whether it is justified, reasonable, or rational; it obviously is. So some beliefs about external reality are well justified, and others are not really justified at all. Or so common sense would have us believe.

Radical skeptics deny this. They think that not a single one of our beliefs about the external world is even prima facie justified, reasonable, or rational. If the radical skeptic is right, your belief that you are reading this book is just as justified as the lunatic's belief that he is an immortal spirit dwelling deep within the stormy eye of Jupiter; they are both epistemically worthless. The radical skeptic thinks that we enjoy no epistemic right or entitlement to believe anything whatsoever about external reality.[1] If you find this shocking, then you understand what the radical skeptic is saying. If you do not find it shocking, reread this paragraph until you do. If the radical skeptic is right, common sense is wildly mistaken.

Why might someone be a radical skeptic? Well, the radical skeptic claims to have a good argument for her shocking conclusion. And if the argument is a good one, then common sense would stand in need of some defense; a rejoinder to the argument would be required. Various chapters in this volume take up and discuss different possible rejoinders. In this chapter, I take up and discuss the relativist reply to the radical skeptic's argument. In particular, I shall examine two different versions of relativism—one about truth and one about justification—to see whether they can provide an adequate defense of common sense. Can the relativist, either about truth or about justification, show that the radical skeptic's argument is not really a good one after all?

To lay my cards on the table right at the start, I shall argue that the relativist about truth holds a deeply implausible view, a view no better than radical skepticism. It may, in a sense, defend common sense, but only at the cost of abandoning common sense in, as it were, another sense. Despite its implausibility, discussing it here has three merits. First, it is a popular (or at least tempting) view in the history of philosophy. It is even tempting today: some philosophers seem to hold it, many humanists profess acceptance, and first-year American college students cannot seem to help voicing at, at least when topics get controversial. Second, if relativism about truth were correct, then it really would undermine the radical skeptic's argument, so showing how it would undermine the skeptic's argument should deepen our understanding of the skeptic's argument. Third, and in so doing, it will help us understand how relativism about justification would work as a reply to the skeptic. And relativism about justification, also a popular view historically and currently, is not nearly as implausible as relativism about truth. Indeed, it may even be true. So if the relativist has a good shot at defending common sense in the face of the skeptic's argument, it will be the relativist about justification, and not about truth. Or so I shall argue.[2]

1. The Structure of the Radical Skeptic's Argument

1.1. Two Analogous "Skeptical" Arguments

The radical skeptic argues for her conclusion using premises she thinks that we would accept. If we really would accept the premises, and the premises support her conclusion, then we really should abandon our common sense conviction that many of our beliefs about the external world are prima facie justified. It is an argument we would like to be able to defuse.

To convey the skeptic's argument, I shall first discuss two other "skeptical" arguments. The first is silly, while the second is not. The structure of the radical skeptic's argument parallels these two arguments.

Here is the silly argument. Suppose that someone claimed that in order to be a teacher, one would have to know all completed physics and the entire history of the world. Since no one knows either, there are no teachers. The first premise sets a standard for what it takes to be a teacher. The second asserts that the standard is not met. To respond, you can deny either the first or the second premise. The first premise is clearly false, while the second is obviously true. So we know how to refute this silly skepticism: deny the first premise. Given what it really takes to be a teacher, there are very many indeed (cf. Edwards 1955). Upon reflection, we would not accept the first premise.

Here is the serious argument. Many philosophers are skeptical about whether we are ever morally responsible for what we do. These skeptics start with the premise that in order to be responsible for what we do, we must have the ability to act otherwise. So to be praiseworthy for giving a needy child monetary assistance, I must have been able to spend the money elsewhere or not spend it at all. If I could not do otherwise, why do I deserve credit? But if causal determinism is true (where everything I do is fixed in advance by the past state of the universe and the laws of nature), I could not have spent the money elsewhere or not at all. And since causal determinism is true, I am never praiseworthy (or blameworthy) for anything I do.[3] Given the standards and the facts, moral responsibility is illusory.

This argument has two premises. The first is a normative claim or theory about what moral responsibility requires: the ability to do otherwise. This places a standard on acts that must be met in order for the subject to responsible for an act. If the standard is never met, the subject is never responsible. The second premise is a factual or metaphysical claim about the nature of the world. If the factual claim is true, the standard set in the first premise is never met. The conclusion follows that we are never responsible for what we do.

There are two ways to respond: first, deny that in order to be responsible, one must have the ability to do otherwise; second, deny that causal determinism is true. Those who take the first route are called "compatibilists"; moral responsibility is compatible with causal determinism. Compatibilists offer a competing standard of moral responsibility to the skeptic's standard; the skeptic, they argue, is wrong about what moral responsibility requires. Given what moral responsibility in fact requires, we are responsible for what we do, regardless of determinism. That is why we can have both.

This first route is a "normative" response to the skeptic. A normative response proposes an alternative norm or standard for responsibility that rivals the skeptic's. Those who take the second route are called "incompatibilists" or "libertarians"; though responsibility and determinism are incompatible, the world is not causally determined; our acts are free; we have the ability to do otherwise. Libertarians accept the skeptic's standard for moral responsibility but insist that it is met nonetheless. This second route is a "metaphysical" response. A metaphysical response proposes an alternative view of the facts that rivals the skeptic's preferred view. On either route, normative or metaphysical, the skeptic is wrong that we are never responsible for what we do.

These two arguments (silly and serious) both have two parts. The first is a normative claim about what standards must be met for a certain "normative" status to obtain. The second claims that the standard is not met. A normative response denies the first part; a metaphysical (or factual) response denies the second. The silly argument is silly because we would never accept the "normative" premise about what it takes to be a teacher. The serious argument is serious because we are strongly pulled to accept both of the skeptic's premises, and because we are strongly inclined to reject the skeptic's conclusion that we are never responsible for what we do. That is why a response to the skeptic's argument is so pressing. Can we avoid the skeptic's conclusion without giving up something that, upon reflection, we find that we really should accept?

1.2. The Radical Skeptic's Metaphysical Premise

The radical skeptic's argument parallels these arguments. The radical skeptic first sets a standard on justified beliefs about the external world (the normative part) and then argues that the standard is not met (the factual part). The radical skeptical conclusion thus follows. What, then, are the radical skeptic's two premises?

The factual or metaphysical part is simply the possibility of massive error, which follows from a realist view of truth, where the facts that make our beliefs true (or false) are one thing, and our beliefs (that are true or false) are another.[4] Given realism about truth, it seems that we might be massively wrong about the external world (envatted like Neo in *The Matrix*), massively wrong about the past (like John Murdoch in *Dark City*), massively wrong about other minds (somewhat like Jim Carrey in *The Truman Show*), or fooled about nearly everything by an all-powerful demon (like Descartes at the end of Meditation 1). All these possibilities rely upon the logical, conceptual, or metaphysical gap between what we believe to be true and the facts that make our beliefs true. The gap between "mind" and "world" allows for the possibility of massive error. These possibilities are often called "skeptical hypotheses" because the skeptic relies upon them when arguing for her conclusion. That the hypotheses are possible is something the skeptic thinks that we would ordinarily, upon reflection, accept.

If this is the factual or metaphysical premise, then what is the skeptic's normative (or "epistemological") premise? Clearly another premise is required, for strictly speaking, nothing follows about justification from the possibility of massive error alone. To reach skepticism, a bridge premise is required that connects the possibility of massive *error* with the lack or impossibility of epistemic *justification*. So what normative standard does the skeptic set for the justification of beliefs about the external world? This question is actually not easy to answer conclusively, as many of the other chapters in this volume demonstrate. But I think that there are at least three straightforward "normative criteria" or "theories of justification" that will do the trick: infalliblism, Cartesianism, and inferentialism.

1.3. Three "Skeptical" Theories of Justification

The infallibilist holds that a belief that P is justified if and only if (iff) the way the subject formed the belief is such that the subject cannot be wrong in any possible circumstance whether P. For example, in thinking that I now exist, I cannot be mistaken, and perhaps my belief that $1 + 1 = 2$ is something I cannot be mistaken about either. Some forms of introspection and reasoning may be "infallible." The infallibilist would count these beliefs as justified. But if massive error—or simply run-of-the-mill, everyday error—about the external world is possible (factual premise), and justified beliefs require immunity from error (normative premise), then no belief about the external world is (even prima facie) justified. Radical skepticism follows from infallibilism combined with the possibility of error.

The Cartesian, like the infallibilist, holds a very demanding view about justification, though the Cartesian is somewhat less demanding.[5] For the Cartesian, a belief that P is prima facie justified iff the process that led to the belief that P is reliable (gets things right most of the time) *in all possible worlds*; that is, the process is *necessarily reliable*. Justification on this view does not require "every-instance" reliability (as the infallibilist thinks) but only requires that the process responsible for the belief be reliable (get things right *most* of the time) *in every possible world*. So *some* justified beliefs may be false on the Cartesian view. The Cartesian may thus call himself a "fallibilist," though the fallibility of justification can only go so far.

Cartesianism clearly supports radical skepticism. If massive error is possible, and justified beliefs are only those based on processes reliable in every possible world, then (almost) no belief about the external world is (even prima facie) justified, for there are possible worlds where perception, ampliative reasoning, and memory are unreliable. Radical skepticism follows from Cartesianism combined with the possibility of massive error, the possibility of wholesale unreliability.[6]

It is widely recognized that infallibilism and Cartesianism have radical skeptical consequences. Though these two views have both had weighty advocates in the history of philosophy, few embrace them today. Among contemporary epistemologists, a third view about justification is widely held that, when combined with an additional "factual" premise, supports radical skepticism. I call this third view "inferentialism" and the further factual premise "pessimism."

The inferentialist requires that for beliefs about the external world—beliefs about tables, computers, soccer games, and pet-show champions—to be prima facie justified, a subject must (be able to) justifiably infer those beliefs from justified beliefs about his own mental states, that is, from justified beliefs about his own perceptual sensations and representations, justified beliefs about his own beliefs and desires. For example, for my belief that I am writing with a blue pen on white paper to be prima facie justified, I would have to (be able to) justifiably infer that I am writing with a blue pen from justified beliefs about how things now perceptually "seem" or "appear" to me and other justified beliefs about what I believe about pens, paper, lighting conditions, and so on. I would have to (be able to) infer something about the external world (there is a blue pen in my hand) from beliefs about my own mind (that it now perceptually appears to me as if there is a blue pen in my hand).

Standardly, the inferentialist thinks that this inference is good only if I can justifiably show that the "real-world hypothesis" best explains my inner psychology. On the real-world hypothesis, I have certain psychological states and experiences *because* I am embodied with sense organs and other cognitive capacities that convey reliable information about the external world. So the beliefs common sense takes to be prima facie justified about the external world really are prima facie justified only if I have good reason to think that the real-world hypothesis best explains my "inner life."[7]

As it stands, inferentialism is not yet a skeptical theory of justification, for maybe I can show that the real-world hypothesis really does best explain why things "seem" to me as they do. To reach the radical skeptic's conclusion from inferentialism and the possibility of massive error, we would have to add the pessimist thought that I cannot actually show that the real-world hypothesis is the best explanation, for rival skeptical hypotheses are just as good at accounting for my inner life. And if they are, then I am not justified in inferring that I really do have hands or write with blue pens. If massive error is possible, if inferentialism is correct, and if the pessimist is right too, then the radical skeptic wins.

The radical skeptic can thus use three different normative criteria (or "theories of justification") to reach her radical conclusion when combined with a second, metaphysical premise: infalliblism, Cartesianism, or inferentialism (plus pessimism).[8]

1.4. How to Respond to the Radical Skeptic

How might one rebut the skeptic's argument? A metaphysical response consists in denying the metaphysical premise: the skeptic is wrong about the nature of truth; massive error (wholesale unreliability) is not possible. A normative (or epistemological) response consists in denying the normative premise: the skeptic is wrong about what justification requires. A third response accepts the metaphysical premise and embraces inferentialism but denies pessimism. Call this the "optimist" response: beliefs about the external world are indeed justified (or at least justifiable) because the real-world hypothesis best explains our "inner" lives. We can think of the second and third responses as "compatibilist": prima facie justified beliefs about the external world are "compatible" with the possibility of massive error.

In the next section, I discuss relativism about truth as a metaphysical response. Later I discuss relativism about justification as a normative response. Though I shall take a dim view of relativism about truth, I shall go on to argue that there is an important truth in relativism about justification. For those who wish to know more about the "optimist" response, see Vogel's chapter in this volume (cf. Vogel 2005). I shall not here discuss whether the pessimist or the optimist is right.

2. RELATIVISM ABOUT TRUTH AS A RESPONSE TO THE RADICAL SKEPTIC

2.1. Relativism about Truth Defined

Relativism about truth is the view that if you believe that P, then P is true for you, and that is all there is to truth. On the relativist view, there is no such thing as "objective" truth, truth independent of what anyone happens to believe. There are two popular versions of relativism about truth, individual relativism and cultural relativism. The individual relativist thinks that all there is to truth is truth for individual subjects: truth for you, truth for me, truth for him, truth for her, and so on. If I believe P, P is true for me. If you believe not-P, not-P is true for you. Since there is no such thing as "objective," nonrelative truth, you and I are both right on the individual relativist view. If the individual relativist is right, no one is ever wrong.

The cultural relativist about truth is not as permissive about truth as the individual relativist, though he is rather permissive for all that. On the cultural relativist view about truth, if a culture believes that P, then P is true for all members of that culture, and there is no such thing as a culture-transcendent truth so that one culture has things "objectively" right and another culture has things "objectively" wrong. So if modern Western civilization believes that the earth is a planet orbiting a sun at the edge of a galaxy, then that belief is true for all members of modern Western civilization. But if ancient Mediteranean culture believes that the earth is a flat body resting motionless at the center of the universe, then that belief is true for all members of that culture. Members of the respective cultures who fail to share that belief have false beliefs. Contemporary flat-earthers living in Los Angeles have a false belief about the earth. Aristotle, who believed the earth to be round, was mistaken if cultural relativism about truth is right. Individual members of cultures who fall out of sync with their culture may have false beliefs. Cultures, however, may not. To be a member of a culture, however, you have to share a good deal of beliefs with other members of your culture. And so on the cultural relativist view of truth, even individuals are guaranteed to have a good number of true beliefs. I shall put aside difficult questions about what a culture is and what it is for a culture to believe this or that. The general idea behind cultural relativism should be clear enough.

2.2. What Relativism about Truth Is Not

Before showing how relativism about truth undermines the skeptic's argument, I should distinguish relativism about truth from other theses with which it is often confused.

Relativism about truth differs from the anthropological observation that different people and different cultures have widely varying beliefs about the world, that is, different views about "what is true." The anthropological observation is one thing, and the philosophical view about truth is another. The realist can say that it is absolutely true that individuals and cultures have widely varying beliefs about all sorts of topics, while denying that *truth* is relative. When cultures disagree, the realist thinks, at least one must be wrong.

Do not confuse relativism about truth with tolerance toward different points of view. It may be morally right to tolerate differences in opinion. If some people believe that Martians live within Lake Michigan, it may be morally wrong to forcibly coerce them to recant their views or to imprison them until they change their minds. It may be impolite or even mean to criticize them. This is probably true for all sorts of beliefs people may hold. But from the fact that it is prima facie wrong to harm people for what they believe, it does not follow that what they believe is true or even reasonable. From the fact that Marty is "entitled" (legally or morally permitted) to believe that Martians live in Lake Michigan, it does not follow that Marty is "entitled" (believes correctly or with good reason) that Martians live in Lake Michigan.

Do not confuse relativism about truth about *all* subject matters (all truth is relative) with relativism about the truth of *certain* subject matters. Take morality, for example. Moral relativists typically hold that moral right and wrong are relative to culture. If culture C says that abortion is morally impermissible, then abortion is morally impermissible for members of that culture. But if culture E says that abortion is morally permissible, then abortion is morally permissible for members of that culture. Moral relativism makes morality look more like legality. Something is legal or not depending upon the laws of the land. Do not confuse relativism about moral truth with relativism about truth across the board. Moral relativists can accept that when it comes to most things—like whether there are apples in the cupboard or neutrinos leaving the sun—the realist is right about truth. And the realist can even accept that truths about morality are relative while denying that truths about all subject matters are relative.

To summarize, philosophical relativism about the nature of truth is not simply the anthropological observation that people and cultures believe all sorts of things. Nor is it the moral or political point that it is prima facie good or right to tolerate differences in points of view. Nor is it simply relativism about the truth of moral claims, where morality works like legality. We might accept any of these other theses without accepting philosophical relativism about truth. Philosophical relativism about truth is the radical view that if an individual (or culture) believes any proposition whatsoever about any subject matter, then that proposition is true for the individual (or culture), and there is no other "objective" or "absolute" truth independent of truth "for" the individual (or culture). Individual relativism about truth makes truth radically subjective, while cultural relativism makes it radically intersubjective.

2.3. How Relativism about Truth Works as a Response

Now that we have a clear idea of philosophical relativism about truth, let us see how it works as a metaphysical reply to the skeptic's argument. Let us start with individual relativism.

Individual relativism clearly implies that the skeptic's metaphysical premise (the possibility of massive error) is mistaken. Any error, not just massive error, is impossible if the individual relativist is right, so the skeptic's argument cannot even get off the ground if the individual relativist is right.

But even if the skeptic's argument cannot get off the ground, is the skeptic's conclusion mistaken if individual relativism is true? Would the skeptic's conclusion follow from the skeptic's view of justification anyway, even if relativism about truth is correct? Is the skeptic still right even if we assume relativism and infalliblism, or relativism and Cartesianism, or relativism and inferentialism? Let us see.

If we assume individual relativism about truth and infalliblism, every belief about the external world is justified, for if relativism is true, then the "process" of believing anything at all is infallible, which is exactly what the infallibilst thinks is sufficient for prima facie justification. So if infalliblism and relativism are both true, all beliefs are justified, and the skeptic's conclusion is mistaken. The reader can clearly see that if Cartesianism is correct, then the same conclusion follows on an individual relativist view of truth.

Matters are not so simple if we assume inferentialism. The inferentialist requires that beliefs about the external world be justifiably *inferred* in a certain way. So from the fact that all beliefs about the external world are true if individual relativism is true, it does not follow on the inferentialist view that those beliefs are justified. The subject would still have to (be able to) justifiably infer the "outer" from the "inner." The question the pessimist raises, then, would reappear: can the subject show that the "real-world hypothesis" best explains his "inner life"? Success at this would require ruling out alternative explanations that involve massive error, that is, alternatives that exploit the gap between what is believed about the external world and the external world itself. But if individual relativism is true, there is no such gap, so there are no such alternative explanations, and so the pessimist cannot get a finger hold. Given individual relativism and inferentialism, there is thus no problem for the justification of beliefs about the external world. So if we assume infalliblism, Cartesianism, or inferentialism, the skeptic is mistaken, given individual relativism about truth.

Furthermore, if the relativist is right about truth, then all that anyone has to believe is that skepticism is false (for that person), and presto, it is false (for that person). If individual relativism is true, and if you believe that your beliefs about the external world are justified, then they are justified (for you). So what if the skeptic believes otherwise.

Therefore, the skeptic does not stand a chance if individual relativism is right. If the individual relativist is right, (a) the skeptic loses her first premise right off the bat, (b) her "skeptical" theories cannot lead to a skeptical conclusion, and (c) her conclusion is false (for a subject) as soon as a subject disbelieves it.

I shall not work through all these points on the assumption that the cultural relativist is right about truth, except to note that matters are more complicated. For example, the skeptic may still be right if infalliblism is correct, for individuals will not have all true beliefs, because they will not agree with everything their culture believes. Furthermore, the skeptic may still have an opening if inferentialism is correct, for the subject will still have to infer from his own inner psychology to the facts that make his beliefs true, which would be what his culture believes. Regardless, all a culture has to believe is that most of its beliefs about the external world are justified, and the game is over.

2.4. Evaluating Relativism about Truth

Though individual relativism undermines the skeptic's argument, it will not pass muster. There are two reasons why this is so. The first is a dilemma: individual relativism is either self-refuting (contradictory) or dialectically ineffective (terminally unconvincing). Here is how Michael Lynch puts it:

> Suppose I am [an individual relativist] and announce that there is no such thing as truth per se, there is only truth-for-me and truth-for-you. A fair question to ask would be whether the statement I just made is true or just true-for-me. If I say that [individual relativism] is simply true, then I have apparently contradicted myself. For if [individual relativism] is true (for everyone, as it were) then it is false—it is not true that all truth is relative. On the other hand, if I go the other way and say that [individual relativism] is only true to me, I am consistent but unable to convince anyone who doesn't already agree with me. You need only remark that [individual relativism] is not true for you, and therefore false. [Individual relativism], therefore, is either contradictory or terminally unconvincing.
> (2004: 32–33)

In short, if individual relativism is absolutely true, then it is false, and if it is only relatively true, then it may be true only for the Relativist, not for anyone else.

The second reason individual relativism will not do—what Lynch calls the really "damning point" against relativism—is that it entails that I never make mistakes. But if "there is one thing I know, it is that I don't know everything" and that some of what I have believed has proven wrong, "and no theory that says otherwise can be true [nonrelatively] or true for me" (2004: 33). Just think of all the false beliefs you have had—for example, about how to get to a party, what kind of food is really good for you, what men (or women) really think about women (or men), what time the movie starts, how old the earth is, or what the Bible really says about divorce. If I know anything at all, I know that not everything I have believed is true, and hence not everything I have believed is true-for-me. The conviction that there is a gap between what we believe and what makes our beliefs true simply will not go away.[9]

These two points against individual relativism apply to cultural relativism as well. Is cultural relativism about truth non relatively true? If it is, then it is false. Is it true only for a culture? If so, it does not follow that it is true for any other cultures. The "relativist" culture will have nothing to say to the "non relativist" culture. And cultures make mistakes and change their minds, so to speak. Just as individuals know that they do not know everything, cultures recognize mistakes as well. If a culture knows anything at all, it knows that not everything it has believed is true, and hence not everything it has believed is true-for-the-culture. The gap between what a culture believes and what makes its beliefs true is just as real as the gap between what I believe and what makes my beliefs true. Once we clearly distinguish relativism about truth from some of the things it might be confused with (such as tolerance for difference, cultural pluralism, or a way of speaking about people's "worlds"), it loses any real appeal it might have had in the first place.

Would weakening the view so that only certain classes of our beliefs are "relatively true" make relativism about truth an effective reply to the skeptic? At best, it would be a first step at rebutting skepticism about those classes of belief. If relativism about morality is true, then perhaps radical skepticism about the jus-tification for moral beliefs will not get off the ground. But the radical skepticism we are interested in here—radical skepticism about the justification for beliefs about the external world—targets just the kind of class of beliefs where relativism about truth seems so implausible.

Relativism about truth is just one of many attempts (such as idealism, phe-nomenalism, and verificationism) designed to circumvent the skeptic's argument by denying the gap between mind and world, the gap between what we believe and the world that makes our beliefs true or false. But the gap, and so the possibility of massive error, is already built into the very nature of our thoughts about reality. There may be good reasons for thinking that *some* of our beliefs must be true, or that they must be true *in certain circumstances when the mind is forming beliefs in a certain way*. Other chapters in this volume discuss some of the various reasons other than relativism why some beliefs must be true, at least in certain circum-stances. Regardless, there are no good reasons for thinking that we cannot be massively mistaken in certain other circumstances, or when the mind is working in other ways, about nearly all subject matters.[10]

Relativism about truth, were it to be true, might defeat the skeptic right at the start. But defeating the skeptic is not so easy, for relativism about truth is not, if anything, true. Upon reflection, we would not accept relativism about truth. The skeptic's metaphysical premise seems secure.

Let me sum up so far. We began with the radical skeptic's claim that nothing we believe about the external world is even prima facie justified. We then examined the skeptic's argument, which essentially relies on (at least) two premises: a metaphysical or factual claim about the nature of truth and a normative or epis-temological claim about the nature of prima facie justification. We then described three normative views about justification that would, combined with the skeptic's view of truth, support the skeptic's radical conclusion: infallibilism, Cartesianism, and inferentialism (plus pessimism). To rebut the skeptic's argument, one would have to rebut either the skeptic's view of truth or the skeptic's view of justification. Relativism about truth was the relativist's attempt to rebut the skeptic's view of truth. But as we just concluded, relativism about truth just will not do. So if the relativist has an effective reply to the skeptic's argument, the relativist must deny the skeptic's theory of justification and offer a relativist theory of justification in its place.

3. Epistemic Principles

But before we turn to relativism about justification, it will prove useful to first talk about epistemic principles and systems. This will help us better understand relativism about justification and so better understand how the relativist about justification would respond to the radical skeptic. Instead of trying to give a general characterization of what I mean by an "epistemic principle," it may be best to just give a list. Here are twelve principles:

AP   If S comes to "see" that P is true based on sufficient understanding of P, and this causes or sustains S's belief that P in the normal way, then S's belief that P is prima facie justified.

INT   If it introspectively seems to S as if S is currently having a sensory, perceptual, or otherwise conscious experience E, and this causes or sustains in the normal way the belief that S is experiencing E, the S's belief that he is experiencing E is prima facie justified.

DED   If S believes P and believes (P entails Q) and believes Q on the basis of inferring Q from P and (P entails Q), then S's belief that Q is conditionally justified.

MEM   If S's memory system presents to S that P, and this causes or sustains in the normal way S's belief that P, then S's belief that P is prima facie justified.

EIND   If S possesses a sufficiently large and representative (nonbiased) inductive base where all (most) F s are G s, and S infers that all (most) F s are G s on that basis, then S's belief that all (most) F s are G s is prima facie justified.

IBE   If S possesses one explanation P that better explains S's evidence E than any other available alternative explanation, and S believes that P on the grounds that P best explains E, then S's belief that P is prima facie justified.

PER   If it perceptually seems to S as if an object x is F (where F is a perceptible property), and this causes or sustains in the normal

> way S's belief of x that it is F, then S's belief of x that it is F is prima facie justified.

TEST   If S (seemingly) comprehends a (seeming) presentation-as-true by a (seeming) speaker that P, and if this causes or sustains in the normal way S's belief that P, then S's belief that P is prima facie justified.

DRM   If S experiences P in a dream and comes to believe that P on the basis of that dream, then S's belief that P is prima facie justified.

REV   If S has a religious experience that P, and S comes to believe that P on the basis of that experience, then S's belief that P is prima facie justified.

ENT   If S cuts open a chicken and comes to believe that P by "reading" the entrails of the chicken, then S's belief that P is prima facie justified.

AST   If S reads an astrological chart and comes to believe P on that basis, then S's belief that P is prima facie justified.

Epistemic principles "govern" belief-forming processes: a priori insight or understanding, introspection of current mental episodes, perception, memory, linguistic comprehension ("testimony"), deductive reasoning, enumerative induction, explanatory inference, dreams, revelation, and reading chicken entrails and astrological charts. If one of these twelve principles is true, then the process it governs is among the "right" ways to form and sustain beliefs.

An epistemic *system* is simply a set of epistemic principles. Although many systems are possible, given the principles just listed, here are five that are commonly discussed, each one more inclusive than the last:

Reactionary	AP, INT, DED
Conservative	AP, INT, DED, MEM, EIND, IBE
Moderate	AP, INT, DED, MEM, EIND, IBE, PER
Liberal	AP, INT, DED, MEM, EIND, IBE, PER, TEST
Permissive	AP, INT, DED, MEM, EIND, IBE, PER, TEST, DRM, REV, ENT, AST

The reactionary system accepts just the first three principles. The conservative system adds the next three. The moderate includes the first seven. The liberal adds the eighth. And the permissive epistemologist includes them all. I am that sure the reader can think of more principles and more systems with even more imaginative labels.

Among contemporary epistemologists, only a few embrace the reactionary view. A good number hold the conservative view. The moderate view is very popular. Some hold the liberal view. Some social theorists and humanist intellectuals find the permissive view attractive.

Disagreements over the very nature of justification drive a good deal of the disagreement over which epistemic system is correct. Given a view about the nature of justification, certain principles turn out true, and others turn out false. We have already seen two views about the nature of justification that have clear consequences for the principles just listed. Recall the infallibilist who holds that justification supervenes on infallibility. The infallibilist thinks that all the principles are false, for none of the processes governed by the principles are infallible, except possibly DED, for deduction is conditionally infallible. The infallibilist holds a "nihilist" epistemic system, so to speak. The Cartesian, on the other hand, might embrace DED and qualified versions of AP and INT, for some very restricted forms of a priori insight and introspection might be reliable in all possible worlds. But the Cartesian will not embrace any of the other principles, for the other belief-forming processes are not apt to be reliable in all possible worlds.

Another view about the nature of justification is reliabilism. Reliabilism, in its simplest form, is the view that a belief-forming process confers prima facie justification on the beliefs it causes and sustains if and only if it is de facto reliable (i.e., as a matter of fact, it produces more true beliefs than not). Which principles are true is fixed by the de facto reliability of the relevant belief-forming processes. Since perception is, as a matter of fact, highly reliable, PER would turn out true if the reliabilist is correct, but DRM and AST clearly would not.[11]

Which principles are true matters for whether beliefs about the external world are prima facie justified. If PER is true, for instance, it pretty clearly follows that beliefs based on the normal functioning of the perceptual system—ordinary beliefs about the immediate external environment—are prima facie justified. So if PER is true, the radical skeptic is mistaken. But if the reactionary is right, then it pretty clearly follows that no belief about the external world is prima facie justified. So if the reactionary is right, the radical skeptic is too. And, as you may have already noticed, the inferentialist view defined earlier is exactly the same as the conservative view. So if the conservative and the pessimist are right, the skeptic wins again.

In the next section, I shall expound the relativist view about the nature of epistemic justification. Relativism about justification, like infalliblism, Cartesianism, and reliabilism, is a theory about the nature of justification, which in turn determines which ways of forming and sustaining beliefs confer prima facie justification. If the relativist is right about justification and if PER (or something very much like it) turns out correct on the relativist view, then the radical skeptic is disarmed.

4. RELATIVISM ABOUT JUSTIFICATION

4.1. Relativism about Justification Defined

Relativists about standards of correctness—about politesse, games, rules for driving a car, or morality, for example—think that what makes a standard true or correct is that it is held or embraced by an agent, whether one person, a group, an entire culture, or an entire species, where the standard applies only to the agent in question. For example, cultural relativists about standards of correct moral behavior think that what makes moral standards true is that the culture says that those are the correct standards, and those standards apply only to the behavior of members of the culture. If you are a member of a culture that says that it is right to tolerate differences in religion, hairstyle, and sexual orientation, then it is wrong for you not to tolerate those differences. But if you are a member of a culture that says that everyone should be Catholic, have short hair, and have sexual relations only with members of the opposite sex, then it is wrong for you to be a Protestant or Jew, grow your hair long, or romantically pursue someone of the same sex.

Relativism about epistemic justification is thus the view that what makes an epistemic principle true for a subject is that the subject (an individual, a group, a discipline, or a culture) embraces it, and the principle applies only to the subject that embraces it. For example, if you are a member of a discipline or culture that says that taking perceptual experience at face value as a guide to the external world confers prima facie justification, then when you noninferentially form the belief that you have hands on the basis of how things perceptually appear to you, your belief is prima facie justified. But if you are a member of a discipline or group that says that perceptual experience fails to prima facie justify beliefs about the external world, then that very same belief would not be prima facie justified. If you are a member of a culture that says that relying on astrological predictions is irrational, then when you read your horoscope in the morning to plan the rest of your day, your beliefs and plans are epistemically irrational. But if, on the other hand, you are a member of a culture that says that astrology is a rational way to form beliefs about the future, then not relying on astrological predictions would be a sign of epistemic irrationality.

Relativism about justification is the view that which epistemic principles are true (for you) depends upon which epistemic principles you (or your discipline or your culture) embrace. To be clear, from here on I will call this view relativism about epistemic principles. Relativism about epistemic prinicples, like relativism about morality, makes justification look a lot like legality. Just as we make laws, and which laws govern our behavior turns on which jurisdiction we are in, so too we "make" epistemic principles, and which principles "govern" your beliefs turns on which "epistemic jurisdiction" you are in. Epistemic principles, like laws, are socially constructed.

In what follows, I shall put individual relativism about epistemic principles to one side and focus on versions that see principles as made true by group acceptance. Cultural relativism is the most popular "group" view.[12]

Be sure not to confuse relativism about epistemic principles with the extremely radical view that a belief is justified for you if you believe it, and that is all there is to justification. On this radical view, everyone's beliefs, no matter what they believe, are all "equally justified" or "just as good as any other." The relativist about epistemic principles rejects this radically permissive view. Relativism about epistemic principles entails that beliefs are prima facie justified if and only if they accord with the principles embraced by a culture. Some beliefs will be held in accord with such principles, and some will not. As a result, some beliefs are prima facie justified, and some are not. Relativism about epistemic principles thus does *not* support the radical view that *any* belief, no matter what is believed, is justified. This extremely radical view, like its twin, individual relativism about truth, simply will not do. Either it is justified full stop, in which case it is false, or it is justified only for those who believe it. And just as we do not believe that everything we have ever believed is true, so too we do not believe that everything we have ever believed is just as justified or rational as everything else we have ever believed. Upon reflection, we would not embrace radical relativism about justification.

If relativism about epistemic principles is a view about what *makes* an epistemic principle true, then given the facts, *which* principles are true? To find out, one would have to find out which principles we embrace. Finding the correct answer might require sociological or anthropological investigation. But depending upon the referent of "we," one might argue that any system might be embraced. There could be groups that embrace only a few of the principles. There could be reactionary or conservative "epistemic communities" that espouse fewer principles. There could be moderate communities that think that perception is okay, but testimony is suspect until proven innocent. There could be liberal, permissive, or any number of other "epistemic" communities. The relativist allows for a whole range of possible epistemic system. We shall return to this possible range later. And, as I noted at the end of the previous section, which system is correct clearly matters for whether the radical skeptic is right. So we want to know whether the relativist about epistemic principles has a good normative reply to the skeptic.

4.2. Contemporary Pragmatism as Relativism about Justification

But before I discuss relativism about epistemic principles as a response to the skeptic, I want to argue that contemporary pragmatists about justification embrace, or are at least sympathetic to, relativism about epistemic principles. Contemporary pragmatists include Richard Rorty, Michael Williams, and Gary

Gutting, among others. Some of their influences include Wittgenstein, Quine, Sellars, and the "classical" pragmatists, James and Dewey.

A central aspect of the (contemporary) pragmatist view is that epistemic justification or rationality is largely an intersubjective affair; justification supervenes on winning agreement (actual or ideal). On this criterion, justification is dialectical. In Rorty's terms, "conversation" replaces "confrontation" (1979a: 170). There is no "ahistorical" ideal of rationality or justification to be discovered and to follow; there is "simply the process of justifying beliefs to audiences" (Rorty 1994: 36). "Justification . . . is just a matter of being able to give good reasons (put forward adequate supporting propositions) for the belief [where] the norms specifying 'good reasons' and 'adequate support' are themselves based on the agreement of an epistemic community" (Gutting 2003: 44). What matters for justification are contingent, contextual, varying features of conversation (Williams 1999: 186–189; 2001: 148–150, 159–162).

Contemporary pragmatists think that the norms specifying good reasons and adequate support are made rather than found; they are constructed by us and not discovered through inquiry into what is there already, independently of our practices. Pragmatists think that we *make* our norms; they are standards we impose on ourselves. The norms are not real features of the mind- or practice-independent world that inquiry might reveal. Here is Michael Williams:

> Norms, including epistemic norms, are standards that we set, not standards imposed on us by "the nature of epistemic justification". A belief is no more justified, wholly independent of human evaluative practices, than a certain kind of tackle in [soccer] is a foul, wholly independent of our practices of judging certain types of tackle to be against the rules. . . . The view I am recommending can be considered a pragmatic conception of norms.
>
> (2001: 170–171)

The pragmatist holds that "there is nothing to be said about . . . rationality apart from descriptions of the familiar procedures of justification which a given society . . . uses in one or another area of inquiry" (Rorty 1985: 23).

Pragmatism is not itself about *which* norms are true, but about *why* any norm is true. "Epistemological [pragmatism] is not a view about the content of the norms involved in our practice of justification, but only about the ultimate basis of these norms. Its claim is that, in the final analysis, there is nothing underlying these norms other than the practice they define" (Gutting 2003: 52). These epistemic "norms have no basis outside of the community itself" (Gutting 2003: 49).

On this view, a belief is prima facie justified just in case it conforms to the epistemic norms of the community, where the norms of the community are patterns of epistemic praise and blame. So, for example, if I believe that there is a blue pen in my hand on the basis of how things perceptually appear to me, then my belief is prima facie justified just in case my community tends to praise beliefs based on perceptual belief as justified. My belief is prima facie justified just in case my community "embraces" the epistemic principle PER. Epistemic principles, if not strictly speaking the *same* as epistemic norms, certainly look like a *species* of epistemic norms, as a part of the entire pragmatist picture. What makes principles true? We do.

We can thus fairly characterize contemporary pragmatism about justification as relativism about epistemic principles. A passage from Rorty should solidify my case:

> "Relativism" is the traditional epithet applied to pragmatism by realists. . . . [Different] views are commonly referred to by ["relativism"]. [One] is the view that every belief is as good as any other. . . . [Another] is the view that there is nothing to be said about . . . rationality apart from descriptions of the familiar procedures of justification which a given society—*ours*—uses in one or another area of inquiry. The pragmatist holds the [latter] . . . view.
>
> (1985: 23; cf. 1979b: 166–169)[13]

Rorty is not a *radical* or *extreme* relativist about justification, where any belief is just as justified as any other, but he is a relativist about what makes epistemic principles true, for all that. Contemporary pragmatists are relativists about epistemic principles.

4.3. Relativism about Justification as a Response to Radical Skepticism

I now discuss how relativism about epistemic principles works as a normative response to radical skepticism. Recall that a normative response challenges the skeptic's view about what justification requires, and so challenges the skeptic's view that either infalliblism or Cartesianism or inferentialism sets the correct standard for prima facie justification, where either the nihilist (infalliblist), reactionary (Cartesian), or conservative (inferentialist) epistemic system is the correct system. An adequate normative response would show that in fact, the moderate epistemic system (or any of the other more inclusive epistemic systems), which includes the epistemic principle PER, is the correct epistemic system. If PER is true, then ordinary perceptual beliefs about the external world are prima facie justified, and the skeptic is mistaken, even if massive error about the external world is possible. So, if relativism about epistemic principles is true, is PER true?

The relativist's answer is yes *and* no. The relativist would say yes because as a matter of fact, every culture that we know of tends to praise beliefs based on perception, and so every culture that we know of embraces PER or something very much like it. Given the sociological, anthropological, and cultural facts, beliefs about the external world based on perception turn out to be prima facie justified if the relativist about epistemic principles is correct.[14]

On the other hand, the relativist also has grounds for saying that PER is false, for there are communities that suspend their ordinary endorsement of PER and embrace a more restrictive epistemic system. One such community, a relativist might suggest, is the "traditional epistemological community." The traditional epistemological community adopts either the reactionary or the conservative epistemic system. It does not praise perceptual beliefs without inferential backing from beliefs about one's own mind. Beliefs about the external world are justified only if the members of the community, when engaged in "traditional epistemological inquiry," can show, on the basis of evidence available to introspection and reflection alone, that the real-world hypothesis best explains their inner lives. In such a community, PER is false. And if the pessimist is right, then members in that community are not entitled to beliefs about the external world. But this is only a small community, and members of this community switch their epistemic systems as soon as they return to ordinary life, life defined (in part) by its acceptance of a more inclusive epistemic system, a system that includes PER. When they are sitting in the office, their beliefs about pens, tables, and chairs are not prima facie justified. But once they turn off the computer and head home, their beliefs about pens, subways, and superhighways are prima facie justified.

So if relativism about epistemic principles is correct, and if as a matter of fact we embrace a moderate or an even more inclusive epistemic system, then our beliefs about the external world are prima facie justified, even if massive error is possible. The skeptic is thus pretty clearly mistaken nearly all the time. However, the skeptic is sometimes right, provided that there are "disciplines" or "domains of inquiry" that embrace a more restrictive epistemic system, and provided that in those domains one cannot inferentially bridge the gap between mind and our ordinary, garden-variety beliefs about the external world.

4.4. Relativism about Justification Evaluated

Relativism about epistemic principles, if true, would undermine the skeptic's normative premise. The skeptic's conclusion, that our beliefs about the external world are not even prima facie justified, would be, for the most part, false. Common sense would turn out correct, where not *every* belief is prima facie justified, but most of our garden-variety beliefs about the external world are. But is relativism about epistemic principles true? Would we, upon reflection, accept it? Or is it just as unpalatable as the skeptical conclusion itself? Evaluating relativism about epistemic principles fairly would, I believe, require at least another chapter as long as this one already is. However, I would like to close by raising two points in its favor and then posing a question for the relativist.

Recall the silly skeptical argument that concluded that there were no teachers because no one knew all completed physics. This argument is silly because it sets a silly standard for what it takes to be a teacher. Knowing completed physics is not *our* standard for being a teacher. A good amount of recent discussion of skeptical arguments about knowledge and justification thinks that for a skeptical argument to be worth taking seriously, it must rely on our ordinary standards for knowledge or justified belief, not artificially high or made-up standards. It must not impose a standard on justified belief that is not *our* standard. To see whether the skeptic has a serious challenge to common sense, we should thus investigate what our standards for justification really are. The relativist's point is that if we really do that—if we really go and look and see which standards we accept and which ones we do not—we shall find that we do not accept any of the skeptic's standards (infallibilism, Cartesianism, or even inferentialism) about justification. If we go and look, we shall find that nearly every culture has no fundamental problem with beliefs about the external world based on perception. The skeptic's standards do not seem to be *our* standards. Upon reflection, we seem to embrace the standards the relativist says we do. The relativist, and not the skeptic, is more in tune with exactly what our standards are.

A second and related point in favor of relativism involves the fact that *sometimes* the skeptic does seem to be right; the skeptic does sometimes hold our attention, though at other times she does not. A good deal of recent discussion in epistemology tries to "explain" just why this is so, to explain why in some contexts we do not find the skeptic's conclusion attractive, but in other contexts we do. The relativist might have a very nice explanation of why this is so. We reject the skeptic's conclusion in ordinary life because there we are (at least) moderates about epistemic justification. But the skeptic is sometimes right because in some contexts we embrace less inclusive epistemic systems that make beliefs about the external world seem hard or even impossible to justify. So I think that there are two points in favor of relativism about epistemic justification: it is in tune with our ordinary standards, and it has a natural explanation for the context sensitivity of skeptical doubts.

I want to end my discussion with a question for the relativist. Recall from section 2.2 that the realist about truth can accept the anthropological claim that the beliefs of individuals and cultures vary greatly without accepting the individual relativist view of truth that all there is to truth is belief. The anthropology of belief is one thing; truth is another. Why cannot a "realist" about justification make a similar point? Why cannot he accept the anthropological discovery that cultures embrace epistemic systems, some more restrictive and others more inclusive, without accepting the relativist view that what *makes* an epistemic system correct is that a culture embraces it? Why cannot perceptual beliefs about the external world be justified even if no culture ever embraced PER? Why is not the truth of PER a "real" fact, independent of culture or group practice? Why is it that epistemic principles are *made* rather than *found*?

NOTES

I am grateful to John Greco and Masahiro Yamada for comments that led to improvements.

1. There are many forms of skepticism. Radical skepticism (as I have defined it) is the view that our beliefs about the external world are not even prima facie justified (they are not even initially credible). A related but weaker kind of skepticism holds that though

ordinary beliefs are prima facie justified and often on balance justified, they are no longer on balance justified once "skeptical" possibilities are mentioned, considered, or even
taken seriously. On this other form of skepticism, common sense comes out right only if
we succeed in ignoring or not considering those possibilities, such as the possibility that
we might all be in the Matrix. I shall table this other form of skepticism and focus instead
on radical skepticism, which would be true (if it is) even if we never even considered
skeptical possibilities. Another form of skepticism is dialectical skepticism, which claims
that one cannot show, on the basis of reflection alone, that one's beliefs about the external
world are justified or true. Still another form of skepticism is just about knowledge; it
grants that many of our beliefs about external reality are justified, all things considered, but
denies that they measure up to knowledge. I shall also table these other two kinds of
skepticism.

2. Since I shall discuss two kinds of relativism, as well as radical skepticism, I shall not
have room to discuss a number of questions an interested reader might want to see me
address. For instance, I shall not discuss the case for relativism about truth or the standard
argument for relativism about justification. And though I shall criticize relativism about
truth, I shall not criticize relativism about justification. For more on relativism generally,
interested readers may wish to consult Swoyer (2003) and Blackburn (2005). For arguments for and against relativism about justification in particular, readers should consult
Boghossian (2005) and Luper (2004).

3. I have compressed two premises here that a more adequate treatment would distinguish: (a) determinism is true, and (b) determinism is incompatible with moral responsibility. For the purpose of illustrating how skeptical arguments go, nothing here
hangs on this.

4. The realist is not, I think, committed to a philosophically loaded correspondence
theory of truth, with "propositions" (understood as a certain kind of abstracta) and "facts"
(understood as entities with logical structure) that "correspond" in some way with one
another. Though a robust or "loaded" correspondence theory of truth is compatible with
realism, all the realist insists is that whatever we say about the nature of truth, we must
allow for the possibility of massive error, on the grounds that our beliefs about the world
are one thing, and the world is another.

5. "Cartesianism" is just a label. I use it intentionally to invoke associations with
Descartes and contemporary philosophers who see themselves as following in Descartes'
footsteps, but I do not mean to imply that Descartes actually held such a view of "epistemic
justification," of reasonable or rational belief.

6. Elsewhere I have lumped the infallibilist and the Cartesian together under the label
"Cartesianism." The general "Cartesian" idea is that justification requires a very high
degree of reliability across possible worlds: either every-instance reliability (infallibility), or
every-possible-world reliability.

7. The inferentialist view is like the Cartesian view in two respects. First, both are
fallibilist; not every justified belief must be true. Second, they agree that any justified beliefs
about the external world must be inferred from beliefs about the subject's own mind. The
Cartesian believes this because the Cartesian thinks that only introspective awareness of
one's own mind is apt to be reliable in all possible worlds, so to justifiably believe anything
about the external world, the subject would have to infer from beliefs about her own mind
to beliefs about the external world. But on the Cartesian view, no such inference will
succeed, for any inference to the external world would involve either enumerative induction or inference to the best explanation, and those two forms of reasoning are not

reliable in all possible worlds. Now we can see where the inferentialist and the Carteisan disagree: the inferentialist allows the use of inference to the best explanation to bridge the gap between the mind (on the one hand) and the world (on the other). The inferentialist, unlike the Cartesian, allows for the possibility of a good inference from how things appear to the subject to how things are in the external world.

8. One might reasonably wonder whether there are other theories of justification that would support the skeptic's conclusion. There clearly are silly ones, like the view that belief is justified iff 2+2=67. But among seriously held views of justification, these three are the only ones, I think, that clearly do support the skeptic's conclusion. For more discussion, see my article "The Theoretical Diagnosis of Skepticism" (Graham 2007).

9. Of course, we might further relativize truth to times (so that all beliefs are true at the times held, so that my belief that p at t is true, and my belief that not-p at $t+1$ is also true, so it turns out that everything I have believed is still "true for me"). But now the view has really gone off the deep end.

10. As Richard Foley puts it, "A plausibility constraint on any proposed account of belief is that it not rule out, *a priori*, the possibility of extensive error" (2001: 38).

11. For additional discussion of the interplay between theories of justification and epistemic systems, see my "Theorizing Justification" (Graham forthcoming b) and "Liberal Fundamentalism and Its Rivals" (Graham 2006).

12. Richard Foley (1993) defends an individual relativist (what he calls "subjectivist foundationalist") view of justification.

13. Michael Williams rejects "relativism" about justification in a number of places (for one, see 1999: chap. 19). He would certainly reject some aspects of my characterization of relativism about justification. But his core reason for preferring the label "pragmatism" or "contextualism" to the label "relativism" seems to be the idea that the relativist thinks that (a) any number of epistemic principles might be true if embraced by a culture, and (b) that these principles are "immune from rational criticism," so that if the relativist is right, there might be any number of uncriticizable "epistemic frameworks" or "normal epistemo-logical views," all just as good as the other, with no possibility of rational criticism. And this very idea, Williams insists, the "contextualist" rejects. So "contextualism" is not relativism.

Since this is not the place to pursue this issue at any length, let me briefly state how I see Williams's position. I think that he really does favor relativism about epistemic principles; he holds a relativist metaepistemological view about what makes epistemic norms true. However, as an anthropological, social, historical matter of fact, Williams thinks that the "core" norms that we embrace are closer to the liberal view, where some of the norms we embrace over time may change because reliance upon one conflicts with reliance upon another. For example, astrology was once practiced, but it fell apart because of advances in physical theory. AST was displaced by reasoning in accord with PER, EIND, IBE, and other forms of reasoning and inquiry. In fact we have a core system that is stable, and other norms get rejected because they conflict with the core. When he rejects "rela-tivism," he is rejecting the anthropological claim that there is a plurality of epistemic systems. He thus accepts relativism as a philosophical view about the grounds of epistemic systems while rejecting it as an anthropological claim about real epistemic systems. Or so it seems to me.

14. If there are cultures that reject this, then radical skepticism is true for them. Maybe some Eastern philosophies or even Greek Pyrrhonists reject PER.

REFERENCES

Blackburn, Simon (2005). *Truth* (Oxford: Oxford University Press).

Boghossian, Paul (2005). *Fear of Knowledge* (Oxford: Oxford University Press).

Edwards, Paul (1955). "Mr. Russell's Doubts about Induction." In A. Flew, ed., *Logic and Language*, First Series (Oxford: Oxford University Press).

Foley, Richard (1993). *Working without a Net* (Oxford: Oxford University Press).

———. (2001). *Intellectual Trust in Oneself and Others* (New York: Cambridge University Press).

Graham, Peter J. (2006). "Liberal Fundamentalism and Its Rivals." In J. Lackey and E. Sosa, eds., *The Epistemology of Testimony* (Oxford: Oxford University Press).

———. (2007). "The Theoretical Diagnosis of Skepticism." *Synthese* 158, no. 1: 19–39.

———. (Forthcoming). "Theorizing Justification." In M. O'Rourke, ed., *Knowledge and Skepticism* (Cambridge, MA: MIT Press).

Gutting, Gary (2003). "Rorty's Critique of Epistemology." In C. Guignon and D. Hiley, eds., *Richard Rorty* (New York: Cambridge University Press).

Luper, Steven (2004). "Epistemic Relativism." *Philosophical Issues* 14, no. 1: 271–95.

Lynch, Michael (2004). *True to Life* (Cambridge, MA: MIT Press).

Rorty, Richard (1979a). *Philosophy and the Mirror of Nature* (Princeton: Princeton University Press).

———. (1979b). "Pragmatism, Relativism, and Irrationalism?" In Rorty 1982.

———. (1982). *Consequences of Pragmatism* (Minneapolis: University of Minnesota Press).

———. (1985). "Solidarity or Objectivity?" In Rorty 1991.

———. (1991). *Objectivity, Relativism, and Truth: Philosophical Papers 1* (Cambridge).

———. (1994). "Truth without Correspondence to Reality." In Rorty 1999.

———. (1999). *Philosophy and Social Hope* (New York: Penguin Books).

Swoyer, Chris, "Relativism," The Stanford Encyclopedia of Philosophy (Spring 2003 Edition), Edward N. Zalta (ed.), URL = <http://plato.stanford.edu/archives/spr2003/entries/relativism/>

Vogel, Jonathan (2005). "The Refutation of Skepticism." In M. Steup and E. Sosa, eds. *Contemporary Debates in Epistemology* (Boston: Blackwell Publishing).

Williams, Michael (1999). *Groundless Belief* (Princeton: Princeton University Press) (originally published 1977).

———. (1991). *Unnatural Doubts: Epistemological Realism and the Basis of Skepticism* (Princeton: Princeton University Press).

———. (2001). *Problems of Knowledge* (Oxford: Oxford University Press).

PART III

CONTEMPORARY ISSUES

CHAPTER 19

ASCRIBER CONTEXTUALISM

STEWART COHEN

1. THE MAIN IDEA

Ascriber contextualism (hereafter "contextualism") in epistemology is the view that the truth conditions for sentences containing "know" and its cognates are context sensitive. For simplicity's sake, let us focus on sentences of the form "S knows P." To say that the truth conditions for a sentence or utterance of the form "S knows P" are context sensitive is to say that the truth conditions of the sentence or utterance will depend on features of the ascriber's situation or context.

We can best understand the distinctiveness of the contextualist view by contrasting it with a traditional invariantist view. According to traditional invariantism, whether an utterance of "S knows P" is true will depend on whether S's epistemic position with respect to P is sufficiently strong. Epistemologists differ on what it is for an epistemic position to be strong. Evidentialists hold that the strength of one's epistemic position with respect to P is a function of the strength of one's evidence for P. Reliabilists hold that the strength of one's epistemic position with respect to P is a function of the reliability of one's belief in P.

How strong does S's epistemic position with respect to P have to be in order to be sufficiently strong—in order for "S knows P" to be true? Although traditional invariantist views may differ in how they answer this question, all invariantist views agree that whatever the required strength is, it is the same for all ascriber contexts. That is, whether or not S is in a sufficiently strong epistemic position with respect to P will not depend in any way on who is uttering the sentence "S knows P."

It is precisely this point that contextualism denies. According to contextualism, how strong S's epistemic position has to be with respect to *P* in order for "S knows *P*" to be true will depend on the context of ascription, that is, on who is uttering the sentence. A striking consequence of this view is that with respect to a subject S, a proposition *P*, and a time *t*, a speaker in one context could say that "S knows *P* at *t*" while another speaker in a different context says that "S does not know *P* at *t*," and each speaker could be speaking the truth. This consequence results from the fact that the truth conditions for "S knows *P*" can differ between the two contexts. That is, the standard for how strong S's epistemic position must be in order for "S knows *P*" to be true can vary between the two contexts. This allows for the possibility that S's epistemic position may meet the standard of one context while failing to meet the standard of the other context.

Fundamentally, contextualism is a semantic thesis, a thesis about the meaning of the word "know" and its cognates. The core idea is that different uses of sentences involving "know" will refer to different standards (for the strength of epistemic position required). Contextualists argue that the way "know" functions can be likened to other words like "flat."[1] Most would agree that sentences of the form "*X* is flat" will have different truth conditions in different contexts. So under ordinary circumstances, one may truly say, "Table *T* is flat." But in another context, where our purpose is to conduct a sensitive scientific experiment, we could truly say, "Table *T* is not flat." We might also be able to truly say, "Table *T* is not flat" in a context where the microscopic variations in the surface of *T* have been made salient. This shows that the standard for how flat a surface *T* must be in order for "*T* is flat" to express a truth will vary across contexts.[2]

2. MOTIVATIONS FOR CONTEXTUALISM

Two main kinds of argument have been given for contextualism. The first argument proceeds from our intuitive reactions to certain cases. Here is one such case:

> Mary and John are at the L.A. airport contemplating taking a certain flight to New York. They want to know whether the flight has a layover in Chicago. They overhear someone ask a passenger Smith if he knows whether the flight stops in Chicago. Smith looks at the flight itinerary he got from the travel agent and responds, "Yes I know—it does stop in Chicago." It turns out that Mary and John have a very important business contact they have to make at the Chicago airport. Mary says, "How reliable is that itinerary? It could contain a misprint. They could have changed the schedule at the last minute. Smith does not know the plane stops in Chicago," John agrees with Mary, and they decide to check with the airline agent.[3]

What should we say about this case? Smith claims to know that the flight stops in Chicago. Mary and John deny that Smith knows this. Mary and John seem to be using a stricter standard than Smith for how good one's reasons have to be in order to know. Whose standard is correct? Let us consider several competing answers:

1. Mary and John's stricter standard is too strong. That is, Smith's standard is correct, and so Smith can know that the flight stops in Chicago (on the basis of consulting the itinerary).

Is this a good answer? If we say that contrary to what both Mary and John presuppose, the weaker standard is correct, then we would have to say that their use of the word "know" is incorrect. But then it is hard to see how Mary and John should describe their situation. Certainly they are being prudent in refusing to rely on the itinerary. They have a very important meeting in Chicago. Yet if Smith knows on the basis of the itinerary that the flight stops in Chicago, what should they have said? "Okay, Smith knows that the flight stops in Chicago, but still, we need to check further." To my ear, it is hard to make sense of that claim. Moreover, if what is printed in the itinerary is a good-enough reason for Smith to know, then it is a good-enough reason for John and Mary to know. Thus Mary should have said, "Okay, *we* know the plane stops in Chicago, but still, we need to check further." Again, it is hard to make sense of such a claim.

Perhaps, then, the correct answer is the following:

2. John and Mary are right, and so Smith's standard is too weak. (Smith cannot know, but John and Mary can know after checking further with the agent.)

I think that this is a natural response to this case as I have described it. But notice that this contrasts with the standards we typically use for knowledge ascriptions. In everyday contexts, we readily ascribe knowledge to someone on the basis of written information contained in things like flight itineraries. If we deny that Smith knows, then we have to deny that we know in many of the everyday cases in which we claim to know. We would have to say that a considerable amount of the time in our everyday lives, we speak falsely when we say that we know things. Moreover, we could describe a case where even Mary and John's standard does not seem strict enough: If someone's life were at stake, we might not even be willing to ascribe knowledge on the basis of the testimony of the airline agent. We might insist on checking with the pilot. This suggests a third alternative:

3. Both Smith's and Mary and John's standards are too weak.

This option leads to skepticism regarding a great deal of what we ordinarily claim to know. Presumably, skepticism is something we want to avoid.

So far, we have examined three different answers to the question of whose standard is correct: (1) Smith's is correct, and so John and Mary's standard is too strong. (2) John and Mary's standard is correct, and so Smith's standard is too weak. (3) Neither Smith's nor John and Mary's standard is correct—both are too weak. None of these answers seems satisfactory. This opens the door for the contextualist to claim that neither standard is simply correct or simply incorrect. Rather, context determines which standard is correct. Since the standards for knowledge ascriptions can vary across contexts, each claim, Smith's, as well as Mary's, can be correct in the context in which it was made. When Smith says, "I know the plane stops in Chicago," what he says is true, given the weaker standard operating in that context. When Mary says, "Smith does not know the plane stops in Chicago," what she says is true, given the stricter standard operating in her context. And there is no context-independent correct standard.[4]

3. SKEPTICAL PARADOXES

The second kind of motivation for contextualism is that it provides a resolution of a difficult skeptical paradox. The paradox comprises three jointly inconsistent propositions, each of which seems intuitively to be true. We can begin to construct the paradox by noting that there are many propositions that ordinarily we claim to know. Consider an example: If I parked my car in lot 2 and remember doing so, then intuitively, I can know that my car is parked in lot 2.

Now consider a skeptical alternative to the proposition that my car is parked in lot 2, namely, that my car has been stolen. Although I have some statistical evidence that my car has not been stolen, intuitively, that is not sufficient for me to know that my car has not been stolen. Finally, consider the proposition that if I know that my car is parked in lot 2, then I know that my car has not been stolen. This proposition seems intuitively compelling. How could I know that my car is parked in lot 2 if I do not know that it has not been stolen? This third proposition follows from what is sometimes called "the deductive closure principle for knowledge":

(DC) If S knows P, and S know that P entails Q, then S knows (or, at least, is in a position to know) Q.

This principle seems very hard to deny, and it explains our acceptance of the proposition that if I know that my car is parked in lot 2, then I know that my car has not been stolen.

These considerations leave us with three propositions, each of which seems intuitively to be true:

1. I know that my car is parked in lot 2.
2. I do not know that my car has not been stolen.
3. If I know that my car is parked in lot 2, then I know that my car has not been stolen.

The paradox arises because these propositions that seem intuitively to be true are jointly inconsistent. This means that we must give up at least one proposition that we find intuitively to be true. The skeptic would enjoin us to give up (1). According to the skeptic, the fact that (2) and (3) are true gives us good reason to deny (1). Because we can construct analogous arguments against almost any claim to empirical knowledge, this view leads to a very general skepticism.[5] But presumably, we want to avoid skepticism.

If we wish to avoid this skeptical result, there are two options. First, we could argue from the fact that (2) is false. But this position seems hard to sustain. Again, although I have some statistical evidence that my car has not been stolen, that does not seem sufficient for me to know that my car has not been stolen.

The other option for avoiding the skeptical result is to deny (3). Denying (3) would entail denying the deductive closure principle for knowledge.[6] But it seems very puzzling how this principle could be false. Many take it as axiomatic. How could I know one proposition, know that it entails a second proposition, yet fail (to at least be in a position) to know the second proposition? In the case we have been considering, how could I know that my car is parked in lot 2 if I do not know that it has not been stolen?

So none of these options for denying one member of the inconsistent triad seems palatable. Of course, this just underscores that we are confronting a paradox. A successful resolution of the paradox must do more than argue that one of the propositions is false. This would leave us with the question why it seems intuitively true. A successful resolution of the paradox must not only deny one proposition from the inconsistent triad, it must explain why we mistakenly thought that the proposition was true.

This is just what contextualists allege that their theory can do. According to contextualism, the sentences that express the inconsistent triad do not have a truth-value *simpliciter*. Rather, each will be true or false in some context. According to contextualism, the paradox results from our shifting contexts as we consider the different members of the triad. I start in an everyday context in which my epistemic position is strong enough for (1) to be true. In that context, my epistemic position is strong enough for (2) to be false as well. But when I actually consider (2), I shift to a context governed by stricter standards. My epistemic position fails to meet the strict standards of this new context. So in this strict context, (2) is true and (1) is false. So according to contextualism, in ordinary contexts, (1) is true and (2) is false, and in stricter contexts, (1) is false and (2) is true. There is no context in which both (1) and (2) are true, so (3) remains true in every context. Thus contextualism can explain why each proposition of the triad seems true while still holding that in every context, at least one member of the triad is false. Although (1) is false in stricter contexts, its intuitive appeal results from our considering it in an ordinary context, and although (2) is false in ordinary contexts, the appeal of (2) results from our considering it in a stricter context. The fact that (3) is true in every context reflects the axiomatic status of the closure principle.

Contextualists use the same strategy for skeptical paradoxes involving global skeptical hypotheses:

4. I know that I have a hand.
5. I do not know that I am not a brain in a vat.
6. If I know that I have a hand, then I do not know that I am not a brain in a vat.

According to contextualism, in everyday contextsm (4) is true and (5) is false. In stricter contexts, (4) is false and (5) is true. And (6) is true in every context.[7]

4. THE MECHANISM OF CONTEXT SHIFTING

We have seen that the contextualist holds that different contexts of ascription can have different standards for the truth of sentences containing "know" and its cognates. In particular, we have seen that certain contexts have standards that are stricter than the standards of typical or ordinary contexts. What explains why some contexts have stricter standards? Although contextualist theories differ on details, a common thread is that the salience of error possibilities in a context tends to drive up the standards.[8] Consider again the case of John and Mary at the airport. When, in response to a normal query, Smith consults his flight itinerary and says, "I know the plane stops in Chicago," intuitively, what he says is true. As we noted earlier, we readily allow that we can come to know things on the basis of written information contained in things like flight itineraries. But when we consider the situation of John and Mary, intuitively, they speak the truth when they say, "Smith does not know the plane stops in Chicago." We can appeal to the mechanism of salience to explain the shift. Because it is very important to John and Mary whether the plane stops in Chicago, error possibilities become salient to them. That is, it is very natural for John and Mary to think about the possibilities that the itinerary contains a misprint or that the route has changed. Because these error possibilities are salient, the standards rise so that when Mary says, "Smith does not know the plane stops in Chicago," what she says is true.

We can also explain how the skeptical paradox arises by appealing to the salience of error possibilities. We normally allow that we can express mundane truths by saying things like "I know my car is parked in lot 2." Given closure, if I know that my car is parked in lot 2, then I know, or at least am in a position to know, that my car has not been stolen. But when we actually consider (2), the possibility that my car has been stolen becomes salient. This raises the standards to the point where "I know my car has not been stolen" and "I know my car is parked in lot 2" are false. So we end up evaluating sentence (2) of the skeptical paradox by a higher standard than the standard by which we initially evaluated sentence (1). Once we are in the high-standards context, sentence (1) will be false. But common sense can reassert itself and lead us to shift back to a context where (1) is true and (2) is false.[9] Positing these kinds of contextual shifts explains why we often vacillate between skepticism and common sense.

5. VERSIONS OF CONTEXTUALISM

Perhaps the three most discussed versions of contextualism are those of David Lewis (1996), Keith DeRose (1995), and myself (Cohen 1988, 1999). I formulate my view in terms of a traditional concept of justification where having justification for believing P is a matter of having good evidence or good reasons for believing P. I attempt to exploit the analogy between "flat" and "justified." Just as we can say that one road is flatter than another, we can also say that one belief is more justified than another. We saw earlier how context determines a standard for how flat a surface T must be in order for "T is flat" to be true. For example, the sentence "The road is flat" might be true in the mouth of a resident of Colorado, but false in the mouth of a resident of Kansas. I claim that analogously, context determines the standard for how justified one's belief P must be in order for "P is justified" to be true. Since "S knows P" is true only if "S's belief in P is justified" is true, we can view the context sensitivity of "knows" as deriving from the context sensitivity of "justified." So on my view, context will determine how justified for S a belief P must be in order for "S knows P" to be true in that context.[10] As we noted earlier, the standards for how justified a belief P must be in order for "S knows P" to be true will rise when error possibilities are salient. So in normal everyday contexts, my belief that my car is parked in lot 2 is sufficiently justified for "I know my car is parked in lot 2" to be true. But when error possibilities become salient, for example, when we focus on the possibility that my car has been stolen, we shift into a stricter context where my belief that my car is parked in lot 2 is no longer sufficiently justified for "I know my car is parked in lot 2" to be true. It is important to note that in the stricter context, my justification is no longer sufficient even though my level of justification remains the same as in the everyday context. What changes is not the level of justification but rather the standard for what counts as sufficient justification.

For David Lewis, the context sensitivity of "know" derives from the natural language phenomenon of quantifier domain restriction. In natural language, the word "every" will range over different domains in different contexts. If I am in a group that is climbing a mountain, and I say, "Everyone made it," what I said is true even if other climbers in other groups did not make it. When I said "everyone," I was talking about only the members of my group. Later on, I might say,

"Everyone was terrified by the avalanche," where I am now talking about everyone on the mountain.

For Lewis, knowledge ascriptions involve an implicit quantification. To say that "S knows P"is to say that S can eliminate every alternative to P except those alternatives that are properly ignored. The second clause makes explicit the restriction on the domain of "every" in the first clause. Instances of "S knows P" come out as context sensitive because of the context sensitivity of "every" in "S can eliminate every alternative." Which alternatives are in the domain of "every," that is, what counts as a relevant alternative, will depend on the context.

Lewis also draws an analogy between "know" and "flat." Following Unger (1975), Lewis claims that we can view ascriptions of flatness as involving an implicit quantification. To say that a surface is flat is to say that it has no bumps. But which bumps are in the domain? That is, what counts as a relevant bump? This is a matter that depends on context.

So for Lewis, when we utter a sentence of the form "S knows P," context will determine which set of alternatives S must be able to eliminate in order for instances of "S knows P" to be true. In different contexts, "S knows P" will refer to different sets of relevant alternatives. For Lewis, the standards for the truth of "S knows P" rise when the domain of relevant alternatives expands, and one way to expand the domain is by making various error possibilities, that is, alternatives, salient.[11] So in a normal everyday context, "I know my car is parked in lot 2" can be true because I can eliminate every relevant alternative. But considering skeptical alternatives, for example, that my car has been stolen, expands the domain of relevant alternatives to include the possibility that my car has been stolen. In this new context, "I know my car is parked in lot 2" will be false because I cannot eliminate this relevant alternative.[12]

DeRose's view exploits Dretske and Nozick's idea of tracking. For DeRose, "S knows P" will be true provided that "one's belief as to whether P is true match[es] the fact of the matter as to whether P is true, not only in the actual world, but also at the worlds sufficiently close to the actual world."[13] How far out from the actual world must one's belief as to whether P matches the fact as to whether P in order for one to know P? On DeRose's view, this will depend on context. Let us say that when one's belief as to whether P matches the fact in a particular world as to whether P, one's belief tracks the truth in that world. According to what DeRose calls "the rule of sensitivity," in contexts where we are considering whether an instance of "S knows P" is true, one's belief as to whether P must track the truth out to the nearest not-P world(s). So suppose that we are considering whether "I know my car is parked in lot 2" is true. On DeRose's view, this creates a context where in order for "I know my car is parked in lot 2" to be true, my belief as to whether my car is parked in lot 2 must track the truth out to the nearest world(s) where my car is not parked in lot 2. Since I would believe that my car is not parked in lot 2 in the nearest world where my car is not parked in lot 2 (a world where I decide to park on the street), in this context "I know my car is parked in lot 2" can be true.

But now suppose that we consider whether "I know my car has not been stolen" is true. According to the rule of sensitivity, we thereby create a context in which, in order for "I know my car has not been stolen" to be true, my belief as to whether my car has not been stolen must track the truth out to the nearest world where it has been stolen. But I would believe that my car has not been stolen in the nearest world where it has been stolen. So in this context, "I know my car has not been stolen" is false. An important element of DeRose's view is that the standard for a context, determined by the rule of sensitivity, applies to any knowledge ascription in that context. So in a context where we are considering whether "S knows P," any belief, to count as an instance of knowledge, must track the truth out to the nearest not-P world. So in the context where we are considering whether "I know my car has not been stolen" is true, "I know my car is parked in lot 2" will be false because in order for "I know my car is parked in lot 2" to be true in this context, my belief that my car is parked in lot 2 must track the truth out to the nearest world in which my car has been stolen. But in the nearest world where my car has been stolen, I would still believe that my car is parked in lot 2. So in the stricter context created by our considering whether "I know my car has not been stolen" is true, "I know my car is parked in lot 2" is false.

6. OBJECTIONS TO CONTEXTUALISM

There have been many objections to contextualism in the recent literature.[14] In this section, I examinesome of the central objections.

6.1. The Gradability Objection

As we have seen, some contextualists appeal to the gradable adjective "flat" as a model for how "know" works. We have noted that flatness ascriptions come in varying degrees of strictness. When a Kansan says, "The road is flat," he makes a stricter claim than a Coloradan who utters the same sentence. Contextualists claim that just as flatness ascriptions come in varying degrees of strictness, so do knowledge ascriptions. In our airport example, Smith's utterance "I know the plane stops in Chicago" makes a weaker claim (about Smith's epistemic position) than John or Mary would make were one of them to utter "Smith knows the plane stops in Chicago." So for contextualists, knowledge ascriptions, like flatness ascriptions, are gradable. In particular, they are gradable along a scale of epistemic strength (of epistemic position).

Jason Stanley (2004) argues that this analogy between "know" and gradable adjectives like "flat" cannot be sustained. He concludes that the fact that gradable adjectives are context sensitive lends no credibility to the thesis that "know" is context sensitive. Moreover, Stanley claims that the ways in which "know" is disanalogous to gradable adjectives undermines the claim that "know" is context sensitive.

According to Stanley, there are two linguistic tests for gradability, both of which "know" fails. First, a gradable expression "should allow for modifiers." So for the comparative adjectives "flat" and "tall," we can say:

(a) X is very flat.

Second, Stanley claims that gradable expressions "should be conceptually linked to a natural comparative construction." So for "flat," we have the following comparative constructions:

(b) X is flatter than Y.
(c) X is the flattest.

But "know" fails both of these tests. It makes no sense to say,

(d) Smith very knows the plane stops in Chicago.

And "know" is not conceptually linked to any comparative construction. We cannot say:

(e) Smith knows the plane stops in Chicago more than Mary knows it.
(f) Smith knows the most that the plane stops in Chicago.

Stanley considers the possibility that the failure of "know" to satisfy these tests admits of a syntactic rather than a semantic explanation. Perhaps (d), (e), and (f) are deviant because "verbs that take sentential complements grammatically do not allow for comparatives or intensifiers."[15] But Stanley shows that this explanation fails. Consider "regret," which is a factive verb like "know." It makes perfect sense to say something of the form "X very much regrets that y" or "X regrets y more than Z does."

Because "know" fails both of his linguistic tests for gradability, Stanley concludes that the context sensitivity of gradable adjectives provides no support for the view that "know" is context sensitive. Moreover, Stanley draws a stronger conclusion. According to Stanley, the fact that "know" fails these tests is positive evidence that "know" is not gradable, that is, that the semantic content of 'know' is not, as contextualism requires, linked to a scale of epistemic strength. For if an expression is linked to degrees on a scale, then "we should expect this link to be exploited in a host of different constructions, such as natural comparatives. The fact that we do not see such behavior should make us at the least very suspicious of the claim of such a semantic link."[16]

Stanley makes a convincing case that any analogy between "know" and gradable adjectives is strained. But having said that, must we agree with Stanley that the fact that "know" fails the two linguistic tests for gradability shows that "know" is not gradable, that is, that the semantic content of "know" is not linked to a scale of epistemic strength? Michael Blome-Tillmann (forthcoming) argues that we need not. Stanley's argument is undermined if there are expressions clearly linked to degrees on a scale that fail to satisfy Stanley's test. And there do appear to be such expressions. Consider the verb "shout."[17] Very plausibly, "shout" is a context-sensitive verb. Suppose that we have two groups of people. The people in the first group tend to speak very quietly, while the people in the second group tend to speak very loudly. The members in the first group would be much more likely to classify a particular vocalization as a shout than would the members of the second group. In the case of a disagreement, clearly it would make no sense to ask which group has it right. There is no unique answer to the question of how loud a vocalization has to be in order to count as a shout. So sentences of the form "X shouts" are context sensitive and thus semantically linked to a scale of loudness.

Now consider how "shout" fares with respect to Stanley's two tests for gradability:

(b) He very shouts.
(c) He shouts more than she does.

Both (b) and (c) are deviant.[18] So "shout" fails Stanley's tests for gradability even though "shout" is context sensitive and so semantically linked to a scale of loudness. Because of this, Blome-Tillmann suggests that the contextualist, rather than drawing an analogy between "know" and gradable adjectives like "flat," should draw an analogy between "know" and verbs like "shout." Both "know" and "shout" are context sensitive and thereby semantically linked to degrees on a scale, yet each fails Stanley's tests for gradability.

Blome-Tillmann notes that although "shout" fails Stanley's tests, it is clear that using adverbial modifiers, we can order instances of shouting along a scale of loudness. Thus we have the following constructions:

(d) He shouts more loudly tham she does.
(e) He shouts the loudest.

But this does not threaten the analogy between "shout" and "know." As Blome-Tillmann points out, we can also use adverbial modifiers to order instances of knowledge along a scale of epistemic strength:

(f) He knows with better evidence/justification than she does.
(g) He knows with the best evidence/justification (available).

This further supports the analogy between "know" and "shout."

6.2. Semantic Blindness

According to contextualism, skeptical paradoxes arise because we fail to see that some of our seemingly conflicting knowledge ascriptions in fact do not conflict. For example, we fail to see that my utterance "I do not know my car is parked in lot 2," made in a high-standards context, does not conflict with my utterance "I know my car is parked in lot 2," made in an everyday low-standards context. Similarly, in the airport case, we fail to see that Mary's utterance "Smith does not know the plane stops in Chicago" does not conflict with Smith's utterance "I know the plane stops in Chicago." Thus the contextualist is committed to the view that although sentences of the form "S knows P" are context sensitive, competent speakers are unaware of this fact. Although their knowledge ascriptions track shifts in context, these speakers are unaware that this is occurring. John Hawthorne (2004a) has referred to this alleged phenomenon as "semantic blindness."

The contextualist's commitment to semantic blindness is further demonstrated by the fact that the following arguments strike us as valid in all contexts:

> S speaks truly when he utters "I know P."
> Therefore S knows P.[19]

> S sincerely utters "I know P."
> Therefore S believes/says that he knows P.[20]

Yet the contextualist must hold that these arguments are invalid in high-standards contexts provided that S made his utterance in a low-standards context. So the contextualist must explain why these arguments strike us as valid in all contexts.[21] And here again, the contextualist must appeal to semantic blindness.[22]

Some philosophers find this semantic blindness thesis implausible.[23] If "know" is context sensitive, competent speakers should be aware of it. What can the contextualist say in defense of the semantic blindness thesis? First of all, we can note that semantic blindness exists for other terms in natural language. Consider "flat." As Peter Unger has noted, by pointing out that microscopic deviations from perfect flatness exist in all physical surfaces, one can get competent speakers to deny that any physical surface is flat.[24] Should we worry that all along we have been speaking falsely when we have called things "flat"? Surely not. Philosophical reflection will convince most persons that ascriptions of flatness are relative to context-sensitive standards. As we have noted, flatness comes in degrees, and how flat a surface must be in order to count as flat *simpliciter* depends on the context. When we are in the kind of strict context induced by Unger-type considerations, our utterance "Nothing is flat" can be true, but the truth of this utterance does not conflict with an utterance of the form "X is flat" made in an everyday context.

But when we are in the grip of "flatness skepticism," we are inclined to deny the truth of our previous utterances of the form "X is flat." That is, we mistakenly think that our utterance "Nothing is flat" conflicts with our (and others') previous utterances of the form "X is flat." This is exactly the same kind of mistake the contextualist attributes to us regarding "knows." So it appears that competent speakers can be blind to the context sensitivity of a term in their language. This lends credibility to the contextualist's claim that competent speakers are semantically blind with respect to "know."

There is, however, a relevant disanalogy between "know" and "flat." Contextualist theories of flatness ascriptions gain easy and widespread acceptance among most people, but contextualist theories of knowledge do not. So the claim that ascriptions of knowledge are context sensitive requires that we posit a much higher degree of semantic blindness than does the claim that ascriptions of flatness are context sensitive. This would appear to be a theoretical cost for the contextualist, for one wonders whether it is plausible to attribute such a high degree of semantic blindness to competent speakers.

Keith DeRose (forthcoming) has argued that the semantic blindness hypothesis has no theoretical cost to the contextualist. He reports that when he presents cases like the airport case to students, a significant number of them will respond by saying that the claims of Smith and Mary do not conflict. They will claim that both are true. But this is impossible if "know" has invariant truth conditions. Thus the invariantist will have to posit semantic blindness on the part of these students. And if the invariantist is stuck with positing semantic blindness, the contextualist's posit of semantic blindness cannot count against the view.

6.3. Knowledge and Practical Reasoning

John Hawthorne (2004a) has held that there is a constitutive connection between what one knows and what one can appeal to in practical reasoning. In particular, Hawthorne endorses the following principle:

(PR) If S knows p, then S may appeal to p as a premise in practical reasoning.

Hawthorne argues that this principle makes trouble for contextualism.[25]

Suppose that I am invited to give the keynote address at the American Philosophical Association, and I am at the airport buying my ticket. The ticket agent offers me flight insurance. I reason as follows:

> I will be giving the keynote address.
> So I will be at the convention.
> So I do not need insurance.
> So do not buy the insurance.

This is uncontroversially bad reasoning. Moreover, it is bad at any context. But given the first premise, the reasoning is impeccable. This means that the problem with the reasoning is the first premise. But notice that if you are in a typical low-standards context, you can truly say, "Cohen knows that he is giving the keynote address." But then the following sentence is true in your low-standards context:

> Cohen knows that he will be giving the keynote address, but he may not appeal to that proposition in his practical reasoning,

Thus contextualism violates the practical reasoning principle.

How should a contextualist reply to this objection?[26] The first thing to note is that this objection applies not just to contextualism but to any view that does not require infallibility for knowledge. Virtually any fallibilist view will face this problem; that is, any view that allows that S can know P on evidence E even though $\Pr(P/E) < 1$ will face this problem.[27] For such views, we can always devise a bet where the payoff structure makes it rational for S to bet against what he knows. For example, a fallibilist view will allow that, having just left my car one hour ago, I can know that my car is parked in lot 2. Suppose that you offer me a bet that pays me one billion dollars if my car is not parked in lot 2, but costs me a penny if it is parked in lot 2. Even though the probability that my car has been stolen in the last hour is small, the payoffs are such that it would be irrational for me to decline to take the bet. Despite the fact that I know that my car is parked in lot 2, I cannot reason that since my car is parked in lot 2, I will be out a penny if I take the bet. I would be engaging in bad practical reasoning, even though according to fallibilism, I would be reasoning from a premise I know to be true.

So virtually any fallibilist theory must reject (PR). But the fact remains that (PR) has considerable intuitive appeal. This places a burden on fallibilist theories to explain why (PR) looks compelling despite the fact that it is false.

How might a fallibilist do this? One way is to hold that "knowledge" talk is a heuristic for simplifying reasoning. If we had a considerably greater capacity for storing and computing probabilities, we could do all our reasoning by relying just on probabilities. But given our actual capacities, we rely on this rough-and-ready, imprecise notion of knowledge and allow as a rule of thumb that when you know P, you can appeal to P in reasoning. So to say that S knows P is to say, in part, that the probability of P on his evidence is close enough to 1 for S to appeal to it in reasoning. This works fine most of the time, except for those rare cases where the extent to which the probability of P falls short of 1 turns out to matter.

This goes some but not all of the way toward explaining the appeal of (PR). For the question remains: Why does the principle seem more like an axiom than a rule of thumb?

Here the contextualist can say that the principle appears to be axiomatic because in general, it will be difficult to say things of the form "S knows P, but S may not appeal to P in his reasoning." When we think about S in those practical situations where intuitively he cannot appeal to P, error possibilities will be salient to us. This means that "S knows P" will be false in our context of ascription. This will make it difficult for us to truly utter a sentence of the form "S knows P, but S may not appeal to P in his practical reasoning." This could account for the apparent axiomatic status of the principle.

7. SUBJECT CONTEXTUALISM— SENSITIVE MODERATE INVARIANTISM

Sensitive moderate invariantism (hereafter SMI), first developed by Hawthorne (2004a), is a theory designed to have the same explanatory power as contextualism without the alleged problems.[28] To get clear on the difference between contextualism and SMI, we need to distinguish with respect to a particular knowledge ascription between the ascriber and the subject. If I say, "John knows his car is parked in lot 2," then I am the speaker/ascriber making the ascription, and John is the subject of the ascription. Contextualism says that the truth-value of a knowledge ascription is sensitive to the context of the *ascriber*. In particular, when error possibilities are salient to the ascriber, the standards for how strong an epistemic position the subject must have in order for the ascriber's utterance "S knows *P*" to be true become strict. So if the possibility that John's car has been stolen is salient to me, then I speak truly when I say, "John does not know his car is in structure 2." This remains true even if this possibility is not salient to John.

SMI denies that there is context sensitivity in the sense of ascriber sensitivity. SMI is an invariantist view. According to invariantism, the truth-value of a knowledge ascription is the same regardless of who is doing the ascribing. So on this view, if I say, "John knows his car is parked in lot 2," and you say, "John does not know his car is parked in lot 2," one of us is speaking falsely. However, SMI says that the truth-value of a knowledge ascription is sensitive to the circumstances or context of the *subject* of the ascription. In particular, when error possibilities are salient to the subject of the knowledge ascription, the standards for how strong the subject's epistemic position must be in order to know become strict. So if the possibility of error is salient to John, then "John fails to know his car is in structure 2" is true *in every ascriber context*. If I say, "John knows his car is parked in lot 2"because no error possibility is salient to me, I speak falsely if some error possibility is salient to him. If I say, "John does not know his car is parked in lot 2" because the possibility of error is salient to me, I speak falsely if no error possibility is salient to him.

So SMI takes a condition that contextualism views as an element of ascriber sensitivity and construes it instead as an element of subject sensitivity—as an element of the subject's context that affects whether the subject knows.[29] Of course, in itself, subject sensitivity is a mundane phenomenon. The truth-value of a knowledge ascription is sensitive to many features of the subject's circumstances, such as whether the proposition is true or whether the subject has evidence. What is distinctive about SMI is that it includes the salience of error possibilities as an important feature of the subject's circumstances. Moreover, according to SMI, the salience of error possibilities differs from other features of the subject's circumstances by determining how strong the subject's epistemic position must be in order to know.

8. SMI and the Airport Case

We previously saw how the airport case provides support for contextualism. Hawthorne has argued that SMI can account equally well for that case. Recall the argument I gave against saying that Smith knows that the plane stops in Chicago. I noted that if that were true, then John and Mary should describe their situation in seemingly incoherent ways. That is, they should say, "Smith knows the plane stops in Chicago, but that is not good enough. We need to check further." Moreover, I argued that if Smith's reasons are good enough for him to know, then they are good enough for John and Mary to know. But then they should say, "*We* know the plane stops in Chicago, but that is not good enough. We need to check further." But it is difficult to make sense of either statement.

Hawthorne argues that SMI can hold that Smith knows that the plane stops in Chicago without allowing John and Mary to describe their situation in these incoherent ways. Consider first my claim that if Smith's reasons are good enough for him to know, then they are good enough for John and Mary to know. Given SMI, this turns out to be false. Because of the importance to John and Mary of the plane stopping in Chicago, certain error possibilities are salient to them that are not salient to Smith, for example, the possibility that the itinerary is mistaken or the possibility that the route has been changed. Thus while Smith is in a normal low-standards context, John and Mary are in a strict-standards context. This means that though Smith's reasons are good enough for him to know, they are not good enough for John and Mary to know. So John and Mary cannot describe their situation by saying, "We know the plane stops in Chicago." Hawthorne argues further that John and Mary cannot even assert that "Smith knows the plane stops in Chicago." Relying on Timothy Williamson's idea that knowledge is the norm of assertion, Hawthorne notes that John and Mary cannot assert that Smith knows that the plane will stop in Chicago unless they know that Smith knows that the plane stops in Chicago. But since knowledge is factive, were they to know that Smith knows that the plane stops in Chicago, they would then be in a position to know themselves that the plan stops in Chicago. But ex hypothesi, John and Mary do not know that the plane stops in Chicago. It follows that John and Marry cannot assert that Smith knows that the plane stops in Chicago. SMI thus avoids the result that John and Mary should describe their situation in seemingly incoherent ways. Hawthorne thus argues that SMI can account for the airport case as well as contextualism can.

9. SMI AND SKEPTICAL PARADOXES

According to SMI, the skeptical paradox results not from shifting ascriber context, as contextualism would have it, but rather from shifts in the subject's context. I know that my car is parked in lot 2 provided the possibility that the car has been stolen is not salient to me. But if the possibility that the car has been stolen becomes salient to me, then I fail to know both that my car is in lot 2 and that my car has not been stolen. Closure is preserved because whenever I fail to know that my car has not been stolen, I fail to know that my car is parked in lot 2.

10. Objections to SMI

10.1. Ascriptions to Others

Consider again the airport case.[30] Recall that John and Mary assert that they fail to know that the plane stops in Chicago. This seems like the correct judgment for them to make. SMI can explain why they would make this assertion about themselves. Given the importance to them of the plane stopping in Chicago, various error possibilities are salient to them. This keeps them from knowing. But when John and Mary deny that they themselves know, they will also deny that Smith knows. If they think that the itinerary cannot give them knowledge that the plane stops in Chicago, they will think that the itinerary cannot give Smith knowledge either. But can SMI explain why they deny knowledge to Smith? According to SMI, it is the salience of error possibilities to the subject of a knowledge ascription that keeps the subject from knowing. But no such error possibility is salient to Smith. Moreover, John and Mary know this. So SMI cannot explain why they deny that Smith knows. It is true that John and Mary are not in a position to make the positive judgment that Smith knows that the plane stops in Chicago. If they knew this, then, given the factivity of knowledge, they themselves would be in a position to know. But ex hypothesi, they are not in a position to know. But even if they are not in a position to assert that Smith knows, SMI cannot explain why they go so far as to deny that Smith knows. Given the truth of SMI, they should suspend judgment about whether Smith knows. They should judge that Smith may or may not know, not that Smith does not know.[31]

Notice that contextualism can explain why John and Mary say, "Smith does not know the plane stops in Chicago." Because they are in a high-standards context, they are speaking the truth.

10.2. The Skeptical Paradoxes

The failure of SMI to adequately explain why John and Mary assert that Smith does not know connects to a more general worry for SMI, namely, that it cannot explain our intuitions that generate skeptical paradoxes.[32] Recall that any nonskeptical response to the paradox must explain the appeal of our skeptical intuitions. But here is a fact about those intuitions. When we are in a skeptical frame of mind, not only do we have a strong intuitive inclination to deny that we know, but also we have the same inclination to deny that others know. Moreover, we are inclined to deny that we ourselves knew previously.

Again, contextualism can explain why this is so. Our skeptical frame of mind tracks the fact that we are in a high-standards context. When we are in such a context, those standards will govern not only our self-ascriptions of knowledge but also our ascriptions to others (and to our earlier selves) as well. So when we judge that others (along with our previous selves) fail to know, we are actually making true judgments.

But SMI is unable to explain why we make these judgments. According to SMI, when we are in a skeptical frame of mind, we fail to know because error possibilities are salient *to us.*But this has no implications for whether others know. That will depend on whether the chance of error is salient *to them*. But we know, even when we are in a skeptical frame of mind, that in many instances, error possibilities are not salient to others or to our previous selves. Yet as we have noted, when we are in a skeptical frame of mind, we have a strong intuitive inclination to deny that others and our previous selves know. But SMI has no explanation for why we are so inclined. Thus SMI does not succeed in explaining our skeptical intuitions and so cannot give a satisfactory resolution of the paradox.

10.3. Absurd Truths

Another objection to SMI is that it makes assertions that seem very peculiar and perhaps even absurd turn out to be true. The truth of these assertions results from the fact that according to SMI, knowledge can come and go. Consider the following:[33]

1. John and Mary do not know that the plane stops in Chicago, but if their important meeting in Chicago were canceled, they would know that the plane stops in Chicago.
2. Smith knows that the plane stops in Chicago, but if he had an important meeting in Chicago, he would not know.

Although both of these statements strike us as absurd, according to SMI, they are true.

It is important to see that ascriber contextualism does have the result that these statements are true because we cannot say that according to ascriber contextualism, knowledge we once had is lost when error possibilities become salient. Rather, when error possibilities become salient, the proposition expressed by our utterances of the form "S knows P" changes. Consider John and Mary before they find out about their important meeting in Chicago. The proposition they express with their utterance "Smith knows the plane stops in Chicago" is true. Moreover, that proposition remains true even after they learn of their important meeting. The change that occurs after they learn of their meeting is that their utterance "Smith knows the plane stops in Chicago" comes to express a different proposition—a proposition involving stricter standards. And that proposition is false.

NOTES

1. Unger (1984), Lewis (1996), and Cohen (1999).
2. Jason Stanley (2004) disputes the analogy between "flat" and "know." I will say more about this in section 6.

3. This case and the ensuing discussion are taken from Cohen (1999). For a similar case, see DeRose (1992).

4. In section 8, I discuss Hawthorne's invariantist treatment of the airport case.

5. Vogel (1990) develops this idea.

6. See Dretske (1970) and Nozick (1981).

7. Sosa (2004) and Feldman (forthcoming) have argued that the skeptical problem arises because it is unclear how, even by ordinary standards, (5) could be false.

8. Cohen (1988), DeRose (1995), and Lewis (1996).

9. Here we must suppose that the intentions of the speaker can sometimes override the salience of error possibilities. Of course, sometimes the shift back to ordinary standards will occur simply because one's attention is no longer focused on the error possibility.

10. Stanley (2004) objects to this approach.

11. For Lewis, a mechanism of context shifting is our attending to error possibilities. This is obviously very close to the notion of error possibilities being salient.

12. For the definition of Lewis's notion of eliminating an alternative, see Lewis (1996).

13. DeRose (1995).

14. Davis (forthcoming), Feldman (forthcoming), Hawthorne (2004a), Sosa (2004), and Stanley (2004).

15. Stanley (2004: 127).

16. Stanley (2004: 130).

17. Blome-Tillmann uses the example of "snore."

18. As Blome-Tillmann notes in connection with his example "snore," we can make sense of (c) if we interpret it as a statement about the frequency with which he shouts rather than the loudness with which he shouts.

19. Davis (1994).

20. Hawthorne (2004a) and Feldman (forthcoming).

21. See Cohen (2005) for an attempt to explain the apparent validity of these arguments along contextualist lines. DeRose (forthcoming) proposes a counterexample to the second argument.

22. In connection with the first argument, if one assumes that knowledge is the norm of assertion (Williamson 2000), then one might think that when one is in a high-standards context, one would not be in a position to assert that S speaks truly when he utters "S knows P." But we could suppose that although one is in a high-standards context, one knows in that context.

23. Schiffer (1996) and Hawthorne (2004a).

24. Unger (1975).

25. Hawthorne endorses the stronger claim that S knows P if and only if S can appeal to P in his practical reasoning. Here I only consider the weaker principle, which I believe to be more plausible.

26. What follows comes from Cohen (2004).

27. Sensitive moderate invariantism (discussed in section 7) is a fallibilist view that avoids this consequence. See also note 29.

28. For another version of SMI, see Stanley (2005).

29. Hawthorne (2004a) and Stanley (2005) also hold that the practical environment of a subject can affect whether the subject knows. This allows them to maintain the connection between knowledge and practical reasoning stated in (PR).

30. Cohen (2004, 2005).

31. Hawthorne (2004a) notes this problem himself and proposes a solution. For a critique of that solution, see Cohen (2004). Hawthorne (2004b) responds to the critique. Cohen (2005) responds to Hawthorne's response.

32. Cohen (2004, 2005).
33. Davis (2007) and Feldman (forthcoming).

REFERENCES

Blome-Tillmann, M. (Forthcoming). "The Indexicality of 'Knowledge.'" *Philosophical Studies*.

Cohen, S. (1988). "How to Be a Falliblist." *Philosophical Perspectives*13 (*Epistemology*): 91–123.

———. (1999). "Contextualism, Skepticism, and the Structure of Reasons." *Philosophical Perspectives* 13 (*Epistemology*): 57–89.

———. (2004). "Knowledge, Assertion, and Practical Reasoning." *Philosophical Issues* 14 (*Epistemology*): 482–491.

———. (2005). "Knowledge, Speaker, and Subject." *Philosophical Quarterly* 55: 199–212.

Davis, W. (2007). "Knowledge Claims and Context: Loose Use." *Philosophical Studies* 132.3: 395–438(44).

DeRose, K. (1992). "Contextualism and Knowledge Attributions." *Philosophy and Phenomenological Research* 52: 913–929.

———. (1995). "Solving the Skeptical Problem." *Philosophical Review* 104: 1–52.

———. (2006). "'Bamboozled by Our Own Words': Semantic Blindness and Some Objections to Contextualism." *Philosophy and Phenomenological Research* 73.2: 316–338.

Dretske, F. (1970). "Epistemic Operators." *Journal of Philosophy*: 1007–1023.

Feldman, R. (2004). "Comments on DeRose's 'Single Scoreboard Semantics.'" *Philosophical Studies* 119: 23–33.

———. (Forthcoming). "Contextualism." In *Blackwell Companion to Epistemology* 2nd ed., ed. J. Dancy.

Hawthorne, J. (2004a). *Knowledge and Lotteries*. Oxford: Clarendon Press.

———. (2004b). "Replies." *Philosophical Issues* 14 (*Epistemology*): 510–523

Lewis, D. (1996). "Elusive Knowledge." *Australasian Journal of Philosophy* 74: 549–567.

Nozick, R. (1981). *Philosophical Explanations*. Oxford: Oxford University Press.

Schiffer, S. (1996). "Contextualist Solutions to Skepticism." *Proceedings of the Aristotelian Society* 96: 317–333.

Sosa, E. (2004). "Relevant Alternatives, Contextualism Included." *Philosophical Studies* 119: 35–65

Stanley, J. (2004). "On the Linguistic Basis for Contextualism." *Philosophical Studies* 119: 119–146.

———. (2005). *Knowledge and Practical Interest*. Oxford: Oxford University Press.

Unger, P. (1975). *Ignorance: A Case for Skepticism*. Oxford: Clarendon Press.

———. (1984). *Philosophical Relativity*. Minneapolis: University of Minnesota Press.

Vogel, J. (1990). "Are There Counterexamples to the Closure Principle?" In *Doubting: Contemporary Perspectives on Skepticism*, ed. M. D. Roth and G. Ross. Dordrecht: Kluwer.

Williamson, T. (2000). *Knowledge and Its Limits*. Oxford: Oxford University Press.

CHAPTER 20

SENSITIVITY, SAFETY, AND ANTILUCK EPISTEMOLOGY

DUNCAN PRITCHARD

EPISTEMOLOGISTS often note that knowledge is, at root, nonlucky or nonaccidental true belief, the point being that what we seek when we try to analyze knowledge is that condition (or set of conditions) that ensures that when our true belief is an instance of knowledge, it is not subject in any substantive way to luck. On the face of it, a justification condition of some sort would seem to achieve this end, since the difference between a justified true belief and a mere true belief is, it seems, that genuine justification eliminates the possibility that one's true belief is only true by accident. Famously, however, the cases cited in Edmund Gettier's (1963) seminal article showed that justification, at least as it is usually understood, cannot achieve this end, and thereby opened up the discussion of a whole range of potential new ways of defining knowledge.

One subclass of proposals in this regard involved offering a *modal* condition (or conditions) on knowledge that captured this antiluck requirement—that is, a condition that was concerned with the way in which one's target belief is responsive to relevant counterfactual circumstances (we will look at some examples in a moment). As we will see, one key motivation for these proposals came from their apparent ability to deal with the skeptical problem, and it is the applicability, or otherwise, of these modal conditions on knowledge to the skeptical problem that will be our primary concern here. In particular, we will be considering the ability of accounts of knowledge of this sort to deal with the skeptical problem concerning our knowledge of contingent facts about the external world.[1]

1. SENSITIVITY-BASED THEORIES

Consider first the idea—prefigured in the work of Fred Dretske (1970), among others, but first clearly outlined by Robert Nozick (1981, chap. 3)—that we should understand knowledge primarily in terms of true belief that meets some sort of *sensitivity* condition.[2] Nozick's insight was to recognize that the antiluck intuition underlying much of our thinking about knowledge was in effect a modal intuition regarding how our beliefs in genuine cases of knowledge should be responsive to the facts not just in the actual world (i.e., be true) but also in a relevant range of possible worlds.

Here, in essence, is how sensitivity is usually understood:

> An agent S has a *sensitive* belief in a true contingent proposition $p=_{df}$ in the nearest possible worlds in which p is not true, S no longer believes p.

Note that the ordering of the possible worlds here is to be understood in the standard way in terms of a "similarity" function: the worlds closest to the actual world will be those worlds most similar to the actual world, that is, where very little is different, while those worlds furthest from the actual world will be those worlds most dissimilar to the actual world, that is, where a great deal is different.

To illustrate this principle, consider my belief right now that I am sitting at my desk. Provided that circumstances are normal, this belief is not only true but also sensitive in the sense that in the nearest possible worlds in which it is not true—those worlds in which I am standing next to my desk, for example—I will no longer believe that I am seated at my desk (but will believe instead that I am standing).

This principle is able, it seems, to deal with a number of problems facing contemporary theories of knowledge. To begin with, note how it copes with the Gettier-style counterexamples. Consider, for example, the following case.[3] Imagine that our protagonist comes downstairs one morning and sees that according to her normally reliable clock in the hall, the time is 8:20 A.M. Moreover, suppose that this belief is true in that it is indeed 8:20 A.M. Here we have a case in which an agent forms a true belief in a way that ensures that her belief is justified, given any normal understanding of what justification might involve. The twist in the tale, however, is that the clock has, in fact, stopped twenty-four hours earlier, and so it is just a matter of luck that the agent happens to look at it at the one time in the day in which it is "telling" the right time. Since, intuitively, one cannot gain knowledge of what the time is by looking at a stopped clock, it follows that the agent in this example does not know what the time is even though she has a justified true belief in this regard.

A common feature of all Gettier-style examples is that they involve an agent who would normally have formed a justified false belief given the circumstances in which she formed that belief and yet, through luck, happened to form a true belief after all. In the case just considered, for example, the agent would normally have formed a false belief by looking at the stopped clock, but by happening to look at the clock at the moment that she did, she ensured that her belief was true after all. As Linda Zagzebski (1999) has neatly put the point, what we have here is a case of bad epistemic luck (the bad epistemic luck of trying to find out the time by looking at a stopped clock) being canceled out by good epistemic luck (the good epistemic luck of happening to look at the clock at the one moment at which it was "telling" the right time).

Sensitivity-based theories of knowledge deal with Gettier-style cases by, in essence, eliminating the possibility that a putative knower could be subject to such an opposing mix of good and bad luck. Consider, for example, how sensitivity-based views respond to the stopped-clock case just described. As we noted, the problem with such examples is that one can form a justified true belief about what the time is by looking at a stopped clock, even though one cannot gain knowledge of what the time is in this way. Sensitivity-based views can account for the lack of knowledge here because forming one's belief about the time by looking at a stopped clock is not a *sensitive* way of forming a true belief and hence cannot on this view qualify as knowledge. After all, although, as in this case, one might happen to form a true belief in the target proposition in the actual world, in the nearest possible worlds in which the target proposition is false—the worlds in which, for example, the time is presently 8:19 A.M. or 8:21 A.M., but everything else is the same—one will continue to form the same belief that one did in the actual world (i.e., that the time is 8:20 A.M.) and hence form a false belief as a result. In essence, what the sensitivity condition ensures (or at any rate is meant to ensure)—in contrast to the justification condition—is that one cannot acquire knowledge simply by accidentally gaining a true belief.

Another key motivation for sensitivity-based theories of knowledge is that they are able to explain why we lack knowledge in the so-called lottery case. This concerns an agent who forms her belief that she is in possession of a losing ticket for a fair lottery with long odds by considering the low probability involved of her winning. Suppose further that the draw has been announced, and the agent's belief is true in that she is indeed in possession of a losing lottery ticket. Given the nature of the odds involved, one would surely regard this agent as being justified in believing what she does. Nevertheless, even though this belief is justified and true, we also have the strong intuition that it is not a case of knowledge.

Although superficially similar to the Gettier-style cases in that it concerns a justified true belief that intuitively is not a case of knowledge, the problem posed by this example is rather different. This is because unlike Gettier-style cases, this is not a situation in which the agent has apparently met the conditions for knowledge through a fortuitous combination of good epistemic luck counteracting bad epistemic luck (and hence has a belief that is only accidentally true). Instead, the way in which the agent is forming her belief in the lottery example is in fact very reliable in at least one sense of the term, in that it will usually enable the agent to form a true belief. Thus the scenario is very unlike, say, the stopped-clock Gettier-style case, where the agent lacks knowledge because although she happens to form a true belief, she does so despite the fact that the way in which the belief is formed is in fact very *un*reliable.

The difficulty posed by the lottery example is thus to explain why, intuitively, the agent lacks knowledge in this case even though she is forming a justified true belief via a highly reliable method. In order to bring this problem into sharp relief, notice that the agent could, again intuitively, gain knowledge of the target proposition by ignoring the odds involved and basing her belief solely on reading the results in a reliable newspaper. Interestingly, however, the probability that she forms a false belief by forming her belief in this way could well be a lot higher than the probability that she forms a false belief by considering only the odds involved in the lottery (note that one can set the odds involved in the lottery as high as one wishes in order to ensure that this is the case). The lottery case thus appears to indicate that knowledge is not—or at least not simply—a function of the strength of one's evidence, where strength here is measured probabilistically. Instead, it seems that evidence of a certain kind can sometimes suffice for knowledge even though, surprisingly, stronger evidence would not suffice.

Sensitivity-based views can accommodate our intuitions in this regard and in doing so can cast some light on why knowledge is not (simply) a function of the strength of one's evidence in this way. Take the agent's true belief that she owns a losing lottery ticket on the basis of her evaluation of the odds involved. Although this belief is true in the actual world, it is not sensitive (and hence on this view not a case of knowledge) in that in the nearest possible world in which the target proposition is false—that is, the world in which she wins the lottery, but everything else consistent with this change stays the same—she will continue to form the same belief and so, as a result, will form a false belief. Thus, although the evidence that the agent has in support of her true belief is probabilistically very strong, it is not evidence that ensures the sensitivity of her belief, and this is what is essential, on this view, for knowledge.

Contrast this case with that of the agent who forms her true belief that she owns a losing lottery ticket by reading the results in a reliable newspaper. This true belief is sensitive since in the nearest possible worlds in which the target proposition is no longer true—again, where she wins the lottery, but everything else consistent with this change stays the same—she will no longer believe that she has lost but will instead believe that she has won (since this is what the reliable newspaper will tell her). On this view, then, there is no bar to the agent being counted as possessing knowledge of this proposition, just as intuition would predict. So although the evidence the agent has in this case may well be probabilistically weaker than the evidence the agent possesses in the previous case, this evidence does suffice to ensure that the agent has a sensitive belief, and this is what is important, it seems, when it comes to knowledge possession.

2. SENSITIVITY AND SKEPTICISM

The main motivation for sensitivity-based theories of knowledge, however, and the motivation that is of most concern to us here, is that they seem to offer a very neat resolution of at least one form of the skeptical problem. We can represent this form of skepticism in terms of two premises and a conclusion. The first premise states that we are unable to know the denials of skeptical hypotheses, such as the skeptical hypothesis that one is presently a brain in a vat (BIV) that is hooked up to supercomputers and is being artificially "fed" its apparently normal experiences. The second premise states that if one is unable to know this, then one does not know any "everyday" proposition (E) that is known to be inconsistent with the relevant skeptical hypothesis, where by an everyday proposition is meant the sort of proposition that we would all typically take ourselves to know in normal circumstances, such as (in my case) that one is seated. Finally, with these two premises in hand, the skeptic validly concludes that one does not know any everyday proposition.

Focusing on the BIV hypothesis, one can thus capture the basic form of this skeptical argument as follows:

(S1)   I do not know that I am not a BIV.
(S2)   If I do not know that I am not a BIV, then I do not know E.
(SC)   I do not know E.

Since this argument could be applied to just about any E-type proposition (one would just have to vary the skeptical hypothesis to suit), one is only a few steps away from concluding that just about any E-type proposition is unknown. Moreover, since the two premises are held to be in some sense necessary truths (we will consider them further in a moment), and the argument is valid, it also follows that we are just a few steps away from the dramatic skeptical conclusion that knowledge of just about any E-type proposition is *impossible* (at least for creatures like us).

Both the premises in this argument are surely intuitive. The first premise is intuitive since skeptical hypotheses are defined such that there is nothing in one's immediate experience that could indicate that one is not the victim of such a skeptical scenario. No matter what the nature of my present experience is, the scenario in which I am a BIV being artificially fed these experiences and the scenario in which I am not a BIV and am experiencing my environment normally are, ex hypothesi, entirely indistinguishable.

The second premise is not immediately intuitive, but it can be made to be intuitive once one reflects that it rests on the principle that knowledge is closed under known entailments, or the "closure" principle for short. This principle can be roughly stated as follows:

For all S, ϕ, and ψ, if S knows ϕ, and S knows that ϕ entails ψ, then S also knows ψ.[4]

In words, closure demands that if one knows one proposition, and one knows that this proposition entails a second proposition, then one knows the second proposition. This principle is certainly intuitive, since it is hard to see how it could possibly fail. For example, if I know that I am seated, and I know that if I am seated, then I am not standing, then surely I also know that I am not standing. What could be more uncontroversial?

The trouble is, however, that one can feed skeptical hypotheses and everyday propositions into this principle with devastating effect. Suppose that I know, for example, that I am seated, and I also know (as surely I do) that if I am seated, then I am not a BIV (since BIVs do not *sit* anywhere). Then it follows via closure that I know that I am not a BIV. Conversely, however, if I am unable to know that I am not a BIV, then I cannot know that I am seated, and hence we get the inference from lack of antiskeptical knowledge to lack of everyday knowledge at issue in (S2). Moreover, since the closure principle is highly intuitive, it follows that (S2) inherits this intuitiveness once the supporting role of closure is made explicit.[5]

Sensitivity-based theorists are quite happy with the first premise of the skeptical argument. Indeed, they claim that they have a very good explanation of why we are unable to know the denials of skeptical hypotheses, which is that the relevant belief in this regard will inevitably be insensitive. Take one's belief that one is not a BIV, for example. Even if this belief is true, in the nearest possible worlds in which what one believes is no longer true—that is, the worlds in which one is a BIV, but everything else consistent with this change remains the same—one will by definition continue to believe that one is not a BIV even though this belief is now false. That is, since there is nothing in one's experience that could enable one to distinguish between BIV and non-BIV experiences, it follows that one's belief in this regard is inevitably insensitive, and hence, since sensitivity is essential for knowledge, one cannot know these antiskeptical propositions, just as the skeptic contends.

We have already noted, however, that our everyday beliefs, such as the belief that one is seated, can be entirely sensitive and so can be candidates for knowledge. The problem premise in the skeptical argument for the sensitivity-based theorist is thus the closure-based second premise. Indeed, defenders of sensitivity, like Nozick, explicitly contend that closure must be rejected and that in its rejection lies the resolution of the skeptical problem. One can know everyday propositions, such as that one is seated, in virtue of possessing a sensitive belief in these propositions, know that they entail the denials of skeptical hypotheses, like the BIV hypothesis, and yet fail to know the denials of skeptical hypotheses, in virtue of lacking a sensitive belief in these propositions.

One can get a sense of why closure fails on this view by noting that sensitivity is a modal principle that demands consideration of very different possible worlds depending on which proposition is at issue. Suppose that the actual world is pretty much as we take it to be. On this supposition, as regards one's knowledge of the everyday proposition that one is seated, the relevant possible worlds will be the relatively nearby worlds in which one is no longer seated but where everything else consistent with this change remains the same. In contrast, as regards one's knowledge that one is not a BIV, the relevant possible worlds will be the relatively far-off worlds in which one is a BIV, worlds in which a great deal would need to be different from the actual world in order to effect the difference. Since on this view different classes of worlds are relevant to the determination of knowledge, it is hardly surprising that a principle like closure will fail, since there will be cases, such as the skeptic's own inference, in which the possible worlds at issue when one considers whether the agent knows the antecedent proposition will be very different from the possible worlds at issue when one considers whether the agent knows the consequent proposition, meaning that the possession of knowledge in the former case tells us very little about whether knowledge is possessed in the latter case, even if the entailment in question is known.

3. Problems for Sensitivity-Based Theories

The obvious problem with responding to radical skepticism in this way is that the closure principle is highly intuitive, so intuitive, in fact, that many feel that rejecting closure is too costly a price to pay for a resolution of the skeptical challenge. After all, can we really make sense of the idea that an agent might know one proposition, know that it entails a second proposition, and yet fail to know the second proposition? As Keith DeRose (1999, 201) has neatly expressed the point, sensitivity-based theorists who deny closure are committed to "the abominable conjunction that while you don't know that you're not a bodiless (and handless!) BIV, still, you know you have hands." There is clearly something bizarre about endorsing a conjunction of this sort.[6]

Intriguingly, however, it may be that one could retain closure *and* endorse a sensitivity-based theory of knowledge that is able to resolve the skeptical problem previously outlined. In order to see how this might be so, we need to consider an essential modification that Nozick makes to the principle of sensitivity that involves relativizing it to a method.

Consider, for example, the following "grandmother" case (cf. Nozick 1981, 179ff.). This involves a grandmother who has a highly reliable ability to tell, by looking at him in good lighting and so forth, that her grandson is well. Crucially, however, in the nearest possible worlds in which her grandson is unwell, he would be kept away from his grandmother and she would be told by his relatives that he is well regardless, so that she would not worry about him. Accordingly, on the version of sensitivity previously outlined, it follows that the grandmother's belief that her grandson is well is insensitive and thus not a case of knowledge, even despite the fact that it is formed in a highly reliable fashion, because in the nearest possible worlds in which the proposition believed is false, she continues to believe it regardless.

Explicitly relativizing the principle of sensitivity to a method solves this problem, since what is crucial to this example is that the method by which the belief is formed—that is, having a good look at her grandson in good environmental conditions—is not the same method by which she forms her belief in the nearest worlds in which the proposition believed is false, which involves the testimony of her relatives. If we keep her method fixed, however, then we are able to retain the intuition that the grandmother has a sensitive belief and thus has knowledge. After all, in the nearest possible worlds in which she gets a good look at her grandson in good environmental conditions and he is unwell, she will recognize that this is the case and no longer believe that he is well.

With the sensitivity principle modified to deal with this problem, however, it is now no longer clear that one gets the counterexamples to closure in the skeptical case that Nozick envisages. After all, the manner in which one forms one's belief that one is not a BIV in the actual (nonskeptical) world is surely, at least in substantial part, via one's normal perceptual faculties, and yet one cannot be forming one's belief that one is not a BIV in this way in the possible worlds in which one *is* a BIV since, ex hypothesi, those perceptual faculties are not available to one in these worlds.[7] If this is right, then one's belief that one is not a BIV can, it seems, be sensitive (and thus, in principle at least, an instance of knowledge), since there cannot be a possible world in which what one believes is false—that is, where one is a BIV—where one continues to form this belief *via the same method as in the actual world.*

The reason that Nozick does not realize that this option of retaining closure exists for his position is that he understands the notion of a method "internalistically." That is, he insists that any two methods that are "experientially the same, the same 'from the inside', will count as the same method" (1981, 184–85). When methods are construed in this way, if one grants that one's experiences are the same in the actual world in which one is not a BIV and the nearest BIV possible world, then it follows that one's method would be the same in both cases. This is an oddly restrictive way of understanding methods, however, especially if, like Nozick, one is in other respects an epistemic externalist.

As an epistemic externalist, Nozick holds that what is most important to knowledge possession is that one's belief stands in an *external* relationship to the world—that is, a relationship that is not reflectively accessible to the subject— where this is cashed out in terms of the agent's belief meeting modal conditions like sensitivity (one cannot come to know by reflection alone that one's belief has met the sensitivity condition).

Consider, for example, the famous "chicken sexer" example. This concerns an agent who has a highly reliable way of distinguishing between male and female chicks, but who is unaware of how reliable she is and, moreover, has false beliefs about how she is making this distinction (she believes that she is touching and seeing something distinctive when in fact there is nothing distinctive to see or touch, and it is her sense of smell that she is employing). Internalists characteristically deny knowledge to this agent on the grounds that she lacks good reflectively accessible grounds in support of her knowledge. In contrast, externalists typically allow that such agents have knowledge on account of how the agent concerned really does have the reliable ability in question. This is certainly the case with sensitivity-based accounts. Consider the chicken sexer's true belief that she is holding two chicks of different sexes. In the nearest possible worlds in which what she believes is no longer true (where she is holding two male chicks rather than a male and female, say), she will no longer believe the target proposition but will instead believe that she is holding chicks of the same sex. Her highly reliable chicken-sexing ability thus suffices to meet the sensitivity condition on knowledge even though she lacks the good reflectively accessible grounds that the internalist demands.

If one is happy to endorse externalism, however—and note that this is not an uncontroversial move to make—then it is not obvious why one should accept that the defining mark of a method should be something that is reflectively accessible, that is, the nature of one's experiences. Why could not one's method be determined by facts that were not reflectively accessible to one as well? Is it not plausible to suppose that a cognitive psychologist could empirically determine that there are two cognitive processes that have the same experiential upshot? Indeed, think again of the chicken sexer. It is not beyond the bounds of plausibility to suppose that there need be no experiential difference between the chicken sexer who is exercising her genuine chicken-sexing ability and someone who lacks this ability but merely thinks that she has it. On the Nozickian conception of methods, however, sameness of experience would entail sameness of method, and this seems counter to the guiding externalist intuition. The chicken sexer has knowledge on the externalist account because she is, as a matter of fact, exercising a highly reliable cognitive ability, even though she lacks good reflectively accessible grounds in favor of her beliefs so formed. In contrast, someone who merely thinks that she has a highly reliable ability, even if she has the same experiences as the genuine chicken sexer, is not a knower. Nozick's account of methods seems unable to allow him to make this central externalist distinction.[8]

There is also a further issue here, which is that although it is uncontroversial to suppose that one would not be able to distinguish between the experiences that one has when one is envatted and the corresponding normal nonenvatted experiences, it *is* controversial to suppose that they are (thereby) the same experiences. Nozick seems to be implicitly supposing that indistinguishability of experiences entails sameness of experiences, but this is not an obvious entailment, especially if one factors in content-externalist considerations. On the content-externalist view, the content of one's experiences can be dependent on "worldly" facts obtaining of which one is entirely unaware, such as facts concerning the relationship between one's experiences and what those experiences are about. On such a picture, it is far from obvious that the content of one's experiences would be exactly the same in the BIV and corresponding non-BIV cases, even though it would still be true that one could not discriminate between the two experiences.[9]

A very different problem for the sensitivity-based account of knowledge is raised by counterexamples that appear to show that sensitivity prevents us from having lots of everyday knowledge. Ernest Sosa (1999), for instance, offers the following example. Imagine someone dropping her rubbish down the rubbish chute in her high-rise condo. Does she know, moments later, that her rubbish is in the basement? According to the sensitivity-based account of knowledge, argues Sosa, the answer to this is no because her belief in this regard is insensitive. After all, were the bag to have somehow snagged on the way down the chute, such that what she believes is false, she would still have continued to believe (via the same method she used in the actual world) that the rubbish is now in the basement regardless. The trouble, claims Sosa, is that this is a fairly paradigmatic instance of everyday knowledge, and if sensitivity-based theories cannot account for cases like this, then the view is in serious trouble. That is, sensitivity-based views are meant at least to have the advantage of ensuring that our everyday knowledge is secure, even if they are not also able to ensure that we have antiskeptical knowledge as well. If Sosa is right, however, then sensitivity-based views cannot accommodate all cases of everyday knowledge, and that would be a fatal blow to the view.[10]

4. SAFETY-BASED THEORIES

Sosa offers a very different modal principle to replace sensitivity, which he refers to as *safety*. Here, in essence, is how safety is usually understood:

> An agent S has a *safe* belief in a true contingent proposition $p =_{df}$ in most nearby possible worlds in which S believes p, p is true.

Note that, as with the sensitivity principle, some sort of relativization to methods will also be required in order to enable safety to deal with potential counterexamples. Furthermore, note that, again like the sensitivity principle, safety aims to capture our intuition that knowledge is nonlucky true belief, the guiding interpretation of that intuition being that one's true beliefs should, if they are to count as knowledge, be safe in the sense that they could not have easily been false.

Safety can account for our putative knowledge in the rubbish-chute case because although there is a possible world in which what is believed is false, yet one believes it anyway (via the same method)—that is, the world in which the rubbish snags on the way down the chute—in most nearby possible worlds one will believe this proposition and one's belief will be true, thereby ensuring that it is safe.

Safety can also be put into service to explain why we have knowledge of the denials of skeptical hypotheses, and thus there is not the same problem regarding closure on this view that sensitivity-based theories have. For example, provided the worlds in which skeptical hypotheses are true are indeed far off, one's true belief that one is not a BIV will be *guaranteed* to be safe, since there will be no nearby possible world in which what is believed is false. Indeed, proponents of safety-based theories of knowledge, like Sosa (1999) and myself (Pritchard 2002b; 2005a, pt. 1; 2007a; 2007b), have made the fact that safety can account for our knowledge of the denials of skeptical hypotheses an explicit part of the motivation for the principle. The antiskeptical view that results is known as "neo-Mooreanism" because, like the commonsense approach to skepticism offered by G. E. Moore (e.g., 1925; 1939), it offers a very straightforward response to the skeptic that treats us as having knowledge of both everyday propositions and the denials of skeptical hypotheses.

5. PROBLEMS FOR SAFETY-BASED THEORIES

There have been two main foci of attack on safety-based views. The first concerns its effectiveness as an antiskeptical strategy on account of its treatment of our putative knowledge of the denials of skeptical hypotheses. The crux of the issue here is that the role of a modal condition on knowledge is usually thought to capture some counterfactual sense in which our beliefs are responsive. In the case of the sensitivity principle, this is clear since it demands that if the fact in question did not obtain, then one would no longer believe that it had obtained. Typically, one also gets a type of responsiveness to the facts by appeal to the safety principle. Take the chicken sexer, for example. There are nearby possible worlds in which what she believes in the actual world is false, and nearby possible worlds in which what she believes in the actual world is true. That she only tends to continue to believe what she does in those worlds where what she believes continues to be true indicates the counterfactual responsiveness of her beliefs.

This sort of picture of knowledge as belief that is suitably counterfactually responsive does not, however, seem to work when it comes to one's putative knowledge of the denials of skeptical hypotheses on the safety-based view. Instead, it seems that one only has such knowledge according to the safety-based theorist in virtue of how one has a counterfactually *stubborn* belief in this regard and there is, as it happens, no wide class of nearby possible worlds in which the proposition believed is false. After all, if there were a wide class of nearby possible worlds in which the relevant skeptical hypothesis obtained, then it would follow that there was a wide class of nearby possible worlds in which one believed the target proposition and yet the belief was false, thereby ensuring that one's belief is unsafe and hence, on this view, that one lacked knowledge. Put simply, whereas in most cases where one has knowledge on the safety-based view—such as chicken-sexer cases—there is a wide class of nearby possible worlds in which what one believes is false and one does not continue to believe the target proposition, this is not so for one's putative safety-based knowledge of the denials of skeptical hypotheses. This makes the knowledge look rather lucky in that it does not appear to be arising out of any cognitive ability that one has but merely to be reflecting a fortunate match across nearby possible worlds between what one believes and the relevant counterfactual circumstances.[11]

We will look at this problem again in the next section. First, however, I want to consider the second main prong of attack against safety-based views—which has been pressed by John Greco (2002, 2007)—to the effect that there is no stable construal of the principle that can accommodate both everyday cases of knowledge and the kind of knowledge that one has in the lottery case.

Recall that the sensitivity principle can deal with the lottery case since the difference between forming your belief that you have lost a lottery simply by reflecting on the odds involved rather than looking up the result in a reliable newspaper is that forming your belief via the former method would lead to an insensitive belief, whereas forming your belief via the latter method would produce a sensitive belief. The problem for safety-based theories of knowledge is that seemingly, they cannot account for our lack of knowledge in the lottery case because, given the probabilities involved, there are very few nearby possible worlds in which one's belief that one has lost is false, and thus in most nearby possible worlds in which one believes that one has lost (on the same basis as in the actual world), one's belief will be true. Thus the belief will be safe and hence, on this score at least, a potential case of knowledge, contrary to intuition.

One way around this problem could be to insist on a further condition on knowledge over and above safety, but one might worry that such an amendment to the view simply to deal with this case would be ad hoc. Alternatively, one could deal with the problem by demanding that one should construe safety so that it requires that one's belief matches the truth not just in most nearby possible worlds, but in all of them, a position for which I have argued (Pritchard 2005a, chap. 6). This would ensure that one's belief that one has lost the lottery is no longer safe and thus not a case of knowledge, but the problem then is to account for the knowledge that is apparently present in the rubbish-chute case. After all, surely there are *some* nearby possible worlds in which the rubbish snags on the way down, yet one continues to believe (on the same basis) that the rubbish is in the basement regardless. The challenge is thus to formulate safety robustly enough to deal with the lottery case while also allowing the formulation to be liberal enough to count agents as having knowledge in cases like the rubbish-chute example.

One could respond to this challenge by claiming that contrary to first appearances on this score, the agent in the rubbish-chute example *does* have a belief that, if it is to count as knowledge at any rate, matches the truth across all nearby possible worlds. After all, suppose for a moment that there is a class of nearby possible worlds in which the bag would snag and yet the agent would continue to believe that it was in the basement (via the same method) regardless, perhaps because there is an imperfection in the lift shaft that the bag is almost snagging on each time it drops. If this is how we are to understand the example, then is it really so plausible to suppose that the agent knows that her rubbish bag is in the base-ment? Indeed, intuitively, one would only suppose the agent to have knowledge in this case provided there really is no nearby possible world in which the bag would undetectably snag. Implicitly, we assume that the shaft is smooth and that there is nothing for the bag to snag on.

Of course, there are possible worlds that are not too far off in which the rubbish bag does snag, such as worlds in which the shaft gets damaged in such a way that there is now an imperfection that the bag can snag on (but which is such that the imperfection would not cause the agent to alter her belief accordingly, as would happen, for example, if the imperfection in the shaft was manifest to the agent or was indicated by a sign next to the shaft warning people of problems with the chute that might prevent the chute working as it should). The point, however, is that there is no obvious reason that we should regard such worlds as close-by worlds, and hence the more robust conception of safety as demanding a belief that matches the truth in all near-by worlds can stand.

6. ANTILUCK EPISTEMOLOGY

One way in which one can motivate the safety-based account—and along the way perhaps offer a more compelling defense of safety-based views against the objection we have just considered—is to explicitly locate the position within an antiluck epistemology. We have already noted that one could regard the sensitivity and safety principles as capturing our intuition that knowledge is nonlucky true belief. The idea behind antiluck epistemology, however, is that one should be more explicit about what this connection involves. In particular, the suggestion—which I have explored at length in Pritchard (2005a; cf. Pritchard 2007a)—is that we should offer an analysis of luck and of the sense in which knowledge is nonlucky, and then, on this basis, explicitly offer an antiluck epistemology. What is salient about this sort of project for our purposes is that it seems to directly lend support for safety-based theories of knowledge.

Consider a paradigmatic case of a lucky event, such as a lottery win. What is it about such an event that makes it lucky? Here, roughly, is one straightforward answer to that question. A lucky event is an event that is of some significance to the agent (or at least in some sense ought to be) and that obtains in the actual world but not in a wide class of nearby possible worlds where the relevant initial con-ditions for that event are the same as in the actual world. For example, the thing about winning a lottery (an event that is clearly of significance to one) is that it is the sort of event that would not normally occur, since normally one would lose. Thus there is a wide class of nearby possible worlds in which the relevant initial conditions for the event are the same as in the actual world—in which one continues to purchase a lottery ticket, for example, and the lottery continues to be fair with long odds—where one is holding the losing lottery ticket right now.

Contrast this case with that of a paradigmatic example of a nonlucky event, such as when a skilled archer hits the target. Here we again have an event that is of significance to the agent, but this time the event obtains not only in the actual world but also in most (if not all) nearby possible worlds in which the relevant initial conditions for that event remain the same (where, for example, the environmental conditions are relevantly similar). It thus is not lucky by the light of this specification of luck, just as intuition would predict.

A great deal more needs to be said about this account in order to flesh it out and provide it with the requisite support, of course, but this crude outline should suffice for our purposes here. This is because with this rough account of luck in mind, we can get a sense of why safety might be the right principle to adopt if one is explicitly seeking to offer antiluck epistemology.

Note that what we want from an antiluck epistemology is an account that ensures that if one has met all the relevant epistemic conditions, one's belief, when true, must be such that it cannot be a matter of luck that it is true. In other words, the epistemic luck that we are most troubled by is luck in the truth of our beliefs. Recall that an inability to eliminate this sort of luck was what was shown to be amiss by the Gettier-style counterexamples to the traditional tripartite account of knowledge in terms of justified true belief, in that one could have a justified true belief, yet it could still be a matter of luck that one's belief was true, as in the stopped-clock example described earlier.

Putting this point together with our rough account of luck indicates that what we want from an antiluck epistemology is a condition on knowledge that ensures that the event of our forming a true belief (an event that we will take for granted is of significance to the agent, in order to simplify matters) is nonlucky. That is, it is not the case that although the relevant event (one's forming a true belief in the target proposition) obtains in the actual world, there is a wide class of nearby possible worlds in which the initial conditions for that event remain fixed and yet the event does not obtain. Turning this around, and taking it as given that the "relevant initial conditions" will tend in this case to be captured by the mechanism through which the belief actually arose, we can recast this antiluck claim as follows: what we seek is a true belief that is such that in most nearby possible worlds in which the mechanism through which the belief actually arose remains the same, the event of believing truly continues to obtain. More simply, what we seek is a true belief that is such that in most nearby possible worlds in which we continue to believe the target proposition in the same way as in the actual world, one's belief continues to be true. But this, of course, is essentially just safety.

Reflection on the antiluck intuition thus seems to directly motivate a safety-based epistemology, and given the prevalence of this intuition in contemporary epistemology, this is strong support indeed for safety-based views. Returning to the skeptical problem that is our primary focus here for a moment, one can see how safety-based theorists might go about responding to the charge, outlined in the last section, that their view offers a very strange picture of our antiskeptical knowledge, such that we seem to be able to know the denials of skeptical hypotheses simply in virtue of a stubborn belief in the target proposition and epistemically friendly nearby possible worlds. The answer to this objection will be to point out that if what is most important to knowledge is possession of a true belief that is not luckily true, then our antiskeptical beliefs, even granted this description of them, can perfectly well meet this rubric. The thought will run that although there may well be something epistemically lacking about our antiskeptical beliefs, this epistemic lack is not decisive when it comes to the issue of knowledge possession, since in this regard mere nonlucky true belief—that is, safe belief—will suffice.

Setting safety-based views within an antiluck epistemology might also enable the proponent of the view to deal with the other key problem we raised earlier, which was the objection that there was no stable account of the safety principle available that could accommodate both the intuition that we have lots of everyday knowledge (such as the knowledge at issue in the rubbish-chute example) and the intuition that we also have knowledge in the lottery case. We dealt with that objection earlier by treating the safety principle as applying to all nearby possible worlds, and this move could be backed up by antiluck considerations. After all, given the honorific status of knowledge, it would not be surprising that when it came to knowledge possession, we wanted a state that ensured that there were no nearby possible worlds in which one continued to form one's belief in the target proposition on the same basis, yet the belief was false.

Perhaps a better way of responding to this difficulty, however, is to note that in our ascriptions of luck, we often put more weight on relevant counterfactual events depending on how modally close they are. For example, consider the following two cases: first, a case in which one is nearly hit by a bullet from a sniper, and the bullet whistles past one's ear; second, an exactly similar case in which one is nearly hit by a bullet from a sniper, with the one difference that this time the bullet does not come quite as close as in the first case but in fact hits a tree a few feet away from one. We would clearly judge one's not being hit by the bullet in question to be lucky in both cases, since in each case there is a wide class of nearby possible worlds in which the relevant initial conditions for the event are the same (the environmental conditions, for example) and the bullet does hit one (moreover, the event of being hit by a bullet is clearly of significance to one). Nevertheless, I think that it is also clear that we would regard the former event as being luckier than the latter event because the possible world in which one gets hit is closer in the former case than in the latter case.

This has a bearing on how one might modify safety in order to deal with Greco's objection. After all, what is salient about the lottery case is that given the nature of how lotteries are decided, the world in which one is presently holding the winning lottery ticket is in fact very close to the actual world in which one is holding the losing ticket. This is in contrast to the rubbish-chute example, since although one might disagree about whether, properly understood, the world in which the bag snags is close enough to count among the nearby worlds, it is certainly true by everyone's lights that it will not be particularly close, since if that were the case, then the agent concerned certainly would not possess knowledge. With this distinction between the two cases in mind, one can thus deal with the problem in hand by sticking to the original formulation of safety in terms of most nearby possible worlds but modifying one's understanding of this principle so that more weight is given to the closest worlds. One could do this, for example, by insisting that there be no very close nearby possible world in which the agent believes the target proposition (on the same basis) and yet forms a false belief (thereby dealing with the lottery case) while also allowing that of the nearby possible worlds as a whole, it need only be the case that one's belief matches the truth in most of them (thereby ensuring knowledge in the rubbish-chute case).[12]

Allying safety-based views to an antiluck epistemology thus highlights some interesting ways in which the view can be defended against some of its most pressing objections.

7. CONCLUDING REMARKS

I want to close by considering two issues of central importance to the sort of views outlined here. The first concerns how this debate connects with one of the dominant research programs of contemporary epistemology, that of "relevant-alternatives" approaches to knowledge. The driving idea behind these proposals is the thought that in acquiring knowledge, one does not need to be infallible in the sense of being able to rule out all error possibilities associated with the proposition known, since that would certainly be far too restrictive and would amount to a clear invitation to radical skepticism. Instead, it is only a subclass of all the associated error possibilities that is relevant, and the task in hand is to offer some plausible and principled specification of what these relevant error possibilities are.

One can regard sensitivity-based views as being within this general program, especially insofar as the view is understood as resulting in the denial of the closure principle. If we take "rule out" here to be broadly equivalent to "know to be false," the thought will be that it is an infallibilist and thus non-relevant-alternatives line of thought that leads us to endorse the skeptic's use of closure and hence require of everyday knowledge that we are also able to have knowledge of the denials of skeptical hypotheses. On this view, then, relevant alternatives and the rejection of closure go hand in hand.

There is reason to be suspicious of this reading of the relevant-alternatives intuition, however. After all, the guiding thought behind this intuition is surely that those error possibilities that are indeed far-fetched are thereby irrelevant to the determination of knowledge and so can be disregarded with impunity. What is odd about the sensitivity-based reading of the relevant-alternatives intuition, however—or at least that reading that results in the denial of closure—is that it does allow far-fetched error possibilities to be sometimes relevant to the determination of knowledge. In deciding whether one knows that one is not a BIV, for example, the relevant possible worlds will be those ex hypothesi far-off worlds in which one is a BIV. But if the possible world in which one is a BIV is indeed far off, then why is it relevant to the determination of any of one's knowledge, even one's knowledge that one is *not* a BIV?

Safety-based views, in contrast, stick to the core rendering of the relevant-alternatives intuition that far-off error possibilities—and thus far-off possible worlds—are always irrelevant to the determination of knowledge. Interestingly, as we saw earlier, if one opts for an "externalist" conception of methods, then it seems that one could retain a sensitivity-based conception of knowledge and hold that far-off skeptical possible worlds, like the BIV world, are always irrelevant to the determination of knowledge. If this is right, then it opens up the possibility that one might be able to stick to this core rendering of the relevant-alternatives intuition while also offering a sensitivity-based account. This raises the intriguing question of how the safety principle and the sensitivity principle on this construal are related, a topic that has been insufficiently explored. Could there be a rendering of these principles on which they are extensionally equivalent? If so, then this would be a fascinating development.

The second issue that I want to raise before closing is whether the skeptical problem as we are understanding it really is the most pressing version of this age-old philosophical conundrum. For if it is not—if there is a more problematic version of the puzzle available—then the antiskeptical appeal of the proposals sketched here will be rather slim. I suggest that this is indeed the case, in that the core skeptical problem is not a problem that turns on closure, and thus on whether we are able in some sense to know the denials of skeptical hypotheses, at all. Instead, I think that there are good reasons to suppose that what really underpins the skeptical argument is an evidential claim to the effect that since our evidence in support of our everyday beliefs does not favor those beliefs over skeptical alternatives, it follows that our evidence is insufficient for knowledge. Rescuing knowledge from the skeptic's grasp in the way that sensitivity- and safety-based theorists do—without in the process explaining what the evidential basis of this knowledge is—thus does not adequately deal with the problem in hand. This, however, is a topic for another occasion.[13]

NOTES

I am grateful to the editor of this volume, John Greco, for his comments on an earlier version of this chapter and also for general discussion, over several years, of the topics related to it.

1. Since it is knowledge of contingent propositions that is our focus here, we will set to one side the vexed issue of how modal accounts of knowledge can deal with our knowledge of necessary truths.

2. Nozick actually imposed two modal conditions on knowledge. However, since only the sensitivity condition is relevant to the problem of skepticism, for the sake of simplicity we will focus on sensitivity here.

3. This example is adapted from one discussed by Russell (1948, 170–71), although it was not explicitly advanced as a Gettier-style case.

4. One might want to modify this principle in a number of ways in order to deal with potential counterexamples of a trivial sort (such as possible cases where the agent does not even believe the entailed proposition), but this unembellished version of closure should suffice for our purposes here.

5. For more on the contemporary debate regarding skepticism, and on treatments of this type of skeptical argument in particular, see Pritchard (2002a).

6. For a recent exchange regarding the merits, or otherwise, of denying closure, see Dretske (2005a, 2005b) and Hawthorne (2005).

7. Williams (1991, chap. 8) was, as far as I am aware, the first to make this point. See also Black (2002) for a recent discussion of this issue.

8. For more on the epistemic externalism/internalism distinction in general, see Kornblith (2001).

9. One type of content externalism that is particularly relevant here is disjunctivism, which holds that the content of one's experiences in cases of veridical perception is different from the content of one's experiences in counterpart cases in which one is deceived, even though one would be unable to distinguish between the two sets of experiences. See, for example, McDowell (1995).

10. For more on sensitivity-based theories of knowledge—and Nozick's view in particular—see Luper-Foy (1987).

11. For more on this point, see Pritchard (2005b).

12. For more on this point, see Pritchard (2007c).

13. I argue that the source of skepticism lies in an evidential principle known as "under determination" rather than in closure in Pritchard (2005a, chap. 4; 2005c).

REFERENCES

Black, T. (2002). "A Moorean Response to Brain-in-a-Vat Scepticism." *Australasian Journal of Philosophy* 80: 148–63.

DeRose, K. (1999). "Solving the Skeptical Problem." In *Skepticism: A Contemporary Reader*, ed. K. DeRose and T. A. Warfield. Oxford: Oxford University Press.

Dretske, F. (1970). "Epistemic Operators." *Journal of Philosophy* 67: 1007–23.

———. (2005a). "The Case against Closure." In *Contemporary Debates in Epistemology*, ed. M. Steup, 13–26. Oxford: Blackwell.

———. (2005b). "Reply to Hawthorne." In *Contemporary Debates in Epistemology*, ed. M. Steup, 43–46. Oxford: Blackwell.

Gettier, E. (1963). "Is Justified True Belief Knowledge?" *Analysis* 23: 121–23.

Greco, J. (2002). "Virtue and Luck, Epistemic and Otherwise." *Metaphilosophy* 34: 353–66.

———. (2007). "Worries about Pritchard's Safety." *Synthese*.

Hawthorne, J. (2005). "The Case for Closure." In *Contemporary Debates in Epistemology*, ed. M. Steup, 26–43. Oxford: Blackwell.

Kornblith, H., ed. (2001). *Epistemology: Internalism and Externalism*. Oxford: Blackwell.

Luper-Foy, S., ed. (1987). *The Possibility of Knowledge: Nozick and His Critics*. Totowa, N.J.: Rowman and Littlefield.

McDowell, J. (1995). "Knowledge and the Internal." *Philosophy and Phenomenological Research* 55: 877–93.

Moore, G. E. (1925). "A Defence of Common Sense." In *Contemporary British Philosophy* (2nd series), ed. J. H. Muirhead. London: Allen and Unwin.

———. (1939). "Proof of an External World." *Proceedings of the British Academy* 25: 273–300.

Nozick, R. (1981). *Philosophical Explanations*. Oxford: Oxford University Press.

Pritchard, D. H. (2002a). "Recent Work on Radical Skepticism." *American Philosophical Quarterly* 39: 215–57.

———. (2002b). "Resurrecting the Moorean Response to Scepticism." *International Journal of Philosophical Studies* 10: 283–307.

———. (2005a). *Epistemic Luck*. Oxford: Oxford University Press.

———. (2005b). "Scepticism, Epistemic Luck and Epistemic *Angst*." *Australasian Journal of Philosophy* 83: 185–206.

———. (2005c). "The Structure of Skeptical Arguments." *Philosophical Quarterly* 55: 37–52.

———. (2007a). "Anti-Luck Epistemology." *Synthese* 158: 277–97.

———. (2007b). "How to Be a Neo-Moorean." In *Internalism and Externalism in Semantics and Epistemology*, ed. S. Goldberg. Oxford: Oxford University Press.

———. (2007c). "Knowledge, Luck, and Lotteries." In *New Waves in Epistemology*, ed. D. H. Pritchard and V. Hendricks, 28–51. London: Palgrave Macmillan.

Russell, B. (1948). *Human Knowledge: Its Scope and Its Limits*. London: George Allen and Unwin.

Sosa, E. (1999). "How to Defeat Opposition to Moore." *Philosophical Perspectives* 13: 141–54.

Williams, M. (1991). *Unnatural Doubts: Epistemological Realism and the Basis of Scepticism*. Oxford: Blackwell.

Zagzebski, L. (1999). "What Is Knowledge?" In *Epistemology*, ed. J. Greco and E. Sosa. Oxford: Blackwell.

CHAPTER 21

CLOSURE AND ALTERNATIVE POSSIBILITIES

JONATHAN KVANVIG

Is it always possible to extend one's knowledge by deducing consequences from what one already knows? Plausibly, the answer is yes. Some versions of skepticism, however, appeal to just such a principle (often called a "closure" principle) to draw radical skeptical consequences. These versions point out that if we know, for example, that we have hands, it follows that we are not being deceived by an evil demon into thinking that we have hands when we do not. Such versions then defend the claim that we cannot know that we are not being so deceived, and hence that we cannot know that we have hands.

This argument appeals centrally to the intuitive idea behind closure principles that knowledge can be extended by deduction. Many epistemologists agree with the skeptic on this principle but disagree with the skeptic about the consequences of accepting closure. Others maintain that the intuitive idea behind closure principles gives inadequate ground for affirming any and instead assert that though extending our knowledge by deduction occurs quite generally, this extension is not limitless in the way required for the truth of closure principles. In the latter group are those who emphasize the importance in knowing of being able to rule out alternative possibilities to what one believes.

In order to understand these disputes properly and provide some clarity concerning them, I will begin with a somewhat extended discussion of the nature of mathematical closure and its application in the context of contemporary epistemology. After this extended introduction, we will be in a position to examine the dispute about the truth of closure principles in epistemology and the role alternative possibilities play in a proper understanding of the nature of knowledge. By way of preview, let me indicate briefly the direction in which I intend to head. The epistemology of the last half century or so has seen an important distinction between the rhetorical context of attempting to answer the skeptic's challenge and the central epistemological task of clarifying the nature of knowledge and the quality of reasons needed in order to know. One assumption being rejected in this discussion is that in order for reasons to be good enough to make knowledge possible, they have to be reasons that would convince a skeptic, or reasons that would be legitimate to cite in the face of a skeptical challenge. This assumption is false. There is no good reason to think that the skeptic must be satisfied with an explanation of how knowledge is possible in order for it to be a good and adequate explanation. Epistemological theorizing should not be done by imagining what a skeptic would or might say and trying to give an adequate conversational response. Once this point is recognized, I will argue, the best arguments against closure are no longer telling. That point does not imply that any closure principle is true, but it does remove the most worrisome roadblock to an adequate defense of the best closure principles.

1. CLOSURE

The mathematical concept of closure at work in epistemological discussions concerning closure and alternative possibilities concerns the closure of sets. For a set to be closed under a particular operation is for nothing beyond the set to be introduced as a result of applying that operation to the members of the original set. For example, the set of whole numbers is closed under addition and multiplication, since adding or multiplying any two whole numbers returns a whole number. The closure of a set O under a particular operation or function is the smallest set that includes the members of O. Given this definition of closure, we can say that a set is closed under some operation or function if and only if it is equal to its closure.

The objects in question for epistemological application are, on first pass, sets of propositions, and the relevant function or operation is deduction. The question under investigation is the question of whether a given set of propositions is closed under deduction. How the set is identified is what makes the discussion relevant to epistemology. Epistemological relevance is furthered by identifying the set of propositions in question with that which is known to be true by a particular person at a particular time. Consider the set of things that you presently know. If this set is deductively closed ("closed," for simplicity), then you know all the deductive consequences of what you know. That is, where "Ksp" is interpreted in terms of some person S and a proposition p and is read as "S knows that p":

> Deductive consequence closure: Where $\Gamma=\{p: Ksp\}$ and $\Gamma \vdash q$, then $q \in \Gamma$.

In deductive consequence closure, '$\Gamma \vdash q$' says that the argument that has as premises some subset of Γ and q as conclusion is valid. In ordinary English, we might gloss deductive consequence closure as follows: If you know some particular claim p, and p implies q, then you know q.

Deductive consequence closure is not the only available deductive closure principle, and other principles can and have been offered. One possibility is to pick an epistemic concept other than knowledge. One might, for example, claim that justification or rationality or warrant is closed under deduction. Here the focus will be on the concept of knowledge, however, for the primary issues associated with such principles can be found here, and the discussion of alternative possibilities is most at home in the arena of knowledge. Another way to generate a different closure principle is to focus on a function or operation other that that involved in the deductive consequence relation.

The formula for offering an alternative is to replace "$\Gamma \vdash q$" in deductive closure with a variable, and then suggest a different value for that variable. That is, we first obtain the following schema:

> Knowledge closure schema: Where $\Gamma=\{p: Ksp\}$ and $\exists R(R\Gamma q)$, then $q \in \Gamma$.

In order to count as a *deductive* closure principle, the relation R that holds between set Γ and proposition q will need to have something to do with the concept of deductive implication. In deductive consequence closure, the relationship to deductive implication is immediate, but there is another common way of achieving the same result. We might interpret the relation R in terms of known deductive consequences, rather than deductive consequences themselves. Such a value for R generates the following principle:

> Known implication closure: Where $\Gamma=\{p: Ksp\}$ and $Ks(\Gamma \vdash q)$, then $q \in \Gamma$.

In slogan form, deductive consequence closure says that knowledge is closed under deduction; known implication closure says that knowledge is closed under known deduction.

We will see later that there are alternatives to these two principles. For now, we will proceed in our discussion with these closure principles, but it is useful at this point to see what kinds of principles can be ruled out as closure principles. Suppose, for example, that an epistemological theory adopts the following principle:

> Deduction extends knowledge sometimes schema: Where $\Gamma=\{p: Ksp\}$ and $Ks(\Gamma \vdash q)$ then $q \in \Gamma$ unless q is a special kind of proposition.

Sometimes epistemologists adopt instances of this schema, one especially prominent version of which will not let us extend knowledge by deduction to the denials of skeptical hypotheses. So, for example, a defender of this schema might grant that you know that you have hands and that you also know that if you have hands, then you are not being deceived by a Cartesian evil demon into thinking that you have hands when you do not. Since the evil-demon hypothesis is a radical skeptical hypothesis, however, some epistemologists think that you do not know that this skeptical hypothesis is false. It is a special kind of proposition that cannot be known, even though you know that its falsity follows from what you know.

Such theorists are deniers of closure, not defenders of it, and in what follows, instances of this schema will not count as closure principles, on the basis of the mathematical character of the initial idea of closure itself. When the object subject to closure is a set of propositions, only instances of the knowledge closure schema, which unrestrictedly quantifies over all propositions when specifying the relation that must hold in order for a given proposition to be a member of the set in question, will count as closure principles. There are tricks, however, that one might use to turn the deduction extends knowledge sometimes schema into the knowledge closure schema. For example, suppose that there is an identifiable characteristic for when the sometimes schema applies. Call that characteristic "C." Then in the knowledge closure schema, we can make the relation R a conditional one where the condition is C itself. We can thus quantify unrestrictedly over all propositions and claim that for all propositions bearing a relation satisfying the following description, we get a real closure principle: "bearing a relation to q having something to do with the deductive consequence relation when the relata have characteristic C." For example, if we suppose that closure works, but only outside the realm of metaphysics, then C would be the property of being a non-metaphysical proposition, and a closure principle could specify R as the relation of known deductive consequence for nonmetaphysical propositions. In this way, even deniers of closure could be accused of being defenders of closure, but this is a result we want to avoid rather than embrace. How to avoid this result by technical gerrymandering is not clear. We will have to place restrictions on what kind of relation R is allowed in the knowledge closure schema, but I will not attempt here to say precisely how one might do so, since the distinction between legitimate closure principles and other principles is clear enough to allow us to focus more directly on the substantive epistemological issues.

The logicomathematical background is the source of the search for closure principles in contemporary epistemology, and it places constraints on what can legitimately count as a closure principle. We need not refuse any and all metaphorical extensions of this idea, and if we do not, we can say something like the following: Suppose that we find an object and then perform some operation on that object and argue that, in some important way, what we end up with can be identified with what we started with. Such a metaphorical extension is legitimate because, to apply it, we still have to argue that something is closed, and for it to be closed, we have to find that what we began with and what we end up with are equal or identified.

Suppose, then, that we have identified a stable of epistemic concepts and a battery of epistemic principles. An epistemic principle is a conditional with epistemic concepts in there somewhere. In order to be a closure principle, the epistemic principle must identify something that is closed. The force of this requirement is that to do so, the principle must cite the same epistemic concept in its antecedent and consequent. That is what makes the following a paradigmatic example of a closure principle:

> If q follows from what you know, then you know q.

It also explains why the following is not a closure principle:

> If a certain group of claims is justified and that group also meets some coherence requirement, then one is in a position to know that the members of that group are true.

The first principle cites the concept of knowledge in both antecedent and consequent. It also identifies some function or operation to perform on items that fall under the concept and says that anything resulting from the application of that function or operation also falls under that concept. So what we are considering before the application of that function or operation can be identified with what we have after this application: we consider the class of things known, create a list of the deductive consequences of the class, and note that the union of this list with what we began is just the same as what we began with (if the principle is true, that is).

As we move away from this paradigmatic closure principle, things get muddier. But if we still insist that something is closed, we can throw out any epistemic principle that does not cite the same epistemic concept in antecedent and consequent. So, for example, the following still passes scrutiny:

> If you know that q follows from what you know, then you know q.

A principle that will play an important role later in our discussion also passes scrutiny, though we may want to whine a bit before letting it in:

> If you competently deduce q from what you know, then you know q.

Notice that this last principle does not involve the application of a mathematical function to the set of things known, but I think that we can live with this level of metaphorical extension. It says that if you start with a body of knowledge and undergo a certain psychological process or operation, then what you end up with is knowledge. I think that we can live with calling this a closure principle for knowledge, because it claims that something is closed with an identification of a certain sort: you start with stuff you know and you end up with stuff you know.

If some wish to be picky and insist that this is not really closure (because there is really no object that is equal to some function on that object), we will understand. It is not really closure. But it bears a strong-enough metaphorical connection to the real thing that it seems not worth arguing about. And the basis for this opinion is that in some way, it is still trying to specify something that is closed.

Think, however, of the array of epistemic principles that do not at all try to specify that something is closed because they do not even use the same epistemic concepts in both antecedent and consequent. Some say that if q follows from what you know, then you are in a position to know that q is true; others say that if you justifiably believe that a conditional is true while justifiably believing its antecedent, the consequent of the conditional is justified for you; still others say that if you know that q follows from what you know, then you have all you need, evidentially speaking, to know that q is true.

Each of these claims has been described as a closure principle, but I can see no good reason to classify them this way. In each case, there is no purchase to be found on the idea that there is something here that is closed. So I say that these are epistemic principles, but they are not closure principles. The alternative is to say that a closure principle in epistemology is any principle that says something about the relationship between deduction and some particular epistemic concept. More generally, we could also talk about inductive closure principles, probabilistic closure principles, and the like. The use of "closure" in such language is, as far as I can see, completely superfluous. If you are not in some way trying to say that something is closed, just say that you have found an important epistemic principle. You might also say that it has something to do with deduction or some other notion of implication. But we should not call these principles "closure principles."

The fundamental objection to widening the scope of what counts as a closure principle is that it makes a mockery of the debate about closure, turning deniers of closure into defenders of such an implausible claim that no one would have thought to deny it. Consider the following principle:

> There is some true epistemic principle that says that if we take a set of propositions that are known by some person, there is some operation or process having to do with deduction that is such that when it is applied so as to produce some proposition q, it implies that q falls into a favorable epistemic category (perhaps involving the concept of knowledge) for that person.

The favorable epistemic category might have to do with being in a position to know, which some would find unproblematic, but it might equally have to do with being justified in the way required for knowledge. To require of closure deniers the intention to undermine this principle is to raise the bar on their objections to such a height that it makes a mockery of the dispute. The proper stance to take on the dispute requires honoring enough of the mathematical home of the concept of closure so that the argument is about whether, in some way, an operation or process on a set of propositions having a certain property yields a result having that same property. If closure is taken in this sense, there is an interesting dispute about whether there are any correct closure principles in epistemology; if it is taken more broadly, as in the last principle just stated, there has not been any such dispute. In what follows, then, the issue of closure will be interpreted in such terms.

Two versions of a closure principle—deductive consequence closure and known entailment closure—are canonical formulations of a closure principle, both being obvious instances of the knowledge closure schema, and both have been attacked from two quite different directions in the history of twentieth-century epistemology. Denials of closure can be found in the context of the epistemic paradoxes, especially the lottery and preface paradoxes, as well as in the work of (what I will term here) modal epistemologists. Modal epistemology understands the truth conditions for knowledge to involve what is true or false across some range of possible worlds.[1] Infallibilism is, on this construal, a version of modal epistemology, for it implies that a particular belief counts as knowledge only when there is no possible world in which that belief is held when it is false. Our focus here, however, will be on more realistic modal epistemologies, and for such epistemologies, knowledge depends on remaining error-free across some smaller sphere of possible worlds. When a theory has this implication, it will count as an instance both of modal epistemology and of alternative-possibilities epistemology. Our goal is to consider carefully the relationship between this latter type of modal epistemology and the question of closure, and I will begin by describing briefly the history of denials of closure.

2. HISTORY OF DENIALS OF CLOSURE

Denials of closure in the context of the paradoxes can be traced easily to the work of Henry Kyburg in his discovery and presentation of the lottery paradox in *Probability and the Logic of Rational Belief* in 1961,[2] though the idea is contained in "Probability and Randomness," which was presented in 1959 at a meeting of the Association for Symbolic Logic and was published in 1963.[3] Even earlier, in 1929, F.P. Ramsey claimed that a closure principle for conjunction is false when he said, "We cannot without self contradiction say p and q and r and . . . and one of p, q, r, . . . is false . . . But we can be nearly certain that one is false and yet nearly certain of each; but p, q, r, are then infected with doubt."[4]

These remarks questioning closure are most at home in discussions of the epistemic paradoxes. Kyburg's denial of closure was explicitly tied to his introduction of the lottery paradox. Though D.C. Makinson is credited with discovering the preface paradox in 1965,[5] it is clear that Ramsey's thought is an important predecessor of the version of this paradox, sometimes called the fallibility paradox, where the book is the set of one's beliefs and one's sense of one's own fallibility is contained in the preface to this book. The element needed for this version of the paradox, an element Ramsey does not mention, is the idea that one can be justified in believing claims that are only "nearly certain" for one.

The other source for denials of closure is found in the development of modal epistemology. The first such explicit denial is found at the end of Dretske's seminal article "Epistemic Operators,"[6] in which Dretske distinguishes between penetrating and semi penetrating operators, where only the first category preserves closure. The knowledge operator, according to Dretske, is only a semi penetrating operator: it preserves closure for some logical connectives (e.g., conjunction) but not for all. Alvin Goldman's "Discrimination and Perceptual Knowledge" is central to the history of modal epistemology as well, refusing to require ruling out all contraries to a given belief as relevant to the question of whether the given belief counts as knowledge.[7] Central to these initial presentations of the relevant-alternatives theory of knowledge is the idea that in order to know, one need not rule out all logical contraries for a given belief. Not all alternatives are *relevant alternatives*, and it is only the relevant alternatives that need to be ruled out in order for one to have knowledge. To get from this point to a denial of closure, one need only add that where *p* entails *q*, the alternatives to *p* that are relevant need not be the same as the alternatives to *q*. In such a case, one might be in a position to rule out the first class of alternatives but not be in a position to rule out the second class of alternatives. To use Dretske's famous example, one might be able to rule out relevant alternatives to the claim that the animal in front of one at the zoo is a zebra without being able to rule out relevant alternatives to the claim that the animal is a cleverly disguised mule.

Viewed in this way, the relevant-alternatives theory has a precursor in Wittgenstein's *On Certainty*. Wittgenstein, in his opposition to Moorean optimism, distinguishes between what we know and the grounds of what we know, where the grounds themselves do not count as knowledge.[8] In applying this distinction, Wittgenstein returns repeatedly to claims of ordinary life for the first category (what we know) and philosophical claims for the second category (the grounds that we take for granted but do not know). Moore notoriously claimed, however, that he could prove and hence know the truth of philosophical claims such as the claim that there is an external world on the basis of knowing claims of ordinary life, such as the claim that here is one hand and here is another. Moorean anti-skepticism is rooted in the idea that we can extend our knowledge by deducing philosophical claims from ordinary items of knowledge, and Wittgenstein's opposition to Moore on this point requires a denial of closure of the same sort defended by the relevant-alternatives theorists who explicitly deny closure.

We have seen that defenders of the relevant-alternatives theory embrace one kind of modal epistemology. A second kind of modal epistemology employs counterfactual connections between a belief and its truth. For example, consider the claim that if *p* were false, then S would not believe that *p*; that is,

$$\sim p \,\square\!\!\rightarrow \sim Bp.$$

Treating the truth of this claim as a requirement for knowledge is said to require that knowledge be *sensitive*, so we can call the requirement itself the sensitivity requirement.

Robert Nozick's theory of knowledge employs just such a sensitivity requirement as the distinctive element that differentiates true belief from knowledge.[9] On the usual semantics for counterfactuals,[10] we interpret a counterfactual by looking for close worlds in which the antecedent is true and check to see whether the consequent is true as well. Even if *p* entails *q*, the close $\sim p$ worlds and the close $\sim q$ worlds need not be the same, and it is this feature that Nozick exploits to deny closure. He says:

So, we must adjust to the fact that sometimes we will know conjunctions without knowing each of the conjuncts. Indeed, we already have adjusted. Let *p* be the statement that I am in Emerson Hall, not-SK be the one that I am not on Alpha Centauri floating in that tank; since *p* entails not-SK, *p* is (necessarily) equivalent to *p* & not-SK. I know that *p*, yet I do not know that not-SK.[11]

Here Nozick explicitly rejects closure on the basis of his preferred sensitivity account of knowledge.

In sum, the sources of denial of closure can be found in literature related to the epistemic paradoxes, as well as in the literature developing the two important versions of modal epistemology. The first version of modal epistemology is the relevant-alternatives theory, and the second is the counterfactual theory.

The failure of closure on these versions of modal epistemology has not been universally welcomed by fans of these theories. In both cases, defenders of such approaches have attempted to present versions of these views that allow them to embrace closure.

3. Defenses of Closure in Relevant-Possibilities Epistemology

3.1. Counterfactual Approaches

Two ways have been developed in the literature for trying to avoid Nozick's rejection of closure while retaining his reliance on counterfactuals in clarifying the nature of knowledge. The first endorses contextualism, the view that the truth or falsity of knowledge attributions depends on the context of utterance. Keith DeRose has defended this approach, claiming that a shift in context explains the apparent loss of closure, and that once the context is held fixed, you either know both that you have hands and that you are not a brain in a vat, or you do not know either of these claims.[12] The strategy involved in this preservation of closure mirrors the strategy used by defenders of closure for the relevant-alternatives theory, and since I will discuss this maneuver at some length later, I will postpone discussion of this contextualist defense of counterfactual modal epistemology until then.

Others, most famously Ernest Sosa, have held that one can embrace a counterfactual theory of knowledge without abandoning closure by replacing Nozick's sensitivity condition with a safety condition.[13] The safety condition is simply the transpositive of sensitivity:

$$Bp \,\square\!\!\rightarrow p.$$

This substitution exploits the fact that transposition is not valid for counterfactual conditionals, and the hope is that the failure of transposition will allow one to preserve closure while still embracing a counterfactual approach to the theory of knowledge.

It would be surprising, however, if all the failures of closure purportedly explained by the sensitivity account just happened to line up with all the failures of transposition between sensitivity and safety, as would be required for the move to safety to salvage closure for the counterfactual approach. We need not wonder at such a possibility, however, for there are counterexamples to closure on the safety approach as well. One is a variant of the fake-barn case. We imagine a region in which real barns are being replaced by fake barns to induce false beliefs in unwary tourists. At each real-barn site, a coin is flipped, and if the coin comes up heads, the real barn is left in place and painted green, and if the coin comes up tails, a fake red barn replaces the real barn. The coin is assumed to be fair, so there is an even chance that when tourists look at what appears to be a barn, they are wrong. That fact makes it false that if they believe that what they are seeing is a barn, it is a barn. Their belief is unsafe. Things are different, however, when we consider the safety counterfactual regarding the claim that what they are seeing is a green barn. If they believe that what they are seeing is a green barn, it is a green barn; their belief is safe. So they can know that the object in their visual field is a green barn, but not a barn.

Sosa takes such examples to be an impetus for theory refinement rather than closure abandonment. It is interesting to consider why a modal epistemologist of the counterfactual variety should have this preference, and we will return to this question a bit later. For now, however, it is worth noting the kind of refinement Sosa suggests. His latest version of the safety condition is this:

> A belief is safe just when the claim in question would be true if it were believed on the basis of the actual reasons for which it is held.

It is important to see the consequences of this new safety condition for the green-barn counterexample to the original proposal. With his original safety condition, one could know that the seen object is a green barn, but not that it is a barn. To get out of that violation of closure, we can distinguish between two different phenomenological backgrounds that might be at play in this case. One way is for us to have two separate appearance states, which we might put in terms of being appeared to barnly and also being appeared to greenly. The other possibility is for there to be one complex appearance state, the state of being appeared to green-barn-ly, or, as I shall grotesquely put it, grarnly.

On the first possibility, the basis of the green-barn belief is two separate appearance states. One plausible way to conceive of how the mechanisms of belief formation work in such a case is as follows: The mechanism of belief formation takes us from each appearance state to two separate beliefs, one about a barn and one about a green object. Then a third belief, that there is only one object here, is used with the other beliefs to arrive at the inferred belief about a green barn. Call the three central beliefs here the "barn belief," the "green belief," and the "green-barn belief."

In this scenario, the barn belief is not safe. Its basis is the appearance state of being appeared to barnly, and the safety of this belief on this basis is ruled out by the devious devices of the denizens of the domain. The green belief is safe, but the inferred green-barn belief cannot undermine any closure principle, since it is inferred from a set of premises one of which is not known to be true (because it is unsafe).

The other phenomenological option involves being appeared to grarnly. In this case, the perceptual belief would be the green-barn belief, and it would be safe (since its basis is both the green appearance and the barn appearance). In this scenario, closure is at stake, since the barn belief is a deductive consequence of the green-barn belief. If the basis of the barn belief is deduction, then Sosa's latest safety condition counts the belief as safe as well.

Both of these ways of describing the process of belief formation yield happy results for Sosa's new safety condition. There are other possibilities here, however, that may not be so kind to it. No matter whether the appearances are distinct or unified, the connections between appearances and beliefs can vary. In describing the two phenomenological possibilities earlier, we assumed that the process of belief formation goes from being appeared to F-ly to believing that something is F, with the rest being a matter of inference. There is no requirement that things work this way, however. The mechanism of belief formation might not go directly from each individual appearance state to belief, but might function to go directly from two individual appearance states to belief. That is, it may be that the default setting for properties registered in multiple appearance states at a given moment is for a belief to be formed that treats all such properties as properties of the same object unless they are accompanied by further appearance states registering distinctness of objects. In such a case, there is a problem for Sosa's latest proposal, since the green-barn belief will be safe, but the barn belief will not. Since the first implies the second and is presumably known to do so, Sosa is required to abandon both deductive consequence closure and known implication closure.

This result would be quite troubling to Sosa if these closure principles were the only ones available, for the motivation for Sosa's particular version of counterfactual epistemology was to preserve closure, which sensitivity versions of the view fail to do. These principles, however, are not the only closure principles available, and it is well known that they fail for more general reasons than those provided by Sosa's epistemology. Deductive consequence closure fails because it requires that anyone who knows anything be logically omniscient, knowing every logical truth whatsoever. Moreover, known implication closure fails as well, since coming to see the implications of one's view is often a reason to abandon that view rather than a reason to come to believe what is implied.

In the face of these difficulties for deductive consequence closure and known implication closure, defenders of closure have looked elsewhere for more defensible instances of the knowledge closure schema. One of the best available is defended by John Hawthorne, building on an idea first suggested by Timothy Williamson to the effect that knowledge should be closed under competent deduction.[14] Hawthorne's principle is the following:

> If one knows P and competently deduces Q from P, thereby coming to believe Q, while retaining one's knowledge that P, one comes to know that Q.[15]

I want to propose a small emendation of this principle in a moment, but it is first worth pointing out how this principle is an instance of the knowledge closure schema. For it to be an instance, we must exclude no propositions whatsoever from the range being considered, and we must find some relation involving deductive consequences. It is clear that there are no restrictions here on propositions considered, and the relation in question is the relation of competent deduction by the person in question of the relevant proposition from the set of knowledge in question. Therefore, Hawthorne's principle counts as a closure principle (and not just some general epistemic principle involving deduction). I will term this principle "Hawthorne competent deduction closure."

The small emendation I will suggest is meant to account for the possibility that one learns a (misleading) defeater for Q while competently deducing it from P. In such a case, one will not be able to come to know Q in this way. The question is whether learning such a misleading defeater would automatically undermine one's knowledge that P. If it would, then Hawthorne's principle is adequate as it stands. If not, the following emendation is needed:

> If one knows P and competently deduces Q from P, thereby coming to believe Q, while retaining one's knowledge that P and learning of no undefeated defeater for Q in the process, one comes to know that Q.

There is little reason to try to avoid this emendation, which I dub "emended competent deduction closure." Rarely do we learn nothing in the process of deducing a claim other than the claim itself. We may be watching television, looking at the clouds in the sky, or any number of other things. In doing these other things, we may, for example, overhear a misleading defeater for what we are inferring, but simply ignore its implications for whether we should believe Q. So we come to believe Q by competently deducing it from P. We do not know Q, however, because we have a defeater for believing Q. As it happens, it is a misleading defeater, but we do not know that part of the story. Depending on what kind of a defeater it is, it may also undermine our knowledge of P, but it need not.

A rebutting defeater is one that is evidence against the claim in question, and it is plausible to think that if E is evidence against Q, and P implies Q, then E is evidence against P as well (because it is evidence for $\sim Q$ and hence evidence for $\sim P$ because $\sim Q$ implies $\sim P$). The same cannot be said for undercutting defeaters, defeaters that threaten the connection between our evidence and what we believe. In the case of deduction, the overheard testimony might be two logicians trying to rob you of knowledge, saying to each other that the inference from P to Q is (subtilely) invalid. You hear what they say and ignore it, forming the belief that Q on the basis of competent deduction from P. But you do not know Q. So Hawthorne competent deduction closure is false.

Emended competent deduction closure fixes this problem. Moreover, both principles give Sosa a closure principle to endorse without being troubled by the green-barn case. In the discussion earlier, the versions of the green-barn case that caused problems were those in which no inference took place between the green-barn belief and the barn belief. Such cases are irrelevant to these principles, since they require competent deduction in their antecedents. Moreover, when the cases involve inference, Sosa's latest safety requirement gives the same epistemological verdict for both the barn belief and the green-barn belief.

Even so, there is a residual worry about Sosa's response here, a worry that I will mention but not press. I do not see why one phenomenological account over the other should somehow indicate a difference in knowledge, as Sosa's view requires. Take two barn believers, one of whom has the conjunctive abstraction experience Sosa indicates, and the other of whom has a unified experience. I do not see why this phenomenological difference should imply knowledge in one case and lack of it in the other. When I look at the cases, I am inclined to think that no matter which of these two phenomenologies is actual, there is no knowledge of a green barn or a barn.

This difficulty is a harbinger of further problems to come. One arises from an example central in the Gettier literature. You see Tim steal a book from the library, and you believe as a result that Tim stole the book.[16] You report Tim to the police, and when they go to Tim's home to arrest him, Tim's mother swears his innocence. She says that Tim has a twin brother, Tom, who is a kleptomaniac, and that Tim is on a safari expedition in Africa. Where is Tom? She claims to have no idea, of course.

This case splits into two. In one case, the police have no past history with Tim's mother. Her claims are persuasive and she appears honest, so the police must check out her story before proceeding with their plans to find Tim and arrest him. In the other case, the police have a long history of acquaintance with Tim's mother and know that she has lied repeatedly to save Tim from trouble. In fact, she has used this precise lie in the past, and the police have investigated the story and learned that Tim does not have a twin but is an only child. In this case, they laugh off the tale and carry on with their plans to arrest Tim.

In the second case, both you and the police have knowledge about who stole the book that is unaffected by the mother's testimony, but not in the first case. In both cases, the mother's testimony is a defeater of your evidence that Tim stole the book, but it has differential significance in the two cases. In the first case, it undermines your knowledge, since it is a possibility that the police must check out. But in the second case, it does not undermine your knowledge.

If this particular case is not convincing, imagine different contexts for the mother to say what she says. Imagine, for example, that the mother's testimony is part of a theater production in which she was acting. Or imagine her saying it in her sleep, as part of a dream, or saying it to convince herself: "He *has* a twin brother! He really does! Tim's in Africa, he *really* is!" And imagine any of these possibilities with no one around at all to hear what she says. Knowledge cannot be so fragile that it disappears just because a normally competent speaker denies what we believe.

Notice that neither safety nor sensitivity can explain the difference between the two cases. In both cases, the mother is failing to tell the truth, and whatever is the proper account of the relevant difference in the two cases, that difference cannot be explained in terms of safety or sensitivity.

Furthermore, notice that there will be cases like this one for any type of belief one wishes to consider. This case involves a perceptual belief, but it could just as easily have been a statistical or inductive belief, a belief based on memory, or a testimonial belief. Safety and sensitivity may be part of the story of what distinguishes knowledge from true belief, though I cannot see at this point what role they might play in that story, but they are not enough of the story to fulfill the promise of Nozickian epistemology. Neither is necessary for knowledge, and together they are not sufficient either.

There is a further problem for Sosa's latest account of safety as well. We can begin to see the problem by noticing the relationship between Sosa's account and Dretske's own version of the counterfactual approach. The difference between this latest safety account and the initial safety account is roughly the same as that between Nozick's simple sensitivity account and Dretske's more refined conclusive reasons account. Nozick's simple account is just the sensitivity condition formulated earlier, whereas Dretske's account claims:

> A belief is sensitive just when one would not have the reasons one has for believing as one does if the claim in question were not true.[17]

Dretske maintains that his account undermines closure just as much as Nozick's does on the basis of the zebra/disguised-mule case. Granting this point and noticing that Sosa's latest condition is the transpositive of Dretske's (if we add to Dretske's account some claim about basing, which can, I think, be viewed as a friendly amendment to his principle), we should still find it a surprising result if the failures of transposition for counterfactuals line up in just the right way so that Sosa's condition preserves closure if Dretske's does not.

Consider Dretske's own example of the cleverly disguised mule. Our perceptual input is the same whether we are looking at a zebra or a cleverly disguised mule. We know, on the basis of these perceptual reasons, that the object is a zebra. We also know that being a zebra entails not being a cleverly disguised mule. But, Dretske holds, we do not know that the object we are seeing is not a cleverly disguised mule. The reason we do not is that we would have the same reasons for believing as we do even if it were not so.

Sosa must claim one of two things about the example. The first option is to deny that we know, on the basis of perceptual reasons, that the object is a zebra. Since Sosa wishes to avoid skepticism, we can abandon this option. Since he cannot deny the entailment claim, he is left having to defend the claim that we can know that the object is a cleverly disguised mule. To defend this position, he must maintain that the following is true: if we were to believe on the basis of the same perceptual reasons we presently experience, the object in question would not be a cleverly disguised mule.

Some will question whether this counterfactual is true, and if it is not, then Sosa's approach yields a denial of closure just as much as Dretske's approach does. Even if we grant that this counterfactual is true, however, there are other difficulties to be faced resulting from noting the obvious point that even if your belief that the animal is not a cleverly disguised mule is a safe belief, there is some chance that it is a cleverly disguised mule. Once we admit this obvious point, the preservation of closure by appeal to safety is going to have problems with lottery cases. You buy a lottery ticket, and the chance of it winning is much lower than the chance that you are looking at a cleverly disguised mule in Dretske's zoo. Given that one has already granted the safety of the belief that you are not looking at a cleverly disguised mule, it will be quite difficult to deny the safety of a belief that your ticket will lose: if you were to believe that your ticket will lose on the basis of the statistical information you possess, you would be right. In the zoo case, you cannot tell perceptually whether the animal is a mule or a zebra, but your belief that it is not a cleverly disguised mule is safe anyway. Similarly, your statistical information remains the same whether your ticket is a loser or a winner, but given what was claimed about the zoo case, that fact cannot be used to say why the belief that your ticket will lose is not safe. But granting the safety of the lottery belief threatens paradox, for the very same statistical information makes any belief to the effect that any particular ticket will lose safe as well. Moreover, since the statistical information itself encodes information about exactly how many tickets there are, the preservation of closure will require that you be able to come to know that every ticket is a loser.

The only way out here is to say that your belief that your ticket will lose is not safe. If that belief is not safe, it is hard to see where to look to explain the lack of safety except at the failure of the statistical information to rule out the chance of error. Yet if that is the explanation here, it will also make trouble for the belief that the object in the zoo is not a cleverly disguised mule, besides making a mockery of the idea of statistical knowledge itself.

It is time to sum up our extended excursion into the tenability of counterfactual theories of knowledge. In an effort to salvage a closure principle, Sosa goes to considerable lengths to propose alterations of the standard counterfactual approaches championed by Nozick and Dretske. To those who favor the idea that there must be some acceptable closure principle and also are attracted to counterfactual approaches to knowledge, Sosa's strategy will be comforting. As we have seen, however, all versions he has proposed of the safety view have problems. The gyrations necessary for salvaging the competent deduction closure principles create problems for the theory in several ways. First, no matter what version of safety we are considering, neither it nor sensitivity will give an adequate explanation of certain kinds of Gettier cases. More important in the present context, however, is that in order to preserve closure, Sosa is required to say things about Dretske's disguised-mule case that appear to land his view in trouble with the lottery paradox.

These difficulties lead one to wonder whether finding an acceptable closure principle is so compelling that counterfactual theorists must travel this road with Sosa. This point is one that I want to press later, but before doing so, I want to show how the relevant-alternatives approach, the other version of modal epistemology under consideration here, ends up at precisely this point as well, the point where we wonder why closure is compelling enough to modal epistemologists to make them attempt the transformations of an intuitive theory that are necessary to provide any hope at all of preserving closure.

3.2. Relevant-Alternatives Theories

We can clarify the relevant-alternatives theory by comparing it with the view that in order to know, one must be able to rule out or eliminate all logical contraries of a given claim. Such a principle is especially attractive to skeptics, who argue that we simply cannot rule out all such alternatives. In response to this skeptical argument, defenders of the relevant-alternatives theory, such as Dretske and Goldman, argue that instead of needing to rule out all logical contraries to a given claim in order to have knowledge, we need to be able to rule out only the relevant contraries or alternatives.[18]

This position obviously needs an explanation of the notion of relevance, but even without an explicit characterization of that notion, it is easy to see why a defender of this view would be attracted to the idea of denying closure. If a radical skeptical hypothesis is not relevant at a particular point in time, one can know without having to rule out that hypothesis, even if the denial of that hypothesis is a deductive consequence of what one knows. For example, when G.E. Moore claims to know that here is one hand and here is another, he may be in a context where the possibility that there is no external world is relevant. Even if he is in such a situation, however, there is no reason to suppose that everyone, everywhere, is in such a situation. So at least sometimes, we can know that here is one hand and here is another without having to rule out external-world skepticism.

In spite of the virtues of this denial of closure, some defenders of the view have been attracted enough to the idea of closure that they have sought to find a way to preserve the theory without embracing the denial of closure. The key to being able to do so is provided by Gail Stine.[19] To preserve closure and yet retain the advantages of the theory in responding to skepticism, the new relevant-alternatives theorist[20] may maintain that one needs evidence to rule out relevant alternatives, but that one can know that an irrelevant alternative is false without evidence. With Stine, one may hold fixed the set of relevant alternatives when engaged in inference and thereby come to know the denial of some skeptical hypothesis *relative to the set of alternatives fixed as relevant*. In this way, it is possible to know that an alternative is false even when the evidence for the proposition that implies that it is false is not sufficient to rule out that alternative. One might put this point as the idea that closure is preserved because one knows that some alternatives are false simply because they are irrelevant, but that is a bit misleading. The more careful point is that one can know that some alternatives are false simply by inferring their falsity from the very claim to which they are an alternative. There is no need to be able to rule them out on any other basis.

There are problems with this view, however, no matter how carefully and charitably it is interpreted. Suppose I know that your pet is a dog, and the situation is one in which the relevant alternatives are the normal ones: your pet is a cat, a bird, a snake, or some other creature often kept as a pet. In such a normal situation, relevant alternatives have to do with other kinds of creatures that are often kept as pets. It is not a relevant alternative, in the usual case, for one to have an inanimate object as a pet. On the new relevant-alternatives theory, however, that does not prevent me from knowing that your pet is not inanimate by inferring it from the claim that your pet is a dog.

There is a problem here, however. When I infer from the claim that your pet is a dog to the claim that your pet is not inanimate, in the ordinary case I end up with a claim for which no relevant alternative to the original claim is an alternative at all to the second claim: being a cat or a parakeet is not an alternative to failing to be inanimate. In such a case, the second claim can be known even in the absence of being able to rule out any alternative whatsoever to it. When the class of relevant alternatives is empty in this way, the appearance of disunity in the theory is rather startling: some knowledge obtains in virtue of having evidence sufficient for eliminating alternative hypotheses, some does not.

There is a legitimate way to arrive at such disunity in this theory. If we begin with careful definitions of the notion of an alternative and the notion of relevance and then apply these definitions in a given case, it may be that there are some propositions that can be known in a given situation without having to rule out anything. But that is not what happens here when a closure principle is applied. The only alternatives that get screened for relevance are the alternatives to the original knowledge claim. Even if there are alternatives to the inferred claim that would count as relevant on the account embraced by the theory in question, those alternatives do not get considered at all. As a result, the disunity of the theory is stark and troubling.

Moreover, and this is the point I want to emphasize, it is hard to see the motivation for a relevant-alternatives theorist to engage in the contortions necessary to preserve some closure principle. Such a theorist is confronted with an argument against closure in which the possibilities relevant to the truth of the first premise differ from the possibilities relevant to the truth of the second premise. The theorist draws the conclusion that the argument against closure must thus be invalid. But there are other cases of precisely the same sort of situation in which none of us are tempted to think that the argument is invalid. Mark Heller uses the example of strengthening the antecedent of a subjunctive conditional as an example of this,[21] and we could use the failure of a hypothetical syllogism on such conditionals for the same purpose. The following inference is invalid:

If I were to jump off a cliff over 300 feet high, I would get hurt.
So, if I were to jump off such a cliff wearing an appropriate parachute, I would get hurt.

So is the following inference invalid:

If Brazil had not won the 2002 World Cup in soccer, Germany would have.
If the U.S. team had won the tournament, Brazil would not have won.
So, if the U.S. team had won, Germany would have won.

The latter example is especially instructive in the present context. In evaluating the first premise of the argument, very nearby worlds are relevant, whereas in evaluating the second premise, quite remote worlds have to be considered. This shift in which worlds are consulted is not normally taken as a sign that it is a mistake to judge both premises true and the conclusion false, however. Instead, we use the shift to explain why the argument is invalid, even though the same kind of argumentative form is valid when it uses material conditionals.

Such considerations are equally relevant to the contextualist attempt to rescue closure for counterfactual modal epistemology. According to this kind of contextualist, abandoning closure is a bad idea, and to avoid it, we should insist that the distance of the worlds at which we evaluate the truth-value of the premises of an argument be held fixed throughout the entire argument. If we do so, then (in a fixed context) we can know that we are not brains in a vat by inferring this from our knowledge that we have hands. The appearance of closure failure is illusory, arising from the failure to hold the context fixed.

Yet no one would suggest that the logic for subjunctives has been mischaracterized by failure to fix context in this way. Instead, we simply conclude that strengthening the antecedent is invalid for subjunctives, as is hypothetical syllogism.

It is, of course, a mistake to conclude that a viewpoint is mistaken by undermining a generalization of that viewpoint. It is not a mistake, however, to wonder about the motivation for a view when the most obvious and plausible generalization of it is obviously false and rejected by the proponents of the view in question. There is little temptation to try to preserve hypothetical syllogism for subjunctives by fixing the class of worlds relevant to the assessment of truth-value for the premises, and yet some are tempted to make this same maneuver when they face an argument against closure.

We thus come to the same point in considering this version of modal epistemology as we did when we considered the version of it that appeals to counterfactuals. In both cases, theorists are motivated to engage in various theoretical maneuvers (contortions?) to try to save closure when a quite intuitive approach to the basic idea of the theory involves denying closure, especially when the context is one of attempting to find a suitable answer to the skeptic. If the case for closure is strong enough, however, the theoretical maneuvers would be well motivated. I turn, then, in the next section to the grounds for adopting closure to see if we can find a suitable basis for this attraction to closure.

4. WHENCE THE ATTRACTION OF CLOSURE?

As I see it, there are several grounds for finding closure attractive. One ground proceeds by consideration of specific cases. You know that Budapest is the capital of Hungary but are uncertain where Hungary is. You find out that it is in Europe, and since the entailment is obvious to you, you come to know that Budapest is in Europe.

Such examination of cases fits a fundamental motivation for adopting closure expressed by Timothy Williamson, to the effect that deduction is a way of extending knowledge.[22] One way to interpret this idea is that there must be some set of conditions that, if met, take one via deduction from things that are already known to knowledge of other things. If this claim is true, then there will be some specifiable operation that takes us from a set of known propositions to another set of known propositions—which is just an intuitive way of expressing the knowledge closure schema.

This argument, however, is not completely persuasive. As I pointed out earlier, we should not count a principle as a closure principle if it restricts the kinds of propositions that can come to be known by application of the given principle. Moreover, the intuitive idea that knowledge is a way of extending knowledge is perfectly compatible with the idea championed by Dretske that there are certain philosophically "heavyweight" propositions that cannot come to be known by deducing them from ordinary pieces of knowledge, for example, that there is an external world, or that I am not a brain in a vat.[23] That deduction is always and everywhere knowledge-extending does not follow from the obviously correct claim that deduction is a way of extending knowledge, and once we have noticed the demand that a closure principle apply to all propositions whatsoever and not merely to some of them, Williamson's adage is far from conclusive in giving one a reason to affirm a closure principle.

A second argument for closure derives from ordinary assertion contexts. Hawthorne presents the argument in an especially pointed way:

> I ask S whether she agrees that P. She asserts that she does: "Yes," she says. I then ask S whether she realizes that Q follows from P. "Yes," she says. I then ask her whether she agrees that Q. "I'm not agreeing to that," she says. I ask her whether she now wishes to retract her earlier claims. "Oh no," she says. "I'm sticking by my claim that P and my claim that P entails Q. I'm just not willing to claim that Q." Our interlocutor now resembles perfectly Lewis Carroll's Tortoise, that familiar object of ridicule who was perfectly willing to accept the premises of a *modus ponens* argument but was unwilling to accept the conclusion.[24]

Hawthorne describes this argument as deriving from the idea that in asserting, we represent ourselves as knowing, and the explanation of this claim as arising from Williamson's idea that knowledge is the norm of assertion.[25] This is a mistake.

Williamson's norm requires that one not assert a claim without knowing it to be true. In the case Hawthorne gives, if a suitable closure principle is true, then S may or may not be asserting something without knowing it to be true. One option is that S knows P and knows that P entails Q. In this case, given a closure principle, her refusal to assert Q is only a matter of her refusing to assert something she knows to be true. That situation, however, is not a situation in which the knowledge norm of assertion is violated. The only way to get a violation of the knowledge norm of assertion is to assume that S does not know Q and hence does not know one of the two things she is asserting to be true.[26]

Moreover, there is a way to show that no impropriety of assertion of any sort needs to be going on in the case in question. If we can add information to Hawthorne's description of the case so that it renders intelligible the assertions made in addition to the reticence expressed, then an interlocutor could speak as imagined without being a legitimate object of ridicule. To see how to render such judgments intelligible, suppose that S has a concept of epistemic priority of the following sort: when Q is epistemically prior to P, then one cannot come to know Q by inferring it from P. For example, suppose that P is the claim that a certain object is red, and Q is the claim that there is no blacklight shining on the object that makes it appear red when it is not. In this case, suppose that S went on to explain her unusual situation as follows: "I know that Q follows from P, and ordinarily that is a decisive reason to believe Q. But I cannot come to know it on that basis, since it is epistemically prior to P. But I do know P and what it entails; so I am left wondering what suitable grounds I have for believing Q. I have no idea what those grounds might be, and without some idea of what they might be, I do not think that I ought to run around asserting Q. I am faced with a puzzle, and to express my intellectual dilemma, I think the best thing to do is to simply stop at asserting P and asserting that Q is entailed by it. Until I have some idea of how I could know that Q, I do not see what else would be reasonable to do right now."

Here S appeals to a version of the problem of easy knowledge,[27] which derives from the fact that "if Q" is itself a skeptical claim of some sort. You cannot defend the claim that there is no blacklight shining on an object that makes it appear red when it is not by remarking that you can infer this from your knowledge that the object is red, which you have on the basis of your visual impression. Someone indicating awareness of the problem might find herself asserting precisely what Hawthorne puts in the mouth of S, and it would be morally and epistemically objectionable to view such a person as an object of ridicule. To feel the force of a philosophical puzzle and end up saying unusual things because of it is a perfectly understandable phenomenon. No one in such a predicament should be thought of as an example of deserved ridicule—every serious philosopher should be balking here, "We do not want to go there!"

Once we see that it is possible to make conversational sense of conversations that violate quite simple closure principles, the argument for closure from the knowledge account of assertion cannot be thought anywhere close to being decisive. It would be a mistake as well to go to the other conclusion—that the conversational possibility shows that closure principles are false. One way to understand the example in a way compatible with the truth of some closure principle is that a person might, in such a situation, know that Q is true and yet balk at asserting it anyway for the reasons given.

Besides these arguments for a closure principle, there is little by way of defense of closure to be found in the literature. In many cases, we encounter merely the argument from befuddlement: how *could* one know some truth and know that it implies some other truth and yet not know the latter? Once the falsity of the closure principle assumed by this rhetorical question is exposed, said befuddled epistemologist will launch off down the road of principle refinement. In many such cases, the refined principle offered is not even a closure principle. For example, in response to counterexamples to the principle presupposed by the befuddlement question, one often gets the claim that one would have to be, at least, in a position to know in such a case. The truth of that claim is no more obvious than the claim that there is some true closure principle, but in any case, it is not itself a closure principle at all, so opponents of closure need not deny it.

5. Closure Reconsidered

The proper conclusion to draw from this discussion is that the positive case for closure is quite a ways from conclusive. In addition, the arguments against closure are equally uncompelling. There are widely shared intuitive reactions to specific cases that lend some credence, on the one hand, to closure and, on the other hand, to its denial. It is hard to make sense of someone balking at the logical consequences of her beliefs without also tending to abandon some of her beliefs. It is hard to make sense, as well, of citing perceptual data to confirm that these very perceptual conditions are not abnormal in a way that makes our perceptual beliefs false. So even the best closure principle we have found, enhanced competent deduction closure, is not obviously correct. Perhaps we are left with an echo from David Lewis: to the winner belong the spoils. That is, perhaps each side should work out a theory of knowledge, and whichever approach turns out to be most successful on general theoretical grounds, that side gets the goods of whether or not there is a true closure principle on the basis of what its theory implies. Closure considerations will still play a role in evaluating such theories, since there are sane examples of closure and its denial and there are idiotic examples of the same. There is a virtue, however, in the approach that gives the spoils to the winner. This conclusion would have the added benefit of pointing away from a lamentable preoccupation in recent epistemology with its metatheory and back to the central task of the discipline, which is that of constructing and defending a theory of knowledge (or whatever other cognitive achievements one wishes to understand).

It would be nice, however, to be able to say something about the issue, even if a bit tentatively, in the absence of a full theory of knowledge. If something can be said here, I think that progress will be found by distinguishing the rhetorical context in which we are imagining trying to answer a challenge to our beliefs from a nonrhetorical context in which we are simply assessing what is true and what is not. When we distinguish these contexts from each other, we have some grounds for affirming emended competent deduction closure (ECDC).

The fundamental objection to ECDC comes from imagining cases like Dretske's disguised-mule example in which a known consequence of something we are quite confident of is challenged. In Dretske's case, we imagine someone asking, "How do you know it is not a cleverly disguised mule?" To respond, "Well, I know that it is a zebra, and I know that if it is a zebra, it is not a cleverly disguised mule; so I know because it follows from other things I know." A sense of shame would be appropriate at putting on such airs.

The context is different, however, when one is casually surveying one's zoo experience after the fact. One can reflect on the carefree afternoon in conversation: "We saw lions, tigers, bears; mountain goats, alligators, bison; what else?" "Oh, lots of things—birds, fish, and snakes." "Zoos are such a—oh, how to put it?—*natural* experience. Well, except for the cages and all that! But what I mean is that what we experienced today was not a human invention, it was not an artifact. We got to see the real thing. We were not looking at *pictures* of animals on TV; we were not seeing fancy *robotics* designed to mimic real animals; we were not seeing *people* dressed in *costumes* to look like the animals. Nature is beautiful and seeing it is so refreshing!" There is no hesitation experienced anywhere in this conversation.

The question is how to explain this difference, and the point I want to stress is that any explanation will favor ECDC over denials of it. These two contexts are ones in which the very same inferences are in question. In both cases, there is an inference from things already known to the target proposition. In the original case, the thing known is that the object is a zebra, and the target proposition is that it is not a cleverly disguised mule. In the second case, we have enumerations of the same kind of thing known, with enumerations of the same kind of target proposition. There is a sense in which the second conversation adverts to background knowledge about zoos in a bit more explicit way than in the first case, but that difference is insignificant since this background information is present, we may assume, in both cases. After all, it is not as if the discomfort in the first case is simply a function of having no prior experience with zoos or awareness of what a zoo is like.

The point to note is that the two cases are structurally isomorphic in terms of inferential structure, background knowledge, initial assumed knowledge, and the kinds of propositions in question. Yet the context difference makes the inference troubling in one case but not in the other. From these facts, we can see that if, perchance, the former case counts against ECDC, it does so in an utterly inexplicable fashion.

Let me explain why. No one can plausibly deny that deduction is a way of extending our knowledge. If there is a failure of closure, the options for explaining the failure are limited in important ways. First, the belief condition for knowledge might fail. That is, one might fail to believe the deductive consequences of what one knows. This problem shows that deductive consequence closure and known implication closure are both false. It does not affect either of the competent deductive closure principles, however, since those principles build into their antecedents that the belief condition is satisfied. Second, one might try to explain closure failure by maintaining that the Gettier condition itself is satisfied for the original belief but not for the target belief. In line with the standard terminology in the literature, let us call this feature an "external defeater" of the epistemic grounds of the target belief (reserving "internal defeater" for those factors within the purview of the cognizer in question that undermine knowledge). Defeaters come in two varieties: rebutters and undercutters.[28] Since one's reason for believing the target proposition is the original proposition from which it logically follows, the external defeater cannot be an undercutter of the connection between these two claims, since the fact that the second follows from the first always and everywhere overrides any such external defeater. That leaves such a defeater to function only as a rebutter, but if there is an external defeater that functions as reason enough against the target proposition to rule out knowledge of it, this same defeater will function as a rebutter of the original proposition as well. A rebutter of P is a reason for $\sim P$, and if a rebutter is reason enough for $\sim Q$ to prevent knowledge of Q, it will be reason enough against $\sim P$ to rule out knowledge of it as well, since $\sim P$ follows from $\sim Q$.

One may object here on two grounds. One may say that this argument begs the question by assuming a closure principle. That complaint is correct; it does assume some kind of closure principle, but not a closure principle about knowledge. The mere fact that some closure principle is assumed is not enough to substantiate the claim that this argument begs the question, and I see no other basis for the charge here.

The other objection is one that Keith DeRose has called the "just barely" objection.[29] Suppose that there is some degree of "drainage" of epistemic support, or accumulation of relevant doubt, when moving from premises to conclusions of even a deductive argument. As John Hawthorne says about multipremise closure principles:

> Deductive inference from multiple premises aggregates risks. The risk accruing to one's belief in each premise may be small enough to be consistent with the belief having the status of knowledge. But the risks may add up, so that the deduced belief may be in too great a danger of being false to count as knowledge.[30]

If this point is true of multipremise inferences, then presumably there is some small risk in any inference. Suppose that this is true here. Suppose that we have a rebutter of the target proposition Q that is just barely enough of an external rebutter to undermine purported knowledge of Q, but that the drainage resulting from the logical connection between $\sim Q$ and $\sim P$ is just enough that this reason for $\sim Q$ is not enough of a reason for $\sim P$ to undermine knowledge of it. In this case, ECDC is false.

A solution to the "just barely" problem can be found, I suggest, by considering the kind of risk that has to be involved for the aggregation of risk to undermine multipremise closure. The risk in question cannot be any kind of objective risk, since the cherished characteristic of deductive consequences is that they are guaranteed to preserve truth. The kind of risk involved must be found elsewhere, in the rational attitude we take toward our own fallibility. That is, the risk involved must depend in some way or other on our own subjective psychological condition. As a result, the "just barely" problem comes into play when a person infers one thing from another, not when it is merely being noted that one thing is a deductive consequence of another. Note that in the earlier argument on behalf of ECDC, no inference from a defeater of Q to a defeater of P is being made: the defeater in question is an external one, and the relationships in question are not inferential but only deductive. So even if there is a "just barely" problem to be solved, it cannot come into play at this stage in undermining my claim that no explanation of the cases above can appeal to differences with respect to satisfying the Gettier requirement for knowledge.

So, as far as I can see, there is no basis for an explanation of the difference in the two examples with which we began this discussion in terms of the belief condition or the Gettier condition that would undermine ECDC. Since the truth condition is guaranteed by the deductive relationship here, the other possibility to consider is that there is some difference with respect to the grounds-of-belief requirement for knowledge to explain the difference. That avenue, however, is closed off because any such explanation would depend on the existence of an internal defeater, and those are already ruled out explicitly in ECDC.

The conclusion we may draw here, then, is that the explanation of the difference cannot appeal to any difference in the usual conditions for knowledge. Moreover, the difference cannot appeal to any difference in the kind of the propositions in question, since the cases are constructed so that there is no such difference. What remains is only other features of the two contexts that do not affect any of the conditions for knowledge and do not depend on any difference in the kind of propositions involved in the deduction.

In the cases we are comparing, there is the Dretske case where one appears to be putting on airs or being pompous in such a way that one ought to be ashamed of oneself for claiming to know what one has derived from one's knowledge gained by perception. In the other case, one infers just as before, but in a reflective moment, registering the joy of life in the experiences of the day. If one does not have knowledge in the first case, we have learned that this lack will be due to some X factor having nothing to do with any of the conditions for knowledge. The most natural way to read the Dretske cases is in terms of some intellectual paroxysm— one recoils from the belief itself, or at least from the kind of full belief, whatever that may be, characteristic of knowledge. Such an interpretation of the X factor leaves ECDC untouched, since one has not truly come to believe the claim in question on the basis of competent deduction.

Suppose, however, that one is blessedly free of this paroxysm and unaffectedly free of the sense of impropriety the rest of us feel in such Dretske situations. Do such epistemic flower children have knowledge in Dretske situations? I will approach this question indirectly. The difference between us normals and such flower children is a *social difference*. We feel the weight of social norms in a Dretske situation in a way they do not. If that is correct, however, the difference between Dretske situations and simple reflective situations is a social difference. I suggest that the most plausible difference to focus on here is the difference in the rhetorical situation in question. In Dretske situations, there is a hint of a challenge to a given belief or inference, and the rules governing rhetorical exchanges are not the same rules that determine whether or not one has knowledge. In a rhetorical situation, certain responses beg the question against one's opponent and are thus inappropriate in the context. To be an epistemic flower child is to be the kind of person whose spontaneity and charm are used to decline the attempt to create just such a rhetorical situation. We may want to criticize such persons on the basis of other social norms, but we should not criticize them on epistemic grounds. The rest of us, shackled by the chains of civilization and having internalized in our doxastic practices the effects of such thorough conditioning, mildly acquiesce to the imposition of such a rhetorical situation and even tend to refrain from forming beliefs for which we have a perfectly legitimate epistemic base.

6. CONCLUSION

Note that the story told about the difference between Dretske cases and reflective-moment cases sustains ECDC. We therefore have an explanation of the difference in the two cases, an explanation that tells us why we should not brashly make the inferences in question in Dretske cases and should feel some discomfort when we do so. Our sensitivity as social animals puts us in just such a position. The important point to recognize is the need to distinguish epistemic norms from social norms, and if we do, we can see that there are good grounds for accepting ECDC in spite of the existence and plausibility of Dretske cases.

NOTES

1. We need not saddle modal epistemologists with the view that this talk about possible worlds must be treated in the most metaphysically serious way. All we need at this point is the heuristic value of such talk.

2. Henry E. Kyburg, Jr., *Probability and the Logic of Rational Belief* (Middletown, CT: Wesleyan University Press, 1961).

3. Henry E. Kyburg, Jr., "Probability and Randomness," *Theoria* 29 (1963): 27–55. I thank Greg Wheeler for pointing out to me the background of Kyburg's denial of closure in the context of the paradox.

4. F.P. Ramsey, "Knowledge," in *F.P. Ramsey: Philosophical Papers*, edited by D.H. Mellor (Cambridge: Cambridge University Press, 1990), pp. 110–111. The original date on this essay is 1929. I thank Horacio Arlo-Costa for pointing out this source to me.

5. D.C. Makinson, "The Paradox of the Preface," *Analysis* 25 (1965): 205–207.

6. Dretske 1970.

7. Goldman 1976.

8. Ludwig Wittgenstein, *On Certainty*, edited by G.E.M. Anscombe and G.H. von Wright, translated by Denis Paul and G.E.M. Anscombe (Oxford: Oxford University Press, 1969). I thank Peter Baumann for bringing to my attention the relevance of Wittgenstein to the issue of closure.

9. Nozick 1981.

10. Developed in detail in David Lewis, *Counterfactuals* (Cambridge: Basil Blackwell, 1973).

11. Nozick 1981, p. 228.

12. See, for example, DeRose 1995.

13. Ernest Sosa is the originator of this approach. See Sosa, "Plantinga on Epistemic Internalism," in *Warrant in Contemporary Epistemology*, edited by Jonathan L. Kvanvig (Lanham, MD, 1996), pp. 73–87.

14. Hawthorne 2005. Williamson's idea is found in Williamson 2000.

15. Hawthorne 2005, p. 29.

16. The case here first appeared in Keith Lehrer and Thomas D. Paxson, Jr., "Knowledge: Undefeated Justified True Belief," *Journal of Philosophy* 66 (1969): 225–237.

17. Dretske's formulation employs an "unless" connective: one would not have one's reasons unless the claim were true. I have interpreted this connective in terms of "if not" because I think that nothing substantive hangs on the distinction.

18. See Dretske 1970 and Goldman 1976.

19. See Stine 1976.

20. This terminology is borrowed from Vogel 1990.

21. See Heller 1989.

22. Williamson 2000, p. 117.

23. Dretske 2005; the term "heavyweight" is first introduced on p. 17.

24. Hawthorne 2005, p. 32.

25. Williamson 2000.

26. I have argued against the knowledge norm of assertion in Jonathan Kvanvig, "Knowledge, Assertion, and Lotteries," in *Williamson on Knowledge*, edited by Duncan Pritchard and Patrick Greenough (Oxford: Oxford University Press, forthcoming), but the dispute on this point makes no difference to the proper evaluation of the argument Hawthorne gives here, so in the text I simply assume that the knowledge account is correct.

27. See Cohen 2002.

28. This is the terminology of John Pollock. See Pollock, *Contemporary Theories of Knowledge* (Totowa, NJ: Rowman and Littlefield, 1986).

29. Keith posted this argument June 24, 2004, at http://bengal-ng.missouri.edu/~kvanvigj/certain_doubts/index.php?p=38, on the epistemology blog Certain Doubts

(which reliable sources say is definitely required reading of anyone seriously interested in epistemology).

  30. Hawthorne 2004, p. 47.

REFERENCES

Audi, Robert. "Deductive Closure, Defeasibility and Scepticism: A Reply to Feldman." *Philosophical Quarterly* 45 (1995): 494–499.

Bogdan, Radu J."Cognition and Epistemic Closure." *American Philosophical Quarterly* 22 (1985): 55–63.

Brueckner, Anthony. "Losing Track of the Sceptic." *Analysis* 45 (1985): 103–104.

———. "Skepticism and Epistemic Closure." *Philosophical Topics* 13 (1985): 89–117.

———. "Transmission for Knowledge Not Established." *Philosophical Quarterly* 35 (1985): 193–196.

Cohen, Stewart. "Basic Knowledge and the Problem of Easy Knowledge." *Philosophy and Phenomenological Research* 65 (2002): 309–329.

———. "Contextualism, Skepticism, and the Structure of Reasons." *Philosophical Perspectives* 13 (1999): 57–89.

———. "How to Be a Fallibilist." *Philosophical Perspectives* 2 (1988): 91–123.

DeRose, Keith. "Solving the Skeptical Problem." *Philosophical Review* 104 (1995): 1–52.

Dretske, Fred. "The Case against Closure." In *Contemporary Debates in Epistemology*, edited by MatthiasSteup and Ernest Sosa. Malden, MA:Blackwell, 2005, 13–25.

———. "Conclusive Reasons." *Australasian Journal of Philosophy* 49 (1971): 1–22.

———. "Epistemic Operators." *Journal of Philosophy* 67 (1970): 1007–1023.

Feldman, Richard. "In Defense of Closure." *Philosophical Quarterly* 45 (1995): 487–494.

Goldman, Alvin. "Discrimination and Perceptual Knowledge." *Journal of Philosophy* 73 (1976): 771–791.

Hawthorne, John. "The Case for Closure." In *Contemporary Debates in Epistemology*, edited by Matthias Steup and Ernest Sosa. Malden, MA, 2005, pp. 26–42.

———. *Knowledge and Lotteries*. Oxford, 2004.

Heller, Mark. "Relevant Alternatives." *Philosophical Studies* 55 (1989): 23–40.

Klein, Peter. "Skepticism and Closure: Why the Evil Genius Argument Fails." *Philosophical Topics* 23 (1995): 213–236.

Lewis, David. "Elusive Knowledge." *Australasian Journal of Philosophy* 74 (1996): 549–567.

Luper-Foy, Stephen, ed. *The Possibility of Knowledge: Nozick and His Critics*. Totowa, NJ, 1987.

McGrath, Matthew, and Fantl, Jeremy. "Evidence, Pragmatics, and Justification." *Philosophical Review* 111, no. 1 (January 2002): 67–74.

Nozick, Robert. *Philosophical Explanations*. Cambridge, 1981.

Schaffer, Jonathan. "From Contextualism to Contrastivism." *Philosophical Studies*, 2003: 73–103.

Sosa, Ernest. "How to Defeat Opposition to Moore." *Philosophical Perspectives* 13 (1999):141–152.

———. "Postscript to 'Proper Functionalism and Virtue Epistemology.'" In *Warrant in Contemporary Epistemology*, edited by Jonathan Kvanvig. Lanham, MD: Rowman & Littlefield, 1996, 271–281.

Stanley, Jason. *Knowledge and Practical Interests*. Oxford: Oxford University Press, 2005.

Stine, G.C. "Skepticism, Relevant Alternatives, and Deductive Closure." *Philosophical Studies* 29 (1976): 249–261.

Vogel, Jonathan. "Are There Counterexamples to the Closure Principle?" In *Doubting: Contemporary Perspectives on Skepticism*, edited by Michael Roth and Glenn Ross. Dordrecht: Kluwer, 1990.

Williamson, Timothy. *Knowledge and Its Limits*. Oxford: Oxford University Press, 2000.

CONTEMPORARY RESPONSES TO AGRIPPA'S TRILEMMA

PETER D. KLEIN

1. INTRODUCTION

In this chapter, I want to explore what can be called "Agrippa's trilemma" or the "epistemic regress problem." I will begin by examining the problem as seen by the ancient skeptics and their opponents, especially Aristotle. The primary purpose for beginning with the ancient view of the regress is to expose some assumptions that were made about the nature of justification that can and have been questioned by some contemporary epistemologists. Once those assumptions are exposed, foundationalism no longer seems the only viable solution to the deepest form of the regress problem. That leaves two other alternatives: coherentism and infinitism. I will provide some reasons for thinking that infinitism should not be dismissed as lightly as it has been.[1]

2. SOME ASPECTS OF THE PROBLEM AS ORIGINALLY FORMULATED

The problem of the epistemic regress is an ancient one. It is addressed by Aristotle, and its most famous presentation is by Sextus Empiricus, who attributes it to the "later skeptics" and, in particular, Agrippa, who probably lived in the first century A.D.

In its simplest form, the regress problem can be put this way:

1. Suppose that S asserts something, say, *p*. Then an interlocutor—or S herself—can ask: Why do you think that *p* is true? *S better have a reason.* S gives the reason r_1. Then the interlocutor asks: Why do you think that r_1 is true? *S better have a reason.* S gives r_2 as the reason for r_1. Then the interlocutor asks: What is your reason for r_2? *S better have a reason.* And so on.
2. There are only three ways to respond to the regress:
   i. Locate a proposition for which no further reason is required.
   ii. Restate one of the reasons given earlier.
   iii. Keep going forever.
3. None of those responses is acceptable.

I say that this is the simplest formulation and put "S better have a reason" in italics in order to highlight an important assumption that is being made, namely, that there is some burden on S to provide reasons for her beliefs. We will have to investigate the source of that burden. But granting for the moment that there is some burden to provide some reasons for our beliefs when asked to do so, why would one think that (3), that is, that none of the responses to the regress is acceptable, is true?

Indeed, Aristotle, when considering the regress in the *Metaphysics*, takes foundationalism to be the obviously correct description of our epistemic practices:

> [There are some people who] . . . demand that a reason shall be given for every-
> thing, for they seek a starting point and they seek to get this by demonstration,
> while it is obvious from their actions that they have no conviction. But their
> mistake is what we have stated it to be: they seek a reason for things for which no
> reason can be given; for the starting point of demonstration is not demonstra-
> tion.[2]

The ancient skeptics had an answer to this foundationalist response. Here is the formulation of the problem as given by Sextus Empiricus in his *Outlines of Pyrrhonism*, in a chapter titled "The Five Modes of Agrippa":

> The later Skeptics hand down Five Modes leading to suspension, namely these: the
> first based on discrepancy, the second on the regress *ad infinitum*, the third on
> relativity, the fourth on hypothesis, the fifth on circular reasoning. That based on
> discrepancy leads us to find that with regard to the object presented there has
> arisen both amongst ordinary people and amongst the philosophers an intermi-

nable conflict because of which we are unable either to choose a thing or reject it, and so fall back on suspension. The Mode based upon regress *ad infinitum* is that whereby we assert that the thing adduced as a proof of the matter proposed needs a further proof, and this again another, and so on *ad infinitum*, so that the consequence is suspension [of assent], as we possess no starting-point for our argument. The Mode based upon relativity . . . is that whereby the object has such or such an appearance in relation to the subject judging and to the concomitant percepts, but as to its real nature we suspend judgement. We have the Mode based upon hypothesis when the Dogmatists, being forced to recede *ad infinitum*, take as their starting-point something which they do not establish but claim to assume as granted simply and without demonstration. The Mode of circular reasoning is the form used when the proof itself which ought to establish the matter of inquiry requires confirmation derived from the matter; in this case, being unable to assume either in order to establish the other, we suspend judgement about both.[3]

Foundationalists, or "Dogmatists," as Sextus labels them in this passage, hold that there are some occasions when we need inquire no further about how the world really is (as opposed to how it merely appears to be) because there is some appropriate starting point that can be taken for granted. But the mode of hypothesis is a method by which the Pyrrhonian can call into question the foundationalists' strategy by pointing out that all such supposed starting points are based either on how things appear to us or on what we believe things to be. The modes of relativity and discrepancy are designed to show that there is no agreement either about how things do (or at least could) appear, because appearances are "relative" to the perceiver and are concomitant perceptions, or about how things really are, because "amongst ordinary people and amongst the philosophers [there is] an interminable conflict."

In order to understand this objection to foundationalism, it is crucial to note that what is often called a "trilemma" is actually a five-horned problem as seen by the Pyrrhonians. The modes of relativity and discrepancy play a crucial role in the *five* modes. Thus, when the dogmatist proposes that the proper starting point is with appearances, the Pyrrhonian can question the probative value of the appearance by pointing out that it is far from settled that there is a good way to reason from how a thing appears to how it actually is. For, as the Pyrrhonians say,

we do not overthrow the affective sense-impressions which induce our assent involuntarily; and these impressions are "the appearances." And when we question whether an underlying object is such as it appears, we grant the fact that it appears, and our doubt does not concern the appearance itself but the account given of that appearance,—and that is a different thing from questioning the appearance itself. For example, honey appears to us to be sweet (and this we grant, for we perceive sweetness through the senses), but whether it is also sweet in its essence is for us a matter of doubt, since this is not an appearance but a judgement regarding the appearance.

(I.19–20)

Appearances are not probative because a thing could appear to have some property and not actually have it or it could appear not to have some property and actually have it. The same would hold with regard to the discrepancy among "intelligible things," such as opinions regarding the nature of proper moral conduct or claims about what is the best explanation of natural phenomena.

Thus the reply to the Aristotelian foundationalist is that there are no unchallengeable starting points from which the dogmatists can provide a good basis for making claims about the nature of the "real" world. It might be that claims about how things appear to us (using "appear" in its broad sense to include how abstract objects and properties appear to us) are unchallengeable, but they cannot provide a basis for believing how things really are.

The foundationalist will attempt to respond by doing one of two things. First, the foundationalist could claim that some propositions about the evidentiary status of a belief are known a priori. That is, we can know a priori that if something looks clear, then most likely it is clear—or even that it is a priori knowable that if something looks clear and we have no reason to think that the perceptual situation (including the status of our perceptual equipment) is distorting how things appear, then it is prima facie reasonable to believe that it is clear. This first response does not seem to have been given by the Aristotelian foundationalists, but it is a view espoused by contemporary foundationalists. I will return to it later.

A second type of response was given by Aristotelian foundationalists and is still employed. Roughly, it goes like this: We have generally reliable faculties that, if used in appropriate circumstances, will deliver knowledge that is not based upon reasoning. Here is a passage from Aristotle's *Posterior Analytics* that provides one such account:

> So out of sense-perception comes to be what we call memory, and out of frequently repeated memories of the same thing develops experience; for a number of memories constitutes a single experience. From experience again . . . originate the skill of the craftsman and the knowledge of the man of science in the sphere of being. . . .
>
>   Thus it is clear that we get the primary premises by induction; for the method by which even sense-perception implants the universal is inductive. . . . From these considerations it follows that there will be no scientific knowledge [demonstrative knowledge] of primary premises, and since except intuition nothing can be truer than scientific knowledge, it will be intuition that apprehends the primary premises—a result which follows from the fact that demonstration cannot be the originative source of demonstration.
>
>   (100a5–9, 100b4–13)

The details of the Aristotelian account are not important here. What is important is that the answer Aristotle favors is that the manner in which we obtain knowledge of the starting points of reasoning cannot involve further reasoning, but rather that the starting points are obtained through highly reliable processes that employ our faculties functioning properly. In other words, Aristotle is giving a reliabilist explanation of the origin of the starting points. As he sees it, the starting points are not claims about how things appear but intuited general principles about how things actually are. Although what Aristotle takes to be the starting points—general principles—are not the favored starting points of most contemporary foundationalists, who would take them to be perceptual judgments, there is much shared common ground, namely, that the starting points are not arrived at by inference. Rather, they are acquired though noninferential reliable processes.

We will return to this general reliabilist form of foundationalism and the skeptic's response when we consider the main focus of this chapter: the contemporary response to the regress problem. To foreshadow that discussion a bit, even if the ancient skeptics were correct that *if* one adopts the general foundationalist picture of warrant, neither foundationalism nor coherentism nor infinitism can provide a solution to the regress problem, there is one option still to be explored, namely, whether that general foundationalist account should be accepted.

That underlying view of warrant needs to be delineated a bit more in order to fully understand the basic thrust of the Pyrrhonian strategy for confronting the three forms of dogmatism: foundationalism, coherentism, and infinitism. All are forms of dogmatism because they are united in holding that among contraries about how things really are, some are justified and others are not. Indeed, some are justified enough that they are worthy of assent. The Pyrrhonian sets out to dispute that claim. Of course, on pain of succumbing to dogmatism, the Pyrrhonian cannot put forth a view about the real nature of justification or warrant.

The underlying view of warrant employed by the ancient dogmatists seems to be that warrant is either (1) a property of beliefs (doxastic warrant) or propositions (propositional warrant) that is transferred from a warranted belief or proposition to another hitherto-unwarranted belief or proposition through good, that is, truth-conducive, reasoning or (2) a property that a proposition or belief has that it does not inherit from another belief or proposition.[4] Put another way, some objects that have warrant have it in virtue of inheriting it from some other object that has warrant; other objects have warrant but not in virtue of inheriting it from something else that already has it. The latter are sometimes referred to by the misleading term "self-warranted" beliefs. It is misleading because such beliefs cannot warrant themselves, for, as we will soon see, that would be impossible according to the foundationalists. Rather, they are warranted, but not in virtue of what warrants nonbasic beliefs or propositions, that is, other beliefs or propositions. They are warranted in virtue of something they possess, that is, a property (perhaps a relational one).

This fits with the general Aristotelian picture of property possession. Either a thing has a certain property, say, P (e.g., motion or heat), by acquiring it from something else that has P, or it has P by virtue of being what it is, that is, its very nature.[5] Heavenly bodies moved in circular paths by nature; sublunary nonanimals did not move unless they were moved by another object that was already moving. Hence if an object acquired P, it must have acquired it from something that already had P. For example, heavenly bodies changed position because it was natural for them to move in circles—no external force was required—whereas the sublunary nonanimal bodies' "natural" state was to be at rest. Hence if they were moving, they had to acquire motion from something that was already moving.

Similarly, a belief or proposition that is nonbasic would have to acquire its warrant from some other belief or proposition; and that one from another belief or proposition, until, as the foundationalists would claim, we arrived at some proposition that was warranted, but not in virtue of acquiring that warrant from some other belief or proposition. That is the only possible explanation because (1) reasons that produce knowledge must be "prior to and better known than the conclusion," and "the same things cannot be simultaneously both prior and posterior to one another, so circular demonstration is not possible" (72b25–28),[6] and (2) providing an infinite set of reasons for our beliefs is not possible because "one cannot traverse an infinite series" (72b10). The only possibility remaining is that there are some beliefs or propositions that do not depend upon other beliefs or propositions for their warrant.

To sum up, foundationalism seems to be the only plausible answer to the regress problem, given the account of warrant that was accepted by both the dogmatists and the skeptics.[7] The other alternatives—infinitism and circular reasoning—are nonstarters.

3. Contemporary Responses

Many contemporary epistemologists take the epistemic regress problem as *a*, if not *the*, central problem in epistemology. BonJour, for example, says when commenting on Anthony Quinton's discussion of the regress problem that "the problem implicit in this passage is perhaps the most crucial in the entire theory of knowledge. The stand which a philosopher takes here will decisively shape the whole structure of his epistemological account."[8] Audi devotes a significant part of a chapter to a discussion of the regress problem and points to its central role in "motivating both foundationalism and coherentism."[9] Ernest Sosa says of the regress that "a main epistemic problematic, found already in Aristotle's *Posterior Analytics*, presents a threefold choice on how a belief may be justified: either through infinitely regressive reasoning, or through circular reasoning, or through reasoning resting ultimately on some foundation."[10] Finally, as is typical with foundationalists, William Alston employs it as the primary motivation in his defense of foundationalism.[11]

Thus the regress problem is a major concern of many contemporary epistemologists, but only two of the three alternative solutions have been developed in any detail, foundationalism and coherentism. A primary reason for not taking infinitism seriously is one of the reasons Aristotle had advanced—the so-called finite-mind objection. For example, BonJour writes that "though it is difficult to state in a really airtight fashion, this argument [the finite-mind argument] seems to me an adequate reason for rejecting [infinitism]."[12] We will discuss the finite-mind objection later; the points here are only that (1) the regress problem is viewed as a central issue by contemporary epistemologists, and (2) one possible solution has not been given much careful consideration.

Although the regress problem remains a major concern of contemporary epistemologists, I think that it is also fair to say about contemporary approaches to the regress problem that some of the assumptions underlying the "ancient" view of the problem have been challenged in a way that reveals new, possible responses to the regress. Let me begin the discussion of these new possibilities by recalling an issue mentioned earlier. Is it the case that S is under some obligation (1) to provide a reason for some, much less all, of her beliefs or (2) to *show* that she is justified in holding the belief?

These are two quite distinct questions. Foundationalists, of course, think that there is no obligation to provide a reason for all our beliefs. That is a central claim of foundationalism. There are some that are basic and do not require that a reason be produced in order for the so-called basic proposition to be fully justified. I will discuss this view in some detail later. Here I want to take up the second question: Is S under some obligation to *show* that she has good reasons for her belief? As Alston has clearly pointed out, being justified in believing something and showing that one is justified in holding the belief are two quite different requirements.[13]

Suppose that one were justified in believing that p just in case the belief has the right kind of causal pedigree—perhaps the process that produced it is such that typically it produces true beliefs in similar circumstances,[14] or perhaps the fact that it is a true belief and not a false one that is possessed by the believer is due to the epistemically virtuous activity of the believer.[15] The particular condition that is taken to be sufficient for a belief to be justified is not important here. What is crucial is that some contemporary epistemologists do not think that S is necessarily under any obligation to attempt to show that her beliefs are justified, much less to succeed in that attempt, in order to obtain knowledge. They would hold, just as Aristotle did, that some beliefs rise to the level of being justified to the degree necessary for knowledge in the absence of reasons for thinking that the belief is justified.

On the other hand, a new, seemingly more vicious regress problem would be created if we were to accept an analysis of inferential justification along the lines suggested by Richard Fumerton:

> To be justified in believing one proposition P on the basis of another proposition E one must be (1) justified in believing that E and (2) justified in believing that E makes probable P.[16]

The "old" regress problem—which is difficult enough—was simply a regress of first-order reasons; here a new problem arises because a more and more complex justified proposition is required in order for S to be justified in believing P: namely, E makes P probable, E^* makes (E makes P probable) probable, E^{**} makes [E^* makes (E makes P probable) probable] probable, and so on. It is doubly vicious, so to speak.

I would like to set aside this seemingly more vicious regress because the original one seems hard enough. In addition, there are many epistemologists who would hold that in order for S to be justified in believing that p on the basis of e, S does not have to be justified in believing that e makes p probable. In other words, my comments will focus on the core regress problem and not the metaproblem that results by accepting a Fumerton-like account of inferential justification.[17] Nevertheless, some of the comments regarding a possible infinitist solution to the core problem will be easily transferable to the meta–regress problem.

The regress problem disappears if one asserts that no proposition requires a reason in order for it to be justified; and one can imagine some reliabilists claiming that. They could point to the fact that children, animals, and even inanimate objects know things. The regress problem, they could claim, presupposes an exalted account of the conditions of knowledge because we can know even relatively complex and abstract propositions without being able to provide reasons.

I think that there is a clear and adequate response to this Procrustean depiction of knowledge. Ever since Plato, philosophers have been seeking to correctly characterize knowledge as that form of true belief that is most highly prized.[18] There is a perfectly legitimate sense of "knowledge" in which S is said to have knowledge that p only if S's belief that p is sufficiently comprehensively justified— taking "a comprehensively justified belief" to be one that possess *all* the features required in order for that belief to satisfy the requirement of being a most highly prized form of true belief.[19] In order to prevent a possible misunderstanding of my use of "comprehensive justification," let me make clear that I do not mean that in order for a belief to be comprehensively justified, it has to have all the epistemically admirable features to the highest degree. Like comprehensive insurance that covers every eventuality, comprehensively justified belief has all the epistemically admirable features, but just as some comprehensive insurance policies provide better overall benefits than others, some comprehensively justified beliefs are better justified with regard to some features than others.

I grant that there is a sense of "know" such that doors that open automatically when they are approached *know* that they are being approached or that dogs *know* their master's voice or that Mr. Truetemp or various unreflective clairvoyants *know* some features of their environments. But the type of knowledge I am concerned with here is the kind that requires that we have good reasons for at least some of our beliefs. Sosa puts the point this way:

> Admittedly, there is a sense in which even a supermarket door "knows" when someone approaches, and in which a heating system "knows" when the temperature in a room rises above a certain setting. Such is "servo-mechanic" knowledge. And there is an immense variety of animal knowledge, instinctive or learned, which facilitates survival and flourishing in an astonishingly rich diversity of modes and environments. Human knowledge is on a higher plane of sophistication, however, precisely because of its enhanced coherence and comprehensiveness and its capacity to satisfy self-reflective curiosity. Pure reliabilism is questionable as an adequate epistemology for such knowledge.[20]

The distinction between types of knowledge is not some philosopher's creation. Here is a quotation from a recent article in the *New York Times*:

> In 10 southwestern counties, he said, the team found thousands of punch card ballots that lacked codes identifying the precinct where the ballot was cast. The codes are typically necessary for the machines processing the ballots to "know" to record which candidate receives the votes.[21]

The shudder quotes around "know" indicate that the reporter is aware that there is something somewhat peculiar in attributing knowledge to machines.

"Pure" reliabilism correctly points to some sui generis features of knowledge shared by supermarket doors, small children, animals, and adult humans. But there are also important differences in what we expect of ourselves. We expect that we have reasons, and good ones at that, for at least some of our beliefs. We are criticized as being epistemically irresponsible for believing some propositions for which we have no good reasons or for denying those propositions for which we have adequate reasons. Of course, we cannot at this point in the discussion claim that we need reasons for each of our beliefs because we would then be assuming that if there is a solution to the regress problem, it will have to be an infinitist one.

Now recall the discussion about how warrant was treated by the Greeks—at least by the Pyrrhonians and Aristotle. Infinitism and coherentism (understood as circular reasoning) were clearly not viable responses, given that view of warrant. Nothing can be "prior to itself," as Aristotle put it; and infinitism (1) cannot account for the origin of warrant and (2) runs into the finite-mind problem. In addition, although the foundationalist can point to our epistemic practices, as Aristotle did, there remains the skeptic's objection that would apply to most contemporary foundationalist accounts of a posteriori knowledge that take first-person psychological reports as basic. That objection, based upon the modes of discrepancy and relativity, is that there are no non-question-begging principles of reasoning that sanction inferences from the basic (evident) propositions to the nonbasic (nonevident) propositions. More simply, we cannot legitimately move from how things appear to us to how they really are. Perhaps propositions of the form "this appears blue" or "*p* or not-*p*" are true and evident, but neither can render propositions about the actual condition of the external world evident.

Contemporary foundationalists who still adhere to the warrant-transfer view will argue along lines similar to those of the Aristotelians. Here is a somewhat extended quotation from Carl Ginet:

> Many of our beliefs are justified beliefs: they are such that epistemic rationality would not forbid our holding them. And often what justifies a belief is the fact that the believer has . . . other justified beliefs from which the belief in question can be properly inferred. That is to say, the justification of many a justified belief is by inference from one or more other beliefs; it is *inferential justification*. . . .
>
> The premise beliefs must, of course, themselves be justified, if belief in what is inferred from them is to be thereby justified; and their justifications may be by inference from still other beliefs; and the justifications of those further beliefs may

be inferential; and so on. Can this go on without end? If not, how can it end? Those questions are the regress problem.[22]

Ginet, as well as many contemporary foundationalists, will take first-person perceptual beliefs as proper ending points of a posteriori reasoning. There are no further reasons that need to be provided. What is sufficient to justify a claim like "I see a blue smear on a white surface in good light a few feet in front of me" is a set of facts, not a set of further beliefs that function as reasons. Here is Ginet again:

> The following two facts are sufficient [to justify the belief that I see a blue smear on a white surface a few feet in front of me]: (1) My visual experience is as if I see a blue smear on a white surface in good light a few feet in front of me and (2) I am not aware of any reason to think that in this instance things may not be what they visually seem to me to be.[23]

Contemporary foundationalists also attempt to provide an answer to the Pyrrhonian worry that there is no good inference available that permits the move from facts about how things appear to me to claims about how things really are. Call the two conditions described in the quotation from Ginet "conditions C." Further, let P be "I see a blue smear on a white surface." The foundationalist can now claim that the following principle is a priori:

J: When C obtains, it is reasonable for me to believe P.

Here is what Ginet says:

> I need no premise from which to infer J. This is because J is a basic *a priori* principle constitutive of the concept of justification for belief in a perceptual proposition like P; it is a principle such that understanding it requires accepting it.[24]

This is classic foundationalism augmented with the claim that J is a priori. There is still the implicit commitment to the originating/transfer view of warrant underlying the ancient view of the regress, and there is the added commitment to the a priori truth of such evidential statements that their looking to be p warrants that they are p (given that I am not aware of any significant contrary evidence). It is, so to speak, built into the concept of justification that such evidential propositions are true. These a priori truths about evidence need not and cannot, on pain of circular reasoning, be verified because such verification would ultimately be circular—relying upon the very truths about evidence that the verification is supposed to verify.

Two comments seem in order. First, the Pyrrhonians would certainly claim that they understand J and that they do not accept it. After all, there are the modes of relatively and discrepancy that seem to provide a good basis for withholding acceptance of J. In other words, there are at least some people who fully understand J but who do not accept it. Hence J is not a priori knowable, at least given the test advocated by Ginet. Second, although contemporary foundationalists still embrace the classical originating/transfer view of warrant, I think that it is fair to say that such a view of warrant is no longer universally accepted.

Contemporary coherentism rejects that transference view of warrant and re-places it with an emergent form.[25] It takes justification to be an emergent property such that when sets of propositions have a certain arrangement—a coherent structure—all members of the set of propositions are justified. *Sets* of propositions are the primary bearers of justification, and individual propositions are justified only in virtue of being members of the set.[26]

The *infinitist* conception of justification is also a radical departure from foundationalism in that it conceives of justification of a proposition *p* as obtaining only when the set of reasons for *p* is nonrepeating and endless. (Note that I am here speaking of propositional justification, not doxastic justification. I will say more about these two forms of justification later.) That is, infinitism does not envision justification as a property of a proposition that can be transferred to another proposition. Rather, it views propositional justification for *p* as emerging when and only when there is an endless set of nonrepeating propositions beginning with *p* such that each succeeding proposition provides an adequate epistemic basis for the previous one. Thus it bears some similarity to the emergent coherentist view because a proposition is justified in virtue of being a member of a set of propo-sitions of a given sort. It differs from emergent coherentism in that it retains a notion of epistemic priority. In that sense, it does bear some similarity to foun-dationalism; but as we will see shortly, infinitism does not require that epistemic priority be a *fixed* relation between propositions.[27]

In order to understand the three concepts of justification—foundationalist, coherentist, and infinitist—it will be useful to say a few more words about *prop-ositional* and *doxastic* justification.

A proposition *p* is *propositionally justified* for a person S *iff* S possesses an overall adequate epistemic basis for accepting the proposition. The proposition would still be justified even if S were to fail to accept the proposition or accept it on some basis that is not adequate. In either of those cases, although the proposition is justified for S, S would not be justified in believing the proposition—either because S does not believe it or believes it for the wrong reasons. Put another way, S could be entitled to believe that *p* without believing it or even if S believed it for the wrong reasons. By contrast, a belief that *p* is *doxastically justified* for S *iff* the belief that *p* satisfies all the conditions required to make the belief comprehensively justified; that is, it is an instance of the most highly prized from of belief.

These definitions are meant to be theory neutral. As we will see, foundation-alists, coherentists, and infinitists differ on what is required in order for a prop-osition or belief to be justified, but all agree that if the belief is justified, then the propositional content of the belief must also be justified. That is, they all agree that if the belief that *p* (B*p*) is doxastically justified, then the proposition *p* is propo-sitionally justified; but the converse does not hold.

A self-conscious, epistemically responsible *foundationalist* (i.e., a founda-tionalist who seeks to practice what she preaches) would seek a belief whose propositional content, say, *p*, is either (1) a basic proposition or (2) such that if *p* is not basic, then p is supported by some path of reasons for p that terminates in basic propositions. Typically, foundationalists will go even further and require that Bp have some sort of appropriate causal pedigree.

For example, Audi takes it for granted that there is such a causal sustaining factor:

> A justified belief is one that is well-grounded; the paradigms of basic grounds are sensory experience, introspection..., memory, and reason; and the paradigm of non-basic grounding is inferential grounding. *Both types of grounding require some kind of causal sustenance.* [italics mine][28]

In other words, not only must S have good reasons for nonbasic beliefs, but also the nonbasic beliefs must be causally based upon other beliefs, and those on others, and so on, with the first (basic) belief in the series being a belief with a basic proposition as its content. If the basic proposition is known a posteriori, then the basic belief with the basic proposition as its content will be caused by either another type of mental state, for example, a perception or a memory (if one is a representational realist), or some nonmental state, for example, a material object (if one is a direct realist). If the basic proposition is known a priori, then, according to Ginet, that proposition is such that understanding it requires accepting it. The belief in that basic proposition will cause or at least causally sustain beliefs for which its content is the reason for the content of the nonbasic beliefs.

This causal requirement seems to me to place the contemporary foundationalist in a very precarious position since it might turn out that the folk assumption about the etiology of our beliefs is false. It seems to me quite risky to build our theories on the existence of wistful mental determinants (WMDs) until we actually discover them.

Transference-type coherentists would take Bp to be doxastically justified just in case we can arrange our beliefs in a circle, one member obtaining its warrant from another that obtains its warrant from another until we arrive back where we started. They, too, are committed to the existence of WMDs that are mutually causally efficacious, and they consequently face the same liability as the foundationalists. But the reason that no one has ever held this view—at least as far as I know—has been given by the Pyrrhonians and Aristotle. If I am wondering whether I have good reasons for believing that p, and I give a set of reasons for p that includes p, I think that we would all say that I have begged the question.

Nevertheless, there is something to be salvaged from this view. It seems that I could offer "It rained last night" as a reason for thinking that there is water on the grass, and I could offer "There is water on the grass" as a reason for thinking that it rained last night. However, what I cannot do is argue in a circle on one and the same occasion. A contextualist could plausibly suggest that epistemic priority depends in part upon what is the issue at hand. That is, there are many pairs of propositions $\{x, y\}$ such that I can offer x as a reason for y when y is being questioned, and I can offer y as a reason for x when x is being questioned.

Foundationalists cannot be that flexible. For example, if they take a proposition like "I am seeing bluely" as basic, then it would violate their conception of propositional justification and, consequently, doxastic justification were I to give "There is a white surface with a blue smear on it" as my reason for thinking that I am seeing a bluely. As Aristotle held, there is a fixed order of epistemic priority among propositions required by foundationalism because if x is a reason for y, x must be prior to and better known than y. This strikes me as another significant problem for foundationalism because it seems easy to imagine circumstances in which the question "Am I seeing bluely?" can be answered affirmatively by "Yes, there is a blue object before me." Suppose that I do not trust my memory regarding what blue smears look like. I could come to believe that there is a white surface with a blue smear on many bases other than my immediate perceptual experience—testimony or the readings on a colorimeter, for example. Then I could use my belief that there is a blue smear on a white surface as a good reason for believing that I am seeing a blue smear.

I will not pursue that difficulty any further here except to say that the infinitist conception of propositional and hence of doxastic justification allows that reasoning need not trace this fixed path. There can be rigid forms of infinitism, but it is not an essential feature of the view.

The contemporary form of coherentism rejects the transference view of warrant. BonJour describes what an *emergent coherentist* would take to be the way in which a belief is doxastically justified.[29] A belief, say, Bp, is justified *iff* its propositional content is a member of a set of coherent propositions that are the contents of my other beliefs (plus perhaps some other more specific conditions satisfied by the coherent set).[30] Doxastic warrant is not transferred from one belief to another via inference; rather, all the beliefs in a set become warranted together because of the inferential relationships among them.

Like the emergent coherentist, an *infinitist* does not accept the foundationalist originating/transfer view of warrant. Beliefs become comprehensively justified only when we provide reasons for them. Justifying a belief is something we do, like acquiring an automobile by paying for it over time. Infinitists will take a belief that p to be sufficiently doxastically justified for S only when S has engaged in providing "enough" reasons along an endless path of reasons. A belief, say, Bp, would be completely doxastically justified only if every reason in the path were provided. By supplying a reason, say, r, for p, S has made Bp partially justified—but note that r is not yet comprehensively justified since no reason for r has yet been provided. Nothing is ever completely settled, because no belief is ever completely comprehensively justified, but as S engages in the process of providing reasons for her beliefs, they become better justified—not because S is getting closer to completing the task, but rather because S has provided more reasons for her belief. How far forward in providing reasons S need go is a matter of the pragmatic features of the epistemic context, just as which beliefs are being questioned or which can be taken as reasons is contextually determined.

4. A Brief Evaluation of Foundationalism, Emergent Coherentism, and Infinitism

Suppose that mental states have causes. That is, suppose something causes S to believe that *p*, and something causes S to believe the proposition, say, *r*, that is S's reason for *p*, and so on. Also suppose that it *could* be, as the foundationalist says that it *must* be, that beliefs with the reasons as their content are the causes of the beliefs whose content is the proposition requiring the reasons. Further, suppose that if one traces the causal chain back to the first mental state in the chain, one discovers, as the foundationalist would have it, that the first mental state is not another belief. It could be a perception or a memory.

Let us grant the truth of foundationalism with regard to the causes of beliefs, namely, that there are some beliefs that are not caused by other beliefs and that those "basic" beliefs cause further beliefs. Does it follow from that supposition that foundationalism has the correct view of doxastic justification?

If a belief becomes comprehensively justified as a result, at least in part, of something we do (in contrast to its simply being caused in the right way), then locating a further reason for a belief need not be equivalent to locating an additional sustaining cause. This is crucial and illustrates what I think is a serious confusion at the core of much foundationalist epistemology, perhaps beginning with Aristotle's arguments in the *Posterior Analytics*. He says that if some knowledge is the result of demonstration, some knowledge is not the result of demonstration. I think that "result" here must mean "causal" result if the reason he gives for rejecting infinitism is compelling. That argument seems to be this: Inferring takes some time. Because we "cannot traverse an infinite series" (since we live for only a finite time), it follows that if there is some knowledge that *causally* results from inference, there must be some knowledge that does not *causally* result from inference. But it does not follow that if we have the kind of knowledge that is distinctive of adult human beings, there is some known proposition for which there is no further reason available or that epistemic responsibility does not, on some occasions, require locating such a reason. In other words, the causal chain resulting in a belief might have a starting point, but it does not follow that locating reasons for our beliefs has a stopping point. There could always be further needed reasons, depending upon what contextually is up for grabs. That is true even if one takes a located reason to be a new sustaining cause. For it could be that if no further reason is located for the initial belief (the belief requiring a reason that initiates the search for reasons) and if S is a responsible epistemic agent, the initial belief might (1) disappear or (2) be modified in content or (3) be modified in degree of credence. My point here is merely that foundationalism does not automatically prevail over either emergent coherentism or infinitism even if we assume that beliefs with reasons as their contents are the originating or sustaining causes of further beliefs.

Nevertheless, the question before us at this point is whether foundationalism or emergent coherentism or infinitism has the best "solution" to the regress problem. Let me briefly attempt to answer that question.[31]

Suppose that Fred (the foundationalist) has offered a reason for his belief and a reason for the reason. Suppose further that Fred, being a foundationalist, eventually arrives at what he takes to be a "basic" belief, b, perhaps "I see a blue smear." When asked his reason for believing b, Fred replies that he has no further reason; what justifies b is some fact or set of facts C. Perhaps C is his experience as if there is a blue smear, and he is not aware of any reason for being wary.

Now Fred can be asked—or can ask himself—whether C is such that when C obtains, b is likely to be true. The Pyrrhonians had some reasons for thinking that one should always be wary, so for them conditions C never obtained. But here the question is whether C is b-truth conducive. If Fred takes that question seriously—and why should he not?—then he has three possible answers: yes, no, or maybe. If he says either maybe or no, then he certainly should refrain from accepting b. If he says yes, then he has provided a reason R for believing b, namely, that C is b-truth conducive and C obtains.

Perhaps, as the foundationalist will claim, there is a sense in which b was justified before Fred proffered R. What justified b is simply that C obtains. Let us grant that, and let us call the type of justification b has "f-justified" (for "foundationally justified"). Now imagine two people, one with the f-justified belief "I see a blue smear" but who either is unable to understand the question posed to Fred or who gives the no or maybe answer, and a second person who has the same f-justified belief and who can provide R and even a further reason for believing R. Which person is acting in a more epistemically responsible manner? I think that the answer is clearly that the second person is. That person has what is distinctive of adult human knowledge that has been the target of analysis by epistemologists since Plato. Put another way, one important feature of comprehensive justification is lacking if a belief is merely f-justified.

Surprisingly, the foundationalists will agree. I say that because the actual C conditions offered by foundationalists are b-truth conducive, and that is not an accident. To see this, imagine what I have referred to in other places as a Wednesday foundationalist.[32] This brand of foundationalism holds that C is the fact that the belief occurred early Wednesday morning. That is, such a foundationalist would hold that if Bb first occurred to S early on a Wednesday, then Bb is basically justified. Of course, no foundationalist would hold such a view precisely because that C condition is not b-truth conducive. As long as we are not skeptics, we all think that if we have experiences as if p and we have no reason to be wary, p is likely to be true. What is important here is that on pain of becoming epistemically irresponsible, we all had better have some story available that provides the reason for thinking that C is truth conducive.[33]

Perhaps it will be objected that the regress has changed to a metalevel when we inquire whether C is b-truth conducive, for here we seem to be questioning whether our reasoning practice is likely to yield truth. I grant that this is a metaquestion, but, pace Alston, I do not see that as an objection.[34] It was Fred, after all, who claimed that b was justified by a fact and not another reason. That opens the door to the metaquestion, and, consequently, it seems perfectly apt.

If the argument up to this point has been correct, then foundationalism is not able to solve the regress, if that regress is seen as one in which the providing of reasons is important to both originating warrant and increasing warrant. Once Fred arrives at the so-called basic proposition b, and if he considers whether he is entitled to accept b, then he had better be able to provide "C is b-truth conducive" as a reason for b, and if he considers whether C is b-truth conducive, he had better have a reason for that, and so on. We can grant that b is f-justified for Fred, but such justifications are not the stuff out of which we get the "most highly prized" form of true beliefs.

I think that it is fairly easy to see that emergent coherentism faces the same type of worry when it tries to solve the regress problem. As Sosa has argued, emergent coherentism is a type of formal foundationalism.[35] What is relevant here is that the emergent coherentist takes C to be a set of facts about the propositional contents of our actual beliefs. If those propositional contents have the appropriate form of coherence, then the beliefs with those contents are justified. In other words, they are all basic. A similar question to the one faced by Fred is appropriate here: Why think that coherent beliefs are likely to be true? Once again, I am not denying that coherence is truth conducive (although I have expressed some doubts about that elsewhere);[36] what I am claiming is that when the emergent coherentist is asked to consider whether coherence is truth conducive, on pain of incoherence, she had better have the right answer: yes. Hence the emergent coherentist must enlarge her set of actual beliefs by including the belief that coherent beliefs are thereby likely to be true in order for her set of beliefs to retain their coherence. The coherentist is forced to the mode of infinitism (just as the Pyrrhonians claimed) because she must add another belief to her system of beliefs. And, of course, the next question that requires an answer is this: Why do you think that C is truth conducive? In other words, the emergent coherentist has no way to stop the regress.

Does this type of objection apply to infinitism? That is, would not the infinitist be required to produce a reason for thinking that the contents of all the beliefs that have the requisite structure are likely to be true? The answer is that the infinitist is required to do so, but, contrary to the foundationalist's predicament, that is just what a self-conscious infinitist would think is consistent with her view of doxastic and propositional justification. For example, suppose that some infinitist thinks that the path of reasons progresses in the way a foundationalist envisions, that is, that the path of reasons for a posteriori justification arrives at what the foundationalist thinks is a basic proposition b. If the argument up to this point has been correct, the infinitist will readily agree that "conditions C are b-truth conducive and conditions C obtain" is a reason for thinking that b is true and that b is the reason for thinking that further propositions are true. In fact, the infinitist has a reason for thinking that each proposition in the chain is true, namely, the next proposition in the path of reasons that is offered as a reason. And since there is a reason available for thinking that each proposition is true, there is a reason, ceteris paribus, for thinking that every proposition in the set is true.[37] Thus the infinitist has an argument for the claim that all the beliefs that have the requisite infinite structure are likely to be true.[38]

There is one objection to infinitism that has been mentioned previously that remains a primary motivation for accepting foundationalism and that I would like to consider before closing, namely, the so-called finite-mind objection. At the heart of foundationalism is the view that justification originates in basic propositions because of the circumstances in which those propositions are accepted and that justification can be transmitted by reasoning from those basic propositions to nonbasic ones. Since this reasoning takes some time, the number of steps cannot be infinite. Thus the objection to infinitism is that it seems to require the impossible.

There are two replies. First, in principle, this does not pose a problem for infinitism any more than a recognition that some of the requirements of some forms of foundationalism might lead to skepticism poses a problem for foundationalism. Suppose that, as Hume might claim, if all our putative knowledge of matters of fact were based upon reasoning about cause and effect, we would have no such knowledge because the normative requirements for such knowledge cannot be fulfilled. It appears that such a foundationalism would require the impossible. Hume, of course, thought that there was another source of such knowledge—custom and habit. Perhaps he was right. My point is merely that it is not an objection to Hume's normative foundationalism that skepticism would follow. Put another way, there can be both skeptical and nonskeptical forms of foundationalism. (Descartes thought that he had discovered a nonskeptical form.) Thus, by parity of reasoning, there can be skeptical and nonskeptical forms of infinitism.

There is, however, a second, more interesting reply based upon the difference between the infinitist conception of comprehensive justification and the foundationalist one that I have been stressing throughout this chapter, namely, that the infinitist holds that an important ingredient of comprehensively justified beliefs arises by the act of producing reasons. That is, producing a reason for a belief that p makes the belief that p at least partially comprehensively justified. And if one produces a reason for the reason for p, the belief that p is even more comprehensively justified. Contra the foundationalist, reasoning helps create this type of most highly prized form of justification—it does not transfer it. Hence it is not necessary to traverse an infinite series of reasons for a belief to be comprehensively justified. Since justification comes in degrees, a belief that p can be both f-justified and justified in the way the infinitist requires without traversing an infinite series of reasons. True, no proposition is ever finally and completely comprehensively justified, but there seems to be no reason for thinking that we are unable to provide enough reasons to make it sufficiently justified for the acquisition of knowledge.[39]

NOTES

1. Some parts of this chapter rely upon other articles I have written: Peter D. Klein, "Human Knowledge and the Infinite Regress of Reasons," *Philosophical Perspectives* 13 (1999): 297–325; "Why Not Infinitism?" in *Epistemology: Proceedings of the Twentieth World Congress in Philosophy*, ed. Richard Cobb-Stevens (Bowling Green: Ohio Philosophy Documentation Center, 2000), 5, 199–208; "Infinitism Is the Solution to the Epistemic Regress Problem," in *Contemporary Debates in Philosophy*, ed. Matthias Steup and Ernest Sosa (Oxford, UK: Blackwell, 2005), 131–140; "Infinitism's Take on Justification, Knowledge, Certainty and Skepticism," in special edition of *Veritas* titled *Perspectives in Contemporary Epistemology*, 50, no. 4 (2005): 153–172, also available at http://revistaseletronicas .pucrs.br/veritas/ojs/viewissue.php?id=4&locale=en; "Human Knowledge and the Infinite Progress of Reasoning," *Philosophical Studies*, 134, no. 1, (2006): 1–17.; "How to Be an Infinitist about Doxastic Justification," *Philosophical Studies*, 134, no.1 (2006): 25–29.

2. Richard McKeon, ed., *Basic Works of Aristotle* (New York: Random House, 1941), 1011a1–14. All quotations from Aristotle will be from this volume.

3. Sextus Empiricus, *Outlines of Pyrrhonism* (Cambridge, MA: Harvard University Press, 1976), I:164–169. All quotations from Sextus will be from this volume.

4. I will have more to say about the importance of the distinction between doxastic and proposition warrant later. This distinction was first introduced by Roderick Firth in "Are Epistemic Concepts Reducible to Ethical Concepts?" in *Values and Morals*, ed. Alvin Goldman and Jaegwon Kim (Dordrecht: D. Reidel, 1978), 215–229.

5. It might be thought that foundational propositions or beliefs are not *by their nature* warranted because they could have a nature that is not dependent upon their causal history. No doubt some conceptions of basic propositions do not take the causal history of basic propositions to be that in virtue of which they are basic. For example, for many contemporary foundationalists, first-person psychological-state reports are basic regardless of their causal history. But given the view in the *Posterior Analytics*, I take it that Aristotle thought that genuine first principles were such that their causal history is that in virtue of which they are basic. A belief with a general principle as its content is a belief in a first principle in virtue of the causal history of the belief, just as a token of a sunburn or Freudian slip is that type of thing in virtue of its causal history.

6. There is one sense in which Aristotle thinks that a proposition might be both prior and posterior to itself, but if I understand him correctly, it is a sense that is not relevant for our purposes. I believe that he thinks that a proposition might be "prior for us" in the sense that we might learn it first but not be "prior in an unqualified sense"—the sense in which something is epistemically prior in demonstrations based upon first principles or what he calls "immediate premises" (72b18). His example is induction. I think that he means that we might come to know that Socrates is a man and Socrates is mortal before coming to know that all men are mortal, but in giving a demonstration of *Socrates is mortal*, the proper way to begin is with *all men are mortal*.

7. As mentioned earlier, the Pyrrhonians would have accepted such an account of warrant in order to meet their opponents on the opponents' own ground. That is, they would accept this account of warrant as part of a *reductio* strategy. They would not assent to the account.

8. Laurence BonJour, *The Structure of Empirical Knowledge* (Cambridge, MA: Harvard University Press, 1985), p. 18. The passage cited from Quinton is from his "The Problem of

Perception," reprinted in *Perceiving, Sensing, and Knowing*, ed. Robert J. Swartz (Garden City, NY: Anchor, 1973), p. 119.

9. Robert Audi, *The Structure of Justification* (New York: Cambridge University Press, 1993), chap. 1, "Overview: The Grounds of Justification and the Epistemic Structure of Rationality," quotation from p. 10.

10. Ernest Sosa, "How to Resolve the Pyrrhonian Problematic: A Lesson from Descartes," *Philosophical Studies* 85 (1997): 229.

11. William Alston, *Epistemic Justification* (Ithaca, NY: Cornell University Press, 1989), p. 55.

12. BonJour, *Structure of Empirical Knowledge*, p. 24.

13. Alston, *Epistemic Justification*, especially pp. 19–38.

14. Alvin Goldman, "What Is Justified Belief?" in *Justification and Knowledge*, ed. G.S. Pappas (Dordrecht: D. Reidel, 1979), 1–23.

15. See Ernest Sosa, *Knowledge in Perspective* (Cambridge: Cambridge University Press, 1991).

16. Richard Fumerton, *Metaphilosophy and Skepticism* (Boston: Rowman & Littlefield, 1985), p. 36.

17. I have discussed this point in more detail elsewhere. See Peter Klein, "Foundationalism and the Infinite Regress of Reasons," *Philosophy and Phenomenological Research* 58, no. 4 (1998): 919–925.

18. Plato, *Meno*, 97a–98d.

19. Of course, various theories of justification (foundationalism, coherentism, and infinitism) will differ on what properties a comprehensively justified belief must have. I will discuss this in some detail later.

20. Ernest Sosa, *Knowledge in Perspective*, p. 95.

21. Ian Urbina, "Ohio to Delay Destruction of Presidential Ballots," *New York Times*, August 31, 2006.

22. Carl Ginet, "Infinitism Is Not the Solution to the Regress Problem," in *Contemporary Debates in Philosophy*, ed. Matthias Steup and Ernest Sosa (Oxford, UK: Blackwell, 2005), 140–141.

23. Ibid., p. 142.

24. Ibid., p. 154. I have changed the name of the principle, J, in order to make it appropriate for our nomenclature. Ginet refers to it as "R1*."

25. This paragraph and several that follow repeat what I have said in Klein, "Human Knowledge and the Infinite Progress of Reasoning."

26. BonJour calls this form of coherentism "holistic coherentism" and defends it in *The Structure of Empirical Knowledge*.

27. In addition to the articles listed in note 1, forms of infinitism are developed and defended in Scott Aikin, "Who's Afraid of Epistemology's Regress Problem?" *Philosophical Studies* 126 (2005): 191–217, and Jeremy Fantl, "Modest Infinitism," *Canadian Journal of Philosophy* 33 (2003): 537–562.

28. Robert Audi, *The Structure of Justification* (Cambridge: Cambridge University Press, 1993), p. 14. The claim is repeated in several passages throughout the book; see pp. 99–105, 334–335.

29. See BonJour, *Structure of Empirical Knowledge*. Also see Lehrer, *Theory of Knowledge*, and Catherine Elgin, "Can Beliefs be Justified through Coherence Alone?" in *Contemporary Debates in Epistemology*, 156–167.

30. I should note in passing that this condition seems too strong because on some occasions it seems that we should retain beliefs that do not cohere with other beliefs, for

example, negative experimental results when testing a previously highly confirmed theory. The coherentist must be able to tell some story that allows for some beliefs to be justified that do not cohere.

31. This paragraph and those immediately following it repeat to some extent what I say in Klein, "Human Knowledge and the Infinite Progress of Reasoning" and in "How to Be an Infinitist about Doxastic Justification."

32. Klein, "Human Knowledge and the Infinite Progress of Reasons."

33. Maybe we would give the story like the one that Ginet gave, namely, that it is constitutive of the concept of justification that when C obtains, b is justified. But then we would need to be able to respond to the Pyrrhonian mode of relativity. I do not claim that that is impossible, just that this response would be the next step in the reasoning.

34. Alston, *Epistemic Justification*, pp. 19–38.

35. Ernest Sosa, "The Raft and the Pyramid: Coherence versus Foundations in the Theory of Knowledge," *Midwest Studies in Philosophy* 5 (1980): 3–25.

36. Peter Klein and Ted Warfield, "What Price Coherence?" *Analysis* 54, no. 3 (1994): 129–132, and Klein and Warfield, "No Help for the Coherentist," *Analysis* 56, no. 2 (1996): 118–121.

37. It is not always the case that if we have a reason for thinking that each member of a set of propositions is true, then we have a reason for thinking that they are all true, as is illustrated by the lottery paradox. But the propositions in the infinite set are not such that if one of them is true, it lowers the probability that others are true.

38. This does hint at an objection to infinitism that I have considered elsewhere: Will there not be an infinite chain of reasons for every proposition? The rough-and-ready answer is that there will be, but not every infinite chain is the right sort to convey propositional justification. See the articles listed in note 1.

39. I have discussed this elsewhere in some depth. See especially Klein, "Infinitism's Take on Justification, Knowledge, Certainty and Skepticism" and "Human Knowledge and the Infinite Progress of Reasoning."

CHAPTER 23

EXTERNALIST RESPONSES TO SKEPTICISM

MICHAEL BERGMANN

1. INTRODUCTION

The goal of this chapter is to consider epistemic externalist responses to skepticism. But what is epistemic externalism? I think that the best way to answer this question is by contrasting externalism with two other views and then giving a few examples.

The other views I have in mind are internalism and mentalism. All three views (internalism, externalism, and mentalism) are views about justification or warrant.[1] For convenience, I will focus mostly on justification. The central thesis of internalism is that a belief is justified only if the person holding the belief is (actually or potentially) *aware* of what that belief has going for it. It is not enough for justification that a belief has something going for it; in addition, the person holding the belief must be (actually or potentially) aware of what her belief has going for it. The central thesis of mentalism is that a belief's justification is a function solely of (1) which mental states the subject is in and (2) which mental states of the subject the belief in question is based on (i.e., if two possible subjects are exactly alike in terms of which mental states they are in and which of their mental states their beliefs are based on, then they are exactly alike justificationally). Mentalism differs from internalism insofar as it imposes no awareness requirement on justification. However, neither does it *reject* an awareness requirement on justification. So some views count as both mentalist and internalist, whereas others are mentalist without being internalist.[2] Externalist views deny both internalism

and mentalism. They deny that there are any awareness requirements on justification. They allow for a belief to be justified even in cases where the believer is not
in any way (actually or potentially) aware of what makes the belief justified. And
they deny that justification supervenes on one's mental states together with which
mental states one's beliefs are based on. They allow that justification can depend on
other factors; they allow that there can be two possible subjects who are exactly
alike mentally and in what their beliefs are based on while differing justificationally.

Standard examples of externalist views are reliabilism, certain virtue theories,
tracking accounts, and proper-function accounts. (These externalist views tend
more often to focus on warrant than justification, though sometimes they focus on
both.) Reliabilists say that justification or warrant depends on the belief's being
formed in a reliable way.[3] The virtue theorists I have in mind say that justification
or warrant depends on the belief's being formed by stable and reliable dispositions
that make up the believer's cognitive character.[4] Tracking accounts say that justification or warrant depends on the belief's tracking the truth (S's belief that p
tracks the truth just in case S would believe p if p were true and S would not believe
p if p were false).[5] Proper-function accounts say that justification or warrant
depends on the belief's being formed by properly functioning cognitive faculties.[6]
There is no requirement that the subject be (actually or potentially) aware of the
reliability, cognitive virtue, tracking, or proper function. Moreover, two possible
subjects can be exactly alike mentally while differing in terms of reliability, cognitive virtue, tracking, or proper function. So these views are neither internalist nor
mentalist. They are typical externalist views.

Now that we have some idea of what externalism is, we are almost ready to
turn to a consideration of how its proponents respond to skepticism. But first, let
us narrow our discussion a little. There are plenty of externalist positions in the
literature. One way of categorizing them is in terms of whether they endorse
reliabilism, a tracking account, a virtue theory, a proper-function account, or some
other externalist analysis of justification or warrant. But they can also be divided
into contextualist, closure-denying, and neo-Moorean camps.[7] Contextualists say
that "knows" functions like an indexical term, with its semantic content varying
across contexts of attribution.[8] Invariantists deny this. Closure *affirmers* endorse
the closure principle according to which knowledge is closed under known
entailment—that is, if one knows that p and believes q because one knows that p
entails q, then one knows that q. Closure *deniers* reject that closure principle.[9] Neo-
Mooreans are invariantists and closure affirmers. Moreover, they are Moorean in a
broad sense, which just means that they think that we know most of the things we
commonsensically take ourselves to know. This threefold division (into contextualists, closure deniers, and neo-Mooreans) is not meant to be exhaustive, but
most externalists fall into one of these three camps.

In this chapter, I will ignore contextualists and closure deniers and focus solely
on neo-Moorean versions of the externalist response to skepticism. There are a
couple of reasons for this. For one thing, other chapters in this volume focus
explicitly on contextualist and closure-denying responses to skepticism, so there is

no need to cover those responses in detail here.[10] In addition, although contextualists and closure deniers are intent on avoiding what they view as weaknesses of neo-Mooreanism—in particular, the neo-Moorean willingness to say that we know that skeptical hypotheses are false—they are still faced with some of the same objections that are directed at the neo-Moorean externalist response to skepticism.[11] And, of course, these alternatives to neo-Mooreanism have incurred some additional costs of their own. In what follows, therefore, when I speak of externalist responses to skepticism, I will have in mind neo-Mooreans externalist responses. But it is worth keeping in mind that the objections I will be considering sometimes apply to contextualists and closure deniers too.

I will focus on two prominent theses about externalist responses to skepticism, one positive and one negative. The positive thesis announces an alleged virtue of externalism: that externalism *alone* avoids skepticism. The negative thesis identifies an alleged defect of externalism: that externalism *implausibly* avoids skepticism. I will be critical of both theses, though I will try to uncover the truth in the neighborhood of each. In section 2, I will examine the positive thesis. In section 3, which will take up the bulk of this chapter, I will evaluate the negative thesis. I will close, in the final section, by arguing briefly that the conclusions reached in sections 2 and 3 give us a reason to endorse externalism.

2. The Positive Thesis: Externalism Alone Avoids Skepticism

In 1985, while trying to identify the main argument for endorsing externalism, diehard internalist Laurence BonJour expressed the positive thesis as follows:

> The basic factual premise of this argument is that in many cases which are commonsensically instances of justified belief and of knowledge, there seem to be no justifying factors present beyond those appealed to by the externalist. An ordinary person in such a case may have no idea at all of the character of his immediate experience, of the coherence of his system of beliefs, or of whatever other basis of justification a nonexternalist position may appeal to, and yet may still have knowledge. Alternative theories, so the argument goes, may perhaps describe correctly cases of knowledge involving a knower who is extremely reflective and sophisticated, but they are obviously too demanding and grandiose when applied to these more mundane cases. In these cases *only* the externalist condition is satisfied, and this shows that no more than that is really necessary for justification, and for knowledge, though more might still be in some sense epistemically desirable.
>
> (1985: 52)

In the very next paragraph, BonJour goes on to concede the basic factual premise he has just described—that is, that only externalist conditions are satisfied in many of the cases commonsensically identified as justified belief or knowledge—though he denies that this gives us a good reason to endorse externalism. Nearly twenty years later, after switching from internalist coherentism to internalist foundationalism, BonJour reaffirms this concession (BonJour 2003a: 199–200), though there too he concludes that "the commonsensical implausibility of skepticism turns out to offer no good reason at all for preferring . . . any broadly externalist view" to his own views.[12] Note that his concession is not just that the falsity of externalism implies that we do not know or justifiably believe quite as much as we thought we did. Rather, he concedes that the falsity of externalism threatens to lead to skepticism, though he insists that that is not a good-enough reason to endorse externalism. Externalists have made this same sort of point (i.e., that the falsity of externalism threatens to lead to skepticism) and have defended it in a variety of ways. In this section, I would like to consider some of those defenses and explain why I think that they fall short of establishing the positive thesis.

Let us look first at Dretske's defense of his conclusion that "if skepticism is false, externalism is true":[13]

> There are always things my knowledge depends on, facts without which my beliefs would be false, that I cannot justify. So the knowledge, if I have it, must be the product of things I need not know or be justified in believing, facts that skeptical possibilities (targeted at what I can justify) do not undermine. This is externalism.
> (Dretske 2003: 106)

The idea here is that first, it is possible (as skeptical hypotheses show us) to have the evidence we do while our perceptual beliefs are false, and second, we cannot justifiably believe that such possibilities are not actualized. Since we cannot justifiably believe that those skeptical possibilities are not actualized, it follows that if such justification is required for knowledge, skepticism is true. And only externalism refrains from requiring such justification for knowledge. So externalism alone avoids skepticism.

The main problem here is that there are internalists who (like externalist neo-Mooreans) reject Dretske's premise that we cannot justifiably believe that those skeptical possibilities are not actualized. Such internalists will not be moved by Dretske's argument. Chisholm, for example, is a clear case of an internalist, but he is also a particularist and a fan of Moore's and Reid's responses to skepticism: he is an internalist neo-Moorean who thinks that we can justifiably believe that skeptical possibilities are not actual.[14] Likewise, an evidentialist such as Moser also clearly rejects externalism while arguing that—because the commonsense view (that our sensory experience is caused by the external world) provides the best explanation of our evidence—we can justifiably believe that skeptical possibilities are not actualized.[15] And Feldman points to internalists like Pryor (who takes a line like Chisholm's) and Vogel (who takes a route similar to Moser's) as examples of those who reject externalism while thinking that we can justifiably believe that skeptical hypotheses are false.[16] Thus, until it can be shown that such philosophers cannot coherently combine their rejection of externalism with their view that (contrary to what Dretske claims) we *can* justifiably believe that skeptical possibilities are not actual, Dretske's argument that externalism alone avoids skepticism will remain unconvincing.

Another argument that externalism is the only way to avoid skepticism is given by Van Cleve. He starts off by saying that the core tenet of internalism is that "there is no first-order knowledge unless there is also higher-order knowledge with respect to the factors that make first-order knowledge possible."[17] He then says that externalism, as he understands it, is "tantamount to the denial of KR,"[18] which is understood as follows:

> KR: A potential knowledge source K can yield knowledge for a subject S only if S knows K is reliable.[19]

Finally, he argues that the only way to avoid skepticism is to deny KR, which, as I just noted, Van Cleve thinks is sufficient to make one an externalist.

The problem here is similar to the problem faced by Dretske's argument. Just as there are internalists who reject the assumption that we cannot justifiably believe that skeptical hypotheses are false, so also there are internalists who reject KR. This is because there are internalists who refrain from imposing *any* higher level requirements on knowledge, contrary to what Van Cleve says in explaining the "core tenet" of internalism. Internalists who are worried about regress problems that arise from imposing such a requirement demand only a sort of awareness that does not involve knowledge or belief or conceiving of any kind. Moser and Fumerton are internalists who require awareness or direct acquaintance with justifiers, but they think that it would be a serious mistake to view this awareness or acquaintance as involving knowledge or belief or conceiving.[20] So even if Van Cleve is right that the only way to avoid skepticism is to reject KR, it does not follow that only externalists can avoid skepticism; for, as we have just seen, some internalists reject KR.

John Greco argues that externalism is "not only sufficient for rejecting skepticism, but necessary as well."[21] To establish this, he argues that each of the following claims is necessary for rejecting skepticism and sufficient for externalism:

> *Rb*. There is no requirement on knowledge that one knows (or even believes) that one's belief is the result of reliable cognitive processes.

> *Rc*. Where S knows p on the basis of reasons R, there need be no necessary relation (logical or quasi-logical) between the truth of R and the truth of p; it is sufficient that the truth of R is a contingently reliable indicator of the truth of p.[22]

In the previous paragraph, I noted that there are internalists (Moser and Fumerton) who reject higher level requirements on knowledge and justification. Because these internalists (along with certain mentalists) consistently affirm Rb, we can see that Greco is mistaken: endorsement of Rb is not sufficient for externalism.

As for Rc, endorsement of it is not sufficient for externalism either. It is true that mentalists such as Feldman and Conee agree that if one's evidence E for a belief B is such that B is a fitting response to E (with the result that believing B on the basis of E makes B justified), then it is a necessary truth that B is a fitting response to E.[23] But although mentalists think that the *fittingness* of B as a response to E is noncontingent, this does not commit them to thinking that E's *truth-indicativeness* with respect to B (supposing that E is a belief whose truth reliably indicates B's truth) is noncontingent. Mentalists will think that B is, of necessity, a fitting response to E even if E is not, of necessity, a reliable indicator of B's truth (though it may in fact be a contingently reliable indicator of B's truth). Mentalists consider this possible separation of truth-indicativeness from fittingness to be a virtue of their accounts because it allows them to say that demon victims with the same type of evidence base we have (whether in terms of experience or inductive reasons) are as justified in their beliefs as we are in ours. So Greco is mistaken about Rc too.

In the spirit of the concern alluded to by BonJour in the quotation at the beginning of this section, Alston and Goldman have objected to internalism on the grounds that internalist standards are often not met by the typical beliefs of ordinary people.[24] However, Alston and Goldman do not give any argument for the conclusion that this is a problem faced by *all* versions of internalism. In fact, one is left with the impression that they think that there are or may be ways of being an internalist that do not commit one to skepticism. And I think that this is the reasonable conclusion to draw from the literature: although externalists rarely if ever seem forced by their positions to admit the truth of skepticism, many (but not all) internalists *do* seem to face this consequence. This is a more modest conclusion than the positive thesis according to which externalism *alone* can avoid skepticism.

It is, however, worth highlighting one form of internalism—strong awareness internalism—that *does* seemed forced to admit the truth of skepticism. The reason this is worth highlighting is that part of the attraction of the positive thesis is due to the temptation to think that (a) internalism is equivalent to strong awareness internalism, and (b) the only way to avoid strong awareness internalism is to be an externalist.[25] And because there is good reason to think that strong awareness internalists cannot avoid skepticism, (a) and (b) will naturally lead one to think that externalists alone can avoid skepticism. Thus understanding why strong awareness internalism cannot avoid skepticism will help us appreciate the appeal of the mistaken positive thesis.

Strong awareness internalism can be stated as follows:

> *Strong awareness internalism*: S's belief B is justified only if (1) S is aware (or potentially aware) of something that contributes to B's justification and (2) this awareness involves either *judging* that the object of that awareness is in some way relevant to the appropriateness of holding B or *conceiving* of the object of that awareness as being in some way relevant to the appropriateness of holding B.

Clause 1 makes it clear that there is an awareness requirement on justification. Clause 2 makes it clear that this awareness requirement is a *strong* awareness requirement. The reason strong awareness internalism results in skepticism is that it implies that the justification for any belief *B* requires the ability to make an infinite number of judgments or concept applications of ever-increasing complexity. But it is clear that we lack that ability. So it follows that if strong awareness internalism is true, none of our beliefs is justified.

To see why it requires this extravagant ability, notice that if the required strong awareness involved actual judging or believing, it would presumably require *justified* belief. (How could an unjustified belief about *B*'s appropriateness help?) But then the regress problem is obvious: S's belief *B* is justified only if S also justifiedly believes that something makes *B* appropriate; and that obviously implies an infinite regress of ever-increasing complexity. Would it help if the required strong awareness required only the *potential* to judge or believe? No, because even then the justification for any belief would require the *ability* to make an infinite number of judgments of ever-increasing complexity.[26] Would the regress problem disappear if we distinguished believing from conceiving (or concept application) and said that what is required is only that S *conceive* of the object of awareness as being something that makes *B* appropriate (rather than that S believe this)? No, because it would still be the case that the justification of any belief requires the ability to apply an infinite number of *concepts* of ever-increasing complexity. This shows that strong awareness internalism implies skepticism.[27]

Regarding the positive thesis, then, we may conclude that there seems to be no good reason for thinking that externalism *alone* avoids skepticism. (I am assuming that good reasons to think that externalism is true and that mentalism and internalism are false do not automatically count as good reasons to think that externalism alone avoids skepticism.) But the truth in the neighborhood of the positive thesis is this: externalists are rarely, if ever, forced by their views to endorse skepticism, while this is a common problem for internalists; and there is one form of internalism—strong awareness internalism—that clearly must be rejected if one is to avoid being committed to skepticism.

3. THE NEGATIVE THESIS: EXTERNALISM IMPLAUSIBLY AVOIDS SKEPTICISM

The positive thesis is an overstatement. It says that externalism *alone* avoids skepticism when in fact some nonexternalist views also avoid it. The negative thesis turns this supposed advantage against externalism by saying that the way in which externalism avoids skepticism is utterly *implausible*, thereby giving us a reason to reject externalism. I will begin our examination of this negative thesis by explaining its motivation, which is evident in the objections that have been proposed against externalist responses to skepticism. Then, before thinking about how externalists can respond to these objections, I will consider whether these same objections apply to *nonexternalist* views that have a chance of avoiding skepticism—that is, to nonexternalist views other than strong awareness internalism. After concluding that they *do* apply, I will respond to these objections on behalf of both externalism and the nonexternalist positions to which they apply.

3.1. Four Objections to Externalism's Handling of Skepticism

The skeptic asks how you know that there is an external world and demands that your answer include a good reason for thinking that when you have sensory experiences of the sort you are having, there really is an external world causing them (rather than the Matrix or a deceptive demon). The reliabilist response is to point out that the skeptic is wrongly assuming that we need such a reason in order to know or justifiably believe that there is an external world. In fact, all we need is reliably formed beliefs that there is an external world: justification and knowledge supervene on reliability, not on our epistemic access to or ability to give good reasons for such reliability.

The main complaint about this externalist response to skepticism is just this: it is philosophically unsatisfying, and that suggests that externalism is false. To understand this reaction, let us consider the case of reliabilism. The reliabilist says that the skeptic is wrong to think that we need a good reason for thinking that our sensory experience is not deceptive—in fact, all that is required is that our beliefs are reliably formed. And, it is added, they *are* reliably formed. Problem solved. The natural response that immediately comes to mind is something like this: "But how do you know that your beliefs are reliably formed? If you cannot answer that in a satisfying way, then you have not adequately responded to skepticism." These very same concerns arise for nonreliabilist versions of externalism as well. They will say that what is required for justification or knowledge is not access to or ability to give good reasons. What is required is cognitive virtue or proper function or truth-tracking, which, in fact, *are* present in our typical belief formation. It is the presence of such things—not good reasons to believe in their presence—that makes skepticism false. But again, the natural question that arises is: "How do you know that your beliefs typically involve cognitive virtue, proper function, or truth-tracking?" The implication behind this question is that the externalist's initial response was unsatisfying, and that if (as seems likely) further externalist responses merely give more of the same, they will be unsatisfying too.

But what exactly is it that makes the externalist's response philosophically unsatisfying? To this question, there are a number of answers in the literature, each of which can be viewed as an objection to externalist responses to skepticism—an objection that supports the main complaint about their being philosophically unsatisfying. I will lay out four such objections here.[28]

1. *Conditional answer*: The externalist's response to skeptical questions merely points out that *if* the beliefs in question satisfy the externalist conditions, then those beliefs are justified. But that conditional answer to the skeptic's question is philosophically unsatisfying. The real question is whether the antecedents of such conditionals are true.[29]

2. *Epistemic circularity (or bootstrapping)*: Externalists are committed to approving of epistemically circular responses to skepticism. We can see this by considering the following track-record argument for the reliability of perception.

> *Track-record argument*: In the past, whenever I was appeared to in this way and formed the belief that there was a tree, I was right—there was a tree there. Something similar applies with respect to my other sense-perceptual beliefs. Therefore, sense perception is reliable.

Notice that this inductive argument relies on memory, introspection, and perception (the latter was used to confirm that there really was a tree there). Now suppose that the memory, perceptual, and introspective beliefs employed as premises in this argument satisfy the conditions the externalist says are required for justification. If that were the case, then the externalist should agree that the beliefs in the premises of that inductive argument were justified. But surely a belief in an argument's conclusion, where that belief is based on a respectable inductive argument relying on justified premises, is itself justified. So the externalist is committed to allowing that one can satisfactorily respond to the skeptic's question (which asks how we know that perception is reliable) by relying on this sort of track-record argument. But there is an obvious problem with this track-record argument: it relies on perception to establish the reliability of perception. This makes that argument, as well as the belief in its conclusion, epistemically circular. (A belief is epistemically circular when one depends on a belief source to sustain a belief that that very belief source is trustworthy.) And being committed to approving of such epistemic circularity, especially in response to the skeptic, is a bad feature of externalism, one that makes it philosophically unsatisfying.[30]

3. *Uncomfortable moving up a level*: Externalist accounts of justification, if true, should apply just as much to higher level beliefs (i.e., beliefs about another belief's epistemic credentials) as they do to lower level beliefs, such as ordinary perceptual beliefs. But when pressed by the skeptic to say how they justifiedly hold the higher level belief that their beliefs are reliably formed, externalists feel uncomfortable appealing to the fact that these higher level beliefs are themselves reliably formed.[31] The fact that externalists feel this discomfort—when, in response to the skeptic, they follow out the implications of their position as it applies to higher level beliefs—reveals how implausible their externalist views seem, even to themselves. That is the basic complaint.

One way to explain this discomfort is to say that it arises simply in virtue of the fact that the externalist realizes that her position (when applied to higher level beliefs) commits her to permitting epistemic circularity of the sort discussed earlier.[32] The problem with that explanation is that just as externalist foundationalists allow that perception can be used to justify the legitimacy of using perception and that memory can be used to justify the legitimacy of using memory, so also certain internalist foundationalists (e.g., Fumerton) allow that direct acquaintance can be used to justify the legitimacy of using direct acquaintance.[33] So why does this sort of internalist position not give rise to the same discomfort that is associated with externalism? The difference, it is argued, is that we are in need of philosophical assurance about the legitimacy of using memory and perception; and we do not get such assurance by appealing to them again in epistemically circular ways. But we are not in need of philosophical assurance about the legitimacy of using direct acquaintance because when we use it, our philosophical curiosity about the justification it produces is fully appeased. It is true that we could get assurance about the legitimacy of direct acquaintance by appealing again to direct acquaintance, and that doing so would itself be philosophically satisfying. But no such assurance is required. Because externalism (unlike internalist positions that appeal to direct acquaintance) fails to appease our curiosity in this way by giving us the assurance we want, it is philosophically unsatisfying. It is their tacit recognition of this fact that explains why externalists are uncomfortable moving up a level.[34]

4. *Anything goes*: The externalist responds to skepticism about the external world by noting that our perceptual beliefs are justified simply in virtue of their satisfying external conditions; there is no need for the believer to prove or know or even be aware that those conditions are satisfied. But if pointing this out is a permissible move in a philosophical exchange with a skeptic, then it seems that almost anything goes. It is easy to see, for example, how a crystal-ball gazer can offer the same kind of externalist response to those who are skeptical of beliefs so formed.[35] Believers in the Great Pumpkin or voodoo might also offer an externalist response to those who find their views doubtful. So long as these nonstandard beliefs are internally consistent and there is no way to falsify or confirm them without appeal to the sorts of faculties allegedly producing these beliefs, it will not be difficult for externalist defenders of them to say, "Look, my crystal-ball (or Great Pumpkin or voodoo) beliefs satisfy externalist conditions, and that is enough to make them justified, even if I cannot offer you any argument proving that those beliefs satisfy those conditions."[36] But that sort of response is philosophically unsatisfying, to say the least. And since there is no relevant difference between such responses and the externalist response to skepticism about the external world, externalism itself is philosophically unsatisfying.

3.2. Applying the Four Objections to Nonexternalist Views

Before looking at how externalists might respond to these four objections, let us consider whether nonexternalist views are similarly vulnerable to such charges. We can begin by dividing nonexternalist views of justification into two mutually exclusive and jointly exhaustive camps: the radicals and the moderates. The radical camp includes all nonexternalist views that endorse either strong awareness internalism or inferentialism—the view that all justification is inferential. (These two positions are classified as "radical" because they lead very quickly to radical skepticism.)[37] All other nonexternalist views count as moderate. We can go on to divide the moderate nonexternalist views into the following three categories:

> *Low standard*: moderate nonexternalist views according to which it is suffi-
> cient, for the justification of S's beliefs, that either (a) S thinks that all is well
> with her beliefs epistemically speaking, or (b) some other equally unde-
> manding (or even less demanding) condition is satisfied
>
> *Medium standard*: moderate nonexternalist views that impose a standard
> more demanding than the one imposed by the low-standard position but
> say that beliefs can be noninferentially justified even if they are not about
> facts that are directly before one's mind (perceptual beliefs are typically
> viewed as beliefs of this kind)
>
> *High standard*: moderate nonexternalist views that impose a standard more
> demanding than the one imposed by the low-standard position and say that
> beliefs can be noninferentially justified only if they are about facts directly
> before one's mind (introspective and a priori beliefs are often viewed as
> beliefs of this kind)

In what follows, I will argue that all three versions of moderate nonexternalism are as philosophically unsatisfying as externalism. (I will be ignoring radical non-externalist views because the fact that they so obviously imply radical skepticism makes them seem rather implausible, even to internalists who want to be open to the truth of skepticism.)[38]

The first thing to notice is that concerns about externalism's allegedly un-satisfying response to skepticism will not be put to rest by turning to the low-standard view. That sort of view attributes justified belief far too liberally. It suggests that the *only* requirement for having justified beliefs is something as undemanding as optimism about the epistemic quality of one's beliefs. Such a response to skepticism will hardly seem like an improvement over externalism in the minds of those concerned about views that seem philosophically unsatisfying. We can, therefore, safely ignore the low-standard position in seeking a version of moderate nonexternalism that avoids the main complaint against externalist re-sponses to skepticism.[39] Our focus should instead be on those views that admit the possibility that although all seems well to the subject epistemically speaking, things are not as they seem. Let us call versions of moderate nonexternalism that admit that possibility—that is, those that reject the low-standard view—"*serious* mod-erate nonexternalist" views.

The problem is that once we allow for that possibility, a worrisome conse-quence arises. We know that all moderate nonexternalists allow for non-inferentially justified beliefs (this follows from the fact that inferentialists are all in the radical camp). This makes it natural for them to think that there is something that counts as a supervenience base for noninferential justification. But if the low-standard view is mistaken, then no matter what is selected as a supervenience base for noninferential justification, it will be possible for it to seem to the subject as if all is well (i.e., for nothing to seem amiss) epistemically speaking with her non-inferential beliefs, even though the supervenience base for their justification is absent.[40] That possibility suggests a troubling sort of skeptical scenario. It is troubling for the serious moderate nonexternalist because her only answer to the question "How do you know that you are not in such a skeptical scenario?" is an answer that is just as philosophically unsatisfying as the answer the externalist gives to the skeptic.

It is easy to see how this problem arises for medium-standard views. Suppose, for example, that the supervenience base for noninferential justification of per-ceptual beliefs is that one's beliefs *fit* the subject's sensory experience or that the sensory experiences in question are *best explained by* the truth of the beliefs based on them.[41] It seems possible for a clever demon to arrange for those supervenience bases to be absent while at the same time guaranteeing that everything seems to the subject to be epistemically hunky-dory: her perceptual beliefs *seem* to her to fit her evidence (though in fact they do not); her perceptual beliefs *seem* to her to be the best explanation of the sensory experiences on which they are based (though in fact they are not). After drawing attention to this possibility, the skeptic will ask the medium-standard moderate nonexternalist how she knows that she is not in such a skeptical scenario, and the skeptic will add that the fact that it seems to this nonexternalist that she is not does not help since that is exactly what one would expect if she were in such a skeptical scenario.

Similar remarks apply to high-standard moderate nonexternalists, for even supporters of high-standard versions of moderate nonexternalism (such as Bon-Jour and Fumerton) acknowledge that one can *think* that one has some fact directly before one's mind when one does not.[42] As a result, one can believe that *p*, thinking that one has the fact that *p* directly before one's mind when in fact one does not. This suggests the following skeptical scenario: a demon arranges for all of one's introspective beliefs to be mistaken because each seems to be a belief about a fact directly before the subject's mind when in fact it is not. How does the supporter of high-standard moderate nonexternalism know that she is not a victim of such a demon? She cannot point out that many of her introspective beliefs seem to be about facts directly before her mind, because that is exactly how things would seem if she were in the skeptical scenario in question.

But are there not some introspective beliefs about which we could not be mistaken—beliefs that a demon could not get us to believe falsely? Consider, for example, the proposition that you are being appeared to redly. Could that be believed falsely by a person who is dead sure that she is believing it truly? Yes. Being appeared to redly is one thing, and believing with complete conviction that you are obviously being appeared to redly is another. Each could occur in a person while the other is absent—there could be the appearing without any belief in such an appearing, and there could be the belief in such an appearing even when no such appearing occurs.[43] But if this could happen while it seems obvious that it is not happening, how do you know that it is not happening to you with your beliefs about how you are being appeared to? Moreover, consider the confidence with which nay sayers insist that this could not happen. How do they know that it *could not* happen—that its occurrence is *impossible*? By a priori intuition, if at all. But it is possible to have an extremely strong a priori seeming in support of a falsehood. It has happened often in the history of philosophy. It would, therefore, be no problem for a demon to arrange for it to happen again. So how do the naysayers who object to what I am claiming here know that that is not happening in them right now? How do they know that they are not being deceived into thinking that such a scenario is impossible? If such a deception were happening effectively, it would certainly seem not to be.

Perhaps the high-standard moderate nonexternalist would insist that it is a mistake to say that *fallible* introspective beliefs can be justified. She could point out that there are some introspective beliefs that are such that it is impossible to even have them unless they are true. An example might be the indexical belief "I am experiencing that" (accompanied by an inner act of "pointing" to a mental state): one might think that in order for S to have that belief, there must exist the experience to which "that" refers.[44] Suppose that this is right, and suppose that the high-standard moderate nonexternalist insists that it is only introspective beliefs of that sort—infallible introspective beliefs—that are justified. We are still left with the following skeptical scenario: Because of the work of a clever demon, the subject is unable to differentiate infallible introspective beliefs from fallible ones. Many introspective beliefs that are admitted by high-standard moderate nonexternalists to be fallible seem to this subject to be obviously infallible. That is, just as it seems obvious to infallibilists that a belief such as "I am experiencing that" could not possibly be false, so also it seems utterly obvious to the subject in this skeptical scenario that a belief like "there are 47 speckles on the visual image before my mind's eye" could not possibly be false. Now the skeptic asks the proponent of the infallibilist high-standard position how she knows that she is not like the person in the skeptical scenario just described. How does she know that her favored introspective beliefs really are infallible—that they do not just wrongly seem to be? The fact that they seem to be infallible is just what she should expect if she were in the skeptical scenario in question.

In each of the skeptical scenarios just described, we have the serious moderate nonexternalist in a situation like that faced by the externalist. The externalist and the serious moderate nonexternalist agree on the following:

> *Inferentialism is false*: There are some conditions that, if satisfied by her noninferential beliefs, would be sufficient for their justification.
>
> *Strong awareness internalism is false*: One's noninferential beliefs can be justified in virtue of satisfying certain conditions even if one neither (a) believes that those conditions are satisfied nor (b) conceives of the fact that those conditions are satisfied as being in any way relevant to the truth or justification of one's beliefs (perhaps because one never applies any concepts to them at all).

The low-standard view is false: It is possible for all to seem well (for nothing to seem amiss) epistemically speaking even when the conditions necessary for noninferential justification are not satisfied.

Because she accepts these three points, the serious moderate nonexternalist will have to grant the possibility of a skeptical scenario in which a person's noninferential beliefs do not seem to the subject to fail to satisfy the conditions necessary for noninferential justification even though they do fail to satisfy them. This is so whether the conditions in question involve the belief's fitting the evidence or its being the best explanation of the evidence; it is so whether the conditions involve having the fact the belief concerns directly before one's mind or the belief's being infallible. But once she grants this possibility, she can be asked how she knows that she is not in such a scenario herself, and she should feel forced to confess that the fact that she seems not to be is exactly what one would expect for someone who is in fact in such a scenario. Moreover, her position forces her to admit that her noninferential beliefs can be justified simply in virtue of satisfying the required conditions; there is no need to believe that she satisfies them—no need to conceive of her beliefs as satisfying conditions relevant to their being justified. All of this places her in a position very much like that of the externalist.[45] Both agree that their noninferential beliefs can be justified in virtue of satisfying conditions they do not conceive of as being relevant to justification—both agree that this justification can be present despite the fact that these conditions could fail to be satisfied without it seeming to them that they are not satisfied. The result is that each of the four objections from the previous subsection can be pressed against serious moderate nonexternalists.

1. *Conditional answer*: The serious moderate nonexternalists' view is that *if* their noninferential beliefs satisfy the relevant conditions, then they are justified. But this is merely a conditional response. The real question is whether that antecedent is satisfied or, instead, they are in a skeptical scenario. Given that things would seem epistemically just fine if they were in a skeptical scenario, the skeptic will think that they cannot tell whether the antecedent is true. Moreover, because serious moderate nonexternalists reject strong awareness internalism, they will insist that they do not *need* to know or believe that the antecedent is true.

2. *Epistemic circularity (or bootstrapping)*: Serious moderate nonexternalists seem forced to allow for epistemically circular track-record arguments. They have no principled way to prevent noninferentially justified "direct-acquaintance" beliefs, for example, from being used as premises in an epistemically circular track-record argument for the reliability of direct acquaintance itself.[46] Both of these first two complaints are as successful at showing that serious moderate nonexternalism is philosophically unsatisfying as they are at showing that externalism is philosophically unsatisfying.

3. *Uncomfortable moving up a level*: Serious moderate nonexternalists should be as uncomfortable as externalists about moving up a level to talk of higher level beliefs satisfying the conditions they think are required for justification. They must

admit that it can merely seem as if their first-order beliefs are justified even when they do not in fact satisfy the conditions necessary for justification. Likewise, they must admit that their higher level beliefs about the justification of their first-order beliefs can also seem to be justified even when they do not in fact satisfy the conditions necessary for justification. Once one realizes that, would not the nonexternalist's philosophical curiosity demand to be assured that both one's higher level beliefs and one's first-order beliefs really did satisfy the relevant conditions—that it did not just mistakenly seem that they did? I should think it would, in which case even high-standard moderate nonexternalists (both fallibilist and infallibilist) should agree that there is some philosophical assurance that they are missing (and wanting) and cannot provide any better than externalists can. This leaves the serious moderate nonexternalist in a position that is just as philosophically unsatisfying as the externalist.

4. *Anything goes*: If the serious moderate nonexternalist is right, then her beliefs can be justified noninferentially even though (a) she does not conceive of them as satisfying any conditions relevant to their justification, and (b) she must admit that all could seem well to her epistemically speaking even though her beliefs fail to satisfy the conditions necessary for justification. Given (a) and (b), she can comfortably assert that she knows via direct acquaintance that her first-order direct-acquaintance beliefs satisfy the conditions of justification and that they would be justified even if she did not know this at all (despite the fact that they could seem justified to her even if they were not). But then it seems that anything goes. Why cannot the crystal-ball gazer claim to know via crystal-ball gazing that her first-order crystal-ball beliefs satisfy the conditions necessary for justification, all the while asserting that her first-order crystal-ball beliefs would be justified even if she did not know this (and despite the fact that they could seem justified to her even if they were not)? This sort of move by the crystal-ball gazer is exactly parallel to what the externalist and the serious moderate nonexternalist say to skeptics about perception and direct acquaintance, respectively. And it is just as philosophically unsatisfying when it is made by the serious moderate nonexternalist as it is when it is made by the externalist.

What we have seen in this subsection is that nonexternalist views can be divided into three groups: radical nonexternalist views, low-standard moderate nonexternalist views, and serious moderate nonexternalist views. Radical nonexternalist views are implausible because they quickly lead to radical skepticism. Low-standard views are implausible because they make justification too easy to come by. And I have argued that serious moderate nonexternalist views are as vulnerable as externalism is to the four objections from the previous subsection.

3.3. Responding to the Four Objections

The fact that the four objections presented in section 3.1 apply just as well to serious moderate nonexternalism as they do to externalism does not by itself help externalism escape the trouble alluded to in those objections. It merely places others in their allegedly bad company. However, once we realize that the alternatives to serious moderate nonexternalism (and externalism) are radical nonexternalism and the low-standard view, we may begin to suspect that facing those four objections is not as problematic as initially supposed. In this subsection, I will briefly explain how externalists can and have responded to these four objections.

1. *Conditional answer*: An initial response to this objection is to note that anyone who rejects radical nonexternalism—that is, anyone who rejects both inferentialism and strong awareness internalism—will think that there can be noninferentially justified belief. When pressed about what makes such beliefs justified, those who reject radical nonexternalism will say that they are justified in virtue of satisfying certain conditions—in other words, they will assert the conditional claim that *if* those beliefs satisfy those conditions, they are justified. If pressed further about whether they know that the antecedent of that conditional is true, the natural thing for the opponents of radical nonexternalism to say is that they do not need to know or even believe that the antecedent is true in order for their noninferential beliefs to be justified. What matters for their justification is that those conditions *are* satisfied, not that they know or believe that they are satisfied. Given that this sort of response makes sense for *all* who reject radical nonexternalism, we can see why both externalists and moderate nonexternalists will find it attractive. The "conditional answer" objection seems, therefore, to depend for at least some of its force on a failure to recognize what rejecting radical nonexternalism requires. And given how common and plausible it is to reject inferentialism, failing to recognize what such a rejection requires is a serious weakness of this objection.[47]

Moreover, as Alston, Sosa, and especially Kornblith have emphasized, there is no reason to think that externalists (or other opponents of radical nonexternalism) will have to *deny* knowledge of the antecedent of conditionals such as "if belief B satisfies condition C, B is justified."[48] It is true that these antecedents *need not* be known in order for a belief like B to be justified. But there is no reason for an externalist to say that the antecedents *cannot* be known. They will be known if they are believed in a way that satisfies whatever conditions are required for knowledge. And, as externalists and moderate nonexternalists will agree, those conditions can be satisfied by a belief—including a higher level belief in the antecedent of the conditional in question—even if the subject does not know or believe that those conditions are satisfied. This is a simple consequence of rejecting inferentialism and strong awareness internalism.

Those who propose the "conditional answer" objection seem sometimes to think that the conditions required for higher level knowledge of the antecedents of such conditionals are not the same ones proposed by externalists or moderate nonexternalists for knowledge generally. They seem to think that for such higher level knowledge, conditions proposed by proponents of inferentialism or strong awareness internalism must be satisfied.[49] But externalists and moderate nonexternalists will think that their favored conditions are sufficient for the justification or warrant of *all* beliefs, including higher level beliefs that some lower level belief satisfies the conditions for justification or warrant.

2. *Epistemic circularity (or bootstrapping)*: The intuition grounding this objection seems to be that a belief source cannot reasonably be relied on to vouch for
its own trustworthiness—that is, a belief in a source's trustworthiness cannot come
to be justified by dependence on beliefs produced by that very belief source. The
alleged problem for externalism is that it seems to contradict this intuition by
allowing for epistemically circular belief justification (or bootstrapping) in responding to skepticism. There have been two main sorts of responses to this
charge.[50]

The first response is to argue that in order to avoid the problem of allowing for
epistemically circular justification, one is forced to hold that knowledge of the
reliability of our belief sources—or even knowledge itself—is impossible. But since
those consequences are so implausible, we should acknowledge that it is not so bad
to admit epistemically circular justification after all. Alston has defended this sort
of response by arguing at length that we cannot know without epistemic circularity
that our faculties are reliable.[51] Sosa argues that looking for someone who knows
without epistemic circularity that her faculties are reliable is like looking for the
patron saint of modesty who blesses all and only those who do not bless themselves. It is silly to bemoan the fact that no one has the feature in question once we
realize that the feature cannot be possessed.[52] The fact that not even God, a perfect
and omniscient knower, could know that his ways of knowing are reliable without
relying on his ways of knowing to do so strongly suggests that epistemic circularity
need not always be problematic.[53]

Others have noted that it is not just externalists who face the problem of
permitting epistemically circular justification. Consider those who allow for *basic*
knowledge—that is, knowledge produced by a belief source S where that knowledge is not preceded by the subject's knowledge that S is reliable.[54] Cohen, Van
Cleve, and Schmitt have argued convincingly that all who say that there is basic
knowledge must permit epistemic circularity.[55] Thus, to avoid permitting epistemically circular justification, one must reject basic knowledge. But to reject basic
knowledge is to say that all beliefs produced by a source must be preceded by (and,
presumably, be at least partially based on) the belief that the source in question is
reliable. Unfortunately, this commits one to inferentialism, which is highly implausible because it so obviously implies that knowledge is impossible. In addition,
I have argued elsewhere, without reference to the basic-knowledge issue, that all
those who reject inferentialism are committed to permitting epistemically circular
justification.[56] Again, given the extreme plausibility of rejecting inferentialism, this
lends support to the conclusion that epistemically circular justification need not be
a bad thing.

The second type of response to the "epistemic circularity" objection is to argue
that we can make sense of the tendency to deny epistemically circular justification
by distinguishing acceptable cases from unacceptable cases of it and noting that
philosophers often focus solely on the unacceptable cases, which they quite naturally and properly find problematic. This is the strategy employed by Pryor,
Schmitt, and me. All three of us agree that when someone believes that a source is

unreliable, an epistemically circular argument for its reliability cannot be of any help.[57] That person's belief in the unreliability of the source functions as an undercutting defeater for all beliefs produced by it, including those relied on in epistemically circular arguments for its reliability. In addition, Pryor and I argue that even doubts about that source's reliability (where those doubts are genuine and strong enough to make one withhold judgment about its reliability—though they may not make one positively suspect unreliability) can serve as undercutting defeaters for all beliefs produced by that source. So, according to us (but contrary to Schmitt), epistemically circular arguments are not useful for helping those who have such doubts come to justifiedly believe in the reliability of the source in question.[58] But Pryor suggests (rightly, I think) that if the doubts in question are merely hypothetical—that is, if the proposition that the source is unreliable is merely being entertained but there is no doubt leading to withholding judgment with respect to that proposition—then an epistemically circular argument for a source's reliability can still be a source of justification.[59]

The upshot of this second response is this. Epistemically circular arguments are useless at convincing skeptics of a source's reliability, but this does not make them intrinsically flawed. They can be used effectively by nonskeptics to come to know that their own faculties are reliable, even when such nonskeptics are entertaining (though remaining unmoved by) skeptical hypotheses. It is true that this will not be philosophically satisfying for the skeptic. But the fault is not with externalism. It is with the skeptic and her tendency to have doubts when she need not—doubts that give rise to a context in which a certain sort of philosophical curiosity cannot be satisfied.

3. *Uncomfortable moving up a level*: Externalists, such as Alston, have expressed misgivings about moving up a level and claiming, in addition to first-order knowledge, higher level knowledge that their faculties are reliable.[60] Fumerton pounced on this as evidence that externalists generally have a reason to feel such discomfort.[61] I have pointed out that Alston's discomfort is due to his discomfort with epistemic circularity, and yet Fumerton also endorses epistemic circularity when he says that we can know by direct acquaintance that direct acquaintance is a legitimate source of justification.[62] In response, Fumerton has offered the additional point (mentioned earlier in laying out this objection) that when the internalist employs direct acquaintance at the first level—to know, for example, that she is being appeared to redly—her philosophical curiosity is fully satisfied in a way it is not when she uses perception to know that there is a red object in her environment. The unfulfilled curiosity in the case of perception gives rise to the need for a higher level belief about the reliability or legitimacy of perception. We have no such need, says Fumerton, in the case of direct acquaintance, though we can easily form a higher level belief in the legitimacy of direct acquaintance by using direct acquaintance itself—and this higher level belief also satisfies our philosophical curiosity. But if we form a higher level belief in the reliability of perception and rely on perception in doing so, we are left with the same unfulfilled philosophical curiosity that we had about the first-level perceptual belief: how do

we know that perception (used this time to legitimate perception) is reliable? According to Fumerton, it is this difference that makes externalism problematic in a way that internalism relying on direct acquaintance is not.[63]

I have already given a partial response to this objection when I argued in section 3.2 that internalists face the same problem, even with regard to direct acquaintance. It seems possible for a person to believe that *p* while assuming that she is directly acquainted with the fact that *p* when, in actuality, she is not so acquainted and there is no such fact. Moreover, it is possible for this to go entirely unnoticed by the person, who may be utterly convinced that all is well with her beliefs, epistemically speaking. But then the skeptic can ask how the direct-acquaintance theorist knows that this is not what is happening with all her current direct-acquaintance beliefs. The fact that it seems not to be happening would seem to be useless comfort for someone who fully understood the problem. In the face of these considerations, such a person's philosophical curiosity should be no more satisfied by claims of direct acquaintance than by claims of perception.

An additional response is this: we can easily explain the externalist's discomfort with epistemically circular track-record arguments without jumping to the conclusion that the externalist is uncomfortable with externalism itself. The discomfort is due to the fact that when someone uses an argument, one typically assumes that it must have some force against a doubter (that is how we tend to think of arguments). But, as already noted, epistemically circular arguments are useless against doubters (since to doubt their conclusions provides an undercutting defeater for some of the premises).[64] Moreover, it seems implausible to suggest that our higher level beliefs in the reliability of our faculties are in fact produced by such arguments. That does not seem to be what is in fact going on when we believe that our faculties are reliable. These two considerations explain the discomfort someone like Alston feels about relying on epistemically circular track-record arguments; and they do so without impugning externalism. Hence the inference from "externalists feel discomfort when moving up a level (and relying on epistemically circular track-record arguments)" to "externalists are uncomfortable with the implications of their externalist principles" is fallacious.[65]

4. *Anything goes.* Sosa considers the charge that if externalist responses to skepticism are appropriate, then crystal-ball gazers can appropriately use the same type of response to skepticism about their crystal-ball beliefs that externalists use in response to skeptics about perception.[66] In response, he says that the externalist is not committed to agreeing, for the externalist can point out that perception is in fact a reliable faculty (known to be reliable in part by depending on perception), whereas crystal-ball gazing is not reliable (though it too may be believed to be reliable in part by depending on crystal-ball gazing).[67]

Of course, the crystal-ball gazer will not be satisfied by this if she thinks about crystal-ball gazing the way typical externalists think about perception. Is there anything that the externalist can say—anything satisfying to the crystal-ball gazer—that will differentiate her views on perceiving from the gazer's views on crystal-ball gazing? I think that the answer may in fact be no, depending on the details of how crystal-ball gazing works. (Does it conflict with itself or with other ways of knowing? Does it confirm itself?) Let us suppose that the crystal ball gazer's beliefs are consistent, self-confirming, and not contradicted by things she knows from other sources. Then it seems that the gazer can mimic exactly the externalist's responses to the skeptic about perception. And just as the typical externalist remains philosophically satisfied despite the skeptic's worries about perception, the externalist gazer can remain philosophically satisfied despite our conviction that she is deluded. Is there any way the externalist can help the gazer see that her views are silly whereas our trust in perception is not? I think that there may be no way to do this—using only the tools of philosophy—that will guarantee that all parties are satisfied.

What does that imply about externalism? Does the externalist's admission that given her externalist principles, she cannot show the externalist crystal-ball gazer that her gazing beliefs are not justified suggest that externalism itself should be dropped? No. First, the same problem arises for serious moderate nonexternalists too—for example, for direct-acquaintance theorists when faced with skeptics about direct acquaintance. The direct-acquaintance theorists cannot noncircularly show that they are not in a skeptical scenario in which their direct-acquaintance beliefs merely seem to be reliably formed when in fact they are not. So they, like externalists about perception, are equally compelled to admit that they cannot satisfyingly explain why the gazer's crystal-ball views are to be rejected while their own (direct-acquaintance) beliefs are not. The only way to avoid this sort of problem is to adopt a radical nonexternalist view such as strong awareness internalism, which is objectionable because it so obviously implies that justification is impossible.

Does it follow that the externalist and the serious moderate nonexternalist must both admit that the gazer's position is just fine? No. They can insist that their position (on perception or direct acquaintance) is correct, while the gazer's position is mistaken. They can admit that they cannot *show* the gazer, using standards both they and the gazer accept, that the gazer's beliefs are unjustified, whereas their own (perceptual or direct-acquaintance) beliefs are justified. But they can satisfy themselves by pointing out that the difference between themselves and the gazers is that their own beliefs really do satisfy justification requirements, whereas the gazer's beliefs only seem to be satisfying them. This is so even though the gazers will not admit it but will instead say that their crystal-ball beliefs do satisfy justification requirements. Moreover, the externalists and serious moderate nonexternalists who think that the gazers are deluded need not show any respect for the gazer's crystal-ball beliefs even though they cannot prove to the gazer's satisfaction that crystal-ball beliefs fail to satisfy justification requirements that are satisfied by perceptual or direct-acquaintance beliefs. Instead, they will just confess that all they can do is hope that the gazer will escape her delusion. Those who find this response unsatisfying need to be reminded that we are forced to choose between that sort of response, on the one hand, and radical nonexternalism or the low-standard view, on the other, and that the former seems preferable by far.[68]

4. THE SUPERIORITY OF EXTERNALISM

In section 3, I argued that externalists can respond to the four objections mentioned in 3.1 by making two points. First, they can argue that those four objections (aimed at supporting the charge that externalism's handling of skepticism is philosophically unsatisfying) apply just as strongly to the only live option for nonexternalists, namely, serious moderate nonexternalism, which rejects both radical nonexternalism and the low-standard view. Second, they can argue that the four objections are either based on some misunderstanding or are focused on alleged problems that are not nearly as bad as the consequences of the only alternatives to those alleged problems (i.e., the consequences of radical nonexternalism or the low-standard view). But I also noted that serious moderate nonexternalists can make this second point in defense of their own views. This may make one think that the discussion in section 3 offers nothing to show that externalism has an advantage over serious moderate nonexternalism. After all, supporters of both positions can offer the replies given in section 3.3 in response to the four objections mentioned in 3.1.

But I think that although serious moderate nonexternalists *could* offer those replies to those objections, doing so will not be tempting to them. They will, I strongly suspect, find those replies philosophically unsatisfying because, although they officially reject radical nonexternalism, they seem to be motivated by a tacit endorsement of the intuitions supporting it. It is the appeal of the intuitions behind radical nonexternalism (supporting either inferentialism or strong awareness internalism or both) that provides one of the main motivations for rejecting externalism, including externalism's reliance on the replies mentioned in 3.1. But once serious moderate nonexternalists are clear about their own rejection of radical nonexternalism, they should feel perfectly comfortable offering the 3.3 replies to the four objections from 3.1. Unfortunately, along with the opportunity to use the 3.1 replies comes the undermining of the main objection to externalism. This, I believe, explains why serious moderate nonexternalists are not tempted by the opportunity to use those replies.

Nonexternalists seem, therefore, to be faced with an uncomfortable dilemma.[69] Either they endorse serious moderate nonexternalism or they do not. If they do not, they face the implausible consequences of either the low-standard view, which makes justification too easy to come by, or radical nonexternalism, which very quickly leads to the radical skeptical results implied by inferentialism or strong awareness internalism. But if instead they *endorse* serious moderate nonexternalism, then they are faced with both the 3.1 objections and the discomfort they feel with the 3.3 replies their position permits. Thus they are caught between facing the implausible consequences of rejecting serious moderate nonexternalism, on the one hand, and ignoring the discomfort that provided their main motivation for rejecting externalism, on the other. The end result is that the arguments of section 3 leave externalists in a better position than serious moderate non-externalists, for although the latter can use the 3.3 replies, doing so forces them to concede that the main reason for preferring their view to externalism fails.

NOTES

My thanks to John Greco, Joel Pust, Matthias Steup, Michael Rea, and the philosophy department at the University of Notre Dame (where I presented a version of this chapter at a colloquium in March 2007) for helpful comments on earlier drafts.

1. By "warrant" I mean whatever, in addition to true belief, is required for knowledge. Gettier (1963) has shown that justification is distinct from (because not sufficient for) warrant so understood.

By "justification" I mean doxastic justification, not propositional justification. Doxastic justification is a property beliefs have only when they are formed in the right way. Propositional justification is a property a proposition p has for a person S if S's evidence is such that if she were to believe p on the basis of the appropriate part of her evidence, that belief that p would be doxastically justified (in other words, her evidence includes what could serve as an appropriate ground for the belief that p). A proposition can be propositionally justified for a person even if that person does not believe that proposition. Moreover, a belief can be propositionally justified for a person (in virtue of its content being so justified) while failing to be doxastically justified; this would happen if the belief is supported by the subject's evidence, but she does not base it on the appropriate part of her evidence (in which case it will not be formed in the right way). See Firth (1978: 217–20) for a discussion of this distinction.

2. Conee and Feldman (2001) are defenders of mentalism, but they want to equate internalism with mentalism as it is defined in the text. For objections to this view of theirs and a defense of the account given in the text (according to which internalism and mentalism are not equivalent), see Bergmann (2006b: chap. 3).

3. Goldman (1979, 1986) and Alston (1985).

4. Sosa (1991) and Greco (1999, 2000).

5. Dretske (1971) and Nozick (1981).

6. Plantinga (1993) and Bergmann (2004b; 2006b: chap. 5). Plantinga focuses on warrant, and I focus on justification.

7. This categorization comes from Pritchard (2002).

8. The most prominent defenders of contextualism are DeRose (1995, 1999), Cohen (1988, 1999), and Lewis (1996). See also Heller (1999), who is quite explicit about combining externalism and contextualism. For an interestingly different view that is similar in spirit to contextualism, see Jonathan Schaffer's articles (2004, 2005) on contrastivism.

9. The most prominent closure deniers are Dretske (1970) and Nozick (1981), both of whom also endorse tracking accounts that naturally fit with the denial of the closure principle.

10. See the chapters in this volume by Stewart Cohen and Jonathan Kvanvig. For the origins of *some* aspects of the neo-Moorean externalist response to skepticism, see the chapters in this volume by James Van Cleve and Noah Lemos.

11. See, for example, Fumerton's objections to externalist responses to skepticism (1995: 173–80)—to be discussed in more detail later—which he applies to Nozick, a closure denier, as well as to neo-Moorean externalists. Fumerton also discusses and criticizes other aspects of Nozick's views (1995: 118–27).

12. BonJour (2003a: 200).

13. Dretske (2003: 105).

14. See Chisholm (1982: chap. 5). For a discussion of particularism, see Richard Fumerton's chapter in this volume.

15. See Moser (1989: 69–77) for his rejection of externalism and Moser (1989: 158–64, 255–65) for his view that we can be justified in believing that skeptical possibilities do not obtain.

16. Feldman (2003: 145–52). See also Pryor (2000, 2004) and Vogel (1990).

17. Van Cleve (2003: 45).

18. Van Cleve (2003: 50). See also Van Cleve (2003: 46), where he says that to be an externalist in the sense that matters for his essay is to say that "there are sources of justification or knowledge that deliver their goods even if the subject does not know they are reliable."

19. This principle, from an article by Cohen (2002), is quoted by Van Cleve (2003: 49). Van Cleve makes it clear on the next page that in characterizing externalism as the denial of KR, he is understanding KR in such a way that the necessary condition it lays down is a *prior* condition saying that S can gain knowledge through K only if S *first* knows that K is reliable.

20. See Fumerton (1995: 60–79) and Moser (1989: 71–88, 173–76).

21. Greco (2004: 54).

22. Rb and Rc appear in Greco (2004: 53–54). For a summary of his argument, see Greco (2004: 62–63, including nn. 21–22).

23. See Conee and Feldman (2001: 232–34) and Feldman (2004: 155). Notice that to say that B is a fitting response to E is not to say B is a fitting response to an evidence base that includes E and more besides.

24. This sort of claim comes up a number of times, for example, in Alston (1986b) and Goldman (1999).

25. The temptation to endorse (a) is evident in Van Cleve (2003), which was discussed earlier. It is also very common to think that all views that are not internalist views are externalist views—which, together with (a), implies (b).

26. An additional worry is that *doxastic* justification (see note 1) requires that one's belief be formed in the right way. Since the mere potential for the relevant awareness seems to have nothing to do with how the belief is formed, it is difficult to see how the mere potential for such awareness will be relevant to doxastic justification. Why think that the fact that one is able, *after* time *t*, to become aware (for the first time) of some reason for believing *p* will have any effect on whether one is doxastically justified in believing *p* at *t*? Clearly, the subject's first-time awareness of that reason after *t* played no role in the formation of the belief at *t*. One could avoid this problem by modifying the potential-awareness requirement so that potential awareness that *p* satisfies the requirement only if the subject was in the past *actually* aware that *p*. But then the potential-awareness requirement would suffer from the same problem as the actual-awareness requirement: it would require actual awareness (now or in the past) involving a degree of complexity humans are incapable of.

27. For a more extended presentation of this argument, see Bergmann (2006a: 140–44; 2006b: 14–19).

28. A fifth objection is proposed and discussed in Bergmann (2006b: 233–38).

29. See BonJour (2002: 236–37) and Stroud (1989: 46).

30. See Fumerton (1995: chap. 6) and Vogel (2000). This objection is sometimes applied independently of worries about responding to skepticism in a philosophically satisfying way. In such cases, the concern is just that by allowing for justified epistemically circular beliefs (whether in response to the skeptic or not), externalism is unacceptable.

31. See Alston (1993: 16–17). It is true that Alston sometimes speaks (see his 1986a) as if an externalist account of the justification of higher level beliefs is perfectly fine. But, as Fumerton notes (1995: 178–79), Alston also seems to show (in his 1993) some discomfort with doing so.

32. Fumerton (1995: 179–80) explains the discomfort in this way.

33. I make this point in Bergmann (2000: 171–72), and Fumerton (2006: 175–77) concedes it.

34. Fumerton (2006: 184–86) offers this amended explanation of the externalist's apparent discomfort.

35. See Alston (1993: 17) and Sosa (1997: sec.6).

36. Examples of voodoo and Great Pumpkin beliefs have come up in connection with Plantinga's externalist defense of noninferentially justified theistic belief, which he develops in response to religious skeptics. See Plantinga (1983: 74–78; 2000: 342–53) for his development of this defense, and see Martin (1990: 266–78) and DeRose (1999) for criticisms. Fumerton has identified Plantinga's externalist response to religious skepticism as one more implausible consequence of externalism (2001: 343–44). Fumerton's suggestion is that if we allow the externalist response to skepticism about the external world, then we have no good principled reason to object to Plantinga's externalist response to religious skepticism.

37. For an argument that strong awareness internalism implies radical skepticism, see the latter part of section 1 of this chapter and also Bergmann (2006a: 140–44; 2006b: 14–19). For an argument that inferentialism implies radical skepticism, see Bergmann (2006b: 185–87). The basic idea of the latter argument is this: If all justification is inferential, then (a) circular reasoning can produce justification, or (b) our beliefs can be justified on the basis of an infinite (nonrepeating) chain of reasoning, or (c) our beliefs can be justified on the basis of inference from unjustified beliefs, or (d) none of our beliefs can be justified. But each of (a)–(c) is manifestly false. Hence if all justification is inferential, (d) is true—which is just to say that inferentialism implies radical skepticism.

38. See Fumerton (1995: 80–81) and BonJour (2003b: 65).

39. Michael Huemer (2001, 2006) defends a view that initially seems to be a low-standard view. It is called "phenomenal conservatism," and he defines it as follows:

> PC: If it seems to S that p, then, in the absence of defeaters, S thereby has at least some degree of justification for believing that p.
>
> (Huemer 2006: 148)

A natural first reading of this principle suggests that it is claiming that a belief is justified so long as it seems to the believer to be true. That *would* be a low-standard view. But a more careful reading of the principle (and the places in which Huemer defends it—see especially Huemer 2006: 156) makes it clear that one's belief that *p* will not be justified (all things considered) if the prima facie justification one has for *p* (derived from how things seem to the believer) is defeated. The factors that can result in defeat are things such as epistemic irresponsibility (Huemer mentioned this factor to me in personal communication) or a failure to cohere with one's other beliefs or seemings (see Huemer 2006: 156). But these are things the believer can *think* are absent—things that can even *seem* to the believer to be absent—when in fact they are present. Hence, according to Huemer's phenomenal conservatism, a believer can think that all is well with her beliefs epistemically speaking (and her beliefs can seem fine to her epistemically speaking) when in fact they are not justified (all things considered) because of the fact that their prima facie justification is defeated by epistemic irresponsibility or a failure to cohere with her other beliefs or seemings. In short, given what Huemer builds into the no-defeater requirement included in PC, that principle demands more for justification (all things considered) than a mere seeming that the belief is true.

40. When I say that "everything seems fine to the subject epistemically speaking," I mean that she has a felt inclination to believe that everything is fine epistemically speaking and no inclination to think otherwise. When I say that "nothing seems amiss epistemically," I mean that she has no inclination to think that something is amiss epistemically.

41. Conee and Feldman (1985: 15–16; 2001: 232–34) think that a belief's noninferential justification supervenes on its fitting the evidence. Moser (1989: chap. 3) thinks that it supervenes on the evidence's being best explained by the truth of the belief in question.

42. See Fumerton (1995: 77) and BonJour (2003a: 192–94).

43. We can see that the latter is true as follows: Suppose that Jack used to be a normal person who regularly formed the belief that he was being appeared to redly when he *was* being appeared to redly, and that in doing so, he picked up the concept of being appeared to redly. Now suppose that because of brain damage or demon influence, he begins to believe that he is being appeared to redly when he is not being so appeared to. He does not *hallucinate* his being appeared to redly—that is, it does not *appear* visually to him that he is being appeared to redly when he is not being so appeared to. Nor does he base his belief that he is being appeared to redly on his acquaintance with how he is being appeared to. What happens is that even when he is not being appeared to redly, he sometimes succumbs to an overpowering *inclination*—caused by brain damage or demon influence—to believe that it is obvious that he is being so appeared to. Given that being appeared to redly is one thing and that believing that one is being appeared to redly is another, the example seems to be a possible one.

44. See McGrew (1999: 228).

45. The only difference is that the mentalist will insist that the conditions for non-inferential justification are determined solely by the subject's mental states, and the internalist will insist that the subject is aware of something that contributes to the belief's justification (even if she need not conceive of that thing as relevant in any way to the belief's justification).

46. See Fumerton (2006: 175–77).

47. See Bergmann (2006b: 227–29) for further elaboration of this response.

48. See Alston (1986a), Sosa (1997), and Kornblith (2004).

49. BonJour, for example, says:

The proper conclusion [for the externalist] is merely that the belief or beliefs originally in question are reliably arrived at (and perhaps thereby are justified or constitute knowledge in externalist senses) *if* the epistemologist's own cognitive process are in fact reliable in the way that he or she no doubt believes them to be. But the only apparent way to arrive at a result that is not ultimately hypothetical in this way is for the reliability of at least some cognitive processes to be establishable *on the basis of what the epistemologist can know directly or immediately from his or her first-person epistemic perspective.*

(2002: 236–37, emphasis added)

Notice that he seems to be stipulating that the higher level beliefs (the contents of which are the antecedents that, according to BonJour, must be known to prevent the externalist response from being merely conditional) count as knowledge only if they are arrived at by something like direct acquaintance.

50. In addition to the works cited in the next eight notes by Alston, Bergmann, Pryor, Schmitt, Sosa, and Van Cleve, defenses of epistemic circularity can also be found in Alston (1986a), Boghossian (2000), Braithwaite (1953), Lemos (2004), Sosa (1997), and Van Cleve (1984).

51. See Alston (1993). Alston focuses mostly on sense perception but makes the argument more generally too in the final chapter.

52. Sosa (1994: 284).

53. Either that or we have an argument for atheism that has not received much attention.

54. In this context, the term "basic" in "basic knowledge" has a different meaning than it does when foundationalists say that there are properly basic beliefs. In that foundationalist claim, "basic" means noninferential. But given the way "basic" is used in this context, even an inferential belief can constitute basic knowledge (e.g., knowledge that is produced by deductive inference prior to the subject's knowledge that deductive inference is a reliable belief source).

55. See Cohen (2002), Van Cleve (2003), and Schmitt (2004). There is a slight complication that arises in defining basic knowledge. Some say, as I did earlier, that basic knowledge occurs if and only if knowledge produced by a source is not *preceded* by the subject's knowledge of that source's reliability. Others (e.g., Cohen) say that basic knowledge occurs if and only if knowledge produced by a source is not *preceded by or produced at the same time as* the subject's knowledge of that source's reliability. I prefer the former definition, given that people (such as Cohen himself) seek to avoid epistemic circularity by denying basic knowledge. On the former definition, denying basic knowledge (i.e., insisting that knowledge produced by a source must be preceded by knowledge of that source's reliability) is enough to avoid epistemically circular knowledge. But on the latter definition, that is not enough. According to the latter definition, it is possible to deny basic knowledge (where this is understood as insisting that knowledge produced by a source must be either preceded by or produced at the same time as knowledge of that source's reliability) while allowing for knowledge of source S's reliability that is produced directly by S itself as its first knowledge output. Since this S-produced knowledge of S's reliability is a case of knowledge via a source whose reliability was not verified before it was employed to produce knowledge of its own reliability—and which continues to be unverified by an independent source—we have a case of epistemically circular knowledge. Thus although Cohen employs the latter definition of basic knowledge, he needs the former definition in order for his rejection of basic knowledge to enable him to avoid epistemic circularity.

56. See Bergmann (2004a; 2006b: chap. 7).

57. See Bergmann (2004a: 717–19; 2006b: 198), Pryor (2004: 365–66), and Schmitt (2004: 392).

58. See Bergmann (2004a: 717–19; 2006b: 198) and Pryor (2004: 366). Schmitt (2004: 392) explicitly rejects this point, insisting to the contrary that merely having doubts that result in withholding judgment about a faculty's reliability is not enough to make epistemically circular arguments for its reliability ineffective.

59. He hints at this point in Pryor (2004: 366–68) and has confirmed it in correspondence.

60. Alston (1993: 16–17).

61. Fumerton (1995: 178–80).

62. Bergmann (2000: 171–72).

63. Fumerton (2006: 184–86).

64. I am thinking here not of hypothetical doubt but of doubt that involves suspecting the falsehood of or disbelieving or withholding the conclusion in question.

65. For further discussion of these points, see Bergmann (2004a: 720–21; 2006b: 200–202).

66. Keep in mind that, as I noted when introducing the "anything goes" worry, we are stipulating that the crystal-ball beliefs in question are internally consistent, and that there is no clear way to falsify or confirm them without appeal to crystal-ball gazing itself.

67. Sosa (1997: sec. 6). Plantinga (1983: 74–78; 2000: 342–53) says something similar in defending his externalist account of noninferentially justified theistic belief against the Great Pumpkin objection.

68. See Bergmann (2006b: 229–33) for further discussion of this reply to the "anything goes" objection.

69. An objection to nonexternalist views that relies on a similar dilemma is developed at length in Bergmann (2006b); see especially chap. 1.

REFERENCES

Alston, William (1985)."Concepts of Epistemic Justification." *The Monist* 68: 57–89. Reprinted in Alston (1989: 81–114).

———. (1986a). "Epistemic Circularity." *Philosophy and Phenomenological Research* 47: 1–30.

———. (1986b). "Internalism and Externalism in Epistemology." *Philosophical Topics* 14: 179–221. Reprinted in Alston (1989: 185–226).

———. (1989). *Epistemic Justification: Essays in the Theory of Knowledge* (Ithaca, NY: Cornell University Press).

———. (1993). *The Reliability of Sense Perception* (Ithaca, NY: Cornell University Press).

Bergmann, Michael (2000). "Externalism and Skepticism." *Philosophical Review* 109: 159–94.

———. (2004a). "Epistemic Circularity: Malignant and Benign." *Philosophy and Phenomenological Research* 69:709–27.

———. (2004b). "Externalist Justification without Reliability." *Philosophical Issues* 14 (*Epistemology*): 35–60.

———. (2006a). "A Dilemma for Internalism." In Crisp, Davidson, and Vanderlaan (2006), 134–74.

———. (2006b). *Justification without Awareness* (New York: Oxford University Press).

Boghossian, Paul (2000). "Knowledge of Logic." In Paul Boghossian and Christopher Peacocke (eds.), *New Essays on the A Priori* (Oxford: Oxford University Press), 229–54.

BonJour, Laurence (1985). *The Structure of Empirical Knowledge* (Cambridge, MA: Harvard University Press).

———. (2002). *Epistemology: Classic Problems and Contemporary Responses* (Lanham, MD: Rowman and Littlefield).

————. (2003a). "Reply to Sosa." In Laurence BonJour and Ernest Sosa, *Epistemic Justification* (Malden, MA: Blackwell Publishing), 173–200.

————. (2003b). "A Version of Internalist Foundationalism." In Laurence BonJour and Ernest Sosa, *Epistemic Justification* (Malden, MA: Blackwell Publishing), 3–96.

Braithwaite, Richard (1953). *Scientific Explanation* (Cambridge: Cambridge University Press).

Chisholm, Richard (1982). *The Foundations of Knowing* (Minneapolis: University of Minnesota Press).

Cohen, Stewart (1988). "How to Be a Fallibilist." *Philosophical Perspectives* 2: 91–123.

————. (1999). "Contextualism, Skepticism, and the Structure of Reasons." *Philosophical Perspectives* 13: 57–90.

————. (2002). "Basic Knowledge and the Problem of Easy Knowledge." *Philosophy and Phenomenological Research* 65: 309–29.

Conee, Earl, and Richard Feldman (1985). "Evidentialism." *Philosophical Studies* 48: 15–34.

————. (2001). "Internalism Defended." In Hilary Kornblith (ed.), *Epistemology: Internalism and Externalism* (Malden, MA: Blackwell Publishers), 230–60.

Crisp, Thomas, Matthew Davidson, and David Vanderlaan (eds.) (2006). *Knowledge and Reality: Essays in Honor of Alvin Plantinga* (Dordrecht: Kluwer Academic Publishers).

DeRose, Keith (1995)."Solving the Skeptical Problem." *Philosophical Review* 104: 1–52.

————. (1999). "Contextualism: An Explanation and Defense." In John Greco and Ernest Sosa (eds.), *The Blackwell Guide to Epistemology* (Oxford: Basil Blackwell), 187–205.

————. (1999). "Voodoo Epistemology." Available online at: http://pantheon.yale.edu/%7Ekd47/voodoo.htm.

Dretske, Fred (1970). "Epistemic Operators." *Journal of Philosophy* 67: 1007–23.

————. (1971)."Conclusive Reasons." *Australasian Journal of Philosophy* 49: 1–22.

————. (2003). "Skepticism: What Perception Teaches." In Stephen Luper (ed.), *The Skeptics: Contemporary Essays* (Aldershot: Ashgate Publishing), 105–118.

Feldman, Richard (2003). *Epistemology* (Upper Saddle River, NJ: Prentice Hall).

————. (2004). "In Search of Internalism and Externalism." In Richard Schantz (ed.), *The Externalist Challenge* (New York: de Gruyter), 143–56.

Firth, Roderick (1978). "Are Epistemic Concepts Reducible to Ethical Concepts?" In Alvin Goldman and Jaegwon Kim (eds.), *Values and Morals* (Dordrecht: D. Reidel), 215–29.

Fumerton, Richard (1995). *Metaepistemology and Skepticism* (Lanham, MD: Rowman and Littlefield).

————. (2001). "Plantinga, Warrant, and Christian Belief." *Philosophia Christi* 3: 341–51.

————. (2006). "Epistemic Internalism, Philosophical Assurance and the Skeptical Predicament." In Crisp, Davidson, and Vanderlaan (2006), 175–87.

Gettier, Edmund (1963). "Is Justified True Belief Knowledge?" *Analysis* 23: 121–23.

Goldman, Alvin (1979). "What Is Justified Belief?" In George Pappas (ed.), *Justification and Knowledge* (Dordrecht: D. Reidel), 1–23.

————. (1986). *Epistemology and Cognition* (Cambridge, MA: Harvard University Press).

————. (1999). "Internalism Exposed." *Journal of Philosophy* 96: 271–93.

Greco, John (1999). "Agent Reliabilism." *Philosophical Perspectives* 13: 273–96.

————. (2000). *Putting Skeptics in Their Place* (New York: Cambridge University Press).

————. (2004). "Externalism and Skepticism." In Richard Schantz (ed.), *The Externalist Challenge* (New York: Walter de Gruyter), 53–63.

Heller, Mark (1999). "The Proper Role for Contextualism in an Anti-luck Epistemology." *Philosophical Perspectives* 13: 115–30.

Huemer, Michael (2001). *Skepticism and the Veil of Perception* (Lanham, MD: Rowman and Littlefield).

———. (2006). "Phenomenal Conservatism and the Internalist Intuition." *American Philosophical Quarterly* 43: 147–58.

Kornblith, Hilary (2004). "Does Reliabilism Make Knowledge Merely Conditional?" *Philosophical Issues* 14 (*Epistemology*): 185–200.

Lemos, Noah (2004). "Epistemic Circularity Again." *Philosophical Issues* 14 (*Epistemology*): 254–70.

Lewis, David (1996). "Elusive Knowledge." *Australasian Journal of Philosophy* 74: 549–67.

Martin, Michael (1990). *Atheism: A Philosophical Justification* (Philadelphia: Temple University Press).

McGrew, Timothy (1999). "A Defense of Classical Foundationalism." In Louis Pojman (ed.), *The Theory of Knowledge: Classical and Contemporary Readings*, 2nd ed. (Belmont, CA: Wadsworth Publishing Company), 224–35.

Moser, Paul (1989). *Knowledge and Evidence* (New York: Cambridge University Press).

Nozick, Robert (1981). *Philosophical Explanations* (Cambridge, MA: Belknap Press).

Plantinga, Alvin (1983). "Reason and Belief in God." In Alvin Plantinga and Nicholas Wolterstorff (eds.), *Faith and Rationality* (Notre Dame, IN: University of Notre Dame Press), 16–93.

———. (1993). *Warrant and Proper Function* (New York: Oxford University Press).

———. (2000). *Warranted Christian Belief* (New York: Oxford University Press).

Pritchard, Duncan (2002). "Recent Work on Radical Skepticism." *American Philosophical Quarterly* 39: 215–57.

Pryor, James (2000). "The Skeptic and the Dogmatist." *Noûs,* 34: 517–49.

———. (2004). "What's Wrong with Moore's Argument?" *Philosophical Issues* 14 (*Epistemology*): 349–78.

Schaffer, Jonathan (2004). "From Contextualism to Contrastivism." *Philosophical Studies* 119: 73–103.

———. (2005). "Contrastive Knowledge." *Oxford Studies in Epistemology* 1: 235–71.

Schmitt, Frederick (2004). "What Is Wrong with Epistemic Circularity?" *Philosophical Issues* 14(*Epistemology*): 379–402.

Sosa, Ernest (1991). *Knowledge in Perspective: Selected Essays in Epistemology* (New York: Cambridge University Press).

———. (1994). "Philosophical Skepticism and Epistemic Circularity." *Proceedings of the Aristotelian Society,* supplementary volume68: 263–90.

———. (1997). "Reflective Knowledge in the Best Circles." *Journal of Philosophy* 94: 410–30.

Stroud, Barry (1989). "Understanding Human Knowledge in General." In Marjorie Clay and Keith Lehrer (eds.), *Knowledge and Skepticism* (Boulder, CO: Westview Press), 31–50.

Van Cleve, James (1984). "Reliability, Justification, and the Problem of Induction." *Midwest Studies in Philosophy* 9: 555–67.

———. (2003). "Is Knowledge Easy—or Impossible? Externalism as the Only Alternative to Skepticism." In Stephen Luper (ed.), *The Skeptics: Contemporary Essays* (Aldershot: Ashgate Publishing), 45–59.

Vogel, Jonathan (1990). "Cartesian Skepticism and Inference to the Best Explanation." *Journal of Philosophy* 87: 658–66.

———. (2000). "Reliabilism Leveled." *Journal of Philosophy* 97: 602–23.

CHAPTER 24

INTERNALIST RESPONSES TO SKEPTICISM

JONATHAN VOGEL

1. INTERNALISM AND SKEPTICISM: THREE APPROACHES

Internalism, as I understand it here, is the doctrine that knowledge requires justified belief. For present purposes, this means that you do not know a proposition X unless you have good reason of some sort to believe X.[1] Justification can be empirical or a priori. You have empirical justification for believing X just in case experience gives you evidence that properly supports X. You have a priori justification for believing X just in case you are justified in believing X, but your justification is not empirical.

Skepticism, as I understand it here, is the doctrine that we have no knowledge of the external world. In an internalist setting, the basic argument for skepticism can be put as follows. Let M be any proposition about the external world.

- 1a. In order to know M, you need to know that various possibilities of massive sensory deception do not obtain.
- 1b. In particular, you need to know that you are not a brain in a vat ($-$BIV) stimulated so that it falsely appears to you that M.
- 1c. In order to know $-$BIV, you have to be justified in believing $-$BIV.
- 1d. But you are not justified in believing $-$BIV.
- 1e. Therefore, you do not know M.

The argument, if sound, yields the conclusion that you do not know any propositions about the external world. That is, the argument, if sound, would establish the doctrine of skepticism. Let us grant (1a).[2] BIV, that you are a brain in a vat, is a representative possibility of massive sensory deception, so (1b) follows from (1a) as an instance.[3] Premise 1c is a direct consequence of the definition of internalism. Premises 1a–1c together imply that in order to know M, you have to be justified in believing –BIV. Thus the status of skepticism turns on whether (1d) is correct. The question is: What justification, if any, do you have for rejecting BIV? The skeptic denies that we have any such justification. An internalist reply to skepticism would show that we do have some such justification after all.

Before proceeding, we need to note that according to many internalists, justification has a characteristic structure. One belief may be justified by or derive its justification from another belief. For example, suppose that you see the fresh footprint of a rabbit in the snow, and you believe that there has recently been a rabbit at this spot. Your belief that there has recently been a rabbit at this spot is justified by your belief that there is a fresh rabbit footprint in the snow. We can say that for you, the latter belief is epistemically prior or antecedent to the former belief.[4] The relation of epistemic priority is antireflexive (A cannot be epistemically prior to A) and antisymmetric (if A is epistemically prior to B, then B cannot be epistemically prior to A).[5]

Another preliminary point is that we can say that if it looks to you that X and it is the case that X, then your experience is *veridical*. If it looks to you that X and X is not the case, then your experience is *unveridical*. These definitions call for some some comments and caveats. First, the formulations are no more than provisional. Instead of "If it looks to you that X, then X," it might be preferable to say, "If it appears to you that X, then X," or "If you seem to perceive that X, then X," or something else. In any case, there would be a further question about what is meant by "its looking to you that X" (or "its appearing to you that X," or "its seeming to you that you perceive X," and so on). One way to answer the question is to maintain that experiences have representational content. Say, for example, that you see a sand dune nearby. Your experience represents that there is a sand dune nearby; that is, the proposition that there is a sand dune nearby is (part of) the content of your experience. We could then understand the variable X in the definitions just given to take such experiential contents as its values.[6] Although this sort of account is controversial, I will assume it here for the sake of exposition.

We should note that experience may be locally or globally unveridical. It may look to you that there is a hand before you, but there really is not (it is a fake hand). Or it may look to you that there is a red table in the room, but there really is not (it is a white table illuminated by red light). If other things are all right, your experience is *locally* unveridical. By contrast, skeptical arguments work by raising the possibility that a person's experience is *globally* unveridical. If someone is a brain in a vat, then (virtually) none of his sensory experiences represents the world as it truly is. That is, for the brain in a vat, it is generally false that if it looks that X, then X.

Now the various internalist approaches to skepticism can be set out. On all the views to be considered here, we have justification for rejecting BIV. There are three main lines of thought.[7] Very briefly sketched, they are as follows:

Apriorism: We are justified in rejecting BIV even though we have no empirical evidence (i.e., evidence from experience) against it. Instead, our justification for holding −BIV is a priori.

Dogmatism: By themselves, particular perceptual experiences in some way justify us in believing various propositions about the world. Each of these propositions entails −BIV, and one's justified belief in such a proposition justifies, in turn, one's belief that −BIV. Thus we have local empirical justification for holding −BIV.

And then there is the position I endorse:

Explanationism: Limited or individual perceptual experiences do not provide justification for believing −BIV; the coherence among those experiences does. More specifically, the regular patterns of one's experience are well explained by the body of one's ordinary beliefs about the world. The BIV hypothesis explains those patterns less well. Hence we are justified in maintaining our ordinary beliefs and in rejecting the skeptical alternative.[8] We have global empirical justification for believing −BIV.

There is another important point of comparison among these approaches. Dogmatism may be seen as a development of G. E. Moore's famous commonsense reply to skepticism.[9] Moore, holding his hands up before him in plain sight, claims that obviously he has a hand. The proposition (H) that Moore has a hand entails the proposition (−BIV) that he is not a brain in a vat to whom it appears falsely that he has a hand. So, according to Moore, his belief that H justifies his belief that −BIV. The proponent of dogmatism agrees that Moore is justified in believing H and justified in believing −BIV, and that the former belief is *epistemically prior* to the latter.[10] The apriorist disagrees with the last of these claims. She holds that Moore, like the rest of us, is entitled a priori to believe −BIV, and that this belief contributes to Moore's justification for believing that H. Thus Moore's belief that −BIV is epistemically prior to his belief that H rather than the other away around (as the dogmatist claims). The explanationist, too, denies that perceptual beliefs, like Moore's belief that H, are epistemically prior to one's belief that −BIV.

To crystallize further the differences among these approaches, consider the following way of supporting premise 1d of the skeptical argument:[11]

2a. Suppose that I have a justified belief that −BIV.
2b. The only way to be justified in believing −BIV is on the basis of some perceptually justified belief PERC.[12]
2c. So PERC is epistemically prior to −BIV.
2d. But since PERC is a perceptually justified belief, it is epistemically posterior to −BIV.

2e. Premises 2c and 2d are inconsistent.

2f. Hence, by reductio ad absurdum, I am not justified in believing −BIV.

The dogmatist accepts (2b) but rejects (2d). For the dogmatist, a perceptually justified belief, like Moore's belief that he has a hand, is epistemically prior (rather than posterior) to his belief that −BIV. The apriorist accepts (2d) but rejects (2b). According to apriorism, we have a priori justification for believing −BIV, so no empirical, perceptually justified belief is needed to support −BIV. But an apriorist may well take the view that if our justification for −BIV had to be empirical, then (2b) would be true, and the skeptical argument would go through. The apriorist thinks that the only way to avoid skepticism is to allow that we are a priori justified in believing −BIV.

The explanationist rejects (2b) and thus disagrees with the dogmatist. However, the explanationist maintains that our justification for −BIV is empirical, and thus disagrees with the apriorist. Since this is such a central issue, it is worth examining in further detail what reason there might be for accepting (2b). One might offer an argument like this one:

3a. −BIV is a contingent proposition about the world.

3b. If S is justified in believing a contingent proposition about the world, then S is justified in believing that proposition either by perception or by inference from some other proposition(s) justified by perception.

3c. Thus if S is justified in believing −BIV, either S has a perceptual belief that −BIV, or S's belief that −BIV is justified by some perceptual belief(s).

3d. We do not see or hear or otherwise perceive that we are not brains in vats, so S does not have a perceptual belief that −BIV.

3e. Hence if S is justified in believing that −BIV, then S has some perceptual belief that is justified and epistemically prior to S's belief that −BIV.

The import of (3c) is that if we cannot somehow perceive that −BIV, the only way to have a justified belief that −BIV is by inference from some perceptual belief(s). If our perceptual beliefs are justified, then presumably any such belief will do. Suppose that you see a sand dune in your vicinity, and you are justified in believing that there is a sand dune nearby. Seemingly, you can deduce −BIV from your belief about the sand dune.[13] This is the dogmatist's picture of how justification accrues to −BIV. The explanationist takes a different view. There are two competing causal accounts of how my experience comes about. One is the body of my ordinary beliefs about the world, including my perceptual beliefs; the other is BIV. The relevant body of evidence, the "data" to be explained, is (E*) the occurrence and nature of my experience.[14] If explanationism is correct, then E^* justifies both our ordinary beliefs about the world (including perceptual beliefs) and the rejection of −BIV. The dilemma set up by (3c) is a false one. E^* can empirically justify −BIV without its being that case that −BIV is a perceptual belief or that −BIV is justified by some perceptual belief(s).

A related false dilemma is at work in the argument 2a–2f. Premises 2b and 2d allow for only two possibilities, namely, that PERC is prior to –BIV or that –BIV is prior to PERC.[15] Let us grant that PERC is justified if and only if –BIV is. Nevertheless, it may be that neither is epistemically prior to the other. PERC does not justify –BIV, nor does –BIV justify PERC. As I will say, PERC and –BIV are *cojustified*.[16] This crucial possibility has generally been overlooked in discussions of skepticism.[17] Once it is recognized, it undercuts the argument 2a–2f, which is important in and of itself. Beyond that, we can better appreciate the distinctiveness of explanationism. Both the apriorist and the dogmatist accept the dilemma that PERC must be epistemically prior to –BIV or vice versa, and they appeal to that dilemma in arguing for their positions. The resulting picture is that if PERC is prior to –BIV, then dogmatism is right; if –BIV is prior to PERC, then we ought to embrace apriorism. By allowing for the possibility that PERC and –BIV are cojustified, the explanationist spikes those arguments and clears space for her own view.[18]

2. VERIDICALITY PRINCIPLES

To understand and evaluate the various internalist responses to skepticism, we need to consider what I will call *veridicality principles*. One is the looks-is principle:

> (Looks-is principle; LIP) One is justified in believing: If it looks to one that X, then X.

Another is the following:

> (–SK) One is justified in believing that BIV is false.

The import of LIP is that a subject is justified in believing with respect to each of his experiences that it is veridical. If LIP is correct, then one is justified in denying that experience is either locally or globally unveridical. -SK is narrower in scope than LIP. -SK says only that one is justified in denying that experience is globally unveridical.[19] But if either LIP or -SK holds, one is justified in rejecting the claim that experience is globally unveridical, which is to say that one is justified in denying BIV. Thus step 1d of the skeptical argument is false, and there is an internalist answer to skepticism.

However, LIP as it stands is obviously too sweeping. For example, suppose that Agnes experiences a mirage. It looks to Agnes that there is an expanse of water before her. LIP entails that if it looks to Agnes that there is an expanse of water before her, then she is justified in believing that there is an expanse of water before her. But suppose that Agnes knows that mirages occur in circumstances like hers. Her background information about mirages makes her unjustified, all things considered, in believing that there is an expanse of water before her. The justification she has for believing that there is an expanse of water before her is merely prima facie justification, which in this instance is defeated by her background information.[20] If we take this qualification into account, LIP can be rewritten as follows:

> (LIP, amended) One is prima facie justified in believing: If it looks to one that X, then X.

It seems advisable to weaken -SK as well. Consider the following example:

> *Waking-up case*:[21] Stan has an apparently normal course of experience until one day, he seems to "wake up" and discover that he is in a laboratory. There are strange creatures who tell Stan that he has been a victim of a brain-in-a-vat experiment that has just concluded. They then affect Stan's experience in various ways to convince him that they are capable of doing what they have described. Perhaps, at that point, Stan is justified in believing that his current experience of the laboratory is veridical and that his previous life was spent as a victim of massive sensory deception. Stan gets accustomed to his new life, but after a while, he has another "waking up" experience in which the experimenters tell him that the first "waking up" experience was delusory, and that Stan has been deceived all along until the present time. Suppose that these "waking up" experiences continue.

Principle -SK says that Stan is justified in believing –BIV, but even so, the repeated disruptions of his sensory life undo that justification. Under these bizarre circumstances, it seems that Stan ought to withhold belief with respect to BIV or even accept BIV. To accommodate this outcome, -SK should be modified:

> (-SK, amended) One is prima facie justified in believing: The brain-in-a-vat hypothesis is false.

The apriorist response to skepticism can be understood as a commitment to either LIP or -SK, with the added specification that the justification in question is a priori:

> (LIP^{AP}) One has a priori, prima facie justification for believing: If it looks to one that X, then X.

> ($-SK^{AP}$) One has a priori, prima facie justification for believing: The brain-in-a-vat hypothesis is false.

Certain ways that experience might fail to be veridical can be rejected, even though experience itself provides no justification for doing so. Moreover, the beliefs licensed by LIP^{AP} or by $-SK^{AP}$ help support, and are epistemically prior to, all our beliefs about the external world. Suppose that I am perceptually justified in believing that there is a cat on the bed. One way things might go, according to apriorism, is that my experience gives me reason to believe (1) that it looks to me that there is a cat on the bed. The relevant instance of LIP^{AP} is (2) that if it looks to me that there is a cat on the bed, then there is a cat on the bed. So both (1) and (2) are prior to, and together justify, my belief that there is a cat on the bed. Alternatively, experience might give me reason to believe (3) that either there is a cat on the bed or I am a brain in a vat. -SK^{AP} provides that I am justified in believing that (4) I am not a brain in a vat. Both (3) and (4) are prior to, and together justify, my belief that there is a cat on the bed.

As I see things, the principal reason for endorsing apriorism is the conviction that there is no empirical evidence against the possibility that one is a brain in a vat.[22] If so, we face a dilemma. Either there is some a priori justification for denying that one is a brain in a vat, or skepticism prevails. Since skepticism is outrageous, we properly take the dilemma's first horn and refuse the second.[23] However, apriorism confronts two difficult, related challenges. The first is a matter of selectivity. Suppose that the beliefs directly licensed by LIP^{AP} or -SK^{AP} have a priori justification. Why do these beliefs and the principles that sanction them enjoy special status, while others do not? Consider the following:

> (SK) One is a priori, prima facie justified in believing that BIV.

According to apriorism, principle -SK^{AP} is legitimate, while SK is not. What makes that so? How can we tell? A second challenge is that it is hard to see how one can have a priori justification for a substantive belief about a contingent matter of fact. The belief that one is not a brain in a vat is of just that sort. The world could be such that you are a normally embodied human veridically perceiving your environment, but then again, the world could be such that you are a brain in a vat. How can reason—or whatever the source of a priori justification may be—pronounce on which way the world actually is?[24] Whether these objections to apriorism can be overcome is a deep issue I will not try to address here. For now, I will just observe that apriorism will be superfluous, if not completely unmotivated, if either dogmatism or explanationism is tenable.

Dogmatism may be understood as endorsing a veridicality principle that is a variant of LIP:

> (DOG) If it looks to one that X, then one is thereby prima facie justified in believing that X.[25]

DOG specifies that its looking that X to someone suffices to make that person justified in believing that X. Nothing else is required. In particular, our perceptual beliefs are justified without support from any other epistemically prior beliefs. Perceptual beliefs are thus *immediately justified* or *basic*. This idea can be developed in two importantly different ways. According to one approach, a belief is justified simply in virtue of its intrinsic features and/or the circumstances in which it arises. I will call beliefs of this sort *endobasic*. If your experience plays any role, the relation between that experience and your belief must be nonepistemic. That is, your sand-dune-esque experience is not evidence that supports your belief that there is a sand dune nearby. An endobasic belief is justified in the absence of anything that is epistemically prior to it.[26] A different approach allows a basic belief to be justified by something epistemically prior to it. I will call a belief of this sort *exobasic*. An exobasic perceptual belief is justified by one's experience. So, for example, its looking to you that there is a sand dune nearby justifies your belief with that content. The experience you have does serve as evidence that supports your belief. However, your belief still counts as basic because it is not supported by any epistemically prior *belief*. My focus here will be on the version of dogmatism that treats perceptual beliefs as exobasic.

The primary appeal of dogmatism is that it that it is meant to be straight-forward and commonsensical. What justifies Moore's belief that he has a hand? His seeing it. The trouble is with what comes next. How does Moore know −BIV? According to the dogmatist, Moore need only infer −BIV from his belief that he has a hand. But it is natural to protest at this point that this inference really does nothing to establish −BIV. Rather, Moore assumes −BIV when he comes to believe that he has a hand in the first place. Moore's belief that he has a hand is not epistemically prior to his belief that −BIV. This impression, if correct, is consistent with apriorism and explanationism, but not with dogmatism.[27]

Misgivings about the Moorean response to skepticism may be sharpened and generalized. The underlying idea is that DOG is too lax. DOG agreeably provides that we are justified in believing −BIV. However, global skepticism aside, DOG would allow that we have justified belief in cases where we manifestly do not.[28] The following is meant to be an example that shows that DOG goes wrong in this way:

> *Red Table Case.*[29] (L) It looks to you that the table before you is red. According to DOG, this experience justifies you in believing that (R) the table before you is red. The proposition that the table before you is red entails that (−W) it's not the case that the table before you is really white but illuminated with red light. So, on the basis of your experience alone, you're justified in believing −W. But that's wrong. Its looking to you that the table before you is red doesn't give you reason to believe that the table isn't really white but illuminated with red light.[30]

We need to proceed with some care here. In the example, you are justified in believing R and −W. If you did not have justification for believing −W, you would not be justified in believing R. All this is quite consistent with DOG. What is at issue, then, is the nature or source of the justification you have for believing R and −W. In situations like the one described, we typically have relevant background information. We know that (B) in ordinary situations (people's homes, furniture stores, and so forth), there generally are not any white tables made to look red by special lighting. The disagreement between the dogmatist and his critic comes down to whether your having the background information B is essential for your being justified in believing −W and thus essential for your being justified in believing R. My sympathies are with the critic, but the Red Table Case is not set up to make that point directly.

The following argument would do the job:

4a. Suppose that you have experience L but lack background information B.
4b. Without B, you are not justified in believing −W.
4c. If you are not justified in believing −W, you are not justified in believing R.
4d. So without B, you are not justified in believing R.

4e. But, according to DOG, your having experience *L* suffices for you to be justified in believing *R*.

4f. Therefore, given (4d), DOG cannot be correct.

The trouble is that in the Red Table Case as given, 4a is false. But a different example supports the construction of an argument along the lines of (4a)–(4f).[31]

> *Absolute-pitch case*: Let us say that Florence has absolute pitch but does not have any background information indicating that she does. She has never been tested and has not otherwise looked into the matter. Florence hears a dial tone at a pitch that sounds to her like C#. Her experience has the content that the dial tone is a C#. By DOG (suitably modified to cover audition), Florence is justified in believing that the dial tone is a C#. But Florence has no reason to believe that her identification of the pitch of the dial-tone is correct.[32] Hence she is not justified in believing that the dial tone is a C# despite the fact that it sounds to her that the dial tone is a C#.

DOG is violated in this instance, so the absolute-pitch case is a counterexample to DOG. The account of perceptual justification that is central to dogmatism proves to be untenable.

I noted earlier that DOG is very closely related to LIP, which figures in one version of apriorism. Let us examine the absolute-pitch case from the apriorist standpoint. According to LIP^{AP}, one would be a priori justified in believing that (1) if it sounds to one that the dial tone is a C#, then the dial tone is a C#. Florence, we may assume, is justified in believing that (2) it sounds to her that the dial-tone is a C#. If the apriorist were right, Florence could infer from (1) and (2) that the dial tone is a C#. She would be justified in believing that the dial tone is a C# despite her having no reason to think that her perception of pitch is accurate. That conclusion seems mistaken. Therefore, the absolute-pitch case presents a difficulty to the apriorist, as well as the dogmatist. The example highlights the point that whether Florence's aural experiences are veridical is a contingent matter, which we can decide only by appeal to empirical evidence. It cannot be settled a priori, contrary to what the apriorist maintains.[33]

Finally, consider another example, which deals with an explicitly skeptical possibility (albeit a limited one):

> *BIV game-show case*: Set general skeptical worries aside and assume that somehow we know in ordinary life that we are not brains in vats. But imagine that the technology exists to create massive sensory deception in a subject by hooking him up to a computer, and this possibility has been made the basis of a television game show. Our contestant Yvonne is told that she will be rendered unconscious and then awakened, after which she will have experience as of an enjoyable vacation in Rome. If she has been chosen by the audience as a game-show winner, she really will be taken to Rome, all expenses paid. If she loses, she will be hooked up to the computer and will merely have delusory experiences as of being in Rome. Yvonne is anesthetized, and when she regains consciousness, it looks to her that she is in Rome.

According to DOG, Yvonne is justified in believing that she is in Rome and so would be justified in believing that she won the contest. She is therefore justified in believing that she did not lose the contest, and that she is not suffering the massive delusions suffered by unfortunate contestants out of favor with the audience. I take it that such a result is thoroughly implausible and calls DOG into question.[34]

The dogmatist would presumably object that Yvonne's perceptual experience gives her only prima facie justification for believing that she is really in Rome. Her information about the game-show arrangements counters or defeats that prima facie justification, so that she is not justified, all things considered, in believing that she is in Rome. This reply raises the question of how the notion of prima facie justification is to be understood. A natural construal is that evidence E prima facie justifies S in believing H just in case E confers some increment of justification on H, such that if sufficient counterevidence is added to E, then S is not justified in believing H.[35] With this account in mind, the BIV game-show case can be elaborated a bit.

> *BIV game-show case, continued*: Suppose that the game-show host is known to be fairly, but not entirely, trustworthy, and he tells Yvonne on the side that she is a winner who will get the real trip to Rome. Things at this point are such that the evidential considerations for and against the claim that Yvonne is a winner exactly balance out. She has no more reason to think that she will be sent to Rome than not. Yvonne is then rendered unconscious and awakes. It looks to her that she is in Rome.

According to DOG, Yvonne's Rome-like perceptual experience gives her prima facie justification for believing that she is in Rome. All the other evidence she has for and against her being in Rome balances out. Therefore, Yvonne has more reason in total to believe that she is in Rome than that she is not. This assessment seems wrong, however, impeaching DOG. Exactly the same sort of difficulty arises for the version of apriorism that incorporates LIP^{AP}.[36]

The absolute-pitch case and the BIV game-show case show that there is something seriously amiss with dogmatism and apriorism. In the former, evidence for the veridicality of one's experience is lacking; in the latter, evidence for the veridicality of one's experience is canceled out by counterevidence. Apriorism and dogmatism treat the claim that one's experience is veridical without any regard for such evidence. The veridicality claim is singled out by special principles (LIP^{AP}, DOG, and in a way $-SK^{AP}$) and given a boost in its epistemic status. As a consequence, dogmatism and apriorism mishandle the problem cases, allowing that the subjects in those cases have justification that they really lack.

3. CONFIRMATION AND COHERENCE

There is another line of argument against dogmatism to consider. For the sake of concreteness, suppose that Jim sees a hand. We will say that its looking to him that there is a hand before him (EXP) justifies Jim in believing that there is a hand before him (HAND). HAND entails that Jim is not seeing a fake hand rather than a real hand (−FAKE). If Jim is justified in believing HAND, then he must be justified in believing −FAKE by the closure principle for justification.[37] The dogmatist may tell us that Jim acquires justification for −FAKE by inferring it from HAND. At any rate, Jim is supposed to be justified in believing −FAKE without coming to possess any other evidence besides EXP, so EXP is the evidence that justifies Jim's belief that −FAKE.

If Jim were seeing a fake hand, it would still look to him that there was a hand before him. A fake hand is something that looks like a real hand but is not one. So FAKE entails EXP. At this point, a widely held tenet of confirmation theory poses a challenge for dogmatism. Evidence e confirms a hypothesis h just in case the conditional probability $\Pr(h|e)$ is greater than the prior probability $\Pr(h)$. It is a theorem of the probability calculus that if h entails e, then e confirms h in this sense.[38] A direct consequence is that if h entails e, then e disconfirms $-h$. We just saw that FAKE entails EXP. It follows that EXP disconfirms −FAKE. Precisely how confirmation is related to epistemic justification is an unresolved question, but one might well think that evidence that disconfirms a hypothesis cannot justify that hypothesis. In that event, the dogmatist errs in saying that EXP justifies −FAKE. Whether dogmatism can be modified or extended so as to overcome this objection remains to be seen.[39]

Confirmation theory yields a further point that bolsters explanationism and counts against dogmatism and apriorism. The latter views credit us with prima facie justification for rejecting the BIV hypothesis. If one's experience takes a nasty turn, that prima facie justification will be defeated, and one will not be justified in believing −BIV (see the waking-up case discussed earlier). Call this sort of experience "rogue experience." As things go, we could have as evidence either that rogue experience is occurring (ROGUE) or that rogue experience is not occurring (−ROGUE). The dogmatist and the apriorist agree that ROGUE is evidence against −BIV. Suppose that this claim implies that ROGUE disconfirms −BIV. If so, by the probability calculus, −ROGUE *confirms* −BIV. And if justification follows confirmation here, −ROGUE counts as justification for −BIV. To say that −ROGUE is the case is to say that your experiences are *coherent* in some way.[40] The upshot is that the coherence of a subject's experiences justifies that subject in believing −BIV. This thesis is a distinctive element of explanationism. Opponents of explanationism will therefore want to deny that −ROGUE confirms −BIV.[41] However, as we have seen, the dogmatist and the apriorist have to concede that −ROGUE confirms −BIV. It follows that the dogmatist or apriorist response to skepticism succeeds only if something like the explanationist response succeeds. This result would be good news for explanationism and less good news for dogmatism and apriorism, insofar as they are meant to be competitors to explanationism.

The preceding line of thought suggests that global features of one's experience provide justification for rejecting BIV regardless of the status of apriorist and dogmatist principles such as −SK^{AP}, LIP^{AP}, and DOG. This point can be sharpened and strengthened. As I said earlier, our ordinary beliefs about the world as a body provide a good explanation of why our experience is the way it is. Call this corpus of beliefs the "real-world hypothesis" (hereafter RWH). But exactly what we believe in toto about the world varies. In that sense, there is more than one version of RWH to consider. For example:

> *Art-attribution case*: Max is an art historian studying an old altarpiece. The best explanation of various features of the painting that he has been able to devise so far is that it was executed by two different painters. Accordingly, Max's initial version of RWH, RWH_1, includes a belief that the altarpiece was due to two different hands. However, reconsidering the available information, Max realizes that a more satisfactory explanation of the data is that the altarpiece was painted by one person over a long period of time. Incorporating that belief into Max's total body of beliefs about the world gives him a new belief corpus, RWH_2. RWH_2 differs from RWH_1, and the former has somewhat more explanatory merit overall than the latter.

Grant that explanatory merit contributes to epistemic justification (I will discuss this later). Then, in general, if two hypotheses are competitors that differ in how well they explain the available data, a subject is justified in rejecting the hypothesis that does worse and in accepting the hypothesis that does better. The data or evidence to which RWH_1 and RWH_2 answer is E^*, the sum of Max's sensory experiences.[42] Ultimately, RWH_2 explains some aspect(s) of E^* better than RWH_1 does, which justifies Max in believing RWH_2 rather than RWH_1. RWH_1 and RWH_2 also compete with BIV. Let us consider Max after he has changed his mind about who painted the altarpiece. Suppose that the skeptic is right and Max has no justification for rejecting BIV at this point. In that case, RWH_2 and BIV must offer equally good explanations of E^*.[43] But then, since BIV explains E^* *just as well* as RWH_2 does, and RWH_2 explains E^* *better* than RWH_1 does, it follows that BIV explains E^* *better* than RWH_1 does. That is, before he changed his mind about who painted the altarpiece, Max was justified in believing that he was a brain in a vat, which surely cannot be right. We have here a reductio ad absurdum of the assumption that Max has no basis for preferring RWH_2 to BIV on explanatory grounds. So explanatory considerations do justify Max's acceptance of RWH_2 and rejection of BIV. This line of thought shows that the explanationist response to skepticism succeeds on its own terms.[44]

4. EXPLANATIONISM

We have seen in general terms how the explanationist means to respond to skepticism. BIV and RWH provide competing explanations of E^*. If RWH explains E^* better than BIV does, we are justified in accepting RWH and rejecting BIV. It follows that premise 1d of the skeptical argument is false, and skepticism is refuted.

Thus the explanationist's chief task is to show that, and how, RWH is a better explanation of E^* than BIV is.

Unfortunately, there is an impediment to proceeding. Explanation and explanatory inference are much less well understood than one would like. There is no uncontroversial list of the criteria of explanatory goodness, let alone precise measures of how well those criteria are satisfied. However, we may hope that it is not far wrong to say that good explanations should be *simple*. Roughly, one account is simpler than another if the first explains everything the second does, but the second deploys more, or more involved, explanatory apparatus than the first deploys. Newtonian mechanics is often presented as a case in point. Earlier accounts used one set of principles to explain celestial motion and another set of principles to explain terrestrial motion, while Newton explained both sorts of motions with just one set of laws. The greater simplicity of Newtonian mechanics made it epistemically preferable to its predecessors. A further criterion of explanatory adequacy is that a hypothesis should not be ad hoc. Very roughly, an ad hoc explanation is one that explains only the phenomena it was introduced to explain and is not otherwise confirmed or testable. Suppose that you observe that salt dissolves in water while charcoal does not, and you want to know why. If I tell you only that salt is soluble and charcoal is not, the explanation I have given is a poor one. It is ad hoc. More generally, according to certain views, good explanations unify either the phenomena or other explanations of the phenomena. Proceeding in this vein, we could say that simpler accounts are more unified than complex ones, while ad hoc accounts are less unified than non–ad hoc accounts.[45]

The idea that RWH has more explanatory merit than BIV, and that we are justified in believing RWH for that reason, was suggested by Bertrand Russell.[46] Two explanationist replies to skepticism have been offered recently by Laurence BonJour and Christopher Peacocke.[47] BonJour distinguishes between what he calls "digital" and "analog" accounts of the contents of experience. Digital explanations "appeal to the combination of something like a *representation* of the sort of world that figures in the quasi-commonsensical hypothesis,[48] together with some agent or mechanism that produces experiences in perceivers." By contrast, analog explanations do their work without invoking representations of the world.[49] Skeptical hypotheses like BIV must be either digital or analog. On the one hand, BonJour thinks that construction of an analog skeptical hypothesis is a hopeless task.[50] On the other, a digital skeptical hypothesis is more encumbered than RWH. The former, but not the latter, includes an extra agent or causal mechanism that mediates between the representation of the world and the occurrence of our experience. Hence, BonJour claims, we are justified in accepting RWH as the best explanation of the contents of our sensory experience.[51]

Peacocke begins by introducing a special notion of complexity. He comments that "complex phenomena are ones which instantiate kinds that are apparently improbable."[52] A satisfactory explanation of the phenomena would be *complexity reducing*; it would explain the more complex by the less complex. According to

Peacocke, perceptual experience (of a specific sort) exhibits a good deal of complexity.[53] The trouble with skeptical hypotheses is that they fail to reduce this complexity. For that reason, at least some nonskeptical explanations are, "other things being equal, more likely to be true" than skeptical explanations. In a certain sense, then, RWH or some version of it is *simpler* than BIV, and we are entitled to reject BIV.[54]

I cannot treat these proposals in anything like the detail they deserve. Instead, I will sketch an explanationist reply to skepticism along the lines I have suggested elsewhere.[55] There are two key points. The first is that the skeptical hypotheses that are actually brought up and discussed by philosophers are impoverished and ad hoc when they are compared with RWH. A somewhat jejune example will help make that clear. Suppose that I am at the zoo, looking at a tiger. An eager zoogoer steps in front of me and blocks my view for a moment, so that I no longer see the tiger, and then I see it again. According to RWH, my tiger experiences are due to the presence of a tiger that I see. My having the sensory sequence consisting of tiger experience, no tiger experience, and then tiger experience again is explained by the zoogoer's walking between the tiger and me. Now suppose that the skeptical competitor to RWH is just the claim that I am a brain in a vat, such that any experience I have is caused by a computer that is hooked up to me. Why do I have a tiger experience, according to the BIV hypothesis? Because there is a computer that causes me to have a tiger experience. This explanation may well seem ad hoc, and in any case things get worse. Why do I have the sequence of tiger experience, no tiger experience, and then tiger experience again? Because the computer causes me to have the sequence of tiger experience, no tiger experience, and then tiger experience again.[56] This explanation is quite clearly deficient. In particular, it seems ad hoc, especially when it is compared with the RWH account that explains the sequence of sensory experiences by reference to the zoogoer's walking between the tiger and me.

This criticism might seem unfair. The skeptical explanation of the sequence of my experiences might instead be something like the following: the computer caused me to have experiences as of a zoogoer walking between the tiger and me (SZ)? This suggestion raises many problems. But compare the explanation SZ with the corresponding RWH explanation, namely, a zoogoer walked between the tiger and me (Z). Within RWH, we can ask why Z, that is, why did the zoogoer walk between the tiger and me? And there can be a satisfactory explanation of Z, for example, that the zoogoer wanted to get a better look at the tiger. Now suppose that we ask, analogously, why SZ, that is, why did the computer cause me to have experiences as of a zoogoer walking between the tiger and me? At this point, it seems, the skeptical explanation runs out. Maybe one might say that the computer causes me to have experiences as of a zoogoer walking between the tiger and me because the computer was programmed to do so. Among other difficulties, this explanation is again ad hoc.

The example I have been discussing is oversimplified in any number of respects, but it serves to bring out something quite important. RWH, our ordinary view of the world, has an elaborated structure that gives it considerable explanatory richness and power. Therefore, it is no surprise that skeptical hypotheses with little or no worked-out structure are inferior to RWH from an explanatory standpoint. This difference justifies us in rejecting such meager skeptical hypotheses on explanatory grounds.

That will be the end of the day for skepticism unless there is some version of BIV that matches RWH in explanatory merit. Only one way of constructing such a skeptical hypothesis suggests itself. The idea is to take over the causal-explanatory structure from RWH itself, but then to fill it in with reference to objects and properties altogether different from those that figure in RWH. Ordinary objects, interacting in ordinary ways, affect your sensory system. Suppose that you are watching a baseball game. Let Ma = the pitcher's arm moves forward; let Nb = the ball speeds toward the batter. According to RWH, Ma causes Nb. Ma also causes EXP (Ma) = you have the experience of seeing the pitcher's arm move. Nb causes EXP (Nb) = you have the experience of the ball speeding toward the batter. Now imagine that the way the computer works is to have some piece of memory a* that has some magnetic configuration M* in virtue of which a* causes you to have EXP (Ma). In addition, the computer has another piece of memory b* that has a magnetic configuration N* in virtue of which b* causes you to have EXP (Nb). Moreover, we can add that M*a* causes N*b*. Call this version of the brain-in-a-vat scenario the "isomorphic skeptical hypothesis" (ISH).[57] What goes on in the world according to ISH mirrors, structurally, what goes on in the world according to RWH. But beyond that causal-explanatory isomorphism, things are utterly different. If RWH holds, there really is a pitcher throwing a baseball, which you see. If ISH holds, that is not true at all. Instead, there is just a computer whose memory elements behave in the manner described. If ISH could be formulated so that its causal-explanatory structure replicates exactly that of RWH, then, plausibly, explanations provided by ISH would be no less simple and no more ad hoc than those provided by RWH. RWH would not be preferable to ISH on explanatory grounds, and the explanationist response to skepticism would stall.

A core part of RWH is our ascription of spatial properties and relations to ordinary objects. If ISH is to serve as a suitable substitute for RWH, then non-spatial properties and relations must be able to do the same explanatory work, in the same way, that spatial properties and relations do. But certain truths about spatial properties and relations are necessary, and such necessary truths enter into RWH explanations. For example, suppose that three material objects a, b, and c—people's houses, for example—are arranged in a triangle. According to RWH, a, b, and c have genuine location properties, L_A, L_B, and L_C. It follows necessarily from the fact that a, b, and c have the locations they do, that Dist (a, b, c), the distance from a to b to c, is at least as great as Dist (a, c), the distance directly from a to c. The difference between these distances would be involved in all sorts of explanations. For example, it might (partly) explain why it takes you longer to walk from a to c by way of b than it takes you to walk directly from a to c. This fact, in turn, has consequences for the character of your mental life. For example, it might (partly) account for (T), that is, why one set of experiences (those you have walking the long way) has greater duration than another set of experiences (those you have walking the direct way). In short, according to RWH, that Dist (a, b, c) is greater than Dist (a, c) at least partly explains T.

How, in this case, would ISH explain what RWH does?[58] The material objects a, b, and c would have counterparts in ISH, which would be material objects radically unlike the real a, b, and c. Imagine that these are chunks of computer disk, a^*, b^*, and c^*. These items have properties corresponding to the genuine locations L_A, L_B, and L_C, which I will denote as L_A^*, L_B^*, and L_C^*. L_A^*, L_B^*, and L_C^* are not genuine locations but rather properties of some other kind—for example, patterns of magnetization at a^*, b^*, and c^*, respectively. Now, RWH explains various things, including T, by reference to the distances between objects. To match the explanatory apparatus of RWH, ISH needs to posit relations Dist$^*(a^*, b^*, c^*)$ and Dist$^*(a^*, c^*)$ corresponding to the genuine distances Dist (a, b, c) and Dist (a, c), respectively. Since ISH is meant to mirror RWH, we will suppose that Dist$^*(a^*, b^*, c^*)$ and Dist$^*(a^*, c^*)$ are magnitudes that are determined by L_A^*, L_B^*, and L_C^*; Dist$^*(a^*, b^*, c^*)$ is greater than Dist$^*(a^*, c^*)$; and the difference between Dist$^*(a^*, b^*, c^*)$ and Dist$^*(a^*, c^*)$ at least partly explains T.

At this point, the question may be asked why the genuine spatial distance Dist (a, b, c) is greater than Dist (a, c). This fact is a consequence of a *necessary* truth about distances among noncollinear points known as the triangle inequality.[59] The corresponding question with respect to ISH would be why the magnitude of Dist$^*(a^*, b^*, c^*)$ is greater than the magnitude of Dist$^*(a^*, c^*)$. According to ISH, the Dist* relations generally are relations among magnetic patterns at various chunks of the computer disk, including L_A^*, L_B^*, and L_C^*, such that these relations are causally efficacious in certain specified ways. What magnitudes are assigned to those relations is a matter of how the computer happens to work. So, according to ISH, the fact that Dist$^*(a^*, b^*, c^*)$ is greater than Dist$^*(a^*, c^*)$ would be *contingent*.[60] If ISH leaves this fact unexplained, it would fail to explain all that RWH does. So it seems that ISH has to introduce some further empirical regularity otherwise analogous to the triangle inequality that has the consequence that Dist$^*(a^*, b^*, c^*)$ is greater than Dist$^*(a^*, c^*)$. ISH might then explain all that RWH does, but its explanatory apparatus would be encumbered by an extra empirical regularity that has no counterpart in RWH. ISH would then be less simple than RWH. Hence RWH would enjoy an explanatory advantage over ISH and would be preferable to ISH on that account.

It should be noted that the details of the foregoing are not essential to the fundamental point at issue. The claims about distance relations and their skeptical substitutes are meant only to illustrate a general line of argument, which goes as follows:[61]

5a. There are necessary truths about spatial/geometrical properties that have no counterparts for non–spatial/geometrical properties.

5b. These necessary truths enter into explanations with respect to spatial/geometrical properties.

5c. If non–spatial/geometrical properties were to discharge the explanatory function of genuinely spatial/geometrical properties, empirical regularities would enter into these alternative explanations in place of the necessary truths that figure in ordinary explanations in terms of spatial/geometrical properties.

5d. Hence the alternative explanations would be less simple than, and inferior to, the ordinary ones.

To sum up, our belief that objects in the world have the shapes and locations we take them to have is not idle or optional. To suppose that the world is laid out in some radically different way, along the lines of BIV, carries with it extra explanatory burdens. RWH is thus preferable to BIV on explanatory grounds, and we are justified in denying BIV.

The success of explanationism as a response to skepticism depends on two theses: (1) RWH is superior to skeptical hypotheses from an explanatory standpoint. (2) Explanatory considerations give us epistemic justification for choosing one hypothesis over another. Critics of explanationism have raised a number of objections to thesis 1. These include the following: (a) The explanationist is committed to a foundationalist model of justification.[62] (b) The explanationist is committed to an unsatisfactory account of perceptual experience and/or perceptual belief.[63] (c) If explanationism were a satisfactory response to skepticism, a similar maneuver could be used to uphold scientific realism, but such a defense of scientific realism is no good.[64] (d) The explanationist response to skepticism brings with it, or exacerbates, the problem of the explanatory gap in the philosophy of mind.[65] Such criticisms can be answered, I believe, but not on this occasion.[66]

There are also attacks on inference to the best explanation as a source of epistemic justification in general. These are objections to thesis 2.[67] One is especially prominent. The worry is that there is no good reason to suppose that the use of explanatory criteria of theory choice, such as simplicity, is truth conducive. Suppose, for example, that we accept a simpler hypothesis rather than a more complex one. Unless we have some grounds for believing that the world itself is simple, in the right way, we have no reason to believe that the simpler hypothesis is true. The thought is then that we have no basis for supposing that the world is simple, in the right way. Therefore, we are not justified in accepting the simpler hypothesis as true.[68] Proponents of inference to the best explanation have attempted to meet this objection and others, and the debate continues.

5. SUMMARY

There are three primary internalist responses to skepticism, namely, apriorism, dogmatism, and explanationism. There are motivations for each view, although I have argued on behalf of explanationism in particular. In my judgment, we are justified on explanatory grounds in believing that skeptical hypotheses are false and that our ordinary beliefs about the world are, by and large, true. Explanationism is the solution to the problem of skepticism about the external world.[69]

NOTES

1. This definition is stipulative and, as it stands, does not capture various aspects of internalism that might be regarded as essential. Obviously, the notion of "having a good reason" is bearing a good deal of weight. It will become clear later that on the views to be discussed, victims of evil demons or brains in vats could have good reasons for believing propositions about the external world. So, by one robust criterion, the positions I characterize as internalist do deserve that label.

2. The first premise follows from the closure principle for justification, which, roughly, states that if S is justified in believing P and knows that P entails Q, then S is justified in believing Q. This principle is controversial, but I will not pursue the question of its status here.

3. To be sure, there are other hypotheses of massive sensory deception besides the familiar brain-in-a-vat story, and the differences among these may have some significance. See Vogel (2004). Here, however, I will treat BIV as the canonical skeptical alternative, standing in for all the others.

4. There are many thorny issues here I would like to avoid, so far as possible. These include the following: How exactly is epistemic priority related to the basing relation? How exactly is epistemic priority related to "inferential" justification? If a proposition A is epistemically prior to proposition B for a subject, must that subject believe A? I do take for granted that sometimes a proposition A is prior to B for a subject even thought that subject has not actually inferred B from A. The very notion of epistemic priority is controversial; see Williams (1992) and Feldman (2004).

5. Perhaps certain foundationalists will allow that beliefs can be self-justifying and so epistemically prior to themselves. And perhaps some coherentists will maintain that there are mutually supporting beliefs for which the antisymmetry condition does not hold.

6. See Pryor (2000).

7. Hilary Putnam (1981) and John McDowell (1982) may be read as providing internalist replies to skepticism that are quite different from the three lines of response discussed in the text.

8. The idea that the explanatory merit of a hypothesis gives us an epistemic reason to accept it falls under the rubric "inference to the best explanation."

9. See Moore (1939). What Moore really thought about these matters is a complex question, and the following is not meant as serious exegesis of what he wrote.

10. One could adopt a variant of dogmatism according to which the contents of one's perceptual experience directly justify −BIV, so that no perceptual belief like "Here is a hand" is epistemically prior to −BIV. −BIV would itself be a basic belief. Perhaps such a view would be committed to the unattractive claim that we can perceive that we are not brains in vats. In any event, I will not pursue this possibility any further.

11. Versions of this argument appear in Pryor (2000), Byrne (2004), Cohen (2002), Bergmann (2004), Van Cleve (2003), Schmitt (2004), and Wright (2004). I think that the

skeptic would do better to argue for (1d) by appeal to underdetermination considerations. See Vogel (2004).

12. Pryor (2000), p. 524.

13. In a series of essays, Crispin Wright has denied that one could acquire justification for −BIV this way. See, inter alia, Wright (2003, 2004).

14. This way of putting things, which I have adopted for the sake of exposition, makes it seem that the explanationist is committed to a pretty traditional form of foundationalism. That is not so, however. See Vogel (1997).

15. Strictly speaking, this claim would need qualification in light of the point made in note 10.

16. The relation of epistemic priority resists successful analysis; so, too, does the relation of cojustification. The following condition is at least necessary: if X and Y are cojustified, then the same evidence justifies each of them, and neither is epistemically prior to the other.

17. Cojustification is not particularly exotic. Suppose that a detective has two suspects for the bank robbery, A and B, and then acquires evidence that clears one and establishes the guilt of the other. The claims that A is innocent and that B is guilty may be cojustified. That is, the detective's belief that A is innocent need not be epistemically prior to his belief that A is guilty, nor vice versa. Some philosophers seem to assume, mistakenly, that when two claims are such that neither would be justified if the other were not, and neither is epistemically prior to the other, then some relation of mutual support obtains between the two. See Cohen (2002), pp. 322–323. That might be the case sometimes, but not always. In particular, it is not the case with PERC and −BIV.

18. This does not follow from explanationism *tout court*. It could be that E^* justifies −BIV on the basis of explanatory considerations, and that −BIV then justifies PERC, so that −BIV is prior to PERC.

19. Again, I am using BIV as a representative for all skeptical hypotheses.

20. For some discussion of what prima facie justification is, see the later discussion, especially note 35.

21. See Vogel (1993).

22. See the argument 2a–2f given earlier.

23. Maybe I am underselling apriorism to some extent. Perhaps there are arguments in a Wittgensteinian spirit that any cognitive practice must incorporate elements that have something like a priori status, immobile "hinges on which the door turns." If that is right, then there could be a more positive motivation for apriorism beyond the claim that it would be the only alternative to skepticism.

24. A helpful treatment of a closely related topic is Hawthorne (2002). The present concern, as well the previous one, might lead some advocates of apriorism toward nonfactualism of one sort or another. See Wright (1985) and Field (2000) for nonfactualist apriorist accounts. Obviously, there is very much more to say about these issues.

25. To be plausible, the principle may need to be restricted in application to only some values of X; see Pryor (2000), pp. 538–539. Finding and motivating a formulation of just the right strength is a serious hurdle for the dogmatist, and presumably for the apriorist as well.

26. One might question whether, under these circumstances, you have good reason to believe that there is a sand dune nearby. If not, then your belief seems to be unjustified according to the definition of internalism given in the text. Various issues arise. What makes a perceptual belief the kind of belief it is? Can its being a belief of that sort provide a good reason to hold it? But these are questions for another occasion. (Thanks here to John Greco).

27. As noted earlier, if DOG holds, then one is justified in rejecting skeptical hypotheses. Pryor (2004) and others have vigorously defended the Moorean response.

28. For an early statement of this line of argument, see the aspirin-LSD case discussed in Vogel (1993).

29. The example appears in Dretske (1970) and is deployed by Cohen (2002) against the dogmatist.

30. At this point, Cohen asserts, "Presumably, I cannot know that it's not the case that the table is white but illuminated by red lights, on the basis of the table's looking red." Cohen (2002), p. 313. I am sympathetic to what Cohen says, but more argument would be desirable, at least. There are certainly various *bad* reasons to say what Cohen does (not that these bad reasons are Cohen's own). For example, one might maintain that since L is consistent with both R and $-W$, L does not give you reason to believe $-W$. Or one might say that since you cannot tell that $-W$ by looking at the table, you need some evidence other than L to justify $-W$.

31. It is not easy to find counterexamples in which it looks to S that X, but S lacks background information about whether it is likely that if it looks to S that X, then X. For example, it can look to you that what you see is blood, but not that what you see is type O blood. We take blood to have a distinctive appearance; generally nothing else appears to us the way blood does. Type O blood, however, does not have a distinctive appearance. Other kinds of blood appear to us just the way type O blood does. Possibly, then, the way we characterize the representational contents of experience is sensitive to the background information available. If so, DOG would be quite unsuitable as a formulation of the dogmatist position.

32. If this is wrong, then the cognitive scientists studying pitch perception are needlessly administering tests to determine whether their subjects accurately identify pitches they hear. The researchers should just ask the subjects instead.

33. Maybe the veridicality of some experiences can be defended on a priori grounds, but that cannot be so in every case.

34. White (2006), pp. 535–536, makes a similar point. Note that the BIV game-show case is simply a variant of the waking-up case.

35. There are weaker construals of prima facie justification. Evidence e prima facie justifies h iff (1) if S has evidence e, and all other considerations for and against h balance out, then S is justified in believing h; or (2) if S has evidence e but has no other evidence at all relevant to h, then S is justified in believing h. The BIV game-show case remains a difficulty for dogmatism on reading 1. Reading 2 is unsuited to the dogmatist's purposes insofar as there are always, or often, some empirical considerations that count for or against the claim that one's experience is veridical.

36. A similar point can be made against the version of apriorism that incorporates $-SK^{AP}$. Suppose that the waking-up case is understood so that the course of Stan's experience gives him no more reason to believe $-BIV$ than BIV. Then the principle $-SK^{AP}$ would put its finger on the scale, so to speak, in favor of $-BIV$, and that seems unacceptable. See Vogel (1993).

37. See note 2.

38. This is subject to certain qualifications. Pr (h) must be less than 1.

39. This criticism is suggested in Cohen (2005). For a careful, extended development, see White (2006). Pryor (2007) responds by deploying a revised account of confirmation. I note, ruefully, that explanationism may confront the same kind of trouble that dogmatism faces. The explanationist claims that the coherence of your experience justifies you in believing $-BIV$ (see the later discussion). However, it is possible to frame a version of BIV

that entails that your experience is coherent. How does the coherence of your experience serve as evidence against that skeptical possibility?

40. That is, your experiences follow the orderly, intelligible pattern they would have if they were veridical perceptions of the external world.

41. There is a gap here. One might deny that in general, confirmation is sufficient for justification. For that reason, among others, the argument of this paragraph is meant to be suggestive rather than conclusive.

42. More precisely, the explanandum is some fact(s) or event(s) involving the body of one's experience E^*, but I will disregard this point in what follows.

43. I take it that no one would want to say that BIV explains E^* *better* than RWH_2 does.

44. The argument just offered is related to one I gave in Vogel (1993). That predecessor was directed against a minimal nonexplanationist view according to which we are entitled to accept RWH if no other epistemic considerations favor RWH over BIV (or vice versa). Here I am arguing that in general, RWH must exceed BIV in explanatory merit and must be preferable to BIV for that reason.

45. This discussion is not meant as a serious account of simplicity, ad hoc–ness, or unification.

46. Russell (1912), p. 24–25.

47. BonJour (2003) and Peacocke (2004); see also BonJour's earlier animadversions on skepticism in his (1985) and (1999). Other authors who advocate an explanationist approach to skepticism include Slote (1970), Harman (1973), Jackson (1977), Bennett (1979), Lycan (1988), and Goldman (1988).

48. What BonJour calls "the quasi-commensensical hypothesis" is more or less what I have termed "RWH."

49. BonJour (2003), p. 93.

50. Ibid., p. 94.

51. Ibid., p. 95.

52. Peacocke (2004), p. 80.

53. Ibid., p. 86.

54. Ibid., p. 95.

55. See Vogel (1990a, 2005).

56. Or, perhaps, the computer causes me to have tiger experience, then does not cause me to have tiger experience, and then causes me to have tiger experience.

57. ISH has considerable limitations as a skeptical hypothesis; see Vogel (1990a). The view that we are in a position to know that either ISH or RWH is true, but not in a position that RWH in particular is true, is akin to structuralism in the philosophy of science.

58. ISH might be set up so that the primary items that occupy the nodes in the explanatory structure correspond to regions of space rather than material objects in RWH, but I think that the line of argument in the text would apply all the same.

59. One version of the triangle inequality is that the length of any one side of a triangle is less than the sum of the lengths of the other two sides.

60. To illustrate further, imagine that the computer keeps a table recording the magnitude of Dist* for the items that have the various L^* properties. This table would be like the table for distances between cities that one often sees in road maps, except that the entries in the computer's table are causally efficacious. According to ISH, the computer does have a greater value for $Dist^*(a^*, b^*, c^*)$ than for $Dist^*(a^*, c^*)$ written in its table. But there is nothing logically or metaphysically impossible in supposing that the computer could have had other values entered in the table, so that $Dist^*(a^*, c^*)$ was not less than $Dist^*(a^*, b^*, c^*)$. So if the world is the way that ISH says it is, the fact that $Dist^*(a^*, b^*, c^*)$ is

greater than Dist*(a^*, c^*) is contingent, as stated in the text. Now ISH does provide that if Dist*(a^*, b^*, c^*) were not greater than Dist*(a^*, c^*), there would be causal consequences for the character of our experience. For example, T might turn out false, in which case ISH would fail to explain the data. Perhaps, then, we have the following: necessarily (if ISH gets the data right, then the value assigned to Dist*(a^*, b^*, c^*) is greater than the value assigned to Dist*(a^*, c^*)). But even so, we do not have the following: (if ISH gets the data right, then (necessarily, the value assigned to Dist*(a^*, b^*, c^*) is greater than the value assigned to Dist*(a^*, c^*))). For ISH to get the data right, it is enough that the value assigned to Dist*(a^*, b^*, c^*) is in fact greater than the value assigned to Dist*(a^*, c^*)—the modal status of that claim does not matter. However, there is more to overall explanatory success than merely getting the data right; higher level explanations matter, too. As I argue next, the modal status of the claim that the value assigned to Dist*(a^*, b^*, c^*) is greater than the value assigned to Dist*(a^*, c^*) does affect the full explanatory adequacy of ISH.

61. For a bit further along these lines, see Vogel (2005). There is clearly much more to say, and I hope to address these issues more fully in future work.

62. See Williams (1992).

63. Especially vigorous statements of this objection are to be found in Williams (1992) and Byrne (2004).

64. See Enç (1990).

65. See Neta (2004).

66. However, see Vogel (1990b, 1997).

67. Van Fraassen's criticisms in this vein are especially well known and widely discussed. See Van Fraassen (1989) and Ladyman et al. (1997). For responses, see Psillos (1996) and Lipton (2004), among others. I would be remiss if I did not mention Harman's pioneering work, in which he argues for the indispensability of inference to the best explanation (1965).

68. One source among very many for this objection is Wright (1992); see also Fumerton (1992). I undertake some defensive maneuvers in Vogel (2004, 2005), somewhat in the spirit of Harman: Seemingly, the complaint that inference to the best explanation is not demonstrably linked to the truth can be lodged against inductive inference of any sort. The objection is either tantamount to skepticism about induction or a demand for a solution to the problem of induction.

For a recent, head-on treatment of the issue, see White (2005).

69. Many thanks to John Campbell, David Christensen, Branden Fitelson, Cody Gilmore, Michael Glanzberg, Kevin Kelly, Jim Pryor, Nate Smith, the members of FERG, and the participants in Philosophy 202. I am grateful to John Greco for his kindness and support as editor of this volume.

REFERENCES

Bennett, Jonathan. 1979. "Analytic Transcendental Arguments." In *Transcendental Arguments and Science*, ed. P. Bieri, R. P. Horstmann, and L. Krueger. Dordrecht: Reidel.

Bergmann, Michael. 2004. "Epistemic Circularity: Malignant and Benign." *Philosophy and Phenomenological Research* 69: 709–727.

BonJour, Laurence. 1985. *The Structure of Empirical Knowledge*. Cambridge, Mass.: Harvard University Press.

———. 1999. "Foundationalism and the External World." *Philosophical Perspectives* 13: 229–249.

———. 2003. "A Version of Internalist Foundationalism." In *Epistemic Justification: Internalism vs. Externalism, Foundations vs. Virtues*, by Laurence BonJour and Ernest Sosa. Malden, Mass.: Blackwell.

Byrne, Alex. 2004. "How Hard Are the Skeptical Paradoxes?" *Noûs* 38: 299–325.

Cohen, Stewart. 2002. "Basic Knowledge and the Problem of Easy Knowledge." *Philosophy and Phenomenological Research* 65: 308–329.

———. 2005. "Why Basic Knowledge Is Easy Knowledge." *Philosophy and Phenomenological Research* 70: 417–430.

Dretske, Fred. 1970. "Epistemic Operators." *Journal of Philosophy* 67: 1007–1023.

Enç, Berent. 1990. "Is Realism Really the Best Hypothesis?" *Journal of Philosophy* 87: 667–668.

Feldman, Richard. 2004. "Foundational Beliefs and Empirical Possibilities." *Philosophical Issues* 14 (*Epistemology*): 132–148.

Field, Hartry. 2000. "Apriority as an Evaluative Notion." In *New Essays on the A Priori*, ed. P. Boghossian and C. Peacocke. New York: Oxford University Press.

Fumerton, Richard. 1992. "Skepticism and Reasoning to the Best Explanation." *Philosophical Issues* 2 (*Rationality in Epistemology*): 149–162.

Goldman, Alan. 1988. *Empirical Knowledge*. Berkeley: University of California Press.

Harman, Gilbert. 1965. "The Inference to the Best Explanation." *Philosophical Review* 74: 88–95.

———. 1973. *Thought*. Princeton, N.J.: Princeton University Press.

Hawthorne, John. 2002. "Deeply Contingent A Priori Knowledge." *Philosophy and Phenomenological Research* 65: 247–269.

Jackson, Frank. 1977. *Perception*. Cambridge: Cambridge University Press.

Ladyman, James, Igor Douven, Leon Horsten, and Bas van Fraassen. 1997. "A Defence of Van Fraassen's Critique of Abductive Inference: Reply to Psillos" *Philosophical Quarterly* 47: 305–321.

Lipton, Peter. 2004. *Inference to the Best Explanation*. 2nd ed. London: Routledge.

Lycan, William. 1988. *Judgment and Justification*. New York: Cambridge University Press.

McDowell, John. 1982. "Criteria, Defeasibility, and Knowledge." *Proceedings of the British Academy* 68: 455–479.

Moore, G. E. 1939. "Proof of an External World." *Proceedings of the British Academy* 25: 273–300.

Neta, Ram. 2004. "Skepticism, Abductivism, and the Explanatory Gap." *Philosophical Issues* 14 (*Epistemology*): 296–325.

Peacocke, Christopher. 2004. *The Realm of Reason*. Oxford: Clarendon Press.

Pryor, James. 2000. "The Skeptic and the Dogmatist." *Nous* 34: 517–549.

———. 2004. "What's Wrong with Moore's Argument?" *Philosophical Issues* 14 (*Epistemology*): 349–378.

———. 2007. "Uncertainty and Undermining." Available at http://www.jimpryor.net/research/papers/Uncertainty.pdf.

Psillos, Stathis. 1996. "On Van Fraassen's Critique of Abductive Reasoning." *Philosophical Quarterly* 46: 31–47.

Putnam, Hilary. 1981. *Reason, Truth, and History*. New York: Cambridge University Press.

Russell, Bertrand. 1912. *The Problems of Philosophy*. Oxford: Oxford University Press.

Schmitt, Frederick. 2004. "What Is Wrong with Epistemic Circularity?" *Philosophical Issues* 14 (*Epistemology*): 379–402.

Slote, Michael. 1970. *Reason and Scepticism*. London: Allen & Unwin.

Van Cleve, James. 2003. "Is Knowledge Easy–or Impossible? Externalism as the Only Alternative to Skepticism." In *The Skeptics: Contemporary Essays*, ed. S. Luper. Aldershot: Ashgate.

Van Fraassen, Bas. 1989. *Laws and Symmetry*. New York: Oxford University Press.

Vogel, Jonathan. 1990a. "Cartesian Skepticism and Inference to the Best Explanation." *Journal of Philosophy* 87: 658–666.

———. 1990b. "Reply to Professor Enç." Unpublished.

———. 1993. "Dismissing Skeptical Possibilities." *Philosophical Studies* 70: 235–250.

———. 1997. "Skepticism and Foundationalism: A Reply to Michael Williams." *Journal of Philosophical Research* 20: 11–28

———. 2004. "Skeptical Arguments." *Philosophical Issues* 14 (*Epistemology*): 426–455.

———. 2005. "The Refutation of Skepticism." In *Contemporary Debates in Epistemology*, ed. E. Sosa and M. Steup. Malden, Mass.: Blackwell.

White, Roger. 2005. "Why Favour Simplicity?" *Analysis* 65: 205–210.

———. 2006. "Problems for Dogmatism." *Philosophical Studies* 131: 525–557.

Williams, Michael. 1992. *Unnatural Doubts*. Oxford: Blackwell.

Wright, Crispin. 1985. "Facts and Certainty." *Proceedings of the British Academy* 71: 429–472.

———. 1992. *Truth and Objectivity*. Cambridge, Mass.: Harvard University Press.

———. 2003. "Some Reflections on the Acquisition of Warrant by Inference." In *New Essays on Semantic Externalism, Skepticism, and Self-Knowledge*, ed. S. Nuccetelli. Cambridge, Mass.: MIT/Bradford.

———. 2004. "Warrant for Nothing (and Foundations for Free)?" *Proceedings of the Aristotelian Society*, supplementary volume 78: 167–212.

CHAPTER 25

VIRTUE-THEORETIC RESPONSES TO SKEPTICISM

GUY AXTELL

VIRTUE theory concerns philosophical evaluation of human agents in their interaction with the world. Because human agents are embedded in a world, both natural and social, their interactions give rise to ethical and to epistemic contexts, which in turn become the primary locus for the descriptive, explanatory, and normative tasks with which philosophy concerns itself. The central focus in virtue theory on understanding agents and the habits and dispositions through which their interactions in the world unfold allows for the acknowledgment of analogies between epistemic and ethical evaluation, but for the acknowledgment of disanalogies as well.

Virtue theory has been applied to numerous domains of philosophic study, and its roots arguably go back to some of the earliest Greek discussions of the motivations to philosophize. Its resurgence over the past four decades has taken place first in the subfield of ethics and since the 1980s in the subfield of epistemology as well.[1] Questions about how to proceed in the study of core epistemic concepts like justification, knowledge, and understanding are ones that contemporary virtue epistemologists quite often engage. Skeptical arguments are another and indeed are closely caught up in discussion of the core epistemic concepts and the problems that surround them. Even where no "true skeptics" are present to support them, skeptical arguments, whether those of "global" (radical) or "local" (domain-specific) import, help uncover the depth in a conception of epistemic agency and allow us to reflect more carefully upon our human epistemic condition.

As John Greco puts it, the study of skeptical arguments "drives positive episte-mology" (2000, 51).

This chapter focuses on the responses that proponents of virtue epistemology (VE) make to radical skepticism and particularly to two related forms of it, Pyr-rhonian skepticism and the "underdetermination-based" argument, both of which have been receiving widening attention in recent debate. Section 1 of the chapter briefly articulates these two skeptical arguments and their interrelationship, while section 2 explains the close connection between a virtue-theoretic and a neo-Moorean response to them. Because I cannot fully canvass the growing field of VE, the focus will primarily be on leading figures such as Ernest Sosa, who develops "virtue perspectivism" in a series of essays and in his 2004 John Locke Lectures, and John Greco, who develops "agent reliabilism" in *Putting Skeptics in Their Place* (2000) and recent essays. In sections 3 and 4, I advance my arguments for improving the prospects of virtue-theoretic responses, sketching a particular version of VE that seeks to recast somewhat how we understand the "externalist turn in epistemology" thereby suggesting ways of improving the adequacy of philosophical responses to skepticism. Section 5 concludes the chapter with some brief suggestions about the direction of future work and additional points about the kind of "expansion" in the theory of knowledge that I think a virtue-theoretic approach argues for.

1. Pyrrhonian Skepticism and the Underdetermination Argument

One type of skepticism that current debate takes especially seriously is expressed in underdetermination-based arguments. According to such arguments, one's total evidence, at least as considered internalistically from a first-person perspective, underdetermines one's judgment in favor of commonsense realism over alternative "hypotheses" that depict us as victims of systematic deception. Here is how Pritchard (2005) more formally articulates UA, the "template underdetermination-based skeptical argument":

(U1)   If my evidence does not favour my belief in everyday propositions over the known to be incompatible skeptical hypotheses, then I am not internalistically justified in believing everyday propositions.

(U2)   My evidence does not favour my belief in everyday propositions over the known to be incompatible skeptical hypotheses.

(UC)   I am not internalistically justified in believing everyday propositions (and thus I lack knowledge of everyday propositions). (2005, 205)

Pritchard takes the underdetermination argument to reflect especially well the motivations behind contemporary neo-Pyrrhonism (see also Sinnott-Armstrong, 2004). He rightly points out that (the explicit appeal to what is "internalistically justified" not withstanding) we can find versions of this argument among the ancients as well. Indeed, I would connect the underdetermination principle[2] with the principle of the *equipollence* (roughly, "justificational equivalence") of theoretical suppositions or "judgments" in the thought of the second-century A.D. skeptic Sextus Empiricus. In *Outlines of Pyrrhonism*, his most basic characterization of skepticism is this:

> Skepticism is an ability, or mental attitude, which opposes appearances to judgments in any way whatsoever, with the result that, owing to the equipollence of the objects and reasons thus opposed, we are brought firstly to a state of mental suspense and next to a state of "unperturbedness" or quietude [*ataraxia*].
>
> (1, 8).

In Sextus and Agrippa's Pyrrhonism, the attempt of antiskeptical philosophers to escape the equipollence of theoretical judgments is found to land them upon one or another point of a trilemma where the philosophic reconstruction of one's ability to know (or, alternatively, one's prerogative to claim rational justification for one's belief) is (a) viciously circular, (b) endlessly regressive, or (c) ultimately arbitrary. "Agrippa's trilemma" remains a matter of deep concern in contemporary epistemology. As Pritchard points out in *Epistemic Luck* (2005), it centrally supports the view "that any claim to know can be called into question via the skeptical techniques the Pyrrhonian skeptics have identified, and [that] this highlights the ultimately 'brute' nature of our epistemic position" (220).

Another reason why Pyrrhonian skepticism and the underdetermination argument are chosen as the focus of our examination is that they allow us to engage the issue of how "the externalist turn in epistemology" over the past several decades affects the prospects of the antiskeptic's path in philosophy. It is clear that the externalist turn and the associated rejection of access internalism have recast the role of positive epistemologists in dialogue with skeptical challengers. But do externalist responses merely change the topic and avoid the real challenge of skepticism, as its critics allege? Or, as their proponents claim, are they highly advantageous by allowing us to see how arguments like UA can appear insurmountable when they are not? These questions are pertinent here because although it would be an overstatement to say that there is a single distinctive virtue-theoretic approach to skepticism, the best known proponents of virtue epistemology clearly take advantage of externalist responses to skepticism, believing that it provides strong resources both for diagnosing the motivations to skepticism and for responding to the skeptic's strongest arguments. In the next section, we canvass some of their views.

2. NATURE AND REASON IN THE COMMONSENSE TRADITION

Philosophers as diverse as Pascal and Hume have seen the primary tension inclining us to radical skepticism as that between "nature" and "reason." "Who will unravel this tangle?" asks Pascal. "Nature confutes the skeptics, and reason confutes the dogmatists . . . [such that a person] can neither avoid these two sects, nor hold fast to either one of them!"[3] Nature inclines us to commonsense beliefs (such as the existence of an external world, of other minds, and of causal regularities in nature), while reason inclines us to take seriously skeptical arguments that would impugn our capacity for knowledge even of these things. The underdetermination argument stated in section 1 expresses one key form of the skeptic's worry. Does not our apparent inability to eliminate known-to-be-incompatible radical skeptical hypotheses by reflectively good reasons demonstrate at least that our human condition is lacking in qualities that are epistemically desirable? Further, does it not impugn our ability to know and our epistemic responsibility in attributing justified belief to ourselves and others?

G. E. Moore's "commonsense realist" reply is to defend our natural confidence in our everyday knowledge and our ability to claim it for ourselves. But critics allege that his reply is question begging and therefore hangs upon the circularity horn of the previously mentioned skeptical trilemma. Contemporary "neo-Moorean" responses argue that Moore's response is actually quite illuminating, but only after it gets a retrofit to reflect a reliabilist stream in modern epistemological thought stretching back to Thomas Reid. Sosa (2000) and Greco (2002a) both discuss how Reid, too, is part of the commonsense tradition, and how certain aspects of his reliabilist orientation are subtly suggested in Moore's better known "defense of common sense" (1925).[4]

For the virtue epistemologists we are considering, developing a neo-Moorean argument with the kind of naturalized conception of reason that can take advantage of the resources of reliabilist externalism would be quite advantageous. Hence Greco finds it illuminating to study the substantive and methodological continuities between Reid and Moore. In his "How to Reid Moore" (2002a), Greco argues that neither was "simply insisting" that we know what the skeptic denies. Rather, both authors are astute critics of skeptical arguments who held that the evidence of sense is no less reasonable than that of demonstration, and for Reid at least, as for contemporary reliabilists and other epistemic externalists, introspective consciousness, perception, memory, testimony, and inductive reasoning are all possible sources of knowledge in addition to deductive or demonstrative reasoning.

In "How to Defeat Opposition to Moore,"[5] Sosa's articulation of a key area of contemporary debate focuses upon the skeptical "argument from ignorance," hereafter AI. This begins with two definitions:

h   I am a handless brain in a vat being fed experiences as if I were normally embodied and situated.

o   I now have hands.

Then follows Sosa's version of the argument:

1. I don't know that not-h
2. If I don't know that not-h, then I don't know that o.

So,

C. I don't know that o

Sosa characterizes the three main positions that have been adopted on AI:

Skeptic	1, 2; therefore C
Nozick et al.	1, Not C; therefore Not 2
Moore	2, Not C; therefore Not 1

The skeptic holds the Moorean escape from skeptical conclusion C to be viciously circular, but the neo-Moorean responds that the logic of the argument cuts in two directions, such that if I know that I have hands, then I do know that skeptical hypotheses inconsistent with this knowledge are false, even if I have not directly considered them all.[6]

Sosa's basic description of knowledge is as "apt performance" in the way of belief. For a belief to be apt, as Sosa puts it in his Locke Lectures, *A Virtue Epistemology*, is for it to be correct in a way creditable to the believer, as determined by the role of the believer's competence in the explanation of his being right (see 2007; see also his 2002a and 2002b). On Sosa's view, epistemic competence is socially, as well as individually, seated, and virtue-theoretic terms better describe this competence than other approaches. Whether we are considering a correct belief due to intellectual virtue or a right action due to practical virtue, the competence and performance of agents are central to our explanations of virtuous success, and a virtuous performance will involve both the agent's constitution and situation.

Since the aptness of the agent's belief entails that its correctness is attributable to a competence exercised in appropriate conditions, the concept of aptness is an externalist one, and the condition is an externalist condition. Yet Sosa accommodates certain intuitions traditionally associated with epistemic internalism by retaining the importance of "reflective coherence" in the individual and a strong sense of human knowledge even at its lowest rungs as an achievement. These concerns with the lasting significance of reflective coherence are developed in the fuller account he describes as "virtue perspectivism," which requires that agents achieve a degree of epistemic "ascent": "reflective knowledge goes beyond animal knowledge, and requires also an apt meta-apprehension that the object-level perceptual belief is apt" (2007, 81).

It is important to point out at this juncture that none of the authors mentioned here see a need to "go internalist" in order to acknowledge and respect "the understanding and coherence dear to intellectuals."[7] Sosa, Greco, Zagzebski, Riggs,

Axtell, and others each adopt what has been called a "compatibilist" view of the relationship between our internalist and externalist interests in explanation. They each articulate a distinction between personal and objective justification that they take to be miscast as a distinction between internalism and externalism conceived, as they typically are, as mutually exclusive and exhaustive accounts of epistemic justification. Epistemic compatibilism and incompatibilism will be more fully discussed later, but Greco's (2005, Sec. 5) description of VE as "mixed theory" is one expression of it, where he writes, "The main idea is that an adequate account of knowledge ought to contain both a responsibility condition and a reliability condition. Moreover, a virtue account can explain how the two are tied together. In cases of knowledge, objective reliability is grounded in epistemically responsible action."

Still, each has distinctive views in this area, and Greco (2004b) worries that Sosa's metarequirement of epistemic perspective makes broader concessions to internalism than are necessary, perhaps hampering rather than improving VE's antiskeptical force.[8] The concern with an epistemically relevant distinction between reflective and animal knowledge and his stratified or "two-tiered" account of justification seems to be a recurring theme in contributors, including Greco, to the watershed volume *Ernest Sosa and His Critics* (Greco 2004a; see Kornblith 2004, for example). But Sosa's "Replies" there and his 2004 Locke Lectures, *A Virtue Epistemology*, engage these concerns quite directly.

In *Putting Skeptics in Their Place*, Greco examines a wide range of skeptical problems and argues that responding to them drives us to a form of reliabilist externalism centered on the cognitive abilities of epistemic agents (compare also Audi 2004). A key thesis in Greco's "agent reliabilism" is that the core "relevant-alternatives intuition" and this form of VE are mutually supportive. The relevant-alternatives intuition as Greco describes it is the commonsense suggestion that modally far-off error possibilities do not present relevant philosophical challenges to our ability to know most of the things we think we know. Philosophers can remain true to this intuition and harness its antiskeptical import by relating it to the settled dispositions and competencies through which agents strive for truth and effective agency in the world in which they find themselves. If the kinds of cognitive dispositions a person must manifest in order for her to meet a normative requirement of reliability are sustained by her thinking conscientiously, then this latter concept is important as well and shows us that issues of motivation and habituation remain important factors in any sound philosophic understanding of our epistemic agency.[9]

Greco thinks that agent reliabilism provides some unique resources for redressing the faulty assumption that for agents to have knowledge, they must be able to discriminate the truth of their beliefs from every alternative skeptical scenario regardless of its modal distance from the actual world. First, we need to understand relevant possibility in terms of the "possible-worlds" semantics of modal logic: A possibility is relevant if it is true in some close-by possible world, and closeness is to be understood in terms of overall world similarity (2000, 206). Second, it is virtue theory that best captures our reasoning about which possibilities are relevant: the very concept of knowledge, and therefore of the relevant possibilities that must be excluded for its possession, involves reference to cognitive abilities and dispositions:

> In the language of possible worlds, someone has an ability to achieve some result under relevant conditions only if the person is very likely to achieve that result across close possible worlds. But if knowledge essentially involves having cognitive abilities, and if abilities are dispositions to achieve results across close possible worlds, then this explains why possibilities are relevant only when they are true in some close possible world. Specifically, only such possibilities as these can undermine one's cognitive abilities. In an environment where deception by demons is actual or probable, I lack the ability to reliably form true beliefs and avoid false beliefs. But if no such demons exist in this world or similar ones, they do not affect my cognitive faculties and habits.
>
> (207)

3. THREE COMPETING ANTISKEPTICAL STRATEGIES

We have focused primarily upon the work of Sosa and Greco because of the direct contributions each has made to a philosophically adequate response to radical skepticism. Turning in this section to points about VE made by its critics, we will describe and engage Sven Bernecker's objections, informed by a kind of austere externalism that rejects epistemic compatibilism, and Richard Foley's objections from an internalist perspective on justification that result in his proposal for "a trial separation between the theory of knowledge and the theory of justified belief." This serves my later purposes, since I want first to defend epistemic compatibilism in this general way before going on to develop philosophical support for its specifically virtue-theoretic versions.

A thoroughgoing externalist, Bernecker considers and rejects Sosa's and Greco's epistemologies as forms of what he characterizes more generally as epistemic compatibilism. This is a useful term but is defined only vaguely by the claim that it is possible to "combine satisfactorily internalist and externalist features in a single theory" (2006, 81). The target indicated by his critique is quite wide, but Bernecker's "Prospects for Epistemic Compatibilism" provides a useful taxonomy of different arguments in the literature supporting distinct versions of compatibilism. Sosa's and Greco's accounts are singled out for extended criticism (the latter in Bernecker 2007) for the reason that the virtue epistemologists offer some of the best sustained defenses in contemporary epistemology of views associated with epistemic compatibilism.

Of course, nobody could hold that what need to be reconciled are internalism and externalism as understood in the usual stipulative definitions of them. Internalism about justification is standardly defined for introductory purposes as the thesis that all the elements that justify a belief must be accessible to the mind upon reflection, and externalism is defined as the negation of that thesis. Notice that this style of definition excludes a middle and leaves the terrain of theories of justification asymmetrically shaped: Internalism is a positive thesis of specified meaning, while externalism, by its purely negative character, is left to a wide parcel that might admit of a plurality of positions once developed as positive epistemologies.

Externalism invites "mixed" theory but does not necessitate it. Compatibilists are those who accept the invitation, while "incompatibilists" are what we can call those (at either end of the scale running from pure internalism to pure externalism) who spurn the invitation to mixed theory. Hence Bernecker's incompatibilist stance is not simply the rejection of internalism, something that is true of all forms of externalism by the definitions he employs. His stance, rather, is that externalists should reject any concerns about epistemic evaluation arising from the first-person perspective. Contrary to the thrust of VE, Bernecker's proposal is that we give up efforts at reconciliation and embrace instead a conception of naturalized epistemology on which only third-person concerns play a central explanatory role.

Besides being able to distinguish different kinds of compatibilism, we should also want a taxonomy that acknowledges as "incompatibilist" such eliminative forms of externalism as the one Bernecker maintains. In order to get a proper handle on the range of positions in the debate, I propose adopting the broadest taxonomy possible, which we might do by adapting the familiar trichotomy among theorists who view themselves as "enemies," "strangers," or "partners" in any given debate. More formally, we will describe these as the "conflict," "independence," and "integration" models of the interests in explanation engaged by the internalist/externalist debate. This threefold taxonomy allows us to see three quite distinct models of the relationship of internalist and externalist interests in explanation, each well represented in present-day debates in analytic epistemology. Moreover, when we extend this taxonomy to inform us specifically about divergent forms of VE, we find a confirmation that few, if any, existing forms of VE adopt the conflict model; instead, most or all support one or another form of epistemic compatibilism.[10]

Finally, we may further explore differences within the "compatibilist" camp. Here positions can be usefully divided between those who adopt the integration model and those who adopt the independence model. This choice between the two models supporting epistemic compatibilism overlaps with a fairly clear distinction between what I will term "strong" and "weak" forms of VE. First, let us refer to any analysis of knowledge that defends an *areteic* (i.e., virtue-theoretic) condition on knowledge as "strong VE." This term is broad enough to include Sosa, Greco, and Zagzebski as proponents despite their outstanding differences. The integrative model suggests that a correct account of knowledge is one that finds epistemic reliability and epistemic responsibility not as sources of antithetical third- and first-person "logics," but as normative concepts mutually presupposed in a proper understanding of self-reflective agents like us. Second, there are today quite a number of authors who can be described as virtue epistemologists because they

Table 1 Three Competing Antiskeptical Discursive Strategies

Metaphor	Model	Description
Enemies	Conflict (or incompatibilism)	Standard access internalism as excluding externalist elements; also "pure" or "eliminative" externalism, as in Bernecker's stance against all forms of compatibilism.
Strangers	Independence (or weak compatibilism)	Foley's compromising "separation proposal," which severs the link between knowledge and justification while maintaining that internalism remains correct when understood as something like a theory of personal justification tied to a general theory of rationality; includes "weak" VE where belief out of intellectual virtue is epistemically desirable, but is not studied for any connection to knowledge possession.
Partners	Integration (or strong compatibilism)	"Mixed theories" of justification that are externalist in character but maintain requirements for personal justification and proper motivation, as well as for agent reliability; includes "strong VE" where the requirement of successful belief out of intellectual virtue carries both kinds of demands.

acknowledge an epistemically central place for the study of the intellectual virtues but see its place lying entirely outside the analysis of knowledge proper.[11] These are, on our taxonomy, proponents of "weak VE," and they have sometimes been the most explicit critics of the preoccupation with analysis of knowledge and justification in epistemology and in strong VE in particular. When our taxonomy is used to illuminate differences within the family of virtue-theoretic epistemologies, it clarifies the point that proponents of strong VE typically maintain integrationist models for epistemic compatibilism, while proponents of weak VE typically subscribe to independence models.[12]

In summary thus far, our proposed taxonomy allows for the fact that independence and integration models are often employed by epistemologists who are not proponents of VE in either the strong or weak sense, but it also identifies under noticed sources of tension among epistemologists and a veiled debate with quite direct implications for how best to respond to radical skepticism. As "models" rather than "theories," conflict, independence, and integration represent in our taxonomy three different *discursive strategies* (table 1), and the choice between them demands that we think closely about which one best serves antiskeptical philosophy.

We can now use this taxonomy to state a stronger thesis: that as an antiskeptical strategy, adoption of the conflict model constitutes a dialectical misstep.

One reason for this that I have already suggested but will continue to develop is that a neo-Moorean argument well serves the interests of an externalist response to skepticism, yet the neo-Moorean approach thrives in an environment of epistemic compatibilism while withering apart from it. More specifically, when starting from incompatibilist assumptions, externalists are tempted to go beyond acknowledging instances of unreflective "brute" knowledge to supposing that most, if not all, human knowledge is merely of this nature. Here the concerns shared predominantly but not exclusively by internalists and skeptics, concerns about our cognitive responsibility in the human modes of inquiry we conduct and the evidence we use when we provide reflective reasons for our beliefs, appear lost or simply given up. The "brute nature" of the human epistemic condition is conceded as we learn to leave first-person perspectives out of the field of the theory of knowledge. Perhaps reflecting this austere form of externalism, Bernecker explicitly rejects Sosa's concern with "so-called reflective knowledge," denying that it amounts to a central concern of epistemology as he defines it and countering it with the suggestion that unreflective "brute" knowledge is simply paradigmatic of what we must take knowledge to be. According to our own compatibilist approach, however, contemporary neo-Pyrrhonists such as Barry Stroud (2004a, 2004b) are actually correct to see the kind of externalist response to skepticism afforded by "unmixed" or "eliminative" forms of externalism as philosophically unsatisfying.[13]

Having considered and briefly responded to eliminative externalist objections to VE, let us briefly look at the problem of the stability of epistemic compatibilism in light of certain objections stemming from an internalist conception of justification. Externalists and internalists are in agreement that questions about agent responsibility in inquiry are distinct from questions about the agent's internal access to reasons. Alvin Goldman (1999) an externalist, rightly points out that access internalism is quite compatible with the "epistemic sloth" of an agent who is subjectively justified only because she shirks her responsibility to carefully investigate or weigh potential counter-evidence to her belief. Laurence BonJour, an internalist/coherentist, recently conceded that although he had earlier conflated these issues, "being epistemically responsible" is neither necessary nor sufficient for "internalist justification" as he continues to use that term (2003, 176). This broad agreement suggests that compatibilists can respond to BonJour's internalism by drawing more fully on the distinction between VE's interest in concerns with epistemic responsibility in personal justification and the strong demand that BonJour allows the skeptic to make, that there be available an "internalist justification" with which to respond to the underdetermination argument.[14]

Another related criticism of strong VE from an internalist perspective is captured by Foley's proposal for a "trial separation between the theory of knowledge and the theory of justified belief." Foley claims that externalism and internalism "need not be competitors at all." He finds their conflict to be due to a major false assumption they share, "that the properties which make a belief justified are by definition such that when a true belief has those properties, it is a good candidate to be an instance of knowledge" (2005, 314). It was this assumption of *logical* connection between knowing and having justified belief, Foley charges, that prompted many externalists who until fairly recently were only reacting against justification-driven accounts of knowledge to seek to reconceive justification externalistically as well.

Foley does indeed provide an interesting reading of the debate by articulating and questioning what he simply calls "the unfortunate assumption" that would have us assess the satisfactoriness of a theory of justification by the service it provides in improving one's analysis of knowledge. The adequacy of an account of justification, at the very least, certainly need not be *restricted* to its contribution to the analysis of propositional knowledge; but Foley's proposal demands more than this, a full (though trial) separation of the two theories. Sosa, he thinks, still makes the unfortunate assumption. But Foley overstates his argument that externalists and internalists "are principally concerned with different issues" by claiming that the one is concerned with the theory of knowledge and the other with the theory of justified belief (2004, 60). It is this division that I take as providing Foley's independence model for epistemic compatibilism.[15]

Although Bernecker's and Foley's objections are both directed against Sosa, it should be clear that they reflect some otherwise quite antagonistic philosophical motivations. In contrast to the stance against strong VE that both authors exhibit, the position for which I will argue in section 5 remains conservative enough to retain a conceptual connection between knowledge and personal justification. In response to Bernecker, I hold that adoption of the conflict model constitutes a dialectical misstep for antiskeptical philosophy; in response to Foley, I point out that there are numerous such "separation proposals" in epistemology today, and many of them upon closer inspection also undermine rather than improve our ability to respond to radical skepticism. The advantage of the integrationist stance in this regard should be readily apparent, and though I have yet to make a positive case to show its philosophical stability in the face of the skeptical challenge, we can at least conclude thus far that the "prospects" for epistemic compatibilism are not something that should be easily dismissed, at least if a philosophically satisfying response to radical skepticism is part of what any theory of knowledge should strive for.

4. Improving the Prospects of Externalist Responses to Skepticism

Edmund Gettier's objections in "Is Justified True Belief Knowledge?" (1963) to the "standard" or justified-true-belief (JTB) analysis of knowledge provided a spur to what has since come to be termed the "externalist turn in epistemology." But the received view of what I will call Gettier's challenge, wherein the task is to produce an analysis of knowledge with true belief and justification as conditions, plus some further condition specifically to handle Gettier cases, is multiply ambiguous. It presupposes that the justification condition remains in place unaffected through the externalist turn in epistemology, with an externalist "Gettier condition" coming only by way of simple addition—as "fourth condition" suggests. It also seems to push at every instance toward "infallibilism," the view that for the challenge to be met, the other conditions in our analysis will not suffice unless they actually *entail* the truth of the target belief.

If this is the way matters stand, they can easily be seen to motivate just the kinds of radical or eliminative externalism that we previously identified and found wanting. But fortunately, this motivation for infallibilism in epistemology depends on a dubious conception of Gettier's challenge. On my view, the externalist turn does not spell the end of the legitimate concern of epistemologists with personal justification but does necessitate its thorough reconceptualization. To help motivate this claim, I want to suggest an alternative construal of Gettier's challenge that accepts its impetus to externalism as a correct implication but provides a quite different understanding of how epistemology needs to change on account of it. On this construal, we can affirm that infallibilism is no part of Gettier's legacy, and we can take the impetus to externalism as genuinely empowering a new mode of response to radical skepticism.

The argument in support of these claims will proceed in three steps. First, contrary to the demand that the received view triggers, a statement of "thick" conditions to inform us what will be sufficient for knowledge in any case whatever, I argue that we need only include "thin" or deflated conditions in our analysis, conditions capable of being flexible enough to take on very different content in response to different cases at hand. This first step is best exemplified in the literature in the proposal made by virtue epistemologist Heather Battaly (2001) in "Thin Concepts to the Rescue: Thinning the Concepts of Epistemic Justification and Intellectual Virtue."

Second, our claim that personal justification remains important but cannot retain its original, internalist construal through the course of the externalist turn will be supported through the work of Michael Williams (2001, 2005). I construe Williams as an integrationist whose form of strong epistemic compatibilism is embodied in his proposal that the "prior-grounding" model of our dialogical obligations (assumed by the skeptic and informing the Agrippan trilemma) be traded in favor of a "default and challenge" model (DCM). The default and challenge model of justification is most evidently responsive to Agrippan concerns, but if the problem of radical scepticism turns on the extreme internalism we will trace to the prior grounding model, then the DCM helps us respond to both, "though in the case of the latter, more by way of showing how we can legitimately set sceptical problems aside than by way of a direct solution" (Williams 2008, 26; see also Axtell 2008)

Third and finally, we develop the symmetries between these two proposals: we spell out the philosophical advantages of "marrying" the thin concept of an epistemic virtue as a condition on knowledge to the DCM as embodying the kind of analysis that should be sought once we have fully eschewed attachment to the traditional, internalistically motivated prior-grounding model. I hope to persuade the reader that it is this third step, our "trial-marriage" proposal of VE to the dictates of the DCM, that provides epistemology with new resources for a more self-consistent form of compatibilism, and through it a more philosophically satisfying response to radical skepticism.

In her essay "Thin Concepts to the Rescue," Battaly argues that we can circumvent much ill-motivated debate "by recognizing that the concepts of justification and intellectual virtue are thin. Each is thin because it has multiple conditions of application . . . [such that] there is no definite answer as to which of these combinations is necessary, or which is sufficient, for its application" (2001, 99). Internalists and externalists (and, sadly, to some extent, virtue epistemologists too) drag out unsupported debates by "picking the poisoned apple" of tacitly thickening these thin concepts in different ways. A "combinatorial vagueness" ensues that spurs heated exchanges and seems to invite still further thickening of a condition as a way to make an analysis more precise and to avoid counterexamples to the necessity and sufficiency of its stated conditions. But just what is this debate over, she asks, if there is "no sharp distinction between the combinations of conditions that are, and those that are not, necessary and sufficient for its application" (104)?

To avoid picking the apple, Battaly prescribes leaving the concepts of justification and intellectual virtue with little pregiven meaning. A thin *areteic* condition is a condition that remains largely formal in character but is for that same reason highly flexible, being able to take on different meanings in different contexts. To place it into one's analysis of knowledge is thereby merely to present the skeptical interrogator with "a roughly drawn sketch that can be completed in different ways" (107).

If this proposal is useful, it is because what epistemologists want to analyze through terms like "justified" and "knows" actually occurs along a range or spectrum.[16] Left in a formal or deflated manner, an *areteic* condition can be "bent" in several directions, allowing it to stand in for a diverse list of possible meanings of justification—items ranging from simple "aptness" that might invite reference to only the faculty virtues in some instances to the complex reason giving and sensitivity to counterevidence that we associate with the application of critical reflective intelligence and with sound reflective intellectual habits and inquisitive methods.

But can this first step of the argument lead us anywhere worth going? By suggesting that we can treat justification this way, are we not conceding that we fail to meet a reasonable demand by the skeptic for a single set of "thick" necessary and sufficient conditions that define knowledge across its entire knowledge spectrum? If so, how can we hold that positive epistemology effectively sidesteps rather than simply ignores the thrust of skeptical arguments? We remain still as if upon the point of the trident and must balance on its edge, explaining both why skeptical arguments have the initial plausibility to deserve serious attention and why they lose their force or do not arise in the same way when we proceed by our own premises. In order to meet this burden, we will need to take a second step involving a more direct examination of just what our dialogical obligations to the skeptic actually are.

Williams's form of epistemic compatibilism makes a crucial contrast between the prior-grounding model of knowledge (hereafter PGM) and the DCM:

> [T]o take account of externalist insights, we have to detach the idea that knowledge is essentially connected with justification, not only from the classical demonstrative ideal and its infallibilist descendants, but also from all conceptions of justification that insist on respecting the Prior Grounding [model]. Effecting this detachment leads us to see justification as exhibiting a Default and Challenge structure, where constraints on the reasonableness of challenges and the appropriateness of justifications are contextually variable along several dimensions.[17]

Not only the Agrippan trilemma but also the traditional internalist conception of justification builds in the PGM, which Williams characterizes as composed of four interrelated theses of an internalist and evidentialist orientation.[18] If we implicitly adopt the PGM from the outset, then we accept an asymmetry of justificational obligations and an unrestricted commitment on the part of claimants to demonstrate entitlement to opinion: "If all reasonable believing is believing-on-evidence, the skeptic is entitled to ask for the evidence to be produced," which generates a vicious regress. But absent this requirement, the skeptic holds no right to issue such "naked challenges" (2001, 150).

Many authors have noticed substantial connections between epistemic internalism and motivations to skepticism. Williams explains this connection by noting that the PGM "both generates the threat of skepticism and constrains our responses to that threat" (2001, 188). On the DCM, by contrast, "questions of justification arise in a definite justificational context, constituted by a complex and in general largely tacit background of entitlements, some of which will be default" (158). What Williams calls our default entitlements are not "mere assumptions" because they are always provisional and backed up by a defense commitment. The most important point of Williams's approach for us to develop is that he thinks that the DCM instantiates a different conception of our discursive obligations, one that "saddles challengers, as well as claimants" to knowledge. Adopting the DCM means that challengers and claimants share justificational responsibilities, and hence that one need not concede the gross asymmetry that the PGM instantiates: "no move in the game of giving and asking for reasons is presuppositionless. On a default and challenge conception of justification, there is no room for either the skeptic's global doubts or the traditional epistemologist's global reassurances" (150).

I think of Williams as proposing a very different reading of Gettier's challenge to the standard analysis of knowledge and a correspondingly different task for the practice of epistemic evaluation in light of it. Williams wants to "preserve the link between knowledge and justification without accepting the prior grounding requirement" (2001, 148). This is what we have called the "integration" position, and it suggests that a shift away from the PGM to the DCM is necessary if we are to find the more stable form of epistemic compatibilism that we seek. But interpreting adoption of the DCM not as optional but as something any self-consistent externalist must do still provides only a partial resolution. What I will insist upon, and what constitutes the third step of my argument, is that what is needed to preserve a conceptual link between knowledge possession and personal justification is to show clearly how our two proposals can be fitted together.

From the one side, the DCM is not only compatible with but seems to require for its completion two distinct functions for philosophical analysis, one for the default mode of inquiry and the other for particular motivated challenges in particular cases. The thin and thick descriptions of intellectual virtues supply the DCM with just the kind of explanations one might intuitively think that the "default" and "challenge" contexts call for: thin descriptions for our default philosophical mode of life and thick descriptions for our more skeptical philosophic mode of life, or simply whenever a defense commitment is engaged for the attributor of knowledge to a particular agent.[19]

In the default situation, by contrast, no particular challenge is set before us, and so one or more "thin" conditions on knowledge suffice; *areteic* and antiluck conditions (one or both) are good candidates for this since they aim to provide what is needed while keeping the focus on naturalistically grounded talk of the agent's cognitive habits and dispositions. "Thin-concept analysis" featuring virtue-theoretic terms, in particular, underscores a naturalistic approach to knowledge (one grounded in our habits and dispositions) that nevertheless preserves the link Williams wants with issues of personal justification (or responsibility). If Battaly shows us that virtue theory is naturally interpreted as providing an analysis of justification in terms of thin, flexible conditions that is not concerned to state sufficient conditions on knowledge in any substantial way, her proposal is just showing us the form of analysis we should expect between antiskeptical and skeptical philosophers were their debate to revolve around the DCM rather than the PGM. In the Default context, a thin *areteic* condition suffices for the expectation that the truth of the agent's belief will be of epistemic credit to her as an agent. By contrast, the dialectical context in which there has arisen a motivated challenge over a particular case calls for a different function for analysis, and in this context, thickly describable dispositions and acquired virtues again seem to provide adherents of the DCM with just the kind of explanation their model calls for.

Adoption of the DCM may also improve the prospects of virtue epistemologies. Proponents of the latter might come to see adoption of the DCM as advantageous if they find that it helps them clarify the very different explanatory roles that thick and thin concepts play in our field. If the DCM supports a more stable form of epistemic compatibilism, as Williams clearly holds, then its adoption and the consequent relinquishing of preconceptions about justification bound up in the PGM may aid inquiries into the relationship between our normative and naturalistic posits and into what Riggs (2007) describes as "the conceptual connections among a family of concepts that include credit, responsibility, attribution, and luck." For in responding to a particular motivated challenge to our attribution of knowledge to an agent, we are essentially responding to concerns that the agent either has a false belief despite her best cognitive effort or else to concerns that the agent should not be accorded the epistemic credit that we normally *would* accord her for her cognitive success—that is, for the truth of her belief (for Greco's account of epistemic credit, see his 2003a and 2003b).

Adoption of the DCM also aids VE by providing another way of understanding the importance of the relevant-alternatives intuition. "It is easy to miss the fact that the practice of justifying is only activated by finding oneself in the context of a properly motivated challenge," and when we miss this, we allow the skeptic "to transform the ever-present possibility of contextually appropriate demands for evidence into an unrestricted insistence on grounds, encouraging us to move from fallibilism to radical skepticism" (Williams 2001, 150). By first accepting the DCM and then tying our obligations under it to a "thin-concept" analysis of knowledge, we still take skepticism seriously but encourage a quite different conception of what was wrong with the standard or JTB analysis of knowledge to which Gettier framed his objections. We avoid altogether what I call the *paradox of general sufficiency* to which debate in the post-Gettier era has apparently led. On the DCM, the demand to provide the skeptic with a set of thick conditions sufficient for knowledge at any point along the spectrum becomes paradoxical. After Williams's proposed dialectical repositioning, the antiskeptical philosopher's inability to answer the skeptic premised upon conditions set forth by the PGM can be acknowledged, but the demand itself can be reasonably set aside.[20]

If the DCM is consistently applied, philosophers should not feel tempted to invoke the PGM even when studying cases from the "high end" of the knowledge spectrum. Nor should they be tempted to reify first- and third-person perspectives of epistemic evaluation into antithetical "logics," as if what is being evaluated were not an agent-inquirer but merely some reasoning-like process "in" him or her.[21] But until our third step is taken, we will likely remain subject to both temptations. Concern over reflective knowledge in particular leads to problems over traditional coherentism, which, according to Williams, accepts the PGM and "is committed to a purely internalist conception of knowledge and justification" (2001, 177).[22] The advice for any who want to pursue the development of a form of VE that takes advantage of Williams's proposal is that they are correct to pursue the importance of personal justification for knowledge possession, but they must at the same time disqualify their special concerns with reflective coherence from leading them to presuppose internalism by building in the PGM.

The view we have arrived at through our three-step argument underlines the pragmatic wisdom behind Battaly's proposal for harnessing the resources of thin-concept analyses of central epistemic terms and acknowledges the force of Williams's demand that self-consistent externalists stop answering to demands whose rationale lies only in the prior-grounding model of our discursive obligations to the skeptic. Epistemological externalists, I now conclude, including the proponents of strong VE on whose work we have focused, would be well served in the future to heed two key points of Williams's account: first, that an analysis of knowledge is only able self-consistently to involve elements of externalism "because it embodies the default and challenge conception" (2001, 177); and second, that if there is a plurality of valuable epistemic aims, or a diverse list of ways in which justification might arise, then "the skeptic's hyper-general questions may be deeply flawed" (2005, 214).[23]

Although we have used Battaly and Williams to illustrate clear lines of argument supporting each of our two proposals, we have taken a step somewhat unique in the literature by intentionally tying them closely together, arguing that doing so multiplies the antiskeptical force of each taken separately. In summary of the arguments in sections 3 and 4, my intention has been to point out how the force of virtue-theoretic responses to skepticism might be substantially enhanced by realizing their symmetries with the DCM of the discursive obligations holding between skeptical interrogators and antiskeptical interlocutors. It is not merely circular reasoning or arbitrary assumption to hold that modally far-off possibilities do not present philosophical objections to our ordinary practices of knowledge attribution. Adoption of the DCM allows us to see this while leading to an understanding of Gettier's challenge that shows the force of neo-Moorean VE and other epistemologies that draw upon the core relevant-alternatives intuition.

5. POSTSCRIPT ON SKEPTICISM AND VIRTUE THEORY.

In canvassing recent work in VE early in this chapter, we found a serious concern with questions about both local and radical skepticism, but also a diversity of opinions about how the resources of virtue theory are best harnessed to address these questions. Much work remains ahead on these and related problems in the theory of knowledge. Indeed, if I have been successful in making the reader take seriously Williams's claim that to be self-consistent, epistemic externalists must adopt the DCM and restate their position accordingly, then the overall implication of this chapter is that there is still a profound dialectical shift that needs to take place before externalist responses to radical skepticism hold the force their proponents so often allege for them even today. Since the issues debated by the conflict, independence, and integration models of section 3 involve diverging conceptions of epistemic normativity, virtue epistemologists also have much work ahead in articulating their own distinctive conceptions of the natural and the normative, and how the rocky relationship between them can also appear to motivate radical skepticism (Stroud). That VE brings unique resources to smooth over these tensions is, I think, well articulated by Greco when he writes:

[E]pistemology is a normative discipline, and a central task of epistemology is to explicate and explain the sort of normativity that is at work in cognitive evaluation . . . [but] we should not expect to solve epistemology's different problems in a piecemeal fashion. Rather, we need a detailed and systematic account of the sort of normativity that is involved in cognitive evaluations.[24]

Finally, in approaching the topic of this chapter, we have had recourse to speaking about "discursive strategies," "dialogical obligations," and "dialectical missteps" and "shifts." This is not (or not merely) an authorial idiosyncrasy; part of any sound response to skepticism is a diagnosis of its driving motivations. When Pyrrhonist arguments are discussed only as logical arguments, and "skeptical hypotheses" inconsistent with our commonsense beliefs are introduced as a potent barrier to those beliefs constituting knowledge despite there being no explanatory *research program* behind them (a usual requirement for describing something as a "hypothesis"), then the more important contrast between the prescribed or implicit associated patterns of living of the philosopher and Pyrrhonian skeptic are neglected. The cost of this neglect is potentially severe, for by it we tacitly assent to a key contention of the skeptic: that her arguments can be raised without committing her to philosophical assumptions of her own.

On the contrary, as Pascal once noted, "to criticize philosophy is already to philosophize," and we have tried to detail by reference to the PGM how contemporary Pyrrhonism and its underdetermination argument stand on unacknowledged and problematic theoretical preconceptions. I want to suggest that future work on radical skepticism needs to display considerably more of that character that authors such as Williams and Pritchard describe as diagnostic, having the intention of exposing to critical evaluation the philosophical presuppositions underlying skeptical arguments. This ties directly into our ability to respond, for as Williams nicely puts it, "We cannot simply confront the skeptic with an externalist reply. We must earn the right to make use of externalist insights by embedding them in a deeper diagnosis of the skeptic's epistemological presuppositions."[25] By ignoring this diagnostic task, we do ourselves the disservice of undermining the crucial interest it has been argued that we have in distancing ourselves from the skeptic's assumptions about the positive philosopher's discursive obligations. Perhaps it also explains why we so often turn a blind eye, though the commonsense tradition from Reid onward advises us we must not, to another related assumption on which the Pyrrhonist deftly plays: the assumption that for us humans to be capable of knowledge and intellectually responsible in attributing it to ourselves, our philosophers must first prove that reason is its own foundation.[26]

NOTES

1. For a fuller account of the emergence of virtue epistemologies, see the introduction to Axtell (2000).

2. "For all S, φ, ψ, if S's evidence for believing φ does not favour φ over some hypothesis ψ that S knows to be incompatible with φ, then S is not internalistically justified in believing φ" (Pritchard 2005, 108). Throughout this chapter, I change "scepticism" to "skepticism" for the sake of continuity.

3. Pascal's *Pensees* 434, my translation.

4. Perhaps the earliest of the virtue epistemologists to draw from Reid was Christopher Hookway in *Skepticism* (1990; see also 2003), where he argues that Reid's approach allows us to recognize the contingency of our confidence in our commonsense beliefs, without denying the legitimacy of that confidence (240).

5. Sosa 1999; compare his "Replies," Sosa 2004a, 276.

6. Sosa 2000. He allows that his virtue perspectivism is thus "structurally" Cartesian while pointing out that "in content it is not" (281), for the agent's epistemic ascent can be understood naturalistically, without Descartes' invocation of a creator-God who benevolently guarantees the truth of what we most clearly and distinctly conceive.

7. Sosa 2004a, 290–291.

8. Sosa's virtue perspectivism has been characterized over the years by its two-tiered or "stratified" conception of justification (1991, 189), where a key distinction is between "externalist, reliability-bound aptness and internalist, rationality-bound justification." The version of strong VE I will sketch is partly intended to show that a troublesome stratification need not be posited.

9. As Sherman and White (2002) put the point somewhat more generally, Aristotle's emphasis on the emotions remains a resource for contemporary VE.

10. For example, Sosa (2004b) argues that internalism/externalism and coherentism/foundationalism are "two false dichotomies" overcome by taking the agent as the "seat of justification," while Greco and Linda Zagzebski, whatever their other differences, both emphasize that the "mixed" character of VE is philosophically crucial rather than detrimental to its ability to respond to the skeptical challenge. James Montmarquet (2007) locates internalist concerns as reflecting interest in "pragmatic epistemic justification" (that is, in acting in a morally satisfactory way on our beliefs) rather than in "pure epistemic justification" and the question of the simple possession of knowledge. Others argue that externalist intuitions track "doxastic justification," while internalist intuitions track "propositional justification." Heather Battaly (2001, 109) argues that the debate between internalists and externalists is misguided insofar as authors fail to see that they are "thickening" a naturally "thin" concept of justification. Wayne Riggs (1998, 453) writes, "The responsibilist and truth-conducivist conceptions of justification define distinct epistemic evaluations, and so are not in any interesting sense rival notions" because each is addressed to a different kind of epistemic luck. Axtell (2001) argues that the truck that internalists and externalists have with filtering out different kinds of epistemic luck shows that each holds an incomplete account, reflecting in part divergent value-charged demands for the intelligibility of all knowledge.

11. These authors are engaged in such projects as the study of "understanding" (Elgin, Kvanvig, Riggs), explanatory stories about the acquisition of knowledge (Eflin, Pritchard, Reed), or theories of pragmatic rationality as contrasted with purely epistemic rationality (Foley, Montmarquet). Alternatively, they describe themselves as "agnostic" about a role for the virtues in analysis of knowledge and simply turn their attention to what they think are other interesting roles that the virtues can play (Roberts and Wood, 2007).

12. On my earlier taxonomic distinction between "reliabilist" and "responsibilist" VE, a responsibilist is free to advocate either weak or strong VE. Kvanvig can be highly critical

of those he says betray "remnants of skeptical shackles that have plagued the history of epistemology" by maintaining a privileged place for the study of knowledge. This includes proponents of (strong) VE who try to locate the place for virtues in epistemology "by defining knowledge or justification in terms of the virtues" (2003, 187). But while on my taxonomy Kvanvig is a weak VE critic of strong VE, it should be noted that he also criticizes Foley's separation proposal as "abandoning the Gettier tradition entirely" (2003, 199).

13. For a fuller defense of this claim and presentation of Stroud's challenge to what he terms "scientific externalism," see Axtell 2006a.

14. Having made his concession, why does BonJour go on to embrace "internalist justification" as the one of epistemic centrality? If BonJour allows that internalist justification and personal justification (qua responsibility) can come apart, "responsibilists" in epistemology might be taken as those who instead choose epistemic responsibility, with its ties to natural dispositions and to acquired habits of inquiry (*hexis* for the Greeks), as the more epistemologically interesting concept. This makes it most plausible to hold that issues of personal justification and of distinctively reflective knowledge and reflective intellectual virtues maintain a continuing importance even after the externalist turn and indeed partly because of it. For responsibilist approaches to problems about religious belief and religious skepticism, see Axtell (2006a) and Roberts and Wood (2007). For more on "responsibilist VE," see Baehr (2006a, 2006b) and the work of other editors of *JanusBlog* at http://janusblog.squarespace.com.

15. Foley and Montmarquet both adopt such an independence model, and with it the weak VE concessionary strategy of endorsing the austere externalist account of knowledge as merely true belief reliably produced. Foley says that he sees no reason "to read back into the account of knowledge some duly externalized notion of justified belief" but rather locates reason-giving explanations elsewhere, in a "general theory of rationality" (2005, 315). Montmarquet (2007) alternatively relocates *his* role for the intellectual virtues in the study of "pragmatic epistemic justification," distinct from "pure epistemic justification"; this makes it a study about *action*, or more specifically about how to evaluate agents with respect to their *acting* in morally satisfactory or unsatisfactory ways on their beliefs. Montmarquet argues that Sosa's influential distinction between animal and reflective knowledge should give way to a distinction between knowledge (animal, mechanical, or human) and the distinctively human form of responsibility (epistemic, as well as moral) involved in acting on one's beliefs.

16. Zagzebski reflects this idea of thin-concept analysis in writing that she wants to construct a virtue-theoretic approach that takes *knowledge* broadly enough "to cover a multitude of states, from the simplest case of ordinary perceptual contact with the physical world, requiring no cognitive effort or skill wherever, to the most impressive cognitive achievements" (1996, 264).

17. Williams 2001, 245. There is "contextualism" in Williams's thought, but it distinguishes between *two different philosophical contexts* for dialogue rather than between an "everyday" and a "skeptical" context, as self-described contextualists typically do.

18. Williams (2001, 147) analyzes the PGM into four interconnected theses: "(PG1) *No Free Lunch Principle*. Epistemic entitlement—personal justification—does not just accrue to us: it must be earned by epistemically responsible behavior. (PG2) *Priority Principle*. It is never epistemically responsible to believe a proposition true when one's grounds for believing it true are less than adequate. (PG3) *Evidentialism*. Grounds are evidence: propositions that count in favour of the truth of the proposition believed. (PG4) *Possession Principle*. For a person's belief to be adequately grounded . . . the believer himself or herself

must possess (and make proper use of) evidence that makes the proposition believed (very) likely to be true."

19. My form of VE is opposed to those who hold that we need to either endorse infallibilism (Zagzebski) or reject the epistemic closure principle. This adds more substance to the claim that we are offering a genuine reinterpretation of Gettier's challenge.

20. Compare this strategy with that of Greco, who until recently has proposed only a "partial" account of knowledge, restricted to stating necessary conditions, but who more recently strengthened his requirements in order to be able to maintain their general sufficiency as well. The present proposal responds to many of the same tensions that previously made Greco reluctant to assert the general sufficiency of his conditions, but it does so by the quite different approach of adopting the DCM and rejecting as unmotivated the claim that an adequate analysis is one that states "general sufficient" conditions on knowledge.

21. Externalist proponents of the conflict model typically insist that personal justification is epistemologically irrelevant because the reflective actions of reason giving are aimed at showing that one possesses a status *fully independent* of this activity. On the present view, however, this objection leans upon the grossest form of what Whitehead called the "fallacy of misplaced concreteness" (see Leite 2004, 231). I am paraphrasing his claim that "basing relations must be attributable to the person and not merely to some process which takes place 'in' him or her."

22. Note that a "Sellarsian" coherentism seems to contrast with rather than exemplify "traditional" coherentism; Williams indeed sites Sellars as a source for the change of venue associated with adoption of the DCM, so there is interesting work to be done in articulating the differences.

23. Williams also expresses doubts about the expectation of providing very precise necessary and sufficient conditions of knowing, but he affirms that subject to that qualification, the account still defends "the standard analysis, which links knowledge with justification"; he therefore, as a defender of ntegration and like my own form of VE, stands sternly in opposition to "purely reliabilist, purely externalist, and thus radically non-justificational accounts of knowledge" (2001, 244).

24. John Greco, "Seminar on Virtue Epistemology," http://www.helsinki.fi/filosofia/k2004/Greco.htm.

25. Skepticism, Williams argues, is best approached not by "the more familiar kinds of positive epistemological theory" but rather by a "more roundabout, diagnostic approach" that refuses to take the arguments at face value, "accepting the skeptic's options while trying to put a better face on one of them" (2001, 122, 124).

26. Special thanks go to Jason Baehr, Sven Bernecker, Juli Eflin, John Greco, and Ernest Sosa for useful and helpful suggestions on this chapter, and to participants of *JanusBlog: The Virtue Theory Discussion Group* for extended discussion of many of the pertinent issues.

REFERENCES

Audi, R. 2004. "Intellectual Virtue and Epistemic Power." In J. Greco (ed.), *Ernest Sosa and His Critics*. Oxford: Blackwell, 3–16.

Axtell, G. 2000. *Knowledge, Belief and Character: Readings in Virtue Epistemology*. Totowa, NJ: Rowman and Littlefield.

———. 2001. "Epistemic Luck in Light of the Virtues." In A. Fairweather and L. Zagzebski (eds.), *Virtue Epistemology: Essays on Epistemic Virtue and Responsibility*. Oxford: Oxford University Press, 158–77.

———. 2003. "Felix Culpa: Luck in Ethics and Epistemology." In M. S. Brady and D. H. Pritchard (eds.), *Moral and Epistemic Virtues*. Oxford: Blackwell, 235–57.

———. 2006a. "Blind Man's Bluff: The Basic Belief Apologetic as Anti-skeptical Stratagem." *Philosophical Studies* 30, no. 1: 131–52.

———. 2006b. "The Present Dilemma in Philosophy." *Contemporary Pragmatism* 3, No.1: 15-35.

———. 2007. "Two for the Show: Anti-luck and Virtue Epistemologies in Consonance." *Synthese* 158: 263-383.

———. 2008. "Expanding Epistemology: A Responsibilist Approach." *Philosophical Papers* 37, no. 1: 57-87.

Baehr, J. 2006a. "Character in Epistemology." *Philosophical Studies*, 128: 479-514.

———. 2006b. "Character, Reliability, and Virtue Epistemology." *Philosophical Quarterly*, 56: 193-212.

Battaly, H. 2001. "Thin Concepts to the Rescue: Thinning the Concepts of Epistemic Justification and Intellectual Virtue." In A. Fairweather and L. Zagzebski (eds.), *Virtue Epistemology: Essays on Epistemic Virtue and Responsibility*. Oxford: Oxford University Press, 98–116.

Bernecker, S. 2006. "Prospects for Epistemic Compatibilism." *Philosophical Studies* 20, no. 1: 81–104.

———. 2007. "Agent Reliabilism and the Problem of Clairvoyance." *Philosophy and Phenomenological Research*, 76, no. 1: 164–172.

BonJour, L. 2003. "Reply to Sosa." In L. BonJour and E. Sosa (eds.), *Epistemic Justification*. Malden, MA: Blackwell, 173–200.

DePaul, M., and Zagzebski, L., (eds.). 2003. *Intellectual Virtue: Perspectives from Ethics and Epistemology*. Oxford: Oxford University Press.

Eflin, J. 2003. "Epistemic Presuppositions and their Consequences." *Metaphilosophy* 34, no. 1-2: 48-68.

Elgin, Catherine. 1996. *Considered Judgment*. Princeton University Press.

Foley, R. 2004. "A Trial Separation between the Theory of Knowledge and the Theory of Justified Belief." In J. Greco (ed.), *Ernest Sosa and His Critics*. Oxford: Blackwell, 59–72.

———. 2005. "Justified Belief as Responsible Belief." In Matthias Steup and Ernest Sosa (eds.), *Contemporary Debates in Epistemology*. Oxford: Blackwell, 313–26.

Gettier, E. 1963. "Is Justified True Belief Knowledge?" *Analysis* 23: 121–23.

Goldman, A. 1999. "Internalism Exposed." *Journal of Philosophy* 96: 271-293.

Greco, J. 2000. *Putting Skeptics in Their Place: The Nature of Skeptical Arguments and Their Role in Philosophical Inquiry*. New York: Cambridge University Press.

———. 2002a. "How to Reid Moore." *Philosophical Quarterly* 52, 544–63.

———. 2002b. "Virtues in Epistemology." In Paul Moser (ed.), *The Oxford Handbook of Epistemology*. Oxford: Oxford University Press, 287–315.

———. 2003a. "Knowledge as Credit for True Belief." In M. DePaul and L. Zagzebski (eds.), *Intellectual Virtue: Perspectives from Ethics and Epistemology*. Oxford: Oxford University Press, 111–34.

———. 2003b. "Virtue and Luck, Epistemic and Otherwise." *Metaphilosophy* 34: 353–66.

————, (ed.). 2004a. *Ernest Sosa and His Critics*. Oxford: Blackwell.

————. 2004b. "How to Preserve Your Virtue While Losing Your Perspective." In J. Greco (ed.), *Ernest Sosa and His Critics*. Oxford: Blackwell, 86–95.

————. 2005. "Virtue Epistemology." *Stanford Encyclopedia of Philosophy*, http://plato.stanford.edu/entries/epistemology-virtue/.

Hookway, C. 1990. *Skepticism*. London: Routledge.

————. 2003. "How to be a Virtue Epistemologist." In M. DePaul and L. Zagzebski (eds.), *Intellectual Virtue: Perspectives from Ethics and Epistemology*. Oxford: Oxford University Press, 183–202.

Kornblith, H. 2004. "Sosa on Human and Animal Knowledge." In J. Greco (ed.), *Ernest Sosa and His Critics*. Oxford: Blackwell, 126–34.

Kvanvig, J. 2003. *The Value of Knowledge and the Pursuit of Understanding*. Cambridge: Cambridge University Press.

Leite, A. 2004. "On Justifying and Being Justified." *Philosophical Issues* 14: 219–53.

Montmarquet, James.2007. "Pure vs. Practical Epistemic Justification." *Metaphilosophy* 38, 1: 71-87.

Moore, G. E. 1925. "A Defence of Common Sense." In J. H. Muirhead (ed.), *Contemporary British Philosophy* (2nd series). London: Allen and Unwin.

————. 1939. "Proof of an External World." *Proceedings of the British Academy* 25, 273–300.

Pritchard, D. 2005. *Epistemic Luck*. Oxford: Oxford University Press.

————. 2006. "Greco on Reliabilism and Epistemic Luck." *Philosophical Studies* 30, no. 1: 35–45.

————. 2007. "Anti-luck Epistemology." *Synthese*, 158: 277–97.

Reed, B. 2001. "Epistemic Agency and the Intellectual Virtues." *Southern Journal of Philosophy* 39: 507–26.

Riggs, W. 1998. "What Are the 'Chances' of Being Justified?" *Monist* 81: 452–72.

————. 2002. "Reliability and the Value of Knowledge." *Philosophy and Phenomenological Research* 64, no. 1: 79–96.

————. 2007. "Why Epistemologists Are So Down on Their Luck." *Synthese*158: 329-344.

Roberts, R. and J. W. Wood. *Intellectual Virtues: An Essay in Regulative Epistemology*. Oxford University Press.

Sextus Empiricus. 1933–1939. *Outlines of Pyrrhonism*. Trans. R. G. Bury. Cambridge, MA: Harvard University Press.

Sinnott-Armstrong. 2004. *Pyrrhonian Skepticism*. Oxford, New York: Oxford University Press.

Sosa, E. 1991. *Knowledge in Perspective*. Cambridge: Cambridge University Press.

————. 1999. "How to Defeat Opposition to Moore." *Philosophical Perspectives* 13: 141–53.

————. 2000. "Reflective Knowledge in the Best Circles." In E. Sosa and J. Kim (eds.), *Epistemology: An Anthology*. Malden, MA: Blackwell, 274–87.

Sosa, E., and J. Van Cleve. 2000. "Thomas Reid." In S. Emmanuel(ed.), *The Modern Philosophers*. Oxford: Blackwell.

————. 2002. "Tracking, Competence, and Knowledge." In Paul Moser (ed.), *The Oxford Handbook on Epistemology*. Oxford: Oxford University Press.

————. 2003. "The Place of Truth in Epistemology." In M. DePaul and L. Zagzebski (eds.), *Intellectual Virtue: Perspectives from Ethics and Epistemology*. Oxford: Oxford University Press, 155–80.

————. 2004a. "Replies." In J. Greco (ed.), *Ernest Sosa and His Critics*. Oxford: Blackwell, 275–325.

————. 2004b. "Two False Dichotomies: Foundationalism/Coherentism and Internalism/Externalism." In W. Sinnott-Armstrong (ed.), *Pyrrhonian Skepticism*. New York: Oxford University Press, 146–60.

————. 2007. *A Virtue Epistemology*. Oxford: Oxford University Press.

Stroud, B. 2004a. "Contemporary Pyrrhonism." In W. Sinnott-Armstrong (ed.), *Pyrrhonian Skepticism*. New York: Oxford University Press, 174–87.

————. 2004b. "Perceptual Knowledge and Epistemological Satisfaction." In J. Greco (ed.), *Ernest Sosa and His Critics*. Oxford: Blackwell, 165–73.

Williams, M. 2001. *Problems of Knowledge*. Oxford: Oxford University Press.

————.2008. "Responsibility and Reliability." *Philosophical Papers* 37, no. 1: 1–26.

————. 2005. "The Agrippan Argument and Two Forms of Skepticism." In W. Sinnott-Armstrong (ed.), *Pyrrhonian Skepticism*. New York: Oxford University Press, 121–45.

Zagzebski, L. 1996. *Virtues of the Mind*. Cambridge: Cambridge University Press.

CHAPTER 26

DISJUNCTIVISM AND SKEPTICISM

ALAN MILLAR

1. INTRODUCTION

Disjunctivism is a way of thinking about perceptual experience and perceptual knowledge. In one central form, it is the view that judgments that characterize how it appears to a subject as if things are have disjunctive truth conditions. To appreciate what is distinctive about disjunctivist thinking and why it is interesting, it is necessary to consider a traditional approach in the theory of perception. This will provide us with the background needed to assess the epistemological significance of disjunctivism and its bearing on philosophical skepticism.

2. DISJUNCTIVISM AND THE TRADITIONAL CONCEPTION OF EXPERIENCE

When I see some physical object, say, a cat on a chair, I have various visual experiences. There is a traditional way of thinking according to which having such experiences always falls short of seeing a cat. Whether (phenomenally) visual experiences are the same or different is determined by whether they are the same or different with respect to how it looks to the subject as if things are. The experiences I have as I look at the cat need not differ in this respect from experiences I might have when hallucinating a cat. But assuming that *seeing* is a success concept, I do not see the cat unless the cat is there. It follows that merely having an experience such that it looks to me as if a cat is there before me does not suffice for seeing the cat, and even in a circumstance in which a cat *is* there, I still might not see it despite having an appropriate experience. If I have the experience because my brain has been cleverly manipulated by neurophysiologists, and the experience just happens to be such that it is as if a cat is there, then surely I do not see the cat. Under the conditions of the example, there is nothing to connect my having the experience with the presence of the cat. Some connection is required for perception. The response to this is to suppose that I see the cat only if

(a) I have an appropriate experience,
(b) a cat is there, and further,
(c) my having the experience is causally dependent on there being this cat before me.[1]

What I shall call *the traditional conception of experience* is the conception of experience that forms part of this way of thinking. Some terminology will help sharpen the exposition. I shall call experiences *perceptual* when their subjects come to have them through the normal operation of the relevant sensory modality in an episode in which they perceive something. Experiences are *phenomenally visual* if they have the sort of phenomenal features that characterize visual perceptual experiences—the kind of features that perceivers can capture by describing how it looks to them as if things are. Experiences can be phenomenally visual by this account even if they are not perceptual. For traditionalists, the same experience I have when looking at the cat could be had by me when I was perfectly hallucinating. So whether an experience is perceptual or hallucinatory has nothing to do with its intrinsic character. The intrinsic character of an experience is its phenomenal character; whether the experience is hallucinatory or perceptual depends on its causation.

In an influential series of articles, Paul Snowdon, drawing upon earlier work by J. M. Hinton, presents a view of phenomenally visual experiences on which a difference in experience need not show up as a phenomenal difference.[2] Even if it is conceded that how it looks to me as if things are in a situation in which I see something can be the same as how it would look to me as if things were in a situation in which I was hallucinating, it does not follow that the experiences in the two situations would be the same. Fundamental to the disjunctivists' way of thinking is a *relational conception of perceptual experiences*. If I see a lemon in a basket on the kitchen table, then under this conception I have an experience that is essentially relational because it is essentially a visual encounter with the lemon. If I were to have a hallucinatory counterpart of that experience—a perfectly hallucinatory experience that does not differ from the perceptual experience with respect to how it looks to me as if things are—this would be a different experience because it would not be essentially an encounter with the lemon. The difference between traditionalists and *relationalists*, as we might call them, is over the conditions under which experiences are the same or different.

Snowdon presents disjunctivism as a view about the truth conditions of sentences or judgments of the form "It looks to S as if *p*." He writes

> That "looks" sentences are true in hallucinations and in perceptions, and are not ambiguous, does not entail that they are made true by (or are true in virtue of) exactly the same kind of occurrence in both cases.
>
> (1990: 129)

He adds that such sentences, and the judgements they can be used to express

> are made true by two types of occurrence: in hallucinations they are made true by some feature of a (non-object-involving) inner experience, whereas in perceptions they are made true by some feature of a certain relation to an object, a non-inner experience, (which does not involve such an inner experience).
>
> (1990: 130)

Arguably, the broader picture to which this kind of disjunctivism is linked is separable from any specific concern to provide truth conditions for looks judgments, if that involves supplying necessary and sufficient conditions for the truth of these judgments in other terms. One might be a relationalist about perceptual experience while not engaging in any such enterprise. What, I think, is at the heart of disjunctivism is a view about what it is for it to be the case that it appears to one as if such and such is there. In relation to visual experiences, it captures at least the following ideas:

(a) Experiences that are such that it looks to the subject just as if an *F* is there include cases in which the subject sees an *F* and cases in which a subject merely hallucinates an *F*.

(b) An experience of seeing an *F* is an essentially relational experience implicating an *F*. Any such experience differs in kind from any experience of hallucinating an *F* even if how it looks as if things are to the subject who sees the *F* is the same as how it looks as if things are to the subject who is hallucinating an *F*.

(c) The experience of seeing an *F* does not break down into (1) the having of an experience that is not essentially relational (an inner experience, in Snowdon's terms) and (2) the satisfaction of further conditions.

3. EPISTEMOLOGICAL DISJUNCTIVISM

Snowdon's interest is not primarily epistemological. He is concerned with how we should conceive of perceptual experiences, and he takes it that a constraint on an adequate conception is that it should make sense of how experiences enable us to think about objects demonstratively. When we perceive objects, we are in a position to have demonstrative thoughts about them. Watching a tennis match, I can think, *That return was good*, where the reference of the demonstrative element of my thought, *that return*, is the very return I have just observed. Here I not only pick out perceptually a particular return, but I am also in a position to think of it, demonstratively, as *that return*. It is my having observed the return in question that enables me to do so. These considerations present a challenge to traditionalists about perceptual experience. If the experience that I have when I see an F is one I could have when not seeing an F, then it is not clear how the experience in the case in which I see an F enables me to think about the F in question demonstratively, never mind how it enables me to acquire knowledge about it. On the traditionalist's account, it is not intrinsic to the experience that it presents an object to the subject, so explanatory work is needed to show how it can contribute to making the object available as an object of demonstrative thought. The attraction of the idea that perceptual experience is essentially relational is that it avoids this problem. Just because the experience is essentially relational, the object is, so to speak, embraced by the experience and thus available to be thought about by suitably equipped subjects.[3] That, at any rate, is the idea. It is clearly of interest for epistemology since any plausible view of perceptual knowledge must be consistent with facts about how perception makes demonstrative thoughts available to us.

In the work of John McDowell, we find a disjunctivist style of thinking recruited to shed light directly on epistemological matters. Although McDowell acknowledges a debt to Snowdon and Hinton, it is not immediately obvious how the disjunctivist strand in his thinking links up with their distinctive concerns about the nature of perceptual experience. I shall first describe a strand in McDowell's epistemological thinking in its own terms and then circle back later, in section 5, to pick up the question of how it relates to the theory of perceptual experience.

In "Criteria, Defeasibility, and Knowledge" (McDowell 1982), McDowell criticizes a way of thinking about knowledge that he thinks plays into the hands of skeptics. The skepticism that is the main target of the article is not "external-world" skepticism but "other-minds" skepticism. This is presented as relying on the following picture:

> Judgements about other minds are, as a class, epistemologically problematic. Judgements about "behaviour" and "bodily" characteristics are, as a class, not epistemologically problematic; or at any rate, if they are, it is because of a different epistemological problem, which can be taken for these purposes to have been separately dealt with. The challenge is to explain how our unproblematic intake of "behavioural" and "bodily" information can adequately warrant our problematic judgements about other minds.

> (1982: 382)

This picture incorporates an *evidentialist* model of knowledge of other minds. On this model, judgments about other minds can be justified and can constitute knowledge in virtue of being based on defeasible evidence relating to behavioral and bodily information that does not itself implicate mentalistic concepts. It is this evidentialist model that McDowell thinks plays into the hands of skeptics. For this purpose, skeptics may be represented as follows:

(a) They accept that if there were knowledge of other minds, it would have to be on the lines of the evidentialist model.
(b) They find the evidentialist model inadequate. Failing to appreciate that an alternative is available, they infer that we lack knowledge of other minds.

In McDowell's view, skeptics are right to find the evidentialist model inadequate. One reason for thinking it inadequate concerns our entitlement to take facts about bodily behavior, conceived in nonmentalistic terms, as evidence for the obtaining of psychological states that are not perceptually manifest. Another concern is focused on the very idea that an adequate view could "envisage ascribing knowledge on the strength of something compatible with the falsity of what is supposedly known" (1982: 372). This latter theme is not pursued in depth in "Criteria, Defeasibility, and Knowledge," though it is always in the background. (I shall defer discussion of it until section 6.) The main strategy in that article has the following three stages:

1. *The diagnosis*: A version of the argument from illusion is viewed as motivating the evidentialist model of knowledge of other minds.
2. *The way out*: It is argued that the argument from illusion is not compelling. This is done with the help of a disjunctivist account of appearances and of a *perceptualist* model of some of our knowledge of other minds.
3. *The response to the skeptic*: The availability of a plausible perceptualist model is taken to show that the skeptic's argument is not compelling.

What is on offer, then, is an attempt to undermine the skeptic's argument. I turn now to a closer look at the diagnostic stage and the way out.

The argument from illusion, under McDowell's conception, runs as follows:

[S]ince there can be deceptive cases experientially indistinguishable from non-deceptive cases, one's experiential intake—what one embraces within the scope of one's consciousness—must be the same in both kinds of case. In a deceptive case, one's experiential intake—what one embraces within the scope of one's consciousness—must be the same in both kinds of case. In a deceptive case, one's experiential intake must *ex hypothesi* fall short of the fact itself, in the sense of being consistent with there being no such fact. So that must be true . . . in a non-deceptive case too. One's capacity is a capacity to tell by looking: that is, on the basis of experiential intake. And even when this capacity does yield knowledge, we have to conceive the basis as a *highest common factor* of what is available to experience in deceptive and non-deceptive cases alike, and hence as something that is a defeasible ground for the knowledge, though available with a certainty independent of whatever might put the knowledge in doubt. . . .
. . . In a deceptive case, what is embraced within the scope of experience is an appearance that such-and-such is the case, falling short of the fact: a *mere*

appearance. So what is experienced in a non-deceptive case is a mere appearance too.

(1982: 386)[4]

The application to other-minds cases is straightforward. Take the nondeceptive case (the good case) to be one in which Bill is anxious and looks it, and the deceptive case (the bad case) to be one in which Bill looks just the same as he does in the other case but is not anxious. In the two cases, according to the argument, what the experience takes in must be the same—Bill's appearing a certain way that could be specified entirely in nonmentalistic terms. But if we assume that what experience takes in must supply the justification of a judgment that Bill is anxious, the justification must be the same in both cases. What experience takes in is the fact that Bill appears as he does. This is at best defeasible evidence that he is anxious. It is defeasible because its evidential value could be undermined by further information, for instance, information to the effect that Bill is fooling around or maliciously deceiving. This is all in keeping with the evidentialist model.

The crucial inference in the argument from illusion, as conceived by McDowell here, is that "since there can be deceptive cases experientially indistinguishable from non-deceptive cases, one's experiential intake—what one embraces within the scope of one's consciousness—must be the same in both kinds of case." The good and the bad cases under consideration are experientially indistinguishable in the sense that Bill looks just the same in the two cases. The conclusion drawn is that what the subject takes in must be the same in these two cases. What is taken in is what is seen to be so. That, according to the argument, has to be the same in the two cases, which is why the only plausible model for knowledge of other minds is an evidentialist one. The basis for a judgment to the effect that Bill is anxious has to be something that is as much available to experience in the bad case as in the good case.[5]

Does McDowell deny the legitimacy of the crucial inference, or does he reject the assumption of the inference? On a certain understanding of "experiential indistinguishability," the right answer seems to be that he challenges the legitimacy of the inference and does not reject the assumption. He thinks that *if* by "experiential indistinguishability" you just mean that there is no difference with respect to how things appear, then the good case and the bad case are experientially indistinguishable (see the middle paragraph of 1982: 389). But we are supposed to resist the conclusion that what the subject takes in is the same in both cases. This takes us to the stage of McDowell's strategy that constitutes what I called *the way out*.

The way out has two complementary strands. The first is a disjunctivist conception of what it is for it to appear to a subject that such and such is the case:

an appearance that such-and-such is the case can be *either* a mere appearance *or* the fact that such-and-such is the case making itself perceptually manifest to someone.

(1982: 386–87)

Notice that here appearances seem to be subjective rather than worldly. The focus is not on how Bill looks, but on how it looks to a subject that Bill is. (I do not think that it distorts McDowell's position to think of subjective appearances in terms of how it appears to a subject *as if* things are.) We are to think of its looking to me as if Bill is anxious in these terms:

(a) Either it is a case in which the fact that Bill is anxious makes itself visibly manifest to me or it is a case in which Bill merely looks to me as if he is anxious (though he is not anxious).

(b) The case in which the fact that Bill is anxious makes itself visibly manifest does not break down into (1) my having visible evidence that would be as much available in a corresponding bad case and (2) making a judgment on the basis of that evidence.

It is noteworthy that thus far there is no reason to think that McDowell is committed to the kind of disjunctivism about perceptual experience considered by Snowdon. The rejection of a common factor in the good and bad cases is not presented as the rejection of the idea that there is an experience common to the two cases. It is presented as a rejection of the idea that what the experiences take in must be the same and, along with that, a rejection of the idea that there is a common evidential base in the two cases. The epistemological disjunctivism exemplified by (a) and (b) allows McDowell to concede that it can be true that it appears to me as if Bill is anxious in both the good case and the bad case and, indeed, that there is no difference with respect to how it appears as if Bill is in the two cases, *even though what the experience takes in is different in the two cases.* For in the good case, what is taken in is that Bill *is* anxious, but in the bad case, what is taken is at best merely that he has a certain look. But it is not clear at this stage whether the difference with respect to what the experiences take in requires that there be a difference in psychological kind between the experiences. It all depends on whether experiences are individuated in terms of what, if anything, they take in. (But see section 5.)

Taken on its own, this disjunctivist maneuver could easily seem like a sleight of hand, for it provides no explanation of *how it is* that what is taken in by an experience gained by looking can be different in the two cases. It should be noted, however, that the disjunctivist maneuver is not supposed to carry the whole weight of the case that is designed to undermine the evidentialist model. It is supplemented by a perceptualist model of some of our knowledge of other minds.

Initially it might not seem promising to treat any knowledge of other minds as perceptual. It might seem bizarre that anyone should suppose that we can see straight off that someone is anxious when it is agreed on all sides that a person can display the demeanor of one who is anxious yet not be anxious. What makes sense of the perceptualist model is a conception of perceptual knowledge as non-inferential knowledge acquired by suitably equipped subjects from what they perceive. Perceptual knowledge under this conception is the kind of knowledge we acquire when we tell from its look that a bird is a magpie or that a flower is an orchid. It is noninferential knowledge in that it is not acquired by reasoning from prior assumptions. It is phenomenologically immediate in that what is known simply strikes the subject as being so. In order to be suitably equipped, subjects need more than the repertoire of concepts required in order to entertain the content of the knowledge. They need to have an appropriate sensibility that incorporates appropriate recognitional abilities. McDowell applies this general conception to cases that philosophical tradition has treated in evidentialist terms. For instance, he applies it to knowledge of what people are saying from hearing what they say. In this case, a prerequisite is obviously knowledge of the language of the speaker. It is entirely plausible that no inference, in any ordinary sense, is involved. Indeed, it looks wrong to suppose that the knowledge that the speaker says that p is in any sense based on evidence pertaining to the speaker's utterance that falls short of saying that p. Yet there is no doubt that knowledge of what people say is a species of knowledge of other minds.[6]

Bringing sensibilities into the picture helps explain why somebody with the appropriate sensibility can detect that Bill is anxious from his look when others lacking those abilities cannot. But what we are most concerned to understand is how somebody who does have the requisite abilities could be in a better epistemic position in the good case than in the corresponding bad case. To address this problem, we need a fuller account of recognitional abilities. McDowell himself does not provide such an account. In the next section, I sketch a way of thinking about the abilities that can be deployed to fill out the perceptualist model.[7]

4. RECOGNITIONAL ABILITIES

I have the ability to tell by looking, in suitable conditions for observation, whether or not something is an orchid. That ability implicates modes of judgment formation whereby I am prepared to judge that something is or is not an orchid in response to suitable prompts. Suppose, for instance, that somebody wants to know whether a flower in a pot is an orchid. If, having looked in the right direction, I have appropriate visual experiences, then, absent countervailing factors, I shall judge that the thing in question is an orchid. It is not that I consider what kind of experiences I have, it is just that what I judge depends on the kinds of experiences I have. If I have a certain different range of experiences, then absent countervailing factors, I shall judge that it is not an orchid. If I do not have a good-enough look, then I shall suspend judgment either way. In some few cases, I would suspend judgment if the thing in question were not close enough to visual type to tell either way. (It might be an orchid that has seen better days.) The modes of judgment formation that are implemented are such that they reliably yield true judgments. But having such modes in my repertoire does not suffice for my having the ability to tell by looking, under suitable conditions for observation, whether or not something is an orchid. The very same modes could come into operation in an unusual environment in which the visually orchidlike things one encounters are at least as likely to be skillfully made from synthetic materials. If I were in such an environment, I would not have the ability to tell of things seen in that environment that they were or were not orchids. To count as having this ability with respect to a given environment, that environment must be favorable—it must not be one in which things that look just like orchids could easily not be or things that are orchids could easily not look like orchids.

When we think of people as having the ability to tell by looking whether or not something is an *F*, we ascribe to them an ability of the sort I have described. But here we come to a couple of important twists. (1) Implementations of the relevant modes of judgment formation can yield false judgments even if the environment is one with respect to which the subject has an ability to tell whether or not it is an *F* that is present. The modes of judgment formation must yield true judgments in such an environment with a high degree of reliability, but that is compatible with their occasionally yielding a false judgment. (That there is the odd thing that is not an *F* but looks just like one does not render the environment unfavorable.) (2) The relevant recognitional ability will have been exercised only if the resulting judgment is true. The ability is an ability to tell, that is, to come to know, by looking whether or not something is an *F*. So if the subject does not come to know one way or the other, then the ability will not have been exercised.

Clearly we have recognitional abilities that enable us to tell by looking that something is so in *some* cases when it is, but that would not generally suffice for telling by looking whether it is so. My ability to tell from his look that Bill is anxious would be like that. We may suppose that Bill has a way of looking—a certain demeanor—such that when he displays that demeanor, I can tell just by looking at him that he is anxious. Even so, I may not in general be able to tell just by looking whether he is anxious. He might not always display his anxiety.

We can now explain why it should be thought that on encountering anxious-looking Bill, I tell that he is anxious despite the fact that he could look just as he does and not be anxious. I tell because I have an appropriate recognitional ability, the environment is favorable to the exercise of that ability, and on the occasion in question, I do exercise it.

The conception of recognitional abilities in play here does not provide the materials for a reductive conceptual analysis of perceptually knowing-that. To exercise such abilities is to come to know something by perceiving it to be so. I have suggested that these abilities implicate reliable modes of judgment formation, but it is not part of the suggested view that we can build up to a conceptual analysis of these abilities from a prior conception of these modes. It is our conceptions of the abilities that are in the driver's seat; our grip on the modes of judgment formation is in terms of those conceptions. For instance, the experiences that are of the right kind for judging that something is an *F* are just the ones that would lead someone with the appropriate ability to judge that it is an *F*. It is doubtful that the range of such experiences is specifiable independently of the concept of the ability in question. Note too that the fact that the abilities are characterized as abilities to know does not undermine their explanatory power. It is not as if they are conceived as powers, but goodness knows what powers, to acquire knowledge. They are powers of which we have commonsense conceptions, and which reflection reveals to implicate reliable modes of judgment formation and to be individuated, in part, in terms of environments. It is informative to know that an item of knowledge has been acquired by one such ability rather than another.

The unavailability of a conceptual analysis of recognitional abilities in nonepistemic terms is in keeping with the fact that our most basic engagement with the acquisition of perceptual knowledge—our own and that of others—is at the level of factive notions like *telling that* (*finding out that*), by means of seeing that, hearing that, and the like. We seem to have learned to apply these notions in a largely satisfactory way without any guidance from reductive-analytical accounts of them. It is arguably in favor of McDowell's way of thinking that these factive notions have this role.[8]

With this picture in place, we can make sense of the idea that I can take in that Bill is anxious by looking. At any rate, if taking this in is a matter of recognizing that Bill is anxious by looking, then I can do that. A crucial difference from standard approaches to epistemology is the rejection of the idea that I know that he is anxious on the basis of evidence that is common to the good and bad cases. My knowing turns on my having exercised an ability to tell that Bill is anxious from his look, but that he looks this way is not to be conceived as evidence on which I base the judgment that he is anxious. This is just as well, since I would be at a loss to sum up how Bill looks in the form of an assumption on the basis of which I judge that he is anxious, and there would be the further problem of explaining what entitles me to connect his look with his mental state. As things are, I simply tell by looking. This is in keeping with McDowell's *way out*. The other-minds skeptic is to be rebuffed by introducing a plausible perceptualist model of some knowledge of other minds. The model helps make sense of McDowell's disjunctivism about appearances and, in particular, of his view that the experiential intake of the subject can be different in the good and bad cases even though how it appears as if things are and, indeed, how the things one sees appear are the same in the two cases.

5. The Character of Experience and What Experience Takes In

As I noted earlier, Snowdon, like Hinton, is primarily concerned with the character of perceptual experiences, not with issues about knowledge.[9] Accepting the kind of epistemological disjunctivism that I have already identified in "Criteria, Defeasibility, and Knowledge" does not in any obvious way commit us to disjunctivism about perceptual experience. In the light of this, it might be wondered whether McDowell need take a stance on the intrinsic character of perceptual experience. Other-minds cases might suggest otherwise. It is not obvious that the view of recognitional abilities I have presented commits us to supposing that the experience I gain when I tell that Bill is anxious is different, qua experience, from the experience I would gain if Bill were feigning anxiety. Nonetheless, McDowell does take a stance on the intrinsic character of perceptual experience. This stance is crucial for his view of what is needed to make sense of what he calls our having a vantage point on the external world. This vantage point is threatened, he suggests, "if subjectivity is confined to a tract of reality whose layout would be exactly as it is however things stood outside it" (1986: 241). The threat comes from a picture of subjectivity on which perception of the world is indirect, being mediated by denizens of inner space. McDowell not only rejects this view but also wishes to replace it with a picture on which experience is essentially world-involving and thus essentially relational.[10] It is at this point that it is natural to think of his epistemological concerns as linking up with Snowdon's concerns. The thought would be that no account of perceptual knowledge will be adequate unless it explains how a suitably equipped subject who has a perceptual experience is put in a position to have demonstrative thoughts about some object. By the light of relationalists about perceptual experience, traditionalists lack the resources to account for how experiences can make objects available for demonstrative thought. If the experience I have as I look at the lemon in the basket could have been had by me if I were perfectly hallucinating, then having the experience does not suffice to explain what makes the lemon available to me as an object of demonstrative thought. Notice that this view invokes a conception of demonstrative *thoughts* as essentially relational and has it that when such thoughts are made available by perception, the implicated experiences must also be essentially relational. It is a further step to suppose that experiences can be essentially takings-in of *facts*, as McDowell often appears to think. Which facts are taken in is, plausibly, determined by which recognitional abilities one exercises. So there is space for a position according to which although *perceptual experiences* are essentially relational, it is not essential to any perceptual experience that any particular recognitional ability has been exercised and any particular fact taken in.

It is important to emphasize that traditionalists agree that perception is a subject-world relation. They may agree that a theory of perceptual knowledge must account for the possibility of perceptual-demonstrative thoughts—demonstrative thoughts about objects perceptually picked out. What they will certainly dispute is that the only plausible explanation will assume that the experiences implicated in perceptions are essentially relational. That leads us to the question whether traditionalists have the resources to account for the availability through perception of demonstrative thoughts.

One way to do so would be to view the sort of recognitional abilities of which I have been speaking as depending on *abilities for perceptual discrimination*. I have in mind here not the ability to discriminate one type of object from another at the level of judgment, but rather a lower level ability to pick out and track objects

perceptually.[11] Think of walking along a corridor and encountering various potential obstacles. You pick them out visually. What this amounts to is that your
visual experiences and dispositions to behavior are shaped in a certain way. How
you move is determined by sense-perceptual and proprioceptive cues. Arguably,
visual discrimination involves *subdoxastic states* that register such cues and prime
subjects for behavior, including *subintentional activity*.[12] We engage in such activity
when we are catching balls, reaching out to pick up objects, playing shots at tennis,
and much else besides. When you catch a ball in a game, you do so intentionally, but
the systems that achieve hand-eye coordination result in small adjustments to the
trajectory of your arm that are not intentional (though neither are they uninten-
tional). Whereas the carrying out of intentions is guided by beliefs, the kind of
subintentional activity of which I am speaking seems to be guided by changes in
subdoxastic states. The activity is responsive to cues that are picked up by sight but
need not be registered at the level of belief. Through the operation of the visual
system, changes in experience and changes in behavioral dispositions vary systematically with changes in the environment and changes in the orientation and
position of the subject so as to enable the subject to move relatively smoothly in that
environment. My picking out Bill by sight is a matter not merely of having a certain
series of experiences, but of an interplay in which my experiences and my behavioral dispositions are shaped as a result of the visual impact of Bill's presence upon
me. It is a relational state targeted on Bill because it is his presence, and possibly
his changing location, that does the shaping and induces dispositions that enable
me to be responsive to the relative positions of him and me in my egocentric space.

I see no reason why traditionalists about experience should not draw upon a
view of visual discrimination along these lines in order to make sense of how
perception makes objects available for demonstrative thought. Traditionalists may
concede that an adequate account of perceptual knowledge must address the issue
of how perception can enable us to have essentially relational demonstrative
thoughts about physical objects, but it is not clear why they need take this to
commit us to an essentially relational view of perceptual experience. Perceptual
experience does enable us to pick out objects perceptually. But what the picking-
out consists in does not seem to require that the experiences themselves be essentially relational. Relationality comes in through the shaping by the object of the
subject's experience and behavioral dispositions.

6. Knowledge, Justification, and Reasons

A central preoccupation of McDowell's *Mind and World* is with understanding
how our thinking can be *rationally* constrained by perceptual experience—how it
can be empirically grounded.[13] His view is that to understand this, we need to

understand how perceptual experience can bear on our justification for believing this and that. To do that, he thinks that we must settle on the right way to think about how experiences give us cognitive access to facts. This in itself hardly seems controversial, for no one is going to disagree that empirical knowledge depends on perceiving things to be thus and so. As McDowell sees it, though, the experiences themselves must be essentially relational. Not only are they essentially pickings-out of objects, but they are also essentially takings-in of facts about these objects. This is open to challenge even if we grant that perception furnishes us with knowledge. We surely do see, and thereby come to know, that this or that is so, and likewise for other modes of perception. But so far as I can see, here too, it is an open question whether such a view demands a conception of experience as essentially relational.

Be that as it may, McDowell has interesting and important things to say about knowledge and rationality that seem to me to be detachable from some of the details of his conception of perceptual experience. We can approach this strand in McDowell's thinking by turning to "Knowledge and the Internal" (McDowell 1995), a difficult article that makes penetrating criticisms of traditional episte-mology. The target of this article is what McDowell calls the interiorization of the space of reasons.

Our thinking operates in the space of reasons in that it is responsive to what there is reason for us to think and do. The interiorization of this space that McDowell envisages is the upshot of a variant of the argument from illusion. Consider a case—a good case—in which I know because I see that, say, Mary has arrived. My knowing involves my taking it that Mary has arrived. By the argument, my taking this to be so is based on an experience such that it looks to me as if she has arrived. But it is possible, even if it is unlikely as things are, that I could have just such an experience and believe accordingly even though Mary has not arrived. This would be the corresponding bad case. In the bad case, by the argument, I have the same basis for thinking that Mary has arrived as in the good case. My standing in the space of reasons is therefore the same in the two cases. That standing has to do with what can be imputed to me as a rational thinker; it cannot turn on whether Mary has or has not arrived but depends on whether my belief is justified. Under the prevailing assumptions, I am justified and, indeed, have the same justification in both the good and bad cases. To take such a view is to interiorize the space of reasons.[14] It straightforwardly follows from this view that whether one knows that something is so is not determined just by a standing in the space of reasons, since knowledge depends on the satisfaction of the truth requirement, and that is being conceived as external to the space of reasons. The upshot of this way of thinking is that knowledge is taken to be a hybrid involving both a suitable standing in the (interiorized) space of reasons and the satisfaction of the truth requirement.

On a variant hybrid approach, knowledge involves the operation of processes that reliably yield true beliefs plus the satisfaction of the truth requirement. A belief might result from a reliable process and yet be false, so the truth requirement is independent of the reliability requirement. On this type of hybrid view, the very idea of the space of reasons plays no role, and so it is even more obvious that the acquisition of knowledge cannot be viewed as an achievement of a rational subject that is secured through operations in that space. The same applies even on a view that retains a role for justified belief but also incorporates a reliability condition, for the satisfaction of the latter condition will be external to the space of reasons: it will depend on factors that are independent of the operations within that space. (For the themes of this paragraph, see McDowell 1995: 400–402.)

It is bedrock for McDowell that knowledge itself is a satisfactory standing in the space of reasons. What is at issue is how this can be so. An important consideration for him is that it cannot be the case that the difference between a good and bad case, for instance, between the cases involving Mary just considered, consists simply in the fact that in the good case the truth requirement is satisfied and in the bad case it is not. He thinks that it makes a difference to our standing in the space of reasons whether or not we have embraced a fact. So it makes a difference to my standing in the space of reasons if I have *seen* that Mary has arrived, as opposed to having a nonveridical experience such that it looks to me as if she has arrived.

Suppose that McDowell is right to reject the view that the only difference between the good and bad cases is that in the latter the belief is false and in the former it is true. Traditionalists about knowledge who adopt an interiorized conception of the space of reasons might well agree, for they might concede that the view in question makes it hard to capture the idea that knowledge is a matter of having a cognitive purchase on, or contact with, a fact. (For this language, see McDowell 1995: 402.) For central cases of knowledge, one might think, there must be some connection between the subject's taking it that something is so and its being so. For cases of perceptual knowledge that p, a natural move is to require that the fact that p should have figured in the explanation of its looking to the subject as if p and thereby in the subject's coming to take it that p. It is open to defenders of the interiorized view of the space of reasons to take this plausible point on board. They might also observe that it is unsurprising that there should be parity with respect to justification in good and bad cases: if justification does not guarantee truth, there will pairs of good and bad cases that are on a par with respect to justification.

McDowell is committed to rejecting these ways of thinking about cognitive contact. The crucial consideration for him is that on the proposed account, the explanatory link is external to the space of reasons. It does not account for what it is to have *cognitive* purchase on a fact just because it does not display the posited explanatory link as relevant to accounting for the subject's achievement of an appropriate standing in the space of reasons. To explain that, according to McDowell, we have to reject the hybrid view.[15]

The concern to do justice to how cognitive purchase on a fact can be a satisfactory standing in the space of reasons might explain McDowell's resistance to the idea that we could have knowledge on the basis of something compatible with the falsity of what is supposedly known. (This takes us back to a point from "Criteria, Defeasibility, and Knowledge" to which I alluded in section 3. See McDowell 1982: 372.) If I judge correctly that Bill is anxious on the basis of behavioral evidence that might obtain even if he is not anxious, then under the hybrid conception, I might have done all that is to be expected of me within the space of reasons. Yet, as McDowell sees it, the fact that Bill is anxious would in that case lie beyond my cognitive reach. This is not an issue that I can pursue here. It raises difficult questions about how to treat evidence-based knowledge within McDowell's framework.

Is it so clear that knowledge can be a satisfactory standing in the space of reasons? The view of perceptual-recognitional abilities introduced earlier enabled us to make some sense of how visual-perceptual knowledge about an object could be acquired on an occasion despite the fact that the object could look the same in a corresponding bad case. But nothing said in outlining the view made clear how the knowledge acquired can meet the requirements for being a standing *in the space of reasons*. To address this matter, we need to look more closely into the links between knowledge, justification, and reasons.

7. How Can Knowledge Be a Satisfactory Standing in the Space of Reasons?

There are two aspects to the standing in the space of reasons in terms of which McDowell conceives of perceptual knowledge. One is that knowing is a state in which what is known is available to the subject so that it can figure as a reason, or an ingredient of a reason, for believing *other* things. The other, more basic aspect is that emphasized in the following passage from "Knowledge by Hearsay":

> If knowledge is a standing in the space of reasons, someone whose taking things to be thus and so is a case of knowledge must have a reason (a justification) for taking things to be that way. But this is allowed for if [for instance] remembering that Clinton is President is itself the relevant standing in the space of reasons. Someone who remembers that things are a certain way, like someone who sees that things are a certain way, has an excellent reason for taking it that things are that way; the excellence comes out in the fact that from the premise that one remembers that things are thus and so, as from the premise that one sees that things are thus and so, it follows that things *are* thus and so.
>
> (McDowell 1993: 427–28.)

In this passage, knowing that *p* through seeing that *p* is conceived as being in a state in which one has a reason to believe *that p* supplied by the fact that one sees that *p*. I shall call this *the basic point*.

To someone schooled in traditional approaches to epistemology, the idea that the basic point could explain how perception furnishes us with reasons, and thus justification, for beliefs could easily look like an abandonment of serious philosophical inquiry. It is hardly a matter of dispute that *if* I have cognitive access to the fact that I see that *p*, then this fact can supply me with a reason to believe that *p*. Having this pointed out might still leave us wondering how we can have cognitive access to such a fact. I am attempting to shed light on the character of perceptual-cognitive access to facts and, in particular, on how such access can be an appropriate standing in the space of reasons. Addressing this issue by appeal to the availability of a fact, access to which seems to be equally problematic, does not initially look like a satisfying response to the problem. Further explanation is surely needed. Nonetheless, the sheer common sense of McDowell's thinking at this point should not be overlooked. In our ordinary thinking about knowledge and the possession of reasons, we regularly treat ourselves as having reasons to believe something because we have seen it to be so. Epistemological theorizing has made this seem problematic.

By reasoning similar to that which McDowell takes to be a species of the argument from illusion, many theorists will no doubt suppose that the only access I have to the fact that I see that *p* is via something that falls short of that fact—the fact that I have an experience such that it looks to me as if *p*. Because this is of a piece with the thinking that informs arguments from illusion, McDowell is committed to rejecting it. How, then, should we think of the access we have to facts as to what we see to be so?

A natural step is to introduce recognitional abilities again. We acquire the ability to tell from its appearance that an *F* is before us by learning when to apply the concept of an *F* in response to what we see. Given that we have such an ability, there is no great mystery to how we could have a second-order ability to apply to oneself the concept of *seeing that an* F *is before one*. The very same experiences that enable us to pick out an F and recognize it to be an F enable us to tell that we see that an F is there provided we have the appropriate second-order recognitional ability. These abilities are just as much tied to favorable environments as are the corresponding first-order abilities. If the environment is not favorable, we may be primed to deploy the mode of judgment formation implicated by the relevant second-order ability and yet lack the ability with respect to that environment. But the environment can be favorable. The environment in which we can tell by looking that an *F* is there can also be an environment in which we are in a position to know that we see that *F* is there.

With the notion of a second-order recognitional ability to hand, the following looks like a plausible position:

(a) We can know that an *F* is there in virtue of seeing (or having seen) an *F* and recognizing (or having recognized) it to be an *F*.

(b) When we know that an *F* is there in this way, we have reason to believe that an *F* is there, constituted by the fact that we see (or saw) that an *F* is there.

(c) We *have* the reason in question simply because the fact that constitutes it is available to us, thanks to our having an appropriate second-order recognitional ability—an ability to tell whether or not we see (or saw) that an *F* is (was) there.

It is not a requirement of this view that the second-order recognitional capacity should actually have been exercised on every occasion on which one knows. Even when it is not exercised, there is a sense in which the corresponding belief is justified. In the usual case, it will be justified in that the fact that provides the justification is readily accessible, and its accessibility has the potential to keep the belief in place.

I do not suggest that McDowell would endorse all the elements of the conception of recognitional abilities that I have been outlining. He would take issue with my view of how traditionalists about experience can do justice to the idea that perceptual knowledge involves cognitive contact with objects and facts (sections 4 and 5). I do think, however, that something like my conception of recognitional abilities, and of how their exercise links up with the possession of justified belief, is required to make sense of the idea that knowledge is itself a standing in the space of reasons. It is crucial to appreciate that as I have presented it, the view does not build up knowledge from justified belief. Rather, the exercise of a recognitional ability explains how we know that *p* on a given occasion, and since on such an occasion we can readily tell how we know—for instance, by seeing that *p*—our believing that *p* can be justified. For all that I have said so far by way of outlining the conception, there could be knowledge without justified belief. This marks a departure from McDowell's own views on the assumption that for him, knowledge is *essentially* a standing in the space of reasons. My conception of recognitional abilities and justified beliefs does not rule out the possibility that there could be creatures with knowledge who lack the second-order recognitional abilities in virtue of which facts as to what we see to be so are available to us. But if knowledge is essentially a standing in the space of reasons, then creatures that lack the second-order abilities do not have knowledge.

8. A SATISFYING RESPONSE TO SKEPTICISM?

McDowell from time to time appears to be dismissive of skepticism. He sometimes gives the impression that once we reinstate a commonsense picture on which we are open to the world, directly embracing worldly facts, skepticism ceases to be of interest.[16] However, we should not underestimate the amount of headway that McDowell makes against certain skeptical arguments and, in particular, those that rest on the style of thinking that he calls the argument from illusion.

Skeptics have models of knowledge—conceptions of what would be required for knowledge of various kinds—in the light of which they claim that the requirements for knowledge are not satisfied. The challenge to skeptics that is discernible in the work of McDowell can be seen as having two components.

The first component is to attack the models of knowledge that underpin the moves that the skeptic makes. Suppose that skeptics devise their models of knowledge, like everybody else, by considering cases that from a pretheoretical standpoint would be judged to be central cases of knowledge and reflecting on why they are counted as cases of knowledge. Then the battle is over whether skeptics are right to think that their models reflect the character of those cases. From McDowell's perspective, as I understand it, skeptics lose this battle so far as perceptual knowledge and knowledge of other minds are concerned because their models of knowledge misrepresent the character of the cases. The idea here is not that skeptics cannot do justice to the fact that the cases *are cases of knowledge*. (That would obviously beg the question.) It is that their models are not supported, and indeed are undermined, by reflection on how in practice we think of knowledge. (I take this to be the thrust of the attack on evidentialist models of knowledge of other minds and, later, on hybrid theories.) This is the first component. To make it convincing, we need alternative models of knowledge that are in keeping with commonsense thinking. McDowell supplies such models, and I have sought to provide additional materials in the form of a conception of recognitional abilities and how they relate to knowledge and justified belief. It is open to skeptics to argue that they do not base their models of knowledge on pretheoretical thinking about knowledge. They may profess to have some different methodology for arriving at models of knowledge. But then we need to know what that methodology is. Otherwise the skeptic stands charged with giving us models of knowledge from nowhere. It is not clear what skeptics can say by way of response.

The second component is simply to point out, from within the stream of life, as it were, that the requirements of knowledge are in fact often satisfied. To take this line is to assume something that the skeptic questions; it is to assume that we know this and that. But if we have the right models of knowledge, we shall still have the dialectical advantage. For if skeptics have lost the battle over models for knowledge, they are in no position to challenge the knowledge claims that in practice we take to be established in the ordinary run of things. That, in broad outline, is the kind of challenge that can be mounted from the resources discernible in McDowell's thinking. It does not set out to give any special philosophical vindication of the claim that there are things we know. It takes on board the task of seeking an understanding of how we know what we profess to know while showing that familiar truths about what we know, at least so far as we have been able to make sense of the knowledge in question, remain untouched by the moves made by skeptics.[17]

The perspective I have suggested on the dialectic between skeptics and anti-skeptics might be questioned. In particular, it might be doubted that skeptics need make use of disputable models of knowledge rather than drawing attention to requirements implicit in our ordinary thinking about knowledge. There is a standard type of skeptical argument that might seem to do just that. The type is represented by the following schema, where not-*H* is the negation of some skeptical hypothesis:

(a) If I know that *p*, then I am in a position to know that not-*H*.

(b) I am not in a position to know that not-*H*.

So,

(c) I do not know that *p*.

Consider, for instance, a famous example discussed by Fred Dretske (1970). At the zoo, you see and recognize zebras in an enclosure. Consider, however, the skeptical hypothesis that the creatures in the enclosure are disguised mules. Do you have any reason to think that this false? On the assumption that they would look just the same if they were disguised mules, it might be thought that you have no reason to believe that they are not disguised mules. But if that is right, then, by the argument, you are not in a position to know that they are not disguised mules, and in that case you do not know that they are zebras. As is well known, some respond to this problem by denying that if you know that the creatures in the enclosure are zebras, then you are in a position to know that they are not disguised mules (Dretske 1970; Nozick 1981). I share the view that this is not a plausible option.

On the view that I outlined earlier, you may be able to know that the creatures are zebras because you have a suitable recognitional ability and have exercised it in an environment that is favorable to doing so. The environment, after all, could easily be one that is not liable to contain mules that are made to look like zebras. Moreover, you can have reason to think that the creatures are zebras because the fact that you have seen that they are zebras can be available to you, thanks to your having a suitable second-order recognitional ability and to your being in an environment that is favorable to its exercise. Against this background, skeptical arguments of the type under consideration can be seen to rely on a contentious assumption that does not drop out of commonsense thinking—the assumption that we do not know that the skeptical hypothesis is false. In the particular case in hand, you can know that it is false that the animals are disguised mules because you can see that they are zebras.

Crispin Wright (2002) presents a challenge to this approach. Suppose, for the sake of argument, that you know that the creatures are zebras and that you are justified (Wright's term is "warranted") in taking them to be. Does your justification transmit to the claim that they are not disguised mules? Surely not, Wright claims. Your justification, he thinks, is provided by the look of the beasts and has no bearing on the possibility that they are disguised mules. Moreover, if you did have justification for thinking that they are not disguised mules, this would need to be independent of your recognition that their being zebras entails that they are not disguised mules. That is because the justification you have for thinking that they are zebras does not transmit to the claim that they are not disguised mules.

Wright's challenge undoubtedly has some bite. At least when one is reflecting philosophically, it is not hard to put oneself in a frame of mind in which it seems puzzling that you can be justified in thinking that the beasts are not disguised mules when (a) all you have done is look at them and (b) they could look as they do and be disguised mules. Nonetheless, the challenge, as so far presented, begs the question against the kind of view I have drawn from McDowell. It assumes that the justification for thinking that the animals are zebras is provided by how they look and thus does not discriminate between the state of affairs in which they are zebras and that in which they are disguised mules. That is, it assumes that the justification would be the same even if the beasts had not been zebras. But on the view I have been taking seriously, the justification for thinking that the animals are zebras derives from your having *seen* that they are zebras. That does discriminate between the state of affairs in which they are zebras and that in which they are disguised mules, for if they had been disguised mules, you would not have seen that they are zebras and would therefore not have had the justification you do for thinking that they are zebras. The trouble now is that although Wright's challenge begs the question, the view challenged seems only to have pushed the problem back onto the question of what entitles you to think that you see that the animals are zebras. For (it might seem) the justification that you have for your thinking that you see that the animals are zebras must derive from or be accessible via how it appears to you as if things are, and that does not discriminate between the state of affairs in which you see that the animals are zebras and that in which you see animals that look just like zebras but are not. The point here, it should be noted, is independent of whether or not a disjunctive conception of appearances is correct. Even if the experience in virtue of which it appears to you just as if the animals are zebras is conceived as essentially one of embracing the fact that they are zebras, your justification for thinking that you are having *that experience* does not discriminate between the case in which you are having that experience and one in which you see animals that look just like zebras, but you are not having that experience. So the argument goes.

Understandable though it is, this last move still begs the question. Wright's challenge assumes that the good case in which you see zebras and the bad case in which you see disguised mules are on a par *both* with respect to justification of the belief that the animals are zebras *and* with respect to justification of the belief that you *see* that they are zebras. But on McDowell's view, there is no parity in either respect. You have a reason to believe that the animals are zebras in the good case that you do not have in the bad case. The reason in the good case is that you see that the animals are zebras. Given the conception of recognitional abilities I have outlined, we can explain your having that reason in terms of the idea that you are in a position to tell that you see that the animals are zebras in virtue of your having an appropriate second-order recognitional ability. Note that thanks to this ability, it is possible for you to have access to your reason for thinking that the animals are zebras.[18]

The central issue, which Wright's discussion undoubtedly serves to bring out, is whether you have a reason to believe that the creatures are zebras in the good case that you do not have in the bad case. On the picture I envisage, you know that the creatures are zebras because you have exercised a first-order ability to tell by looking that they are. What explains your acquiring knowledge on a given occasion is your having exercised such an ability. The ability is tied to the environment you are actually in and environments like it. You do not have this ability with respect to an unfavorable environment in which there is a decent chance that what look like zebras are not. On this picture, knowledge is not built up from justified true belief. But rational agents like ourselves, who have access to facts about what we think and what we see, have a reason to believe that p when we know that p through seeing that p. The reason consists in the fact that we see that p. This by itself will seem to skirt around the real issues if one insists that such facts are not readily available to us. But, arguably, they are readily available to us through the exercise of second-order recognitional abilities. On this view, knowledge acquisition is possible only because various conditions are satisfied that we have done nothing to check out. That you know that the animals are zebras and know that you see that they are depends on your not being in a weird environment in which there is a decent chance that things looking like them are disguised mules. You need have done nothing to satisfy yourself that you are not in such an environment. For some, this latter claim will be the stumbling block. But it can reasonably seem to be a stumbling block only if it is assumed that knowing that the creatures are zebras would require independent assurance that one is not in a weird environment. That assumption is not obviously true. Indeed, if the model of perceptual knowledge in terms of recognitional abilities is correct, then it is false.

Does this general approach help at all with radical skepticism about the external world, induced by instances of the skeptical-argument schema in which the skeptical hypothesis puts in question all knowledge of the external world? Arguably, it does. Radical skepticism, as much as skepticism linked to less radical skeptical hypotheses, rests on models of knowledge that are disputable since they impose requirements on knowing that it is not clear need be met. Because the models of knowledge are disputable, they do not subvert the assumption that the cases we count as central cases of knowledge are actual cases of knowledge. Better still, it is arguable that the model of perceptual knowledge that draws upon recognitional abilities more adequately fits our pretheoretical thinking.[19]

NOTES

1. It is not easy to spell out the nature of the required causal dependence. The problem is noted in Grice 1961.

2. My exposition is based principally on Snowdon 1980–81 and 1990. Snowdon has further commented on disjunctivism in his 2002 and 2005. For Hinton's ideas, see his 1973. The character of disjunctivist thinking about experience is lucidly explained and discussed in Child 1994. Haddock and Macpherson 2008 has articles on all aspects of disjunctivist thinking.

3. See Snowdon 1990: sec. 6. That demonstrative thought is philosophically important is emphasized by Strawson 1959 and later in Evans 1982. The view is explored in McDowell 1986 and figures crucially in Brewer 1999 and Campbell 2002.

4. In its classic form, the argument from illusion is not directly epistemological and is not about which facts experiences "take in." It is about the objects of perception in the sense of "object" in which a thing is the object of perception when it is perceived.

5. See Williamson 2000: chap. 8 for further pertinent reflections on evidence in relation to pairs of good and bad cases.

6. See McDowell 1981. For a discussion of related issues concerning the scope of perceptual knowledge, see Millar 2000.

7. I deploy the notion of a recognitional ability in Millar 2007 and 2008.

8. The same applies to the thinking of Williamson 2000, which I have not been able to discuss here.

9. The same may be said of Michael Martin, who has developed disjunctivist thinking in ways that are akin to, but differ from, that of Snowdon's disjunctivists. See Martin 1997, 2004, and 2006. Snowdon 2006 comments on the variety of disjunctivist thinking.

10. This is the burden of the portions of McDowell 1986 that deal with experience. See especially sections 5–8. A similar theme is in play with the use of the metaphor of openness to the world in McDowell 1994, especially lectures 1, 2, and 6 and the afterword to part 1, 140–41.

11. I draw on such a view in Millar 2007.

12. I put the notions of subintentional activity and subdoxastic states to work at various points in Millar 2004.

13. McDowell 1994. For critical discussions of this book, see Smith 2002 and Macdonald and Macdonald 2006.

14. I take the line of thought just set out to be the gist of the exposition of the argument from illusion in McDowell 1995.

15. Juan Comesaña (2005) takes McDowell to task for assuming that his opponents are committed to holding that the truth-value of a belief can be the only epistemically relevant difference between a good case and a corresponding bad case. I do not think that McDowell makes, or need rely on, any such assumption. It is open to him to concede that hybrid theorists may invoke differences other than truth-value between good and bad cases. So far as he is concerned, that will not help if the differences concern factors external to the space of reasons.

16. See, for instance, McDowell 1994: 113.

17. John Greco (2004) criticizes McDowell for arguing, in effect, that content externalism is sufficient for rejection of skepticism. If the view I have been outlining is correct, content externalism is not the only weapon in McDowell's armory against skepticism. There are resources for a challenge to the skeptic's models of knowledge backed up by a plausible model of perceptual knowledge and justified belief. Duncan Pritchard (2003) and David McArthur (2003) also seem to me to underplay the dialectical value attaching to the case that can be made for thinking that McDowell finds fault with the skeptic's models *and* replaces their models with one that more adequately captures our pretheoretical thinking about knowledge. Pritchard raises interesting issues about the role of luck in McDowell's epistemology that I cannot pursue here.

18. The relation between McDowell's views and internalist/externalist debates, and issues about reflective access, are explored in Neta and Pritchard 2007.

19. For further critical discussions bearing on disjunctivism, see Haddock and Macpherson 2008. Work for this chapter contributed to a project on the value of knowledge

generously funded by the Arts and Humanities Research Council. I am grateful to the council for its support and to coparticants, Duncan Pritchard, and Adrian Haddock for regular discussion of the issues. I also thank John Greco for comments on an earlier version that helped improve this chapter.

REFERENCES

Brewer, B. (1999). *Perception and Reason* (Oxford: Clarendon Press).

Campbell, J. (2002). *Reference and Attention* (Oxford: Clarendon Press).

Child, W. (1994). *Causality, Interpretation and the Mind* (Oxford: Clarendon Press).

Comesaña, J. (2005). "Justified vs. Warranted Belief: Resisting Disjunctivism." *Philosophy and Phenomenological Research* 72: 367–83.

Dretske, F. (1970). "Epistemic Operators." *Journal of Philosophy* 67: 1007–23.

Evans, G. (1982). *The Varieties of Reference* (Oxford: Clarendon Press).

Greco, J. (2004). "Externalism and Scepticism." In R. Shantz (ed.), *The Externalist Challenge: New Studies on Cognition and Intentionality* (New York: De Gruyter).

Grice, H. P. (1961). "The Causal Theory of Perception." *Proceedings of the Aristotelian Society*, supplementary volume 35: 121–52.

Haddock, A., and Macpherson, F. (eds.). (2008). *Disjunctivism: Perception, Action, Knowledge* (Oxford: Clarendon Press).

Hinton, J. (1973). *Experiences* (Oxford: Clarendon Press).

Macdonald, C., and Macdonald, G. (2006). *McDowell and His Critics* (Oxford: Blackwell).

Martin, M. G. F. (1997). "The Reality of Appearances." In Mark Sainsbury (ed.), *Thought and Ontology* (Milan: FancoAngeli), 81–106.

———. (2004). "The Limits of Self-Awareness." *Philosophical Studies* 120: 37–89.

———. (2006). "On Being Alienated." In Tamar Szabó Gendler and John Hawthorne (eds.), *Perceptual Experience* (Oxford: Clarendon Press).

McArthur, D. (2003). "McDowell, Scepticism, and the 'Veil of Perception.'" *Australasian Journal of Philosophy* 81: 175–90.

McDowell, J. (1981). "Anti-realism and the Epistemology of Understanding." In Hermann Parret and Jacques Bouvresse (eds.), *Meaning and Understanding* (Berlin: Walter de Gruyter), 228–48. Reprinted in McDowell (1998), 314–43.

———. (1982). "Criteria, Defeasibility, and Knowledge." *Proceedings of the British Academy* 68: 455-79. Reprinted in McDowell (1998), to which page numbers refer.

———. (1986). "Singular Thought and the Extent of Inner Space." In Philip Pettit and Crispin Wright (eds.), *Subject, Thought and Context* (Oxford: Clarendon Press), 137–68. Reprinted in McDowell (1998), 228–59, to which page numbers refer.

———. (1993). "Knowledge by Hearsay." In B. K. Matilal and A, Chakrabarti (eds.), *Knowing from Words: Western and Indian Philosophical Analyses of Understanding and Testimony* (Dordrecht: Kluwer), 195–224. Reprinted in McDowell (1998), 414–43, to which page numbers refer.

———. (1994). *Mind and World* (Cambridge, MA: Harvard University Press).

———. (1995). "Knowledge and the Internal." *Philosophy and Phenomenological Research* 55: 877–93. Reprinted in McDowell (1998), 395–413, to which page numbers refer.

———. (1998). *Meaning, Knowledge and Reality* (Cambridge, MA: Harvard University Press).

Millar, A. (2000). "The Scope of Perceptual Knowledge." *Philosophy* 75: 73–88.

———. (2004). *Understanding People: Normativity and Rationalizing Explanation* (Oxford: Clarendon Press).

———. (2007). "What the Disjunctivist Is Right About." *Philosophy and Phenomenological Research* 74: 176–98.

———. (2008). "Perceptual-Recognitional Abilities and Perceptual Knowledge." In Haddock and Macpherson (2008).

Neta, R., and Pritchard, D. (2007). "McDowell and the New Evil Genius." *Philosophy and Phenomenological Research* 74, 381–96.

Nozick, R. (1981). *Philosophical Explanations* (Oxford: Oxford University Press).

Pritchard, D. (2003). "McDowell on Reasons, Externalism and Scepticism." *European Journal of Philosophy* 11: 273–94.

Smith, N. H. (2002). *Reading McDowell: On Mind and World* (London: Routledge).

Snowdon, P. (1980–81). "Perception, Vision and Causation." *Proceedings of the Aristotelian Society* 81: 175–92.

———. (1990). "The Objects of Perceptual Experience." *Proceedings of the Aristotelian Society*, supplementary volume 64: 121–50.

———. (2002). "What Is Realism?" *Proceedings of the Aristotelian Society* 102: 201–28.

———. (2005). "The Formulation of Disjunctivism: A Response to Fish." *Proceedings of the Aristotelian Society* 105: 129–41.

Strawson, P. F. (1959). *Individuals* (London: Methuen).

Williamson, T. (2000). *Knowledge and Its Limits* (Oxford: Oxford University Press).

Wright, C. (2002). "(Anti-)Sceptics Simple and Subtle: G. E. Moore and John McDowell." *Philosophy and Phenomenological Research* 65: 330–48.

INDEX

....